Defending Politics:
Bernard Crick at *The Political Quarterly*

WILEY-
BLACKWELL

To Audrey Coppard

Defending Politics: Bernard Crick at *The Political Quarterly*

Edited and with an Introduction by
Stephen Ball

Wiley-Blackwell
In association with *The Political Quarterly*

This edition first published 2015
© 2015 The Political Quarterly Publishing Co. Ltd
Preface, Introduction and this arrangement © 2015 Stephen Ball

Registered Office
John Wiley & Sons Ltd, The Atrium, Southern Gate, Chichester, West Sussex, PO19 8SQ, UK

Editorial Offices
350 Main Street, Malden, MA 02148-5020, USA
9600 Garsington Road, Oxford, OX4 2DQ, UK
The Atrium, Southern Gate, Chichester, West Sussex, PO19 8SQ, UK

For details of our global editorial offices, for customer services, and for information about how to apply for permission to reuse the copyright material in this book please see our website at www.wiley.com/wiley-blackwell.

The right of Stephen Ball to be identified as the editor of the editorial material in this work has been asserted in accordance with the UK Copyright, Designs and Patents Act 1988.

Library of Congress Cataloging-in-Publication Data
Crick, Bernard, 1929–2008.
  [Works. Selections]
  Defending politics : Bernard Crick at the
political quarterly / edited by Stephen Ball.
    pages cm
  Includes index.
  1. Political science. 2. Great Britain—
Politics and government—1945– I. Ball,
Stephen, 1961– II. Title.
  JA71.C732 2014
  320–dc23

  2014028618

A catalogue record for this book is available from the British Library.

Cover image: Front cover photo of Bernard Crick used with permission granted by Tom and Olly Crick

Cover design by Raven Designs
Set in 10.5/12pt Palatino by Anne Joshua, Oxford
Printed in the UK by Hobbs the Printers Ltd

1 2015

Contents

CONTENTS

1960s

1970s

1980s

Preface

THIS collection brings together everything that Bernard Crick wrote for *The Political Quarterly* during his long association with the journal, from his first review for it, published in 1957, to his final *PQ* articles and reviews of 2008, the year of his death. For much of this long period he was not simply a prolific author for the journal but was active at various times as a board member, its coeditor (1966–1980), board chairman (1981–1993) and Literary Editor (1993–2000). He was also the principal creator of the Orwell Prize, with which *PQ* has been organically linked as a major sponsor and key supporter since the award's foundation in the 1990s.

A collection of Bernard Crick's *PQ* writings could be justified on several grounds: for a demonstration of political writing as an art, or in defence of politics, for an insight into *PQ* or the *PQ* project, or for various political-historical or historical-political reasons, and so on. From any such vantage point it would be possible to make a selection of articles to produce some kind of themed volume—Crick on politics or the study of politics, Crick on the Left, Crick on the nature of the UK and the Union, or on citizenship, or even as a road map for the evolution of Bernard Crick's thought or career. But none of these suggested themselves as more important or interesting than any of the others, so I decided—without knowing what I was letting myself in for—that the best option would be the complete *PQ* Crick. Before I started digging I thought the project might stretch to about 120,000 words. It turned out to be more than twice that.

Political writing often dates badly—and sometimes very quickly. That risk is heightened where the writing comes from a journal concerned with issues of policy and practical politics that are often transient and sometimes fiercely topical. Material that goes stale in this way retains at best only a specialist historical interest and normally dies a death, never to be read again, as do so many dusty books in the politics sections of the dwindling number of secondhand bookshops. I can't envisage an equivalent complete collection of William Robson's *PQ* writing, for example, though a selected slim volume might well appeal to a small readership interested in, say, the evolution of administrative law; it would be robustly plain fare.

Most of Bernard Crick's writings in this collection avoid this trap and remain remarkably fresh. While not many of us eagerly leaf through Sir Charles Webster's *Art and Practice of Diplomacy* or Arthur Schlesinger's *Politics of Upheaval* on a daily basis (to take at random two of Bernard's review subjects from the early 1960s), there are two aspects of Bernard's writing that ensure very little of this collection can be consigned to the status of dusty relic or mere historical curiosity.

One of these saving graces is that nearly everything he writes is shot

© Stephen Ball 2014
Published by Blackwell Publishing Ltd, 9600 Garsington Road, Oxford OX4 2DQ, UK and 350 Main Street, Malden, MA 02148, USA

through with one or more of the underlying themes of the Crickian outlook on politics. Whether he is writing on the nature of politics or the condition of the Left, or reflecting on the state of the Union or Britishness, or engaging with a grand figure like Ernest Gellner or Hannah Arendt, there is always evidence of a genuine passion for politics and the study of politics. And this is the intrinsically messy, real-world politics of *In Defence of Politics*, not something contrived in a remote cave for the amusement of other cave-dwellers. This means that even where the immediate subject of the piece has drifted out of currency, there is usually at least something of current significance worth taking for our own time.

The other defence against obsolescence is that Crick the writer, the self-conscious stylist and wit, is usually worth reading whatever the subject. From the earliest reviews and articles in the late 1950s and early 1960s, he is recognisably Bernard—confident and fluent, and of course at times cocky and a bit of a show-off. He is not like the conventional young academic who learns the essential survival skill of writing for the examiner (or referee, which is much the same thing) but who never learns—or never feels able—to write for the world. This is impressive given BRC's youth when he first comes to *PQ*— 27 and newly started in his first British academic job when he writes his first review, still only 30 at the time of his first article, and coeditor by 36—and the more so given that what we see now from that period is Bernard after he had been reined in by his editors, particularly William Robson. Later still, his coeditors had moved aside and he could write more freely without fear of the chilling touch of Robson's green ink. And he was able to merge Orwell into his (and to a certain extent *PQ*'s) outlook as he began work on his celebrated biography through the 1970s. It suited Bernard's approach to follow the Orwell dictum of making political writing an art, which he would later make the theme of his Orwell Prize.

Another, minor, risk is that to claim completeness for this collection is to offer a hostage to fortune; there's a danger that somebody will find something in a dark corner of *PQ* with Bernard's name on it and insist that it should have been included. But even if that were to happen the omission would be relatively tiny; the collection is effectively complete and reliably depicts Bernard in full spate across his entire professional career. It also shows him writing with more freedom than is usual in conventional academic journals because of the rather special context of *The Political Quarterly*, a journal with an unusual provenance and distinct publication policy that sets it apart from its more orthodox cousins across the spectrum of political studies.

What this collection includes

There are four main groups of content in this collection, arranged in chrono-logical order in four corresponding parts. The two most obvious ones are Bernard's main articles, of which there are 25, and his reviews for *PQ*, of which there are 52 though many of these cover more than one book. The third group is a series of Commentaries from journal issues during Bernard's editorship that I have been able to identify as his own rather than his coeditor's or the result of a collaborative effort. *PQ* has always run with two coeditors,[a] apart from a few years during the Second World War when William Robson was doing war work and Leonard Woolf effectively acted on his own. The fourth and final element in this book is the early part of Bernard's unfinished history of *PQ*.

The articles nearly all appeared as independent pieces in the quarterly issues of the journal, but include the occasional book chapter; I have numbered them to help with navigation and cross-referencing. Since the late 1980s *PQ* has produced a fifth book issue each year, under the guidance of either the journal's own editors or specialist guest editors whom they invite and appoint. Technically, this collection is in that tradition. Also among the 25 are two Reports and Surveys articles—a separate category of usually shorter pieces that the journal maintains for commentaries on and critiques of government reports, think-tank studies, survey results and so on.

Commentaries appeared as a regular feature at the start of 1950, first as 'Notes and Comments', then later as pieces labelled 'Editorial' or as short topical lead articles whose status is less clear but whose lack of a by-line identifies them as (mostly) in the Commentaries tradition. Since their introduction they have not normally been signed or initialled so their authorship is not reliably assignable even if it is sometimes guessable. But a shift of editorial policy in the 1970s—very much the result of disagreements between Bernard and his coeditor that I say more about in the Introduction—saw names or initials added to these editorial contributions for several years. That is fortunate for this collection as it means I've been able to include here all Commentaries that carry Bernard's name or the initials BRC between 1974 and 1981. Since that time, successive *PQ* editors have once again accepted joint responsibility for Commentaries regardless of which editor was involved in writing the piece.

I was tempted to include a couple of other examples of Commentaries that are full of Bernardian themes or language, but eventually decided that there was too much of a risk that they are either Bernard plus another or Bernard in Robsonian chains. This was highly likely in the first years of his coeditorship with William Robson, where the latter's influence was still strong and Bernard was but a promising young man; WAR's green ink would have struck through anything he deemed a little wild or colloquial from his ambitious young partner. But the caution needs to be extended to pieces from the early 1970s too: in his Introduction to *Seventy Serious Years* (see below) Bernard complains that '"Good prose need not be unlively", I would often sigh to myself as he [Robson] toned me down in the 1970s'.

But I did weaken once and have included a single unsigned Commentary—

---

[a] The usual term among *PQ* insiders is 'joint editor', which is how William Robson and Bernard Crick normally described themselves, but I use the briefer 'coeditor' in this book.

'Political Reviews' from issue 3 of 1978. As I point out in a footnote to that piece, there is enough Crickian content and Bernardian style there to make it almost certain that he wrote it without constraint. By that time Robson had retired as coeditor and Bernard's new partner was John Mackintosh, so though the lack of declared ownership of the piece may be a reflection of both editors sharing responsibility for it I don't think Mackintosh would have interfered beyond commenting on his coeditor's piece as a colleague might.

Several of the Commentaries included in this collection are complete for that issue; that is, they were all that appeared under the Commentary heading or as the opening editorial element in that number of the journal. Some other Commentaries through the period were composed of separate sections written by others, usually but not always the coeditor of the day. For example, the 'Euro-Communism' piece from the last issue of 1978 included here is actually the first of two sections, the second written by James Cornford who was a Literary Editor but never a coeditor. Wherever Bernard's Commentary is part of one of these I mention it in an editorial footnote.

The fourth element of this collection is Bernard's unfinished history of *PQ*, eventually entitled *Seventy Serious Years*—a publisher-depressing title that was unlikely to attract droves of readers, intelligent, general or otherwise. This book never progressed beyond an introduction and a first chapter, which together were circulated in a stapled and partly corrected proof form, complete with draft cover, at the Orwell prize event in spring 2000. That's as far as it got. By this time the first Blair government was in office and Bernard was immersed in his well-known citizenship work. In spite of gentle and repeated inquiries from the editors, and later myself too, Bernard never resumed work on the book. Given the pull of his public political engagement, and later his declining health, it was never able to command enough of his time and attention.

Book chapters and external pieces

In the interests of keeping this already long collection within bounds I excluded a small amount of Bernard's *PQ* linked material, usually on the grounds that its association with the journal was secondary and not part of the central effort of the quarterly issues or of the later annual 'fifth issue' books published from the end of the 1980s onwards. One example is the collection that he edited in 1967 for OUP commemorating the second Reform Act of 1867, *Essays on Reform, 1967: A Centenary Tribute*. By this time he was newly installed as a coeditor of *PQ*; also, several of the book's contributors had *PQ* connections, the most prominent of these being founding editor William Robson. Bernard's own contribution included a short introduction and a final chapter on 'Parliament and the Matter of Britain', some of which is taken directly from his 1965 *PQ* article 'The Prospects for Parliamentary Reform' as included in the present collection (as Article 4).

Bernard coedited four other collections of *PQ* articles with Robson; three of these were published by Penguin and branded as 'Pelican Originals'—not quite convincingly, given that most of the content was reprinted from journal issues and that all pieces carried the *PQ* copyright—and one by Sage. Two of the Penguins—*The Future of the Social Services* and *Protest and Discontent*—were largely composed of articles from two 1969 issues of the journal, more or less revised, topped up with three or four others newly commissioned for the books. These two were published in 1970 and helped to mark *PQ's* fortieth anniversary. Bernard was enthusiastic about celebrating decades and special occasions and centenaries—more so than his predecessors. *Protest and Discontent* was further dedicated to the memory of Leonard Woolf, Robson's long-serving coeditor, who had died in 1969. *The Future of the Social Services* carried a brief 'housekeeping' preface signed by both editors but there is no other identifiable Crickian content.

Protest and Discontent is different: although there is a joint preface, a full-length Introduction from Bernard takes the place of the unsigned introductory article that appeared in the original *PQ* version of the collection from the last quarter of 1969. (In these thematic collections the journal editorial was directly related to the following articles, unlike the topical and frequently independent content of the normal Commentaries.) Judging from its style and content, the introduction to the *PQ* issue appears to be very much Bernard's, but the book's signed Introduction makes its authorship clear, and as revised is a slightly better piece. Hence in this one instance I've used the book version of the article rather than the journal original, with the kind permission of Penguin Publishers.

The 1973 Penguin volume *Taxation Policy* has an introduction by William Robson alone. Although unhelpfully there is no preface or other description of provenance, and in spite of Robson's introduction to the book talking of 'this symposium', combined with a copyright date of 1972 on the book's title verso, the collection is based on the articles in *PQ* issue 1 of 1971, a special issue on taxation, in the same order but with three added chapters along the lines of the other Penguins. But there is no trace of Bernard in the collection, who doesn't talk about taxation at length in his *PQ* writings. Nor—perhaps unsurprisingly—is Bernard in evidence in the Sage volume *China in Transition*, which reprints *PQ's* issue 1 of 1974 and whose unsigned introduction is plain, sober and decidedly Robsonian. This view is confirmed by its attribution to Robson in the bibliography of his writings,[b] though that volume unfortunately doesn't add much to attributions of other *PQ* material in the Robson–Crick years beyond the fairly obvious examples of *Taxation Policy* and *China in Transition* together with a few of Robson's Commentaries.

Bernard does appear in the 1981 edited collection for Methuen, *Unemployment*, which reprinted a 1981 special issue (vol. 52, no. 1) of *PQ* together with an article on the same theme added from the immediately previous issue. In

[b] C. E. Hill, *A Bibliography of the Writings of W. A. Robson*, Greater London Papers no. 17, London, LSE, 1986.

his Preface to the *Unemployment* book Bernard announced: 'I sadly chose this sombre theme to mark my retirement after fifteen years in the *Political Quarterly*'s editorial chair'. He also notes that the chapters are now unrevised reprints of the original journal articles, unlike those in the earlier Penguin collections which had varying degrees of later intervention; the emphasis now is on speed, 'the publishers and ourselves believing in the urgency of giving this material wider circulation'. His own contribution to it, the Commentary that introduced the special issue and hence formed the Introduction to the book, is reproduced here in its *PQ* rather than book-specific form (though the two appear to be substantially the same). After this Methuen collection, Bernard's contributions to *PQ* books fall within the journal's own 'fifth issue' cycle, yielding the pieces reprinted here as Articles 18, 22 and 24.

Editorial intervention

One reason for the substantial nature of this collection is that Bernard Crick's association with *PQ* was a very long one. Another is that Bernard always had a great deal to say and *PQ* presented rich and varied opportunities to say it. A consequence of this long span is that authorial, editorial and typographical fashions and preferences have changed a lot over the 50+ years from Bernard's first review to the time of this collection. I therefore had to bring some kind of editorial consistency, mostly by applying present day *PQ* style but with some deliberate Bernard-indulging variations.

The first variation concerns the position of notes. Following a redesign in 1996, *PQ*'s notes—always strictly rationed, and fiercely so under Bernard— mutated from the footnotes that had ruled from 1930 to endnotes, appearing at the ends of articles. I decided to revert to the earlier form and use footnotes throughout. This makes it easier for readers to glance down and see what sources or (subtly breaching *PQ* style) asides Bernard has served up; as I mention in the Introduction and as his long-term readers will be aware, asides are an integral Bernardian feature.

I should mention the way in which the text in this book was generated. The traditional way to do a new edition of an academic book was to break up a couple of copies and stick the pages down on sheets of paper so that any changes and new copy could be written in the extra space. The whole book was then rekeyed. Now there's an alternative. Some years ago *PQ* digitised its entire backstock so I used this digital resource as raw material instead. I was able to OCR the stock files—that is, convert them to text via optical character recognition—to create new text files for re-editing in a wordprocessor. The method avoids rekeying but has the drawback that the raw files it creates usually contain many errors, especially where the original pages used small type or are otherwise less distinct, as is true of material from issues in the fifties and sixties. The process creates many near misses that have to be edited out, so 'modern' could end up as 'modem', 'I', 'l' and '1' get confused and so on, and it's not at all good at recognising italic. However, I hope all of these snags were picked up during my re-editing, or if a few escaped that the proofreader found them.

More generally, I have made occasional corrections to the original text where there are clearly unintended slips of authorship, editing or typesetting (usually, it's not possible to say which), and impliedly of proofreading. To give one typical example, in Article 23 there was the phrase 'not just by killing one or two its officials' where there is clearly an 'of' missing and it should read 'one or two of its officials'. The change is uncontroversial so it remains silent: I haven't annotated these corrections of obvious errors—after all, this isn't an exercise in the minute exegesis of Bernard's First Folio but the revival and celebration of a significant selection of his writing over a professional lifetime. However, on the few occasions where the sense *is* changed by one of my amendments, or where a change is less clear-cut and open to debate, then I have mentioned it in one of my editorial notes (see below).

Taken together these changes are few and far between, and beyond the updates to present-day *PQ* style I have not indulged in any intrusive editing on stylistic or any other grounds. Readers can be confident that although the originally published piece must remain as the version of record, for referencing purposes they can cite the reprinted pieces in this collection as exactly equivalent. This also applies to the annotation throughout, so a note 1 from Bernard in this collection always matches a note 1 in the original.

My notes are in a different series. To mark some corrections and to make the occasional comment I have added editorial notes, and of course had to distinguish these from Bernard's own. I decided that the best way to do this was via a separate set of footnotes cued by lower case letters, like those to this Preface. Thus any conventional number-cued footnotes (1, 2, 3 etc.) are Bernard's throughout, whereas all letter-cued footnotes (a, b, c etc.) are mine. I have tried to keep these editorial notes to a minimum. This has much to do with *PQ*'s general disdain for notes and other apparatus—a position that Bernard championed but didn't always follow to the letter—and the journal's parallel assumption that its readers already understand the background and context of what is under discussion. The ideal number of notes for a *PQ* article is none, though few authors can manage that and the journal does allow authors a restricted number of bibliographic—but not substantive—notes. Academic authors sometimes have a problem with this, brought up as they are to mark their tracks with great care.

The '*PQ* reader knows what we're talking about' assumption goes back to the journal's beginnings in the lost world before the internet. It applied equally in 1930, 1960 and even 1990, though risks the charge that it is a policy that selects in favour of an elite readership and ignores everybody else—I pick up this theme again in the Introduction in connection with Bernard's musings on *PQ* as an elite journal. But if that charge was ever justified it has little impact now. Pretty well anything mysterious that readers encounter is now just a few mouse clicks away on the Web or can be casually thumbed up on a smartphone, hence this contextual assumption is much less forbidding than it was at times when looking things up meant long spells digging in libraries.

There are times when Bernard alludes to something that may not be immediately apparent or Google-obvious, in which case I do add comments. For example, whereas it would be absurd for me to add a note to explain who Tam Dalyell is, I should and do provide a note to explain that when Bernard mentions 'the Laird o' the Binns' he's referring to Tam Dalyell. I also add *PQ* specific information from time to time, filling out journal cross-references or adding a few details about the *PQ* significance of people mentioned along the way.

Capital punishment

Bernard had strong views about the quality of writing and editing, which included the detail of his own writing and the policy of the journal. This concern extended to the minutiae of punctuation and the use of initial capitals, and he would push a point when it mattered to him Although he was not a pedant or mindless defender of mere forms, he sometimes took issue with a copy-editor for what was done to his writing, or what was not done to somebody else's.

PQ's later house style, which I've largely employed in this collection, embodies many aspects of what is now commonplace in UK publishing practice, including less fussy punctuation and fewer initial caps than was standard when Bernard began his professional life. So, to use an invented example, something that in 1965 would have appeared in the journal as:

The Labour Party's response to the B.B.C. was to say "We are on your side," so to speak.

would appear in the new style as:

The Labour party's response to the BBC was to say 'We are on your side', so to speak.

Bernard liked his initial capitals, though, and would insist on the 'P' in 'Labour Party' and other party names. (The rationale against the capital is that short party names are often not official party titles. So, for example, in the days of that happy union 'The Conservative and Unionist Party of Great Britain and Northern Ireland' would be referred to as the 'Conservative party', but as a shorthand in place of the unwieldy official party name. The other objection is that caps are 'shouty' and noisy.) Accordingly, one of the Bernardisms that I've preserved—or reinstated in some cases—is his usually careful and sometimes idiosyncratic use of initial capitals. It's actually more complicated than this, and not just a question of whether or not to follow some arbitrary rule: this was an area that Bernard liked to finesse in a way that could create traps for unwary or mechanical copy-editors, such as here from his 'A Meditation on Socialism and Nine Theories' (reprinted in this collection as Article 13):

Does it matter at all what name one gives to the cluster of perceptions and theories by which one defines what is possible and desirable: Labourite, social democrat, Social Democrat, Democratic Socialist, democratic socialist, marxist or Marxist?

In November 1995, while Bernard was still Literary Editor of the journal, Gillian Somerscales (then Bromley, and the first professional copy-editor to work long term for the journal) created a new stylesheet. Some of his concerns (and his less than impeccable typing) are evident in a reply he sent her after he received a draft:

. . . in my own writing I find it helpfull [sic] to capitalise the Left and the Right, as well as definite movements (you have that) like New Left and even New Right, if only to avoid absurdities like 'what is left of the left' or real amiguities [sic] like the former Irish nationalist slogan 'God defend the right!' (in case anyone thought the Fenians meant the Tories), and more than once I have enjoyed the pun 'the Right are too confident that they know what is right'. Poor moral 'right' needs clearly separating from the political Right, or right turns. There is a point here to consider. I want to stick to that in the Review section, but promise not to scream if they get decapitated.

The upshot of all this is that I have preserved (and sometimes added back) as many of Bernard's concerned capitals as possible rather than sacrifice them all to the present journal style. This did not mean a blanket search and replace. The danger of subtle capitalisation systems is that they can be too complicated for their own good: it can be unclear to an editor what is intended and systematic and what may be just an unintended oversight or lapse. For the reader, too, there is a related problem in that subtle schemes can fail to register or may just look like inconsistencies. Also, when re-editing, as I have done, the problem is compounded because there is a layer of prior copy-editing and possibly proofreading to penetrate too: I'm able to reinstate the cap P in 'Labour Party' in a broadly systematic way, for example, but I'm unable to second-guess whether all lower case initialled terms are Bernard originals or have simply been decapitated without him screaming.

Another area that creates pitfalls for an editor is Crickian punctuation. As I point out in the Introduction, although he writes in clear English within the *PQ* tradition, with a flair that is all his own, Bernard does not write *plain* English—certainly not in the sense that William Robson wrote plain English or the Plain English campaign might like to see it. His love of asides, and asides within asides, creates complicated sentences and often complicated punctuation to support them.

Very occasionally I have clarified some of the punctuation of Bernard's characteristic parentheses, particularly when these are nested two or more deep, or where they use his idiosyncratic and occasionally misleading dash–semi-colon pair in a way that creates ambiguity. To show what I mean by these, here's a very simple example from his Article 20 on Hannah Arendt, which is one that I haven't amended:

Only recently have Arendt conferences broken out here—in the States they have been legion; and probably the best of many books and symposia about her, certainly the best for clear exposition and good judgement, has come from an English author.

Normally, of course, if dashes are used to mark out a parenthesis like 'in the States they have been legion' they should appear both fore and aft, but Bernard would very often use a semi-colon instead of a second dash. Usually it's clear enough what he means, so I've left most of them on the grounds that it's his readers' privilege to unravel Bernard's doubly or triply nested parentheses.

At one level this is all very trivial, but someone as significant to *The Political Quarterly* as Bernard deserves care and attention in an area that was important to him. The best thing that an editor of somebody so voluble and self-assured can do is keep well out of the way. My editorial policy was not to impose a ruthlessly uniform and consistent style on every scrap of detail throughout the whole book, hence readers will find small variations between chapters or over the decades. I've aimed instead at a working consistency that accords with current *PQ* style as much as possible but that allows the Bernardisms to shine through. Anything more than this I leave to little statesmen and philosophers and divines.

One more thing: to everybody associated with *PQ* the name 'Bernard' has a particular resonance. It would seem strange for me always to use the 'Crick' of army, public school and orthodox academic discourse when writing about him in this celebratory collection—as if 'Crick clashed with his coeditor in the 1970s' speaks true but 'Bernard clashed with his coeditor in the 1970s' counts for no more than a rumour. Of course, he described himself as 'Crick' often enough for that form to earn its keep too, but I hope my talking of Bernard this and Bernard that doesn't cause the punctilious William Robson any undue grave-spinning.

Sources and acknowledgements

Inevitably, I have had to use many sources when working on this collection and in writing the Introduction.

First there are the minutes, internal documents and correspondence of *The Political Quarterly* and the associated company that are not generally available. These include the minutes of what were originally two separate boards—one editorial and one company—that later combined into one working board. There is no central and continuous collection of *PQ* documents, only broken series and fragments still in need of further rediscovery and organisation—more jobs for the future. Naturally, the record is more complete as it gets up to date. The earlier records are generally lost or interrupted, except where preserved by good fortune in the collected papers of PQ's founders, board members and others. A deep search through these—and the new archive of Bernard Crick's own material—is something that I have not had the time or resources to undertake now and will have to wait for the longer, slower process of writing the journal's history, for example, so I have not attempted it here and simply dived into documents that apply to the immediate story.

I'd like to thank my own subject librarian Chris Fowler and also the special collections librarians at the University of Sussex, PQ's former editorial assistant Gillian Somerscales, and Bernard's sons Tom and Ollie Crick for their support. Thanks are certainly due to PQ's Emma Anderson, who after my first sketch of the contents made an initial foray to seek Bernard's material in PQ's digitised backstock and has also been brave enough to read the proofs. I'd also like to thank Rachel Smith and colleagues at Wiley Blackwell for tracking down the original 'official' status of *Seventy Serious Years*, and I am very grateful to Henry Hardy for permission to use an extract from Isaiah Berlin's 1959 letter to Leonard Woolf at the start of my Introduction.

I am very grateful to Audrey Coppard, long time (and thus frequently heroic) associate of Bernard from her days as research assistant at Birkbeck, then as editorial assistant and later assistant editor and company secretary for *The Political Quarterly*, both for saving and passing on many official documents and for information and conversations over some ten years—and especially from my visit to talk about this project in November 2011. This book is dedicated to her.

My particular thanks go to the editors of the journal at the time of this collection's first approval and later gestation, Andrew Gamble and Tony Wright. I thank them for indulging my long project, and for being gracious as it grew from small beginnings into an ever larger (and alas slower) beast.

Any errors that remain are of course entirely my own responsibility. The views expressed in the editorial writing and selection in this book are my own, and I do not offer them as the views of *The Political Quarterly* or of its past or present editors or board members or anybody else connected with the journal.

SB, August 2012

Introduction

STEPHEN BALL

Dear Mr Woolf

I would rather not review *The American Science of Politics* for anyone if you will forgive me. I am in bed with a sprained sacroiliac joint, and as soon as this is over shall go to Italy, and would rather not read books for review, especially by Mr Crick, whom I have met and thought not over-intelligent. I may well be wrong about this, but I do not feel anxious to test my view by this degree of exhaustion. . . .[a]

So began Isaiah Berlin on 8 July 1959 at the start of a long reply to Leonard Woolf, who had written two days earlier. He had asked Berlin whether he would review Bernard Crick's first book, *The American Science of Politics*, for *The Political Quarterly* (*PQ*), before offering a series of comments on *Two Concepts of Liberty* that had produced the rest of Berlin's reply. At the time Woolf was the journal's first Literary Editor (that is, reviews editor), having stepped down the previous year after 27 years as its coeditor.

This would prove no setback for Bernard Crick. After spending a couple of years moving between US universities, he was now established at the LSE at the beginning of his British academic career. That first book, a revised version of his 1956 London doctoral thesis, drew on his US experience and reflections. It's quite possible that he was aware of the rebuff by Berlin, if not the details, as he had already written reviews for *PQ* by that time (included here as the first five in the collection) and Woolf may have passed on the news. Besides, *PQ* coeditor William Robson was also at the LSE as a senior colleague of Bernard's until 1962.

During the development of his career Bernard appears to have measured himself against the public-facing political intellectuals of the day. He naturally sought success in academic political studies, but this very ambitious and driven young man would not be content with a life in the cloister. Nor would a consistent application of his view of politics permit it: 'I wanted to argue that the study of politics is necessarily part of politics', he said in the fourth edition of his most famous book.[b] As some of the writings in the collection reveal, he deliberately aimed for a significant public profile too, both as public intellectual and stylish writer. I believe that during this rise Berlin was a particular marker for him, as if to say 'When I am regularly

---

[a] Accessed at Leonard Woolf Archive, University of Sussex special collections, SxMs13, General Correspondence. Collected in Isaiah Berlin, *Enlightening: Letters 1946–1960*, ed. Henry Hardy and Jennifer Holmes, Chatto and Windus, 2009, pp. 693–5.
[b] Bernard Crick, *In Defence of Politics*, Penguin, 1962 and later editions; Preface to fourth edition, 1991, p. 8.

© Stephen Ball 2014
Published by John Wiley & Sons, 9600 Garsington Road, Oxford OX4 2DQ, UK and 350 Main Street, Malden, MA 02148, USA

spoken of in the same breath as Isaiah Berlin then I too will have become a major public figure'. Perhaps the early rejection of the review, if he knew about it, may have provided a small stimulant to that.

This process, both in style and substance, is already evident at the time of his first encounters with *PQ*. In a typically Crickian touch, Bernard added a verse appendix to his Sheffield inaugural of 1966, delivered in the same year that he would join William Robson as coeditor of *The Political Quarterly*. It's sprinkled with literary references and knowing gags, and drops names and allusions, both ancient and modern, in every other line.[c] If you want to be harsh, this is the Bernard of many of his critics, too clever for his own good and desperate to show us just how much he knows. But if you're prepared to forgive him his compulsive showing off and fondness for a joke, his mixed-metre verse is sharp and provides both a gloss and critique of Berlin's ideas. As in so much of Bernard's writing, the humour—for better or worse—grabs your attention, and draws you into the concentrated substance beneath.

His appendix brings to mind a music hall comic who decides to end with a humorous recitation. Much of it concerns Berlin's *Two Concepts of Liberty*, critiquing as so many have its rather limp concept of negative liberty ('Liberty is surely not just taking care / But taking care at least to get somewhere'). It also reinforces the sense that Berlin—'my craft-master and elder brother'—is a key point of comparison for Bernard's early career and a landmark for his own progress. Here's the opening of the appendix, which is already indulging in fancy allusion (*The Beggar's Opera*) by line 3:

> Pick a big one when, with academic sagacity,
> One attacks to hide one's own inadequacy;
> So, like Peachum to Lockitt, I abuse another
> Who is my craft-master and elder brother,
> No less than Professor Sir Isaiah Berlin
> Picked for being, like a Liberal in love,
> Reluctant to go far enough,
> Sensing an impropriety in every call
> On freedom made by rough political.

Here he may be contrasting his 'rough political' self with the gilded pedigree of 'Sir Isaiah, Oxford but modest', but he also implies that their relative standing has become something like that of master and journeyman. At the very least he is no longer the rejected supplicant who is unworthy of the great man's attention. Bernard the would-be public intellectual is catching up.

He has to wait nearly ten years before he has the chance to deal directly with his touchstone in *PQ*. His 1969 review of *Four Essays on Liberty* (included in this collection) perhaps tries a little too hard; and whether his fantasy of

[c] Bernard Crick, 'Freedom as Politics', Inaugural Lecture, University of Sheffield, 1966; reprinted in revised form in Preston King, ed., *The Study of Politics: A Collection of Inaugural Lectures*, Frank Cass, 1977, pp. 301–22.

2

Berlin's encounters with political thinkers such as Hegel and Comte in his morning promenade down the 'historical High' is seen as a miniature *tour de force* or merely over-clever and irritating, it certainly shows our young professor in full, stylish and confident flight. It also presents Bernard as feeling significant enough to claim to be on Berlin's radar: 'It is hardly odd that some of us enjoy being knocked down by Berlin more than being hoisted on the shoulders of the rest of the philosophical Fancy.'

As with so many aspects of Bernard's professional life and writings, it is possible to trace the shape of this and other developments through the 52 years of his writings in this collection. By the time of his 1976 article 'The Strange Death of the American Theory of Consensus' (Article 9 in this volume), Bernard is able to name-drop himself into Berlin's company, effectively as an equal, courtesy of Ernest Gellner, a figure he also admired greatly and, as I claim later, another significant influence:

In this journal's special issue on *Protest and Discontent*, Ernest Gellner lumped me together with Popper and Berlin, a back-handed compliment for holding this view: that simply a respect for politics, for the open society and for liberty, respectively, could solve our problems, whereas those very problems might be a condition of our dilemmas of indecision.

Gellner's original roll-call in the passage from his chapter 'Myth, Ideology and Revolution' was actually longer ('In social theory alone, one can find monism eloquently condemned in Berlin, Oakeshott, Crick, Gallie, Popper, and others'),[d] but Bernard edits out Oakeshott and Gallie (and 'others') and narrows the association to the two favoured heavyweights in the extract above—three if you count Gellner.

Berlin would also contribute directly to Bernard's progress. He reputedly supported his approaches for Oxford jobs that never came his way, and the covers of the later editions of Bernard's classic *In Defence of Politics* carried selected fragments from Berlin's review of it in *20th Century*—'Written with verve and brilliance', it is a 'clever and disturbing book', say the extracts. Bernard's writing is 'alive' and that 'much of what he says', even if at first sight 'perversely provocative', turns out to be 'penetrating and serious' (the essence of Bernard the gadfly, as many saw him).

And in a much later *PQ* article, 'Hannah Arendt and the Burden of Our Times' from 1997 (Article 20 in this volume), Bernard finesses another Isaiah Berlin reference that portrays them not just as matched thinkers but as friends sharing an equal public standing, this time conveyed by one of Bernard's favourite literary devices—dramatically reconstructed dialogue, for want of a better term (and more on this later too):

When political theorists did come to look at it [Arendt's original *Burden of Our Time*] the then prevailing tone of logical positivism or linguistic analysis would have inclined many to share Isaiah Berlin's *ex cathedra* judgement. He once said to me,

---

[d] *Protest and Discontent*, PQ/Penguin, 1970, p. 212. See my Preface for the origins of this book.

3

apropos of kind words about my *In Defence of Politics* . . . 'We seem to agree on most things except your admiration for de Jouvenel and Miss Arendt. Could you summarise either of their arguments for me in brief propositions?'

'That's a tall order.'

'Indeed, can't be done. Sheer metaphysical free-association. Fairy gold, Bernard, fairy gold, I beg you to notice.'

But I still beg to differ.

These extracts illustrate the transformation of Bernard: whereas at first the illustrious scholar who refuses to review his first book could dismiss the young Crick with a patrician wave as perhaps 'not over-intelligent', Bernard is now a widely known figure who has contributed to many areas of political learning and political life. He is a public intellectual and can hold his own with any other public political figure of his time.

Both Crick and Berlin finished as 'Professor Sir', but the capricious nature of the honours system means that this tells us little about their relative standing and longer legacy. Bernard was genuinely upset that he did not become a lord, something reported in his obituaries but also experienced first-hand by Audrey Coppard—his long suffering research assistant from his early days at Birkbeck, and subsequently brought in by Bernard to take various editorial and administrative roles at *PQ*.

Whether or not Bernard Crick and Isaiah Berlin finished honours-even in the fame and influence stakes—and a reasonable view would be that there are incommensurables as well as parallels—the immediate responses to their deaths couldn't have been more different. A not untypical response to Berlin's death is Henry Hardy's glowing 'great man' tribute in the *Independent* of 7 November 1997 ('one of the most remarkable men of his time, and one of the leading liberal thinkers of the century'), but in the days following Bernard's death all of his obituarists felt obliged to mention some of his more difficult qualities as much as they celebrated his achievements. He is *almost* a great man, as it were, *if only* it hadn't been for those 'other things'.

It is true that there was a difficult side to Bernard Crick, and it was far from hidden: anybody who worked or spent time with him would see it soon enough—the drive, challenging personality, relentless self-interest and attention-seeking, attitudes to relationships and women in general, manoeuvring, behaviour in meetings and committees. Many who encountered him have stories, sometimes scars, to show for it. Audrey quoted to me a colleague of theirs from Birkbeck days who had said Bernard Crick was 'selfish to the point of solipsism'. At times he was not simply Bernard but Bloody Bernard—demanding and manipulative, inclined to walk away from anything that did not go his way, and in the eyes of some a bully.

We can imagine how these traits would dominate a newspaper serialisation of a Crick biography to the point of serious distortion of his life and legacy, but they raise an intriguing question in the context of this collection: why did such a self-interested person throw in his lot with the unusual quarterly journal that is *PQ*? This would not prove to be a transient association, cynically contrived as a career enhancing move in his early days, but was deep, sustained and long term to the extent of him becoming part of the *PQ* 'family' and a most significant champion of the journal. Beyond the 52-year span as an author for the journal, mapped by the contributions collected here, his richer association with it as coeditor, Chair and Literary Editor ran from 1966 to 2000—a total of 34 years right at the centre of the journal's existence. This is far longer than any of the other major professional or even personal associations of his life. Not only that, but *PQ* insiders generally viewed him with affection and appreciation as well as with sometimes inevitable exasperation. And still do.

A first inference from the view of a self-interested Bernard would be that he joined *PQ* because it gave him some control over a convenient forum that he could use for his own nefarious purposes—especially as somewhere to write what he wanted with more freedom than was possible in a purely academic journal. This could be a marginally convincing argument for his first few articles and the early years of his coeditorship, but it doesn't get us very far. Bernard could have built every aspect of his career and reputation without the aid of *The Political Quarterly*, though it was undoubtedly a useful vehicle for many kinds of his writing, as this volume testifies.

His tenure as editor alone was nearly 15 years, not at that time especially long in *PQ* terms given that his coeditor in 1966 was a principal founder who had been in place since 1930, and would serve for another nine years. This length of editorial service is now rare in journals, even in the slower-moving worlds of arts and humanities publishing, and is unthinkable in science and technology journals where strictly policed three-year terms are the norm. By the mid-1970s, when tensions were growing between Bernard and others about the journal's direction and editorial policy, he had already long ago written his landmark *In Defence of Politics*, whose first edition pre-dated his *PQ* editorship, and was well into his work for the Orwell biography. Neither of these was dependent on his *PQ* roles, which if anything probably stole time from them.

Yet the journal did provide him with more opportunities to write in the way that he liked, essentially as an essayist with a tendency to be provocative. It wasn't that he had to take on the editorship to establish himself as a *PQ* author—he had already been writing for the journal for nine years when he became coeditor and had contributed four articles and a dozen reviews. But now that he was an editor, in theory he could drop in a piece largely when he wanted to. Besides, although not exactly a mass media outlet, *PQ* provided a far more public space than an academic journal could, especially at a time when there was no scope to be a TV academic beyond the occasional archaeologist, astronomer or *Brains Trust* participant, and few opportunities to be a regular newspaper columnist—certainly not in the way there is now. The ubiquitous celebrity columnist was yet to appear, and most people writing comment pieces in newspapers were career journalists writing editorials or regular columns, or people who had managed to straddle press and parliament, such as Tom Driberg. For an academic looking for places to write for a *PQ*-like audience—more on what this means later—and beyond the strictures of the formal journals, there were the *Spectator* and the 'Staggers and Naggers', or reviewing for dailies and other weeklies like the *Listener*, but few other opportunities for somebody like Bernard to fire off ideas at a few thousand words in length and get them out in the world within a reasonable time.

So there is a limited case for saying that at first *PQ* served Bernard's purpose in giving him better access to a wider public for what was often his more strident writing. (*PQ* has no problem with intelligent polemic provided it is well argued and clearly written.) An added benefit of his editorial stint was that he was able to produce the shorter and more topical Commentaries, some of which are in this collection, as well as contribute articles.

But this still only gets us so far. First, had the journal been no more than an exploitable resource during a time when Bernard was building a career in political studies and a reputation in the wider political world, he could simply have abandoned it when it had served its purpose. Long though his editorial term was, its end in 1980 would have provided a natural point to leave the journal behind completely by dropping off the board, as his predecessor Tom McKitterick had done. The major landmarks of his career were already established by then, with the Orwell biography newly published and Bernard in the midst of his second professorship.

Second, it was entirely his own decision to stand down as coeditor when he did at the age of 50—the journal then and even now not stipulating any limit to an editorial term. (See Table 1 for the main dates linking Bernard Crick and *PQ*.) If he'd become editor simply to publish articles at will and to have a free quarterly 'column' in the form of Commentaries, then he could have stayed put indefinitely, or at least until the board called time. In fact, the evidence suggests the contrary: he didn't increase his contributions to the journal during his time as editor. He wrote eight or nine articles between 1966 and 1980, two of them shorter Reports and Surveys pieces, which works out at one every couple of years—hardly greedy and opportunistic. And his reviewing fell away sharply too, no doubt constrained by the demands of his new role at Birkbeck and his work on the Orwell project through the 1970s. He had already written a dozen reviews in the 1960s up to the point at which he becomes editor, but he only contributes seven more from 1966 through the 1970s, and after that no more until 1983. Again, this hardly adds up to using the journal as a convenient mouthpiece. Only the Commentaries represent an extra outlet, which Bernard was able to use more freely after the mid-1970s when Robson had retired. Yet even here all is not what it seems: if anything, many of the Commentaries in this collection are where Bernard is at his most restrained compared to the articles and reviews. In spite of his protracted fight to be able to author his own Commentaries (see below), it's as though he feels he is speaking on behalf of the journal, and he reins himself in a little.

Far from following McKitterick and leaving the board when he stood down as editor, Bernard took on in turn two other important roles on for the next 20

Table 1: Bernard Crick (BRC) and *The Political Quarterly*: some key dates

	BRC and *PQ* events	BRC and other events
1957–9	First review for *PQ* (1957); in 1958 Leonard Woolf retires as coeditor and is replaced by Tom McKitterick	LSE lectureships, starting as assistant lecturer; publishes *The American Science of Politics*, 1959
1960–4	First article for *PQ*	Publishes *In Defence of Politics*, 1962; *The Reform of Parliament*, 1964
1965		Appointed to Chair of new politics department at University of Sheffield
1966	Joins *PQ* editorial board (January); McKitterick retires; BRC appointed coeditor alongside founding editor William Robson (November)	
1971–3		Becomes Professor of Politics (1971) in new politics department at Birkbeck; begins work on Orwell biography
1975	Robson retires from the editorship (dies 1980); BRC's new coeditor is John Mackintosh MP	
1978	Mackintosh dies; BRC's next coeditor is David Watt	
1980	BRC retires as coeditor and is replaced by Rudolf Klein	Publishes *George Orwell: A Life*, 1980
1981	Becomes Chair of the *PQ* editorial board	
1984		Retires from Birkbeck Chair and moves to Edinburgh
1985	As Chair, oversees shift of *PQ* publisher from Thomson to Blackwell	
1993	Stands down as Chair of *PQ* board; becomes Literary Editor and thus exchanges roles with new Chair James Cornford	Sets up present version of Orwell Prize
1998	Proposes and begins *Seventy Serious Years*, a history of *PQ* (never finished)	Begins involvement with David Blunkett and the Blair governments, and work on citizenship
2000	Stands down as Literary Editor and is replaced by Donald Sassoon; leaves *PQ* board after 34 years	
2006		Stands down as director of the Orwell Prize and is replaced by Jean Seaton
2008	Final articles and reviews for *PQ*; dies December	

Note: the dates of *PQ* roles are sometimes imprecise because there can be several months between an original decision or announcement of a change—for example, in meeting minutes or correspondence, or on the journal cover—and the start or end of work in the role.

years, and remained part of the *PQ* family for the rest of his life. This can only be because the flourishing of the journal itself was important to him for more than just selfish reasons. There are at least three aspects to this: the importance and suitability of the journal as a vehicle for the Crickian enterprise of defending politics, Bernard's strong belief in the value of high-quality political writing—paralleling the Orwellian project of trying to make political writing into an art—and from 1993 *PQ*'s all-important sponsorship of his new-format Orwell prize, which was dear to his heart and linked back to his Orwell biography and the founding of the Orwell Trust.

This belief in the journal worked both ways, as he gave a great deal back to it. At the very least his intelligence, flair and energy helped to modernise and revitalise it, and there is a good case for saying that at a critical phase in its evolution he helped to save it from two possible threats, either of which could have been terminal. One was to drift towards becoming a conventional academic journal like so many others, a forum for insiders only; the other would have been to stagnate in the face of a changing political, cultural and media environment some decades on from the founding, to end as a kind of quarterly and politicised *Listener*, fighting the good fight but fading into genteel obscurity as its subscribers died out. Without going as far as making the strong claim that without Bernard there would be no *PQ* today—perhaps other figures could have emerged when the founders moved on—his contribution was exceptional. His importance to *PQ* is second only to that of Willie Robson himself, and if we set on one side the latter's status as founder then Bernard has a strong claim to be of equal importance.

In the confined space of this Introduction my aim is to provide a context for this collection of Bernard Crick's involvement with *The Political Quarterly* as coeditor, Chair and of course author, and perhaps in the process to throw a little more light on the apparent contradiction I mentioned—of 'selfish' Bernard's long association with a journal that had become something of an institution even by the 1960s. It is not a biography of the author or a history of the journal, both of which I provisionally set aside for another time; nor can it include a theme by theme gloss of the very large number of subjects he covered during the 52-year span of this collection. I assume that most readers will leap fearlessly into this collection and see what Bernard has to say first hand. After all, he does have a great deal to say. However, it's worth looking in more detail at the way he conducted himself in his rapid rise through the journal's ranks, and at how his prowess as writer and thinker fed back into the journal's fortunes.

From Robson to Crick

The 'promising young man' becomes coeditor

The journal that Bernard Crick joined as coeditor was in nearly all respects unchanged from that of its founding years three and a half decades earlier.

Something of how its founders saw the original project can be found in Bernard's *Seventy Serious Years* fragment in this collection. Its function as a vehicle for political ideas and debate was endlessly discussed by the founding group, and as soon as it was up and running the 1930s provided a ready-made and volatile period through which it could display its credentials. Yet its wider character, beyond the core elements of its political mission and insistence on clear writing and argument, is less evident from those discussions.

The journal had something of a hybrid soul. While clearly a vehicle for political ideas and the discussion of public policy, it also had some 'literary' overtones as a quarterly and at the same time a journalistic approach to its editorial policy. Shaw's teasing of the founders, in the story told and refined by Robson and then retold by Crick in *Seventy Serious Years*, does have some justification. It was perhaps incongruous for young 'Fabians' (as Shaw saw the founders, and many of them were) to choose to express themselves through a quarterly, a form that was already something of a throwback to earlier times and if not managed well could have risked the journal spiralling off into a self-conscious literary gentility—stylish but politically impotent. In the event it didn't go far down that road; perhaps the presence of Leonard Woolf, initially associated with the founding group and then very soon as coeditor, suggests the journal would start life with its head in clouds of Bloomsburyite incense smoke, but that wasn't the case, and if it had a base at all then the LSE had the strongest claim to be it. Where the journal did adopt a consciously elitist stance it was not in an aesthetic direction but linked to its expressed aims to take political ideas into the wider public view. Besides, Woolf's work was to one side of the literary Bloomsbury, and what he brought to the journal apart from his everyday work as coeditor would have been his status as a public figure—far better known at the time than Robson—and also his publishing experience. The other aspect that saved *PQ* from sliding back into Edwardian gentility right at the start was not just the editorial policy, requiring that authors write clearly and without jargon, but also the robust and often journalistic approach to the editing. The editors behaved like subs on a newspaper, awarding themselves an unrestricted licence to recast and rework any material that came their way, however exalted the author. This created a rather authoritarian editorial style and potentially a high degree of intervention, certainly when compared to what is common in journals now. I shouldn't overstate this because it wouldn't have seemed very unusual at the time, but it does show the editors as entirely confident in their ability to know what was best in terms of clarity and style; it also created implications for the editorial process and a high workload that would eventually lead to friction and change in Bernard's time.

PQ's editorship had remained substantially unchanged throughout the journal's first thirty years. The first coeditors, William Robson and Kingsley Martin, oversaw a handful of issues but Martin soon stood down in 1931 to concentrate on his other work, including of course the *New Statesman*. He was involved in the founding and remained on the journal board throughout his life, contributing articles in the 1930s and 40s, and Bernard awards him moderately large text in the visual pecking order on his cover of *Seventy Serious Years* (see below). But Martin barely mentions *PQ* at all in his volumes of autobiography, and his biographer C. M. Rolph says equally little, so while he supported the journal it certainly wasn't a priority for him. Leonard Woolf immediately took his place, and these two, Robson and Woolf, were to continue as coeditors from 1931 until 1958, when Woolf stood down. By the time Bernard became coeditor in 1966 Robson was still there, having served continuously as the editor of the journal he helped to found except for his withdrawal into various Whitehall roles during the war years, finishing as Secretary to the Air Ministry.[e] Perhaps it was there that Willie Robson developed the taste for his trademark green ink.

A tradition of coeditorship was established from the beginning and continues to this day with at least one of the editors normally an academic—although not an academic journal *PQ* runs under watchful academic eyes—though by Bernard's accession Robson was an emeritus professor, having retired from LSE in 1962. In his detailed reply to Bernard's strong criticisms during the editorial rift in the 1970s that preceded his resignation, Robson summarised the coeditorship thus:

From the beginning the Board has always wanted there to be two joint editors. This has many advantages. It widens the scope of knowledge and ideas available to the editors; it provides continuity in the case of absence abroad (a frequent occurrence with academics), illness etc. Above all it affords a surer judgement of the quality of articles and contributors than a single editor might possess.

It was still squarely the *PQ* of Robson and Woolf that published Bernard's first contributions to the journal—initially a handful of reviews—but by the time of his first full *PQ* article in 1960 (Article 1 in this volume), Leonard Woolf had retired to become the journal's first Literary Editor, a position he held from 1958 to 1962; this originally bespoke and somewhat grand title for the journal's reviews editorship would remain in place for all later incumbents. Woolf was replaced as coeditor by the Fabian ex-MP and international specialist Tom McKitterick.

During the next few years Bernard increased his contribution rate to *PQ* considerably, with four articles and 16 reviews in the journal by the mid-1960s. But by this time Tom McKitterick was finding the role of *PQ* coeditor onerous and he would soon stand down. As an indicator of things to come he recommended very strongly to the board that the journal should appoint an assistant editor to ease some of the editorial workload, but this fell on deaf ears. This factor would become progressively more important as the sixties wore on, with the labour-intensive editorial methods essentially the same in 1965 as they had been in 1930. Although the coeditors finally shed direct

---

[e] In *A Bibliography of the Writings of W. A. Robson*, LSE Greater London Paper No. 17, 1986, compiler Clive Hill gives the period as October 1940 to July 1946; see pp. 11, 15.

responsibility for reviews when Woolf moved across in 1958, with these now handled by Richard Greaves—Woolf's successor as Literary Editor—the job of *PQ* coeditor remained decidedly laborious. Both editors had to be 'hands on' at all stages from author to reader—commissioning and reviewing the articles and other contributions, writing the editorial matter, and undertaking the general publishing supervision as well as all the copy-editing, a role that both Leonard Woolf and Willie Robson performed with great—some might say excessive—diligence. They read the proofs too. There was no editorial support of the kind familiar in journals publishing today. Robson was strongly in favour of this approach throughout his tenure and was dismayed by its erosion after he stood down: 'he was quite distressed to discover that Mackintosh and I had farmed out the proof-reading', Bernard noted in his 1980 Commentary marking Robson's death.

By the middle of 1966 McKitterick had had enough. He tendered his resignation as coeditor and also left the board, pleading the demands of his other work as his public reason for standing down but confiding in a letter to Leonard Woolf that the real reason was the deterioration in his working relationship with Willie Robson. He said he had always found the editorial partnership difficult but felt it had now become unworkable in the space of a few months. In his reply Woolf very delicately but firmly agreed.

In the autumn of 1966 Robson and the board had to find a new editor and Bernard Crick rapidly became the favourite for the job. Now newly installed as professor at Sheffield and still only 36, Bernard had been on the *PQ* board since January. He was of course known to Robson at least from his LSE days, also sending him an inscribed copy of his *American Science of Politics* in July 1959. (Robson replied to thank him in a short, typed note signed—and at one point self-corrected—in his favoured green ink.[f]) Bernard's age and energy were prime attractions, potentially vital inputs to a journal that was strong on continuity and 'mission' but drifting into a real danger of stagnation under a founding editor who had first taken on the role 36 years earlier.[g] In many respects, Robson had become *PQ*'s very own John Reith, towering over the journal as an internal driving force and tireless advocate of its cause, and at the same time as closely identified with his creature as was Reith with the BBC. To his credit, and in spite of an apparent reluctance to step aside himself, Robson remained forward-looking and was well aware of the value of new blood. In a letter written to Leonard Woolf in September 1966 and copied to the journal board he recommends Bernard as 'the best possible choice' and 'younger than any recent Editor', and in his opinion 'one of the ablest political scientists in this country and full of energy and creative ability'. He had

[f] I needed to buy a copy of the scarce *American Science of Politics* to use when writing this Introduction. I found only one rather expensive copy via the internet in a bookshop in Scotland, so I bought that. Remarkably, it turned out to be Bernard's own copy, with materials slipped inside its covers including congratulatory letters from Robson (with green ink), Elie Kedourie and others.

[g] It was never lost on Bernard that he and *PQ* were of the same age.

already sounded out Bernard about the possibility (in a handwritten letter in green ink), who replied on 8 September:

I've given the matter much anxious thought and have come to the conclusion that I cannot refuse to take up such an important task. This may sound peculiar to put it backwards in the rather Irish way, but I don't underestimate the responsibility and the amount of work involved. But my respect for the journal and your judgement is such, that if you are sure, then I am very willing to be your nominee and drop things elsewhere so that I will have time to give to the journal.

Nothing has delighted me so much for years, not even my chair; PQ seems to bring all my interests together. But I quite understand of course, that the appointment is by no means automatic. . . .

Almost all of the board agreed with the recommendation. 'I would agree to the appointment of Crick. I am sure you know best', Woolf had said rather enigmatically in a brief reply to Robson's letter. Typical comments from other board members included 'Bernard Crick would be absolutely first rate' and 'happy that you want Bernard Crick'. Another on the board remarks that 'What is particularly important for the Quarterly is Crick's abounding energy and resourcefulness'. This recognised the need for somebody who could not only continue Robson's grand project but bring new life to a journal that risked settling into a rut if the editorship were renewed on a 'more of the same' basis. He adds 'Most important of all, however, is that fact that you are happy to have him as joint editor'.

The support was therefore strong; but it was not unanimous. There was a note of caution in another board member's reply, who though generally enthusiastic and hopes 'that it may even produce an improvement which we can—I am pretty sure you agree—well afford', feels he should add his one concern that 'I do wish he could learn to discipline his style'. And there was one very strong objection from a board member who instead recommended David Marquand—who would become a coeditor but not for another 21 years—strongly counselling against the appointment of Bernard Crick and threatening resignation if he became editor:

I agree that he is able and intelligent and that he writes in a lively style, but in my opinion he lacks judgement and he is often personally extremely offensive. . . . I feel sure that if the Political Quarterly is placed in the hands of Crick there is a real danger that [it] becomes a vehicle for the pursuit of whatever particular cause he has embraced.

Two months later, following Bernard's appointment as coeditor at a board meeting in November 1966, the dissenter duly sent Robson his letter of resignation in protest at this 'profound mistake', in evidence also citing Bernard's *New Statesman* article of that week, a piece that in his opinion 'glaringly displays all the faults of judgement and all the personal qualities that I think are so much wanting in Crick'. But the deed was done; and with hindsight, far from it being a profound mistake, Bernard's editorship and other subsequent roles on the journal may well have helped to save it.

The journal now embarked on a period of joint editorship by William Robson and Bernard Crick that survived until Robson's retirement in 1975. By then Robson had served as an editor and been the dominant force on the journal for the best part of 45 years, with the exception of his war service; it was only as the 1970s progressed that the grip of *PQ*'s Reith over all things was finally loosened by the increasingly powerful presence of his new coeditor.

There was steady innovation during the period, not least in the content of the journal itself. Meeting minutes and *PQ* correspondence of the period show Bernard suggesting new ideas for themed and special issues of the journal. Into the 1970s there are other ideas—a new prize for political writing, a concern for the importance of effective promotion and PR, and in 1979 the publication of the journal's first general index. This last publication listed all main articles and some other material from 1930 to 1978. It was compiled by Julian Singer—'Under the Guidance of Bernard Crick', proclaims the title page ominously—and included both an article and an author index in a rather idiosyncratic form. At an editorial board meeting in July 1978 the project had been envisaged as something that would 'provide substantial revenue at a modest investment'. 'Substantial revenue' was decidedly optimistic: by commercial standards it was overproduced in quality terms—as a hardback on good quality paper—and quantity—not just with a bullish first print run, but with an additional run-on that could be bound up later in the event of a fondly imagined future demand. But as the first index covering the whole run of *PQ* to that date it was a welcome addition. In the General Manager's report to the editorial board of 14 October 1980, sales of the index are even held to be largely responsible for the (very modest) profit predicted for that year, though the following years would show holdings of unsold stock and it probably never sold out. The profit concern was real enough: for much of its existence, the journal had bumped along just above or below the break-even point, and it was not until Bernard oversaw a change of publishing partner in 1985 that *PQ* was established on more comfortable financial foundations.

Bernard was keen to make more of the journal and expand its influence. Although the everyday aspects of editing remained largely as before for the rest of the 1960s, dominated by Robson's hands-on approach and control, *PQ* entered a much noisier phase under the guidance of the brash new coeditor. There were new collaborations with book publishers, especially with Penguin, Bernard's publisher for *In Defence of Politics*, and an increase in the number of *PQ*-organised or *PQ*-sponsored events that could yield a special issued or a themed set of papers. This began a tradition that continues today, and includes the annual book issues that began in 1989 during Bernard's stint as Chair.

Bernard believed that *PQ* and its project were interesting in their own right and needed celebrating, and his editorship marks the start of a tradition of retrospective articles, themed collections and books at anniversaries and other suitable points—yet another tradition that continues. As I mentioned in the

Preface, the two Penguins *The Future of the Social Services* and *Protest and Discontent* appeared during the year as part of the festivities. Two other less welcome markers of the passage of time were the deaths in 1969 of Kingsley Martin, briefly William Robson's first coeditor, and later in the year of Robson's principal editorial partner Leonard Woolf. As one of his celebratory projects Bernard had proposed a collection of *PQ* content from the 1930s, to be jointly selected and edited by Robson and Woolf. Events overtook this collection, which was published by Allen Lane as *The Political Quarterly in the Thirties* in 1971, but it was edited by Robson alone as Woolf died before it got under way.

The first journal issue of 1970 was Bernard's first real opportunity to write something of his own to celebrate a *PQ* milestone, in this case the journal's fortieth anniversary, to which he responded with the lead article 'The 1970s in Retrospect' (Article 7 in this collection). This jokey 'look back' at the 1970s is written from the imagined vantage point of the end of the decade and a more high-tech future. The article runs the gamut of Bernardian tropes likely both to appeal to his admirers—sharp observation, wit and style—and to bait his detractors—self-indulgence, and the schoolboy humour of some of the acronyms (RAPE, DIM). No doubt it raised a Robsonian eyebrow behind the scenes and confirmed the worst fears of the resigned board critic if he was still reading the journal. As the only sustained and deliberately comic piece in this whole collection, it doesn't quite work—even as something intended to amuse rather than offer an effective satire or angst-ridden 'The Machine Stops' dystopian view of the future. Yet in its view of imagined future technologies it is surprising prescient in places.

At the time of this article Bernard still had another decade to serve as coeditor, but as the 1970s progressed there were now definite strains between Robson and Crick, the chalk and cheese of coeditors, and eventually— inevitably—large cracks appeared and the relationship broke down. When Tom McKitterick resigned in 1966 Willie Robson had recommended Bernard as somebody he could work with, which he clearly believed, and the board accepted this view. But subsequent events and surviving documents show that whether or not Robson was content with the arrangement, now that Bernard was fully settled into the role he was finding it hugely difficult to carry on playing second fiddle and being reined in by his senior partner. For as long as this grand founding figure remained as coeditor it was still Robson's *PQ*, whether or not he was completely aware of the extent of his own domination of the journal's editorial policy and wider activities.

A shift of power

Things came to a head in 1973–74, by which time Bernard was well into his new professorship at Birkbeck and was also beginning work on the Orwell biography that would occupy him for the rest of the decade. It was a busy time for him, during which his reviews for *PQ* all but dried up and he produced few other articles for the journal. His patience, or forbearance, finally snapped, and on 10 December 1973 he sent a disgruntled letter to Robson that raised various dissatisfactions, especially about his role as coeditor and the direction of the journal. There would also be strong disagreements with the reviews policy and Literary Editorship, which I'll return to in the Reviews and Reviewing section below. His complaints initiated a series of tetchy exchanges by letter, together with a number of unrecorded face to face meetings, that would carry on into the new year and culminated in Bernard producing a long memorandum outlining his position and demanding changes if he was to remain in the editorial chair. Seemingly surprised by the turn of events, Robson matched this with a memorandum of his own in reply.

Bernard was now clearly thinking very carefully about the allocation of his time: in his first letter of 10 December he begins by postponing an appointment for later that day, pointing out that 'It is the one day that I set aside for my Orwell work', adding that 'my department is very demanding' and 'I try rather desperately to preserve weekends for my sons and family'. This opening salvo appears to be a reminder to the long-retired Robson that, for Crick, the journal was one among many pressing demands on his time.

The series of letters, self-typed and much corrected, were sent on *PQ*'s headed notepaper. It seems likely that the two also met around the turn of the year—a meeting that was unlikely to be harmonious. In a letter of 19 December Bernard writes 'As our next meeting will be a difficult one, I would rather meet after Christmas and not at your home, where I am always at a disadvantage in speaking my mind freely.' This was followed by another of 28 December clarifying some points, and an even longer one of 25 January 1974 that again revisited the earlier points but added new ones. Robson had replied to the early ones straight away, and then later to summarise his position on 23 February.

The differences between the two men's views were not just about the journal content; the evidence of the letter exchanges of 1973–4 is that they were about editorial policy and procedure too, as well as strongly personal in places. The core of the problem, and probably the trigger for the disputes, was the working of the coeditorship. Bernard was no longer prepared to be the *de facto* junior partner. He wanted both more editorial independence and the freedom to write more of his own content in the Commentaries than his coeditor could countenance, as he pointed out in his first letter:

You must realise, William, that in being, as people are kind enough to say, a good and loyal joint editor, I have to restrain or divert what would otherwise be energy in perhaps rather different directions. . . . we should . . . seek a wider readership, otherwise we are getting pushed back and back into political science . . . rather than left wing politics; and I would like to [be] able regularly to write commentary on the quarter's affairs in a much more personal and polemical tone than you would accept as editorials. Evidently I'm too young to be fully trusted, but I'm certainly too old to [be] happy just jogging along with the old formula.

15

In the letter of 19 December he is even more direct and his tone is full of irritation:

In several ways recently my subordinate position in this journal has been made so apparent, that my mind is quite clearly that I either want a greater independence of action, including complete responsibility for half the issues including the editorials without consultation (as you did on the China issue),[h] or a clear date when you will become chairman of the board, but to leave me as full editor, perhaps then with a more active board . . . I am not willing to continue giving so much of my time in my best years for something over which I have so little control. Otherwise I must give up the editorship, but would remain on the board . . .

This second and fiercest of the December letters seems to have been triggered by a Robson-approved article being queue-jumped by its patron without consultation, ahead of pieces by 'younger' authors that Bernard had been dealing with—authors 'who deal through me rather than directly with the "real editor"', he adds in irritation—before complaining about the unequal nature of decision-taking compared with the actual workload. He finishes by pointing out that he has served his apprenticeship, adding that he is 'now owed some of the thanks, respect and trust that I have given you'.

It appears that the two men had already discussed the succession, with the idea already mooted in principle that Robson—who was by now approaching his 80th birthday—would stand down as coeditor to chair the board instead, but Bernard has lost patience with this by his letter of 28 December, which he starts by saying 'Perhaps I imagined that you would want to retire from being joint editor to being chairman of the board'. It's also interesting to note that although in his letter of the 19th Bernard is prepared to give up the coeditorship if things don't go his way, he is not threatening to march out of *PQ* altogether. Just 'walking away' does appear to have been something of a Bernard speciality: Audrey Coppard says he was a man who would storm out of rooms—meaning that if he wanted to finish with something (or somebody) he would often simply walk away from it completely and leave others to clear up the mess. Some of Bernard's past collaborators would know this, and Audrey more than most.

By 28 December Bernard writes again with slightly less irritation, apologising for his 'temper or rudeness over meeting', which had obviously taken place by then, and suggesting that they still can work together with surprisingly few differences and irritations considering they 'are both rather firm characters'. At this point a new editor is definitely under active discussion, with the Labour MP John Mackintosh a prime candidate and indeed the eventual successor to Robson. Bernard also suggests, rather unrealistically and against the run of the other reasoning, that the two of them could take back the responsibility for reviews themselves—something

[h] The 'China issue' is the first one of 1974 and would be reprinted as the Sage volume *China in Transition*, as I mention in the Preface. There is nothing of Bernard in it, which is not surprising, but it seems from this comment that he wasn't even consulted about it, which is surprising.

that didn't happen and would not have been wise. *PQ* still retains its separate Literary Editor.

A later letter of the series from 25 January 1974 is longer and more considered. This time it appears to have been professionally typed for him, and is also copied to the Literary Editor Richard Greaves, but it is still strong in its demands. Bernard picks up his themes again—he wants a lot more responsibility, a discussion of editorial policy and scope to find ways of reaching a wide readership and avoiding an academic narrowing. There is also more about the poverty of the reviews section (hence the inclusion of Greaves in the correspondence), and further discussion of the succession to include Rudolf Klein as well as John Mackintosh as potential future editors. He also asks Robson not to stand down before the summer of 1975, mainly because of Mackintosh's unavailability before then, which is how the timing eventually worked out. He reiterates his claim for more independence as coeditor, admitting to his 'irritation and impatience' at the status quo and pointing out again that he has 'served his apprenticeship'. He also offers himself as a conduit to new kinds of writing and younger authors:

I feel that I can fairly claim to have a very wide range of acquaintance both in university and public life, in London and outside, perhaps to be more in touch than any of us with new writers and tendencies, and generally feel that I shouldn't have to make a special case every time my two editorial colleagues [Robson and Greaves] haven't heard of someone.

Another theme Bernard introduces for the first time at this point is that he has not written much for *PQ* since his coeditorship began: 'I admit to feeling unhappy that most of my best writing over the last three years has gone elsewhere . . .', he says. This dip in Bernard's submissions is evident from the contents list of this collection, and I revisit it below when talking about Bernard as reviewer and Literary Editor. Robson politely rejected many of Bernard's concerns in a reply dated 23 February, insisting in particular that the principles of the joint editorship were 'absolutely essential' and, as central to his concerns about Bernard's intentions, that '*PQ* is a forum rather than a vehicle for the personal views of the editors, except in their own contributions'.

However, he was sympathetic to Bernard's lament about writing for the journal: 'I certainly think you should write more in the PQ than you have in the past', and agreed to another of his ideas: 'I would like to try out your suggestion for a Commentary on several themes, signed or initialled by you', provided that this still left room for unsigned editorials if required. Bernard had asked for this expressly in his letter of 25 January:

I would like to write regular 'Comments' in the editorial space—this was done in the past: it hasn't always been a joint long piece or nothing. To be always more than one theme, sometimes several: a mixture of the fully serious and some slightly lighter— examples of notable follies as well as problems. These could be initialled.

17

Hence one side-effect of this serious editorial dispute was the appearance of initialled Commentaries written by individual editors—in the event a transient change but one that has made it possible to include the examples of Bernard's Commentaries in this collection, even if many of them are fairly restrained pieces of writing by his standards.

Memorandum wars, 1973–4, and the passing of the crown

The Robson–Crick correspondence of 1973–4 displayed the elements of the growing dispute between the two that rumbled on into the first half of 1974 and presaged Robson's departure as coeditor, but the dispute found its more explicit and rehearsed voice in the two draft memorandums, one from each man. Both of these are undated and it's difficult to know how far they were circulated to others at *PQ*, yet each is written to appeal to third parties who must have been *PQ* insiders. If in the end they didn't reach everybody else on the board, it is clear that it was originally intended that they should. As for the dates, Robson's 'Memorandum on the Editorial Control and Policy of Political Quarterly' seems to be from the first quarter or so of 1974 judging from its opening sentence:

Until a few months ago I had reason to believe that the collaboration of the joint editors had been satisfactory to both of them. In December 1973, however, I received two letters from Crick expressing great dissatisfaction with the existing arrangements and making proposals which appeared to be not in the interests of the Political Quarterly.

Later on it mentions 'Crick's memorandum', showing that the latter had already appeared and that Robson's memorandum was to a certain extent a reply to it. For its part, Bernard's 'Memorandum on Policy and Development of Political Quarterly' has few clues to its date beyond the opening sentence, 'Having been joint editor now for over seven years . . .', putting it as expected in late 1973 or early 1974.

They are both neatly typed, double spaced and error free, which suggests at least in Bernard's case that they were produced by a typist for circulation, presumably to the *PQ* board. This is reinforced in the case of Bernard's memorandum as he adds at one point 'I have side-scored matters in which I want the Board's guidance or decision'; but even so it's not clear whether they were ever sent in full to the whole board for discussion, or just remained as draft green papers that were overtaken by events. It's probable that they were seen by selected board members for private comment, though.

Bernard's memorandum that so exercised Robson runs to seven pages and lays down a sharp, wide-ranging critique of *PQ*'s general policy, editorial arrangements and content. He summarises his grievances and requests for change under several main areas: the working of the joint editorship; that *PQ*'s content was becoming too narrow in subject matter, authorship and readership; a need to expand the circulation; a more 'committed editorial line' ('middle of the radical road' and 'a truculent and rather noisy moderation', or the centre of the then Labour party), and a change to editorial policy to allow each coeditor to commission two articles per issue without consulting the other. Later he also wades into the 'literary section' (the reviews), about which Bernard had long held strong views, attacking both the Literary Editor and the reviews ('some of the reviews are appalling; pointless academic writing at its worst').

It's not possible to say precisely how far Bernard's challenging letters and memorandum of 1973–4 were simply disinterestedly offered as vital for the future of *PQ*, and how much was just a petulant overflowing of frustration or the laying down of bargaining counters—or even just a determination to break things for the sake of provoking any kind of change as better than doing nothing. I think there was something of each of these in what he did. There was an element of conscious politicking that was intended to bring about change, and part of that change was a desire to make the editorial role a fitting use of his own time. The frustration of being left out of decision making, as for the China collection, or irritation at the 'queue jumping' of Robson-approved pet projects, may have been the immediate triggers during a period of high workload and other pressures, but the dispute had probably been simmering for some time on Bernard's side.

On the other hand, the two men had worked together as coeditors for more than seven years by this time, with Robson the first among equals and Bernard apparently tolerating the arrangement. This gives the lie to the simple idea that 'Bad Bernard' was so obsessively selfish that he was impossible to work with in any collective context unless he always got his way. Also, the evidence of the succeeding years suggests Bernard was genuinely concerned for the journal and that it should have a healthy future as a platform for intelligent debate and the exchange of ideas in politics, considered broadly. This fatal breakdown in coeditorial harmony may have reflected an 'end of tether' moment in Bernard's position, but it doesn't look like a foot-stamping Crickian tantrum simply designed to get him his own way.

Robson's memorandum in reply was shorter and he mainly confined himself to responding point by point. It's evident right from the surprised tone of the opening sentence quoted above that he is genuinely shocked by the whole episode of the letters and memorandum, and there are clues—such as the use of the unadorned 'Crick', even making due allowance for the impersonal conventions of the time, without 'Professor' or even the 'Bernard' that would have been appropriate after such a long acquaintance—that he was hurt, annoyed or both. His response throughout is clear and shot through with wounded dignity, but his tone is as pointed as his critic's:

These proposals were so unacceptable to me that I wrote to Crick on 22 December saying that I would resign at a convenient date in 1974, meaning by that as soon as someone could be appointed to take my place. Crick replied that 'it would be very bad for the journal' if I were to resign this year. . . . I agreed to continue if we could agree on general policies but Crick's memorandum appears to show that this cannot be achieved.

He then immediately raises the tradition and benefits of the joint editorship, observing that it 'has always been the practice in the past but Crick now finds it burdensome and irritating' and claiming that Bernard's demand for editorial independence is 'incompatible with the concept and practice of joint editorship'. He objects to most of Bernard's requests for change here, such as the idea of each coeditor commissioning two articles per issue without consultation or one editor being able to have sole responsibility for an issue, on the grounds that these changes would risk overlap, inconsistency, and eventually loss of identity for the journal.

The rest of the memorandum is concerned with Bernard's suggestion of a Reports and Surveys editor—which he opposes as unnecessary as well as adding a fourth editor, though the post would eventually be created many years later—and a strong rejection of claims about narrowing of content. In his memorandum Bernard had said 'we give too much emphasis to institutional reform', which was a barbed implication that the journal content was heavily linked to Robson's own areas of interest and expertise. Even if this was as important an area as people had thought, which Bernard was beginning to doubt,

now there are so many other journals in these fields: *Public Policy*, *Policy and Politics*, *Public Administration* and *Parliamentary Affairs*. I think we should carry more matter on politics interesting to general intellectuals, raising more often issues of social justice, fairness, what is fashionable to call 'qualitative issues', less on institutional reform.

Robson rejected this outright: '[PQ] has at no time concentrated on institutional reforms but has always been glad to publish articles on political issues, international issues, social affairs, etc.', listing his China collection and Bernard's own 'Protest and Discontent' issue as counterexamples. He finished by reiterating the importance of the joint editorship and, pointedly, that the journal 'should not express the persona of a particular editor, who publicises the periodical and himself'.

It's unlikely that Robson's defence of the journal's content would have satisfied Bernard, who wanted more 'general essays on political directions and problems' and to 'tempt out the more literate of the New Left . . . both to get the more rational of them out of the sects and coverns [sic] and to inform our readers'. He also wanted to expand the content to attract 'general intellectuals', such as the political themes and biases of contemporary literature and theatre', displaying his own interests at the time by offering some of his *THES* theatre pieces.

Whatever the circulation of these documents and the precise timing of their delivery—and there's no real trace in the meeting minutes of the time—they mark a tipping point for *PQ* between old and new as the crown passed from one powerful personality to another and the journal entered a new phase. The disagreements and tensions were only finally defused—or at least redirected—when Robson confirmed that he would be standing down the following year. From that point, sometime in May 1974, their discussion shifted back to the talk of who would become Bernard's new coeditor.

Bernard eventually did place a memorandum before the board in May 1974 but it was a tame thing by comparison with the earlier one. The 'Memorandum to the Board on Literary Policy' is much reduced in scope and covers only one point of the original dispute—his old bugbear of the content and management of the review pages—though he first sets out his view of *PQ* editorial policy at the start. The charges against the reviews (the 'Literary Section') were that they were of too narrow a range of books—professional academic politics and contemporary history—written by a too small band of LSE based reviewers, and that they were going through largely unedited, which set them in unwelcome contrast to the articles at the front of the journal. Looked at from a distance, these problems seem to be about the reviews editor having insufficient time to do more than passively accept whatever publishers submitted, send the copies out to one of a small band of reliable reviewers, and finally pass the reviews on for typesetting with minimal intervention. This is not an uncommon position for busy reviews editors of journals to be in. Bernard's implied critique of the Literary Editor really harks back to a highly interventionist Robsonian editorial strategy that would be unworkable on any major journal nowadays but was becoming unsustainable even then.

William Robson retired as joint editor in the summer of 1975 at the age of 80, with meeting minutes suggesting that issue 3 was his last, and became Chair of the editorial board. The new coeditor was John Mackintosh, whose tenure was destined to be short: he died in office in 1978 to be succeeded by the defence historian David Watt. Serving until 1985 Watt was to be Bernard Crick's final coeditorial partner on the journal. Bernard himself stood down at the end of the decade and was replaced by Rudolf Klein, his own recommendation as coeditor but not Robson's choice for the post.

This is not the place to talk at length about William Robson but it's important to say something about his status and position on the journal: to understand the importance of Crick to *PQ* it is first necessary to understand the importance of Robson. By present-day standards his 45 year stint as a journal editor is ludicrously long. The risks of such long tenure are obvious, though there's no reason to suppose that Robson stereotypically embodied all of these: first, there's a founder's drive and energy, sustaining and pushing forward the journal through those early stages; then there may be a tendency to stick with what has worked well so far and seek 'more of the same'; later there may be a growing inability to let go as newcomers and new tendencies threaten change; and then later still there is the possibility of stagnation or even decline if the world moves on but the journal does not. What's not uncommon with people who start journals and remain with them over a long time is an understandable desire for control to keep the original vision intact. But this can lead to a tendency to micromanage and intervene in everything: as time goes on it's easy to develop fears that anything you can't control will be wrong or not good enough for the journal, so you make sure that all channels come through you. The problem was probably even more acute for *PQ*, because regardless of intention the original *PQ* editorial process and workflow meant that all channels always did flow through the two coeditors.

By reputation a dry and punctilious man, Robson seems to have had an unshakeable confidence in his own judgement about the contents of the journal and its articles—his blue pencil, or green pen, always at the ready to correct transgressions. There may have a been a strong element of 'Après moi, le déluge' in his private thoughts about *PQ* as he came towards the end of his tenure, but it's more complex than that. Nor do the memorandums show a self-seeking young Bernard cynically making a move for increasing power, or that this was simply a 'battle of generations'—the cliché of a conservative old dinosaur resisting the new ideas of a young rival who alone can see what is needed. For his part, it's highly unlikely that Robson simply wanted to keep everything the same: he may have been in his 80th year, almost twice the age of his colleague, but was perfectly aware that the journal needed new blood to survive and that he would have to stand down soon regardless. At one point in his 1974 letter he tells Bernard 'we should invite some really good and active men [sic] of about your generation to join the Board—people who are likely to be able and willing to contribute both ideas and writing'.

But by placing himself at the intersection of all lines of decision and editorial intervention Robson became a bottleneck. One of the frequent criticisms of him was that he was slow—slow to decide, slow to deliver. When confiding in Leonard Woolf his reasons for standing down as coeditor in 1966, Tom McKitterick had said 'I would make time to do the job properly were it not that everything takes so long to decide and were it not that my enthusiasm for it has been largely eaten away'. This got a sympathetic ear from Woolf, whose brief reply acknowledged diplomatically and a little intriguingly that 'Willie is a difficult person to work with because of his slowness and, of course, other things'. This is also a valuable reminder that it was not just Bernard who could be difficult to work with.

The Reithian aspects of Robson's highly controlling approach and close identification with the journal may have prevented him from seeing some of the problems others had when working with him. He seemed genuinely surprised to find that others had difficulties, even in the rather obvious case of Bernard after several years of collaboration. He also appeared to be blissfully unaware of Leonard Woolf's view that 'Willie is a difficult person to work with', or his perceived slowness, or the 'other things' enigmatically intimated to Tom McKitterick. In his retrospective article 'The Founding of the Political Quarterly' in the first issue of *PQ* in 1970, Robson paints an entirely different picture: 'I worked with Leonard Woolf in complete harmony for the 23 years[i] of our association as joint editors. I can remember only one serious difference of opinion which arose over the abdication of Edward VIII.'

On this evidence, the two coeditorial tactics for working with Willie Robson appear to have been either diplomacy and quiet toleration (Woolf—who of course had impeccable credentials for dealing with difficult personal circumstances) or a strained tolerance leading to eventual withdrawal rather than confrontation (McKitterick). Neither of these approaches would be likely to appeal to Bernard, who was not a natural candidate for long-suffering silence. Yet he does seem to have shown a great deal of tolerance in the early years of his editorship; either that, or Robson was particularly thick skinned or too wrapped up in 'his' journal to be aware of the tensions. In the event Bernard did not just walk away, which is what the Crick of his obituarists might have been expected to do.

Not only did he not walk away from *PQ* and Willie Robson, in spite of this appearing likely at times during 1974, he actually saw the crisis through, albeit that it all worked out in his favour. He stayed on as coeditor to work with Robson in the chair for a further five years, then continued in two other roles until 2000. What Bernard said and did at *PQ*—episodes of local politicking aside—suggest that he genuinely cared about the journal and was prepared to put up with a lot to work with it; and that caring was more than just about having a vehicle for his own views in the way that his detractors (and perhaps at times Robson) feared. Bernard was willing to be identified with the journal as something bigger than himself, as well as caring about it for its own sake and to improve it. For example, in his draft memorandum of 1974 he had said as much while setting out the Robson–Crick problem as he saw it:

I have very much identified myself with the journal. I frankly enjoy both editorial work and the modest power and notoriety very much. But it is a big burden, particularly with so much need for joint consultation, never being able to say 'yes' only 'may be, if Robson likes it' etc.

Once Robson stood down, the endless consultation aspect of the 'big burden' went with him, but other aspects remained. The editorial workload—with the inevitable delays as all content queued in orderly procession through the editors—was a principal reason for McKitterick's resignation in 1966. It was only overcome by the progressive modernisation of the journal at Bernard's hands, slowly at first in the years immediately after Robson's retirement as editor but more rapidly after his death. By that time Bernard Crick had moved from coeditor to become Chair of the editorial board.

---

[i] The span is not as inaccurate as it seems because it allows for Robson's years out on war service.

Bernard in the Chair: managing change

After some 15 influential years as an editor of the journal, Bernard took on the first of his two subsequent roles, succeeding Robson as the Chair of the editorial board. Robson was effectively the first to make the role of Chair a named role rather than simply the person who agreed to chair board meetings on the day, but Bernard would regularise and strengthen the position still further after relinquishing his coeditorship. He saw himself as a natural successor, having just stepped down as editor with a wealth of understanding of the nature and the running of the journal. It was a good time to have an energetic person overseeing the journal's general direction and the company behind it. The world was a very different place from that of *PQ*'s first decades, with Robson now dead and a comparatively new editorial team in charge, but there was also a great deal of change afoot in the wider world of journal publishing.

Natural successor or not, the chairmanship was by no means an automatic shoe-in for him, and in Bernard's eyes there was at least one other candidate. On 23 September 1980 he typed a letter to 'Peter', the perceived rival, initially to talk about what *PQ* should do as a suitable memorial for the recently deceased William Robson. This was Peter Self, a *PQ* stalwart and originally another LSE man, who had been on the board even longer than Bernard and was then at the ANU in Canberra. The letter eventually strays on to *PQ* topics and the editorial succession, in the process revealing Bernard's support for a permanent Chair and his eagerness to fill it himself. He also knows this may produce nervousness in some quarters: that he would be 'too active', thus cramping the editors' style and also echoing the concerns raised in 1966 when he was proposed as editor. Yet although as Chair he did keep an eye on the editors of the day it would be his express policy to leave them entirely alone to determine the content of the journal—provided they didn't mind the occasional comment. Bernard's letter to Self is also an artful piece of politicking, politely deferring to his colleague's potential claim while at the same time making it clear that he alone was the natural choice.

A more delicate matter. David Watt and I are nominating Rudolf Klein, as you know, for joint editor of PQ. The chairmanship of the Board then comes up. David, myself and the Thomson [then *PQ*'s publisher] Manager all agree that there should be a chairman of the Board, if only to cope with meetings and succession crises. . . . David seems a little nervous that I mean more than that, and would be too active. I readily agreed with him that you, if approached by him and willing, would be readily acceptable by me, without rancour, as chairman. However, I do want to be chairman, after all those years, knowing the Thomson people and actually believing, as I grow older, that I wouldn't interfere with the editors, but be reasonably active on the promotion side. So I am going to be nominated, by James [Cornford] and Rudolf [Klein], even if you are too. But I want to say that I wont [sic] be in the least upset if you are put forward, you've been on the Board and known William far longer than I; and if the Board elects you, I'll put all my support and contacts your way. . . .

Peter Self wrote back from Canberra on 3 October with some ideas for the memorial and added a postscript on *PQ* matters, offering his support to Bernard as Chair:

I'm sorry as you know that you are retiring as editor—it will be a great loss to the journal although I'm sure that Rudolf will do it well. . . . As you are set on going I can well appreciate the value of keeping your experience and wisdom in play in the role of chairman even though the roles are different. I suspect it's none too easy for an active, innovative editor to become an elder statesman. . . .

This was Bernard's desired outcome. In any case, Peter Self would be more deeply established in Canberra by 1982 and could never have taken the role himself. The changes soon went through as planned. In a letter to the Thomson organisation of 14 October, Bernard confirmed the arrangements had been approved, with Rudolf Klein as the new coeditor and himself Chair. Then, rounding off the correspondence he replies to Peter Self on 20 October to pass on the same news and apologises in typically Crickian fashion for getting 'wires crossed' (and playfully crosses his metaphors too):

I think David Watt and I got our wires crossed. No approach was made to you, so I apologise for stirring up what must have seemed like a straw man in a mare's nest! Thank you very much for your kind word.

Rudolf Klein was elected unanimously as the new Joint Editor. . . . and I was elected as Chairman of the Board, that to be held on an annual but renewable basis.

In the same letter he also mentions that the board agreed to look at a suitable time scale for editorial appointments at a future meeting, 'so that they don't simply go on for ever by inertia'—an obvious reference to Willie Robson—though this if this ever happened it didn't result in any new policy. The newly consolidated position of Chair was an important one. As the founding generation withdrew or died, taking their tight controls and interventionist ways with them, it's not clear that any succession by gentle evolution would have been equal to new challenges. The position, though now a fixture, was relatively undefined in scope, and hence offered an opportunity for somebody free of editorial responsibilities to take a wider view. Bernard took the role seriously and presided over a period of evolution and modernisation that continued the kind of change he'd overseen towards the end of his coeditorship and helped to cement the future of the journal.

There were two main areas that needed particular attention. One was to do with editorial process and personnel—as we have seen, then a bottleneck for the main journal content but also causing problems with reports and reviews, leaving little time to do much more than put the journal together on a hand-to-mouth basis. In time this would mean putting more of the everyday editorial work, and not just the proofreading, out for others to work on rather than expect the editors to do this themselves. The journal would retain its coediting tradition and Literary Editor for reviews and in the years to come would eventually add a Reports and Surveys Editor to spread the load still further. As well as further administrative streamlining, another innovation was the appointment of Bernard's long term associate Audrey Coppard as Assistant Editor, given the title officially in 1989 though she'd been at *PQ* for many years before that. Still later came the hiring of Gillian Bromley (later Somerscales) in the 1990s as an editorial assistant; her main role was the copy-editing but she would take on a lot of the editorial administration too.

These innovations could not simply be introduced by fiat. In spite of the founding editors' beliefs in a fully hands-on approach, it wasn't dogged institutional conservatism that had allowed the old, slow methods to survive into the 1980s. The problem was that there was no reliable annual financial surplus that could pay for the necessary editorial and administrative support to change the way everybody worked. Hence the desired modernisation of function and process was linked to the other area in need of attention—the publishing partner and the journal's overall profitability. *PQ* had worked with a number of different publishers throughout its history, starting with Macmillan in the 1930s, and was with Thomson by the time Bernard was in the chair. Although these partnerships had brought some incremental advances in their train, linked to their own production systems and the technology of the day, there was now an opportunity to take stock of the journal's place in the contemporary publishing environment. By now its methods marked it out as fairly inefficient and something of an anachronism in production terms. There were still a lot of piecemeal processes, with much time-consuming toing and froing that all had to go through the editors. Besides, the journal's finances, as mentioned above, were often precarious; each year the income was never more than modest, and in some years *PQ* made almost nothing or a loss.

Through the 1970s and 1980s a vigorous new approach had been evolving in mainstream academic journal publishing, and several publishers were to invest heavily in that sector over the period with some going on to become the dominant journal publishers of the present day. This new environment offered many attractions to *PQ*, as a well-designed partnership with one of these publishers would allow the journal to tap into their economies of scale, more efficient editorial and production processing, and advantages in dis-tribution and marketing. The suitor that eventually came to win the hand of *PQ* was Basil Blackwell Ltd (as they then were), who stood out with a growing reputation as the leading 'society' publisher among its rivals. This means not that they were rivals to Debrett's or *The Lady* but that their business extended beyond the journals they owned outright to contract publishing for independent journals, learned societies, associations and small operations like *PQ*. As far as its size and the requirements of running a large publisher allowed, their claim to fame was that they offered a bespoke publishing service for each of hundreds of different associations and societies.

As Chair, Bernard oversaw *PQ*'s switch of contracted publishing partner from Thomson to Blackwell, and was in the thick of the negotiations, hammering out details on the phone to the publisher right up to the eventual signing. The change finally came about in 1985 after a period of due diligence, and led *PQ* to adopt a new set of articles for its underlying publishing company, as well as appoint its first company secretary (another task for the ever-dependable Audrey Coppard). After some teething troubles the partnership proved highly successful, putting the journal on a more secure financial basis but also streamlining many of the editorial and production chores. Together with the coming of a reliable annual surplus for the first time and its role in paying for editorial support, these changes reduced the chores expected of *PQ*'s editors and—in theory at any rate—freed them up to give more time to the main business of commissioning and evaluating the journal's content. William Robson would very probably not have approved, but the changes really were necessary if *PQ* was going to attract busy people as editors and serve it in an era very different from the founders' own. There were other innovations too, with in 1989 the appearance of the first of the annual book issues of the journal. For its part, particularly during the decades of expansion and acquisition, Blackwell would have valued the reputation and cachet of the then 55-year-old journal as a welcome addition to its politics portfolio.

Such moves are not entirely risk free. This kind of agreement between a journal and a publisher is always renewable rather than permanent, typically for five years at a time, but for *PQ* even over that relatively short timescale there was an ever-present risk of being drawn too far into a uniform style of academic journals publishing. The large majority of journals owned by or contracted with a publisher like Blackwell are conventional academic publications in subjects across the disciplinary spectrum, so the whole operation, from production systems to marketing, is geared towards that kind of journal. Further, much of the energy, drive and innovation in journals comes from fields in science, technology and medicine, which further shapes the mainstream approach to journal publishing. For *PQ*, with its distinct character and deliberately aimed at a wide non-academic readership, the challenge was (and still is) to derive the maximum benefit from a publisher partnership without the journal losing its soul. But if anybody was going to be able to steer this difficult course, Bernard was the ideal choice. His deep identification with *PQ* and its founding principles, and strong views on the dissemination of political ideas and thinking through writing and publishing, meant that he was better placed than anybody to keep that kind of assimilation at bay. The ways of working established during that transition under Bernard's guidance remained in place with only minor adjustments for another 25 years, until the era of online journals publishing introduced many new challenges. He also found himself in the position of defending the Blackwell connection when others at *PQ* later suggested severing it. On 11 November 1989 he replied (from Edinburgh) to a letter from the editors expressing their concerns with problems over the first five years that they felt were more than just teething troubles, problems they felt should require *PQ* to look for another publisher at the next AGM (when the arrangement was up for renewal):

27

I do appreciate the difficulties. But this year has been a difficult year with each side scoreing [sic] a splendid Own Goal [that is, production slips on both *PQ*'s and Blackwell's sides]; and I am very impressed that for the first time in the PQ's history we are out of the red, well in the black and able to pay for real assistance and nice extras. So think carefully, says he irritatingly.

Bernard would remain as a very influential Chair for almost as long as he had been editor, stepping down in 1993 to take on his final *PQ* role, that of Literary Editor. This move, undertaken around the time that his new Orwell Prize was launched, was a straight swap. He simply exchanged his position with James Cornford, who had been the Literary Editor since 1977, and Cornford took over as Chair. The new role had perhaps less direct influence than the main editorship or the Chair, but it reconnected him with the journal's content, and at last gave him the chance to put into practice his ideas about political reviewing. These had exercised him ever since he joined the journal and featured heavily in the editorial disputes of the 1970s. He was able to produce a new Notes for Reviewers that included his succinct view of the journal's nature for those reviewers who didn't know it well, and had a major say in a style sheet that Gillian Bromley produced for the journal during the 1990s.

I return to the importance of reviewing for Bernard in the section on Reviews and Reviewing below. Taken together, his successive occupation of the three roles meant that he had been at the centre of the journal's life and activity from 1966 until at least 2000, when he finally left the board. This was a very long period of influence—rivalling Woolf's stay at the centre of things if not Robson's. And to return to that theme again, in spite of Bernard's oft-discussed reputation for a prodigious selfishness and shortcomings as a team player, it was an almost entirely beneficial association for journal. The journal not only survived but gently prospered, repositioning itself in a new journals environment while striving to retain the essential *PQ* virtues and principles.

Bernard as author: *PQ* and plain speaking

Above all else, this collections celebrates Bernard as an author who (usually) manages to combine academic rigour with self-conscious style and wit, as it featured in a journal designed to reach an audience beyond the narrowly academic or professional. Hence before looking at aspects of Bernard's own writing style and approach it's useful to review the authorial context that *PQ* offers.

From its foundation, *PQ* has always had a strong editorial presumption in favour of clear prose. This was both explicit policy and a reflection of the founding editors' own styles and outlook, and has evolved to remain in place in the present journal. As a policy, it relates to the belief that there is a wide audience for intelligent and informed political writing beyond a narrow professional elite and their dense insider-speak. The *PQ* view, to which I'll return at the end of this Introduction, is that no matter how complex or abstruse the topic or argument, a good and knowledgeable writer can present it in such a way that an intelligent non-specialist audience will understand it.

In its original form this policy rested firmly not only on the belief in a gifted elite who could write for the journal, but on the idea of an educated (or 'intelligent' etc.) general reader who would take the ideas found in *PQ* and help disseminate or implement them in the world at large. The existence of this target life-form was perhaps easier to assume in the 1930s when *PQ* first saw the light of day. (As we shall see, the primary target audience was and is not the intelligent general public considered widely—whether or not they are inclined to ride upstairs on buses in south London—but something altogether narrower.) At that time, although there was an increasingly well educated population at large, the overwhelming majority of British people did not go to university. The proportion was still only 4 per cent by the time of the Robbins Report in the early 1960s and was no more than 2–3 per cent at the time of the journal's launch. Besides, the study of politics as a separate discipline, rather than via a sideways glance during the study of, say, philosophy or economics, was still in its infancy even inside the university. Beyond the newspapers and the occasional weekly there was little available for those seeking to be 'informed' about current affairs, politics and policy, certainly not for those who were unwilling to swallow off-the-shelf ideology and who wanted more depth than newspaper articles could offer. Even the 'wireless' was a relatively new medium. *PQ*, as a kind of non-aligned but progressive think-tank at a time before there were think-tanks, was created to meet that need. Later, other possibilities would emerge, first in the form of books from publishers like Allen Lane and Victor Gollancz as well as initiatives like the Left Book Club, and later still with the coming of other media.

Once the journal was established the practice of plain speaking through plain prose was ensured by Robson and Woolf, the two editors at the helm during its first decades. Their own writings in their different ways displayed variations on the theme of cultivated Edwardian gentlemanly prose, but they also applied the journal's standards fiercely. Contributors who could not write naturally in *PQ*'s plain-speaking way but who still had valuable things to say would be ruthlessly edited. Then as now, jargon, officialese and convoluted professional discourse were anathema; anything not immediately intelligible to the educated lay audience, as imagined by the editors, was cut or recast. In Bernard's 1998 revision of his Notes for Reviewers, where he was able to present his distilled experience and deep understanding of the journal to potential contributors, he put it thus:

Therefore write at the utmost demanding level of intelligence, but without neo-logisms, polysyllabic linguistic entrapments or technical vocabulary: no social-scienceese [sic] please. . . . The Literary Editor reserves the right and power to translate into plain English any occasional lapses.

What constitutes plain English is of course open to debate. At a minimum there must be clarity in both style and subject matter. It would be good to see

29

elegance and other aesthetic virtues too, but not every plain author can manage that. For some, plain English conjures up images of unambiguous but characterless fare of a kind suitable for official documents and statements, which is where campaigners have traditionally concentrated their attention. The Plain English Campaign is in this tradition, as it makes clear on its website: 'Since 1979, we have been campaigning against gobbledygook, jargon and misleading public information. . . . We believe that everyone should have access to clear and concise information.'

There is something of the *PQ* mission there, but the journal is not just about 'information', and the Plain English approach alone would make for a rather boring journal. In the Faustian pact at the centre of Max Beerbohm's story 'Enoch Soames', the devil offers dismal poet Enoch the chance to go forward 100 years (to 1997) to look himself up in the British Museum reading room. There he finds the uniformed and regimented population using a lifeless phonetic prose, and in a literary history text he discovers Beerbohm's story itself described as 'sumwot labud sattire'. The best *PQ* writers have always managed to add style to clarity and create text that is as pleasing and engaging to read as it is informative. For over 50 years Bernard effortlessly fell into that category, as an author taking a very different approach to his predecessors. Of the two grand coeditors during the first decades of the journal, Leonard Woolf was the greater stylist, and as a public figure the more widely known among the readers *PQ* sought. It is arguably his coeditor Willie Robson who presents *PQ* prose at its most economical and austere—not by any means boring or 'labud' but certainly unornamented. Robson's predilection for plainness and clarity carried over into his editing during his time on the journal, even when *PQ* and the world were moving into a very different era. This would add to the friction with Bernard and contribute to the final breakdown in the mid-1970s.

Political studies and political writing

That there was an evident tension between the two men does not mean there was a sharp discontinuity between Robsonian and Crickian editorial policy in regard to the journal's prose. Bernard was an ardent supporter of the *PQ* clear-speaking tradition—it would not still be in place today otherwise. By his time as coeditor, the challenges to clarity in *PQ* content were more than ever from the ingrowing language of the academy rather than from officialese or pompous politicians. Political studies (or political science if you prefer) had fully come of age and by the end of his editorship most present day UK departments were already in place—two of them via Bernard himself as foundation professor. The relentless professionalisation of the scholarly world that continues today was gathering pace, and an increasingly formulaic writing style had evolved to go with it. An ingrained habit of writing for the examiner, as I mention in the Preface, is one aspect of this; another is the convoluted and self-consciously technical nature of much writing in the social sciences, something that Bernard frequently savaged.

One factor to tempt social science authors beyond the normal requirements of academic rigour into an impersonal sterility and technical complexity may be the desire to create a code that distinguishes them from other 'lighter' denizens of the arts and humanities. When this happens, insiders may deliberately—not just unwittingly—write to keep the wider population at bay. On top of this, highly controlled funding systems and a profession that depends on them for its existence add an even greater pressure in this direction. In the UK, for example, the ever more Gradgrindian approach to the allocation of funds for research and teaching forces academics to emphasise the use value for their work, and hence make everything look as 'scientific' as possible.

Whatever the reason, these tendencies are not conducive to clear, publicly accessible writing of the kind championed by *PQ*. For Bernard the nature and wider dissemination of political studies remained constant concerns, and a descent into scientism or an empty if data-packed pseudo-science of politics had to be resisted. Scientism in political studies is of course something that he had critiqued sharply from the start of his career, beginning with *The American Science of Politics*. His 'Inconclusion' to that book (a very Bernardian title that he'd use again elsewhere) starts with an epigraph from Collingwood on idealism, that 'it was a revolt against the theory that limited the intellect to the kind of thinking characteristic of natural science'. A good early distillation of Bernard's outlook and a guide to his stance on both political enquiry and political writing can be found in the *PQ* review[j] of that now largely forgotten first book. After Isaiah Berlin turned him down, Leonard Woolf had found a sympathetic reviewer in the person of the Americanist Denis Brogan, who was presumably not suffering from a bad back at the time.

Brogan held the chair of Political Science at Cambridge. His own war-delayed inaugural of 1945, 'The Study of Politics', suggests that he would be sympathetic to Bernard's position and approach.[k] There he showed he had doubts about a simple science of politics ('Politics may have all the potentialities of the atomic bomb, but those potentialities are not the result of the activities of political scientists . . .') and also shared Bernard's belief in the importance of history in the study and understanding of politics ('"History is past politics", said a Cambridge professor. He was only very partially right, but present politics is always at least half history.') Compare this with Bernard's oft repeated (with variations) epigram on the importance of maintaining a historical perspective: that one does not have to be a bad historian to be a good X. In 'Scotching the Scots', Bernard's last ever review for *PQ* from 2008, he links to his 'Four Nations' article to parade this favourite one last time: 'I remember saying in my Mackintosh memorial lecture . . . that one does not have to be a bad historian to be a good nationalist'.

[j] *The Political Quarterly*, vol. 31, no. 1, 1960.
[k] Reprinted in Preston King, ed., *The Study of Politics*, pp. 35–45.

Brogan evidently also enjoyed Bernard's approach as a wit and dispenser of asides—'a most acute, elegant, witty, and timely assessment of a dominant tradition in American intellectual (or, at any rate academic) life':

(Dr Crick 'throws away,' as they say of actors, enough ideas to stock a conference at Aspen.) He is a wit and a wit of the best kind; he justifies a smile and he adds to understanding at the same time.

He summed up Bernard's approach as follows: 'Dr Crick believes in politics not as a science, not as an art, but as a craft and in the necessity of a political theory and a political ethics.' Not everybody would be quite as partial to Bernard's parenthetical wit: in a contemporary review of the book in the *New Statesman*,[1] Marcus Cunliffe, though generally positive, was more cautious about this aspect of 'Dr Crick's cheerfully ferocious volume':

His book has a few minor faults. He is sometimes a sucker for an aphorism, and the early chapters—in which he develops a historical genealogy of 'scientism'—are not always sharply relevant.

This difference of views about Bernard's approach—the political craftsman who is a 'wit of the best kind', or the 'sucker for an aphorism' who can't resist asides—would surface throughout his career. But his support for open and inclusive forms of writing was unwavering. He didn't promote lively, open writing simply because he adhered to some aesthetic theory on the nature of writing, but because it has intrinsic importance to his view of political thinking and political practice. The understanding of politics is for everybody, and vitally so. This is not to say that Bernard was anti-science or anti-theory, which would be a nonsensical gloss of his position, nor that he regarded everything that comes from academic politics as worthless, which would be entirely implausible given that he was very much part of that world at least until his retirement. What he objected to, as the example of his 1998 *PQ* review of Quentin Skinner's *Liberty before Liberalism* reveals, is an academic or professional isolationism, especially where shored up by dead, obscurantist or jargon-ridden prose:

Politicians and even reading journalists don't know it, but we are in a great age of political thinking—of academic political thinking. Elsewhere and often I have railed against the tragic chasm between academic and practical political thinking (if a politics of soundbites and sentimental generalities can be dignified as thinking).

Bernard's view of this interplay between politics, reason and clear language—whether threatened by academic tendencies, lazy editors or shallow politicians—can be found throughout this collection. Here's a relatively early (and typically parenthetical) example from Article 6 of 1970:

We must no longer confuse social toleration with any unnecessary and self-destroying intellectual tolerance of nonsense, as Gellner argues so well; particularly, I would only add, when so much nonsense gets written, not even in plain English for ordinary

[1] *New Statesman*, 22 August 1959, p. 227.

people, but in the barbaric abstractions of the dialectic (*le mot juste*?) fusion of American social science and an equally abstract translator's Marxism. (What is clear can be said clearly.)

A few years later in Article 12, his 1977 report on socialist books, he promotes the familiar line on readership ('my main point as ever') and berates sterile academic modes of expression. But he also tells us that clarity is as important for the dissemination of politics as it is for political studies—and by this time, well into the period of his work on the biography, he is able to introduce Orwell as an exemplar too:

[N]ot all socialist books are likely to appear—to our readers at least—as either serious or aimed at the intelligent non-specialist, which politically (my main point as ever) is to say much the same thing. . . .
[T]he language of translated Marxism, never famous either for clarity or literary merit, is now largely embedded in a meta-jargon of the social sciences spoken only on the campuses, never on the shop-floor, itself suffering from neologism posing as knowledge and noun-phrases restating a problem but posing as solutions. . . .
So I take the old Orwellian line that serious socialists should write plain English and appeal to the ordinary experiences and the commonsense morality of ordinary people.

In the following year he showed that his view of the dissemination of political thought and practical politics is not simply a matter of authorship and literary style. In his 1978 Commentary 'Political Reviews' (see the section on Reviews and Reviewing below) he is critical of the literary establishment's disdain for political writing, and in the same year he adds publishing to the charge sheet in his review of Sheila Hodges' history of the publisher Gollancz:

For political publishing, indeed political writing, in both Gollancz's and Orwell's sense, is now in sad decline. The safe pickings of the university and polytechnic social science market, producing so much needlessly technical, internalised, neologistic, a-political bad writing, have led most publishers to abandon the kind of general reader who was the target on whom Gollancz's eyes were set.

This appears to be a charge laid against the UK in particular: in his 1997 article on Hannah Arendt (Article 20) he refers to the apparent 'openness of American higher education to thinkers who do not fit easily in the procrustean beds of academic disciplines, and the consequently greater interchange there between academia and quality or intellectual journalism' and contrasts that with 'what here in the UK is still that great editorial divide (despite Orwell, or why he is still held in despite by some) between politics and literature, not to mention a certain lingering intellectual parochialism'.

So by now it has become a question of both the nature of political writing and also of political publishing and its reception, two themes that Bernard revisited on regular occasions throughout his life. *PQ* provided many opportunities for involvement with both, of course. From the publishing side, his comments from the Hodges review on the promotion of supposed 'easy' textbook pickings at the expense of more difficult publishing—including that aimed at the fabled 'general reader' who was so much a staple of *PQ*'s own approach—appear to suggest the root problem is a loss of editorial nerve in publishers. Yet he would give grudging praise to publishers at times and acknowledge that the problem was not just about them, as here in his 1992 *PQ* Northern Ireland books review:

The Oxford University Press can, of course, offload some of the risk on libraries; but nonetheless they stubbornly and properly think that the matter is important and the thought and scholarship on offer proportionate. In other words, even academics write clearly and not just for themselves when they have something to say and want to be heard. Even so, alas, they seldom are. These books rarely if ever get reviewed even in the quality Press.

In fact, these tendencies were symptoms of a much broader large-scale shift: the balance of power and decision making in publishing was moving inexorably away from editorial towards marketing, a move that went further in some areas of publishing than others but is now essentially complete. In other words, in terms of the kind of writing and publishing that he valued, things were worse than Bernard suspected. A book proposal that offered itself as principally aimed at 'the general reader'—educated, intelligent or other-wise—would now be laughed out of court by a present day marketing department, to be rejected completely or sent back to editorial for a major rethink. Some areas of academic publishing are now decidedly marginal, with doubts as to whether traditional monographs can survive at all. Beyond academic publishing, Bernard-style complaints about politics for the wider consumer market are now commonplace: that there is a dearth of 'intelligent' political publishing for wider public sale unless the content is salacious, scandal ridden, written by a current and preferably controversial political celebrity, or preferably all three. Arguably, such publications are hardly political at all, at least in the sense that Bernard would have wished. As for the exclusion of dirty old contemporary politics from the precious realm of the 'literary', that practice seems to be as deeply embedded as ever.

At the same time as these strong themes are emerging in his writing—the 1970s—Bernard was working on his Orwell biography. Unsurprisingly, as the decade progressed Orwell began to feature regularly in what he has to say about politics and political writing. George Orwell would seem to be a natural bedfellow and supporter of both Bernard as an author and the *Political Quarterly* as a project. In an often-quoted sentence from his 1946 essay 'Why I write', from the short-lived *Gangrel*, Orwell said that 'What I have most wanted to do throughout the past ten years is make political writing into an art'; a shortened version of this would become the motto of Bernard's Orwell Prize. *PQ*'s stylistic openness gave Bernard more freedom for his writing than any conventional academic journal could; he too strongly believed in the possibilities of political writing as an art, and most of his writing through this collection reveals him trying to put that into practice.

This apparent natural affinity between Orwell and *PQ* may imply that they had progressed hand in hand from the early 1930s, a time when the young

Orwell's writing had started to appear in a small way and the new journal was embarking on its first and highly influential decade. But that's an illusion. *PQ*'s plain speaking tradition emerged independently under the tutelage of Robson and Woolf. Indeed, Orwell's name and Orwell's writing are almost entirely absent from *PQ* during its first 45 years or so, apart from a 1961 article by Michael Maddison examining James Burnham's influence on *1984*. Regular mentions in *PQ* really only start after Bernard introduces them in earnest in his 1976 piece 'The Character of a Moderate' (Article 11 in this collection). After that, Bernard helps to encourage the naturalness of fit between *PQ* and Orwell: there was an obvious common approach, and as well as more explicitly adding him as another strand in his own writings, it was relatively easy to graft Orwell on to the *PQ* 'mission'. I think there is a case for saying that as well as Bernard measuring himself as a public intellectual *à la* Berlin, and as a purveyor of heavyweight but accessible political content *à la* Gellner (see below), he also came to see himself as a kind of academic mirror of Orwell.

Bernard as stylist and wit

All this talk of clarity and *PQ*'s plain-speaking mission to reach a wide audience should not conceal the fact that Bernard does not write as his editorial predecessors had done. In fact, he does not write plain English at all. Whether the witty and conversational style he cultivated, both in person and in print, was natural for him or something he worked hard on initially, by his later years it was probably an ingrained habit he couldn't help. There is a clue to how he saw his own writing when he complained during the mid-1970s editorial battles that Robson did not approve of his 'rather personal style of polemical serious-satire, that other journals seem to appreciate' (see the section on Reviews and Reviewing below). Later would come the Orwellian overtones; and twenty years after his memorandum wars with Robson there is another clue to the kind of writing he valued in his review from *PQ*'s first issue of 1995: 'And I ask myself uncertainly if the style of my first paragraph is affectionate irony or loving emulation of Richard Hoggart, his easy mix of the informal and the formal, of cultural references and colloquial tone?'

These stylistic tendencies are strongly linked to Bernard's preference for short forms of writing. Whether in reviews or articles he was essentially an essayist, not somebody who was happiest writing at great length. By the time he had reached the fourth edition of *In Defence of Politics*, whose editions had grown not by revision of the original text but by the additions of new sections and chapters, he was apologising (with Crickian nested parentheses) for the extra length this produced:

So the brevity of which I was once so proud, always enjoying the speculative essay more than the monograph (I have only written two monographs, one a doctoral thesis and the other a biography of a great essayist), has suffered.[m]

[m] These were the thesis that would become *The American Science of Politics* (1959), and *George Orwell: A Life* (1980).

His very first review for *PQ* and hence in this collection, published 51 years before his last, is already recognisably Bernardian—confident, waspish, with a self-conscious flair and wit. These characteristics stayed with his writing throughout his life, and when he was at his best and most fluent they gave it a rare sparkle and impact. He not only wrote this way in his public-facing writings but also, albeit in a more measured way, in his academic prose, something that only the most confident and/or defiant person would dare to do. The academic propriety was all there, but he added a flourish that made what he was saying far more appealing to read. The conversational inform-ality of his *PQ* contributions must have raised regular frowns in the Robson era. A third important factor that drove his writing style was a general intensity, what Audrey Coppard describes as the 'fire in his belly' that she felt set him apart from the vast majority of his academic contemporaries: he couldn't help but write in a spirited way.

The confidence is there from the earliest days, if not the polish, which would come later. It is confidence that is on show in his first *PQ* article in 1960 (Article 1), where the 30 year old Crick feels able to talk, with precocious avuncularity, of 'poor Laski' dying ten years before, and in the same piece about the follies of youth—to which group in this and other pieces of the time Bernard makes clear he does not belong. '[N]othing is more boring and more ephemeral than the strident voice of professional youth', he says, incidentally showing his credentials as something of a young fogey long before the term was invented.

From the earliest his confidence—or unabashed bravado—also extended to him making grand and sweeping statements, at least when he was being 'literary' rather than constrained to the purely academic. Here his reviews offered an extra freedom. Such swashbuckling declarations can be found throughout his writings; to take just a couple from his early contributions to this collection, they vary from offhand one-liners such as 'David Urquhart, that greatest of eccentrics ever to plague the Foreign Office from within' from his 1962 review of Webster's *Art and Practice of Diplomacy*, to more elaborate and entirely unsupported glosses such as this from his review in the last issue of 1964 (Bernard's italics):

But his artistic awareness is helped by a simple social fact: he is a Scot from Glasgow—they are much *more like* the Americans than the English are. Americanism is the ideology of the North British middle class without either the vices or virtues of being squeezed by aristocracy or proletariat.

For Bernard the jokes and caustic comments usually come in asides like those on display in 'The parenthetical Crick' below, not in pieces that try to be funny from start to finish. Of all the many items in this collection, in only one does he attempt to sustain a piece of humorous writing from start to finish—'The 1970s in Retrospect' of 1970 (Article 7), which as I mentioned above is not a complete success. Humour in otherwise straight writing is always risky, and will not be to everybody's taste. But Bernard's humour and love of clever ornament doesn't undermine what lies beneath; whether his style or humour amuse or irritate, he gets your attention. And he is never completely over the top: even at his most polemical or boisterous his style is, as it were, more mannerist than rococo. What saves him from charges of superficiality and cleverness for its own sake are the clarity of his ideas and reasoning or the evident intensity of his underlying beliefs, and the fluent and approachable nature of his narrative prose.

Some of the specifics of Bernard's stylistic approach are not hard to find. There are everyday flourishes such as alliteration in the service of political critique, as in 'Best brute British blinkered empiricism' in his review in issue 4 of 1960, which is a more elaborate variation of his frequent charge of 'blinkered empiricism' for the British. There are also some favourite expressions that recur, such as the 'one does not have to be a bad historian to be a good X' form, and two or three instances of 'feet planted firmly in mid air' that Bernard attributes to Laski. In several places, such as in his 1996 review of two books by Ernest Gellner, there appear variations on 'Which the rider, which the horse?' that he attributes to Yeats (though is this a misremembered reworking of 'How can we know the dancer from the dance?'). Two larger characteristics are his tendency to launch into dialogue at times (see his Burns-flavoured first paragraph to Article 19 of 1995, for example) and his delight in subordinate clauses, often in the form of parentheses ('the parenthetical Crick', as I have called him). These are worth a little more discussion.

Crickumentary reconstruction

Bernard's dramatised conversation with Isaiah Berlin that I quoted at the start of this Introduction ('Fairy gold, Bernard, fairy gold, I beg you to notice') reveals a favourite Crickian device in action. Long before drama-document-ary, 'faction' and other blendings of fact, re-enactment and total invention became a staple of the visual media, Bernard often used an equivalent form of reconstruction as a narrative device. To add colour to a discussion or an event, he sometimes produces an apparently verbatim dialogue. Unless we are to believe that he had a photographic memory, a constantly running tape recorder or a capacity for concealed shorthand writing, these are clearly dramatic reconstructions, the indulgence of authorial licence for added effect.

They fall naturally into the conversational fluency of Bernard's normal style at its best, and there are plenty of examples in this collection. This is hardly a conventional academic device, to put it mildly, though Bernard does tend to use the device more in reviews and less formal contexts. At its most innocuous, it's simply a device to add a little colour to the narrative, such as here when he is claiming to report an encounter with 'a figure that Richard Hoggart would treasure as from a bygone age' that took place over 50 years in the past (review of Rose in issue 1 of 2002):

I remember around about 1950 someone staggering from a pub on to the top deck of a bus with his arms full of books from the Holborn Public Library. 'It's all here,' he told us all in old Cockney, 'all here. Everything the working man needs to know. All in the books of H. G. Wells.'

The detail is characteristic: in the repetition of 'It's all here, . . . all here', he 'recalls' every nuance of the conversation. But whereas in his later writings his reconstructions have become purely literary devices—Bernard the stylist in full and gleeful flow—there appears to have been another motive in earlier times when Bernard the public intellectual in waiting, measuring himself against admired figures of the day, is still on his way up. Here is one from that period, along the lines of Berlin's 'fairy gold', from his review of C. H. Rolph's biography *Kingsley* (issue 3 of 1972):

Come and have dinner with me at the Savile, I want to pick your wits. You know my old *Magic of Monarchy* book? I'm so glad. Yes, I think it stands up well, too. But I'm going to revise it and update it. I want to pick your wits on the changing role of the Crown in the Commonwealth.

This scenario has Kingsley Martin inviting Bernard to lunch at what would become his own club too. Once again all the nuances and details are there, but this time there's added dramatic technique in the form of establishing dialogue. Bernard's response of 'I think it stands up well' is ghosted into the conversation in a way that wouldn't be out of place in a telephone call to persons-off in the first act of a genteel play in rep. In this example, as in 'fairy gold', there is more to it than stylistic flourish. The message is clear: Bernard is so evidently on the same level as these grand figures—Kingsley Martin in this case—that he is on chatty speaking terms with them, socialises and dines with them, and is even invited to advise them.

The parenthetical Crick

It's not an original observation that Bernard Crick enjoyed peppering his lectures and conversations with asides designed to inform, impress or amuse. These are everywhere: a glance at any of the pieces in this collection will reveal that this was a lifelong habit in his writing too, and nothing he writes is without them. This is where Bernard the gadfly was often in full view, with stinging or mischievous irruptions that could lie anywhere along a scale from tightly relevant to entirely off the point.

This aspect of Bernard's style grew more polished over time, though the kind of audience that appreciates this kind of writing may well have declined over the same period. An Amazon customer review of his *Democracy: A Very Short Introduction* written around the time of its publication in 2002—markedly untypical of online comment in that it is both signed and fairly thoughtful—adds an alternative view of the developed Crick style:

Where he does stray, however, is in a propensity to, if not digress, bring in extraneous information but make little of the point. Too often an analogy or obscure reference is cited only to be almost instantly dropped. It is as if the author were trying to show off his breadth of knowledge, or perhaps more like listening to the rambling anecdotes of an aged lecturer—whose meanderings, while interesting and informative, sometimes obscure the point he is trying to make.[n]

This chimes with a comment on Bernard's lecturing habits from his *Independent* obituary:

His off-the-cuff lectures were educative but also at times self-indulgent. Brighter students appreciated the asides—mischievous, indiscreet, brilliant and only sometimes relevant. Less sophisticated students found them difficult to follow as he argued with himself.

The tradition of the student having to make what they can of an uncompromising lecturer, for better or worse, is of course extinct in today's customer-driven universities. Anybody, however grand, found behaving in this way would be invited to tend their garden indefinitely. Bernard's retirement in 1984 meant that he was long gone before this transition had become universal. In his writing the asides are naturally more controlled and less spur-of-the-moment than his lecture ad libs, but they are no less frequent. Every piece in this collection contains examples. At its most general, this Bernardian trait reveals itself through a pronounced tendency to adorn his sentences with subordinate clauses, whether to add qualifying detail to prevent misunderstanding, or to get a defence in first, or as a device to display a grand academic dilatoriness—'to show off his breadth of knowledge' in the Amazonian's words. Or because he is a natural comedian who can't resist a gag and the attention it brings. Whatever the reason in any particular sentence, he uses the technique to great effect. But as my label 'the parenthetical Crick' suggests, his favourite and trademark device among all his subordinate clausal adventures was the parenthesis, sometimes nested two or three deep.

At the level of the paragraph, he would sometimes make a whole sentence serve as a functional parenthesis and use parentheses (the brackets, that is) to flag it up, such as in this early example from his 1959 *PQ* review of Simone Weil and Hannah Arendt: '(Her quotation is actually from Adam Smith who, like Marx, was more of a humanist than his followers.)'. In a much later example, his 1995 review of Richard Hoggart's *Townscape with Figures*, his whole-sentence parenthesis has become a typically Crickian jest about his use of 'God' in the review: '(I'm sure Hoggart would agree, out of respect for other people's feelings, to give a capital to a non-existent entity.)' At the other extreme, the device could be just a few words as part of a one-liner, as in this sentence that contributes to the grim humour of a paragraph in his 1992 *PQ* Northern Ireland book review: 'McGarry and O'Leary include one non-

[n] Amazon customer review of *Democracy: A Very Short Introduction* (Oxford, 2002) by Ben Saunders, 19 December 2002.

academic contributor, Charles Graham of the New Ulster Political Research Group (the spiritual arm of the UDA).'

But the commonest manifestation of Bernard's love of a more complex textual weave is a sentence like this one, from his final 'Four Nations' piece (Article 25), with its characteristically nested parentheses:

Now one must notice that the SNP itself, since its stormy days in the late 1970s, has, very much, due to Alex Salmond's clarity and tenacity (from the time when he was nearly expelled from the party for being both too left wing and pro-Europe), begun to move from rhetoric of 'separation' to the more relative term of 'independence'.

Here's another example from his 1995 piece on the Scottish Act 1998 (Article 19). Whereas the plain-writing mortal might say 'When the anti-devolution argument gets put in a general election, the present size of the pro-devolution vote will undoubtedly diminish', this is not enough for Bernard:

Undoubtedly, as in the past, when the anti-devolution argument gets put in a general election (or perhaps in a referendum; for if the parliamentary going really gets tough, that escape hatch could be uncovered again), especially when it gets put in such terms, the present size of the pro-devolution vote will undoubtedly diminish.

It's arguable that in some of his more complex sentences he did sail perilously close to stylistic tendencies that he freely criticised in others, such as in his 1964 review of Hannah Arendt's *Eichmann in Jerusalem* ('The thesis is made no easier by Arendt's famously complex style, her inability to pursue a firm, clear line of argument without learned digression'). But if Bernard was prone to digression, learned or otherwise, he could never be accused of an inability to pursue a clear line of argument, nor of being 'almost irresponsibly obscure'—his charge against Arendt. Another trait that could be considered a bit risky for Bernard to raise appears in his 1993 review of two biographies of Harold Laski: 'The problem [of Laski's alleged predilection for inexactitude] now appears more that of a storyteller's exuberance, or the highly embellished anecdote-from-life . . . Both biographers are understanding of Laski's half boastful, half didactic but always entertaining foibles, if, quite rightly, not wholly forgiving.' The risk here is not so much being associated with tall tales (not generally a Bernardian characteristic) but the resonances in 'storyteller's exuberance', 'highly embellished anecdote', and whether he too is prone to 'half boastful, half didactic but always entertaining foibles'.

Bernard nearly always gets away with his ardently complex style of plain speaking, but in a 1997 article that again sets out his considerable if tempered admiration for Hannah Arendt (Article 20) there is a reminder that his love of subordinate clauses and nested parentheses can occasionally produce a rather unlovely sentence:

Thus, though she is often thought of as a modern Aristotelian, she rejects his teleology—even a polis with well-ordered institutions will not necessarily increase in betterment; so much depends on free human action (and sometimes accident,

Machiavelli would add—say, Cesare Borgia's sudden death or, for example, John Smith's)—and she rejects what is perhaps his instrumentalism: that free political action in the long run ordinarily succeeds (he might have noticed, under the pikes of Macedonia, that it didn't).

Yet even here, given careful reading and an understanding that orthodox punctuation would put a dash rather than a semi-colon after 'betterment', this sentence is clear enough. It's not a question of clarity, a *PQ* virtue that Bernard nearly always displays, but of complexity. It's nothing like plain English—the plain English of Orwell, say—yet for the reader who takes the trouble it's easy enough to follow. Of course, he sometimes uses a parenthesis merely as a qualifying device, as any other author might, but in Bernard's trademark uses it yields a richer prose texture and is an ideal vehicle for his love of a caustic or sardonic aside. What the parenthetical Crick reveals is a concentrated form of writing: a compression of several ideas into a space that another writer might take three or four paragraphs—or a whole section—to express. This is the Bernard who '"throws away" . . . enough ideas to stock a conference at Aspen'.

It would be easy to read a lot more into this, perhaps through some casual biographical psychologising that would see his writing as a symptom of a hyper-confident but ultimately insecure person—the insider–outsider again, grandee and gadfly both—finding disparate ways to say 'I am clever'. This is admittedly one way to see an author whose first inaugural lecture ends up in print with a long wandering piece of verse—accomplished comic verse if you like it or unfunny doggerel if you don't—sprinkled with allusions in Latin, French and German. But then again showing off and excesses of vanity are not exactly rare in either the academic or literary worlds.

If Bernard came to see himself as a kind of academic Orwell—and I think to some extent he did—then the parallel can only go so far. Undoubtedly he shared the objectives of political writing as an art and the importance of making it accessible to a wide readership. As an editor and *PQ* insider he was able to graft Orwell's approach quite naturally on to *PQ*'s in his (and its) later years; but as an author he was an extravagantly different creature from his biographical subject. Orwell lauded and wrote a deliberately plain and unornamented prose, but Bernard did not.

Reviews and reviewing, 1957 to 2008

It would be a mistake to see the reviews in this collection as merely a sideshow to the articles, a manifestation of a secondary activity distinct from the main article- and book-writing business of being an academic or public intellectual. Bernard Crick held reviews and reviewing in high esteem, certainly when they are done well. While it's true that his *PQ* articles show him immersed in subjects of importance to him at a time of his choosing, and may serve as a potential marker of the development of his ideas as for any academic author, his *PQ* reviews contain much first class political writing and large doses of vintage Crick. He also had strong views on the management of reviews, both in the wider world—where the activities of newspaper and periodical reviews editors regularly came in for some sharp comment—and on *PQ* and its reviews editors, finally put into practice when he became Literary Editor himself as his last major role on the journal.

Bernard remained an excellent and prolific reviewer throughout his life, as the 52 examples in this collection testify. His reviewing wasn't restricted to *PQ* and if anything was even more plentiful elsewhere: in the Notes to Reviewers he produced while he was Literary Editor, he describes himself as 'at various times . . . a regular reviewer for the *Observer*, the *Guardian* and the *New Statesman*'. The Bernard Crick archive created at Birkbeck contains hundreds of reviews for the *Guardian*, *Observer*, *Listener*, *New Society*, *New Statesman* and *TES*, together with other newspapers and periodicals, and a considerable number of theatre reviews for the *THES*.

Yet even when he had become a moderately grand figure his reviews never descend into mere vanity projects, where the subject of the review occupies a few lines at the start of the piece and the rest becomes a convenient stepping off point for a lecture, in the grandiose literary supplement review tradition. However, the 1998 version of his Notes for Reviewers showed that he did expect reviewers to use the opportunity to express their own agenda provided they presented the core of the book too: '*Be as critical as you like and push your own ideas, but always give the reader a fair summary, however brief, of what the book's thesis and grounding may be*' (Bernard's italics). As Literary Editor he was happy to write short cameo reviews at the end of the section, or sweep up the ones that he couldn't place with others. His reviews are also useful sources for his views on contemporary publishing—as I have already noted a strong interest for Bernard—whether of the books themselves or of the editors or periodicals that reviewed (or failed to review) them.

His first contribution for *PQ* was a review of *Fabian International Essays*, a collection edited by Tom McKitterick and Kenneth Younger, both of whom became *PQ* board members; as I noted above, McKitterick would succeed Leonard Woolf as the first new coeditor after the long Woolf–Robson partnership ended. Bernard is only 27 and newly returned from the USA at the very beginning of his UK academic career, but the piece is recognisably and confidently Crick, with no sign of nerves or (never a Bernardian trait) false modesty. Perhaps he is more reined in than he is in later reviews at this time before reputation had been established. Crick the deliberate stylist and wit was still developing—and we can guess that some Woolfian delicacy if not Robsonian green ink had been expended on the piece—but it's definitely not a cautious apprentice piece. He doesn't seem to be looking over his shoulder at anybody, whether for approval or censure.

A glance at the Contents list for this collection confirms what I have already mentioned, that the spread of Bernard's reviews for *PQ* is uneven across the years. The number of reviews tails off sharply when he becomes coeditor of the journal, and particularly as the 1970s progressed and the journal's centre of gravity moved ever further from Willie Robson towards his brasher heir. His *PQ* review tally reaches its lowest point in the 1970s and 1980s. Between his 1969 piece on Berlin's *Four Essays on Liberty* and his 1983 review of a collection of books on the character of the UK—a major Crickian theme in subsequent years—he produced only four reviews for the journal, and for the remainder of the 1980s only three more. Part of this falling off is likely to be down to the workload and demands of two successive foundation chairs in new politics departments from the mid-sixties through the seventies, together with the long years of work on the Orwell biography up to 1980. But a passage from one of his letters during the 'editorial wars' of 1973–4 shows that there was more to it—and in the process reveals Bernard's high regard for the importance of reviewing. In the long letter of 25 January 1974, after starting with a paragraph on the main theme of editorial differences with William Robson he turns to his own writing for the journal:

Also I admit to feeling unhappy that most of my best writing over the last three years has gone elsewhere than *PQ*—*New Society*, *TLS*, *THES*, *New Statesman*[—]simply because I don't get the kind of books I want to review from Richard unlike from Leonard (quite apart from the chore of Shorter Notices), and that my rather personal style of polemical serious-satire, that other journals seem to appreciate, is never quite that which I feel you approve of for unsigned editorials.

This single sentence—also a typically Crickian concentration of several separate issues—expresses a series of exasperations: for example, that it's only Robson whose editorial style is at odds with Bernard's writing; that Bernard is at odds with the reviews editor who replaced Leonard Woolf; and given that his own writing is 'polemical serious-satire', surely *PQ* should provide a more natural home than 'other journals'? But there is another strand to this: in talking about *PQ* being uncongenial and his having to write elsewhere, he chooses to mention not articles but Commentaries and reviews. On Commentaries, he is implying that as coeditor he would expect to be able to work within the *PQ* context to have his say in his own style—not an unreasonable perk for the labour of that role. But, revealingly, he is strongly implying that reviews are a mainstay and at the centre of his own writing: 'most of my best writing . . . has gone elsewhere . . . simply because I don't get the kind of books I want to review from Richard'.

The unhappiness about the books he received can only be part of the story for the beginning of the 1970s ('the last three years') because Richard Greaves, the reviews editor he is criticising, had been in post for the eight years before that and wouldn't hand over to his successor James Cornford until 1977. Bernard had written some significant reviews for Greaves throughout that period to date, including some of books by major figures such as Gellner, Berlin and Alan Taylor. Workload aside, he probably wrote fewer reviews than might be expected from the number he produced earlier for Leonard Woolf, whom he greatly respected, but those came from an earlier and presumably simpler phase of his career. His output doesn't really increase under Cornford's reign as Literary Editor, even after the Orwell biography is published, and doesn't pick up again until the 1990s. By this time, Bernard has long retired from full-time academic life—and from 1993 he is reviews editor himself.

Bernard's strong views about reviewing at *PQ* and equally strong reservations about Greaves's tenure as Literary Editor had spilled over into open criticism during the editorial skirmishes with Robson. Already in 1973 the editorial board had discussed the review section, Bernard and Richard Greaves coming down on different sides—the latter favouring a small number of high quality reviews against Bernard's request to revive the old 'shorter notices' section, with the rest of the board holding variations on these positions. In one of his December 1973 letters, Bernard had offered to take over the reviews role himself 'if, say, Mackintosh would be prepared to take over my shoes [i.e. as coeditor] and I would become literary editor—if the range of books could be widened'. He was thus now actively thinking about standing down from a position that he had said in 1966 meant more to him than his professorship, and it seems to have been more than a bargaining counter. The range of books was a major part of the problem for Bernard: during this period of memorandums and other broadsides he also produced a list of some 40 books that he believed *PQ* should have reviewed but didn't. By the end of month he made the proposal that the literary editorship should be reabsorbed into the main coeditorship: 'It could be that two of us could do the whole thing between us', he says in the letter of 28 December.

In January 1974 the Literary Editor is still squarely in Bernard's firing line. Richard Greaves was a professor in the LSE's Government department and had taken over the reviews role from Leonard Woolf in 1962 at a time it was a relatively new post, only four years from inception. He handed over to James Cornford in 1977, two years after he retired from the LSE; he died in 1981. In his letter of 25 January Bernard tells Robson that 'There is no disguising that amid my great affection for Richard, I have too much disagreement with the running of the literary section to make things comfortable', referring to a view that had come not from themselves but from the board two years before, that 'too many important books were getting missed and that too few reviewers, drawn from much too narrow a circle were being used'. This wasn't really new: before the days of the Literary Editor the reviews were managed by the two coeditors alone and a great many were written by a fairly small coterie of *PQ* insiders and board members. The expectation was that a dedicated reviews editor would cast the net more widely, but it's likely that at busy times books would go to familiar contacts who could reliably produce copy in time for the next deadline. Bernard asked Robson if the three of them could meet to discuss it: 'I'm desperately sorry to have smouldered irritably behind Richard's back—than whom no more honest man I know'.

The matter was not resolved and bursts out again in Bernard's letter of 25 March to William Robson with the journal contents and cover copy for the

April issue. After complaining that some of the review copy appears to have gone forward from the Literary Editor 'unedited via his secretary to the printer' as he can't believe it was intentionally edited that way, he notes that this 'exposes the root cause of my discontent. The review section is now so awful, really ask anyone what they think'. Then he again lays himself on the line to Robson:

If this [asking Greaves to stand down] is not possible for you to do, then I must as[k] for a special board meeting to discuss the Review Section, on which occasion I would make clear that it was he or I, and the board can choose; and you would defend Richard or keep a neutral position as you chose. I would neither expect support nor resent opposition.

This shows that the issue was intertwined with the wider Robson–Crick disputes, although it was still a separate concern; it also seems that Bernard's views on the literary editorship were not necessarily shared by others. In passing, it also shows him in action, harrying and chipping away at his opponents, and not afraid to indulge in the occasional bit of grandstanding. In the event, the 'he or I' showdown didn't happen—the Literary Editor would survive the change of coeditor and carry on for another two years after Robson stepped down. Instead Bernard prepared the memorandum to the board that I mentioned above in connection with the editorial wars. By now, the end of May 1974, it is all about the literary section, the 'back half' to borrow *New Statesmen* terminology, though it also carries an appendix proposing a best book competition that he'd raised with the board in October of the previous year and that they'd agreed to 'after considerable discussion' by a modest three votes to one.

What we see here and throughout this period is Bernard's constant affirmation of the importance of reviewing both as serving the journal's purpose and as a vehicle for some of what he saw as his best writing: as well as engaging its readers directly through its main articles, *PQ* must also show them the best political books out there via the reviews pages. In a further extension of this idea, the *PQ* award he had proposed in the appendix would be for the 'best book on British politics published in the previous year'. To win, the book should be the one that 'best combines literary merit with an understanding of any aspect of British politics, politics considered in the broadest sense, whether treating of problems, ideas or institutions, whether contemporary or in recent history, where aimed at a learned, an informed or a popular audience'. He acknowledges that the case for doing this was partly publicity for the journal, but importantly it was also 'to try and encourage interest in good political writing, especially in our review columns'. Although the idea was received sympathetically by board members it effectively remained dormant until Bernard's launch of the present-day Orwell Prize in 1993.

The May complaints were not just about the Literary Editor; he also launched into the weaknesses of political reviewing in general, which went beyond the journal's management and processes. He claimed that the system was too passive, relying only on books sent by publishers who 'plainly don't understand how general we are' and 'think that we are Political Science'; that the reviews almost all went to academics instead of the more balanced range of contributors to the front half of the journal, and that they miss 'important' books 'because they're not political science': '[s]horter notices in the last few issues have included far too many books only of interest to academic students of political science'.

Coupled with this was his strong view of what a good review should be, and how the wider press in its reviewing failed the non-specialist intelligent reader of politics that *PQ* stalked. Bernard felt that the problem had much to do with literary snobbery and political ignorance on the part of reviews editors. Among the pieces in this collection, these views are expressed most directly in his 1978 Commentary on political reviewing and its importance:

Book reviews, after all, are about something more than the likelihood that readers will actually buy the book: they are a vital form of publicising knowledge, including knowledge about ideas and ideas about ideas.

For Bernard, reviews perform this valuable purpose—though it's worth remembering that even the shortest review in Bernard's sense is a world away from the dismal customer comments that have substantially usurped the meaning of 'review' in today's Amazonian and trip-advised world. In the same Commentary he is scathing about the place of politics in the literary establishment, and also offers an interesting aside on politics in theatre:

Among the literary intelligentsia can be found a philistinism about politics to match anything that politicians can show towards the arts. It usually takes, even in classically minded men, a romantic form: politics is seen as a realm of force and will, mitigated only by personality and sincerity. Most politics in the theatre is of this kind.

In that closed world, politics can only feature in mainstream literary environments when it's safely tucked into the past, hence contemporary political publications are largely ignored:

Literary editors will, indeed, look back to anything on politics and literature in the 1930s with pleasure, but anyone trying to be a political writer today finds it hard to get a hearing outside the sectarian little magazines.

He saw a greater willingness to cross this 'great editorial divide' in the USA, as he remarked in his 1997 piece on Hannah Arendt (Article 20). And he felt that the weaknesses of narrow categorisation and closed thinking were not just confined to newspapers and weeklies. Academic journals get criticised for a parallel to this 'lingering intellectual parochialism' raised in his Arendt piece, and as here in his 1986 review of Colls's and Dodds's *Englishness* collection:

I'm going to be lavish in my praise for this book for I suspect that, falling between English, Social History and Politics, it will get struck by all in the wretchedly narrow professional journals.

Bernard's reviews in this collection track several aspects of his own evolution, such as from promising young man (as he had described his former self sarcastically in the memorandum wars) to established professor, and at the same time the development of Crick the stylist in a medium that he regarded as extremely important for the art of political writing and its dissemination. In his 1998 Notes for Reviewers he is able to summarise these ideas in a concentrated, if gentler, form for potential contributors:

PQ tries hard only to review books of real importance with something to say, and hopes that reviews will reflect that aim. We try to look for books of political importance, whether directly for their proposals or indirectly for their analysis and ideas; especially those which, all too often alas, get passed over by the literary editors of the quality Press whose concern with politics or whose political judgement could sometimes be better.

Towards his last years Bernard's *PQ* reviews reveal the established public figure and grand old man of political studies, easy in his talent to inform, analyse and amuse. Lying behind this evolution as *PQ* reviewer there is the incidental effect of the Literary Editor of the day and the route by which the titles came to Bernard for review. He is happy writing for Woolf, everything from impatient to disappointed to angry under Greaves, content under Cornford, and happy again under his own literary editorship and finally that of Donald Sassoon.

If the young Crick was immediately into his stride as a *PQ* reviewer, by the time he is part of the journal family as coeditor he is taking on major reviews, or at least reviews of major authors. The last issue of 1969 carries the Berlin review I mention at the start of this Introduction, though it is short and placed right at the end of the section. After that, although as we've seen his *PQ* reviewing almost dries up in the busy 1970s he did produce four main reviews—two of books by major figures he admired (Ernest Gellner and Hannah Arendt), and two with publishing connections (C. H. Rolph's biography of Kingsley Martin and Sheila Hodges' history of Gollancz, the publisher). These were natural subjects for him (though it's reasonable to assume that Robson would have known Kingsley Martin better than did Bernard), and may have been at his request.

Bernard was effectively *PQ*'s Arendt and Gellner specialist; he had already reviewed Arendt's *The Human Condition* in 1959 and *Eichmann in Jerusalem* in 1964 by the time of his 1971 review of *On Violence* (all included in this collection), and would later make plain his admiration of her—albeit with irritations duly acknowledged—in his 1997 article 'Hannah Arendt and the Burden of Our Times' (Article 20). She was clearly an inspiring figure of lifelong interest to Bernard, and is among the few annotated sources mentioned in *In Defence of Politics*, as well as featuring in the acknowledgements of subsequent editions of the book: 'By the second edition I was aware of how much in debt I had been to the late Carl Joachim Friedrich at Harvard and to the writings of Hannah Arendt.'

Just after that acknowledgement of Arendt is one of thanks to the equally admired Ernest Gellner, who 'gave me stern and helpful criticism of my first draft' (presumably of the fourth edition), and who as we've already seen included his one-time LSE colleague Bernard in satisfyingly illustrious company in his *Protest and Discontent* article. The admiration is still evident in Bernard's 1996 *PQ* review of two of Gellner's later books, *Postmodernism, Reason and Religion* and *Anthropology and Politics*. There Bernard says of Gellner, who had died only a few months earlier, that he 'will remain one of the greatest voices for truth and reason within the academy of our times'.

I believe that *Words and Things* was a key inspiration for *In Defence of Politics*. Bernard does not make the connection explicit, and says in a later Preface only that he wrote his book as an extended essay 'to share with a German friend' in part to exorcise the past of her people. It would also take more research time than I can muster for this book to take that claim beyond circumstantially supported conjecture. I don't mean that particular themes and arguments in Gellner's book can be neatly mapped on to equivalent examples in Bernard's—though no doubt some can—but that the scope and character of the whole project of *Words and Things*, as a sustained and reasoned polemic that took on a whole academic establishment, would have appealed to Bernard with its verve, clarity and power. Both authors would be on the same side in condemning anything like the 'argument from impotence' that Gellner saw underpinning the ordinary language Oxford philosophy of his day, and Gellner's iconoclastic tone would appeal to Bernard, already blooded in that approach via his critique of US political science in his first book. To that extent, *In Defence of Politics* is Bernard's own *Words and Things*, a warning shot across the bows of political studies.

We know what Bernard thought of *Words and Things* because it is the subject of one of his first reviews for *PQ* and in this collection, from the first issue of 1960, presumably offered to him by Leonard Woolf. It is extraordinary to think now of the reaction this classic book once provoked, partly because its target has now largely disappeared to become just a brief interlude in the history of ideas. There were fierce exchanges in *The Times*, and Gilbert Ryle as editor of *Mind* famously refused to have anything by Gellner reviewed in the journal—a shameful response from an academic establishment that, far from appearing as champions of reason and reasoned discourse, come across as a group of smug insiders who spent their days congratulating each other on their empty 'brilliance' and proudly leaving no mark on the world whatsoever, fulfilling Bernard's prophecy in his review that 'The rest of the educated public may grow bored with them and forget about them.'

If 'metaphysical truths' are no longer fashionable (which has created rather a shortage of straw-men for dissection), then there are scientific truths being actively canvassed in the universities and also, growingly, those of social research and speculation. If linguistic philosophy is irrelevant to both these activities, then it is irrelevant indeed. Mr Gellner has not cried 'trahison des clercs' once again; he has simply shown that linguistic philosophy has nothing to offer him as a sociologist. Its prestige is now shattered. Perhaps political and social philosophy will now pick up the old traces.

Once he became established his featured reviews were of two main types: those on grand persons such as Arendt and Gellner and those on themes that were of interest to him. So, for example, in the early days he receives American-themed books to review, such as those by Arthur Schlesinger; later on, especially when Bernard finally takes control of the reviews section, there is much on the nature of the UK and its constituent parts, such as books on Northern Ireland and on Scotland, where he lived from the mid-1980s.

The nature, character and positioning of his reviews varies too. Unsurprisingly, the early reviews are often short and tend to appear in the middle or towards the end of the reviews section as the Literary Editor of the day saw fit. Later, he would take the lead spot, as in his 1986 reviews that included Beatrice Webb's diaries, and two considerable portmanteau reviews: one from 1990 of several books on a Britishness theme, and a similar *tour de force* (or reckless attempt) to cover nine Irish themed books in 1994; the latter was from his time as Literary Editor so presumably he gave it to himself to do. In his Notes for Reviewers of 1998 he set out his requirements for such multi-title reviews, adding a typically mischievous mixed metaphor along the way: 'Composite reviews can be useful, so long as the review itself remains an organic whole and not a caterpillar crawling over closed-spaced hurdles.'

From the time he became Literary Editor in 1993 and for the rest of his life, a Bernard review was once more a frequent feature of the back half of the journal. When he took over the review section he seems to have concentrated on books on his major late-career themes, such as the UK and the Union, Ireland, Britishness and citizenship. Or he chose to review whatever was interesting to him, especially if quirky and regardless of grand provenance or names, and would put those anywhere. This sometimes meant Bernard turning up as the last review in the section, as in 1995, which could be seen as modesty but equally as a cameo appearance from the 'special guest star' the elder Crick had become.

Threescore years and ten

According to Bernard's *Guardian* obituary he wrote a history of the *PQ*'s first seventy years, and indeed it is possible to find this history listed on Amazon. When I looked in 2012, just before sending the edited part of this book for production, its publication date had been pushed out from the originally projected 2000 to 2006 and it came a splendid 5,519,389th in the bestseller rankings. I could have bought it new at £25 and, remarkably, second-hand from a store in the USA at £42.85 and have it delivered within three weeks. By autumn 2013 it had slipped a mere million or so places to 6,579,284th in the

49

bestseller lists and was no longer available, as if out of print ('We don't know when or if this item will be back in stock'). These are all impressive statistics given that the book doesn't exist: Bernard started it but never got beyond the first chapter.

The same age as the journal, give or take a few months, Bernard was not only keen to celebrate another anniversary in the millennium year—their 70th—but also to mark his standing down from the journal in all capacities. In a postscript to his proposal to write the book, he said 'by 2000 I too will be 70 and have irrevocably decided to retire both from the Literary Editorship and the Board to try to set a precedent in order to avoid for the future some problems of the past concerning longevity'. It's not hard to see here a strong reference to Robson's prodigious tenure as editor and the eventual clashes of the 1970s. Although by the time he stood down Bernard had also served and influenced *PQ* for a very long time—nearly 35 years—this had been in three different capacities.

The proposal was intended for the *PQ* board meeting of 20 October 1997. 'I would like to write a history of *Political Quarterly* as part of whatever we may plan for the journal's 70th birthday in 2000', he began the five-page document, hoping that 'this will be enough for the Board to give me a go-ahead':

While the occasion of publication would be *PQ*'s 70th birthday, I neither plan, promise nor threaten a piece of celebratory 'company history' (which would be of little interest beyond ourselves); rather[,] a serious intellectual history or the biography of a journal in the context of its times.

Unsurprisingly, the board and editors supported the proposal and Bernard set to work. He was the ideal person to write a broad review of *PQ* and its evolution: he had been in the thick of it all for such a long time, had taken three major roles, and presided over periods of change, and had worked with everybody from the then current board and editors all the way back to the founders and especially Robson and Woolf.

He was also vitally interested in the journal as a force for discussion and change in politics, and in its past, present and future as evidenced by the special issues he suggested or promoted during his period of influence. It was understandable that following his retirement from an active role on the journal he would want to write a celebration of the *PQ* story to date. The coincidence of the approaching millennium and the journal's (and Bernard's) seventieth made the timing even more appealing.

Alas, it was not to be. Initially because of his citizenship work in Blair's first administration and his association with his former student David Blunkett as Home Secretary, the time evaporated. Perhaps the significance of *PQ* receded for him too as the years went by, and after the main elements of his citizenship work were over he was diagnosed with cancer and life became more complicated. Failing health became a new concern, which with the other demands on his time pushed the history of the journal down the list of priorities. It didn't resurface. At intervals the editors would ask him when he would deliver the finished book, but as time went by it became increasingly forlorn. At intervals from 2003 I asked him too; I do believe he very much wanted to write the book and still planned to do it, up to the point at which his health failed completely and it became impossible.

Although it was never produced, the book started off well enough and with due propriety. Bernard received a contract, discussing how the book would work as both a fifth issue of the journal and as a standalone volume for the retail trade. The publisher sent him cover design visuals for approval, with the draft design resembling one of those tag clouds now familiar from web pages, based on the names of *PQ*'s great and good over the 70 years. Bernard approved one version of the design in principle but felt that, rather as in tag clouds, the size and weight of each name should reflect their importance to the journal. In a reply to Blackwell of 20 February 2000 he said:

I like the general concept very much . . . But the names *must* be changed around so that it is William Robson and Leonard Woolf who stand out big and bold as Kingsley Martin and H. L. Beales now do but should be reduced. Woolf and Robson were the great long partnership, Robson well-known to our readership and Woolf to everyone else and quite a surprise in this context. Beales could well come down to the present Grossman size and Grossman could come up a bit. That would be an optional improvement, but the upgrading of Robson and Woolf is essential.

And so it came to pass. The revised cover used on a circulated proof chapter in 2000 was adapted to match Bernard's rebalancing of *PQ*'s historic heroes. It was true that Woolf and Robson's names should be relatively enormous if proportional sizes were to be used, but it would be difficult to take this too far without spoiling the design. Kingsley Martin, for example, was a well known figure and after his few months as Robson's first coeditor remained on the journal board throughout his life, but as I mentioned earlier, apart from writing some articles in the 1930s and 40s it is clear that *PQ* was not a principal factor in his life. Figure 1 shows the pre- and post-Bernard versions of the proposed cover for comparison. Unfortunately, while everybody was busy fiddling with the relative sizes of names it was a pity that they overlooked something that should have been more obvious—as so often happens with these things. Nobody noticed that Barbara Wootton appears in both versions as 'Barbard Wooton'.

The title *Seventy Serious Years* doesn't exactly set the blood racing—a Blackwell editor had described it as 'a little sombre'—but it was one that evolved from earlier drafts. The question of the title was still unresolved at the end of May 1998, when in a letter responding to some suggested alternatives, Bernard shared his thoughts with Stephan Chambers, his editor at Blackwell:

I still think that 'Seventy Serious Years: The Political Quarterly, 1930–2000' has a main title that will attract attention, an engaging touch of humour or sardonic truth. 'Political Thought' is wrong, conveys the academic discipline. 'Political Thinking: Seventy Years of the PQ' is possible. Or brazenly to stirr reviwers [sic]: 'Talking to the Few: Political quarterly, 1930–2000'. You see it was and is an elite journal, but a

51

Seventy Serious Years:
The Political Quarterly
1930–2000

William Robson
Kingsley Martin
GEORGE BERNARD SHAW
J.M. Keynes Sidney Webb
H.L. Beales
R.H. Tawney HAROLD LASKI
Barbard Wooton
RICHARD CROSSMAN
Beatrice Webb **David Watt**
JOHN MACKINTOSH

By Bernard Crick

Seventy Serious Years:
The Political Quarterly
1930–2000

J.M. Keynes **Leonard Woolf**
Kingsley Martin HAROLD LASKI
GEORGE BERNARD SHAW
William Robson
Sidney Webb RICHARD CROSSMAN
R.H. Tawney **David Watt**
Barbard Wooton
Beatrice Webb H.L. Beales
JOHN MACKINTOSH

By Bernard Crick

Figure 1: Bernard Crick liked the first cover design for his *Seventy Serious Years* (left) but insisted that some of the names be resized to reflect their relative importance to the journal, resulting in the revised version used for the chapter circulated in 2000 (right). During all this earnest adjustment nobody noticed the grand error in the lower part of both versions, where Barbara Wootton appears as 'Barbard Wooton'.

changing elite, originally the marriage to two kinds of elitism, Leonard Woolf and William Robson.

As for the text, all that remains is what appears here in this collection. There is a Preface, an Introduction and Chapter 1, which covers the story of the journal's foundation. This portion was typeset then circulated as a printed proof of single sided A4 pages stapled together with a cover page carrying the post-Bernard design, 'Barbard Wooton' and all, in time for the Orwell Prize celebrations of April 2000. These early elements were completed by 1998–9, which would have been on track for the original publishing deadline for the whole book.

There is no evidence to suggest that Bernard wrote any other chapters, even in draft, though he had definitely planned the book's structure and fixed the main chapter plan (which I have included in the version in this collection). For each chapter he had created a separate folder and suspension file, but most of these were almost empty except for the materials that he used to complete the Introduction and Chapter 1, a bundle of materials for the Wilson/Heath era chapter (6), and a few photocopies of meeting minutes and other oddments slipped into the folder for the final chapter. In a covering letter to a questionnaire of September 1999 that he sent to *PQ* editors past and present, he went so far as to declare that he was 'getting near the post-war section'. This suggests he was about to write chapter 4, but as nothing has turned up from chapters 2 and 3 and the corresponding folders were almost empty it could well have been *pour encourager les autres*, or just as plausibly *lui-même*, that the project was still on track.

On 3 June 2002 Bernard emailed the editors and Blackwell to say the book project could just possibly be revived, but that there were many obstacles and it was looking less likely:

Everyone has been tactful enough not to raise the matter with me. As most of you know when I got my 'K' I had thought that was Blunkett's farewell gift and that I only had some commitments to the 16–19 years citizenship proposals to wind up, but he drew me back this last January into making the first draft . . . of the proposed curriculum for the immigrants' naturalisation test . . . [Hence] I have been pretty busy, not to mention the Orwell prize . . . In other words, since 2000 when I was to present those two chapters [that is, the materials in this collection] . . . I have done nothing and you/we probably assumed the project is dropped. . . .

I feel some sense of duty that the tale should be told and am happy to do it. . . But sometimes projects have to be abandoned and I have a much bigger contract to fulfil by the end of 2003 . . . If you think better not to go ahead, regret on my part but not great disappointment just acceptance that I may have missed the boat.

In reproducing the surviving fragment of *Seventy Serious Years* for this collection I have simplified the opening extracts from Robson and Woolf, reducing one of the latter, and moved them from the separate page they occupied in the privately distributed proof edition. They now appear at the start of the Introduction, which already mentioned 'the above legends' at the start of its first sentence. The text of *SSY* has remained largely unedited—unlike the already published material in the rest of this collection it has not yet appeared in a published 'version of record' until now—hence I felt able to make a few more editorial improvements as well as corrections, but these were still minor and few and far between. I also needed to add fuller notes to this part of Bernard's legacy to provide some missing context.

A postscript to the founding

Is Bernard's unwritten book a significant loss? In some ways, inevitably, yes. The fragment that we have is characteristically stylish and illuminating but revisits a well trodden part of *PQ*'s past, if gently suggesting along the way that it is a past very much shaped by William Robson's progressively more polished—and increasingly Robson-centred—accounts of it. Beyond the founding there would have been more to say on the 1930s, a decade ripe for the *PQ* treatment if ever there was one and already celebrated in the Robson-edited collection *The Political Quarterly in the Thirties*; and then would come the challenge of how to organise the subsequent history. We know from Bernard's provisional chapter titles what each would cover, but there are few clues beyond that.

A key question is what would he have said about his own time on the journal? As a major figure in its evolution with a stature to rival the founders' own, and possibly even crucial to its survival, how would he present himself and his contribution from his accounts of the 1960s onwards? It's not that we could expect him to be unduly modest about it—as I've already said and many will know, self-effacement and false modesty are not part of the Crick canon. On the other hand, would Bad Bernard emerge and overstate his importance, both during his editorship and his later stints as Chair and Literary Editor? I don't think so, and if anything understatement would be the greater risk. Modesty aside, I think it far more likely that Crick the punctilious academic would have won out over Crick the showman and he would have tried to present a balanced view of his time at *PQ*. In the process he may have undersold himself; he certainly wouldn't have had the reflective distance on himself that he was able to apply to Robson and Woolf.

As an example of the value of this perspective, in finessing his own retelling of the story that Robson had presented more than once before, he does try to rein in his predecessor's increasingly self-centred view of the founding that would culminate in his 1980 version beginning 'I conceived the idea in 1927 of a serious political review'. Hence his warning in the first paragraph of the Introduction that any contemporary reprint of Robson's 1970 'The Founding of *The Political Quarterly*' would need heavy footnoting, given the that '[o]ver forty years perspectives can change and memory, as I warn myself looking back . . ., is an active substance, growing as well as decaying'. So if nothing else, at least we have Bernard's cautionary take on the founding, which has the merit of preventing the later Robson story from hardening off into a kind of foundation myth.

And now to add one more element to this postscript on Bernard's *Seventy Serious Years*. One thing has always puzzled me about both the Robson and Crick accounts of the genesis of *PQ*. Why does nobody ever mention the previous but unrelated *Political Quarterly*, a short-lived journal of exactly the same name founded a dozen or so years earlier? That *PQ* is now almost entirely forgotten, but when people come across it they naturally assume it is the first incarnation of the present journal. Preston King in his Introduction to *The Study of Politics*, his 1977 collection of politics inaugurals, says of *PQ* I's editor William Adams that 'he was the founder and editor of *Political Quarterly*', and a reader would naturally suppose that this means the present-day journal. King may have believed this himself. But there is no indication that Adams had any part in the founding of the Robson–Woolf *PQ*, nor, as far as I can tell, did he ever write for it. They are entirely separate journals.

Founded in the dreadfully inauspicious year of 1914, the ur-*PQ* staggered on for two years and eight issues before succumbing to the inevitable curses of its time. If the present-day *PQ* was hatched within the precincts of LSE, lightly brushed by the winds of literary quarterlies, a bracing draught from Fleet Street and a fragrant whiff of Bloomsbury, its earlier namesake was very much an Oxford creature under the editorship of William Adams, the All Souls based Gladstone Professor of Political Theory and Institutions. A founding father of the fledgling discipline of what is now usually called political science, he was installed in its first British chair in 1912.

PQ I is a different kind of journal from *PQ* II and if anything is more of a precursor to present day academic journals in political science. Even so, although it was not ostensibly seeking the same general readership as the present journal, it did carry pieces on pressing practical problems of the day, such as (inevitably) war and unemployment, and there are reviews of parliamentary sessions and judicial decisions. It surely rates a mention in any history of *PQ* II, but doesn't get one. In spite of its identical title there is nothing about this first journal in any of Robson's *PQ* pieces on the founding of the journal he was to edit, from 'Bernard Shaw and *The Political Quarterly*' of 1951 onwards. Nor does Bernard mention it anywhere in his writings for *PQ*, including the existing elements of *Seventy Serious Years*.

We can understand Willie Robson not having any direct contemporary experience of the first journal, given that he was in the air over France or otherwise involved at the time, but he would surely have known about it and perhaps would have referred to its articles in his lecturing. And wouldn't the older Woolf know? One person who certainly did know was Harold Laski, a member of the *PQ* II's founding group whatever his true influence on the course of the journal might have been. (In Bernard's 1993 *PQ* review of the Kramnick and Sheerman biography of Laski he says 'they exaggerate the role of Laski in the founding of this journal (true, he had a finger in every pie)'.)

By 1927, the start of the period that Bernard picks up in his first chapter of *SSY*, Robson was a young lecturer at the LSE and Laski was already installed as professor there. In the latter's 1926 inaugural, 'On the Study of Politics', Laski explicitly refers to his 'friend' Adams's journal. After lamenting that 'the sister social sciences have all of them the media of discussion and publication; we have been the Cinderella of the family', he then goes on to say: 'I am not unmindful of the gallant effort made before the War by my friend Professor Adams to found a journal; but it did not survive the difficulties of the post-war epoch.'° It's unclear what he means by the 'difficulties of the post-war epoch' as the last issue of *PQ* I appeared during the thick of the war in 1916, but it could be that Adams originally intended to revive the journal once peace returned rather than abandon it completely. Whatever the case, *PQ* I either was discreetly airbrushed out of the foundation story as it hardened off over the decades or, less conspiratorially, has simply been forgotten.

Inconclusions: defending politics and the 'elite' journal

Within the necessarily limited confines of this Introduction I've concentrated on Bernard's contribution to *PQ* via such Crickian strands as defending politics, making political writing into an art, and this unusual journal's intended role in the dissemination of political ideas to a wide audience as a contribution towards political understanding and engagement. I've also looked at how *PQ* provided a platform for Bernard's writing. It's now time to draw this Introduction to a close and in the process take one final look from the other direction. In asking again what Bernard did for the journal we inevitably return to the background question I posed at the start: how did legendarily selfish Bad Bernard come to settle for so long at *The Political Quarterly* and appear to give so much back to it?

For example, he was a moderniser—and had to be—but how far did he preserve and continue with the journal of Robson and Woolf? Given the pronounced editorial discord of the mid-1970s and his reputation for selfishness, did he take *PQ* in a new direction to suit himself? What was Bernard supporting and defending through his long association with the journal, or to put it counterfactually, what would the journal have looked like without Bernard? A full answer to these questions would need another whole book to work out, or perhaps would make a nice PhD topic for somebody. My short summary answer is that Bernard did not change the journal for his own selfish purposes, and that he could have left it completely at any time during his career—as many other good servants of *PQ* had done after stepping down

---

° Harold Laski, 'The Study of Politics', an inaugural lecture delivered before the London School of Economics in 1926, London, Humphrey Milford. (As OUP's publisher Milford had also produced Adams's original *Political Quarterly*.) Reprinted in Preston King, *The Study of Politics*, pp. 1–15.

from their particular roles. He did not reshape it to make his own style of prose the principal medium, nor did he exploit it by writing articles or even reviews on a continuous basis, and indeed there were longish periods when he wrote little for the journal. I have also suggested that although there is no way to show categorically that without him the journal would have withered or even closed, it remains a distinct possibility that these would have come about without his drive and energy but also without his take on politics, political studies and political writing.

With that generality in mind, I thought it best to close by briefly sampling just one aspect of *PQ* through the decades as an exemplar, one that both he and Robson were explicit about and where Bernard expressly states that he was working in the tradition that Robson had identified. The one I chose is the claim that *PQ* was and is by its very nature an elite journal, which first means clarifying what 'elite' might signify here. This in turn brings us back to the characteristics that distinguish *PQ* from 'the wretchedly narrow professional journals' that Bernard lamented—the mainstream journals across political studies and beyond that continue the everyday business of affording space for purely professional exchanges. From the outset, *The Political Quarterly* was going be written *by* professionals, experts, specialists of all kind, but not *for* them. The target reader was to be outside the 'profession', particularly beyond the academic profession of political studies. Instead, the journal was designed to reach the wider politically interested public, whether deemed 'intellectual', 'educated' or not, both to inform and to seed the widest possible debate on policy and practice.

This aim continues to set challenges for authors, who must write in a clear, jargon-free way, however abstruse and tricky the subject matter, and for the journal's editors, who must find, nurture and shape an appropriately strong content for an audience that is not narrowly professional. In that sense, being an editor of *PQ* is far harder than being the editor of a mainstream journal where the constraints and characteristics are much easier to define, especially as academic careers become ever more rigidly circumscribed by a massive bureaucracy of target setting and REF-like cost-benefit exercises, and 'quality' is reduced to such absurdities as impact factor.

So how does this make *PQ* an elite journal? Let's take Robson's view on this first, via his reflections on the journal's evolution as expressed in his 1970 article on the founding of *PQ* written when the journal—and Robson's editorship of it—was now 40 years old.[P] For him, *PQ*'s elite status had always been straightforward and not at all something to be embarrassed about: the journal's founders had 'the belief that all or nearly all new ideas or progressive policies begin with discussions among a very restricted circle of persons of exceptional ability and concentrated interests'. Hence, the journal positioned itself as a channel between this core of special people and a wider non-specialist but interested public. In other words, the founders' view as

[P] William Robson, 'The Founding of *The Political Quarterly*', vol. 41, no. 1, 1970.

expressed by William Robson is that *PQ* should function as both proving ground for political ideas and policy and as a channel for their wider dissemination. *PQ* is not only a kind of think-tank before there were any, but also engaged in a supposed intellectual trickle-down of progressive ideas.

A progressive and 'left of centre' journal?

As to whether *PQ* is of the left and progressive, there was certainly a leftish aura about it from the start, much of that to do with the personalities and leanings of its founding group. Bernard says much about this progressive tendency in his Introduction to *Seventy Serious Years*, '*PQ* from the very beginning takes both an unashamedly elitist and a "centre Left" or simply "progressive" stance, broadly sympathetic to but firmly distanced from the internal politics and the leading figures of the Labour movement'. This leftish foundation, which as Bernard says is not explicit in *PQ*'s public descriptions of itself, remains intrinsically associated with the journal in the eyes of many people and is has been a contingent feature of much of its content and a good many of its personnel through the years. If the leftness is more implicit than explicit, a deliberate focus on progressive ideas and policy has remained a declared characteristic, even though the battered term 'progressive' is now regularly subject to dreadful indignities at the hands of marketers from at all points on the political spectrum. By the time of his 1980 piece 'A Meditation on Socialism and Nine Theories' (Article 13), Bernard expresses it thus, putting himself into the equation too, and in the 'obsession with institutions' having a retrospective dig at the Robson years:

The Political Quarterly is to the left in the total spectrum but to the right of the spectrum of the left, myself equally ambivalent, walking in two worlds, a left-wing heart but a right-wing head; yet editorially always trying to resist, with little success, consensual reductionism and obsession with institutions.

There may appear to be an incongruity here, though. If we are in the realm of leftish, progressive thinking, why would the journal associate itself with elites or elitism? And why would two of the most dominant figures in the journal's history set out to defend *PQ* as an *elite* journal? From our present vantage point, at a time when the identification of elites and elitism is routinely associated with reproach rather than praise, it may seem odd that this was ever the declared aim of a self-styled progressive journal. But it was, and openly so, and didn't end with the Robson era. Bernard took on the mantle himself. He did not simply acknowledge the elite character of *PQ* as proposed unashamedly by Robson, or excuse it as a transient cultural phenomenon that belonged to an earlier time when people didn't know any better; he actively supported and promoted the view himself as essential for *PQ*'s survival. He expresses this clearly in his 1980 Commentary 'William Robson (1895–1980)', written to mark Robson's death, and coincidentally at a time when he too is standing down as editor and no doubt in reflective mood in relation to the journal:

Standards were at the heart of the matter. I admire the professed elitism of Robson and Woolf's theory of public opinion so frankly stated. New ideas do filter down. Mr Benn may deceive himself that he is the *vox populi*; he is simply a tribune among the people—and why not? Robson was well aware that the formation and dissemination of new ideas is only part of politics; they have to prove acceptable to and even workable among ordinary people.

So *PQ* is an elite journal because of its declared function: it disseminates ideas generated within an elite theory of opinion formation and development that 'ordinary people' then adopt. But Bernard's 1980 support for the elite journal was not just a passing fancy triggered by fond reflections at the time of Robson's death. At the turn of the millennium some 20 years later, at the end of his surviving fragment of *PQ*'s history, Bernard's view hasn't changed and if anything is even more forthright:

I am sure that at the end [*sc.* by the end of *Seventy Serious Years*] I will vindicate Woolf and Robson's view that *PQ* was, is and must be, an elite journal. Ideas and policies must be acceptable in a democracy, but they do trickle down, not up. There is much phoney populism in intellectual rhetoric today: too many know-all columnists and presenters who know so little and read so little, but are never at a loss for a striking opinion. But it is now a different kind of elite, more professionalised, more dispersed, and perhaps bewildered by a multiplicity of sources: not clustering to a few, not even to *PQ*.

This represents the same idea, brought more up to date while recognising that *PQ* is now just one among countless plausible-seeming outlets for political ideas and opinion. It's still a knowledge elite rather than a power elite that's at issue (though it's doubtful the two can ever be neatly separated). But whereas the attraction of—even desperate need for—rational political discussion in the 1930s was to combat the threatening character and disorder of the time between the wars, Bernard now offers it as a defence against a rising tide of instant communication, throwaway opinion and—already in full swing by the end of millennium—the growing Babel of multiple sources ever more bloated by the internet, which for all its benefits is also a force for the dissemination, entrenchment and celebration of unreason. And, together with the rise of the activist-driven single issues over broad-church party politics, it is surely another factor in widespread political disengagement.

This unashamed defence of the elite journal should not come as too much of a surprise. For one thing, it fits nicely with Bernard's view of politics and its defence, and is partly why *PQ* was such a congenial home for him. The unkind might even say it sits squarely in the tradition of the patrician left, which always knows what's best for us if only we'd listen. For another, in spite of his leftism (whether he's describing himself as an 'old socialist', or contrasting his 'left-wing heart but a right-wing head'), being associated with various elites did not represent a personal inconsistency for Bernard. A first and rather superficial *ad hominem* view might be that he was part of a social elite himself—not simply through working in the relatively privileged world of academe, but as a fast-rising star in academic politics and twice a foundation professor of a new department who would become a public intellectual, a noted author, a government adviser and finally a knight of the realm.

In later life he had a series of ready put-downs for anybody who accused him of elitism, and appeared to enjoy using them. Nor was he—the insider–outsider again—averse to becoming a member of some establishment elites. During his first professorship at Sheffield he may famously have dossed down in the Politics tower rather than rent somewhere locally or move permanently out of London, but by the time he had moved to Edinburgh in the 1980s he would enjoy the benefits of his Savile Club membership and always stay there on his trips south. And as I mentioned earlier, Audrey Coppard says how extremely disappointed he was not to be ennobled after the citizenship work for the Blair government that rounded off his career, having to make do with a paltry knighthood instead. She tells how the would-be Lord Crick used to complain bitterly about it, comparing himself with others recently ennobled for a life of political service of one kind or another and fiercely insisting his claim was stronger than any of theirs.

Given his apparent regard for titles, he certainly didn't support the 'unelitist' editorial policy that later editors brought to the journal. This turned its pages into a title-free zone, and still remains in force today: in *PQ*, lords, dames, professors and other entitled folk revert to their simple *ur* forenames and surnames at the heads of articles and in the contents or contributor pages. Bernard wasn't happy and at one point went so far as to complain to the editors of the day about this.

So in terms of this one sample dimension, the 'elite' tradition, Bernard explicitly continued the model of *PQ*'s founders that Robson had progressively distilled into the form he described in 1970. But can it work now? The biggest problem with *PQ*'s elite dissemination model is the other side of it—the imagined audience, the intended receivers of the carefully crafted wisdom that the elite purports to create or collate. Who is listening? And now it has the newer problem of trying to distinguish itself from the mass of blogs and other outlets that also claim to be disseminating political ideas, which is difficult to do without heading off in the other direction and increasing the risk of convergence with the 'wretchedly narrow' academic journals.

It's now less clear how a journal like *PQ* can turn people away from 'phoney populism' and the 'know-all columnists and presenters'. For one thing, it can only talk to those who are disposed and in a position to listen—the already engaged, not the disengaged who wouldn't dream of reading it in the first place. In an era of widespread disengagement from mainstream politics it's not clear that anybody who is not already close to Robson's elite would share that elite's view of itself or assign any wisdom to it at all, still less assign it authority. Besides, the same people who reject politics are not likely to respect elites in general terms either, and may well back their judgement with the recent public failings of power elites such as 'bankers' or 'politicians', or of knowledge elites such as 'economists'. *PQ* can hardly reach such an audience by offering its elite credentials to people who reject the notion of elites altogether. Who is going to be swayed by the message: 'Read us. We stand apart from the general background noise of opinionated bloggers, think tanks with axes to grind, columnists and the rest because we are persons of exceptional ability'?

But these are problems for Bernard's successors—*PQ*'s present and future editors—and represent a major challenge for the coming years of *PQ* and publications with a similar aim. At least the journal is still here to carry on the battle. What Bernard did was take Robson's model and adapt it through changing times, helping to keep the journal's unique character alive into the twenty-first century—a new era but one with uncertain outcomes. It needed somebody with enough self-belief and confidence to keep the important ideas of the founders alive in a shifting world.

And a still-closer look at the elite view shows that it was never intended to be about the mightily wise magnanimously distributing intellectual largesse to the unknowing masses. There's a clue in Bernard's exchange with Black-well about the title of *Seventy Serious Years*, when he joked that he would call it *Talking to the Few*: Political Quarterly, *1930–2000* to stir up reviewers. That is, the elitism of Robson and Crick is of an elite talking *to* the few. If the language of elites is apt at all, it's more to do with a specialist elite engaged in study and reflection talking to a generalist elite that can act in the world. This echoes what Robson had said about *PQ* decades before, that it was a journal that connects the world of ideas with the world of action: that is, the people who receive *PQ* wisdom are those who may be in a position to act on it. Bernard didn't manage to write enough of *Seventy Serious Years* to give his promised defence of the elite view, but his Notes for Reviewers of 1998, written at about the same time, put it very succinctly. In a section headed 'Audience', he first notes that 'A recent advertisement drafted by the editors described us as "a bridge between specialised knowledge in the social sciences and opinion and policy-makers"', and then gives his reviewers their target:

Imagine that you are writing not for an academic specialist in a discipline but for that old mythic British animal to whose preservation we are dedicated: the general educated reader—more specifically, leader and feature writers in the quality Press, producers and presenters in TV and radio, MPs and MEPs, civil servants, foreign diplomats and sixth form teachers.

This collection shows a multiplicity of Cricks—including the development of a political thinker, the rise of an academic career and a public one, the growth of an establishment figure who could never give up his role as a gadfly, and the political writer who took considerable pride in his craft for its clarity and aesthetic worth as well as the quality of his thinking. It also shows him in the context of a journal that he nurtured and helped to keep alive, and that was really important to him. To return full circle to the question near the start of this Introduction—how did self-interested Bad Bernard come to be associated for so long with the idiosyncratic journal that is *PQ*?—it was not because it offered him a ready platform for the dissemination of his own writing. There were times when he wrote less for *PQ* than he wanted to, and as this collection shows for many years his contributions were relatively scarce. Also, there were several natural break points in his association with the journal when he could have left completely, in the way that other *PQ* insiders had done over the years when their terms of office had ended. This would be even more understandable when these natural breaks coincided with his lean periods of writing for the journal. But he stayed. Above all, this was because he believed in the journal not primarily as a vehicle for Crick the author but because it embodied and enabled his ideas on politics, political studies, and the political writing that should convey and celebrate them.

Nothing shows his continuing attachment to the journal better than a piece of ephemera that has survived by pure chance—a Savile Club compliments slip attached to the amended copy of his 2003 *PQ* review of the books by Colls and Weight that he was submitting for publication. He had stuck his Edinburgh address label in the corner and scribbled a few lines on it for copy-editor and Editorial Assistant Gillian Bromley, who was leaving the journal. It reveals his deep affection for *PQ* (and in passing that his plan to write *Seventy Serious Years* was not entirely dead): 'This may be the last time we have dealings. Can I thank you warmly and sincerely for all you've done for my beloved journal (I *will* finish its history)'.

Part I
Articles and book chapters, 1960 to 2009

1 Socialist Literature in the 1950s

Vol. 31, no. 3, July–September 1960

THE DAYS of the giants seem over. Even a handful of young angries and a quorum of old Marxists boiled together in an anthology do not emerge as one giant—and Fabians, who no longer hope for painful miracles, do no better at building cooperative Valhallahs. Most socialist writers in the last decade have been content to be all too human dwellers on a middle earth inhabited by particular, not general, truths. This is a time, in the language of Isaiah Berlin's fable for the 'fifties', for foxes not hedgehogs.

Ten years ago poor Laski died. It is strange to think, purely in my local terms, that only this year would he have been retiring from his chair of Political Science. In 1952 the unfinished manuscript of his *The Dilemma of Our Times* was published, a perhaps questionable act of friendship, for it was a book sprawling and diffuse, the work of a man already too tired to think sharply rather than just largely—open to all the charges of internal contradiction which have been levelled at books that attack a contradictory system, accepting parts and rejecting parts, ever since the time of Rousseau. But, none the less, it was the work of a man who still had vision and conviction, a testament which was finally that of the moralist, not the quasi-Marxist, of a man who, while he knew that politics was politics, knew also, equally empirically, that, in those words of the Psalmist he so loved to quote, 'Where there is no vision, the people perish.' Laski would not have been surprised or discomfited to hear, as we've so often heard in the last decade, that socialism is a 'creed' or 'ideology'; he would have mocked anyone who thought that it could be anything else. He was not an original political philosopher; he was simply a great publicist and a very great teacher.

The character of socialist literature

Laski was almost the last author of what can strictly be called socialist literature: a style of expression and argument, free from technicality and comprehensive in content, which was read by all those who were open to argument at all. R. H. Tawney, true, is still with us. A collection of Tawney's past essays made early in the decade, *The Attack* (1953), should have reminded many that his *Acquisitive Society* and his *Equality* should stand with Laski's *Grammar of Politics* as the great landmarks of the British socialist mind.

Strictly speaking, the 1950s have seen the demise of socialist *literature*—particularly if achievement as well as form is considered. Perhaps big books now carry less weight than the plethora of repetition in the weeklies and monthlies. But whatever and wherever the literature, two clear characteristics emerge. First, fragmentation, both in source and substance, has been one of the marks of the 1950s. Serious and solid work is being done—in bits and

Published by Blackwell Publishing Ltd, 9600 Garsington Road, Oxford OX4 2DQ, UK and 350 Main Street, Malden, MA 02148, USA

pieces: Fabianism without Shaw, that British empiricism whose advantages are obvious and whose defects, if fatal, are subtle. Secondly, the primacy of economics has been replaced by sociology as the centre of the socialist imagination. To some extent these two things are connected, for sociology to sociologists has meant sociological investigation; it is only Professor C. Wright Mills and naive laymen, as the editors of *Twentieth Century* recently exposed, who think that academic sociology is, or should be, a body of theory which explains the working and predicts the future of society in the way economists once, but no longer, claimed to do. From Left to Right, however, a solid revival takes place of the early socialist perception that the social factors, in all times but those of emergency, condition and control both the 'narrow' political and economic factors. Educational policy is seen as at least as significant a technique of social engineering as nationalisation. There is some reason for the Establishment to suspect that the growth of sociology in the universities is a form of 'socialism of the Chair'. The revival of old Cobbett's use of the term 'the Establishment', not simply as in the 1930s 'the Tory Party', 'the cartels' or 'big business', is itself a case in point. The special number of *The Political Quarterly* last year on 'British Attitudes to Politics' is another example.[1] But all this is, as yet, a perception, a drift of opinion, a sentiment; it is not a body of theory. The various unreconstructed advocates of reconstructed Marxism know that; but it is no reason to return to dead theory simply because new theory is as yet inchoate, implied and immanent rather than actual.

Even the appearance of Professor Titmuss's *Essays on the Welfare State* (1958) and his already influential Fabian lecture, *The Irresponsible Society*, of this year, does not alter the point. He stimulates interest in the sociology of the 'Welfare State'; but his very strength is his refusal to generalise. Even in his *Irresponsible Society*, the strongest general point is simply and strongly a condemnation of a 'retreat from government'. Certainly, no one can read Titmuss, the very humanistic warmth and clarity of his style, without feeling that there is a general theory of social planning struggling for emergence; but it has not yet emerged—and the suppression may even be deliberate.

The vices of socialist literature

Two more preliminary points: the characteristic vices of any socialist literature (amply illustrated of late) are rhetoric and exposure, just as the characteristic vices of conservative writing are platitude and paradox. Certainly by comparison with conservative, socialist writing has had little to be ashamed of—the trouble is only that the case is more urgent for the Left, it depends more upon persuasion; being more scattered, even in its leadership, it depends more upon explicit public communication than does the Establishment. How many times have conservative sages, native and

[1] *The Political Quarterly*, vol. 30, n. XX, 1959, pp. X–X.

imported, been praised by the *Times Literary Supplement* for oracular platitudes like 'government must govern'—a good point—or for the deeper kind
of paradox like 'good government rests upon necessary evils' or that 'politics
is a voyage without a destination'?

But, to return to the task at hand, is this reviewer alone in finding the
rhetoric of *Conviction*—which was the first deliberate attempt to 'revive'
socialist thought and faith—embarrassing, superficial and in parts, alas,
even silly? An anthology of ex-communists like R. H. Crossman's *The God
That Failed* tells one something, but Norman Mackenzie's anthology of
socialist revivalists told one little except that the authors were better socialists
than most of us poor Hamlets—which one knew already. (Besides, nothing is
more boring and more ephemeral than the strident voice of professional
youth.) Two glaring exceptions did stand out from *Conviction*. First, there was
the hesitant and thoughtful persuasion of Iris Murdoch on the relatively
technical matter of the relationship of modern philosophy to social action. It
was one of those indirect stimulants to our intelligence which may have more
ultimate effect than many direct assaults on our emotions; Mr Gellner's *Words
and Things* may find a place in a history of reformist thought more secure than
many obvious candidates. Secondly, there was Mr Brian Abel-Smith's careful
and unrhetorical demonstration that the cost of the welfare state falls
disproportionately high on the working classes who are popularly supposed
to benefit from it most. But Smith's essay could equally well have kept other
company and was itself on the perilous borderline of the Fabian vice of mere
exposure. There is a parallelism in English Fabian thought, as also in much
academic sociological work, with the American liberal fallacy of 'worthiness
through facts', the product, via the journalists, of old 'muckraking' days, and
via the social scientists, of their retreat from politics into projects: the belief
that the mere uncovering of hidden anomalies will somehow, in society as in
individual psychoanalysis, lead to reform. Now this wonderful natural
mechanism of research, publicity, and public reaction may or may not be
so; and there is no need to deny that work that stops short of showing its
relevance to future reform, but concentrates on exposing a present abuse, is
not admirably humanitarian; but it is not specifically socialist. Of course, this
is why many who are nominally called 'socialists' are, from the highest
motives, not willing to sacrifice immediate help, influence and involvement—
liberalism—for the difficulties and delay of creating a socialist literature. For
the same reason the Establishment may well restrain some of its fears of the
influence of sociology; for sociology may equally well, as has largely
happened in the United States, find itself, in the name of science, objectivity
and impartiality, acting as the defender of all existing facts. 'Factualism' or
empiricism inevitably becomes the ideology of an existing system—if it is
held alone, if it is unrelated to any even tentative general theory of reform.

The quality which should redeem these vices of socialist literature is simply
'comprehension': simply the ability to comprehend more by approaching
society at its social roots. Socialist literature should be able to draw more

things together because it is concerned with the democratic roots of a mass society, hence ripe for generalisation, and not with the personal politics of even an expanding oligarchy. 'Comprehension' goes further than the conservative virtue or concept of 'understanding'; unlike 'understanding' it renders relationships explicit, it does not merely stick with intuition and the men who are supposed to 'know by experience'; being explicit, it is susceptible to manipulation, it is a way of thinking that makes society susceptible to deliberate changes. Hence the conservative 'understands' that radical change is not possible, when he means, on quite other grounds, that it is undesirable.

Revising Crosland

I take it to be beyond dispute that the most comprehensive work of the 1950s is C. A. R. Crosland's *The Future of Socialism* (1956). The angry, almost obsessive, attacks on it in *Tribune* and the author's almost diabolical status in the mythology of the 'New Left' are as clear a witness to this as his virtual canonisation in the quiet and gentle pages of *Socialist Commentary*. (Indeed, a re-reading of the old *Universities and Left Review* reveals a tendency to lapse into blaming him, and 'people like him', for creating the social circumstances which, otherwise, they are accused of accepting too readily.) But neither view seems necessary.

Crosland's book can now be seen as existing on two levels. First, it is an extraordinarily able analysis, synthesising both economic and social factors, of the broad changes in British society since the war. If his thesis that 'capitalism has been reformed almost out of recognition' is not acceptable as a statement of the basic dilemma confronting the Labour Party, one humbly wonders what is. The passion of the 'New Left' for remedying the very real poverty of many old age pensioners is, by itself, generous; but in the rhetorical use that is made of it, it is ludicrous and misleading. They are not a 'symbol of capitalist civilisation', as one writer puts it; they are simply, and harshly, an anomaly. (One is tempted to define a symbol, *ULR*-wise, as a generalisation which one wishes were true.) When the Conservative Party feels that it needs their votes, it will give them something more; the country can afford such things but will only act when pushed—the politics of what is growingly a pressure-group society. The motives will be those of buy-and-sell but the political fact will be absolute, and the Labour Party will be once again just left in the position of someone who would offer more if only he were in a position to do so. Time and time again Crosland's critics have themselves shown the truth of his fear of a 'hostility to economic progress within the Labour movement'. But the second level of Crosland's case—his statement of socialist aims in relation to these social changes and to the fortunes of the Labour Party—is more questionable.

Ultimately, strategy is compounded of tactics. Ends are an orchestration of means. But, the argument is familiar—it probably runs, one way or another, through most of the pages of this issue—if Crosland is so right on tactics, on means, on inevitable adjustments, does he still leave sufficient comprehension, commitment, vision, to work a British party in British terms? Put in purely constitutional terms: does Mr Hugh Gaitskell's determination to make the socialist movement a responsible alternative government give it sufficient scope to be an effective opposition? Put in political terms: does it give sufficient electoral *élan* to make it likely to move public opinion when the other party seems just as capable, or more so, of making the purely tactical adjustments which will better mirror public opinion? The American example, so dominant in Crosland's writings, makes much sense economically, but does it make equal sense politically and socially? 'Revisionist' socialist thought may be in as great a danger of making an untenable 'comparative' inference as American reformers once did when they regarded the irrelevant beauties of the English Cabinet system. The case against Crosland on grounds of realism was put at its strongest by Richard Crossman in the March issue of *Encounter* this year—which Crosland had chosen as a suitable forum the month before to write on 'The Future of the Left'.

Crosland may well be right to argue that those who talk of 'fundamental beliefs' usually mean quite specific bits and pieces of outmoded economic planning. But when William James addressed himself to the problem of war, he called his great essay 'The Moral Equivalent for War'. There is some doubt that without a moral equivalent for the idea of public ownership, the Labour movement could not hold together. Mr Crosland is in favour, all right, of equality; but there is some doubt as to quite what he means by this. Men and theories, it is a harsh but evident truth, are judged by the company they keep. Could it not be that he has, indeed, by trying to reconcile his Fabian pamphlet *Can Labour Win?* with *The Future of Socialism*, set himself, for the next few years at least, an impossible task? The things that may hold the Labour movement together at all may not be the things that look like winning the next election. The electoral statistics of the Nuffield school have encouraged, knowingly or not, a kind of 'marginal analysis', somewhat borrowed from pure economic theory, which is possibly only of limited applicability to political arguments based on social structure. Small shifts on the margin do not alter the electoral price of every unit: vast rigidities, immobilities, inelasticities still remain. Even in tactical terms, one might gain the margin and lose the bulk if one ceased to talk the kind of language, and to be the kind of people, the bulk expect. This is not a question of the Labour Party remaining true to 'fundamental socialism', but of it remaining representative of its clientele.

Crosland, of course, shines best by comparison. Where is the equivalent hard and comprehensive analysis by those who talk of nothing but 'fundamentals'—as if bent on proving, as an old anarchist once said, that mind was but a disease of matter? He has himself reminded us of Max Weber's distinction between the 'ethics of ultimate ends' and the 'ethics of responsibility'. This is a proper theoretical and polemical distinction. Many of his critics simply do not seem to care for politics, will not tolerate what they call 'purely political' considerations: the fact that there are, in any free community, a variety of different interests and moral ends which must be reconciled, if one is to act politically at all, factors which must never simply be ignored—or destroyed. The idealists of the rank-and-file of the *New Left Review* will remain inevitable dupes of the old Marxists so long as they believe in being absolutely right—about somebody else's business. They do not believe in political action—which is, indeed, compromise, even though it should be creative compromise: to build the future out of a wide sympathy for all the best elements in the past. The ethic of ultimate ends in politics is, at its best, the phariseeism latent in pacifism; at its worst, it is the ruthlessness of Stalinism. Vision is needed, but it needs to be a persuasive vision, not a strident, intolerant, denunciatory vision. The vision must be of people as they are—so hard to love—not the perverse desire to offend and denounce them in favour of a vision of an abstract people who will gamble, telly-view, and motor-mortgage themselves no more. Which is the truer and more humane morality, their bastard Platonism or my bastard Aristoteleanism? There are only ever two views tenable.

But Crosland finally falls short, by his own standards, of the claims of a socialist literature. As much as he preaches 'tactics, reconciliation and compromise', he himself forgets these virtues in his obvious and unbending revulsion from the silly sympathies of youth. Many of us are also not impressed at the spectacle of mature men gushing over the impossible, ignorant nonsense of those too young, or too prudish, to have worked in politics (demonstrations do not count), too wilful, convicted and conceited to have read much. But some sympathy is called for, some amusement, some pleasure (for they are not dull), some thought as to what the disease is, however bizarre the symptoms. There are, figuratively speaking, young people praying to be led—and the official leaders tell them to wash their faces, to go away and bury themselves in a Young Socialist basement and stop rocking the boat, or to stop rocking at all. A few well-washed stooges, horrible with unction, are paraded at Election Telly time as 'typical youth'—which thank God they are not, but these are even less reading types than the cellar population—so all this is getting rather irrelevant. But clearly there is close to hand a theme of traditional socialist literature which would rally, because it already permeates, the rank-and-file of the New Left, even if not their rusty old Marxist leadership: sheer dislike of the Establishment, sheer contempt for the conceit and constraint of class.

But somehow this theme embarrasses writers like Crosland. When Crosland talks of equality he means simply, as he says, 'equality of opportunity' (Mr Michael Young's *Meritocracy* was surely in part provoked by *The Future of Socialism* itself?). He is more keen to expose error, as a matter of principle, than to channel and reconcile it as a matter of politics. Is he in earnest with his own appearance of comprehensiveness, or is he simply a doctrinaire of the Right engaged in mutual caricature with the doctrinaires of the Left? If his sense of politics and compromise is as great as he tries to demonstrate, why denounce one's leader in such an offended and priggish manner as in the sudden footnote in his *Can Labour Win?*—'I personally strongly disapproved of the tax-pledges made during the 1959 election.' Does he indeed? Poor, pure soul. Socialist literature is, however, not a product of an author's simon-pure integrity—some great books have been written by great scoundrels—but rather of a content which can raise itself above such momentary and petulant detail, stuff woven for a decade not a season.

Two more tries

By way of contrast, John Strachey's Contemporary Capitalism (1956) as the classic look of something built to last. One only treats his book second to Crosland's because of a suspicion that it has, for all its clear merits, been little read. Strachey is now a man whose fame is greater than his following, who has more respect for his writings than he has readers. He suffers from the general decline in interest in comprehensive writings: the over-great absorption with the snip-snap of periodicals rather than the long judgements of volumes. But his developed argument that socialism must be a development of democratic society, a product of democratic institutions, not a sudden scheme of economic planning, this is important. It would seem, tactically, to link the sense for sociology of the New Left with the realisation of the 'revisionists' that nationalisation is not the only, and may sometimes be the worst, means of control. If this sounds like a platitude, then read Strachey; he makes it pregnant. Socialism, he argues, is not feasible until society has passed through a far more democratic stage of liberal-capitalism than it has yet reached, From within the liberal-democratic ethos there is, he would suggest, still ample need and leverage for an anti-Establishment politics, for a discrediting of educational privilege, gentlemanly incompetence in business, and all that conceit and constraint of class which the old radical held in contempt sometimes more than the modern socialist. This is not, to Strachey, an end in itself; it is the point at which socialism can begin. 'How can one be a socialist', he seems to ask, 'without first being a democrat?' He strikes against both the intolerance of the Left and the excessive respectability of the Right. He knows what is wanted, historically and tactically, but he is not able to say so with quite that precision or command of subordinate detail which might break his book through the youthful barrier of resistance to anything—except a novel—over twenty pages.

Another brave attempt at comprehensiveness was *Twentieth Century Socialism*, a Penguin Special written by Socialist Union in 1956. Rarely has anything ever walked the high road of generality so earnestly and deliberately. Though it was, in some manner, infused with Christian socialist ideas of fellowship, yet its underlying wish to heal immediate rifts in the Labour Party had the well-meaning but fatal effect of squeezing it dry of all real content or controversy. Even socialist committees cannot write books—'one man one book', I say.

71

Anthologies and histories

The easiest substitute for attempts at a general theory are anthologies or symposiums. When the New *Fabian Essays* appeared in 1952, edited by Richard Crossman, the universal comment was of the diffuseness of their viewpoint—in contrast, it was said, to the influence and coherence of the original *Fabian Essays* of 1889. Now it is at least interesting that two recent scholarly studies of the origins of the Labour Party, discussed below, leave one almost no ground for perpetuating the Fabian legend of the vast importance of the original *Fabian Essays*. If one reads them one finds that they mirror, rather than comprehend and synthesise, their contemporary differences in socialist thought; and, in so far as they had a unity, it was that of one sect in the socialist camp whose gradualism was already a commonplace in the real Labour movement, but whose lack of contact with that movement was exceptional and remarkable. The latter part of this charge would not, of course, apply anything like as strongly to the *New Fabian Essays*. But if we get the facts right about the influence of the original essays, we need not despair so much over what is, in its essence, still minority writing; and nor need we look for a coherence of viewpoint which is simply not obtainable. It is enough to name the contributors: Richard Crossman, C. A. R. Crosland, Roy Jenkins, Margaret Cole, Austen Albu, Ian Mikardo, Denis Healey and John Strachey. The centre of gravity leans leftwards, but if there is any equilibrium, it could only be expressed in a most complicated model of nine different fields of atomic attraction (and repulsion) held together only by the thick lead walls of a political party. Reading it all again, the wonder not of theory, but of politics, fills one's mind; the historical achievement of a party that can bind these forces together—and a party of which, all too obviously, intellectual socialism is only one part. It is an essential part; it is the driving force, but not the machine. The editor himself, in a manner, saw this: 'To realise that the socialist society is not the norm, evolved by material conditions, but the exception, is not to emasculate our socialism, but to set ourselves a challenge.'

Socialist thought will, perhaps, be far more influenced by two remarkable histories, than by the attempted works of comprehension and the intellectual stocktakings of the anthologies: Henry Pelling's *Labour and Politics, 1900–1906* and Philip Poirier's *The Advent of the Labour Party*, both published in 1958. The authors are supposed to be at war with each other over intricate questions of who used what archive. But their basic agreement is remarkable. First, they agree that the founding of the Labour Party was predominately an urge of the Trades Unions to get labour representation in Parliament—not to build a new Jerusalem. Secondly, they agree that in the wider Labour movement theoretical socialism, of many varieties, was always a driving force, but never more than a minority opinion. Thirdly, they agree that within these rival socialisms, the evangelical style of the ILP was far more influential on the new party than either Fabianism or, still less, Marxism. One might offer the summary that the

Labour movement was a remarkably wide coalition both of interests and ideals, held together by a common sense of injustice arising from the monopoly of power held by the Conservative and Liberal Parties. To some, of course, this sense of injustice was or became a quest for some ideal justice; but to most working class leaders justice simply meant 'getting their due', getting a fair share of representation and influence in Parliament and local government. Why is this so very relevant? Because, taken in conjunction with Crossman's realistic idealism, quoted above, it should exorcise the curse of present-day socialist thinking: the myth that at some period the Labour movement was 'truly socialist' and that all is cured by getting back to the primitive foundations of the uncorrupted Labour church. Keir Hardie was, after all, Keir Hardie—a wonderful impossible person, not some protean Solon / Aeneas / John the Baptist / King Arthur giving the Law to a chosen people. The Labour movement has never been socialist. And socialists may stand on firmer ground if they do not sacrifice themselves to bad history and if they do not forget that while they are the keepers of our conscience, they are not the sinews of our body. Too many socialist theorists seem prone not merely to put actual democratic values a poor second to hypothetical socialist ones, as Crossman warned against so brilliantly in his *Socialism and the New Despotism*, but to put political values a very poor third.

'Out of Apathy'

This is the sad and inescapable conclusion from reading *Out of Apathy*, edited by E. P. Thompson, the first of New Left Books series to be published by Stevens & Sons under the general editorship of Dr Norman Birnbaum. It is a series sponsored by the editors of the *New Left Review*, itself the merger—oh, the crazy pace of contemporary history—of the *New Reasoner* and the famed *Universities and Left Review*. All this is necessary because I am reading an advance copy which will be published long before this appears. It will be enthusiastically reviewed by all those tired and guilty minds who prefer anything to apathy—but they will not be thanked for it, for the slightest quibbles of self-respecting criticism will be out of order; and the few unfavourable reviews will strengthen no end the apparent persecution mania of the editors and contributors. For it represents a complete rejection of political values. All is denunciation and sectarian polemic. It is, brothers, the revolution or nothing; damn your mess of pottage and God bless mine. The editor, Mr E. P. Thompson, modestly contributing three out of the eight articles, hops wildly from theme to theme—in one essay polishing off, in this order: T. S. Eliot, NATO, Mr Alistair Cooke, the *Manchester Guardian*, the Bomb, apathy, Mr W. H. Auden, Christianity, the *New Statesman*, *Encounter*, George Orwell, anti-Soviet intellectuals, Wordsworth, Mr Kingsley Amis, Stalinist intellectuals, Orwell again, Mr Michael Young, Professor Shils, the Natopolitan ideology, the Korean War, Matthew Arnold, Hugh Gaitskell—and a third of the way still to go. But always his red thread is a rejustification of Marx. Alasdair MacIntyre ends, *inter alia*, an excellent criticism of the ideological bias of Professor Popper's 'methodological individualism' with a demand that we make the 'intellectual choice' between 'two images': 'Keynes with his peerage, Trotsky with an icepick in his skull'—but the editor has already warned us that MacIntyre 'as a Trotskyite differs in some ways from all the other contributors'. And, on the less frequented level of factual exposure, not all this wind of rhetoric, we have Mr Stuart Hall assuring us in 'The Supply of Demand' that we spend 'nearly two-thirds as much on advertising as we spend on education; as much on packaging as on industrial research'; and Mr Ralph Samuel assuring us in '"Bastard" Capitalism' that 'packaging expenditure equalled the amount spent by the government on education; as much money was spent on advertising as on industrial and scientific research'. A moment's algebra will convince any brother that something has, indeed, gone horribly wrong with the national economy. As Dr Birnbaum remarks, *'New Left Books* is not an academic series.' 'We have been enjoined', he says, 'to celebrate Britain's tin-plate version of the affluent society at the same moment as well-paid professors at Harvard turn against their own.' This, in its odd way, is the equivalent in a normal book to a footnote acknowledgment to Galbraith for ideas borrowed (though one does wonder what Dr. Birnbaum means by drawing attention to his interest in the salary of a former colleague).

The ranting near-hysteria, the self-righteousness, the good old Marxist style of souped up violence, the quick dash of irrelevant literary polemic, all this would be a bit of a joke, rather than a serious topic for review, if it did not demonstrate, as the authors themselves revealingly harp upon, the vacuum of ideas in the rank and file of the old *Universities and Left Review*. Their fund of inchoate idealism has been taken for a ride by a few old Marxists who know what they want—the shipwrecked survivors of *The Reasoner*, which Dr. Birnbaum calls a former 'journal of opposition within the Communist Party'.

Inconclusion

The kind of writing that more truly represents the literary interests of the rank-and-file is in fact more eclectic. Raymond Williams's *Society and Culture* and Richard Hoggart's *The Uses of Literary* strike a genuine chord of sympathy among those who dislike genteel culture, particularly southern-English, even in its most sophisticated forms. These books have both, perhaps a little to the dismay of the authors, been appropriated to the New Left. 'Culture', wrote Williams in *Conviction*, striking a conscious slogan 'is ordinary.' But most of all, it is provincial or, if London at all, cockney not West End. For what is virtually a provincial or East End school of theatre has probably been the greatest intellectual absorption of the actual rank-and-file of the New Left— whose publicists accuse them of holding such tortuous and preposterous political views. The Royal Court and the Theatre Royal may prove to be quite as significant as *Conviction* and *Out of Apathy* in shaping the prejudices of the younger generation of socialists.

Suppose one took for granted that many young 'socialists' are not directly interested in politics; one is still left with something quite formidable, of great indirect relevance to politics. They dislike the Establishment. They may leave, but they do not dislike the provinces—indeed, a regional accent is rather 'in'. They are interested in society, in social structure—though seldom in politics. They are greatly stirred by the Nuclear Deterrent issue and by any tale of racial oppression or discrimination. They are interested in welfare problems, particularly housing problems, of which they often have some experience. They are nominally politically anti-American, but they have the greatest fascination with America, Americans and American things. Here is a set of attitudes ready to be taken up, made use of and assisted. There is no lack of a sense of service which could be invoked, even if not directly for politics. Let there be no doubt about it, *Out of Apathy* does not represent these people—if anything they are closer to the tempo of mind of *Conviction*. If they have not provoked a genuine socialist literature, in a curious but true way they *are* socialists—but at the cost of turning their backs on ordinary society.

Perhaps, after all, there are virtues in fragmentation. General theory will have to wait upon a still growing dominance of the 'sense for society' over the old 'sense of economics'. What has to be seen is that each section of the Labour movement will throw up its distinctive literature—but that two general truths, nonetheless, emerge. First, that British socialism must be inherently pluralistic—since the British Labour movement is inherently a coalition; secondly, that good use can be made of any form of writing which is prepared to recognise that fact. Perhaps neither 'reconstruction' nor 'revision' is required; but simply a more careful attention to relevance. Socialist literature exists already, for those who care to read. The recent inquests and recriminations have, fortunately, added or subtracted nothing. 'He that striveth for the mastery is temperate in all things'—if he is really concerned with 'the mastery' and not just with expressing his all too common 'personality'.

2 The Campus and the Caucus

Vol. 33, no. 2, April–June 1962

THE MOST practical application of a country's political thought is to be found in the relationship between its recruitment of political leadership and its educational system. The most powerful influence on social change may still be, as Aristotle first argued, ideas about education. Political education is everywhere, of course, part tradition, part accident and part design. The United States has had its full share of accidents, good and bad; and the present electoral accident of an unashamedly well-educated man in the White House reminds us of the importance in politics, above all else, of example. But example can only be followed if there are people prepared to follow—that is, both willing and able. The election of President Kennedy cannot by itself explain, any more than could the election of Professor Wilson fifty years before, the sudden and remarkable spectacle of one of those rare waves of revolt by educated Americans against their normal condition of political alienation. Mr Kennedy's election is not the cause of such a revolt, nor is it simply the product of such changes already afoot; but real changes are likely to follow from the heartening conjunction of his election with the ascendancy of a long period of conscious design on the campuses for some such assault on the caucuses.

Politics as a career

Many things have cut against the well-educated American regarding politics as a vocation or even as a normal career. He has had to contend with the normal pharisaism and prudery of liberals about politics itself: politics is something intrinsically base and venal, the 'badge of man's lost innocence', a reminder of the depravity of human nature and thus a standing affront to the optimism of Americanism. The very word 'politician' is invidious—in America 'statesmen' are live, not dead, politicians. There has also been, among the politically less inhibited classes, a fierce democratic dislike and distrust of the 'stuffed shirt' and the 'silk stocking' in politics, all those who would feel, with that former Tammany statesman Alderman George Washington Plunkett, that 'Shakespeare was all right in his way, but he didn't know anything about Fifteenth District politics' (views which make very old hat of the pretentious debates about 'the crisis of the intellectual in modern America', which are such sturdy space-fillers in the great American cultural quarterlies). There is the uncertainly of service when one's political career is tied to the fortunes of one and only one area. There is the lack of a system of honorific patronage to compensate the frustrated faithful and to solace the still ambitious when longevity finally outvotes the sovereign people. There is the lack of a genuine national capital: Washington plus New York might equal London or Paris, but Washington is too exclusively political to be the centre of the national mind—apart from politics it is a provincial Southern city, genteel and philistine. New York is, indeed, New York, yet its huge financial, cultural and opinion-making capital has no political counter-part—its political energies are sapped and diverted by a system of city, local and state government almost unbelievably chaotic and inequitable. The lack of a national Press has made the emergence of a national political class, as we know it in Britain, all that more difficult. The pull of business as a career is greater, not in a narrow sense of profit, but in a wider sense of being a more esteemed activity. And there are many other reasons besides these why normally, as Bryce put it, 'the best men do not go into politics'.

The 'best men', however, have themselves been long and morbidly conscious of this fact: indeed, the most commonly and the most strongly expressed *purpose* behind the great wave of university expansion and founding, which began immediately after the Civil War and has continued ever since, was that—in the language of the day—of educating 'a respectable and responsible political class'. Andrew D. White, the historian and first President of Cornell, typically bewailed 'the frequent want among political leaders of adequate training for discussion'; and he urged the new campuses to send forth 'well-trained young men, sturdy in the town meeting, patriotic in the caucus'. Precisely because of the difficulties, the colleges must fire youth with the enthusiasm as well as we fill them with the information thought necessary for regular political involvement. By the 1940s a refugee German scholar would sadly tell his questionnaire : 'It takes a long time for anyone not born or brought up in this country to realise . . . that . . . the primary aim of a college, at least potentially, is to educate members of a democratic society.'[1]

Political education in college

Nowhere in the world but in America is there such a concern for educating youth to show an active interest in politics. The Soviets may expend equal learned energy in teaching good citizenship and party spirit, but this is not politics. In the United States, despite local lapses into mere indoctrination, the professed aim, at least, is procedural and not substantive: to get people interested and into politics, not to get them of one mind. *Every* American youth who goes to college—and over eight times as many, in proportion to population, go to college than in Britain—will have studied in some form or other, whatever his eventual 'major' or his scatter of eclectic curiosities,

---

[1] See Maurice R. Davie, ed., *Refugees in America*, Report of the Committee for the Study of Recent Immigration from Europe, New Haven, 1943, p. 307; and on the same page the editor sums up many such statements: 'Whereas in Europe education for scholarship is the primary aim, in America the emphasis is on education for citizenship.'

something intended as 'citizenship', whether in the disguise of American History, Political Science, Social Studies, or subjects even more generous and comprehensive like American Studies or American Civilisation. So this is not a question of Political Science studies alone, even though the 'profession' is uniquely large, having at least 5,000 full-time teachers who dispense, in an average year, some 7,000 degrees.

Teaching the immigrants

Now there is, of course, a vital distinction between citizenship training and political education. Such a distinction may be the real issue at hand. But that there came to be in America some such training or education at all, even on such a vast scale, is not as such a subject for criticism; it arose from the public high schools as a condition of American life. For as soon as mass immigration began, and for as long as it continued, there was a need to Americanise the immigrants. When polyglot masses could become Americans by act of will and for the price of their Atlantic passage, there was a need to teach, if not the immigrants then their children, what it was to be an American. And there was a national moral identity, universally shared, exclusively and inflexibly liberal, which could be learned and had to be taught. The national identity, before the ending of mass immigration, consisted of a set of moral beliefs and a known style of doing things democratically; it was not thought to be a product of language, religion, custom, circumstances hallowed by time, or of a peculiar geographical limitation. If the unity of these beliefs was always greater than their clarity, yet their existence could hardly be doubted, if only in the hostility to them of European conservatives, and finally even of European socialists. But there was always an element of paradox in the deliberate teaching of a doctrine of individualism and freedom: every individual was absolutely free only to become a liberal. Americanism was liberalism, and the clearest example of advanced liberalism was America. But the existence of the doctrine could hardly be doubted. And the vast expansion of what Jefferson had called 'the American experiment' in geographical scope and in size of numbers (the factors which have made space and movement, not time and measure, the metaphysic of the American imagination), these made inevitable a greater substitution of doctrine for tradition than in Britain.

Training for citizenship

So citizenship training has commonly been concerned with means and not ends, not out of any academic modesty before the complicated world of the politician, nor out of any philosophic doubt that 'ends' can be rationally delineated, but on the contrary because these 'ends' could be so massively taken for granted. 'These truths' have continued to be held as 'self-evident'. This is, of course, a not entirely novel situation: English empiricism, like

American pragmatism, is a political doctrine disguised as a methodology. But in England once empiricism is exposed as conservatism, there are other doctrines to espouse which do not make one, *ipso facto*, un-English. The American, however, if he exposes the intrinsic liberalism of his pragmatism, or the underlying democratic assumptions of his 'neutral and objective' political science or citizenship training, has nowhere else to turn without becoming un-American. He cannot reject liberalism, he can only refine or reorder it; but he finds it hard to do even this because the belief that there should be a 'consensus of values' is far stronger than any urge to see precisely what they are and how far they are, in the forms in which they have been held, still relevant to an America who closed her doors at about the very time when she became permanently involved in the outside world. The international appeal of a particular nationalism no longer makes sense when natural Americans everywhere can no longer easily become actual Americans. The ending of mass immigration marked the end of 'Americanism' as an international principle.

Thus the teaching of citizenship has carried with it, over the last forty years, two purely political dangers—leaving aside for the moment what are called 'purely educational' criticisms. Citizenship training has become a ritual and an incantation imposed upon a generation whose parents are already Americanised, through the experience, possibly more complex and compelling than any training or education, simply of living in America as Americans. This has served only to strengthen an already existing conformity. And the continuance of this rigid doctrine, which made sense when America was the isolated haven of liberalism, into an era when, first, Americans decided to act with the national self-interest of any other nationality by limiting mass immigration and, secondly, when Americans faced the unwanted ending of isolation as a condition of American life, this has led to a lack of relativism in dealings with the outside world. No amount of enthusiasm—and the enthusiasm is great and commendable compared to this country—for including an endless series of topical areas of the world in the undergraduate syllabus can prevent all this exciting and miscellaneous information from being interpreted in the light of a single doctrine, if the doctrine itself is treated as above or beyond dispute. Information about foreign systems, of which there is more in American education than anywhere else, is mistaken for knowledge, just as internally the neutrality about 'value judgments' in citizenship instruction is mistaken for objectivity. Traditional values are taken too much and too uncritically for granted; there is a kind of 'traditionalism of anti-traditionalism' in American political thought which masks an intense conservatism. More research is held to be the answer to nearly everything; there is a kind of idea of 'worthiness through facts' in American political thought which depends upon the taking of traditional values completely for granted. The object of reformers has been, in the words of Lincoln Steffans, 'to put the facts before the people' so that, in the words of Justice Brandeis, 'the people will judge'; moral argument is not needed since the people are of one mind; there are no genuine differences of policy, only corruption of and falling off from the single national purpose.

These traditional values, happy and appropriate though once they were, now hinder imagination and the understanding of very foreign systems. So to the uniformity of American individualism is added the attempted 'internationalism of a particular nationalism'. The basic fact is that while the American experience and condition is still much to be envied, for its very middle-class classlessness and the very exclusiveness of its liberalism, it is less likely than ever to be repeated or emulated—indeed it was never really possible to emulate it elsewhere (not even in the Philippines or in Liberia); it was only possible—once—for individuals to join it. One concrete illustration should suffice of this curious blending of factual information and liberal idealism that is citizenship training. A book called *Goals for Political Science* was published in 1951 by the American Political Science Association, a learned body, as the Report of their Committee for the Advancement of Teaching. The committee discovered, from answers to questionnaires they sent out, that 'among political scientists in the United States training for intelligent citizenship is the predominant interest and emphasis'. Most of the book is then concerned with technical ways and means of teaching. The committee was content to define its task from the majority opinion of the questionnaires: 'If citizenship is the primary objective, then more attention should be given to instrumenting the objective.' It had relatively little to say about the content of citizenship training, except a brief, frank, startling and categorical statement of the need for indoctrination. They quoted at length from an article of Professor Clinton Rossiter's called 'Characteristics of the Good Democratic Citizen'.[2] The first two of these recommended characteristics are somewhat general: he '1. Believes in equality of opportunity for all people. 2. Values, respects, and defends basic human rights and privileges guaranteed by the United States Constitution.' The final characteristic is very specific: he '24. Recognises taxes as payment for community services and pays them promptly.' An interesting group rests somewhere between the general and the specific: he '14. Respects property rights, meets his obligations in contracts, and obeys regulations governing the use of property. 15. Supports fair business practices and fair relations between employers and employees. 16. Assumes a personal responsibility for the wise use of natural resources. 17. Accepts responsibility for the maintenance and improvement of a competitive economic system assisted and regulated when necessary by government action.'

It should be gladly said that this well-meaning nonsense proved too much for most prominent American political scientists to stomach. A large symposium devoted to the book in the *American Political Science Review* was nearly unanimous in denouncing such aims and in thinking that any 'goals for political science' were worth deriving from questionnaires—though no one

---

[2] *Social Education*, XIV, November 1948, pp. 310–13.

questioned the accuracy of its reportage of opinion. Professor Louis Hartz of Harvard commented: 'The first thing we must do, it seems to me, is to give up the proposition that the function of political science education, even on the undergraduate plane, is the creation of good citizens. Its function, like that of other types of liberal education, is to communicate to students the experience of thought.'

Now there are some grounds for thinking that this report may well represent, to some future historian of ideas, the point of time at which this belief in citizenship *training* began to lose its hold over the imagination of the best men. All this has had to be said; for in America this is the burden of tradition against which present stirrings have to struggle. It is the instinctive reflex of Americanism in time of trouble: to reiterate and reindoctrinate the hallowed shibboleths.[3] But there are signs that the troubles of our time are leading to some view of the relationship between education and politics more subtle than this.

It is here that the election of Mr Kennedy plays a symbolic role—not so much in that he is an educated man, but that he is the grandson of an Irish immigrant. If the Catholic grandson of a Boston Irish immigrant politician can come to the White House via Harvard Yard, it should demonstrate that there is no more need to continue to Americanise the immigrant. And if he has been able to take with him his Dean of the Faculty of Arts and Sciences, two Professors of Economics, and one Professor of History, not counting small fry, as well as other people equally likely to be famous and popular in the city wards and the rural counties, such as the former Director of the Rockefeller Foundation to head the State Department, and all this without rousing one-hundredth of the yammer and clamour which struck FDR's 'brainstrust' (who, incidentally, were a far less erudite and far more politically experienced bunch), then this shows that it *is* now possible 'to speak Shakespeare in the Fifteenth District'. University teachers of even 'citizenship' are beginning to feel that they do not just have to mirror public opinion, handing it back packeted in glittering technicalities, but may even think for themselves, thus communicating to students 'the experience of thought' and the curiosity to ask whether things are true, not merely popular. And when such an activity begins, a free society does have an immense initial advantage.

The rise and fall of McCarthyism

The rise and fall of McCarthyism, compared to which the antics of John Birch Societies are, however theoretically interesting, politically insignificant, may

---

[3] See, for instance, George S. Counts—Professor of Education at the Teachers' College, Columbia University—*Education and American Civilisation*, New York, 1952, p. ix: 'This volume represents . . . an effort to develop a conception of American education which will support the values of a free society in the present troubled age as effectively and vigorously as the educational conceptions of totalitarian states support the purposes of despotism.'

mark the end of the era of a civic religion, rather than of a political education, such as we have described and criticised above. For the plausibility of McCarthyism was fundamentally an unwillingness to recognise that, for the first time in history, American progress and security could no longer be maintained in purely American terms. McCarthy appealed to those to whom isolation had become a dogma outliving its demise as a fact. Because Americans had hitherto controlled their own destinies, threat and danger could only occur through internal treachery and conspiracy; if China had gone communist, this was not because there were forces in Asia possibly beyond the control of even a perfectly wise and sternly belligerent United States, but because of treason at home. And this treason was a product of everything which threatened, or even witnessed, the ability of the American people to control by democratic means their safety and their sense of inevitable progress. So all the *effects* of American involvement in the outside world became treated as the *causes* of that involvement: the United Nations Organisation, college courses on Soviet government or on communism, and above all, in a thousand manifestations, internationalism and foreign spending—meaning any realism about the need to treat foreign powers in foreign terms.

Surely the most remarkable phenomenon of the last ten years has been the willingness of American public opinion to drop this dogmatic belief in isolationism. But McCarthy might have lasted longer, though time was against him, had he stuck to his original attack on education, and had not, through fatal pride, taken on the army. For teachers could not answer his attacks that they were indoctrinating communism by claiming that they were not indoctrinating anything at all; they were forced to prove that the Americanism which they were indoctrinating was pure. But even to argue that it was a tolerant, liberty-loving Americanism compared to his was to stand on the slippery slope of public opinion. All this, in essence, seems over and past, though fragments linger on in wounds still easy to irritate, though no longer easy to open.

A new outlook

The essence of true political education is indirection, not the direct assault. And political education is as strong as education in general. Books like *Why Johnnie Can't Read*, Professor Arthur Bestor's *Educational Wastelands*, are signs of new times more heartening than any of the many 'urgent'—and tedious—attempts to restate and reaffirm traditional Americanism. The battle for learning and imagination has to be won in the public high schools before it can be consolidated in the leading universities. Parent Teacher Associations have hit the local headlines throughout the country with criticisms of 'professional educators' who still hold that 'democracy means', as this author was once assured by the principal of a large public high school in a middle-class suburb of Boston, 'giving all the children in our care exactly the same educational experience'. (The degree of 'streaming' in an English comprehensive school would have horrified this educator quite as much as the more obvious horrors of the English un-public schools.) These PTAs are applying a good old American pragmatic standard of criticism to the schools; but now 'the results' which pragmatism demands are levels of education relevant to different levels of ability, not the continuance of the integration or 'socialisation' of an already quite well-socialised population. Professional educators are even having conferences and symposia on the *problem of the gifted child*'; they will move slowly, but so long as they can have their conferences they will move if public opinion changes. And on the campuses there is a distinct trend, something more than one of the many fashions which from time to time sweep American higher education, for the students to demand—and in the long run they get what they demand—'problem' and 'content' courses in the social sciences, rather than the great fashion of the 1930s and 1940s for 'method' courses. There are rumours of war even in the high citadel of debased Deweyism, the Columbia Teachers' Training College; that content is being talked about as well as method, and that teaching *the subject* may well emerge as part of what is necessary—'in a democratic age, etc.'—to teach *the child*. So influential is this institution in the vastly over-professionalised American teaching profession that it is not too extravagant to say that a change in their ideas of education could affect the future history of the whole free world.

Everywhere there is evidence both of a revival of true learning—of a scope and importance which, certainly in history and political science, makes most contemporary British work appear, by comparison, almost desperately parochial and unadventurous—and, more specifically, of the revival of a truly critical spirit applied to the political problems of our times. This spirit does not reject traditional American liberalism—which would be impossible; indeed, in some respects, it is more secure in it than ever before. Sense can be talked about the American party system now that it is seen as something purely American, and not as a debased example of an allegedly pure case of (British) two-party responsible and ideological politics. But this spirit is almost wholly critical of the belief that Americanism is a potentially universal phenomenon. World politics can now be seen in political terms—of compromise and conflict between things which are essentially different—and diplomacy can be seen as diplomacy, not as the technique of a moral crusade.

For all the silliness of the deep shelter craze, there is more serious and reputable study of the problem of arms control than anywhere in the free world. For all the craziness of small-town anti-communism, there is more objective and scholarly study of the Soviet Union than anywhere in the world. For all the recurrent political struggles about 'foreign spending' there is developing more serious study of the political and economic problems of the former colonial areas of the world than can easily be found in the countries that were formerly imperial powers.

Thus political problems are at last being taken seriously as political problems, demanding both knowledge and a sense of prudence and relativity, not in terms of a stark contrast between good and evil, or in terms of the theoretical extremes of absolute military power or an absolutely convincing ideology. Communism may still be the devil of our times (as, indeed, in its totalitarianism it is—as we in this country[a] are often flabbily reluctant to admit); but the devil can now be negotiated with by statesmen of either party without the moralistic accusation, far more deadly than the political charge of appeasement, of contamination. Politics is reborn. The 'hack politician' no longer disbelieves that America is permanently involved in the outside world; and the educated man can now feel that he has some role to play in politics. In the 1950s David Riesman's *The Lonely Crowd* had to defend the values of civilisation against philistine conformity by praising the 'autonomous individual' in terms that were then essentially apolitical. This is already dated. The free man in the 1960s will feel free to enter politics without too much fear of sacrificing either his freedom or his intelligence; he may even come to feel, as in high periods of political culture, that this is the life and that he can gain by it.

[a] It is common to find 'in this country' in *PQ* articles of the time, and indeed later, reflecting the fact that authors assumed their readers to be the British in Britain, the English in England (or even the educated general reader in London). Nowadays, journal authors would be unwise to assume such a localised readership.

3 What Should the Lords Be Doing?

Vol. 34, no. 2, April–June 1963

ONCE more the mountain has laboured and has brought forth a mouse. The Parliament Act of 1948 brought life peers and peeresses into the Constitution to strengthen the repute and efficiency of the House of Lords. And now the Joint Committee on House of Lords Reform[1] has proposed that hereditary peers may renounce their titles and status for life, thus removing an injustice for some reluctant elder sons and, in some cases, for their loyal and unhappy constituents. Perhaps the government may even accept its recommendations—they are, as we will see, modest enough. Certainly the government will go no further. So another piece of patchwork is added to the already crazy quilt of modern government in feudal dress. A British Parliament can bring itself to tear apart and rebuild the whole administration of our largest urban area (albeit with a typical reprieve for the pageantry and futility of the City itself), but it still allows the mouse of reform only the smallest nibble at the ermine. The way in which the whole question of the House of Lords has been handled is now either beyond a joke or beneath contempt.

No lasting solution to the resulting set of anomalies, contradictions, privileges and inefficiencies will be achieved until both political parties are willing to look, not just at the question of powers and composition of the chamber, either separately—which has been foolish enough—or even together, which has been deliberately avoided, but at the basic question of the function and utility of the second chamber in the context of the work of Parliament as a whole, indeed of the whole framework of British government and administration.

The Wedgwood Benn affair

It is hard to keep a sense of proportion about the Wedgwood Benn affair. A personal wrong may soon be righted and perhaps it is a kind of victory for democracy that peers may soon be able to divest themselves of nobility and run for the Commons. Even in our mundane politics there is a bit of the romantic in us all which is joyful that a personal campaign such as Benn's can get so near success at all, amid the frozen prejudices and the well-disciplined party fears that have surrounded this whole problem. But the campaign was fought and won on a very narrow front. It was important not for its cause or effect so much as for the conditions it revealed.

Let us recall the main facts of the case. The First Viscount Stansgate was created in unusual circumstances. On 21 December 1941 a statement was

---

[1] HL 23, HC 38 (Session 1962–63).

issued from 10 Downing Street: 'The King, on the advice of HM Government, has been graciously pleased to confer peerages upon four members of the Labour Party. These creations are not made as political honours or rewards, but as a special measure of state policy. They are designed to strengthen the Labour Party in the Upper House . . . at a time when a coalition Government of three parties is charged with the direction of affairs.' He would certainly have been a life peer had the recent Act been then in force (or had an attack of the gout not afflicted Sir James Parke—later Lord Wensleydale—on the first day of Session 1856, preventing him from taking his seat and thus giving their Lordships time for second thoughts about accepting him as a baron for life). Since this was a 'special measure of state policy' there was an element of ungenerosity throughout in successive governments invoking heraldic precedent, rather than using the sovereign power of the Crown in Parliament to find some relief for the Member for Bristol South-East, before the crisis came. A private bill and a public bill promoted by Benn were both rejected. Then, on 17 November 1960, the first Viscount died. The House of Commons referred to the Committee of Privileges Anthony Wedgwood Benn's claim that he was not disqualified.[2]

The Committee reported against Benn: that his 'instrument of renunciation' had no legal effect; that his status disabled him, not the Writ of Summons to the Lords for which he had not applied;[3] and that the issue of such a writ, while plainly forcing someone to leave the Commons, yet constituted no breach of the Commons privileges.[4] And they rather gratuitously added, after voting on straight party lines, that they neither recommended the introduction of a special bill to help Benn, nor were they called upon to express any view about the desirability of general legislation. The Committee, while accepting the view that the House of Commons is the sole judge of the qualification of its members, yet hid behind the law. (And the story went around that one Conservative member of the committee persistently committed the politically Freudian slip of saying 'Hogg' for 'Benn'.) When the report was debated and accepted, the House refused permission, voting again on strict party lines and against several clear precedents, for Benn to address them from the bar of the House on his own behalf. But on this division twelve truly honourable Conservative Members voted against the government. Certainly, as one of the editors of *Public Law* wrote: 'such a refusal must . . . have injured the reputation of the House for generosity, courtesy and fair play'.[5]

Public opinion now entered into it, and Conservative MPs were left in no doubt from press, radio and television that Parliament had acted foolishly in

---

[2] 631 HC Debate, 171–74.

[3] The current *Roll of the Lords Spiritual and Temporal*, (1) HL, 1962–63, shows 68 peers who have never bothered to collect their Writs of Summons, without which they cannot sit.

[4] *Report from the Committee on Privileges*, 142 HC, 1960–61.

[5] Gordon Borrie, 'The Wedgwood Benn Case', *Public Law*, Winter 1961, pp. 349–61; see also Peter Bromhead, 'Mr Wedgwood Benn, the Peerage and the Constitution', *Parliamentary Affairs*, Autumn 1961, pp. 493–506—both excellent accounts of the whole case.

the eyes of the public. It is hard to think of a case in which Parliament was so much at odds with an aroused and informed public opinion. The new writ was at last issued for a by-election and Benn determined to stand. The Returning Officers have statutory power to refuse a nomination paper only if the formal particulars of the candidates and other persons subscribing the paper are not as required by law. Many odd holes in the Constitution began to appear. On 4 May 1961 Bristol returned Benn by 23,275 votes to 10,231, *double* his majority at the general election, despite much publicity by his opponent that his election would be invalid. And so the Election Court found when his opponent, Mr Malcolm St Clair, petitioned it. Meanwhile the House, on 8 May 1961, yet again refused admission to Benn, though with growing ill-temper and doubt as it realised how clearly it was challenging the rights of the constituency; here was, indeed, the clearest clash between Parliament and a constituency since the days of Wilkes and the Middlesex elections in the 1760s and between the hereditary and the democratic elements in the Constitution since 1911. But the Commons sheltered behind the court.

There is no reasonable doubt of the legal soundness of the first part of the Court's judgment: that Benn was not elected because under a disability. He had argued that the disability of a peer only arose from the incompatibility of duties imposed by the Writ of Summons. In practice the Crown only issues a writ when applied for, and he had neither applied for nor received one. There were precedents on his side—the whole status of peerage was much more uncertain and flexible until the mid-seventeenth century than today. But it is hard not to follow Victorian judges who held that these precedents and practices had fallen into desuetude (there is now, as with modern ceremonial, a kind of bureaucratic freezing and codification of customs and pageants once far more fluid). The modern law was quite clear. But what were the sources of the law? Nothing was to be found in statute. The sources were, of course, the decisions of the courts; the opinions of writers of authority; and the reports of the committees of both Houses. This reveals what was shabby in the whole affair. Clearly the Election Court would give most weight to modern decisions of Parliament itself. But the Committee on Privileges had itself refused to contemplate change or innovation. What was, in the eyes of the Court, the only unchallengeable source of new law in these matters, itself took political shelter behind a refusal to consider anything except the precedents and the opinions of writers of authority.[6] This was to the discredit of Parliament.

But the Court went further. It declared that votes for Benn did not count and that, therefore, Mr St Clair was the Member for Bristol South-East—an injustice and a political absurdity. The Court relied on *Beresford-Hope* v. *Lady Sandhurst*,[7] which had found that when the fact of incapacity was well known,

---

[6] The tautologous character of the doctrine of parliamentary supremacy has never been made more clear: Parliament is even supreme to ignore its own supremacy—but surely not its political duty?

[7] (1889) 23 Queen's Bench Division 79.

votes for that candidate were thrown away. But was it as 'clear and notorious' that a peer was disqualified in 1961, when seemingly allowed to stand at all, as was a woman in 1889—particularly when it was well known that a case was pending? The public might well suspect, wrongly, that if electoral law were not in a thorough muddle, an action would take place at the time of nomination, not after a campaign and the declaration of the poll. The Court could easily have avoided the absurdity and injustice of declaring Mr St Clair elected. On this matter of opinion it could have declared the election invalid and ordered a new writ to be issued. It was the first time—and one hopes the last—in which a candidate with a minority has been seated by order of a court (the House of Commons acted directly in the case of Wilkes).

The latest nibble at the ermine

Two days after Wedgwood Benn (Viscount Stansgate) had been nominated for the by-election, Mr Butler announced in the House of Commons that the government intended to set up a Joint Select Committee (that is, of both Houses) to consider: (i) the composition of the House of Lords; (ii) whether peers should have the right to sit in either House, to vote at elections or to surrender their peerages; and (iii) remuneration.

The terms of reference were subsequently narrowed to the second point alone. The Labour Party simply refused to join a committee on such terms. Perhaps the wonder is that they joined it at all, but for the fact that they had already fully committed themselves on the Benn case, albeit Mr Gaitskell himself had from the beginning shown far less enthusiasm than most of his followers, both on points of law and policy. For the Labour Party had and has no policy whatever on the House of Lords. The impetus for reform in recent years has been, with the single exception of the Benn case, Conservative. Since the breakdown of the 1947 Conference of Party Leaders and Mr Attlee's refusal to enter into fresh talks in 1953, Labour had pursued a resolutely conservative policy of letting sleeping top-dogs lie. They feared that any reform or rationalisation of the Upper House would strengthen its prestige even if the powers were left as now, or even reduced. And this was probably sound sociological sense; but it is political cowardice and, in the long run, politically untenable. It will be remembered that the Labour Party opposed the Life Peerages Act of 1958, though immediately cooperated in its working. Clearly it was absurd, theoretically and politically, for Mr Butler to expect Labour to discuss the question of composition without discussing the question of powers. It is normally thought that the nature of a job is relevant to the selection of personnel. But the real objection was to discussing the problem at all. One supposes that the government refrained from calling Labour's bluff by including 'powers' in the terms of reference only because they actually did want some result and not another stalemate. They were under, as usual, far more backbench pressure from their own supporters to provide some remedy for reluctant peers—after all, they have more of them—than was apparent in the Parliamentary debates on the Benn affair.

If the subsequent report of the Joint Committee on House of Lords was a mouse, yet it was a very pretty one—well suited to pseudo-gothic surroundings. The Select Committee on Public Accounts should reprimand Her Majesty's Stationery Office for not advertising it in the hopes of wide commercial sales among all the many literate eccentrics and men of humour still in the realm. The printed evidence showed the Lord Lyon King of Arms taking the committee relentlessly through the history of 'hereditary tribal representation' in the second of the Scottish 'Thrie Estaits'; Lyon showed that the Scottish Peerage had had the undoubted right of resignation *in favorem* and even powers of Nomination and Tailzie. Our own Garter Principal King of Arms struck closer to the eventual recommendations of the Committee; Garter did, however, find need to solemnly reject 'the genetic argument', but to weigh judiciously the 'social argument' as being 'too deeply embedded in human nature to be changed easily'. And much more of the same—including several disingenuous proposals, notably from Lord Salisbury, that peers should be allowed to stand for the Commons without renouncing their titles.

The report of the Joint Select Committee

The report recommended that:

1. Peerages may be surrendered. Existing peers will be given six months to make up their mind from the date when the new law comes into effect; newly succeeding peers one year, except if they are already in the Commons, then one month. The resignation will be for life, complete and irrevocable in every respect of title, dignity, precedence and privileges, but will be resumed by the heir on the death of the 'holder' of the dormant title (the Labour minority on the committee had voted for the extinction—technically, the 'drowning'—of such peerages).
2. The Peerage of Scotland (that is those created before the Act of Union of 1706) should all be admitted to the House of Lords. At present they elect sixteen representative peers; the additional number will be only fifteen. So here is an actual increase in hereditary numbers!
3. The Peerage of Ireland (that is those created before the Act of Union of 1800) have had no representative peers since 1919; so they should now be able to stand for any constituency in the United Kingdom and to vote if they fulfil normal residence requirements (previously they were excluded from election in Northern Ireland). This removes an anomaly without increasing (by about seventy) numbers in the Lords; but it emphasises the remaining absurdity that some people *with* titles may stand for election and sit in the Commons. This seems, for obvious reasons, inequitable.
4. Peeresses in their own right (at present some seventeen ladies) of England,

the United Kingdom and of Scotland should be allowed to sit in the Lords, or to surrender their titles on the same terms as all other peers.

Well, justice may be done—to peers. And once again it is done without infringing the right of hereditary peers to sit in the Lords. And no one questioned the continuing undemocratic habit of Irish peers and of holders of courtesy titles (many eldest sons of the senior peerage) being able to use their titles in Parliamentary elections. This is a pretty small point; but it is a pretty small-minded report. Mr Wedgwood Benn may have succeeded in his personal case; but both parties saw to it that no thin end of the wedge would be made towards an agreed and genuine reform of the Lords. Yet his fight could have very great political significance. His remarkable majority in the Bristol by-election should convince any future Labour government that public opinion is not so wedded to the Lords as the Lords make out. If public opinion remains in this mood, may prior agreement between the parties prove politically necessary at all? Would there be much risk in a unilateral Labour House of Lords Reform Bill?

Agreement as to reform

It is not too difficult to see a clear way to reform in the sense of improving the utility of the second chamber. It may perhaps well be, as Lord Chorley has asked in a tone of amused despair, 'quite unrealistic to think that any such agreement can be reached'.[8] Let us grant that the Preamble to the Parliament Act of 1911 was a quite unrealistic red herring;[9] no one now wants a 'popular . . . basis' for the chamber; the Commons is and should remain the only elected, national body in the Constitution. But agreement about the function of a second chamber is, in principle, great.

Let us go back to Lord Bryce's report of 1918 on the 'Conference on the Reform of the Second Chamber' of 1917—which is still the classic study of the function of the Lords. He distinguished four functions:

(i) 'The examination and revision of Bills brought from the Commons.'
(ii) 'The initiation of Bills of a comparatively non-controversial character.'
(iii) 'The interposition of so much delay (and no more) in the passing of a Bill into law as may enable the opinion of the nation to be adequately expressed upon it.'
(iv) 'Full and free discussion of the large and important questions . . . at moments when the House of Commons . . . cannot find sufficient time for them.'[10]

---

[8] See his thoughtful 'The House of Lords Controversy', *Public Law*, Autumn 1958, pp. 216–35.

[9] 'Whereas it is intended to substitute for the House of Lords as at present constituted a second chamber constituted on a popular instead of a hereditary basis, but such a substitution cannot immediately be bought into operation . . .'

[10] HC 9038 of 1918.

It is commonly agreed that the value of work in the first two categories is now actually greater than in Bryce's time, in terms of the time saved to the Commons, indeed for clauses of bills and statutory instruments that often would not have been examined at all but for the Lords.[11] (There is simply *no* case whatever for abolishing a second chamber.) The third function has been modified drastically by the Parliament Act of 1949. And the fourth function of general debate seems to do no one any harm and may sometimes do some good. The essential thing is that Bryce's first two categories point to the use of the Lords as an efficient working body.

The 'Agreed Statement on Conclusion of Conference of Party Leaders'[12] in 1948 stated that: 'The Second Chamber should be complementary to and not a rival to the Lower House and, with this end in view, the reform of the House of Lords should be based on a modification of its existing constitution as opposed to the construction of a Second Chamber of a completely new type based on some system of election.' The full concept imminent in the word 'complementary' is yet to be explored.

The Parliament Act, 1958

Then came the Parliament Act of 1958. It must be remembered that this was a Conservative measure, introduced without interparty agreement and without any mandate (the Conservatives, like ancient Chartists, invoked 'the mandate' in 1948). It was clearly intended to restore the efficiency of the House of Lords without diluting the hereditary vintage. The repute of the House of Lords depends upon its efficiency, and upon its repute depends the social esteem that the public give to the peerage.

Conservatives are well aware of the truth of Tocqueville's great maxim that aristocracies without function wither into contempt.[13] And the Act might have killed the two birds with one stone. But the use made of it has been both half-hearted and contradictory.

Forty-five life peers have been created (including seven peeresses), of whom 43 are still alive. It was said by the government in the debates on the bill that they would all be people who would be willing to play a regular part in the work of the House. In most of the cases this has been true, but not in all. There has been a tendency for the list to degenerate into, if not window dressing, then a supplementary form of patronage; and appointments have been made of people already so impossibly distinguished and busy that they have had little time for their duties. They seem to play no more or less a role in the recent life of the House than the other peers of first creation who provide

---

[11] See P. A. Bromhead, *The House of Lords and Contemporary Politics*, Part III: The Lords at Work, Routledge, 1958; and Chorley, Crick and Chapman, *Reform of the Lords*, Fabian Society, 1954, pp. 11–21.

[12] HC 7380 of 1948.

[13] See my 'The Life Peerages Act', *Parliamentary Affairs*, Autumn 1958, pp. 455–65.

most of the hard core of sixty–seventy regular attenders who do the honourable donkey work.[14]

About the same time the Standing Orders of the House were amended so that a peer *may* apply for leave of absence for either a session or a Parliament, and will be deemed to have applied if he doesn't turn up at all. Then he 'is expected not to attend the sitting' and 'he is expected to give notice . . . at least one month' before he might subsequently attend. At the moment 62 peers have leave of absence for the Session and 156 for the Parliament. But this is a purely informal and legally quite unenforceable tidying up—'is expected' forsooth! The Crown's Writ of Attendance is absolute. There is no legal power to stop any absentee turning up if the spirit moves him.

Clearly the Life Peers Act could be an effective instrument to create a chamber of men and women experienced in the administration of matters likely to come before the House for scrutiny and revision. And the stress should be on relevant experience rather than on 'public distinction' in the conventional way of the New Year and Birthday honours lists. It can be said that no one has been made a life peer who could not, with propriety, have been made an ordinary hereditary peer, were they willing. Yet a few good town clerks would do far better service than most of the already over-busy people of public distinction who have been appointed. If an element in a reformed House should continue to be retired MPs and failed ministers, yet at least an equal element of it could be, if properly paid, almost a career service, certainly something to fill an important stage in the career of a lawyer, civil servant, public official, some businessmen and some people in education: not all appointments need be for life, nor need 'nomination' preclude application.

A house of scrutiny

The true function of the Upper House is to save time for the Commons; to give more time than can the Commons for the scrutiny and suggested revision of complex public bills and of statutory instruments; and to discuss and debate not so much great issues of public policy but matters of administration and of the working of social policies for which the Commons seemingly has little time, or even, with the declining use of Select Committees, inclination.[15] If this administrative, bureaucratic, scrutinising conception of an Upper House as a Chamber of Review (or House of Correction?) could be grasped, and the

---

[14] See Bromhead, *House of Lords*, pp. 31 ff; and Chorley, Crick and Chapman, ibid., pp. 9–10. Some newer figures: the average attendance of all peers in the 1961–62 session was 143; the total number attending at least once was 578 (of whom 56 attended only once); and only 123 attended more than half the sittings. Of the 32 life peers who sat for the whole session, the frequency of attendance was: up to 115 times (4 peers), 100 (3), 80 (7), 60 (7), 40 (3), 20 (8), and two peers attended once only.

[15] See my *Reform of the Commons*, Fabian Society, 1959, pp. 18–20; and 'A House of Scrutiny?', *Observer*, 1 April 1962.

composition made appropriate, then one could envisage many useful *additional* functions being undertaken by such a thoroughly depoliticised 'Lords'. Committees could undertake work of investigation as well as scrutiny, to allay the continued public worry, and to fill the real gap in ministerial accountability, about the workings not merely of systems of public tribunals and enquiries, *vide* the Franks Report, but also the greater un-tribunaled areas of ordinary administration, *vide* the Whyatt Report. It would be a proper place for the Standing Council on Tribunals envisaged by the Franks Report, and even, with Law Lords active, a final Court of Administrative Appeals. Many forms of public enquiry, even many topics handled by interdepartmental committees, at the moment completely outside the scope or control of Parliament, could be undertaken or reviewed by such a second chamber. In this context the composition and work of the *Conseil d'Etat* of the French Fourth Republic deserves far more sympathetic study from British parliamentarians. And to press to the uttermost bounds of political imagination, could not the Commons, if the second chamber is both depoliticised and de-Lorded, pass on to it some of the detail of financial scrutiny of which it is more important that it should be done adequately than who does it.

But the main point is that the functions of a reformed and efficient second chamber should be studied in relation to the work of the Commons. It is for the Commons to use the Upper House as a policy-making body uses committees of consultants, advisers and scrutineers. The solution to the House of Lords problem will not be found until the next Select Committee on Procedure of the House of Commons has, in its terms of reference, the function of the House of Lords.

As for composition, the Labour Party must nerve itself, as Mr Benn has just suggested,[16] to cut the Gordian knot and divorce membership of the peerage of the realm from membership of the Upper House of Parliament. Halfway houses, such as Lord Salisbury has been fertile in planning, all have the same object: to preserve the social and political esteem of the Order of Peerage. This consideration is simply irrelevant to the work of Parliament—though it is relevant to the social mechanics of Conservative electoral prospects. And if this is so, as most politicians would agree it is (even though different conclusions can be drawn from the observation), the Labour Party should attack the inequity of the Order of Peerage having any special role in Parliament at all. Since they may now lay down their rank and run for the Commons, let them do so. They could be appointed to serve in a nominated Upper House the same as anyone else; and they are likely to furnish more than their share of people with the right kind of experience of service on public bodies and in local government.

The Labour Party has been wise not to be affronted by the hereditary principle as such in relation to the work of the Lords. But the Life Peers Act

---

[16] Anthony Wedgwood Benn, 'The Labour Party and Lords Reform', *Guardian*, 28 January 1963.

recognised that the peerage could no longer perform this work. And the peerage is, after all, part of an undemocratic system of social influence exploited by the Conservative Party. Social esteem may be, as the worthy Garter argued, 'part of human nature'; but there is no justice in continuing to give it constitutional sanction.

The House of Commons could well, as Benn argues,[17] be given power to override the decisions of the Lords by simple affirmative resolution. But his suggestion to leave the peers of first creation, together with the life peers, the bishops and the Law Lords, would still leave a chamber of about 250 members. If Mr Benn would consider what the functions should be, rather than putting composition first (in his admirable animus against the hereditary principle), he might think that something far smaller was appropriate— perhaps no more than 100 if most were genuinely full time, not Lords but Councillors of Parliament.

So the House of Lords should be radically reformed for two reasons, which perhaps up until now have only been implicit in this argument, but reasons which should make the Labour Party think the question part of the matter of Britain and not just a silly, quite useful anomaly which can be ignored on sufferance. First, that the House of Commons is overburdened with work and thus drowned in detail. Second, that the prestige of the peerage helps to perpetuate the undemocratic character of British life.

[17] 'The Labour Party and Lords Reform', ibid.

4 The Prospects for Parliamentary Reform

Vol. 36, no. 3, July–September 1965

SINCE there is in fact surprisingly wide agreement among those who have thought about the problem at all as to the broad character of what needs to be done, one may sensibly pause to ask, why is nothing done?

It seems agreed that four types of change or adjustment need to be made in order that the things we value most in the traditional system of British government can be preserved in new circumstances.

1. To decrease the amount of time the House of Commons spends in consideration of legislation (which is going to pass anyway, by virtue of parties fighting elections with programmes) and to increase both the amount of time it can spend examining and publicising the broad outlines of future legislation and policy, and the amount of time it can spend (particularly by Select Committee procedure) examining the efficiency and effectiveness of the day-to-day administration of the country.
2. To establish facilities to enable individual MPs to participate in these processes more fully and be more fully informed, most important of which would be a parliamentary library with greatly expanded research services.
3. To turn the House of Lords into a genuine Upper House for and to the Commons; that is, to do those things which the Commons leave undone rather than to presume to censure those things which it ought not to have done.
4. To increase the experience, adaptability and flexibility of the higher administration by increasing the amount of horizontal mobility between it and other professions. (I am well aware that most people say that they are more concerned with entrance qualifications and internal training, but I think that these considerations are derived from an unstated major premise: that 'bureaucracy' means the settled expectation of being in the same job for forty years. But here is not the place to argue this, except in that it is relevant to the question of the function and composition of a reformed Upper House.)

To these four broad areas of actual or virtual agreement,[1] I would only add one personal (that is, equally true but not so often admitted) point: that people

---

[1] See *Change or Decay: Parliament and Government in our Industrial Society*, by a group of Conservative MPs, Conservative Political Centre, 1963; 'Three Dozen Parliamentary Reforms', by one dozen parliamentary socialists, supplement to *Socialist Commentary*, July 1964; and Part I of *The Liberal Challenge*, Jo Grimond MP, Hollis and Carter, 1964.

need to get their theory right, but just the theory of how things actually work. Lord Campion, a former Clerk of the House of Commons, once complained that Members tended more and more to 'speak over the heads of the benches opposite them and directly to the public'. This is, of course, what actually happens.

British government is stable government and strong government because it is *not* normally threatened by parliamentary defeat (Gladstone in 1886 was the last Prime Minister who had a majority when elected to be then overthrown by the Commons, in peacetime at least). Governments are overthrown by the electorate. Thus we have strong and responsible government because electorates can get at governments when Parliaments so rarely do. The 'sovereignty of Parliament' men and the Hansard Society mentality cannot have it both ways: Parliament is so important because it is the link of communication between government and people, not because it does itself (in some strained sense) govern and also holds some normally quite useless, because indiscriminate, 'ultimate deterrent' in the division lobbies.

So, if that much can be taken for granted—certainly that agreement is fairly widespread, both inside and outside the House, that there should be reform— why, after all, does reform not take place?

Entrenched attitudes: the executive mind

There are certain deeply entrenched attitudes which delay reform, and of these the 'executive mind' is by far the most important. This is something that carries to an extreme the undoubted virtue of both Tories and Socialists in not being diffident about taking up and using power. The very success of British government as a continuous historical force has blinded many of those who work it to one of the most important explanations for the continuity of our institutions. Governments gave way in time to give some share of power to new elements. In allowing the successive reforms of the franchise, governments gave way—though they always gave less than the reformers hoped for—because they could see no *political* alternative, but in doing so they discovered that governments more broadly based in popular support are actually stronger—as Machiavelli taught in the great *Discourses*.

The reforms of the franchise were relatively simple: social crises took on, at least, superficially, an almost purely and narrowly constitutional form. But we are now in the middle of, nearly everyone admits, another kind of crisis, one quite as great but much less clearly formulated, quite impervious to any great legislative stroke. A seeming loss of energy in business and commerce; a widespread acceptance of economic planning, but confused and fragmentary application; and deep worries about the availability and use of knowledge. Many of these problems appear to be related to the class structure and the educational system, which we are then oddly reluctant to involve in politics (as if it ever was not). These problems are quite as real as anything in the decades before the two great Reform Bills. The polity could founder on them, or certainly run down to an intolerable level of bicker, inflation and emigration.

The problem is a social problem of making existing knowledge available. It is not really a problem of lack of the right kinds of knowledge. But we seem to lack the ability to involve people who already know how to do things, in the professions and occupations, in the *political* processes of administration. Laski's famous quip or dictum can be as misleading as the thing he rightly attacked: 'the expert on tap', he said, 'but not on top'. For experts on top notoriously cease to be experts and also lose touch with the key experts-perforce-administrators-also in their professional or scientific field. And questions are rarely simply one of technical feasibility, but of whether the experts or authorities in a field think that the project is a particularly pressing priority on which to apply their always scarce time, manpower and resources. Otherwise they will drag their feet unless convinced politically. The expert must be kept in touch with the political processes, not left just 'on tap'.

It is profoundly important to see that distinctions between pure and applied knowledge, between politics and administration, and between expert, political and lay opinion are all ultimately relative, not absolute. In other and more familiar words, any small group of people of different skills and backgrounds involved in a common problem is worth a whole wilderness of administrative sages demarcating functions.

To come down to earth, I can make a prediction based on this analysis: that such a typical (if unconscious) exponent of the 'executive mind' as Mr George Brown will become an advocate for parliamentary reform once the Incomes Policy by means of central planning and national exhortation has failed—which it plainly will. All our statesmen have suddenly discovered technology (even in administration and politics, as well as industry). Mr Brown exhorts people to be technology minded, Mr Wilson sets a good example; but neither man apparently sees this as connected with parliamentary reform and—in its broadest sense—representation. Parliamentary reform to them is a matter of fiddling with Standing Orders to make things more easy or more difficult for the government. They do not appear to see some paths of parliamentary reform as being a way of involving different scientists, technologists, experts and specialists of all kinds in the processes that go to make political decisions. On the contrary, the instinct is usually to try to keep these things 'out of politics'—which only means frustrating the things themselves and narrowing politics to what the House of Commons far too often gets up to on wet afternoons.

But first things first. The 'executive mind' on both sides of the House has little patience with even the existing opportunities of parliamentary participation. One thinks (to take worthy examples) of the procedural reforms of Attlee's administration all being aimed simply to put through government business more quickly, and of his later counsel to MPs not to waste time on constituency work, for 'Government Departments deal, I think, with cases on their merits, and intervention by an MP is often quite unnecessary'.[2] *Noblesse oblige*, indeed, and this kind of old Fabian trust of government is by no means passed away. Or one thinks of Lord Butler, when Leader of the House, speaking in the debate on the report of the Select Committee on Procedure, 1959, and going it strong against 'their proposal' to establish a Select Committee on Colonial Affairs, but having to be interrupted and reminded that they had *not* (cautious men) made this proposal, rather had voted it down. But he knew what to expect if such things were allowed discussion at all.

Now to some extent this kind of thing is endemic to government. A little pride in their own ability and a little indifference to control and criticism is part of the confidence needed to govern firmly at all a complicated and prickly country. But this proper pride of office has grown beyond tolerable limits in Britain due to the conjunction of three circumstances. First, the very success, stability and continuity of British parliamentary government since at least the Glorious Revolution; secondly, the mutual aid between the new public schools and the Northcote–Trevelyan reformers to create not so much a subservient as a super-servant class, not so much a non-political as an above-politics 'intellectual' (they said) or administrative class; and thirdly, the great effect of the two world wars on British administration: strengthening their prestige, increasing their size and seemingly validating their most disputable characteristics—secrecy, discretion, initiative and freedom from detailed parliamentary control.

These attitudes usually combine a great public spiritedness with considerable distrust of the actual public and, above all, dislike of publicity. Hence such different things as the concentration of the administrative class in Whitehall, rather than its dispersal in the field; the fifty-year rule relating to the study of public documents; and the lack of realistic studies of administration by civil servants. Some academics do not see this at all. One can be very impressed, on the contrary, by how 'incredibly freely' public servants will talk, even leading statesmen—if they are sure they will not be quoted. I can think of several political scientists who 'know everything' but whose lips are always sealed—sometimes one suspects by confidences intended to muzzle. For statesmen and civil servants to trot up to Oxford high tables or even LSE seminars and talk off the record is no great use to anyone except themselves; and it encourages some academics both to feel that publication is something vulgar and inaccurate as well as indiscreet (if you really know the subtleties of what you are talking about, you could not publish); and that they are only really concerned with educating the future governing class—who happen to be their students—and not with discovering and publicising truths.

---

[2] *Fabian Journal*, November 1958, p. 6.

Entrenched attitudes: mere politics

All this works against bridging the gulf between Parliament and the public and between both and expert opinion, which is the true object of both administrative and parliamentary reform. Another powerful factor is the habit of 'keeping things out of politics'. In this century it has meant, for instance, the replacement of the late nineteenth-century Select Committee as an instrument of advice and investigation on current social problems by either departmental committees or by the many types of advisory committees with independent chairmen, either of which may be hybrids of civil servants and our strange race of 'public servants' (usually people paid by universities for not doing what they should do in order to do work for government bodies who won't pay them at all), but very rarely will they include MPs.

This example seems infectious; recently there has been a rare old crop of demands to take things out of politics. 'Immigration' is the favourite of the moment,[3] but Cardinal Heenan unexpectedly led the field by devoting most of his first sermon, on return from Rome after elevation to the Sacred College, to suggesting that education be taken out politics: 'And if education, why not national defence and social security? The safety of our land and the well being of the sick and aged are of equal concern to us all.'[4] Indeed they are, which is precisely why one wants to keep them in the hands of Lord Denning, Lord Franks, Lord Plowden, Lord Reith, Lord Robbins, Lord Shawcross and all the other able non-politicals available. If I appear to be rude (which I am) it is because I do not think it always a public duty to help governments and Parliaments to shuffle off their responsibility.

Great issues are inevitably political. Even if both Parties decide to take an issue out of politics (which is surely Cardinal Heenan's real complaint?), it is unlikely that this will produce more realistic advice and more information than the traditional Select Committee procedure in which witnesses appear, make their record, but are examined searchingly by a committee aware of political factors (that is, whether people are likely to stand for particular solutions) and can then, if necessary, produce a minority report as well. It is impossible to divorce political considerations from planning, so the best way to include political considerations is to include the experts and specialists at politics—politicians; just as the best way to include scientific considerations is to include scientists.[5]

The habit of 'taking things out' of politics also makes it easier to hamper parliamentary politics in another way: by narrowing it. The debate on the

---

[3] See a letter from Donald Chapman MP, Eric Lubbock MP and Joan Vickers MP, *The Times*, 5 March 1965; and 'Our Political Correspondent' on 6 March 1965.

[4] See *The Times*, 2 March 1965.

[5] Some recent articles in *Parliamentary Affairs*, by Mr S. Walkland, on the work of the Parliamentary Labour Party's 'Scientific Committee', a hybrid of Members and others, deserves close study.

Machinery of Government Bill, 1964, is a splendidly sad example of this. Mr Grimond made the only speech that got an inch and more below the surface: he spoke of the fundamental lack of interest of the House in constitutional matters. 'The combination of the tradition of the British Civil Service and the laxity of this House in probing into government has meant that most people have no knowledge of how it works.'[6] The size of the Ministry is felt to be something, for instance, domestic to the government.

Some MPs and some Officers of the House still view with deep constitutional suspicion the efforts of the meagre six research clerks in the House of Commons Library—for, it is said, half the questions they answer are *political*, not House matters or—Lord save us—'purely factual'. The postage and travel allowances of MPs are related solely to their individual dealings with constituents or their constituency; even Burke's perception that MPs are political members of an omnicompetent national Parliament does not seem to have sunk in yet. And I will continue to hound and nettle Dr Eric Taylor until he either changes the title of his *The House of Commons at Work* (to *An Introduction to the Procedure of the House of Commons*), or, better still, expands subsequent editions to include an account of the work of the House of Commons, including the vital work of Private Members' Committees— which he regards as not part of the official 'House'.[7]

Portents of change

It would be unfair, however, to imply that what seems out of sight to the present government is out of mind—on the contrary. I am well aware that *The Political Quarterly* is a journal of sound comment and original opinion, not a journal of documentation. But I must ask pardon for now quoting a report and a speech at unusual length because otherwise they might now seem fantastic inventions.

On 23 February 23 1963 the Political Correspondent of *The Times* began:

Although he has been in the saddle no more than a week Mr. Harold Wilson, the Opposition leader, has already settled on a practical decision in readiness for the day when a Labour Government is returned to power.

Knowing that a change-over of Administrations will involve a delay before parliamentary draftsmen can produce the first batch of Labour Bills, he has provisionally planned to fill the legislative gap by bringing in immediate proposals for the reform of Parliament itself.

The *Times* man was not the only well-placed person taken in. A 'working party' did indeed get to work under the able chairmanship of Mr Charles Pannell, but they were soon told that they should concentrate on control of the

---

[6] 702 HC Deb, 19 November 1964, col. 684. See also William A. Robson, 'The Reform of Government', *The Political Quarterly*, vol. 35, no. 2, 1964.

[7] Because the book is such an excellent guide to procedure and is widely read as a Pelican, this is a matter of some importance: people read the book but come away awed but exasperated with the House. See our exchange of letters in *The Times*, 7 and 9 June 1964.

Palace of Westminster, quite an important matter, and that broader issues were so important that the National Executive Committee itself would deal with them as part of the programme. RIP. But not quite.

Mr Wilson did in fact make one remarkable speech on parliamentary reform during the actual campaign. Nearly all that was reported was his pledge to create an Ombudsman. I remain unrepentantly of the view that Ombudsman has become a gimmickry: Ombudsman is newsworthy. He might even be quite a useful fellow, but he is no substitute for increased parliamentary scrutiny and investigation of the administration as regards efficiency, not just abuses. There is a real danger that he will be used, if at all, as a substitute for parliamentary reform; and that his elevation as saviour represents a brand of legalistic thinking, more subtle than the old Common Lawyers' legalism it attacked, but legalistic none the less in its hope to turn political issues into matters for impartial adjudication. But be that as it may, my point is that only Ombudsman got reported. However:

The Commissioner's report would be to Parliament and would, of course, be debatable by Parliament. But, in addition, there would be a high-powered Select Committee of the House who would make it their business to go through the periodic reports of the Commissioner and report to Parliament on them.

The Committee would also be free to initiate inquiries which had not been the subject of a report by the Commissioner. . . .

Now I turn to the wider aspect of the work of the House of Commons. In recent years, the balance of power between the Executive and the Legislature has shifted in favour of the machine. This is perhaps inevitable, but much more thought needs to be given to enabling MPs—of all Parties—to make a greater contribution to the formation of policy, including legislation. I should like to see more free votes in the House of Commons, instead of the present system whereby every detailed amendment to a measure dealing with the regulation of the wine trade or some aspect of the criminal law is regarded as an issue on confidence in the Government, involving its fall in case of defeat, even in Committee. . . .

But I should like to go further. In the past year or two, we have seen how effective certain Select Committees—Estimates, Public Accounts, Nationalised Industries— have been in getting to the heart of some national problem by summoning witnesses, taking evidence and reaching agreed conclusions, cutting right across Party con- troversies. I believe this could be taken further.

Many years ago, I did a study of railway legislation in the nineteenth century and was struck that with the new problem which the coming of the railways presented to Parliament, the major piece of legislation was prepared by a Select Committee of all Parties under the chairmanship of the Minister, William Ewart Gladstone. This committee took the decision to produce its report with a draft Bill as an appendix. Now I do not consider for one moment that this should be done with the greater part of economic and social legislation which a modern government must introduce or, indeed, on any issue which involves Party principles and Party controversy. But I believe that this technique could be used more and more for non-controversial measures, particularly those within the field of the Home Office.

In recent years we have seen the wider use of departmental committees, consisting mainly of outside experts, with the Parliamentary Secretary of the Ministry concerned as Chairman. I am extremely dubious about this kind of mixed committee. Both Parliament and public administration would gain from the appointment of parliamentary committees, under ministerial chairmanship, with power to take evidence from experts and outside bodies.[8]

I hope someone at Stowmarket understood enough of this to applaud with more than usual fervour.

There are some points with which one might gently take issue. Mr Wilson might consider whether there really is any ultimate or worthwhile (certainly any predictable) distinction between matters which involve 'Party controversy' and 'non-controversial matters'. At some stage his qualification might either take everything away (just depending on the political climate at the moment), or else it opens the door generally, with proper caution and gradualnesss. But the important thing is his clear and unequivocal statement of the functional relationship between changes in the 'machine' of government and the need for Parliament to change correspondingly. That is the whole point—and the correct assumption that Parliament no longer adjusts, on this scale, naturally, informally, and inevitably. Modernisation of the one, in other words, is not possible without modernisation of the other.

A somewhat similar perception of the need for modernisation, if not immediately, at least not to be put off for ever, is growing in the Conservative leadership. Partly this is just a natural response to being in Opposition, so now there is a revival of some rather antique notions of parliamentary control of the Executive. But something extremely important has taken place already. Reforms, let it be remembered, rarely follow from conversion to 'bright ideas', but from changing political needs; the only advocacy for reform worth anything is the attempt to show that present institutions serve actual political needs rather badly. Now the Conservatives have discovered this at the heart of their own internal system of politics. The lesson of the Vassal case and the Profumo affair sunk in, doubly and bitterly reinforced by the *public* controversy (how else when private trust had been broken?) over the odd manner in which the Earl of Home was 'evolved' as leader. These incidents demonstrated that even the oligarchical and informal, known-to-each-other and trusting, discrete and clubbable parliamentary Conservatives now needed to 'police the deal' when it came to running a Cabinet and choosing a new leader and had to introduce some element of public law into their family concerns. This I take to be a sign that the old Conservative system of government by friendship, what the Romans called *amicium*, where publicity was unnecessary because people knew each other's minds already, where controversy could be contained within four walls, this has ended with Vassal and Profumo. Conservatives are becoming more aware of the need for formal restraints, not just informal processes, delvings and soundings; the need to institutionalise restraints is becoming clear.

So I take perfectly seriously the changing Conservative attitude to parlia-

---

[8] Mr Harold Wilson, 3 July 1964, at Stowmarket, Labour Party News Release, S/279.

mentary and administrative reform. It is not just that these are good sticks to use in opposition; it is that many Conservatives realise that part of the reason they are in opposition is because they ignored and scorned them when in government.

There are, then, some middle-term factors on both sides which make the prospects good that the entrenched attitudes against reform may be losing their dominancy.

Immediate political factors

The return of a government pledged to parliamentary reform[9] does raise some hopes. One does not expect the reformers in the Party to win their way by truth and advocacy, but it does mean that there is a background of real thinking ready to supply precise proposals once political events bring on the need to do something. For this is in fact happening.

The government's slender majority makes some procedural changes more likely and more urgent rather than not at all. For the government is determined to govern. That much was plain almost at once, however much a silly and quite unconstitutional howl went up for a few weeks that a government with such a slender majority had 'no right' to bring in big legislation (as for a few days the Tory press clamoured that it couldn't). But the Queen's government is carried on and it always has been so. And since 1867 governments have known that the grand accounting for what they do is with the electorate; only very rarely indeed, if ever, with Parliament—even though Parliament has the greatest single, though not the only, influence on how the account is drawn up. The limits for manoeuvre, even with the financial crisis, were much greater than at first supposed. And this for many obvious reasons to do with the system of government in Britain and the practices of politics.[10] But most important of all were three factors: that government Party discipline would be stronger, not weaker, on such a slim lead; that the Liberals could not afford to create for themselves a purely negative image by helping to defeat, even by accident, the government; and, thirdly, that any government is quite safe until the opposition is ready to fight a general election (with the added and peculiar contingency that many Conservative MPs plainly are waiting not just for the public to come to its senses again, but for their leader to somehow vanish).[11]

[9] Actually furnishing the closing paragraphs of *New Britain: the Labour Party's Manifesto*, see pp. 23–24; and also the last section of the Conservative *Manifesto*, see pp. 29–30. Both gave poor old Parliament respectful pride of place, at any rate.

[10] May I claim credit for dully and academically setting down the grounds as early as November as to why *any* British Government with *any* majority whatever is still one of the strongest types of government known to man? See my 'The Limits of Manoeuvre', *Socialist Commentary*, December 1964.

[11] As the last verse of the modern *Ballad of Chevy Chase* has it: 'For when they rode against the foe / The Earl was cast to the ground, / So they'll nae pick another fight / 'Til they've a new leader found.'

Since the government does intend to govern, not surprisingly, it does mean that it needs to take steps to secure its majority in standing committees; perhaps to remove some opportunities for mere obstruction (though one suspects that public opinion is a better safeguard there, perhaps coupled with the threat of morning sittings); and, generally, by several possible means, to speed up the process of legislation—not because of the present political situation but simply because, as in 1945, the government has a big programme. Some or all of these things will be done. But they are likely to involve a political price, even if Mr Wilson were further away than he is from July nights at Stowmarket. If the government wish to speed up the legislative process, they will almost certainly be accused—and rightly so—of gross Executive bias against Parliament and the rights of Englishmen (one can already hear Hogg getting up steam as Hampden, a role that suits him). So they must, even just as a political sop, or to keep the lads busy, strengthen parliamentary powers of scrutiny and investigation over the administration. Members are unlikely to be put off with opportunities for more debate, deeply though some of them thirst for that and that alone.

So the reports of the current Select Committee on Procedure will be eagerly awaited, in political as well as procedural terms. It is some hope that there is such a committee at all. But its terms of reference preclude it from considering accommodation, facilities, research and information, and anything as exotic as the relationships between the two Houses.

For there is still a great reluctance to look at the problem as a whole. There are little huffs and puffs of reform around. Strong back-bench pressure for a committee on Research and Information to encompass the Library; threats against the powers of the House of Lords; but there are no schemes to create a rational allocation of functions between the two Houses—which is the real matter;[12] and little agitations to televise Parliament—a matter whose importance it is very easy to exaggerate (and to underestimate the difficulties).[13] But of much more potential importance have been two short reports from the Estimates Committee[14] asking for technical and scientific assistance to be given to them, and for facilities to travel overseas on the work of the committee. Increased activity by and facilities for the Estimates Committee is the only possible path of 'spontaneous adaptation' at all likely, with some strong nudges, if anyone still really believes in the metaphysics of parliamentary antiquarianism: that Executive challenge always brings forth parliamentary response (perhaps it does, but sometimes the response is to go into hiding). A greatly expanded Estimates Committee could begin to specialise in its subcommittees and to cover the whole field of administration on some regular basis.

On the other hand, the Lawrence Report and its acceptance is a retrograde step. Certainly MPs needed salary increases, at least that small band who do

---

[12] See chapter 6, 'Nibbling at the Ermine', of my *The Reform of Parliament*.

[13] Ibid., App. G, by Allan Segal, 'The Case for Not Televising Parliament'.

[14] *Fifth Special Report* and *Sixth Special Report*, Estimates Committee, Session 1964–65.

work full time, but it was sad and bad, both in common sense and politics, to keep separate questions of facilities from those of salary. The Report, indeed, though it inquired into such matters, did not release to the saucy public any figures whatever on the actual burden of work of MPs and the facilities that are, informally as well as formally, in fact available to them. Would their release have been too embarrassing?

Theoretical conclusion

Perhaps there can only be a theoretical conclusion. First, that political events will force some 'reforms' on the government and may force them to make them politically palatable: to increase the speed with which legislation is considered, but to increase occasions and facilities for scrutiny and investigation. Secondly, that informal changes are likely to come the more MPs come to see that all these problems are related.

The British system of government is subject only to political restraints. But political restraints will not be effective or regularly acceptable unless they operate in some fairly settled and established institutional framework. We tend to call these institutional arrangements 'constitutional', but this adds nothing but a mark of (revocable) sanctification. Government and politics are closely related (for all politics is a form of control upon government). This is obvious. But it is also obvious that they can be considered apart, and that changes in either, whether conscious or unconscious, can take place without any immediate adjustments in the other. Consider, for instance, the change in the size of governments relative to control by their own supporters.

The politician will find this banal social theory: what gives political science a bad name. But, on the contrary, I think there are many 'stout government men' in both Parties who do believe, in face of the facts, that it is possible to change the machinery of government without in the long run creating changes in the character of politics and of its main (but far from exclusive) forum or context, Parliament. And also there are reformers who talk as if parliamentary reform was a matter of standing outside actual political processes and measuring everything up to some self-evident 'first principles': 'individual freedom', 'science', 'democracy' and 'standards of business efficiency' are some of them. In fact, one must look at the system as a whole simply because the parts of it affect each other. Parliamentary reform becomes almost inevitable because there has been such great institutional reform of the machinery of government.

Some changes will come simply as MPs realise what they are in fact doing and not what the older academic writings say they are doing. Parliamentary control is effective not because of the division lobbies but because debates are aimed at the electorate. 'Parliamentary control' is not a legal and coercive category whose concrete actuality is the vote in the division lobby; but it is a political category of publicity and persuasion whose concrete actuality is the vote in the ballot box. Parliament is not—and has not been for almost a century—a direct restraint upon the government, but rather the focus and the prime (but not sole) disseminator of political opinion and information to the electorate.

The need is not to reform technical details of procedure, but to expand those 'digesting' and 'publicising' aspects of Parliament. To be very proper and mod, Parliament is both the output and the feedback information centre relating to policy decisions in the whole communications system of society. So almost anything is relevant to reform, wherever it comes from, which would deepen debate and make MPs (not outside committees) better informed. Devices to enable MPs to specialise and to rub shoulders with experts are, however, more useful than devices for making more experts either MPs or administrators. Politics is itself a valuable expertise.

Thus ideas about what MPs should be doing are likely to change more radically than is the working environment of MPs. They will get the facilities they rationally need to increase scrutiny and investigation some time after, by hook or by crook, they have actually been doing it. But the pace of change could be greater if a government was willing to look at all these problems as a whole—not just a second Haldane Commission before the twentieth century is gone, but one that could survey the work of Parliament as well. However, better still for Everyman just to be his own commission and to think in these slightly more comprehensive terms.

5 The Future of the Labour Government

Vol. 38, no. 4, October–December 1967

AT THE moment one cannot open a newspaper without discovering that the Labour Party is in fratricidal agony once again. Now in Britain we have many extremely good and awesomely well-informed political journalists; but it may be that their, and their papers', involvement in politics is greater than the understanding they are able to convey to their readers of the dominant and recurrent factors in British politics.

How the press misleads

The very demands of the medium are to blame: having to appear to say something new every day, the journalist exaggerates the importance of day-by-day events; and he moves from personality to personality rather than identifying and following administrative policies. The demands of Juggernaut for novelty and drama can even affect writers of the less secure of the weeklies. Out of a swallow they make a summer and from the last point on the curve they extrapolate a tendency. Some journalists may itch to write 'background pieces', to remind their readers of what they may well never have known; but editors will normally only stand for this in the most disguised, dilute or titivated form.

Political correspondents should, however, have learned at least three lessons in recent years on the dangers of taking too short-term a view and of 'taking for granted' (or ignoring completely) certain relatively fixed and long-term factors in British politics. For, after all, British political habits and voting behaviour are, by almost any comparisons, very rigid and depressingly predictable (except to those who spend too much time talking to politicians before ever they read books about what happened yesterday).

'Suez' was hammered pro and con in the press; but whether pro or con, no political writer or committed proprietor seemed to doubt that the ghastly incident could not but have a great effect on public opinion and party fortunes: in fact, it appeared to have practically no effect at all—at the time it rallied people back (from apathy not apostasy) to their habitual parties, there was little crossing of lines, and the influence on the next election was negligible (as Leon Epstein's book, *British Politics and the Suez Crisis*, showed). Then the 1964 election result, the 'knife-edge majority' and all that, was held by all papers either to give Mr Wilson no mandate to govern or else to make government impossible—and dramatic day-to-day reporting heightened the plausibility of the latter view. I hardly went near the House of Commons that first winter but felt confident (like a good bookmaker studying form and wasting no time looking at horses) to argue publicly[1] that Wilson was actually in a very strong position, because of the nature of party discipline and the respect the British public shows for firm government (since no British government elected with a majority had been defeated in peacetime as the result of a vote in the House of Commons since 1886). And the third object lesson is the current hammering at, or bewailing of, the Parliamentary Labour Party and their leaders.

I want to disinter, at the risk of being boring and simple-minded, those long-term factors which make these present squabbles seem (if looking for political growth stock and not playing the market) eminently discountable. To this end, so as not to take the most important things for granted (those things which are the most permanent, recurrent and unnewsworthy), I will attempt to foretell the probable future of the Labour Party in government *as if for some intelligent foreign journalist and visitor* who has little knowledge of English history except what he may infer from reading the pulsing dailies and the exciting weeklies (rather than the dull quarterlies). And I will assume that such a detached visitor is not interested in Westminster personalities and plots of the moment, and that he will miss nothing by this lack of interest: on the contrary, will see things more clearly. (But do not think me critical of the press for dealing in personalities, for we are all, unless very austere indeed, interested in them for their own picaresque sake; I only criticise those who think that this kind of thing has any effect on long-term political fortunes.)

I will suggest to him that the chances of Labour's return for a third term are very favourable indeed and that 'the threat of socialism' (of which he may read in the *Express*) is as unlikely to materialise as is its 'betrayal' (of which he may read in *Tribune*).

Historical factors

Do not believe, my friend, most of what you read in the newspapers. The Party is not uniquely and fatally split: it has always thrived in public quarrel with itself. Keep in mind three basic historical factors. Forgive me if they are familiar, but they appear unknown to many of us. *First*, the Labour Party and the *coalition* of the wider Labour movement (of the Trades Unions and Cooperatives, etc.) was never and is most unlikely to be ever predominantly socialist. *Second*, the Labour government of 1945 was the product of abnormal wartime circumstances; the governments of 1924 and 1928 were minority governments; so that of 1964 was the *first time* that the Labour Party had ever, in normal circumstances, won an absolute majority in Parliament (even then a majority of only four, diminishing to one). So 1966, with its majority of ninety, represents something highly exceptional in British politics. Normally the Conservatives have governed Britain, it taking the effects of war or mass

---

[1] 'The Limits of Manoeuvre', *Socialist Commentary*, December 1964, based on a Fabian Autumn lecture given in November.

unemployment to get them out. *The question is whether 1966 represents something accidental, or a new pattern of forces? Third,* that despite the origins of the Labour Party, as an extra-parliamentary force it has both accepted the ways of behaviour that comprise the traditional constitution and has also developed an internal power structure of which the final result (but not the manner in which the decisions are reached) is very close to that of the Conservative Party.

A Labour Representation Committee was founded in 1900 in order 'to increase the representation of Labouring men in Parliament'. A specifically socialist programme was rejected, though most of those most active in calling the originating meeting were socialists of one kind or another. The new party was to be representative of the political interests of organised labour—see as Trades Unions. The balance of forces at the inaugural meeting is worth recalling: delegates represented 22,861 members of specifically socialist societies or small parties, but also 353,000 trades unionists. From the beginning the leadership of the party were socialist, and not merely *democratic-socialist*, but socialists who realised (in Ramsay MacDonald's words in 1906) that 'in British conditions socialism will be the last form of a successful labour movement, not the first'. One could say that the brains of the labour movement were socialist, but its political and industrial power rested with trade union leadership always more interested in immediate practical reforms than in social revolution. And even the socialism was markedly different from the continental Marxist tradition. It was predominantly a moral tradition of protest at the inequalities and hardships of the capitalist system, rather than a positive theory of equality. Indeed, one should always say in England 'socialisms' rather than socialism. Marxism had some influence, but a small one—even after 1917. As influential was positivism and secularism, but even more influential was Christian socialism, which survives as a style of idealism even among socialists who are no longer Christians: it is idealistic in theory, but very realistic in practice. The secretary of the Labour Party rightly said in 1948 that 'the Labour Party owes more to Methodism than to Marx', but it owed more to other mixed sources than to either alone or even to both together.

So in continental terms of France and Germany, the English Labour Party was right from the beginning a *coalition* both of interests and doctrines. Some Marxists, some Fabian socialists (few in number but influential with their doctrine of permeating and influencing the administration), many Christian socialists, many democratic socialists of differing viewpoints, more and more taking over the radical elements of the old Liberal Party which split in the First World War, and always absolutely dependent on practical trade unionism. It was united not by doctrine, but by common antagonism to the social establishment and the Conservative Party. And being united by a common enemy it drew great strength from the poorer regions of Great Britain, Wales, Scotland and the North of England, who had always been antagonistic to the power and culture of the London-based and predominantly Home Counties establishment. Hence a great potential political power, but a doctrinal vagueness or flexibility. A famous Scottish left-winger in the 1920s, James Maxton, once said of the task of any leader of the Labour Party: 'the man who cannot ride two bloody horses at once doesn't deserve a job in the bloody circus'.

Only after 1918 did the party adopt a specifically socialist constitution. Give yourself an unfair advantage over English commentators by actually reading these famous words:

1. To organise and maintain in Parliament and in the country a political Labour Party.
2. To co-operate with the General Council of the Trades Union Congress, or other kindred organisations, in joint political or other action in harmony with the Party constitution and standing orders.
3. To give effect as far as may be practicable to the principles from time to time approved by the Party Conference.
4. To secure for the workers by hand or by brain the full fruits of their industry and the most equitable distribution thereof that may be possible, upon the basis of the common ownership of the means of production, distribution and exchange, and the best obtainable system of popular administration and control of each industry and service.
5. Generally to promote the Political, Social, and Economic emancipation of the people, and more particularly of those who depend directly upon their own exertions by hand or by brain for the means of life.

Notice the very sensible mixture of idealism and caution. And remember that the making of a specifically socialist constitution did not alter the real social basis of power in the Labour Party. Even today trade unionist membership is six times as great as individual membership of constituency parties.

The doctrinal basis

The conclusion to be drawn from this simple history lesson is that the debate in the English and international left-wing socialist press about *how* and *when* the Labour Party deserted its 'original socialist principles' is either ignorant or wilful nonsense. It never was, in that sense, purely socialist, and in left-wing Marxist senses of socialism, never even near to being predominantly socialist. 'Parliamentary socialism' did not destroy 'revolutionary socialism'; it was there from the beginning, firmly in the saddle. Pardon this perhaps familiar detail, but so many of the popular books and articles on the history of the Labour Party have claimed that the party was or 'naturally is' (if not constantly betrayed by its leaders, etc.) 'truly socialist'. This was the argument, for instance, of Dr Ralph Miliband's widely translated *Parliamentary Socialism*—a piece of protracted teleology, rather like Arthur Schlesinger Jr's notorious history of the New Deal. (One does not need to be a bad historian in order to be a good socialist or democrat: I myself, for instance, would like the

Labour government to be more radical than I think it likely to be, but on grounds of principle, reason and prediction about social changes, not in order to be true to its history—I wish it could break from much of its history, which is just what we English find it so hard to do.) And this mythological view of the Labour Party is also given currency by Tory writers trying to create a fear of socialism under Labour governments. The *Daily Express*, for example, habitually calls the Labour Party 'the Socialist Party' and calls individual Labour MPs, even Mr Wyatt and Mr Donnelly, 'Socialists'. This is either abuse or unintended flattery; I wonder no one has sued them.

My point is that the basic ideological position of the Labour Party is remarkably unchanged since its foundation, either for the better or worse. It is a distinct viewpoint from that of the Conservative Party, but its views on what it is possible to achieve are very much affected by its acceptance of the Parliamentary system. Here the left-wing critics are quite correct. Even to speak of 'ideology' is perhaps to exaggerate if by ideology is meant something fully comprehensive or something derived deductively from first principles. Very often of recent years it is some Conservative leaders in Britain who have appeared ideological more than any in the Labour Party.

Nationalisation of the basic industries is unlikely to go further. Even the recent nationalisation of steel was really a hangover from the legislative programme of 1945–50. If there is, in general terms, a Labour Party economic doctrine of the moment it would be that of 'the mixed economy' (using the term to apply to the economy as a whole, not necessarily to individual industries). But it would be hard to describe any non-Communist industrial state as anything else, certainly Britain from 1951 to 1964 under Conservative governments. Yet there is a real psychological difference of emphasis: the Conservative still views government control and intervention as a regrettable necessity (but one to which he himself is well used); while the Labour politician sees it as the legitimate assertion of public power against private interests (but to limit the market mechanism, not to destroy it).

Wilson's election campaigns of 1964 and 1966 placed far more emphasis on the expansion of 'science and technology' than on specifically socialist controls. He attacked the incompetence of Conservative governments largely in social rather than specifically class terms: that too many unbusinesslike gentlemen (specifically the old Tory landowning families) were in charge and were hopelessly out of touch with modern science and modern business methods. And he levelled the same attacks at the 'boards of directors' of industry. This has, after all, a large element of truth in it in England; and it appealed to many of the more hard-working expansive and modern-minded elements in business. They saw—and to only a slightly diminished extent still do—Wilson as a technologist more than a socialist, and to be preferred to the Macmillan and Home aristocratic type of leadership. You should think of the doctrines of the American New Deal, rather than of the few socialist revolutions.

The Conservative Party is, of course, aware of this and most of its internal struggles over leadership in the last five years have been attempts to find more 'businesslike' leaders rather than people identified with the old territorial aristocracy of the country gentry. But their difficulty is that the constituency parties who nominate candidates persistently choose candidates on social grounds and this snobbery spoils the image of the whole party, which the Parliamentary party is trying to change (though it is not clear whether this is, in fact, an electoral liability—perhaps the contrary). This social cleavage helps to keep the morale of the Labour Party as a national party high, even during a period of disappointment with their leadership; and the continuing struggle over leadership in the Conservative Party gives Wilson valuable time and tactical advantage.

The personal factor of Wilson

As well as 'science and technology', one other theme, or group of themes, dominated Wilson's two campaigns: special care for minorities. Wilson seemed intent to picture the Labour Party as the 'majority party of all minorities' snubbed, ignored or cheated by the hierarchy of the establishment. The special problems of the aged and of the young were put prominently, as were appeals to specific occupational groups popularly regarded as under-paid: teachers and nurses, for instance. This was in tune with Wilson's 'American style' of campaigning, at times almost painfully copied from John F. Kennedy.

But it also revealed his basic understanding of the nature of the Labour movement: that it was a coalition, not just doctrinally but regionally and socially as well. Wilson has rarely wasted words on interparty debate: Gaitskell at one time felt that he led a right wing which should and could win; Aneurin Bevan at one time felt that he led a left wing which should and could (in the long run) win. Wilson led the party from the centre, spoke to the public and has usually stifled internal quarrels by ignoring them, or actually claiming that the diversity of the Labour movement gives it its strength. This simple but profoundly correct appreciation makes a secure basis of power, if a leader recognises it. Certainly one can now discount entirely both left-wing and Conservative views that the Labour Party is 'hopelessly split' and 'too divided' to govern. When Wilson has answered back publicly his critics within the Parliamentary Party (perhaps not always wisely, but then canine metaphors are like-coin for, if taken literally, accusations of 'betrayal'), he has done so not to support one wing against another, but to show the party and the public that leadership is undaunted by controversy. (And, after all, his party does contain more than a few splendid souls who would react that way to any government, let alone the present generous degree of provocation.)

The Parliamentary Labour Party's meetings, like the Annual Conference, are no real restraint on the Government, except in the general political sense that there is a level of unpopularity attached to certain possible actions which might still not split the party, but which might nevertheless destroy its morale. Recently Mr Wilson has on two occasions given the press exact copies of speeches he has made at these private meetings when resolutions critical of his policies came up; thus he gets his share of national publicity, and seems quite glad for the opportunity to show the public how firmly he deals with his own temporary rebels.

It is worth recalling yet again that no modern government elected with a working majority has fallen as a result of internal dissension except Gladstone's in 1886 over his proposal to give independence to Ireland (the bitterest issue ever in modern British politics), and Chamberlain's in 1940 over his failure as a war leader at a moment of unparalleled crisis. And there is nothing of such scale in the specific events of the moment to threaten Wilson's dominance over his colleagues, however much the rank-and-file of the Parliamentary Labour Party are disappointed at the economic cutbacks and the apparent ineptness or exhaustion of new ideas. But again, even to judge by lack of new ideas is a very intellectual way of looking at politics—to which both the new Labour MPs and the university-educated press are prone; but most of the electorate appear to judge on much more generalised grounds of a government 'doing well' or 'doing badly' (presumably, and quite sensibly, in the whole business of government). If we are disappointed at programmes and policies not being carried out, we should also realise that such disappointment is relative to unreal expectations, and is partly the product of the folly of trying to be too comprehensive and specific. (It has been an odd result of the international fashion for manifestos in the 1930s that few of us can get away from the idea that good government is somehow the fulfilling of *a priori* prophecies.)

Prime Minister and colleagues

In evaluating British tendencies it must also be recognised how misleading is the common description of the system of government as 'Cabinet government'. The Cabinet now rarely, if ever, makes decisions; it registers and coordinates decisions made by subcommittees (of ministers and civil servants) all picked and given their agenda (from which they must not stray) by the Prime Minister. He is no longer 'first among equals'; if they are sages then he is a demigod at least. This is now common knowledge.[2]

His power comes basically from the power of appointment in the Queen's name. He appoints all his colleagues, and is directly interested in all senior appointments in the Civil Service and the other government boards. In appointing his colleagues, rarely, if ever, does he consult. He alone decides when a general election will be fought, etc., etc. And the Prime Minister and the Leader of the Opposition play an ever greater role in campaigning.

But here there is some room for misunderstanding amid the new and better conventional wisdom. If people say that the British system is now 'presidential' or 'almost presidential', this should *not* be taken to mean that there is any

[2] But not before J. P. Mackintosh's book, *The British Cabinet*.

evidence that even Wilson, certainly not Churchill, could attract votes which would not otherwise come to his party (as plainly happens in the United States). To say that British general elections are now personalised is *not* to say that people will change their normal vote according to the personality or character of the party leader, but simply that one man, rather than many, comes to represent his party in the public eye. The character of the leader may have an important effect on how many of his party's normal followers actually vote (the Conservative turnout obviously suffered from Home in 1964 and Labour's benefited from Wilson in 1966). But even if people do not switch their vote for a personality, yet this personalisation gives the leader far more control than in the past over his own colleagues and his party's policy.

Wilson's popularity in the country is the basis of his exceptional power over his parliamentary colleagues. Only if the former declined would the latter be imperilled. Westminster is a very small and gossipy island, but it is surrounded by a cruel and demanding sea (a fact that some political correspondents appear to forget except when by-elections or general elections are pending). Wilson is very aware of this and is very skilful and deliberate indeed in placating the waves or running before them. The electoral prospects of the Labour Party are not going to suffer through either incompetent or insufficiently dramatised leadership.

The danger for Britain is the contrary, that a conventional reading of 'political factors' and 'public opinion' will make the Prime Minister reluctant to embark on basic economic reforms, designed—whatever their pattern of ownership or control—to get rid of stagnant and declining industries and to accelerate growth industries. Normally a Prime Minister would tackle unpopular actions in the first two years of office, but these two years have now been taken up with short-term unpopular measures stemming from the balance of payments crisis of 1966. Now the Prime Minister is wholly right to see that his primary relationship is with the public, not with his colleagues on the island of Westminster. But I have the heretical wonder as to why this relationship should apparently be seen by him as so much one of listening rather than of leading. You will see that the British press commonly blame Wilson for using so much power and ignoring public opinion. I think the boot is, in fact, on the other foot. The power of office is only formal power, a lack of effective rivalry, not a guarantee that if a leader leads he will be followed. The strangest thing about the famous power and stability of the British 'Cabinet system' is how little effect actually it has on maladies of basic social behaviour and working habits. Most of our economic difficulties are at that level, not that of the institutions of government. Personally I wish that he would, as I think he could, demand more from his supporters, and not try to follow them so much. Only liberals are against power as such; it depends to what use it is put.

Labour's support

But who are the followers who should be led decisively, not just governed strongly? The social diversity of the Labour Party is important, in its MPs a strength, but in its electoral support a limiting factor. For from the point of view of its support, the Labour Party is a class party with a huge exception.

Table 1 makes obvious the basic factors of British practical politics: the significant percentage of the working classes who do not regularly vote Labour. And there has been little significant shift in any such survey conducted between 1945 and the present day; and only a surprisingly small shift in numbers between 2 and 5 per cent according to different assumptions. This makes nonsense of widely expressed views in the British press and by foreign observers based in London and the South of England that, as the *New York Times* said after the 1959 election: 'the working class is in rapid decline as more and more people achieve middle class status'. Subjective feelings of status are much stronger in England than objective shifts in income redistribution (though these have, in fact, been painfully small). The Conservative Party has to avoid policies which might drive away its big working class following, and equally while so many working-class people vote Conservative, the Labour Party needs middle-class votes. And consider this in light of the *extremely narrow margin* of popular support which separates the two major parties.

Various surveys all agree that, roughly speaking, a third of the whole working class regularly vote Conservative with very little change in voting habits of individuals. The British voter is astonishingly fixed in his habits. If the Labour Party were able to carry even 5 per cent more votes from the working classes alone, it would be sure of something like the 'permanent majority' that commentators in the United States ascribe to the Democratic Party. It could win on any or on no programme.

Since the war neither the Labour Party nor the Conservative Party has ever gained an absolute majority of the popular vote. The highest Labour percentage was 48.3 per cent in 1945, and the highest Conservative vote was 49.7 per cent in 1955. By comparison with any other large country with real party

Table 1: Class and voting in Britain, 1964 (per cent)

	Upper middle class	Lower middle class	Skilled working class	Unskilled working class
(of total population)	(10)	(20)	(39)	(31)
Conservative	75	60	34	31
Labour	9	25	54	59
Liberal	15	14	11	9

Source: National Opinion Polls Ltd.

competition, the margin between the two parties has remained astonishingly small.

The Labour majority in 1964 was the result of a marked reduction in Conservative support rather than any sharp rise in Labour support (only increasing in 1959 by 0.3 per cent). Only in 1966 did Labour make significant gains, increasing its vote by 3.8 per cent, while the Conservatives declined to their lowest vote (41.9 per cent) since 1945. But Labour did not get as large a share of the total vote as in 1945 or 1951, and the turnout of total numbers voting (while high by comparative standards, 75.8 per cent) was the lowest in Britain since 1945.

A qualified prophecy

So on the face of it there is no basic change in the political allegiances of the British public. It is almost certain that the 1964 election was largely determined by regular Conservatives not voting at all, or voting Liberal, in protest at the seeming incompetence (and ill fortune) of their own leaders; and a good deal of this must have carried over into 1966. Many commentators said that the 1964 vote almost perfectly expressed what the British public appeared to want: a new and more professional-looking government with a very narrow majority, so able to carry out some relatively minor reforms, but not to make basic changes.

Add to this two more facts: (1) that in Britain individual voters rarely change their allegiance; and (2) the few who do change (or who do not vote on vital occasions) seem more affected by 'the conduct of the late administration' than by the announced policies or by the propaganda of the parties. Then the prospect (with all the economic difficulties of the moment) of Labour returning to power might seem doubtful (1966 then appearing as an exception, not a new trend).

But there are four strong contrary factors. (i) Labour does not need to fight a general election until the spring of 1971 (though it is more likely to fight in 1970). This gives plenty of time for recovery from the immediate crisis *if* long-term economic difficulties can be put off (not even to think of solving them). Commentators in the press at the moment are taking far too short-term and immediate a view of things, as over 1964 and over Suez. (ii) Wilson has twice destroyed the deeply rooted belief that Labour cannot win except in circumstances as unusual as 1945: psychologically this is vital; many undecided voters can now view Labour as a governing party of equal status with the Conservatives, not just a perpetual and natural opposition. (iii) The mess that the Conservative Parliamentary Party is in. The Profumo crisis and the controversy over the ambiguous manner in which Macmillan resigned and in which Home was chosen as leader seem to have destroyed their old habits of loyalty to their leader and of disputing only privately. It is *not* accepted by senior Conservative politicians that Heath will necessarily lead them in the next election. Like Eden he seems to have been born a brilliant and tough

'No. 2', but a very indecisive leader for a party now as riven with internal dissent as ever the Labour Party was in the mid-1950s. (iv) Wilson may be in a position to attract to the Labour Party some of this vital third of the working-class electorate who regularly vote Conservative.

Several solemn academic studies of the Tory working man all agree that his primary motivation is 'deference': he prefers to vote for his social superior, whom he acknowledges as such, rather than his class equals. But this 'deference vote' has been unquestioningly accepted as pro-Conservative, simply because it has voted Conservative. But what if much of it, even some of it, has in fact been 'pro-government' when Conservatives have normally been the government? Here Wilson's great personal standing in the opinion polls (still) and style of 'strong government' politics are highly important. The many jokes that Wilson is 'the best Tory Prime Minister we have had' have *a* truth in them. But it does not refer to the content so much as the manner of his politics. And this is likely to appeal to the 'deference voters'. There are some indications that Wilson is not unaware of this. Certainly he has gone very far to make clear that Labour has no shyness in acting like 'Her Majesty's Government' and exercising all the power *and* exhibiting all the dignity that goes with it. No one denies that in domestic affairs he at least looks and acts like a great Prime Minister. He must at least put the deferential in a quandary.

So I hazard the prediction that unless there is some economic catastrophe (as there could well be), causing mass unemployment, Labour under Wilson has made a fundamental electoral breakthrough. The Labour Party will fight the next election with all the advantages of being 'the government' which, in a highly deferential society, have been normally attached to the Conservatives: Wilson will fight when he wants to, picking the most favourable moment, helping by budgetary policies to stimulate that moment (as the Conservatives did in 1955 and 1959 with well-timed public investments, though they bungled it in 1963–64); and he will fight against a Conservative Party which has lost its invaluable reputation for doing 'nothing in particular' but doing it 'very well'.

Looking over a long period of British politics, since the beginnings of a mass franchise which followed the Reform Act of 1867, one sees that quite long periods of dominance by one party are typical, followed by a period of dominance by another. There is no natural tendency towards alternation: quite the contrary—that was a liberal myth. Governments, bar economic recessions involving unemployment, have a built-in advantage in general elections and the British public has always seemed reluctant to dismiss a government which is at least 'not doing too badly'.

So one must discount both all newspaper tales of fatal 'splits' and all left-wing nonsense that Labour can only win with a fully socialist programme. The key to British politics is still the working-class Conservative vote, and Wilson's style of governing seems likely to woo it, if not wisely, at least well. The influence of the constituency parties could wither away (as the decline in membership might argue) and yet Labour still be returned by the electorate as the party of strong government, the manager of structural changes in industry, the stimulator of technology and the provider of welfare. The Conservatives, their Parliamentary leadership faced by a third big defeat, may (as happened after 1945) become more and more dependent for their survival and dynamic on their constituency organisations; but Labour, meanwhile, less and less. Here is a possible reversal of historic roles—although the net public benefit either way is hard to assess since neither Party's activities are closely representative of the electorate. (Perhaps they should not bother to be representative, should simply be concerned with being right; but certainly it is nonsense for Labour's activists to presume to evangelise their leaders when they have so obviously failed to make socialists of their constituents.) Ultimately one must judge, however, by *what* is done, not by who or how. Labour may win and win again, but one may still be left wondering, like the doomed lovers in the poem, 'Have we come all the way for this?'

If Wilson has fundamental reforms in mind, they could come in the third term. Yet the full truth could be that programmes affect electoral results so little, and even actual policies scarcely more so, that the government could, in fact, do far more (or far less) if it chose without endangering its political survival. We are unduly pessimistic to think that there are many things which are needed for the country but which are 'politically' (that is, electorally) impossible; for at any time there are obviously more measures, large and small, good and bad, which are electorally perfectly irrelevant. But this matter of what should be done is another—and more important—matter. As to what is likely to happen, the fortune-teller's safest bet here fits well: 'a long life but little change in the way it is led'.

6 A Time to Reason

Book chapter; Introduction to Bernard Crick and William A. Robson, eds, *Protest and Discontent*, Penguin (*The Political Quarterly*), 1970, pp. ix–xx.[a]

'WHICH of us', said the Lord Hamlet, 'shall 'scape whipping?'[b] One of the contributors may have been too polite to mention us as among the fossils of Social Democracy which seem inadequate to give a sense of purpose or direction to so many radicals and socialists at the moment. *The Political Quarterly* solidly and stolidly hoes a hard row: reason applied to practical social reforms; a desire to change, but to change by political means; the illumination of desires to achieve a far greater equality and social justice, but working with the materials that are at hand; so in this sense, perhaps, irredeemably of the centre of the Left, but a centre that can, when stung to life, be as truculent as any in its self-defence and advocacies for the future. We believe, as the life of our late colleague Leonard Woolf[c] so well exemplified, both in reason and in being reasonable; but it is never reasonable, hence the waspishness as well as the gentleness in Leonard Woolf, to compromise reason to forces of irrationality, whether of Left or Right.

There is no party line and only the occasional bracing whiff of sectarian ferocity in this book: most of the contributors share a recognition that these troubles are likely to be with us a long time; that they are a mixed bag, some destructive, some stimulating, some bewilderingly inchoate; and so they had better be looked at coolly. Perhaps John Griffith provides a provoking exception to this latter maxim, and Peter Sedgwick carefully and sympathetically attempts to sort out the various schools of advanced socialist thought today, both from each other and from the backsliders. But there have been many symposia lately of exemplary writings of the radical protestors (though more, it is necessary to remind ourselves, from the Left than from the Right—however many stirrings are equally apparent there, as James Jupp brings out in his essay on youth). The views of the *enragés* and the *ultras* are not under-publicised. The general object in this book has been something more square and solid: to analyse critically.

Not everything has been covered by any means, and it is not claimed that the book is a fully comprehensive (or superficial?) international survey; some countries feature but not others, and we have neglected specifically

---

[a] A revised version of 'The Time for Reason', the lead article in *PQ*, vol. 40, no. 4, October–December 1969, but unlike that piece directly attributed to Bernard Crick (see my Preface).

[b] Well, not quite. The Lord Hamlet actually said '. . . use every man after his desert, and who should 'scape whipping?' But rather than amend the quotation or move the quotation marks around I thought it more fitting to leave Bernard's new edition intact.

[c] Coeditor of *PQ* from 1931 to 1958 and Literary Editor for four years after that, Leonard Woolf had died in the previous August and the book was dedicated to him.

nationalist influences even within the United Kingdom,[1] despite our deliberate concentration on our own immediate problems in Britain. Even so, 'what about the rest of us?', it may be asked. Protests of consumers, taxpayers, managers, professionals and the middle class are not without their interest and patronage; Young Liberals are a strange and interesting lot, worth treatment on their own; Michael Young's 'Open Group' has just rallied some of these inchoate forces into some kind of doctrinal utterance. And Edward Goodman's recent Acton Society pamphlet deserves close attention by any worried about both the technical and the qualitative problems of scale: his radical liberalism has many points of contact with those socialists who still think, or think again, of the small group as well as the central plan.[2] Obviously there is a danger in this book, as always, that in examining interesting extremes, one exaggerates their importance—as the Press has shown in building up a few self-styled student leaders and, more generally, in persistently referring to a very few extremists as 'the students', seeming to accept their own analysis that they are the leading point of a trend which only fails to touch the mass of students because of sloth and deceit. In fact, as Trevor Fisk brings out, students contain many subcultures; they are almost as mixed a lot as the rest of us; and many of the self-styled 'advanced elements' are in fact simply 'way out', sadly directionless and tragically lost.

Certainly the ideologies of the extremists are an extremely bad guide to the reasons why they suddenly appear to flourish. Their explanatory value is low and even their prescriptions have to be taken with some salt as a guide to the actual or probable behaviour of their advocates. They thrive not through their own merits, but by the prior failure of the established order of society to carry conviction. The revolutionary would not agree, but the theorist of the revolutions might, that it is the declining self-confidence of, and the growing internal discontent within, a governing order that create the conditions for effective revolutionary protest. Revolutions take place when governments break down, not just by purposeful and heroic struggles from below. And those who fortunately seize the chance of power are, certainly in their ideologies and their historical writings, far too obsessed with themselves and their opportunities to understand the basic reasons for the decline of the old order. Only if those are understood will 'the new men', if ever they come to power, cease to act so remarkably and depressingly like the old. I admire Peter Sedgwick's careful analysis of the varieties of current socialist thought, but I must remain more sceptical than he about both their novelty and, quite simply, their clarity and truth.

Certainly our times appear to be, now and rather suddenly, uniquely troubled: the students, eastern Europe, China, Vietnam, 'Biafra', Castroism,

[1] But see in recent issues of *The Political Quarterly*, Cornelius O'Leary, 'Northern Ireland: The Politics of Illusion' (July–September 1969); E. Hudson Davies, MP, 'Welsh Nationalism' (July–September 1968); J. B. Mackintosh, MP, 'Scottish Nationalism (October–December 1967).
[2] Edward Goodman, *The Impact of Size: A Study of Human and Economic Values in Modern Industrial Society*, Acton Society, 1969.

'Black Power' and militant civil rights movements in the United States and now Northern Ireland, and, more humbly domestic but equally surprising, the sudden convergence of demands for reform of some of our basic institutions (Parliament, the Civil Service, Local Government, town planning, etc.) and some steps taken. It would be foolish not to see something unique in the convergence of so many currents, but it is possible—as Margaret Cole hints—to exaggerate the uniqueness of these events. So many of the young rebels have so little sense of history. The whole modern world has been turbulent and unsettled since the time of the French and industrial revolutions—if one defines modernity itself in terms of high rates of change of material environment and social values and, still more, in terms of a growing expectation of change. There is, by contrast, often depressingly little real change in the so-called 'development territories', but the expectations are great and men are governed by their expectations of what will happen quite as much as by their beliefs as to what is the case at the transitory moment.

During these times of great change, legality and constitutionalism have also made great strides, so that in Britain we now have a very low tolerance of disorder and public violence compared to our eighteenth-century ancestors (or, for that matter, to modern Americans). One has only to recall the lack of police in old London, the constant threats to the person in the street and the recurrent riots. The Gordon Riots were, after all, for a country at war, a remarkable event. And the conduct of elections right up until the 1890s, longer in Ireland, hardly shared the respectable dullness of today. Sometimes for 'student' one is tempted to read 'apprentice' and, recalling seventeenth- and eighteenth-century history, to murmur '*Déjà vu*'. Days of misrule and riots were once much more common and yet governments, let alone 'society', did not feel threatened by them in general, only particularly and personally. Would some of our political leaders who now deplore 'apathy' really like to have stood amid the shower of animal, vegetable and mineral matter of the nineteenth-century hustings? Perhaps for too long now we have become habituated to these forms of public participation turning entirely to football and scarcely even marginally to politics.

So let us beware, without becoming complacent, of exaggeration. Youth has usually been a somewhat nasty and threatening spectacle to middle age. The problem is not that of one generation supplanting another—unless some Rousseau–Herod were to arise—but is one, as David Rapoport argues so well, of the relationship between generations. And we are also apt to draw too sharp a line between order and violence. Politics is, in fact, rich with intermediate gradations between compliance and killing. Dr Johnson was going too far to say that behind every state must stand the public hangman (although the anarchists would agree with Duncan Sandys in this, at least); but equally rebellion usually has its limits, and its ritual. The eighteenth-century mob, for instance, smashed windows which were not illuminated in honour of popular heroes, but there is much negative evidence that the householders had due warning to get into the back rooms. Levels of violence can increase drastically, but usually violence is of specific kinds: it need not, as again the high Tory and the bomb-anarchist both believe, escalate comprehensively. Collective violence has far more tradition in its varied forms than the traumas of individual psychosis (which is one reason why psychoanalysis is a poor guide to history). There is a difference, after all, between assassination of individuals, terrorism against a class, and communal massacres—just as with individual political failure there is a difference between execution, imprisonment, exile, retirement and a seat in the Lords. Some of our worries arise because of an inadequate vocabulary to conceptualise modern politics: opinion, pressure, threat, strike, demonstration, parade, riot, rebellion, *coup d'état*, civil war and revolution all need distinguishing as, in some way, different forces with different conventions. Until we can be a little more precise in some of these respects, defenders of the status quo, reformers and revolutionaries all very often confuse and alarm themselves quite as much as their opponents. 'Revolution', or anything as clear cut, is simply not the issue in Britain, nor is it to be found in the cards before us and nor are there any but a handful of highly debatable and historically specific examples anywhere in the modern world.

What are typical of the modern world are not clear and unique threats or hopes, but the bewildering number of alternatives and the unprecedented intermingling of different time-scales of social and economic change. We all know now, thanks to television even more than the Press, 'how the other half lives'. *Seeing* how so many other kinds of people live, people conclude that things could so easily be different, here and there, were there a concerted will. So we all become disappointed, aggrieved and restless to an extraordinary degree: not just 'Youth', but even those older ones who see this Youth as either a UNIQUE PROMISE or a UNIQUE THREAT. It was, after all, *The Times*, not the *Black Dwarf*, which had an editorial in May 1968 on 'The Sickness of a Capitalist Civilization'. It did not mean to imply that the disease was fatal, but it did assert that the sickness was radical: no amount of material prosperity could make up for what seemed to be a qualitative hole right in the heart of our culture. Some of us had heard that before, but not from such a quarter. And if the editorial writers of *The Times* had stayed a little frightened—which is, at times, a good stimulus to thought—they might have come to see that the problem of conflict between the generations, if such it is, is unlikely to be solved by playing-fields, adventure playgrounds, fresh air and the Duke of Edinburgh or even Prince Charles.

Even on the level of the consumption of goods, there is something both very enjoyable and plainly decadent in the prodigality of alternatives that our society showers upon us. It is becoming hard even to choose with any rational consistency—and most of the choices are trivial. Even 'fashionable' is now too rigid a concept for the trendy: the future is anticipated, but then neglected for yet another possible trend. And with ideas as for goods, everything is tasted but nothing is digested.

On top of these cultural tendencies, there is the greater uncertainty of the international situation. But, it is worth pointing out, there is also perhaps less real fear. The political events of 1956 meant the breakdown of the international Communist movement, or certainly of the Russian hegemony in it. Looking back to the 1945–55 era, this was a fantastic thing that no one dared to predict; and still more fantastic would have been the idea of a Russian–American 'understanding' growing out of mutual fear of China and distrust of the endless exactions of their own nominal allies. In the 'bipolar' world of the Cold War, there was the Great Fear of atomic warfare. The possibility remains, but—one dares to say, even to protesting Youth—the great and pressing fear has gone: the situation has now grown too complicated to think that there are any longer two clear sides of which one could knock out the other to ensure both world power and peace. But also, amid the great nuclear fear, there was a kind of clarity and, even if an unwanted certainty about where the world stood, a certainty nevertheless. Now that has gone. And, further, the break-up of so many international Communist parties released so many activists in so many different directions, but yet gave no focus to the generation just then growing up. If the youth of today had grown up in a world in which, as so very recently, the Communist Party dominated the Left, many would have looked at it eagerly, rejecting their present society as hollow or inadequate, but few would have joined it with its grim record of subservience to Russia and internal corruption. Those few, however, would have been the tough ones and their joining tended to push the rest, however uneasily, into organisations either specifically anti-Communist or lamely fellow-travelling.

Now a whole generation has grown up since 1956 into this fragmented and diffused stock of dissent. It was always easier to define one's enemies than one's concrete objectives; but, in the past, the objectives were provided either by the Communist Party or, in Britain, by the Labour Party—even if there had been for long a myth that Labour once had had genuinely socialist objectives away from which it was constantly backsliding but towards which it could be brought back again. Rebels were left without a cause, indeed. CND broke up as the Great Fear diminished, or rather grew so complicated; and suddenly the conviction grew that the real antagonisms were those of generation rather than of economic class, status or the possession of political power. Plainly there is something in this theory of generation conflict, but equally plainly it is, as both French and American experience suggest, a convenient doctrine for middle-class socialists rebelling against the gradualism and indulgence of their middle-class and socialist parents, as well as a side-effect of the fantastic concentration of commercial advertising upon the teenage generation. There has been, as it were, a conspiracy of flattery that equates inexperience with political purity and urges the young to try, by deeds if not in years, to stay young for ever. One feels as hypocritically sorry for the ageing revolutionary lecturer trying to keep up with his students as one does for the bank manager under orders to hook 'the spenders of tomorrow' however wobbly is their credit today.

123

In this context in Great Britain must be seen the colossal failure of the Labour Party in the 1950s to endure, at the very moment when the Communists had played into their hands, the verbal assaults of the Labour League of Youth and then the Young Socialists. So touchy were the Party leaders at internal criticism, so unperceptive were they of the consequences of 1956, that instead of pursuing a cynical or indulgent policy of letting little dogs bark, or of wading in and arguing with them, but keeping them in touch with the rank-and-file of the Labour movement at almost any cost, they took them at their word; even though they disbelieved in ideologies themselves, they rose to every verbal provocation and expelled them or murmured 'good riddance . . .' as they withdrew. And in power the Labour government has done no better. Let us sadly admit an element of theatricality—almost of escapism—in the great youth causes of Vietnam, Cuba, Rhodesia and 'Biafra' (with no international brigades as for Spain in the 1930s, only weekend demonstrations under the tolerant eye of the London police); but none of the Labour leaders had even the most cynical perception of what even apparent concern for these problems might have done to mend their domestic political fences. Must the voice of Britain in foreign affairs always be so uniquely and deadeningly diplomatic? And must the deep concern of so many young people for international problems—as witnessed in the huge oversubscription for Voluntary Service Overseas, or membership of the United Nations Association—be steered only into such impeccably non-political channels? For there is now a Labour Party in Great Britain virtually without young members or influence on youth, and this is at a time when, even though let down by their government, there is, at least, a great radical ferment among young people—but one going in fragmented and wildly disparate directions through lack of any intelligent and perceptive leadership (some even leaning more towards Powell than socialism). The young will not thank the government simply for giving them votes: they want something more compelling to vote about.

But see all this also in a still wider context. What price now the much-vaunted 'end of ideology'? It did not take CIA money to make the regular contributors of *Encounter*, for instance, picture the Cold War as a contrast between a practical-minded empiricism (or was it pragmatism?) and ideology. They already believed, as part of a Mandarin upper-middle-class liberal culture, that positive beliefs were positively harmful. The polemic against ideology as something comprehensive and actually or potentially totalitarian was justified, but all forms of doctrine were then seen as ideological: the whole vast middle ground of reform between empiricism (that is, acceptance of the present order) and compulsive, total alternatives was almost wilfully obscured. The effect of bad ideas in the 1930s and 1940s made men frightened in the 1950s and early 1960s of ideas at all—even the good revolutionary ideas of liberty, equality and fraternity as restated in Democratic Socialism. Moreover, philosophy, it was held, should not deal with value-questions, and social philosophy was a very funny kind of discipline at best concerned to stop one believing in anything. British academic philosophy is much to blame in helping to create that unnatural vacuum in education, an almost complete lack of challenge to the young or visible concern with the great issues of humanity, which both Ernest Gellner and Arthur Koestler discuss and deplore in different ways. So far from being at 'the end of ideology' we may hopefully be at the beginning of a revival of a recognition of the importance of social and political theory, both to show us how much we assume already (even the most practical of us) and to point new goals and new directions. We British have been blinkered empiricists for too long. Never has there been a time more ripe for constructive social and political thinking. As vast dogmatic alternatives collapse and as 'the merely practical' stands discredited, there is need to pick and choose rationally and qualitatively amid the debris and the mud (as the Czechs attempted so brilliantly and bravely in 1968 and, indeed—on the level of theory—succeeded: a true statement of the necessary relationship between freedom and economic planning). For any of us to talk of action and to reject rational understanding is madness, but for us to cultivate understanding and to divorce it from progressive action is wickedness.

If the effects of protest vary in each country and culture, it is hard to read, as here, of France, India, Japan and the USA (and we could well have added Germany and Italy too) without being aware of astonishingly similar forms but also, of much more significance, of broadly similar failures of the established regimes—failures so acute as to give the protests, often not so novel in themselves, both their unique opportunity and often their frustratingly irrational character. But in Britain, sad for the revolutionary and cold comfort for the reformer, we are not threatened with breakdown, simply with moral failure. It may almost be worse to have to go on living with ourselves than to fail after having tried for something radically better—this is plainly Professor Griffith's basic assumption: he comes to revolution out of pessimism, not from an impatient optimism. The protests of the moment arise from a society in which quality and quantity have become not conditions of each other, but bitter enemies. The scale and cynicism of things have grown too large to be endured. Revolutionary remedies are offered. But few of these would be listened to for five minutes if a reforming government had been able to carry conviction, even on certain elementary levels. 'Democracy' as well as 'technology' was one of Mr Wilson's catchphrases in both 1964 and 1966. We have had a frustrated and hobbled phase of parliamentary reform, good words about 'openness' in the Civil Service, good words (in the Skeffington Report) about popular participation in planning. But the last mentioned is worth pausing upon—as does Professor Page—as a classic case of the Anglican grin of good intentions while the teeth remain papier-mâché or rubber. Democratic participation has degenerated into mere public relations. The trade union movement *should* so enter into management that industrial democracy would emerge—says a Labour Party policy statement. Would it not be nice, says the Skeffington report, if local authorities acted in all these

125

new publicising and participative ways? But it suggests not the slightest new power to ministers or inspectors to see that these good things are done. If the Joint Statement of the Committee of University Vice-Chancellors and the National Union of Students (October 1968), at one end of the scale, and the Plowden Report on Primary Schools, at the other, should also turn out to be 'polite, meaningless words', as may parliamentary reform itself (which should tie all these things together), the fat may well be in the fire. Not the fire of revolution or even revolt, but of that utter cynicism and frustration which arises from glibly aroused expectations and results in exoticism, delinquency, decadence and decline of any concern for real public issues. There is no risk of revolution, only of a moral seediness, a collapse of civic spirit and political concern, and an ever-increasingly competitive materialism and a trivialised mechanism[d]—nonetheless dehumanised for now—operating in personalised or christian-name terms. 'Keep telling a man that he is nothing but an oversized rat', as Koestler puts it, 'and he will start growing whiskers and bite your finger.'

We have more time than we think if our nerves are strong, our sympathies eclectic and tolerant; but it is time that needs spending deliberately, visibly, energetically and sincerely to make the world better in such a way that the imagination of people is stirred to participate in politics in a freely moved and rational manner. We must no longer confuse social toleration with any unnecessary and self-destroying intellectual tolerance of nonsense, as Gellner argues so well; particularly, I would only add, when so much nonsense gets written, not even in plain English for ordinary people, but in the barbaric abstractions of the dialectic (*le mot juste*?) fusion of American social science and an equally abstract translator's Marxism. (What is clear can be said clearly.) To hold strong views and to remain silent is not to be especially tolerant: it is to be peculiarly foolish or cowardly. Intolerance arises from the manner in which we act, not from action itself. The time has come to argue back against irrationalism of both Right and Left, and to change the conditions in which it can flourish. Have we grown too frightened of the worst in men any longer to dare to call forth the best? And are the Left doomed to quarrel amongst themselves for ever more effectively than they can persuade the others? This I will not believe—whatever the present facts.

---

[d] The following dash embodies my judgement as to the correct end to the parenthesis, which is missing in both the book and journal versions. I also replaced the 'mechanism' of the book version with the 'mechanicism' of the original journal version, which seems to be the right form.

7 The 1970s in Retrospect

Vol. 41, no. 1, January–March 1970

WE LIVE, indeed, in times of change. Can the 1980s bring anything to match what we have seen in the 1970s? Could anyone writing in the fortieth birthday number have foreseen, albeit that he was then on the verge of decimalisation and halfway through the decade towards the coming of the 'Keep Right' signs, that this fiftieth birthday[a] number would be, because of our increased circulation and modest prosperity, the last to appear? Subscribers will see through this unhappy joke: they will already know that on 1 April 1980, volume 51 no. 5 will not have to be fetched from the nearest of the seventy splendid new RESSPOs (Regional Enclave Self-Service Post Offices), but will appear promptly on their table from the 'mouth'—as we still prefer to call it—of their personalised DTs (Domestic Telex), together with all the national briefings and random individuated impulses. We guarantee that our impulses will be on the line in the early hours of each Quarter Day, but it is, of course, purely the decision of each individuated participant-consumer what impulse-priority to give it if he has, as we are proud to say most of our 'subscribers' have, an overloaded line. Of course, when SOBSs (Self-Operating Backlog Selectors) come generally into play, we can only modestly hope that many will pick out our codes ahead of the previous week's print-out of Sunday pop-papers.

Casual purchasers of single-unit issues can also save themselves a pedestration to one of the remaining bookshops, so ably preserved the Publishers' Association and the CPRE, simply by dialling our NOSPIC (National Organisation of Small Purchases Indexing Computer) current single-purchases code 011-6938-67924-690345-23956478, and, of course, punching in their own Personalised Identificatory National Home Expenditures Disc while *the last eight* digits are 'going in'. They will then receive either a 'table of contents' as a print-out on their DTs or else as a micro-tapelet which can be activated at any time on any standard Japanese Regurgitating Machine. If they wish to purchase, by dialling the indicated purchasing code (as an addition to the above) the cost of the first inquiry will be automatically cancelled by QIRC (Question and Inquiry Repayment Computer). And in common with all other reputable and licensed Digested Information Media we include, even before the passing of the new Consumers' Protection Bill, an underprinted code *gratis* to a free Accidental Computer Over-Charging Underwriting Policy.[b]

---

[a] This is not, of course, from the fiftieth issue. Just in case it's not obvious, this article is an extended joke written from the vantage point of an imagined issue 1 in 1980. In spite of the obvious schoolboy humour of some of the acronyms and abbreviations, there is much that is more subtle here and Bernard displays a good deal of prescience. (See my Introduction.)

[b] I didn't go for a foolish consistency of hyphenation here and make 'Over-Charging' consistent with 'Underwriting' because the application of that hobgoblin of little minds would have spoiled the (admittedly not very good) acronym gag.

In some ways, of course, it is sad that the slight reservations of a few of the older members of the Board did not delay the change from magazine-format to telex-format, until at least one last issue had appeared still in the good old bindings but with spellings and typography in the new Rationally Aggregated Phonetic Enunciation, which is to be compulsory in four years' time. We are not thinking simply of the economic advantages of a 'spelling' or transliteration convention that enables Dictatype to function satisfactorily, thus dispensing for ever with both secretaries and printers, but as a vindication of what was for long felt to be the silliest view of the man who, fifty years ago, put up the money which eased the birth of this journal, George Bernard Shaw. So now both Dictatype and Telex messages can be fed under RAPE into translating machines, so that either way we play our part in continuing to strengthen Britain's case to be admitted to EEC.

Looking back on the 1970s, we can now see it as the epoch of POC—Participation-Openness-Communication. How hard to have foreseen in 1970 the long-term effects of the founding of the London and Manchester Business Schools in the mid-sixties and the beginnings of Civil Service reform in the late sixties. Only a few extremists of left and right now deplore the arrived-at functional PA[1] of enterprise into *public* and *private* sectors. It is curious to think that even in the 1960s these words still had almost precisely the opposite meaning to what they now carry, representing a curious and basically mid-Victorian attempt to distinguish between ownership by the 'state' and ownership by 'private persons', an almost meaningless distinction, of course, compared to that between those enterprises which can best operate publicly and those which can best operate privately. Second thoughts on Fulton, like second thoughts on Skeffington, were, of course, almost as important in the mid-seventies as the first thoughts; a tighter and more precise definition was achieved of those aspects of either joint-stock or national government which for functional-operative efficiency need privacy and those which need publicity. It would be too crude for our readers to say that 'the government', old style, is now firmly seen as the cost-effective sphere of privacy, and 'business', old style, as the cost-effective sphere of nationally supported publicity (and how long it took the BBC to come round), but not too crude for everyone else. There is still some distance to go. As Mr Benn remarked in a recent *Observer* 'Sayings of the Week' competition, 'The country cannot move from the PR of the 1960s out of the PA of the 1970s immediately into what I may call the PTC, or "Pure Technical Competence", of the 1980s. Some of the facts do not yet fit all of the theories.'

---

[1] 'Persuasive Analysis'. The habit has grown, unhappily in *The Times*, of translating 'PA' as 'Persuasive Admin', but this is an error. The Prime Minister used the correct phrase originally in his 'Words Speak Louder than Actions' speech to the Inter-Party Agents' Summer School at Nuffield College, 1973. 'Persuasive Admin' is, in fact, the title of a compulsory learning-programme at the Civil Service Staff College, but is, to avoid confusion, never abbreviated.

POC (Participation-Openness-Communication)[2] may take new directions, now that the National Suggestions Council has been turned into a Public Corporation, under the able chairmanship of the first of the new Honorary Bishops, Mr Humphry Berkeley, but it is clear that Mr Wilson's 1975 Sark by-election speech has become part of the constitution: 'Never again can it be said that a government should "make up its mind" when the continuing debate on whether to implement the far-reaching provisions of the Radcliffe-Maude, the Crowther and the Donoughmore Reports has become the first and the continually urgent task of each of the new Grand Regional Consultative Grievances Councils.' Some sceptics claim to see inner contradictions between PTC and POC, but we must retain an element of faith in a rational age that publicity, applied under the new concept of compulsory availability, will eventually produce a creative as well as an informed public opinion, or else weary most people into compliance with decisions of pure Technical Competence arrived at after confrontation with, in Mr Crossman's famous last words (or were they really his?), 'the maximised continuum of unpremeditated public dialogue'.

Some problems will always remain. Perhaps on a broad historical view one has not been surprised that the GRCGCs or the Consultative Grievances Council for Scotland and Wales continue to be frustrated in their search for unanimous agreement to the often repeated offers, made in such good faith by Mr Callaghan and his many successors, of a status identical with that proffered to the Stormont Parliament: 'national guidance with local initiative', which Stormont itself may even now, under the wise statesmanship of Lady Devlin, be on the edge of accepting. At least the need for another Constitutional Commission may become clear to revive the somewhat flagging debate on the regions (from which some English regional consciousness may in time emerge), if the election of a second Nationalist MP in both Scotland and Wales has not recently made the point 'politically'—as used to be said.

Equally, on a broad historical view, there is much to be said for Mr Wilson's making moral capital out of unhelpful criticism by describing the Labour Party as 'indeed a holding operation, and proud of it', just as his description of the Heath–Powell Progressive Party has stuck: 'still, despite nomenclature, a profoundly conservative party: a withholding party'. Certainly Mr Wilson has shown philosophical depths unsuspected in the 1960s by his systematic development of 'PA' (Persuasive Analysis) both as a tool of planning and as, at least among the new Hampstead Garden Suburb set of young PEP dons around him, as a radical attack on the age-old—and now almost universally discredited—distinction between fact and value. This is sometimes called 'neo-pragmatism', but, of course, as Professor Gellner demonstrates, there is a

---

[2] We use POC here and throughout to stand for the concept and not the new Ministry of that name (MOPOC, but more generally known as MOCOP, for the sake of euphony), but would not apply 'PTC' in capitals to a person who does not hold the award of that name, thus being an automatic member of all Advisory Committees and Commissions (like the VIPs of the 1960s and the IBPs —Impossibly Busy People—of the 1970s) and also entitled to vote but not speak in the Lords.

world of distinction between the crude 'what works is true' and the infinitely more subtle 'what can persuade is real'. It was one of the last great parliamentary occasions of the unreformed Commons, before the House sensibly curtailed its proceedings to fit in with the technical demands of TT (Telly and Telex), when Wilson, on introducing the famous eighth Green Paper on Pensions, and being heckled by the cry 'But "selective universality" is a purely persuasive definition', replied with such ready wit and massive common sense, 'Yes, Sir, indeed'. Not since Dr Johnson kicked the stone[c] has action so perfectly validated a concept. And Mr Wilson has by no means been extreme—as witness his continued and patient dialogue with the Labour wing of the Old Age Pensioners' Association (which has so splendidly revived the local organisations of both Parties—of such historical and intrinsic value) about the distinction between, but the equal importance of, Faith and Words in Socialist theory. He has not repeated Hugh Gaitskell's mistake of attacking things he disbelieves in. When PA was seized on crudely and overenthusiastically, he was right, however painful personally it must have been to him, not to prevent the final hounding of Mr George Brown from political life for shouting out in the annual Balance of Payments Emergency Debate: 'If they want bloody good figures, let's give 'em them'. One has some sympathy with Mr Brown, perhaps; but he fails to see the lingering, but still real, need to have occasional bad figures while the Trades Union movement remains so stubbornly obdurate to the truth behind Mr Wilson's distinction between Faith and Works. 'Ritualistic Socialism', a once invidious phrase which Mr Crosland has done so much to rehabilitate, is not for the unsubtle mind. But this is no excuse for Mr Brown's belated attack on the whole anti-ideology of PA, his attempting as it were to don the historical mantle of Mr Bevan by his famous outburst at Belper, 'Drown them with consultation and to hell with decisions. Just keep reshuffling along.'

There does remain, we would be the last not to admit, some grain of truth in his recidivism. Perhaps he took too literally Mr Wilson's classic utterances of the 1960s that 'the first duty of a government is to govern'—so often then facetiously attributed to the first Duke of Wellington; for he was then thinking of government as the making of decisions in the general interest, perhaps subject to some periodic reviews of popular opinion or interest, and not, simply and subtly as we have all come to see, as the self-perpetuation of what the American political scientists well called 'processes' or, more simply yet, 'styles' of intergroup consultation—put slightly more crudely, but proudly, by the current chairman of the Parliamentary Labour Party as 'our way of doing things'.[d] However, if it does not sound undemocratic to say so,

[c] This of course refers to the bluff doctor's supposed demolition of Berkeleyan idealism by kicking a stone and saying 'I refute it thus'. As with G. E. Moore's 'Here is a hand . . .', and depending on your point of view, Johnson and Moore either exemplify the doughty roast beef virtues of British empiricism or they just didn't get it.

[d] With its nested parentheses and complex punctuation this is a wonderful example of one of the more convoluted Bernardian sentences.

occasionally we feel in ourselves the old anthropolitical pull of 'matter' and 'substance' rather than of process and methods. Perhaps it is *The Political Quarterly*'s role to say unpopular things and occasionally to get back to things that used to be called 'matters of public policy', occasionally to open our coded-keys to unsolicited-impulse-sheets which seem premised, however crudely, though sincerely, on the old either defeatist or utopian disjunction between the 'is' and the 'ought' (or what the Russian Federation still calls 'reformism'). One can still, perhaps, just be understood when one says that things could be better than they are, and better perhaps in some consistent sense, 'patterned visions' as social psychologists now say—or what used to be called 'political doctrines'.

We raise this old-fashioned speculation with some diffidence, fully grant- ing that 'democracy as the right to differ' must, in modern processes of institutionalised debate, in fact strive to obliterate significant differences. We only take advantage of a fiftieth birthday (personal, by coincidence, to the writer as to *The Political Quarterly*)[e] to muse back through the history of the journal to raise the point, provocatively, that the obliteration of differences may, in part at least, as the founders clearly believed, be a function of physical and institutional changes as well as of circular processes of communication and feedback. By 'physical' we mean such things as the reallocation of resources and incomes, even at the humble level of regressive taxation systems, when looked at as a whole to include all social insurance payments as well as rates and taxes. There was a stir of such debate in the 1970s when some of the old—how shall we call them?—'moralistic socialists' sat down for a while with the new economists (who, after all, would turn their objective intelligences to anything intellectually stimulating) to see if taxation (in the broadest sense), wages, incomes and prices could not be looked at together in the light of such old-fashioned concepts as social justice and equality. We now grant—as the founders seemed to do implicitly—that 'equality' is a relative concept; but one can still sensibly hold that inequalities of income are far too great and may have something to do, whatever the scepticism of modern economists, with the problem of incentives and productivity, perhaps even with something even more immeasurable, not exactly 'justice', but still a recurrent sense of injustice, or to put it in more trendworthy terms, plain communications-breakdown. Certainly there seems some disjunction between the economic incentives which we accept as necessary for manage- ment and the professions, and the theory that the nature of these tasks makes them more attractive anyway. The repeated general strikes of teachers and nurses in the 1970s (we may ignore the famous 'troubled generation' of students, since we have now seen how easily they became socialised upon graduation) may seem to refute this; but their gradual dying down may, after all, have had something to do with the monetary element involved in the wise

[e] Bernard, born in December 1929, was almost exactly the same age as *PQ*, which launched at the beginning of 1930.

131

policies of 'giving them professional status' rather than, or at least as well as, the greater control they have themselves gained of the processes of becoming a profession.

This may have some moral for our continued 'industrial problems' or, however much the term is now disliked (as in the renaming of several university chairs recently), 'labour relations'. Granted that the moves to 'give the worker status' of the early 1970s have had some effect—the very word 'worker' is now being replaced by 'junior staff' or 'management probationary'—but one still wonders, looking back over the pages of this journal over the forty years before the beginning of post-Fulton Persuasive Analysis, whether this avoids all the problems unsolved by the qualified success of the era of PR in the 1960s. Might not either real income have something to do with it, particularly in relation to differentiated environmental factors (or 'bad conditions'); or, if this sounds too like the old crude distributivist argument (still found and refuted in some of the older textbooks), might not the accidental, perhaps even, in some sense, the unjustifiable character of some of the differentials continue to promote unrest?

Amid such continuous debate, it seems ungrateful to all the new public opinion engineers to say that reform of the educational system is still needed in crude terms of resources. We may, as the Opposition continually warned, actually be building up greater resentments by having granted self-government to teachers in secondary and further education, rather as they have it in the unmerged universities, medicine and the law, but without having given them resources commensurate with what they feel to be their task. They are a new type of Englishman, basically the product of the old Industrial Training Act's unexpectedly great stimulus to occupational mobility, who are not, as they say, to be 'fobbed off' by consultative processes which involve them in compromising with every element which has an economic interest not to increase public expenditure in education—whatever the good words—and involve them with every interest but that of the state itself.

In the fields of planning and of housing a similar case could have been made even in the early and mid-1970s, when the well-meant processes of consultation and open planning were first put into operation. Perhaps the odds were always against 'the tenants' in dealing with other local interests, however strongly the Ministry's 'missionaries' strove to set up spontaneous neighbourhood groups in cooperation with the already semi-official National Suggestions Centre. It may not merely have been 'the last political vicissitude', as Mr Taverne called it, that the state was forced—as a temporary measure to alleviate the intractable race relations problem[3] and the stubborn refusal of labour to become mobile (despite the wide and constant re-debating of the Hunt Report)—itself to allocate directly one-tenth of the Local

---

[3] When it became clear that one of the greatest early victories of PA or Persuasive Analysis had somehow misfired—that the redefinition of 'assimilation' as 'integration' and then 'integration' as 'segregation' had not, in fact, removed all the causes of discontent.

Government houses for which it pays, but it might well be a piece of national machinery that we should defend as if permanent; and should resist talk of returning these houses to the local authorities. Some old methods have a way of not quite dying off. This was a field of institutional change which events appeared to force upon us. Perhaps in some fields there is something to be said for that old type of planning theory that sought to identify objectives rationally (and usually with some ill-digested moral assumptions too) and to construct machinery to achieve them. There may be unexpected limits to the 'consultative-goal-formation' of PA as the method by which public policy adjusts to social change.

Certainly PA in the 1970s has not solved everything. The 1980s will see continued or revived demands, certainly in our pages (whatever the views of the Press Council), for what we can only still call institutional change of certain key institutions: the pay-as-you-learn educational sector, free higher and further education, the legal profession, Parliament—particularly the House of Lords, the nationalised industries, the trades unions, administrative justice, the mass media themselves, etc. By 1990 we may well feel, *plus changes, même choses*, but by then this may only betray our stubbornly old-fashioned socialist way of looking at things.

It would be too unfashionable, even for *The Political Quarterly* in 1980, to suggest without qualification that deliberate change, rather than democratic adjustment, should be the object of public policy, subject to the review of general elections, but there may be a residual germ of truth in this.[4] And the objects of change, even if it is hard to demonstrate much success in specific terms over fifty years, may emerge occasionally from what is to be frankly called intellectual debate—and by using, still more unfashionably, non-measurable concepts of what the old subjectivist school called 'moral principles'. Certainly over fifty years it is hard to see the changes for the good that have taken place as having come entirely from consultative processes of political adjustment. Someone must occasionally reach into the future above what is immediately agreeable. The parties could perhaps consider that there are advantages in 'product differentiation' as well as dangers; that there are dangers as well as advantages in the attempt to pursue a consensus politics before there is the economic and educational basis for consensus. In British politics it has sometimes proved the case, as with the Nationalisation Acts of the late 1940s and the National Health Scheme, that things are acceptable, *ex post propter hoc*, which are not always generally agreeable at the time. By 1980 it is clear that the masses are still not socialist and that the country still has to trade to live and has to finance that trade. But it is not clear that the masses would not respond to a socialist programme—since they have responded to little else except matching materialism with materialism, and since if, as is

---

[4] As perhaps shown in two slogans in a recent anonymous letter to the *Guardian*, presumably by a moderate member of one of the certified Anarchist Groups: 'Problems exist to be solved, not perpetuated' and 'Evolutionary Socialism must evolve—socialistically'.

said, 'Labour governments can get away with anything', then they might as well try to get away with socialism; and that a socialist programme might not do more for the expansive forces of British industry than it has already done so ably for the restrictive forces of City of London finance. A socialist programme could be put through if systematic leadership were given on the shop floor: the point on which everything depends. And the only natural and effective leaders lie, we suspect, in the backbenchers of a Labour government. Far from further reducing the size of Parliament, we would wish to see the government party's backbenchers being consulted and being used to gain the government the kind of support and response it needs for structural changes which involve not merely the consent of the trades unions but also, far more profoundly, changed patterns of behaviour among those who do the real work. Perhaps the continued impotence of Labour governments to do anything except stay in power will lead to a revival of the Labour Party—as an influence on the population as well as on the Cabinet. Perhaps some distrust is growing of the national communications networks. Populations by themselves are powerless to formulate or define policies, sometimes even powerless to change a policy with a government; but governments are powerless to do anything novel, except to sit there adjusting and watching the weather, unless they have the imagination, the authority and the voluntary local support to use their office to mobilise popular power. Politicians may still need vision and courage as well as common sense—and others may occasionally influence them, however indirectly, in different proportions towards these two great attributes. Intellectuals are not always to be despised, for they try to think ahead; and trouble-makers are not always to be reproved, for they force real decisions.

8 Social Trends and Statistical Services

Reports and Surveys, vol. 42, no. 2, April–June 1971

THE EDITORIAL of this important new annual publication begins:

The growing realisation in Parliament, the Press and elsewhere that economic progress must be measured, in part at least, in terms of social benefits makes it the more important that the available key figures about our society should be readily accessible. *Social Trends* is intended to meet this need by drawing together, initially once a year, some of the more significant statistical series relating to social policies and conditions. The emphasis is on trends, though there are also tables showing differentials and distributions at a particular time. The underlying theme is information about people, rather than about governments or institutions.[1]

So now as well as the justly famous *Economics Trends* there is to be *Social Trends*, both of which should be a compulsory free issue of equipment to every executive and administrative class civil servant (sorry, I haven't got the new coinage right yet), to every teacher of the social sciences whether in higher, further or secondary education, to every journalist, councillor and Member of Parliament. The actual circulation is likely to be a bit smaller, but it will at least be a great help to the compilers of annual surveys and almanacs.

Much praise

The publication is in many ways a brilliant vindication of the expansion and reorganisation of the government statistical services associated with the appointment of Professor C. A. Moser to be Director of the Central Statistical Office, after he had been research officer for Robbins: the very model of the new style, research-minded commission of inquiry. If social scientists believe that theory is divinely or necessarily related to practice, it is more likely that Claus Moser and Jeremy Bray will sit sifting the academic sheep from the academic goats at the portals of heaven than Tariq Ali and Rudi Dutschke.

The new volume reflects the increasing interest in Whitehall in social statistics and social research, and also Whitehall's new—and as yet still continuing—post-Plowden and post-Fulton desire to communicate. And communicate it does. The designers have, with few exceptions, done them proud in the easily comprehended hundred or so charts and diagrams which match the 108 tables in the book. The intelligent layman would only recoil screaming 'Stats' if he happened, by ill luck, to open the lucky bag on page B7, which gives the cumulative distribution of personal incomes by size, in Pareto curves on a logarithmic scale (but I'm going to take one of my students aside,

---

[1] Muriel Nissel, ed., *Social Trends*, No. 1, 1970 (HMSO for the Central Statistical Office), £3.25.

now that Sebastian has done his job and gone, to explain this to me). Otherwise the bomb is remarkably clean.

As well as tables, there are three articles about trends in social statistics and problems of interpreting them. Professor Brian Abel-Smith writes on 'Public Expenditure on the Social Services'; Jean Thompson (of the Office of Population Census and Surveys) writes on 'The Growth of Population to the End of the Century'; and A. E. Holmans (of the Ministry of Housing and Local Government) writes on 'A Forecast of Effective Demand for Housing in Great Britain in the 1970s'. Each of these articles is highly interesting in its own right, and all are topical and deal with highly contentious areas of policy. One admires the mixture of caution and boldness both in the choice of contributors and the themes. A contentious academic can help break the old ice, and civil servants, of two rather different organisations, can now be shown thinking in public. They are thinking not about policy, of course, but about the grounds on which policy is (or ought to be) based, rather like the remit of the new Expenditures Committee of the House of Commons.

The categories of tables are as follows: public expenditure, population and environment ('environment' is a rather pathetic little table on atmospheric pollution), employment, leisure, personal income and expenditure, social security, welfare services, health, education, housing, and justice and law (mainly criminal statistics). There are three appendices: Statistical Notes, Definitions and Terms, and Sources and Further References. And there is a rather undifferentiated index (i.e., more entries under subheadings than under main headings, a common enough fault of a rapidly declining craft). As we have said, the whole volume is attractively produced, with a gay photographic cover.

Some minor faults

With such a large potential audience, it is a great pity, however, that it is so expensive. Three pounds and twenty-five pence is a bit off-putting for 181 pages, even if quarto, double-columned, in a print size larger than this[a] and with so many coloured diagrams and tables, etc. The almost extravagant layout and the price suggest that HMSO are not optimistic about the number of sales, or are not equipped to get the large number of sales for such an almost indispensable reference work which Penguin or any big educational publisher would attain. This is an old problem and a sad one. HMSO have so few outlets, ordinary bookshops are so loath to search their lists and carry their matter, that a great deal of beautifully prepared and widely interesting and useful matter gets only very small sales. And they have to carry so much else, that generally one hardly blames them for not being able to promote a few books as commercial publishers would, although sometimes they seem neither to care nor try. Only very occasionally does HMSO act as if it was on

---

[a] That is, when compared to the relatively small typeface used in the original journal article.

to a good thing in selling, not just producing, books. They were reprimanded over ten years ago by the Estimates Committee for lack of commercial zeal, and they appeared to retaliate, shortly afterwards, by advertising on a very large scale to 'Read Lord Denning's Report'. Amid all the talk of hiving-off anything profitable, of ruining the public farm to feather private mansions (to paraphrase the Poet Laureate in his youth),[b] there might be a real and sensible case for the HMSO to issue some of its books jointly with a commercial publisher, someone more geared to selling and promotion.

Notes should be on the page in a publication of this complexity, not in an appendix. Many of the notes are absolutely essential to understanding the tables, so the reader should have his eyes caught firmly. Here, I suspect, the 'book designer' has an aesthetic of clean typography[c] that is remarkably divorced from the real needs of the reader and customer—again, an all too common and growing fault. The basic categories used in the Health and the Education sections are both terribly misleading if the explanatory notes are passed over. The appendix on 'Definitions and Terms' should also be up front and not hidden behind. As the complete statistical layman, I found this appendix clear, fascinating and helpful, emphatically not to be de-emphasised. And also the one genuine appendix, that of 'Sources and Further References', is set out vertically up the page in some trendy, hard to read because over-spaced, book designer's style, utterly eccentric to any ordinary bibliographic conventions. And these sources are all official: no references to learned journals, trade publications or books at all (the *Current Awareness Bulletin* might never have existed, and the House of Commons Library can give MPs far fuller and more helpful bibliographies. I suspect that they are a source unknown to the compilers of this volume).

Some middling faults

Generally there is a weakness in the lack of any comparative figures, or even references. Obviously such figures are neither relevant nor possible to produce all through, but there are some tables which are virtually meaningless unless some comparative yardstick is produced. 'Work stoppages due to industrial disputes' shows 6,925,000 days lost in 1969, rising from 1,710,000 in 1951, which quite takes the breath away. But are the figures large even in 1969—call it one day a year lost on average by one worker in four? And what is happening in the EEC? Is the increase and the aggregate anything like comparable? Numbers in further and higher education and criminal statistics are also obvious candidates for even the briefest comparisons.

[b] The reference is to Cecil Day-Lewis and his communist past.
[c] It's quite likely that the endnotes and some other aspects of the design were chosen for economic reasons—endnotes, for example, were cheaper to set than footnotes at that time—so it may not simply be the designer's choice (though notes in tables should certainly stay with tables, regardless of the design).

More disappointing, as the editor admits, is the inability to produce United Kingdom series in many places, only figures for Great Britain. And generally regional variations are only lightly touched upon outside obvious population figures. Northern Ireland, Scotland and Wales are producing political problems which make comparison and projection of social statistics particularly important. Here perhaps (and I will return to the point) statistical neatness and completeness of series triumph over political relevance; and I suspect that careful combing of written answers to Parliamentary Questions would fill several obvious gaps, as would searches through (if permissible) the House of Commons Library's Reference Department's files of answers to MPs' queries.

Statistics on manpower resources are promised in the next issue. 'Work on a social services manpower account is now proceeding', we are told; so we look forward to seeing if this necessary part of any national planning really exists or not, certainly in any manner subject to control of any kind. Again lack of complete series may inhibit the CSO from putting forward what bits and pieces there are relevant to policy; or it may be the limitation to 'official', virtually departmental (that is, not parliamentary at all), sources.

Some worry

Professor Moser himself contributes an interesting chapter on 'Some General Developments in Social Statistics'. 'We decided two years ago', he tells us, 'that there would be merit in producing a publication parallel to *Economic Trends*. . . . Our aim is to bring together a number of significant statistical series relating to social policies and conditions.' A doubt arises simply because all social *series* are not significant, and many social problems which are significant have no regular statistical series. And the 'parallel' to *Economic Trends* can hardly be exact. The whole object of that publication is to show how projections are made, and the interrelation of various indicators. But here long-term projections are not in every case relevant, rates of change vary greatly and vary in importance, and sometimes one feels that there is too much stress on trends. A lot of immediate problems get completely passed over, not because there are no statistics on them, but because they do not form part of any regular series, indeed of any official series. Certainly it is very useful indeed that, for instance, the General Household Survey is now being developed as well as the Family Expenditure Survey (which has been going since 1957) as a continuing series; but Professor Moser seems to forget that the demand for statistics is so often a response to highly unpredictable political changes, so it is either a chimera to hope that supply can ever fully anticipate demand, or a very high-level way of trying to influence demand (another case of high technologists being able to conceal—often from themselves—their own political values). I am not arguing against longitudinal studies, but just raising a warning that the very high financial and mental investment in them could make administrative reformers of one decade singularly rigid in the next, if problems appear to occur outside the parameters of the main, interrelated series. A more flexible strategy may help the decision-makers more. Social trends are bound to be less systematically connected, more full of discontinuities and incongruences than are economic statistics of the type found in *Economic Trends*. I suspect that most readers of *The Political Quarterly* (whom I imagine to be civil servants, MPs, journalists or teachers) would have preferred something less neat and systematic; not just complete series, but a couple of pages of miscellaneous statistics on current problems under each of the main headings.

'The aim', says Moser, 'is to construct a system in which the many statistics bearing on social conditions, social resources, and the flows of people through various activities and institutions are brought together coherently and meaningfully.' He aims eventually at nothing less than 'a system of social statistics', something fully integrated and interrelated, a difficult object to achieve, he admits, but even to fall short 'should yield statistical benefits in showing up gaps, harmonising concepts and classifications, setting up standard definitions'. Again, I doubt if there is such a parallel with economic statistics, and still more whether the construction of such a system is a high priority in relation to the kind of statistics we need of relevance to policy-making in the short and middle periods. Perhaps, unlike the departmental civil servants, the CSO is not guided in its own priorities by political priorities. On the one hand it is more free, but on the other it is less relevant and too academic in its choice of topics and tables. There is a danger that this annual, like the CSO, could take off into a rarefied world of 'basic prerequisites for planning', prerequisites which the actual planners never, in the nature of things, have time to consult. There is a danger of a kind of paper planning emerging which will in fact benefit statistical theory more than public policy. The danger is perhaps not very likely to arise, and it could only be a disaster if any politician came to believe in following the projections, rather than seeing them as social forces to be influenced, balanced and adjusted (and nothing will ever happen again as crude as the way the Robbins' figures were projected as demands for expansion of university places without a parallel debate being engendered about the quality and kind of education in relation to such great numbers— more should have meant different, neither 'worse' nor, almost worse than 'worse', the same).

In other words, I hope very strongly that the utility of these figures will always be considered more important than the hunt for 'system', for the system does not exist in society, but only in the eye of the planner or the statistician. If the needs of policy-making more than an aesthetic of 'system' guide the next annual edition, then it will use more sources and contain more relevant but scrappy information. So good it is, however, and educationally useful, so wonderfully better than anything else before, that it seems wrong to grumble. I only wish to pick a bone with Professor Moser in case the great reorganisation of central government statistical services which he has undertaken, together with the increasing sophistication of economic statistics, should lead to hopes for the same degree of cohesion in other social indicators. This I would think to be politically dangerous. So important and skilful is the enterprise that it demands the most basic criticism. If I, as a politically alert statistical layman or ignoramus, have in fact misunderstood what this new venture is about, I can only say, in apology, that this shows how difficult is their task.

9 The Strange Death of the American Theory of Consensus

Vol. 43, no. 1, January–March 1972

MY POINT of departure in events is somewhat personal and accidental: four years spent in the United States as a postgraduate and a young teacher in the 1950s, during the first Eisenhower Administration. This was the time of McCarthyism and the Korean War, and one felt that America was under great domestic strain, certainly as at no time since the Great Depression and before that the Civil War, perhaps even set on a collision course with the Soviet Union *and* (in those far off times) China. But it was also a time when one did not doubt American power and self-confidence and they did not doubt it themselves, regardless of whether the Senator from Wisconsin won or lost. One did not like the official version of the unique American mission; so one applauded Adlai Stevenson's version, as later—for a while—one applauded that of John F. Kennedy. But now one goes back to a land in which one can reluctantly but all too readily perceive a growing chaos, rather than simply strain; and, indeed, in a new Atlantic situation in which the old desire to know America well, above all other places, as the centre of events, whatever was to happen, is now mitigated by a self-annoyance at a lost opportunity, when a young man, to have really lived in Europe, in France or Germany, which at the time seemed a dull and purely traditional thing for a student of politics to do, rather than a commitment towards understanding the future. However, one also now goes back to a land whose fearsome sense of imperial mission is much diluted, and much for the better: far from the collision course of the bipolar world. An old and frankly rather unpopular Harvard acquaintance, who was writing a thesis on Metternich of all people, not on Jefferson or Woodrow Wilson, now flies like a wise owl, neither hawk nor dove, into China on the President's business (that same man who as a Senator . . . etc.). Then there was domestic tension and the fear of world war, now there is much internal disorder, some terrible local wars, but a clear determination by the Great Powers to isolate these wars, to prevent escalation, to preserve world peace. The fear of a world war recedes. (I would say in an aside to 'the students' that we were not unaware in the 1950s of population, pollution and participation, but we did attach a higher value to survival while learning to live with the bomb.)

The Hegelian democracy

My point of departure in ideas is, however, less personal. Even in the 1950s, living in America one was able to accept, indeed relish, a strange paradox, though strange only to Europeans ignorant of American history. Hegel's account of states as embodiments and expeditors of a single idea of moral order seemed a ludicrous description of actual European history since his time—a history infinitely complicated by rival ideas and interests within each nation; and attempts to impose such a unity led to disaster—but, to be fair, disaster of a kind that Hegel would have recognised as disaster. His account, however, seemed to fit exactly 'these United States' that became 'the American Union'. 'Where in the world but in America', indeed, was there a country that so clearly pursued a self-conscious and self-willed civic religion, so tenaciously and—in the sense that it had no rivals—successfully? Every university textbook in political science, which was and is a compulsory course in all state universities and in most others, began with a statement of 'the American Way', which was only more sophisticated than the doctrines already imbibed by the whole population in high schools, not merely in compulsory civics but spilling over into most other subjects.

Less contentious, perhaps, to put all this in terms of Tocqueville rather than Hegel: but Tocqueville painted a picture of a country of unified values, which had indeed fought a 'revolution' because its values were threatened, not to establish new ones. 'The great advantage of the American', he said, 'is that he has arrived at a state of democracy without having to endure a democratic revolution: that he is born equal without having to become so.' 'This nation conceived in liberty', said Lincoln, 'and dedicated to a proposition . . .'—not a platitude then, but a brilliant simplification. Liberalism was universal: there were dangers in this as well as merits, there could be a tyranny of public opinion grimmer even than that of old autocracy; but on the whole, Tocqueville thought not; he wrote to exhort and reprove extremists of both wings in France, not to provide wounds for the salt of modern American intellectuals. True, a unique 'American dilemma' became apparent; but the whole point of Gunnar Myrdal's argument of the late 1940s was that the white American did not treat the black American by his own professed standards, and that the black American only wanted to be treated as an American and that he was nothing else but an American. It is an argument still not to be scorned, but after 'Black Power' it is at least a damned sight less obvious. And less obvious both empirically and morally: are they of the same culture? Should they necessarily be of the same culture?

America was profoundly conservative, we used to say, but the actual content of American conservatism was *liberal*. Self-styled American conservatives were either *laissez-faire* ultras, who had come to wear proudly a sobriquet of domestic political abuse, or else they were a few malcontented intellectuals, enjoying a fantasy that the Irishman Edmund Burke could have migrated in the other direction. They were forced into a quite unconservative stand on first principles rather than on history. In actual American history, the civic religion of nineteenth-century liberal republicanism was inculcated into the immigrants through the schools. No genuine American political philosophy emerged, precisely because values were taken for granted and the motive was nation-building, not contemplative, but there was always a vastly able civic or patriotic literature, a great middle ground of publicists between philosophy and the rhetoric of politicians. It was needed for 'nation-building'—I deliberately use the same phrase that American political scientists apply to nationalism in contemporary Africa. What has perhaps been less considered has been the effect of continuing to teach the civic religion of unity long after the closing of the doors to the mass immigration of the poor in the early 1920s: it is one thing to indoctrinate those who wish to become citizens, quite another to continue to do so with those who are spontaneously, habitually and socially—I say this, I hope, with irony and not sarcasm—American enough already.

The thesis of liberal unity

The best expression of the thesis of America as exhibiting a unity of liberalism is to be found in Professor Louis Hartz's *The Liberal Tradition in America*, published in 1955. It is a book which, while little known outside the United States and though overwritten with an extraordinary disorderly energy, yet has had a profound effect on many American historians. For one thing, it poured scorn on what could be called the half-dialectic theory of American history: that American politics has been a struggle between reactionaries and progressives—but progressives, of course, in a very special and relative sense. This is brought out almost as self-parody in the title of Arthur Schlesinger Jr's first big book, not the dead but *The Vital Centre*, in which he did not in fact leave room for any real left. Hartz had little difficulty in showing that by any possible European comparisons these two alleged traditions look almost identical; they even looked remarkably similar in American terms; and he suggested that many of the genealogies of goodies and baddies (stemming from 'Jefferson and Hamilton') were extremely suspect—different croups at different times had crossed the largely rhetorical floor of 'Left' and 'Right'. He argued that this unity of American liberalism was not a product of reason, but of an historical accident of immigration by 'Lockean' Englishmen, and that it was so remorseless and ingrained as to blot out any alternative sets of concepts and of values. This 'irrational liberalism' proved myopic in perceiving differences in the outside world—so much so that Hartz agonised whether any 'transcendence' of this liberal claustrophobia was possible at all. Hartz felt driven to use such an unhistorical term. He has been accused of being fatuously complacent or bleakly pessimistic—but in fact he displayed a very rare and dispassionate kind of passion for objectivity.

Hartz admitted that American liberalism as it faced the outside world could adopt two stances:

'Americanism' has a dual life . . . it has been characterised by a strong isolationist impulse: the sense that America's very liberal joy lay in escape from a decadent old world. . . . And yet . . . 'Americanism' has also crusaded abroad in a Wilsonian way, projecting itself headlong over the strange and ancient societies of Europe and Asia.

And, indeed, the compulsive anti-Americanism one had argued against in Europe had the very same ambivalence, always shifting ground between 'rash interventionism' and 'selfish isolationism'. But what Hartz's thesis of the essential unity of American political ideas very much suggested was that it was an all or nothing proposition: either a liberal conduct of foreign relations, or as few foreign relations as possible—so as to preserve liberalism at home from contamination: to greet the immigrant, either the symbol of the Statue of Liberty (built for that purpose) or that of Ellis Island (although unhappily one stands on the other). Woodrow Wilson, the internationalist, *and* Robert LaFollette, the pacifist and radical isolationist; Robert Taft, the business liberal and isolationist, and the same Robert Taft in favour of an aggressive China policy (to use the bomb) during the Korean War, to get the thing over, once and for all. They are all equally representative of the true American tradition. So isolationism and internationalism could both be authentic variants of liberalism, but what was not to be contemplated was what Washington had famously warned against (and Jefferson, too), 'entangling alliances', any permanent involvement in the endless business of diplomacy and balancing of power with power.

On an economic level, the thesis of unity of American liberalism appeared almost unassailable. Despite all the literature on the few authentic American socialists, there has never been any serious challenge to a liberal economic system—using the word 'liberal' in an historical sense, for in terms of strict economic theory of liberalism there has never been a wholly 'free economy' anyway, anywhere. Jackson stood for the small businessman against the banks, Wilson for the small businessman against the big businessman, and FDR for 'the people against the interests', but it meant little more in the New Deal than it had to Woodrow Wilson: to restore individualistic capitalism against the monopolies. If a 'Fair Deal' and a 'Square Deal' failed, then—God willing—a 'New Deal', but the same cards and the same players, only a need to redistribute the alleged run of worthiness and luck, 'from rags to riches in one generation' (and back again) more quickly. Even the most strident free-enterprise fanatics, who might grotesquely call Roosevelt 'a socialist', depended on state and federal law for their mining rights, their rights of way, their licences and their tariffs. Gabriel Kolko, in his misleadingly titled *The Triumph of Conservatism*, has well called the American economy 'political capitalism': a capitalism dependent on playing politics, he means, but by the same token also a highly political capitalism. And as well as the lack of any fundamental disagreements about how to organise the American economy, there has been the almost universal belief in its ever-expansive power and affluence. It is a biting shame, said Galbraith, that in an *Affluent Society* something cannot be done for the pockets of poverty, done for them from all this wealth; but not the shadow of a suspicion that the continuation of economic expansion in a highly complex society may not be limited by such deformities or running sores, rendered inefficient because of them. Until these last few years, a myth of infinite expansion and abundance has dominated American economic thinking. It is strange to think that the resources of the planet are finite . . . 'O.K., then we'll take off to the Moon, and then . . .'

On a political level, American politics had to be understood realistically in terms of interest groups. Political parties on the European model did not exist. Indeed, perhaps it also worked the other way. Might not consideration of the American party system lead one to see that the role of ideas or of ideology was not as great as had been painted, both by rivals and zealots, among European parties? Might not the Labour Party look more like the Democratic Party, even, than the Democratic Party could ever look like the idealised picture of the Labour Party? Perhaps not a question of American parties not having any ideas, but simply of not differing in their ideas? Certainly this is how H. G. Wells saw it in his slickly titled *The Future in America* of 1906 (a book already getting near to the end of the tradition of *optimistic* futurology books about America):

the two great political parties in America represent only one English party, the middle-class Liberal Party, the party of industrialism and freedom. There are no Tories to represent the feudal system, and no Labour Party. . . . All Americans are, from the English point of view, Liberals of one sort or another.

The style of politics was called purely pragmatic and one noted how ruthlessly realistic Americans themselves became in giving an account of politics purely in terms of 'who gets what, when and how?', the politics of spoils, the pork barrel, of interests—things not unknown elsewhere, but somehow felt in America to be the rule, rather than the exception. And the descriptions became justifications. Political justice must exist in the rules of the political process, not in its objects. Now in fact it was always fairly easy to expose that pragmatic whores had hearts of gold, that muckrakers and realists, whether in those huge thick novels or in the new algebraic mono-graphs of political science, were in fact raddled with good democratic values, occasionally rather affected Comtean elitist ones (for the people, but not of them), but anyway values, big as your fist, warm as your heart. *A pragmatic politics could be assumed and practised not because of the absence of values, but precisely because of their presence and unity.*

Now strictly speaking this has made Americans adept in practising and describing bargaining, but not compromise. Amid a unity of values, conflicts of interest can be resolved, either by counting votes or hard cash; that is, horse-trading or bargaining (game-theory, to some). But amid a conflict of values, something is called for which cannot always be satisfied in cash or accepted as the result of votes—compromise: when one knowingly allows a value that one holds, and will not readily give up holding, to be diluted in a given circumstance (usually because of some other value that one also holds, respect for law, peace, stability, sometimes even because of respect for the sincerity of another of whose values and objectives one disapproves). Perhaps I put this over crudely, but to begin to make the point: bargaining works

145

within a culture, but not among cultures; among cultures a mixture of empathy and realism is called for.

The breakdown of unity

So it is almost bewildering to pass quite suddenly into an America where the habitual processes of bargaining appear to have broken down, when the majority is being asked to compromise with aroused and articulate minorities in a way that it feels affects its principles. It was said of Herbert Spencer that his only idea of tragedy was a theory killed by a fact: this could be cruelly said of the Hartz thesis nowadays—at least we await a reply. Certainly the historical unity of American liberalism has broken down. Internationally, the abandonment of the idea of victory, even of forward containment, still less of ideological victory or even of great influence through liberalism in South America—and memories of the hope for such influence for such reasons in Asia and Africa now seem a bitter joke. And also, quite simply, defeat. Mr Dooley once remarked, when the British declared the South African War at an end and that henceforward anyone found under arms would be shot as an outlaw and not interned as a soldier, that all other nations had to defeat their enemies, but the English merely disqualified them. The Americans have now declared the Vietnamese War at an end and have disqualified the Vietcong, but they have left the field; and left it, moreover, with very little assurance that this style of communism will not spread. The 'domino theory' was not absurd, only not necessarily true; but the communists appear to believe in it.

Politically, the party system and the Federal machinery of government failed to produce programmes to deal with the great social problems, or even to generate confidence that they could be ameliorated, contained—'solved' seems an almost utopian term. Such problems as were exposed on that one hot August night in 1965 in Watts, the negro ghetto of Los Angeles, when the attempt by the police to arrest a youth for a traffic violation set off a six-day riot which resulted in 34 deaths and property damage estimated at forty million dollars—in a district which had reached 30 per cent unemployment on the eve of the trouble. A season of race riots followed, a flood of statistics, radical then official, revealing the size of these pockets of 'residual poverty' amid the automobile opulence—'residual' very literally in the sense of being left behind without very much hope of catching up; the assassinations came and then the riots at the Democratic Party Convention in Chicago revealed basic problems of law and order, of police as well as mob violence; and all this was illustrated nightly on the television screens amid the endless reportage of the brutal war. For the first time open opposition to the war arose, in Congress as well as among minority groups; and then, to crown all, the great anti-war movement emerged on the proudly favoured campuses, the Kent State killings and all that, revealing a sudden empirical intensity in hitherto highly intellectual concepts like 'anomie' and 'alienation'. And amid all this, the sudden blossoming of an exotic literature of protest, of which the recent *Greening of America* was only a second-generation prototype, a literature far removed from old populist and progressive literature of dissent, itself proudly historical; now came fantastical intellectual missiles and turgid prophecies of woe and apocalypse, eagerly popularised on the screens and in the syndicated columns: the time when Marcuse incredibly became a household word.

Economically, on top of all that, there was the beginning of inflation and fears of recession, mild by some past standards, but vastly unnerving in relative terms compared with the expectations and experience that had gone before; and which led to the present economic policies of President Nixon, the *de facto* if not the *de jure* deflation of the mighty dollar and the jeopardising of America's international strength—perhaps more apparent than real, but the reputation for power, as Hobbes pointed out, is a great part of the possession of power, and it is likely that America may never quite recover the previous ascendancy she had in the non-communist world; nor even want to do so. Deflationary policies are pursued at the very moment when it was always said that vast Federal expenditure would be needed, if ever there was a victory in or a withdrawal from Vietnam, to replace the underpinning of the economy by war expenditure. The victory of the students in driving Pentagon money from the campuses can be seen to have had its price—and, sad but probable, tighter budgets, reduced expenditure and graduate unemployment may actually damp down superficial campus unrest; but when the same process spreads into Detroit, Pittsburgh and Los Angeles, industrial troubles may follow in comparison with which the campus uproars will seem but puny stirrings. Could these things radicalise the Democratic Party and motivate the great industrial unions politically? Somehow no one seems to put much money nowadays on that one hallowed chimera. Some reactions to the students by the workers have showed that a radicalised working force is a somewhat ambiguous prospect.

Astonishingly exotic brands of socialism, anarchism and even rejections of any political action in Hippiedom and now Yippiedom currently flourish. They have few roots, if any, in the population; even among the campuses and the university educated they thrive on acquiescence out of disgust with the parties, rather than on positive agreement; but the spectacle of their being taken so seriously is at least impressive, if not alarming—perhaps, if one's nerves are still reasonably strong, 'impressive' because they do represent an attempt to question some of the basic assumptions of an acquisitive society. If there seemed any hope of getting results through the established political system, the conditions would seem to be ripe for the coming of social democracy to America. Perhaps the radicals exaggerate the hopelessness of working through the political system—there is more than a touch of Pharisaism and an almost deliberately self-isolating elitism about many of the advanced radicals of the moment—but certainly no political leaders have yet emerged who seem willing to channel these new divergences and discontents constructively, simply because it would involve surrendering their own values of individualistic success. They cannot yet face the fact that so many young Americans have turned sour on this basic premise, are almost glorifying failure, at least lack of conventional success. The puritan religion of work and labour as the highest values now has many vociferous critics. In fact it always had some serious critics, Niebuhr and Arendt to name only two, but then nobody was listening to such humanistic critics of 'possessive individualism'.

Into an unconsensual polity

So, both to many Americans and to former visitors, the country is now an unfamiliar-familiar landscape, like having jumped through the mirror: realism has suddenly come close to surrealism: art somehow does seem to anticipate both social action and social philosophy. But if the old pragmatism and realism were only possible because of unified values, perhaps much of the present malaise is no more than that Americans are having to adjust, rather suddenly, to a condition long familiar to inhabitants of many other countries: living in a society that can no longer pretend to be a nation in the sense of a unified culture agreeing on basic values. The consensus has broken down. But did the consensus ever have to be that consensual? Perhaps once, in the new nation and the nation of mass immigration; but plenty of states have survived amid a plurality of values, have seen their consensus and sense of nationality narrowly but strongly in the political institutions themselves, neither in something that is compulsive and compulsory, as in communist states, nor perhaps as meaninglessly vague as the late General Eisenhower's frequent appeals to 'our common Hebraic-Christian-Graeco-Romano civilisation'. When that kind of rhetoric was needed, perhaps the old unity had nearly withered away. If one takes only such differences as the General mentioned, even leaving aside political ideologies and doctrines, perhaps the best description is not synthesis and sameness, but is tolerance and difference. The formal values of the narrowly political may have been lost in cascades of traditional rhetoric, even by those who would now defend them against others who seem, some who perhaps indeed are, anti-political.

The political institutions have to be adequate, however, to the task of conciliating and compromising genuine differences of morality and policy, as such there now are. Living with divergence in the USA is infinitely complicated by the lack of strong and consistent central government—a rather conventional remark. It has to be central, for the problems of race and poverty, of urban decay and of law and order, are on too great a scale to be dealt with locally—or else the result is gross inequity in what is in fact economically a national system. Institutional reforms never precede social needs—that is what made so much of the old literature of constitutional reform seem so academic, abstract, remote and even Anglophile; but sometimes the structure is not so rigid that it cannot adjust. Some great adjustments have certainly taken place.

In foreign relations the contrast between the mid-1950s and the end of the 1960s is almost unimaginable: the point at which we began. What Brogan called 'the illusion of American omnipotence' has now vanished. Even in the early 1960s the Pentagon was spending money on the campuses fairly freely on political and social studies of 'stability' in far-off lands, a preoccupation which would have seemed defeatist and treasonable in the days of both Joseph McCarthy and John Foster Dulles. The 'bipolar' and the convergence theses of world politics had become implausible. Vietnam went against this tide, revealed grim inadequacies of political control over the military, but was never the ruthlessly premeditated policy that some critics claimed. Nixon could negotiate, Nixon could claim credit for bringing the boys home, Nixon can visit China and Russia; for he is ever the pure politician, inadequate as a leader, certainly, but ever restlessly searching for the dead-centre of a now highly confused and somewhat volatile public opinion. Of course the war could have been won, but at a cost in terms of world politics that both Johnson and Nixon, a pretty pair of arch-realists, clearly realised could not be paid. John Kennedy was in many ways a lapse back into the Wilsonian idealism and democratic imperialism of the unique American mission, just as in domestic politics he was an embodiment of ruthless money-power as well as of Harvard sophomore liberalism; but Nixon has not lapsed back into a Taft or Dulles version of the unique American mission. He seems to learn to coexist, much as the Soviet leaders are doing, and in domestic politics he is too much in love with power to be the tool of 'the interests', who themselves appear frightened and ready to be led into reforms if a lead is given. But also he seems too much in love with power for its own sake to be willing, unless forced by events, to do much with this power.

Some equivalence in domestic politics is now needed to the hard lesson that is being learned of living with and managing diversities of interests *and* values in foreign politics. Perhaps some progress had already been made, even amid the troubles already related: certainly extremes have been avoided, with some luck but also some public judgement—Goldwater was defeated and the student militants seem to have drawn back in fear and puzzlement from further exercise of the undoubted negative power they showed two seasons ago to break down their own American universities and colleges. There is a programmatic literature of reform emerging, not so much in the fashionable way-out books, but in a remarkable shift of social scientists from the old 'value-free' assumptions, not just into 'policy science' (an old slogan which simply assumed a basic agreement as the starting points and goals), but into the canvassing of policy alternatives based upon different hypotheses as to motives and goals. It stops short of the absolute commitment demanded by some, but is probably the better for that; for absolute commitment to what?—there is little agreement, and absolute commitment is so terribly blinding when the whole problem may now be the development, recognition and creative compromising of different values.

A new consciousness of the need for coherent public policies is emerging.

In crude terms, public administration can never be so dull again, nor political theory so woolly. The old realism still has some virtues, if it can be realistic about different values as well as different interests. Certainly the old, crude dichotomy of ideas versus interests seems to have been discarded. What perceptions do people have of their differing interests? Understanding that perceptions differ—and a little about why they differ—how should priorities be arrived at? Questions like these are beginning to be asked. And the theory of consensus as a necessary social cement is beginning to be abandoned. Even political scientists come to believe that strong government has something to do with the cohesion of society.

Fear of breakdown or of continued levels of nearly intolerable trouble may assert a general interest to conciliate differences—if first they are recognised. Even grass-roots politicians may come to feel this, else the grass will wither, dry and catch fire easily—even if as bush fires and not revolutionary conflagrations. Otherwise there may be no alternative but breakdown and decay, not even revolution or radical change: the legions and the commissariats will have to be called back from the outside world to police and feed the inner cities. Domestic and foreign politics are inextricably intermingled. And already the American-trained troops of the client powers will be mending their own fences, 'neutralism' not achieved, but often thrust upon them. And we may be seeing, through all the anguish and confusion, a genuine pluralism thrust upon America itself: not a total moral repudiation of the old thesis of liberal unity, but a recognition that it long ago served its purpose in building up a young nation, now grown mature and complex.

Pluralism: hard and soft

The concept of pluralism is ambiguous and contentious. One hesitates whether or not to abandon it, but it is too established and expressive, so much better to distinguish a soft from a hard sense. The soft sense is everything that is simply an acceptance of diversity for the sake of diversity, a fatuous belief—based on a vague analogy from classical liberal economics— that the political economy is a self-rectifying system, that every challenge has its response, that every interest group is balanced by another. This is what Marcuse rails against as 'toleration' and his disciple, John Paul Woolfe, attacks by its own name, but sees as a failure to choose, to make qualitative decisions, and as a pseudo-social science and a destructive politics in which, in fact, the organised interests always defeat the unorganised majorities; and in which the substance of social justice is smothered in procedural rules. In this journal's special issue on *Protest and Discontent*,[a] Ernest Gellner lumped

[a] Vol. 40, no. 1, 1969; Bernard's introduction to the book version of the collection from the following year is reproduced in this volume as article 6. Note too the subtle name dropping that follows: 'Ernest Gellner lumped me together with Popper and Berlin . . .', with its implication that already by the age of 42 Bernard is fit to be mentioned in the same breath as these two grand figures (and by no less a figure than Ernest Gellner).

me together with Popper and Berlin, a back-handed compliment for holding this view: that simply a respect for politics, for the open society and for liberty, respectively, could solve our problems, whereas those very problems might be a condition of our dilemmas of indecision. If indeed we held that view, it is an inadequate one.

But there are radicals who praise pluralism. I notice, to take one advantage of having read the other contributions, that James Glass fetes the Yippie as at least an apostle of pluralism as against conformity. I find this, personally, an extreme but important and interesting case—more like a symptom than a cure, yet a telling symptom of the disease. And for the same reason, to take only one other advantage, that I must basically differ from Esmond Wright's reinvocation of the spirit of American history as the answer, I must also believe that Americans are, indeed, beginning to discover a hard and sensible, not amorphous, sense of pluralism. For the old unity has gone, and it has not led to the absence of doctrine, rather to a plethora. Opinion is beginning to form as to radical alternatives—but the plural is important. There is no clear radical alternative, but a bewilderingly rich variety of alternatives, many too eccentric and fragile to survive, but some of which will almost certainly coalesce into a limited number of schools of thought and policy. In so far as they do become fewer in number, it will be because they correspond to different kinds of widespread support and to different social bases. They aim at change or at different patterns of conservation. But they exist. Each wishes to predominate. They will be serious about national policy, not just sectional interests. They are dreadfully and properly in earnest. But it is overwhelmingly likely that none alone can prevail, short of force and coercion. What is needed is not acceptance of a plurality of values and interests as such, but a toleration of necessary differences that are based on real diversities of the dimension of cultures, or at least of subcultures. Even Britain begins to see this in relation to problems of race relations and has, in fact, long practised such a hard pluralism, fairly knowledgeably and successfully in relation to Wales and Scotland, very ignorantly and ineptly in relation to Ireland. Toleration, Marcuse is wrong, is not acceptance of everything—he should attack old-fashioned liberalism instead; toleration is the limited acceptance that one extends, out of a mixture of policy and humanity, to those things of which one disapproves.

Perhaps an odd conclusion, that Americans have to learn to disapprove openly of each other. But such a disapproval is less strident and hysterical if it is not assumed that everyone should be conforming to one unified set of values, or else the nation is in danger and they are perverts or traitors. Government can be more measured and creative in its policies and compromises if it recognises liberalism will and should assure that none of these emerging communities restricts the opportunities of their young, for such is always the crucial point; let them move into other modes of life if they wish; but that they should pursue openly different goals should be seen as no threat to the survival of the polity. Disapproval does not imply persecution among

151

civilised men; national survival does not imply unity of belief; but tolerance does imply intolerance towards discrimination and social and economic inequalities of the kind that permanently doom an individual to remain always a member of what is ascribed to him as 'his community', whether he wishes to or not, however eager he is for some community amid the anonymous world of thrusting individuals. A plurality of values simply based upon hardship and oppression is the seed-ground of rebellion; but if based upon public concern and real help for minorities, it is the basis of practical allegiance to any state.

The end of consensus is the beginning of political doctrine. How facile now seems the 'end of ideology' thesis. Perhaps it was only ever an attack on a false thesis, the pseudo-dialectic account of American history and the extension of it to the rest of the world. The real ending of ideology has been the end of a particular ideology, that of the necessary unity of American liberalism. Now the era of doctrines will begin. Since the moral guidelines are now gone, that were needed to make a purely interest group work, qualitative choices about priorities of social action will have to be made. I choose the word 'doctrine' rather than 'ideology' as implying sets of concrete policy-objectives based upon theory—each group may have its 'ideology', but no more ideologies, indeed, either as single total solutions, or as the total complacency—as it now seems—of the belief in a unified liberalism. Hard choices which will conflict with the values of others now have to be made, but they can be made—if only America will realise that the incantatory rhetoric of the old American liberalism will now summon no legislators from the dead. *Ex unibus plures!*

10 Paying for the Parties: a Review

Vol. 46, no. 4, October–December 1975

Mr Dick Leonard's paper *Paying for Party Politics*[1] gives a mass of useful, clear and reliable information about some foreign systems of subsidy in competitive party situations. The author, who was Labour MP for Romford between 1970 and 1974 and is now Home Affairs editor of *The Economist*, is the soul of independence. But he must forgive us saying that the conclusions of the report could equally well have been a well-researched joint brief to the Houghton Committee by Transport House and the Conservative Central Office. Its aim is preservationist. But what about public amenity and access?

The whole concept is very new in British politics. Only in January 1973 did Dick Leonard himself raise the issue in a speech to the Fabian Society; later in the year Dick Crossman praised the Federal German Republic system in *The Times*, and in 1974 the House of Lords (15 May) and this journal (July–September)[a] gave it an airing. To any who did not know how near bankruptcy the two major parties were, it might have seemed surprising for the House of Commons to welcome Mr Edward Short MP (19 December 1974) setting up a committee under the chairmanship of Lord Houghton:

To consider whether, in the interests of parliamentary democracy, provision should be made from public funds to assist political parties in carrying out their functions outside Parliament; to examine the practices of other parliamentary democracies in this field, and to make recommendations as to the scope of political activities to which any such provision should relate and the method of its allocation.

The committee aims to report by the end of the year. Its membership is wide. The parties are directly represented on it, but do not predominate. Lord Houghton is a wise and tough old bird, born and bred in the Labour Movement but no party hack; indeed a patriotic, shrewd, independent and honourable man. He may have, in other words, some faint inkling of the public storm of contempt that would arise if a straight subsidy, in whatever form, were voted in Parliament by the parties for themselves.

The need is great, but the basic cause needs to be pondered. Is the right question being answered? Even before inflation and the year of two general elections, the finances of the two main parties, let alone the Liberals, were in poor shape. In the year 1972–73 the Conservative Central Funds had an income of £1,199,198 and the Labour Party's General Fund in 1973 had £869,027. The smallest university or polytechnic could not run on that: the

---

[1] Dick Leonard, *Paying for Party Politics: The Case for Public Subsidies*, PEP broadsheet no. 554, July 1975.

[a] That is, vol. 46, no. 4, the immediately previous issue.

sums are indeed, as Leonard says, ridiculously small. In the same year, 74.5 per cent of Conservative incomes came from donations (business firms) and 72.2 per cent of Labour's income from trade union affiliations. Only 22.3 per cent of Conservative income and 8.9 per cent of Labour's came from the constituencies. The incompetence of the parties to raise income from the real members makes the task of Lord Houghton's committee somewhat like the celebrated excuse of the other Marx when caught red-handed, amorously assaulting the rich widow: 'I was only fighting to preserve the honour of this woman—a thing she has seldom done for herself.'

Basic assumptions

Mr Leonard says that there is a case for making the parties less dependent on 'pressure groups'—that is, big business and the big unions. But he does not care to mention the late Richard Crossman's robust line that subsidies could save the Labour Party from the jealous and restrictive embrace of the trades unions. 'There is no good case', Dick Leonard asserts without argument, 'for severing this financial connection, but it would be healthier if the burden of support for the two main parties could be spread more evenly'. Healthier than now, certainly, but how healthy is 'healthier'? Still more healthy if they were given some incentive to recruit members or even to win back the vote. And if there was adequate public funding and more public confidence in the parties, there might be a case not just to publicise but to forbid all large donations.

For many have long suspected what has now been proved by Dick Leonard: the incredible decline in membership of the Conservative and Labour Parties—even if, as we will see, he does not draw the right inferences.

Neither party now makes it easy to calculate what is their individual membership. Both hide these figures—even from themselves. Leonard convinces one that the Labour Party has fallen from its 1953 peak of just over one million to somewhere between 300,000 and 250,000 today. And the Conservatives fell from 2,805,032 in 1953 to about half that number currently. Leonard uses these figures mainly to suggest that the parties cannot finance themselves and that increased membership is a vain solution in the changing society of today. Indeed it is. But what question is being asked 'in the interests of parliamentary democracy'?

Lord Houghton's committee should think very, very hard about the significance of such a decline. Here the PEP pamphlet is sadly and disappointingly superficial. All sorts of ills follow from declining membership. The parties are no longer effective in influencing or mobilising public opinion. The selection of MPs tends to be in fewer and fewer hands, and it is likely that these hands are those of (a) the grim old 'my party right or wrong' regulars, hanging on and still talking (despite the Referendum result) of being 'the voice of the people'; and (b) of new extremists and fierce hermit-crabs who find the emptying shells easy to infiltrate. There is a public interest, indeed, in trying to arrest and reverse declining membership of the parties. Money should be used to that, and other, ends.

This PEP pamphlet simply assumes that things should go on as before, even if the public does not appear to want it. Cause and effect are neatly reversed. 'The inescapable conclusion, therefore, is that, left to their own resources, both major political parties will be unable to raise sufficient funds to fulfil the functions which society expects of them.'

That last phrase deserves to be a classic of question-begging[b] and pretentious, muddled thinking—with its echoes of Hegel ('society'), Talcott Parsons ('the functions') and Lord Nelson ('expects of them'). All it really means is that, left to their own resources, both major parties will be unable to raise the money to pay for their functionaries, The press and the public will weep great crocodile tears at this! What society? What functions? There are, indeed, tasks that the parties still fulfil for which no clear substitutes can as yet be imagined or seen emerging. So let us be at least cautious and critical supporters of Mr Leonard's and Mr Short's 'Society for the Preservation of Old Parties'. We need some coherence and consistency in the formation of policy and some way of recruiting and selecting, first, MPs and then ministers.

Why the decline?

But the question of why membership has declined should be faced. And to face the fact that membership of other voluntary bodies is *not* declining, but to follow (a) the Social Survey figures for the Redcliffe–Maude report on local government management, and (b) the great increase in pressure-group activity, people are joining voluntary societies on a large scale. Pictures of an anomic, alienated society are rubbish. Hardly a person does not belong to some kind of voluntary body. One adult in five is a member of some kind of committee. And the last way a person would ever feel 'lonely' is in *not* being a member of a political party.

People do not join parties presumably because they do not want to—there are all kinds of explanations as to why people do not want to do things; and probably because they do not think that parties are *as important* as in the past. If a young person is politically interested, it is now far more likely that he or she will join a pressure group. And this may not be a feckless or romantic mistake: it may be quite rational behaviour. Many of these groups, operating directly on Town Halls, Whitehall or Westminster, may now be more effective in influencing decisions than any other agency or group other than ministers themselves. In some ways we are now living in a politically far more pluralistic society than one with simply a two-party system. The very textbooks are being rewritten to take out the absurd 1950s picture of pressure

---

[b] In the traditional and meaningful sense of 'question begging', of course.

groups threatening 'our two-party system' and are trying to paint a more complex shaded picture of a political system composed of both parties and pressure groups, the former still predominant, if far from omnipotent, but the latter relatively far more important than twenty years ago. Even on that narrow score, not one word of the PEP study considers whether the case for subsidising parties has anything to do with the dismally reduced share of the popular vote that the two main parties possess, or whether (as is surely likely) the Ulster, Welsh and Scottish nationalist groups are not likely to be around, with the Liberals, for longer than the old party regulars still care to face.

If the parties are that much less important, and are seen to be by the public, measured both by membership and electoral support, it is hardly surprising that donations from big business and unions also decline, a process unlikely to reverse itself. Therefore any scheme of subsidy must offer incentives either to genuine individual membership or to voting support.

On the contrary, the PEP scheme suggests that a global sum should be equally divided between the national parties (in proportion to seats in the House of Commons) and the parties in the constituencies in proportion to votes. The argument here is not merely flimsy but embarrassingly transparent. If, as in Germany, Mr Leonard says, money was divided in proportion to votes rather than to seats, it would not make much difference between the Conservative and Labour parties, 'but the Liberals would . . . stand to gain about nine times as much . . . . But:

Whatever the theoretical justification for relating the allocation to seats in Parliament, in practice this is likely to be regarded as highly unfair and it would disproportionately reward the two parties with the largest existing resources. Yet to relate the allocation entirely to votes would be illogical in the absence of a system of proportional representation.

So he proposes a crude compromise: fifty–fifty. Half a pork barrel is better than none, presumably. 'Likely to be regarded as unfair' indeed—no mean understatement. Is Dick Leonard an innocent or is he a reformer—of the kind that Ted Short is likely to be? 'Reform in order to preserve', as Edmund Burke once remarked; but to preserve the present dominance of the two main parties? Sheer preservationism. This kind of happy handout might be what the two-party offices wish for, but it is unlikely that Lord Houghton's committee would fall for anything as crude in effect and superficial in analysis.

If the problem arises because both public and pressure groups are less keen on the parties than once they were, then that basic problem has to be grappled with, not the symptom.

Subsidise the parties, certainly, get them free from their big friends, but only in such a way that 'the interests of parliamentary democracy' in the broadest sense, not just the interests of the party machines, are enhanced. When Mr Leonard says that it would be 'illogical' to give money in proportion to votes 'in the absence of a system for proportional representation', he lets the practical cat out of the theoretical bag. Things that affect each other must somewhere be considered together. It is either crazily short-sighted or wickedly partial to advocate a straight subsidy as if the issue was a self-contained one. Precisely because the present voting system is increasingly seen to be unfair, it would be illogical to give money in any other way than in proportion to the vote—unless one actually wants to increase public antagonism to the party system. A Speaker's Conference may soon be looking at electoral reform. All these strange things are in the air, for the system is not working well. But Lord Houghton's committee could stop short of saying 'No electoral reform, no subsidy' by simply saying 'Any subsidy, only in proportion to the vote'. That might give the unreformed system a last chance—if the Liberals and the Nats of various hues at least got a rough monetary justice.

The price for subsidies

This leads to a still wider consideration. 'Should there be control over how the money is spent?', the study asks. 'It is, in my view', says Mr Leonard, *ipse dixit*, 'objectionable in principle and would lead to manifold difficulties in practice, for the state to seek to control in any detailed way the manner in which parties might seek to expend the money they received in subsidies.' It is in our view, say we, objectionable in principle if there were no public control of public funds. Would they vote themselves, as the Italian Parliament seems now to do, as much money as they themselves think they need? What—to use an old-fashioned expression—a job that would be.

The only *quid pro quo* for which Mr Leonard sees a strong case is for publication of full accounts with lists of all donors of over £50. How public-spirited it would be if the parties agreed to that.

Actually this matters little, nor does control in the sense of deciding whether parties should spend 'their' or 'the' money on platforms, propaganda or picnics. That really is their business. The 'control' that public funds should bring with them is an attempt by public law to democratise the parties, indeed all voluntary bodies that benefit by public subsidy, whether direct as here proposed, or indirect as in bodies with charitable status. The number of trade union election cases that have been before the courts; the impotence of shareholders to control company donations to parties or political pressure groups; indeed, the impotence of millions of members of bodies like, say, the AA and RAC which they joined in case their cars broke down, and yet hear these officials speaking in their names on matters of public policy. The whole question of superveillance of 'private jurisdictions' needs joining to the enactment of general public rights for members to be consulted before important decisions are made and to be protected from indirect processes of election or nomination by officials or committees who can achieve results quite different from the views of the membership, if they were ever asked, polled or balloted. The problems raised by the old Industrial Relations Act are

157

general—it was prejudicial to limit such first attempts at public accountability of private power simply to trade unions.

Certainly the case for interparty primaries is now very strong—perhaps even for public primaries among those who—as is common in America—register as regular supporters. These things are all part and parcel of the same considerations. This is what public control should mean. Would Mr Short think this a fair price for a public handout to Mr Haywood?

Political imagination is needed from independent bodies—not such sober party line stuff, even if a rather new party line that some of the regulars have not digested yet. Take the most basic point of all that underlies the declining membership and income of the parties: that political influence has shifted from being a monopoly of the parties to being shared with pressure groups—not just unions and business, but 'good causes' as well as interest groups. Should not this be recognised if there is to be some general reform of political institutions to meet new conditions?

Currently there is a committee sitting on Charity Law Reform. It seems bogged down with the dilemma that if the scope of charitable (thus tax-free) status is broadened, groups may use their funds for direct political purposes, not even generalised campaigning for law reform. But the answer may be, why not? Politics is not the preserve of the two main parties, or even of two and a half, or several halves. All voluntary bodies are political.

If the three main parties need public subsidy and two are determined to get it, the price that should be extracted is a double one: (i) new laws creating a new jurisdiction to implement general principles for equitable procedures by which voluntary bodies of all kinds pass resolutions and elect officials and delegates; (ii) the extension of the tax relief at present enjoyed by charities to all bodies open to public membership which are non-profit-making and which claim to be advancing the public interest—whether by education, prayer or political pressure or propaganda. It would cost a little, but it might revivify British democracy, or rather go far to creating it. The role of the main parties would be much as now, to recruit leaders and form governments, but policy would come from where policy would come. If the need for subsidy is because of public withdrawal of support for either the parties or their policies, the answer cannot simply be to subsidise the parties without conditions. Conditions must be created to make it easier for the public to participate in politics *both* through parties and through pressure groups, and for all these bodies to be subject to public law, acknowledging some basic democratic principles of procedure. By all means let the public pay for the parties since they can no longer pay for themselves; but let us see how to get better value for money.

11 The Character of a Moderate (Socialist)

Vol. 47, no. 1, January–March 1976

> *Gilnockie*: Aha, ha. But you *are* ane whoor?
> *Lady*: I'm no *your* whoor.
> From John Arden, *Armstrong's Last Night*.

'MODERATES stand up!', indeed—as Mr Roy Hattersley has just cried.[1] I am a moderate, indeed a rather truculent and aggressive moderate, someone who has always thought that the average citizen should have his sleeves rolled up and his fists lightly clenched, not sit wincing behind this or that newspaper. But I want to say something before I stand up: that I am a moderate *Socialist*, or rather a Socialist who is moderate. I hope I am still with Mr Hattersley, or probably a bit beyond him, keeping my distance but not too far ahead.[2] I am not moderate, however, in the sense that the editor of *The Times*, Mr David Wood, Mr Ronald Butt, Miss Nora Beloff, Mr Robert McKenzie, even, and all in the Liberal Party over the age of 40 are moderate. And Roy Hattersley should beware of the motives of these Greeks when they come bearing gifts, praising him as moderate. They have damaged the repute of Reg Prentice in the Labour Party by this. And when in September *The Times* called Mario Soares a moderate (catching correctly that he believes in parliaments and persuasion, but missing utterly that he wishes to achieve a planned egalitarian society) they drove the editor of *Tribune* into acute dialectical contortions: for Dick Clements seemed to accept that anyone whom *The Times* called moderate is not fit to be thought of as a Socialist.

This silliest usage of 'moderate', however, is simply to mean 'what I approve of'—or as the *Daily Telegraph* editorial writers use it to refer to any *others* whom they can on occasion mildly tolerate. The commonest use is to define an alleged centre of the political spectrum. (I always remember that Arthur Schlesinger Jr once wrote a book called *The Vital Centre*, which seemed to me to be simply dead centre.) This dead-centre-of-the-political-spectrum view soon gets muddied up with talk of coalition (immediately jerking several points to the Right all those radicals who are flattered into that premature senility of being 'responsible fellows', that is unresponsive to popular pressures). What would they do with a coalition if they had one? Or 'moderate' can be given the more theoretical-seeming and less practical-politics import of 'consensus'—a belief that we must have 'fundamental

---

[1] This is a much-revised and expanded version of five short articles which appeared in the *New Statesman* in August and September [1975].

[2] Roy Hattersley, 'The Radical Alternative', in *New Statesman*, 31 October 1975.

values' in common in order to survive. This view is usually advocated by people without any belief in clear values themselves: so probably the moderate-as-consensus-politician needs to reformulate his case to say that other people, that is the People, should hold values in common (like a bit in the mouth of a horse), but that they are not necessary for us, pragmatists all. Values should restrain (difficult) people, not animate them into positive citizenship.

Modes of moderation

The confusions arise because 'moderate' can be applied either to means or to ends, to goals or to values. And when it refers to substantive goals, it can refer to the centre of the national spectrum or to the centre of the Labour Party—a rather different calculation. And when it refers to means or to procedural values (like parliamentarianism, toleration, respect for simple truth, liberty and democracy, not the contortions of ideology), it can treat them simply as means towards many different ends or it can treat them as ends in themselves—which is the most sophisticated argument, the argument that any pursuit of rational and clearly defined goals is ultimately going to prove coercive, so we should best carry on simply managing, administering, politicising, with decency and humanity, not hope for too much, and never treating men as if they could be better, either more altruistic or more rational, than they are.

Now there is much to be said for this view, if we believe in the myth of the Fall, are naturally pessimistic or rationally believe, through reading what Sir Keith Joseph calls 'the noble philosophy of Hayek', that there is little chance of us all bettering our lot in this world of scarce, indeed, diminishing resources, particularly in our British economy of today. I simply want to say that as a moderate and a socialist this is not my view for one. I believe that our society needs to be changed, should be changed and can be changed. But that it can only be changed in desirable directions through time and by what are essentially moderate means. When this has happened, there may be a point at which we can look back and say that there has been a revolution (as for world health or scientific technology, for example), that is both a change in the conditions that shape social and economic arrangements and in human consciousness. But revolution is rarely the most probable means to ensure a good end. Violent revolutions are a response either to the breakdown of government or to intolerable oppression: at best they create the opportunity, which then has to be taken deliberately and carefully, for comprehensive social change. More often revolution can only sensibly be understood as a process and not an event. In other words, moderate but naked and quite unashamed, I am an evolutionary (that is, revolution-through-time) Socialist. Please do not call me moderate at all, though call me tolerant and libertarian (if I deserve it) any day, if this then leads you to believe that I want to maintain the same kind of present society (cleaned up a little) as the centre of the political spectrum both desire and enjoy. Which of us would then have been deceiving the other? And please will the Left stop deceiving themselves that socialist legislation without mass support can transform society (at least without an intolerably—and usually self-defeating—degree of coercion); and will they stop calling any who doubt this either backsliders or Fascist beasts? Ordinary people still need convincing, and convincing freely, that socialist ideals are worth trying, perhaps not necessarily only in alternating electoral spasms, but always in such a way that while advance continues, the possibility of peaceful retreat is never closed. Yet if once ordinary people were convinced, then a democratic socialist regime would have far more power behind it to transform society genuinely than have the imposed socialist regimes of East Europe.

So let me try to restate in its broadest and most commonsensical terms the case for democratic Socialism (to use George Orwell's careful lower and upper case). But is this necessary—when we have had a Labour government for about a decade, with one short interruption?

Lack of thought

They (I mean the leaders of the Labour Party) find it hard to think at all (apart from being too busy, except perhaps in August) because of (a) a constitutional debility; and (b) a mistake in logic. The constitutional debility is the castrating or muzzling (as the case may be) of leadership by the doctrine of collective responsibility. No minister may safely state any principles that the Prime Minister might dislike or might feel put himself in the shade, nor apparently produce any evidence which might ruffle the belief of the Sir John Hunts of that world that the least said the better. The Prime Minister himself may break the doctrine (a) by writing his memoirs (which contain no thought in the whole of the book, only a day-to-day celebration of his own cleverness); and (b) by the agreement to differ in the Common Market referendum campaign. But the others may not break it. And civil servants watch that they do not.

The others, it is said, collectively constitute (with a bit of ballast) the most intelligent, certainly the most highly educated, Cabinet in British political history; and yet they cannot talk freely and speculate publicly about the aims of political activity. They may only, by permission, defend set positions. Only the briefest and most enigmatic signals are allowed of what their basic beliefs and working theories may be. Whatever one thinks of Tony Crosland's general views or of those of Tony Benn (and I am a very tolerant moderate who can see the intense plausibility of both), there is no doubt that each of them would be more influential if out of government, perhaps even out of the House. The pen is mightier than the mace. We do not lack good administrators: we lack thinkers with an empathy towards real, ordinary people; and we lack sufficient politicians with integrity and almost any with a clear sense of purpose—or if they have it, we can only surmise it by occasional discordant phrases cutting across cautious department briefs, or by knowledge of what they said before they went silent and underground in high office.

The mistake in logic is, however, an even more important factor in explaining why a Labour government which has had the lion's share of power for the last decade yet lacks any publicly comprehensible sense of direction. 'Pragmatism' is believed to be a thing that wins elections (but only just, it seems). Pragmatism apparently means being practical, or vulgarly that 'truth is what works': the pseudo-philosophy of the careerist or of the manager of a going concern (and if it is not 'going', then not to question if one is in the right trade or working in the best way, but to borrow more and to pray for more oil). The fallacy of pragmatism is that it can only work within a known and accepted context of moral habits, beliefs and principles. It is not self-validating. To be 'purely practical', even, assumes that there are under-lying values which are known, shared and understood. If there is no such consensus, then pragmatism is fraudulent—both in the sense of being self-deceiving and of being imposed on others, itself masking an ideology while pretending only to mirror public opinion. The question may indeed be one, as the Archbishop has remarked, of basic values; but whose values and what values? It may not be a problem of the decay of 'good old values' (of competitiveness and individualism?), but of changing values—a search for more fraternity and sociability.

The pragmatist in a changing world is likely to make great mistakes by attempting, for all his hyperactivity, to conserve the unconservable. Pragmat-ists wasted our national resources by trying, like Alice, to run very fast to stay put in one moving place: the hanging on to 'East of Suez' for so long after there was anything to defend; the defence of the pound in the late 1960s; the belief in a free market for wages amid falling productivity; and the eco-nomically crippling belief that houses and jobs should be brought to people and all movements of population, as far as possible, frozen.

The pragmatic politician's contempt for doctrine is almost as misleading as the journalist's habitual attempt to reduce every idea to a personal interest. Journalists often say that the public will only grasp issues if they are personalised, but more often they themselves believe —as the daily quest for novelty amid long-term problems conditions them to believe—that personal factors predominate. So deep is this contempt for ideas and resulting ignorance about them that it is leading people to call almost any manifestation of real socialist thought 'Marxist'—as if the tradition of the Webbs, Cole, Tawney and Laski had never existed. Indeed, the genuine Marxists of the book had better watch out, for the very word is shifting its colloquial meaning to refer to anyone who believes in Liberty, Equality, Fraternity.

I am not a Marxist. I hold the amiable view that on some things that very great man was profound and right, on others wrong and that on still more issues he was so overgeneralised and abstract as to be virtually meaningless. If Marxism is a 'growing method', then it may just become another word for socialism. If Michael Foot is persistently called a Marxist by the right wing press (moderates?), he will end up by believing that, after all (all those long battles with his friends Bevan and Orwell against the Communist Marxists), he really is one. I do not much care. One can be a good man without being a follower of Christ, and a good democratic Socialist with or without the blessing of the censorious pedantic priests of Marxism. But I do care intensely for the theory and spirit of Enlightenment and of the French Revolution: that mankind will progress by applying reason to the ideals of liberty, equality and fraternity. Yet revolution is to be seen as a long and deliberate process of government and popular education and persuasion, not as a dramatic single event. And I am angry when non-Marxist social democrats refuse to argue with Marxists and take refuge behind a shallow technological scepticism about the importance of ideas at all—just as angry as when quests for doctrinal purity disallow any practical political action.

Socialism implies reason and example from both leaders and followers—not secrecy and perpetual personal exceptions. (That a *Labour* government could prosecute publishers of a book by a colleague[a] and that a *Labour* government should flinch at limiting high incomes!) But a practical socialism means an intelligent appreciation of the different demands of the short-run and the long-run factors, the pursuit of neither without the other and also a tolerant recognition that a socialist party must act on different levels simultaneously. Great changes need more planning and time than do immediate responses to short-term problems. If it has been decided to rehouse the area completely in ten years' time, the ancillary services can be prepared; but in the meantime redecoration and repairs must continue, especially if the roof is blown off by one of those intercontinental storms really beyond the control of any government.

The right wing of the Labour Party is in danger of making a cult of pragmatism and of realism not as means to ends, but as ends in them-selves—an hermaphrodite chasing its own tail. The left wing is in danger of forsaking political means to their ends, which is, in fact, recurrently destructive of these ends—a phoenix far too frequent. Too many right wingers have become, indeed, simply careerist smoothies. Too many left wingers have simply retreated into sectarian fanaticism rather than face the lapsed, but perpetual and necessary, task of converting the public to socialist principles.

What is the common core of all types of genuine socialism? Basically it is both a theory and a doctrine. The theory is that the rise and fall of societies is best explained not by the experience of cleverness of elites (Conservatism), nor by the initiative and invention of individuals (Liberalism), but by the social relationships of the primary producers of wealth—in an industrial society, the skilled manual worker. The doctrine is that a greater equality will lead to more cooperation rather than competition, and that this will

[a] The Crossman Diaries affair. See Bernard's 1975 Commentary 'Opening the Crossman Diaries' in this volume.

enhance fraternity and thus liberate from inhibition and restriction both individual personality and the productive potential of a society.

In the 1930s the Labour Party had a bad spell when it wanted both to fight fascism and to disarm. We have recently been in a bad spell when we wanted both to maintain free collective bargaining and to obtain social justice for all. This may only have been a temporary aberration. Socialism began and rests on the belief that a free market in wages leads both to intolerable injustice and to a limitation both of productive and of human potential. But the message still has to be got across. A resolute socialist programme would still lose votes.

So if the politics of self-interest is not working and if people are plainly fed up with the ping-pong party electoral battle of 'Who's the better manager of the shop?', let us explore (if only for a New Year's Resolution) what a realistic and immediately relevant democratic socialist argument would be in terms likely to convince the unconvinced, not just the dwindling and thus somewhat touchy party faithful. Let us have a little less on programmes and manifestos and a little more on principles and long-term objectives.

Principles and directions

So I want to consider what a democratic Socialist (to use again Orwell's careful emphasis, the adjective distinguished from the noun, the means from the end) or a moderate Socialist (that is moderate about means, but not necessarily about ends) should be doing to develop his three basic values of liberty, equality and fraternity. I say 'develop', not work towards 'the goal', because values are not a kind of distant beacon that one day we may reach, thereupon rest, and in the meantime ignore: they are constant companions (if often quarrelsome among themselves and of varying influence upon oneself) on a journey which, while it progresses, yet never ceases. And this journey is governed not by some predetermined selection of an arbitrary point on a dubious map, but simply by agreement about a general sense of direction and how to behave towards each other on the way. Strictly speaking our goals are specifically socialist, but our values are not all specifically socialist—they include such values, good and common values, as truth, freedom, tolerance and fairness, none of which rules out our goals, but all of which may affect the means towards these goals.

Is any sense of direction realistic, however? Before a moderate socialist charges he wants (a) some idea of where he is going; and (b) some hope of being followed. Cromwell once remarked that an army never goeth so far as when it knows not where it is going. And there is an argument against any such politics of purpose at all. Is not the best any government can do simply to keep the ship afloat—as Oakeshott has taught (and Wilson is more the Oakeshott figure of a statesman than ever a Heath or a Thatcher)? The actual Labour Party is, indeed, to be understood historically as a coalition of interests, primarily the wage-politics of trade unions, and any specifically socialist influence has been at the best marginal. Certainly it is untrue that once upon a time, in the days of the banners and the brass bands, it was socialist; and that it has fallen away by treachery, careerism and parliamentary nice-Nellyism. The myth of the Fall is poor history. There is no need to be a bad historian to be a good socialist. Look for socialism in the future of the Labour Party, not in the past. For socialism is not a movement; it is a theory which sees the key to social progress in the character of the skilled working man's relations to the factors of production. The Labour Party may not be socialist, but socialism may be more illuminating of its dilemmas and more useful in giving it self-respect and a sense of direction than the non-theory or the 'pragmatism' of the leaders of the moment.

The dilemmas of the Labour Party, loss of membership, loss of support, loss of heart, increasing internal intolerance, may arise not from the lack of realism of its leaders but from their lack of theory and doctrine. Realism and pragmatism must be about something, they cannot feed of themselves; and plainly the customs and habits of the past are failing lamentably. Pragmatism, at the moment, is only concerned with how to keep the party in power. Reducing politics to that level, the electorate will simply judge in terms of immediate management of conventional values, self-interest and prosperity. And since no one can fully control the weather, not even Harold Wilson or Margaret Thatcher, each government will in turn, in these hard times for our country, be judged to have failed: so periods of alternating power will follow, rendering almost impossible any fundamental changes—which is just what opponents of adversary politics seem to want. Doctrine and publicly argued principles must be replenished and revivified if only to break from this truly liberal, capitalist, utilitarian vicious circle. Such doctrines must be realistic as well as heart-felt and clear—and the more heart-felt they are, the more one can compromise in the short run without destroying long-term hopes and integrity.

Socialist ideals are not to be restored; they are yet to be adopted. As one of the founding fathers wrote in 1911 in a once-famous Home University Library book, *The Socialist Movement*:

The Labour Party is not Socialist. It is a union of Socialist and trade union bodies for immediate political work. . . . But it is the only political form which evolutionary Socialism can take in a country with the political traditions and methods of Great Britain. Under British conditions, a Socialist Party is the last, not the first, form of the Socialist movement in politics.

Hardly strengthening my case to quote Ramsay MacDonald. But if he did not last the course himself, back then he happened to be right. Short-run realism and long-run idealism (plus middle-term planning) do not exclude or contradict each other: they complement each other. Even our short-run factors need not be a retreat from Socialism (as cuts in public expenditure are seen) but could be made a prelude to a more socialist system of rewards. A declining economy in crisis may yet produce strident calls for an equality-fraternity of sacrifice. Such a siege-socialism could prove social fascism, unless we look to our liberties too. But even given the opportunity, the worst of conditions and the best of motives, am I too not falling into the trap of advocating something that would hearten the faithful and lose the elections? What will it benefit a politician if he finds his own soul and loses the whole world? We are indeed fed up with the pharisaism and self-indulgent purity of so much left wing sectarian thought. But I am not arguing against their ideals, only against their believing that they can achieve them all at once or not at all. We have all been talking to each other in the Labour movement too long if we cannot see that long before the public will ever want nuances of socialist principle, they are right now very hungry for almost any kind of principles in politics. So great dangers as well as opportunities appear. Some sense of integrity, some sense of movement, some sense of common purposes and fraternity, some lessening of injustices in rewards—never mind quite precisely what—is what the public seems hungry for at this very time. The public seem to thirst for something positive, but all they get is people knocking on the doors with questionnaires asking them what policies they want their leaders to lead them with—some leaders! The present leader of the Labour Party seems like an ignorant nurse who believes that constant application of a thermometer will lower the patient's temperature.

Liberty

Leaders should just try what they believe in and find out if it is popular. But the manner in which socialist leaders try and in which they find out should be distinctively open, participative and subject to correction. The one easily recognisable mark of a democratic Socialist movement should be its almost fanatic commitment to more liberty and openness. The means are not the ends but they can make or break the ends. And even Rosa Luxemburg said of Lenin, a socialism that does not proceed through freedom becomes oppression. All talk of 'socialist liberty', as if it were different in kind from any other, is dangerous nonsense, often deliberate obfuscation. Far-away thoughts? I am no longer sure when one thinks of students howling down Sir Keith Joseph; or of campus bookshop assistants refusing to stock, order or handle books hostile to what they judge to be 'the student' cause.

More immediately, official talk of 'open government' is rhetorical nonsense when it goes with the maintenance of traditional, conservative controls over publicity: the belief of all autocracies and autocrats that government cannot work well if the reasons why decisions are made can be publicly known. In fact, there is a kind of British half-autocracy: Tony, Alan, Bernard, John, Robin, David, Peter and the statutory woman could have always read—and did—Crossman's *Diaries* without the Attorney-General or a High Court Judge's permission; but not the rest of you. And all schoolkids in the country can be taught that the ombudsman is a 'good thing'—they and their teachers seem captivated by him—but the government could reply to his criticisms last year of Mr Benn and Mr Shore not with honest and beguiling admissions, nor with reasoned rebuttals, but with the ignorant and ignoring contempt that seems to possess modern governments with even the slenderest of mere parliamentary majorities. And the government damps down the Poulson inquiries. And the Labour Party National Executive refused even a party inquiry into the affairs of the NE England Labour Party. Have we come all the way for this?

The right wing think that they can pick and choose what liberties to adopt, in their own interests—sound on Clay Cross, but hostile to workers' control: very few are libertarians at heart. But those of the left wing who are libertarians at heart often get themselves trapped in bad Marxist logic: that only in the classless society after the revolution can there be true liberty—until then all we have is an instrumental 'bourgeois liberty' or an 'oppressive tolerance'. (Therefore no holds barred in your own strategies, but tactical howls of 'liberty in danger' every time the law comes near you.) But active liberty has a long history, and it was bourgeois in its origins. The fault is not in its paternity but in its prudishness. Liberty is all very well for the likes of us, but impossible *en masse*, for all of them. But we must be promiscuous in liberty if we have any faith in reason and human nature. 'The liberal bourgeois is genuinely liberal', said Orwell, 'up to the point where his own interests stop.'

What we must do is constantly to try to persuade people that their idea of self-interest is self-defeatingly narrow; and that ideals widen our horizon into the future, particularly our children's future. 'Do you want *them* to grow up into a world like *this*?' is the strongest practical socialist idealism. It is not so much that the impractical of today can be practical tomorrow, but that in the modern world the practical of today is always the impractical of tomorrow.

Socialist liberty is no different from liberal liberty, except that there is more of it for all: a humanistic faith that ordinary working people have to be drawn into participation and decision-making too, and not just in leisure time but in working life. Of course an incomes policy under Socialism, but ultimately a voluntary one—how else? How else, that is, without ever greater centralised controls and oppression in fewer and fewer hands. If from political democracy we cannot also create economic, industrial and occupational democracy, then we drift towards a 1984 kind of society—though more likely to be one, as Tocqueville imagined, in which the elite dole out welfare rather than privation; so long as they can make the decisions, the masses can have everything possible given to them, except freedom.

If socialist liberty does differ from liberal liberty in one respect, it is in that it goes back, like the men of the French Revolution, to a classical or Roman concept of liberty more than a *laissez-faire* one: not just being left free by the state, which is often to be left high and dry; but that each man and woman should exercise freedom aggressively. A state is neither as strong nor as just as it can be if its inhabitants do not act like citizens—nor is a union, a firm or a school. Citizenship and liberty is enhanced by example and by multiplying participative institutions in all spheres. We could stop short of 'extremist'

Socialism and yet make some public stir about that. But what a long way from the practical policies of our great leader's fourth administration.

Equality

Equality is a value basic to any possible kind of socialism. Without a real desire to achieve an egalitarian society, any democratic Socialist movement loses its dynamic and lapses back into the alternating ping-pong politics of the 'I'm a better manager of the shop than Fred' kind (whatever trash the shop is selling, however badly built it is). But the concept has its difficulties. Literal equality, whether of opportunity, treatment or result (or of all three), is almost as undesirable as it is plainly impossible. But an egalitarian society is both possible and desirable. By an egalitarian society I mean a classless society, one in which every man would see every other man as a brother, a genuinely fraternal society with no conceit or constraint of class to limit fraternity. But it would not be a society in which everyone was exactly equal in power, status, wealth and ability, still less in humane end-products of happiness.

No difficulties about the concept are, however, so great as to warrant abandoning it or treating it as pure ritual of the Labour church—unless one wants to abandon it. One difficulty is that we want, rhetorically, to make something sound positive which is, intellectually, at heart a negative matter. There is no 'complete equality' which can 'finally be realised', unless genetic engineering was to come to the aid of economic planning (with about equal accuracy and predictability, one would hope). But there are so many unjustifiable inequalities—not just in theory but so flagrantly in practice. The boot should be worn on that foot. If we believe in the moral equality or the fraternity of all mankind, then all inequalities of power, status and wealth need explaining and justifying. They can be justified (here I follow Rawls and Runciman) only if these inequalities can be shown to be of positive advantage to the less advantaged. Some inequalities can be justified, more not—particularly if one adds the vital condition of liberty, actually to ask the disadvantaged. No precise agreement can ever be reached or, if so, for no more than a transitory time and a particular place. Nor can philosophy supply incontrovertible criteria for what is an unjustifiable inequality. But in an egalitarian society *all* inequalities will be called into question, constantly questioned and criticised: they will have to be justified precisely and for themselves; not as an acceptable, general side-product of status or power.

'Less Unjustifiable Inequalities!' may not be a slogan that warms the blood like wine, but that is as well. For there are other values to be preserved, which is always the difficulty. No one value, be it liberty, equality, fraternity, love, reason, even life itself, can at all times override all the others or be sure never to contradict them. Equality could certainly be maximised in a totalitarian society—but only at the expense of liberty so that genuine fraternity is destroyed. The Socialist, having a theory of society, looks at values together, in their social setting and in relation to each other. He no more postpones liberty *until* the classless society than he reserves egalitarian and fraternal behaviour and example *until* the classless society. If he does, he will not get there; and when he does, classlessness by itself will not have solved all problems and removed all possibilities of tyranny.

The moderate socialist as egalitarian should not get drawn into the parody argument of exact equality of income and wealth: that is somebody else's nightmare not his dream. Literal minded distributive socialism is very hard to find—since the time of the Gracchi at least. 'Soak the fat boys and spread it thin' may be good rhetoric, but most people know how thin it would be. Industrial relations are not as bad as they are because the men on the shop floor believe that the cow can make milk without grass or that 'vast profits' are there to be distributed to our direct advantage—about 6p a week more all round, once and for all, on Friday and bust by Monday—but they are bad because men think that it is *unfair* that they should be restrained while their bosses actually write to tell newspapers that in their cases incentives to do better do not begin until about £15,000 a year; and that they have no real incentive to work anyway if their children or the cats' homes cannot freely inherit all their wealth. Workers, oddly, use their eyes and see how much patriotic restraint is practised by those who at least look like ruling classes. They see clearly the gross extravagance of Ascot, of the West End and of the fashionable residential areas. (Photographs of such should be forbidden— they do far more harm 'our civilisation' than do those pictures of which Lord Longford complains and blames.) And working men do not miss the claim of top civil servants that their salaries should be competitive with industry (as if they, too, shared the Marxist–capitalist view of the exclusive importance of economic motivation), and should be inflation proof even, on top of a non-contributory pension. What servants of the state! What example! *Quis custodiet custodes*, indeed. Nothing better illustrates the decline of the traditional restraints of the cult of the gentlemen and the growth of the moral standards of the speculators and developers.

Equality is, then, a demand for equal justice not for proportional distribution. But the parody is sometimes accepted, perhaps because some Labour leaders begin to have doubts, from the company they keep, as to the potential popularity of the ideal at all. Most people, they feel, want no more than equality of opportunity; and only then if they are among the disadvantaged in 'the great game', to transfer Kipling's phrase to the happy world of Keith Joseph. This destruction of socialist morals and morale earns newspaper praise as 'realism' or 'pragmatism'. Here the moderate socialist parts company with many right wing Labour MPs.

True, ordinary people will commonly get no further than 'equality of opportunity', if you put the question to them in such an abstract and general way. But suppose you ask them if they think it right that the top 20 per cent of incomes (before tax) had seven times greater a share in the total income than the bottom 20 per cent? Or (findings of the recent Royal Commission on the Distribution of Income and Wealth) that 67 per cent of the personal wealth in the country is possessed by the top 10 per cent? The answer may then differ. And answers will certainly differ in terms of perceptions of the justice or not of particular rewards and relativities. Here is an incredibly undeveloped area of liberty and openness. We are so full of taboos about disclosing incomes, even though civil servants and teachers are among obvious exceptions. Suppose all incomes were disclosed. Suppose it was a constant topic of debate in the mass media: 'Here's what this man or woman does, here's what they do, here's what they get. Is it fair?' If this happened, justifications for differences would have to be produced and discussed seriously—not as easy, however, as to knock the miners for their muscle tactics, or praise them for their temporary restraint, or to knock MPs for the crass folly of the timing of their own pay award last year.

Amid full openness, many differences and some injustices would remain. Surveys show that many unskilled and poorly paid people seem to believe that almost no salary is too high for the greedy medical consultants—so socialised have we all been about the long and worthy tribulations (invest-ment) of medical education. (Do not let them leave the country, I say, unless they pay it back.) But it is likely that genuine knowledge, publicity and debate would help to raise the floor and bring down the ceiling. By itself it could not create an egalitarian society, but it would be a condition for it. There would emerge, whatever the justifications for particular inequalities and relativities, a public view of a minimum and a maximum income. An incomes policy would be acceptable if it was, thus, a genuinely socialist one; establishing what range of differentiation is tolerable to an informed majority.

Are there still some primitives who think that any income differentials are contrary to socialist principles? If there are, they are less in number, I suspect, than the hypocrites and careerists who can always find some reason for a Labour government not to enforce some fairly modest, middle middle-class income as a maximum income.

If socialism means anything, the theory is that with greater equality there can be greater fraternity, hence greater cooperation, hence greater productiv-ity—since wealth basically comes from the worker. The record of British management of late hardly impresses one with the claim that only ever-continuing economic incentives lead to efficient management. Power and status count for a lot and so does having a clear and worthwhile job. Real managers like to produce, but the English upper middle class now prefer the City to industry. Their kind of mentality led even a Labour government to leave 'the white-hot heat of the technological revolution' for the paper battle of saving the pound. (The class of men who would do it better and do it for less are from the foremen, the junior managers, the technical teachers, that borderland between the old skilled workers and the old lower middle class, so many of whose sons and daughters are now, in beliefs and behaviour, so unexpectedly but clearly if precariously classless.)

So much scope for action remains in the direction of greater equality: not to be represented or misrepresented as levelling but rather as a constant, aggressive questioning of the reasons for and the justifications of both existing distribution of incomes and wealth and existing divisions of responsibility between 'workers' and 'management'. Such questioning could prove as popular as it is right. More important for socialism than abstract arguments about formal ownership is progress towards taking all wages and incomes out of the market and determining them by representative arbitration and open comparison of relativities. The media, even now, could give a lead in popularising knowledge of differences between jobs and of different incomes. People are surely fascinated by this. And public policy should work towards complete openness of all incomes. Many differences can be justified. But they must be. We need to develop this as a whole new branch of applied social philosophy rather than of traditional economics. If we had shown one half of the energy in this direction that we have shown in educational policies, an egalitarian society would be appreciably nearer. Indeed, we must beware that, perhaps mainly out of frustration with national economic policies, we do not hope for too much from mere education nor drop out, as it were, from political economy into a fantasy of the comprehensive school as a model of the Socialist commonwealth. Especially in education we should not confuse literal equality of treatment with true egalitarianism. For true egalitarianism is no more—but no less—than the removal of unjustifiable inequalities; and it is a necessary condition, but not a sufficient condition, for fraternity.

Fraternity

To appeal for more fraternity and less fratricide within the Labour movement needs a thick skin as well as a clear head. The Labour movement used to be proud of exhibiting within itself the very fraternity it wished to create in society as a whole, but of late brother seems more eager to revile brother and sister sister than to argue with opponents and to seek to persuade the vast majority of the unconvinced.

Any advance towards a Socialist Britain needs, first, more democracy; a greater opening up to popular influence and knowledge of all the institutions that shape our lives—'liberty'. Secondly, it requires a constant public demand for justification (if any) of each particular inequality of reward, together with gradual but systematic and determined action to reduce those inequalities— not equality but 'egalitarianism'. But, thirdly, it requires an attitude of mind, a morality, a psychology, which gives equal respect and care to everyone, irrespective of class, kin, race, religion, office, talent or learning—'fraternity'. Our preachers should say: 'And now abideth liberty, equality, fraternity, these three; but the greatest of these is fraternity . . .'

Equality of respect does not, however, imply either—as Runciman puts it— 'equality of praise' or the confusion of sincerity with truth. Is it rational to treat all opinions as equal? And is it brotherly to treat all people as one would ideally have them rather than as they themselves are? Big brotherly, perhaps. But fraternity is treating all men as ends and not means, not just all societies. It

171

does not mean treating everybody the same but according to their different personalities and needs; and it means reconciling conflicts by mutually acceptable, public political institutions.

An enforced equality is the destruction of brotherhood—the dark warning of Orwell's *1984*. Fraternity can, indeed, exist amid great inequality, but only in times of emergency: the comradeship of the trenches, the Dunkirk spirit, and 'the years of struggle' of both left wing and right wing political movements. But a fraternity for everyday wear in all seasons is hardly imaginable amid great inequalities which limit common purposes. Doing things together for ourselves in common enhances fraternity—unlike having equal welfare given to us which, if personal involvement is lacking, too often creates jealousies rather than comradeship. Economic controls by themselves can never guarantee a more fraternal society. Simple arithmetical equality could create even fiercer competition. We must not oversociologise. Social conditions can help or hinder but they can neither guarantee the consumption of fraternity—nor even ensure its destruction. Fraternity is an ethic that can and should be chosen and pursued freely. It goes with simplicity, lack of ostentation, friendliness, helpfulness, kindliness and restraint between individuals, not just with the fierce memories of the great occasions, the times of struggle or the Sunday 'socialism' of Saturday afternoon demos.

Fraternity does not mean no leadership; it only means no permanent class of leaders tomorrow and no *noblesse oblige* today—no condescension, no giving favours, but rather receiving trust on account of peculiar skills of both empathy and action in helping common and commonly defined purposes. In Beethoven's *Fidelio* the king hails all men as his brothers. But the power and arrogance of a king or a modern leader who thinks that he had such a gift to bestow will of itself negate the brotherhood. Even Edmund Burke said that it is hard to argue on one's knees. Some still try. The boss in a small firm or office who drinks with the men and chats with the girls is only being matey, perhaps even condescending or politic, but not genuinely fraternal unless he seeks for their opinions and takes them seriously about how things should be run.

Nor does fraternity imply the necessity of pseudo-proletarian behaviour. Society is not altered as quickly as a change of costume on a bare stage. The oldest blue jeans will now attempt to hide the newest wealth. But that leaders of working-class parties are commonly bourgeois is neither surprising nor reprehensible. For bourgeois culture stresses individualistic skills of initiative, while working-class culture, in response to exploitation and oppression, stresses solidarity. The culture of the classless society is, indeed, more likely to be bourgeois in the best sense than proletarian. It will encourage and respect individual skills, talents, personality, character; not a new iron mould of conformity, however better than the one that went before. The virtue of class solidarity was an adaptation to class injustice and would become regressive if ever class differentiation vanishes to the point of irrelevance. So the cultural ideals of a democratic socialist movement must be more than the revival of a few folk songs and dialects: amid the new we should sift, refine, adapt, but offer the best of the old to all. And that best includes the moral seriousness of the puritan tradition of individualism as found in Lawrence and in Orwell, neither the purely acquisitive, competitive individualism of capitalism nor the indulgent, permissive, irresponsible individualism of anarchic socialism. Seriousness tempers personality into sociability.

Fraternity must begin at home but be extended to the workplace. It is not simply a luxury for schools or an indulgence for radical teachers. Indeed, beware of overstating the relevance of education to achieving an egalitarian and fraternal society. Far from being the spearhead of Socialist advance, as some hope and others fear, schools may be in danger of becoming the last refuge of noble and frustrated Socialist minds, baffled at the seeming uncontrollability of the national economy or of their national leadership. Beware of hoping for too much from schools and of overburdening them with the type of concern for 'character education' we all once attacked—not just because it was the wrong kind of character.

As I wrote the original articles on which this essay is based as serial parts in the *New Statesman* last August,[b] correspondence almost entirely concentrated on the fact that I had admitted openly in a newspaper to sending my sons to a private school. My difficulty was (and still is) that I just do not see the issue as that important compared to gross inequalities of income and housing. State education is not yet a necessary shibboleth of Socialism. As a scholar, I have scholarly values. Some comprehensive schools do, some do not. Amid conflicting values, I make a local choice. I assume that scholarship is among the permitted range of human choices which will be found in a democratic Socialist society. But my generous critics seem to admit only one possible kind of motive in wanting such an education, that of social advance. Their sociology tells them that there is only one real reason for going to public schools; mine tells me that, in any case, the home is more important socially than the school. Fellow socialists seem more worried at individual cash choices involving education than about those involving housing. I am simply not as sure as my critics why, within the higher minimum income and the lower maximum income which I advocate as a socialist wages policy and as our first priority for action, some such choices are thought legitimate, some not; they would matter less if we had such a programme.

I am more worried at the educational fashion for 'mixed ability groups' right down the line in LEA schools. In some subjects the state sector is now almost doomed to inferiority. We may have got the worst of both worlds by leaving the private sector free but seeking to abolish the direct-grant grammar schools. I would hesitate long, however, in the name of liberty before

---

[b] That is, in 1975. The 'Why send your children to private schools?' accusation of a kind that would become more common against leftish figures in the Blair era gets an early airing here, and a characteristically Bernardian response.

abolishing the private sector in the name of equality until the public sector returns to the original ideal of the comprehensive school: that under one roof pupils would be treated differently according to their different abilities in different subjects or different skills, but never all in the same class for everything, never treated *en masse*. The doctrine of 'mixed ability' classes is either a bad confusion between literal equality and egalitarianism, or more likely a rationalisation of despair at having too few teachers and too many children to make the old ideal of 'to each according to his abilities' work. Knowledge can be used for social status, but limiting access to knowledge will not create equality of status. Do not destroy anything unless there is something better to put in its place, and do not let us destroy education as we destroy privilege. My socialist ideal is a common educational system; but my moderation makes me see this as coming through time and through infinite gradations of different forms of both control and content in education, not through expropriation and proscription. These points are worth labouring because they touch on liberty as well as equality in a way difficult for many Socialists.

The state system has its problems too. Perhaps it is sometimes justifiable to bus children against their will away from their neighbourhood to satisfy intelligence-quotient planning. But at least recognise that 'community' suffers, which is also a great Socialist value (we may be making the same mistake as in the new towns policy and the high-rise flats); and recognise that no one knows if the policy of an initial equal distribution leads to a less discriminatory final result overall than would positive discrimination in the supply of teachers and resources for the less-favoured schools.

Of course, if all housing were state-owned and equitably distributed and if all environments were made equal. . . .

What we do know is that social stratification is still acute inside schools, not surprisingly, for the evidence is strong that schools have little effect on basic values and behaviour patterns compared to the influence of home, the media and society at large. Educational systems work badly, it is good to know, as vehicles for deliberate indoctrination, whether of the Rhodes Boyson and Ronald Butt variety or of the Revolutionary Socialist kind. Most guff is like unto water off a duck's back. Pupils react sceptically against any such abuse or extension of authority. But the schools work better at developing skills to understand the world: they are rather unlikely instruments to change it. If one wants an egalitarian educational system, first we must change society.

Let us get our priorities right. Fraternity is not something to be thrust on kids as a sacred episode before they are pitchforked into the real industrial word; it is something that has to be applied in the real industrial world. And fraternity is more concerned with individuality than is literal equality: but it is always endangered or frustrated by gross inequalities of power, wealth or status. Certainly education is among these inequalities. But as we are now and will be for some decades at least, once we leave the classroom or the ward meeting, the illusion is over. In the real world, however, there is vast scope for making far more of what is there already—the expertise and experience of the man who knows the job and who cares for the persons and views of his colleagues or workmates. Fraternity is simply taking common sense and common concern seriously.

The second chance

The long summer of national power, prosperity and self-conceit is nearly over and socialists in the Labour Party must face the fact that in times of relative ease we have failed; but that during a winter of crisis we may be given a second chance. (The first chance was squandered from 1945 to 1950.) We have failed not merely through failures of governments to use their power in socialist directions, but more basically through a failure in the days of affluence of the Labour movement itself to persuade an effective majority of the electorate that we should build a better Britain, not just on occasion manage the shop better. Our declining share of the vote (39.2 cent in October 1974) is a pitiful basis for radical and freely willed social change. Individual membership of the party, even, continues to decline (probably now no more than a quarter of a million compared to a million in 1953)—despite the help of all those Reds whom Miss Beloff finds under other people's beds. The party now is too small either to reflect public opinion or to be able to influence it.

A genuinely socialist society needs the resolute use of centralised power, but that power is itself powerless, in any modern industrial society, unless it can carry with it popular support. And such support must be found both in the grass roots and in all those groups in which we work or spend our leisure, where our opinions do count (somewhat) and in which our opinions are influenced (somewhat) by our fellows. Only in war did we achieve a unity of purpose, great productive efficiency and (for a brief and memorable moment) a sense of fraternity. Yes, indeed, a fraternity that largely depended on external threat: none the less, it was on the home front between 1940 and 1945 that both the need and the practicality of a welfare state were proved. 'Equity of sacrifice' and 'Fair shares for all' became, instead of competitive individualism, both the official ideology of work and popular belief and behaviour.

We could be close to such a situation again. 'Equality of sacrifice' may be both a national need and a genuinely popular slogan. Perhaps it was always unlikely that the average person would be converted to socialism in relatively affluent times. Socialism does not aim at austerity, but it becomes plausible (particularly its value of fraternity), the idealistic suddenly appears practical, indeed necessary, in times of enforced austerity. Perhaps Socialism is, at heart, a prophecy of what could happen if the capitalist economy breaks down, rather than a safe prediction that it will. But while the free market in wages may not yet be quite beyond repair, its defects have proved so strong, both in terms of uncertainty and injustice, that many could now be persuaded that it is not worth repairing. A more planned and egalitarian society, albeit one hungry for and jealous of liberty, will avoid these savage oscillations of prosperity and depression which marked and marred classical capitalism and which now threaten even that minimal certainty of expectations on which the mental health of societies, as well as individuals, depends.

Ordinary working people cannot be expected to practise self-restraint and to suffer or to watch mass unemployment grow while businessmen and top civil servants enjoy huge salaries and the perquisites of office far beyond even middle-class standards; such luxury amid deprivation is not merely indecent and immoral, it grows politically untenable. If governing elites still wish to govern, they must set an example in the patriotism, public spirit and austerity that they preach to others, not themselves get in first in the endless claims for socially useless personal material advantage. The wiser of those new right-wing intellectuals of free-market liberalism see the difficulty and preach the need for restraint and example to the businessmen. But without sanctions they could save their breath to cool their porridge: they become either naive or hypocritical.

So an egalitarian incomes policy, setting a national maximum and minimum and establishing public machinery to arbitrate relativities between severe limits, should be Labour's policy for the crisis, and the greatest step forward ever towards democratic Socialism. Such arbitration would not be the bureaucratic imposition of 'objective' criteria, but rather publicity for and public discussion of what other people do and get. The object is to establish what people *think* to be fair and will accept as fair, to educate us all in making genuine comparisons, not to pretend that full objective criteria are possible, either of national need or of job specification. Such factors of job evaluation and of statistical evaluations of differentials are highly relevant, but not decisive; a greater sense of fairness is the greatest need. Complete openness about incomes and wealth and constant public debate would create the voluntary basis to emerge for an enforceable consensus on outer limits. And with lower and upper limits there could be a vast simplification of tax and welfare structures. Within such limits, market forces would work; prices can only reflect what people actually want to buy and sell.

A Socialist incomes policy calls for a Left and Centre alliance in the Labour Party. As a moderate Socialist I find *Tribune* too wild and woolly and the Social Democratic alliance too class-conscious and complacent. The Left at last begins to emerge from the temporary delusion that a free market for wages and the industrial power of a few unions on behalf of their own members can lead towards social justice, or that prices can be controlled when we live by export and import. The Left and the unions will accept incomes policy only if it strikes hard at high incomes and in this they are both just and sensible. The right of the party would regard this as impractical. Their version of incomes policy has only been aimed at the unions; and they have for long indeed abandoned any talk of Socialism—except for party workers at weekends—in favour of a kind of John F. Kennedy Democratic Party fantasy complex or complex fantasy.

176

Some of the Right would actually prefer to do without the party at all and appeal directly to the electorate, rather as some of the Left, for all their rhetoric of 'the people' (remember the Referendum) would prefer to do without the electorate (or elect another one). The Centre of the Labour Party is still warmly but rather vaguely socialist, but has, of late, either been too absorbed in practical work to think very much, living off some very run-down mental capital, or has actually lost hope of the practicality of Socialism in British conditions, but without quite losing their faith. This sleeping giant could be woken by the economic crisis.

Even the Fabian Society shows some glimpses of trying to think about general principles again, rather than the constant administrative war-game of arguing that this or that social service is scandalously underfinanced and if given more would be the key to a more healthy and salubrious future (the worst legacy—someone had to say it sometime—of the Titmuss school: worthiness, energy, dedication, indeed; but a complete lack of theory, hence of direction: *noblesse oblige* plus BSc (Econ)).

What the press call 'moderate' is usually the right of the Labour Party; that is, the centre of the national spectrum. The true moderate in the Labour Party, however, is anyone, whether of the Left or the Centre, who aims at transforming our society to a better one *by political means* and who sees the main priority as themselves persuading the unconvinced, not as enforcing dogmatic purity within the ranks or as threatening freedom of the press—as if a press wholly controlled by unions or syndics could convert a pliant public to Socialism, rather than that a more socialist public should be demanding, by how they spend their 10ps, a more socialist press. Political means are the acceptance of effective representative institutions, including Parliament, above all, but now needing to reach far more people in their own neighbourhoods and workplaces than ever Parliament did; and the need to persuade people openly and fairly; not to deceive or coerce them, even for their own good.

Democratic procedures cannot allow, for instance, MPs a property right in their seats; but equally parties must be no more immune than unions, indeed voluntary bodies of all kinds, from reform to ensure a greater and wider democracy (the only answer to infiltration is not less membership and less democracy, but more). But politics and democratic procedures are not ends in themselves. They are ways of pursuing ends. And fairness or social justice is not just the perpetual patchwork fairness of the best possible as we are: it could be something permanently better. All kinds of disputes may always remain; but they can be lifted to a higher level.

The opportunity now presents itself in crisis and in need. The affluent spree is over for ever. Guilt and remorse begin to replace sheer bewilderment; even some fear arises. For even if we can learn to live easily with ourselves again, Europe as a whole still has to come to terms with the Third World. But some hope, too, for there is a mood of seriousness and a thirst for principles. Clear and simple formulations of doctrine are needed as never before. Labour finds its basic principles in trying to create more fraternity and liberty for all, in denying all democratically unjustifiable inequalities, and in acting on the belief that ultimately it is the worker who creates wealth and that his cooperation and mutual aid create fraternity. If the party can show by behaviour and policy that it follows these, then it has a much more compelling and relevant rhetoric than the precarious 'our man is a better manager than yours' into which we have so despicably and foolishly descended.

The pure idealist is useless, but so is the pure pragmatist. We have to work on different levels, to look far ahead as we try to do the best we can right now; to imagine people as they could be, while we deal with them as they are. Political compromises are not sell-outs nor debased pragmatism if the long-term sense of purpose is clear and if we are taking clear steps forward. 'The man who striveth for the mastery', said St Paul (himself no mean prosely-tiser), 'is temperate in all things'—if he is really interested in mastery, not just in the negative power of keeping a label saying 'leader' on a private door or 'pure Socialist' on a banner of a purely propagandist weekly. Genuine Socialist leadership is collective. The 'long term' is being quickened by the crisis more than by our own exertions. But can the Labour Party be ready to seize the chance to demonstrate, for the first time since 1945, the relevance of Socialism to the majority not yet convinced? Advance by 'small steps' by all means, as Roy Hattersley argued, echoing Willi Brandt, but steps need to be placed deliberately on top of each other, not scattered surrealistically, one by one, over a landscape as opportunity arises. And we build at a moderate pace towards *Socialism*, not 'radicalism', please. Radicalism is only an attitude of mind, a style, an itch: Socialism is both a theory of society and a moral doctrine. It only needs to be taken seriously.

It needs to be argued. At a time of crisis and national self-doubt, the public are no longer impressed by the shopping-list electoral arguments of 'we did' and 'you didn't', whether based on left- or right-wing manifestos. It would be a grim irony if the Powells and the Keith Josephs carried greater weight, because of the greater clarity of their principles, than those of the traditional men of doctrine, the socialists of the Labour Party, suddenly turned prag-matic, practical, that is with nothing to offer unless the winds blow fair— which they do not. And so much extreme ideology is the souring of good doctrine by the bland or contemptuous refusal of practical men of politics or administration to think long, to think systematically, to think morally, almost to think at all.

12 Some Socialist Books

Reports and Surveys article; vol. 48, no. 1, January–March 1977

LOOKING back at our review pages in the 1930s, most specifically socialist books were reviewed which even looked important. The journal stood more clearly to the left then and was both plainly democratic Socialist, despite the scepticism of Keynes and the wavering of the Webbs, as well as decidedly anti-Communist. The literary pages could then, however, look with some hope, even if admittedly a somewhat cautious and critical hope, at whatever came up, be it Fabian, Social Democratic, Communist or the then rare heterodox Marxism. Leonard Woolf sat, it seemed, in secular judgement on whatever was published that appeared to be serious and aimed at an intelligent but non-specialist reading public. Even in the 1950s to be sent a book to review by Leonard Woolf was as much an examination of oneself as of the author. It seemed a very important business, as if one had been lent the keys of heaven for an evening, subject to good behaviour, to spread news of interesting speculative and theoretical books and to save our readers' time from reading the bad and the pretentious.

Writing in 1960 a similar but more elaborate mass review to this, so writing after 1956 which marked the revival or the dispersal from the Communist Party's discipline of the Marxist left but before the vast expansion of social science publishing in the 1960s, I bewailed the lack of theory and theorising: 'the characteristic vices of any socialist literature . . . are rhetoric and exposure, just as the characteristic vices of conservative writing are platitude and paradox'.[1] Then there were a limited number of books to review, including solid if already slightly dull and secondary democratic socialist demi-classics such as John Strachey's *Contemporary Capitalism* (his final twist), Tony Crosland's *The Future of Capitalism* and Richard Titmuss's *Essays on the Welfare State*. One noted the style and broad content of the *Universities and Left Review*, failed to note the purer Marxist *New Reasoner* (which may have proved to be the real red mole), but still dismissed both Norman MacKenzie's anthology *Conviction* and Edward Thompson's *Out of Apathy* as basically old 'rhetoric and exposure' books, underestimating the beginnings at least of the formidable shift that was to follow from their still quite public language to the internalised one bred of the strange marriage in the 1960s of free Marxism and structural social science. I was serious and not frivolous in 1960 (if only half right) to conclude with the judgement that 'the Royal Court and the Theatre Royal may prove to be quite as significant as *Conviction* and *Out of Apathy* in shaping the prejudices of the younger generation of socialists'.

[1] 'Socialist Literature in the 1950s', *The Political Quarterly*, vol. 31, no. 3, 1960, pp. 361–73 (reprinted above as article 1).

Now, however, all is changed, 'changed utterly' in Yeats's words, though I am not sure that all the terribleness is beautiful. The problem of what to select for review must be almost insoluble, not just because so many more books are published, but because not all socialist books are likely to appear—to our readers at least—as either serious or aimed at the intelligent non-specialist, which politically (my main point as ever) is to say much the same thing. The problem is, to coin a phrase, that of a routinised and compulsive internalisation of sectarian dialogue. So much that is written by authors who see themselves as above all else socialist authors is written only for fellow socialists, nearly always meaning Marxists. Problems are seen as problems within a Marxist perspective. The continued growth of nationalism, of military rule with little or no regard for economic rationality (whether of socialist or capitalist varieties), and the continuance of despotic unfreedom in the nominally socialist states, these are deemed (quite rightly, in a sense) to pose problems for 'Marxist theory'—as once they would have been seen, in the tradition of the Enlightenment, as problems for humanity. But Poulanztas in *Political Power and Social Classes* (1973) has now added 'humanism' (soft) to 'positivism' (empirical evidence) and 'historicism' (that there is no human knowledge before the birth of Marx) as proscribed categories of thought for serious socialists!

If some Marxists still have a lingering belief in an empirical outside world, the foremost files have convinced themselves that the world only exists in terms of systematic theoretical perspectives which are sometimes called ideologies, sometimes philosophies but most audaciously and ludicrously are called by some 'Science'—as if (as in the church of St Louis Althusser) science was an a priori, rational and deductive version of Thomism.

So in the 1960s, the habit grew up among socialist authors, in sad contrast to the 1930s, of making the prime test of their books an ability to talk wholly to themselves ('authenticity'), in contrast to the more common self-evaluation of the 1930s, 'have I convinced an opponent or someone as yet uncommitted?' The tone, the style, the comprehensibility and even the manners of genuine polemical books (which seek to persuade backsliders and the unconvinced) are very different from most contemporary polemic (which seeks to parade virtue among the already faithful—who now constitute a publishers' market in their own right). Most Marxist socialist authors now view any attempt to reason and argue in a way that might convince a non-believer as exposing oneself almost fatally to compromise, corruption and loss of authenticity and integrity—false consciousness 'personified' or even, to be really rude, 'reified'. And the Pharisees write fluently in esoteric dialects.

Religious metaphor is apt because reasoning is no longer looked for as the bridge from non-belief to conviction, but rather conversion and total commitment (well, total on weekends and Tuesdays, anyway). Once the leap has been made, the reborn man may learn and even in time hope to add to the rational theology. And add to all this internalising of the Marxist dialogue the fact that the language of translated Marxism, never famous either for clarity or literary merit, is now largely embedded in a meta-jargon of the social sciences spoken only on the campuses, never on the shop-floor, itself suffering from neologism posing as knowledge and noun-phrases restating a problem but posing as solutions. Thus a fervid professional desire is born, rivalled only by liberal economists, not to be understood by any other intelligent man who has not already soaked himself in the language and culture of Marxism. The internalising has gone so far, indeed, that there are now some scholarly sects of Marxists who seem to wish neither to proselytise, nor ever to risk applying high theory to contingent practice, but simply to preserve the purity of the texts and of authentic commentaries.

Perhaps our readers should be more 'serious' and perhaps I should not mock rigid and overly systematic theory when I so often denounce blind, blinkered empiricism (contemporary Fabianism indeed) and ask for a little systematic thought about socialist values (such as, after all, liberty, equality and fraternity) in terms of observable social *trends* (not laws). But I do take the simple view, often so complexly expressed, that language is rooted in culture, so that any political, social and economic philosophy is suspect which either cannot come down to earth or which presents (as Marxism now begins to) a radical dualism of theory and practice in which never the twain shall meet (except by incantation of the spell, '*Praxis*'). So I take the old Orwellian line that serious socialists should write plain English and appeal to the ordinary experiences and the common-sense morality of ordinary people. And I tend to suspect that anything concerning social order and moral principles that cannot be expressed simply is usually meaningless. How odd a paradox it is that those who talk most of 'the People' (however much the actual, false-conscienced people vote against them or only give them a conditional trust) have lost both the common touch and the common style.

So let us just note, from the large number of specifically socialist books that now reach us (and from doubtless the larger number that are never even sent to such a bourgeois, middle-left journal), a few that are more approachable and possibly significant—if much time and some pain are granted.

An annual collection of essays of great interest is, of course, *The Socialist Register* (Merlin Press, 1975, paperback), edited by Ralph Miliband and John Saville.[2] They are broad-bottomed or liberty-conscious Marxists ('liberal minded' would be subtly wrong) who keep high editorial standards, suffer jargon less readily than most, and offer the prime venue for much original writing and specially commissioned translations of a kind that seeks revolutionary transformation of society, but through time and with a sense of difficulty or 'problematic'. It is a reasonably flexible, historical Marxism that fills most of the *Register's* pages, one in which the word 'critical' (as in 'towards a critical sociology', '. . . a critical history' or a 'critical medicine'

[2] The extraordinarily interesting 1976 number on '1956' arrived too late to review in this number.

181

even) has not entirely shifted its meaning to 'uncritically committed', but keeps up some vestige of humanistic self-criticism. The pressing need for action and the duty of doubt mingle, as a rule, reasonably congruously. Certainly, like the *New Left Review*, it is all argument within the (they sometimes use the word to accommodate the odd non-Marxist anarchist) radical socialist camp, and social democrats either do not dare to argue or are not welcome within these holy precincts; but the editors' own concept of the camp is still that of the left wing version of the broad Labour movement in Great Britain—'for all its faults', they seem to say. And their continued criticism of the Soviet Union (often just 'Russia') and their attempts to account for what went wrong in Marxist terms, this makes them very different people from the parody view of the editorial pages of *The Times* and all those Solzhenitsyn-buffs and Keith Joseph (or rather Hayek) fans who so stubbornly and ignorantly identify all Marxism with apology for Soviet despotism. These old thunderers are just as internalised as most Marxists. Both should be sentenced to the socially useful labour of reading each other's works and then be assessed for remission of sentence on their ability, for a momentary suspension of disbelief, to empathise thereon. Know your opponents, said Silone, Borkenau, Orwell and Koestler. *The Socialist Register* is a useful and interesting book to buy. If there are book-reading intellectuals still at large in the *Tribune* Left (for at the moment the oral and the exhortatory journalistic traditions, almost the philistine and the populist, seem far stronger), then a fairly complete set of *The Socialist Register* will be found on their shelves. And if they will forgive my saying so (perhaps a kiss of death), both the editors can write clear English: example is infectious, though not always infectious enough; and some of their authors are prone to believe that any editing is either oppressive censorship or else violence to their authenticity, or both.

Several recent books have set out to give the kind of tour of the horizon of contemporary socialist thought that reading regularly *The Socialist Register* might also, over time, provide. A combination of sponsorship between the Graduate School of Contemporary European Studies of Reading University and Sir George Weidenfeld (Sir Harold Wilson's publisher) produced a conference and a book, *The Socialist Idea: A Reappraisal* (Weidenfeld, 1974), edited by Leszek Kolakowski and Stuart Hampshire. The idea of the conference was to gather a broad spectrum of socialist thinkers to consider whether the quarrels among contemporary socialists and the contradictions between their writings are a product mainly of changing circumstances or of original ambiguities in the theories or even contradictions in the values. Alas, as often happens with conference papers and proceedings, the balance of argument turns out to be very uneven, with some people coming and some not and additional pieces being added from people who did not attend at all; and the level and seriousness of the contributions vary greatly. Perhaps conferences are useful preliminaries to anthologies if people will talk first and then go away and write something, rather than defending already well-known positions. It is a good source-book for the student of socialist ideas and it does raise questions of moral philosophy that the economic, materialist tradition has so often skated over; but it is not a comprehensive or particularly well-balanced survey of schools and doctrines. An editor or author working on his own, without so much dependency on whether distinguished lions will come and if so roar, can usually do better. *The Concept of Socialism* (Croom Helm, London, 1975); edited by Bhikhu Parekh of Hull University, contains some good writing, by no means all of one stamp or camp. Antony Arblaster, while sympathetic to the Marxist contribution to socialism, questions its claim to be or even to supplant 'science'. David McLellan, the scholarly biographer of Marx, contributes a short and beautifully clear account of Marx's view of 'the whole man' (so much more pointed, incidentally, than John Plamenatz's posthumous large book, *Karl Marx's Philosophy of Man* (Clarendon Press, 1975)). The author's own introduction is excellent, achieving subtlety as well as true theoretical simplicity, that is an ability to reduce an assertion to its most generalised form: 'socialists reject the bourgeois view that the pursuit of self-interest was natural to man and maintained that it was planted by capitalist society'. (A bit difficult as a question at A Level, but I'd like to see students tackle it in an 'Explain and Discuss' mode.) And Raymond Williams in an essay nicely called 'You're a Marxist, Aren't You?' generously, but rather interestingly, airs his muddles and ambivalences. Another super examination quotation: 'I believe that it is not necessary to abandon a parliamentary perspective as a matter of principle, but as a matter of practice I am quite sure that we have to begin to look beyond it'. I would agree wholeheartedly, if quite sure what he meant by 'beyond'.

A man on his own two feet, however, can best survey a field. R. N. Berki's *Socialism* (Dent, 1975) is a modest little student introductory book in appearance; but as in the best of the old Home University Library books, before the market became flooded and anybody thought that they could do the most difficult thing of all—write a simple introduction—Berki shows great analytic intelligence. He displays the presuppositions of all the main schools of socialist thought in a way that, while unlikely to be wholly acceptable to any of the different adherents, yet is always fair, perceptive and recognisable. It is the best short, general guide over the whole field of socialist thought that I know. It is an ideal Winter Festival present to a radical son or daughter. And it would help a Tory understand a little bit more of what he faces.

Two theoretical books which are not surveys deserve note, neither of which raises intractable problems of understanding. They are both in an interesting new series called 'Controversies in Sociology', edited by Professor Tom Bottomore and Dr Michael Mulkay (which could just as well be called 'Problems in Socialism' or '. . . in Society', and which will do even more to increase paranoia among educational authorities that Socialism and Sociology are synonyms). Professor Zygmunt Bauman of Leeds (a Polish exile, like Kolakowski), in *Socialism: The Active Utopia* (Allen & Unwin, 1976), tries to purge Marxism of its determinism and to restore a sense of quest for values or

183

at least to institute a debate, as some Yugoslav anti-Party Marxists would, about what moral values should be / can be / will be in a classless society. Brian Fay in *Social Theory and Political Practice* (Allen & Unwin, 1975) delivers a sermon to social scientists about their inextricable involvement in political practice. He shows how analytic (political philosophy) is needed to explicate the concepts involved in the sociology of the neo-Marxist Frankfurt school. He demonstrates his main thesis admirably that the relationship of theory to practice is a perpetual, revolving mutual influence; but oddly seems to assume, rather than argue, that only Marxists hold this position. A lot of political philosophers have been saying this for years, but perhaps in less formal (pretentious?) terms. Precisely because values affect what we study and how we study affects values, there is need to keep debate and political institutions open.

Two particular studies are especially interesting. David Lane in *The Socialist Industrial State: Towards a Political Sociology of State Socialism* (Allen & Unwin, 1976) seeks to examine the role of the state in socialism mainly in Russia and Eastern Europe. A lot of interesting material on stratification and bureaucracy is drawn together, although non-Marxist readers may think that some of the need to explain 'the relative autonomy of the state' is a bit of a non-problem to them. They may, wickedly perhaps, never have expected more than that 'servants of a state' or 'a party' develop interests of their own unless checked (the simple, good old theory) by popular and representative institutions. But a bad example of research on an important subject almost completely vitiated by 'locating the discussion within a clear theoretical framework' is a study of attitudes to wages: Richard Hyman and Ian Brough's *Social Values and Industrial Relations* (Basil Blackwell, 1975). This is basically an attempt to refute W. G. Runciman's *Relative Deprivation and Social Justice*, which sought to show that there was little egalitarian impulse in wage negotiations and attitudes to rewards, but rather a broad desire for 'fairness'; and that this desire, accepting relativities and differentials, takes many unexpected forms, but is generally compatible with the philosopher Rawls's position that people should dislike 'unjustifiable inequalities' but would be mistaken to desire simply 'equality'. The authors reject all ideas of more or less 'fair' differentials and of 'relative deprivation' as being part of the manipulation of the working classes by the power elite. This is a sad come-down for the Warwick Studies in Industrial Relations for, however legitimate the authors' viewpoint may be, the confusion of ideology and research takes us back to our starting point: a lament that so much socialist theory is in danger of becoming, as Berki puts it: 'an inward-looking, self-sufficient literary culture, way above the heads of ordinary mortals'. 'And this', he adds, 'is scarcely what Marx himself seems to have intended.'

Many of the *Tribune* Left regard *the* theory-to-practice book of the decade as Stuart Holland's *The Socialist Challenge* (Quartet Books, 1975). He has a First in economics, has worked in the Cabinet Office, for the Labour Party NEC, for the Commons' Expenditure Committee, was a special adviser to MOD and is active in the Institute for Workers' Control. And since *The Socialist Challenge* he has published two books on regional problems and the new capitalist economy of the multinationals, what he chooses to call *meso-economic power* between Keynesian macro- and micro-economics. But it is odd that his demonstration of the economic power of multinationals leads him not forward into seeing 'the struggle' as international, or more immediately as of a whole European dimension (as Tom Nairn and Ernest Mandel have bravely argued), but back into talk about national sovereignty—which is about the most reactionary and regressive concept that a socialist could still adhere to—as Laski had at least and long ago, I thought, convinced the Left. That theory and practice should be close is one thing, but I do not give much odds for the future theoretical reputation of an argument which seems to be simply a response to the *Tribune* group's tactics over the referendum—tactics which have become, as the saying is, qualitatively transcended with chauvinism. Again, I do not think any kind of socialist was looking for that.

13 A Meditation on Socialism and Nine Theories

Vol. 51, no. 1, January–March 1980

A JOURNAL at 50 and oneself at the same age, almost more easy to change one's own character than that of a long-established journal. *The Political Quarterly* is to the left in the total spectrum but to the right of the spectrum of the left, myself equally ambivalent, walking in two worlds, a left-wing heart but a right-wing head; yet editorially always trying to resist, with little success, consensual reductionism and obsession with institutions. For pragmatic leadership has failed both in policies and in loss of public principles, without which ability to persuade is simply ephemeral PR, while the left wing are rhetorically splendid but still hopelessly vague on theories and policies. Country, party, journal, self, to stand still now, even running very fast like Alice (or whoever) to do so, is to risk running downhill rapidly, perhaps disastrously.

So a suitable time to stop and consider where I really stand, or should move. When I was 21 I believed that I would see the Republic before I died. No longer, but does that mean that I have changed my values or simply my sense of time-scales? Realist or time-server? The 'good old cause' is also 'the long revolution', yet I'll never believe in 'the last fight'. I am at heart a critic and not an activist. What has happened, by the way, to 'socialist intellectuals'? They have all suddenly become 'Labour Party activists'. The word 'activist' has a different image. The activist lives for the battle, the clamour of the trumpets and the neighing of the horses, he knows that he is right and is impatient of being asked why he fights. I suspect that he has few books on his mantelpiece compared with Aneurin Bevan's generation: 'you don't look at the mantelpiece when you poke the fire'. The activist is obsessed by 'where one stands'; but, after all, one may not always be standing in the right place in the present to realise one's future-looking ideals. True theory deals both in time-scales and in truth: the activist is too tempted by symbolic gestures, many of which isolate him from those he must convince if the republic (or something far, far more republican) is ever to come.

So 'where do I stand?' is not the best way to put the question: too subjective, too narcissistic and, anyway, who cares? There is much too much worrying about where one stands: thought then becomes reduced to honouring or deceiving the shibboleths of those with a compulsion to write Manifestos and who believe that through small majorities big legislation can be imposed on apathetic people to make them happy. One would end up thinking about the present quarrels and calamities of the Labour Party and the struggle for leadership, or democracy. I try to think about all that as little as possible; for the theorist there is, as Kraus said of Hitler, 'nothing to say'.

The only sensible way to put the question is 'what do I *think*'? I think a lot of things at once, for values and theories cross-cut each other, supporting and complementing, as well as modifying and contradicting: it is not reasonable, only loyal or lonely, to 'adopt', as people quaintly say, a single unifying paradigm, whether a variety (for unifiers are many and are often mutually intolerant) of Marxism or of liberalism. Does it matter at all what name one gives to the cluster of perceptions and theories by which one defines what is possible and desirable: Labourite, social democrat, Social Democrat, Democratic Socialist, democratic socialist, marxist or Marxist? But theories have names and names have associations: established usage needs to be made more precise, but can neither be ignored nor can all its ambiguities be affably accepted. 'Socialist', to me, is still the simplest. To believe in the primacy of theory at all, however, while not believing in total explanations or that social systems are as systematic as either Hayek or Engels have said, is to risk from the pragmatists one mocks, to whom thought is merely compromise, tactics or PR, the puzzled or ironic response, 'what theory?' 'Always connect', yes; but always specify. A right wing realism towards a left wing ideal?

What *do* I think? While I do not think that one can reach down from the peg any ready-made suit, I do think one knows what a good suit looks like and has some idea of how to go about making it. Basically socialism is a cluster of doctrines derived from a core of theory. The theory is that the rise and fall or stability of societies is best explained not by considering the experience and ability of ruling elites (Conservatism) nor by the initiative and invention of individuals competing in a natural market (Liberalism), but by considering the social relationships of the primary producers of wealth—in an industrial society, this is the skilled worker (who for the first time in history can give leadership for and from the majority), elsewhere the peasant. The doctrine has a critical and an affirmative side: it is a critique both of the injustice and the inefficiency of the distribution of wages and rewards in both traditional and market societies; and it affirms that greater social and economic equality would lead to cooperation and mutual aid replacing competitiveness and acquisitiveness, and that this will enhance fraternity and hence liberate from inhibition both the individuality and the productive potential of a poverty-less and fully employed society.

Words may differ, but some such synthesis is not hard to state. The difficulty is that general theories are necessarily abstract, and though they point in a definite direction and exclude some alternatives, they cannot tell the cadres or the guides which are the best routes. The theory itself is not dangerous to liberty, indeed it has a prospect of genuine freedom for all: what is dangerous is any belief that a particular tactic or policy is necessarily the best route, that there is only one way in which the kingdom of ends can be reached. The theory cannot contain the conditions for the realisation of the doctrine, and doctrinaires are those who try to build into the theory the necessary justification of their own favoured route. The theory, in other words, is neither self-sufficient nor self-contained. So to assert socialist

187

values and begin to think from basic principles all over again. For the Social Democrats have reached a dead end and the Labour Left indulge in activity almost as a substitute for, almost as if haunted by, thought—thoughts on what socialism should say about all the other general theories of society through which we perceive, by which we move towards policy and action. The great difficulty with socialist theory and finding a popular articulation of it is that theorists have tried to make it self-sufficient, even using it as a refuge from the world, rather than a critique of other beliefs and a core of persuasive guiding principles for public bodies.

Again, I don't think there is much mystery about what socialist values are, only a certain amount of social democratic embarrassment. The principles are those of 'the Revolution': Liberty, Equality, Fraternity. The three must be taken together, for each alone defeats itself. *Liberty* alone is selfishness, competitiveness and the acceptance of poverty and failure-in-life as perennial; but liberty alongside fraternity is the ancient, pre-capitalist republican tradition: the free man as citizen. This freedom has to be encouraged, even if its results are always unpredictable and often disliked. Freedom is not being left alone; it is political action with and among others. Perhaps ancient liberty and citizenship did depend upon slavery for its leisure, its space to move. There would have to be slavery, said Aristotle, until the machines of Prometheus come to life. But now for the first time in human history all men could be citizens, if the machines are kept working for the good of all. *Equality* may best be seen negatively, as Rawls has argued: the absence of inequalities that cannot be justified in terms of benefits to others. What a different society it would be if all inequalities of wealth and power had to be publicly justified. Meanwhile we just keep up the critique. Equality of respect, said Runciman, does not imply equality of praise. It is the democratic fallacy, said Aristotle, to believe that since men are equal in some respects, they are equal in all. But those 'some respects' are primary and cannot be negated by the inequalities. *Fraternity* diminishes and civilises what inequalities there must be and gives a context to freedom. Fraternity needs to be stressed, exhibited and lived, indeed enjoyed. Again, to think of all men as brothers is not to think of them as the same. Example is so important—and lacking: simplicity, non-ostentation, friendliness and not condescension. Men who live differently think differently. Labour leaders are simply not socialists when their life-style aspires to that of their opponents. Only in times of war and crisis do King Harry and his soldiers believe, or think it politic to believe, that they are brothers. Only Dunkirks create the Dunkirk spirit.

Back to basic principles? Yes, but in a logical sense, not a temporal one. There was no socialist Eden nor party pure with missed opportunities for revolution from which we fell away; and there may be, in the world economy, no immediate chance of a fully planned or wholly controllable national economy, one that was not simply a self-induced siege-economy. None the less, we could take the chance of a society with specifically socialist responses to international conditions. Will international trade, for instance, change the basic character of Chinese Communism? Surely not, unless they want it to.

So let me meditate on what socialism should have to say about all plausible theories of the rise, fall and stability of societies. General theories of social change are more clear and common than we often imagine; the difficulties lie in their relationships both to each other and to the political doctrines of what ought to be done. I can identify nine general theories, not of equal importance, certainly not when taken each on its own, but each held by learned people and plausible at some level to ordinary people; and each needing some kind of response from socialists, a possible beginning for rethinking. Before doing so, one assumption that is so often neglected: one must think both for the short and for the middle and long term. Politics, planning ahead, social transformation, they do not negate each other, a man is not a hypocrite if he shores up a bad house before he gets ready to rebuild it (people are living in it). People may properly concentrate on being politicians, planners or revolutionaries, but to do so to the total exclusion of the other time-scales is self-defeating. In meditation one can move freely, though without conclusion, from one level to another, whereas a political argument, a legislative policy or a scientific explanation can only be said to work or not to work within its defined context. Yet I speculate mainly about what could and should be done in the long run, irrespective of scepticism about whether central planning, physical or fiscal, can control anything like as much as once hoped or feared; and speculate not in hope of finding a pure and all-embracing socialist theory (still less revisionism revised), but to show how a socialist perspective is still relevant to all other theories. So some suggested beginnings for a long march of rethinking.

1 *Many believe that the rise and fall or stability of a society is best understood in terms of the role of the inhabitants.* Socialists were the first to say that not merely could and should all inhabitants of states be citizens but that maximum participation from free men and women was needed if societies were to prosper and be just. High theory went together with a belief in the common sense of the common man. Government by the people, not just for the people; but not simply government either, the workplace, too. Industrial discipline and industrial unrest? But isn't there a fairly obvious hypothesis as to why people so often kick against the pricks irrationally? Consultation, of course, is a proper, perhaps often necessary, first step; but as a substitute—deceit and delusion. Yet the difficulty in the Labour movement is that historically it arose as a force led by and for the skilled worker. What of the unskilled? Too much union power? 'Free collective bargaining' and 'social justice for all'—won't someone tell him / them that this is impossible (that is how socialism began, a critique of the liberal theory of wages). Why don't the unions use their power to gain a minimum income for all and to impose a maximum, too? 'Mini-max' as a slogan? The cow's udder cannot be milked for ever without killing the cow, but it is not easy for people to hold back and to think of fattening up the

cow while others, even a few, flaunt such conspicuous consumption, are correctly felt to have more than their fair share of the cream and the gravy. Relativities should be diminished and should be determined politically. Economically the unions are too purely defensive (they have had to be) and naively distributionist. Could they not become productivity minded?— probably not, as they have been and are organised. But is it utopian to think that ordinary workers, if they thought that their firms were indeed theirs, would have new ideas and consistent energy?

More participation is needed in a socialist society than in either capitalist or pre-industrial republican states, but it must stop short of being compulsory. Yet when voluntary abstention is actually induced a new form of despotism arises. Objectively we already have all the prerequisites for general participation, yet is the stultifying 'prolecult' of the entertainment media chosen or imposed? Partly imposed, one hopes it will entertain the unemployed adequately. The system does without their participation.

Beware of 'From each according to his abilities, to each according to his work'. If that was Lenin for the transition, it is also capitalism for everyday life (minus the unemployed). 'From each according to his abilities, to each according to his needs' must be both the process and the goal, otherwise we make a god of work for the sake of work, in reality for an infinity of consumer goods, far, far beyond need. Consider the popular contempt for those who find no work. Do we then amidst new technologies insist on finding or keeping up meaningless work for the sake of *wages*, or not think rather of a guaranteed income, of maximising wealth as efficiently as we can, however labour intensive, but sharing the proceeds by criteria of need and through taxation? If there is a psychological demand by all to participate in work, then is not the answer to extend what we can do for ourselves in our home environment, not enforced and uninteresting commercial or public employment?

Socialism must be democratic, but we need to think carefully about *duties* of participation as well as rights to elect. The model of the jury system could be extended. Aristotle observed (not liking it) that the democratic way of filling office must be by lot, for elections are usually *won* by the most able or the most rich, call them demagogues.

2 *Many believe that the rise and fall or stability of a society is best understood in terms of its ideology or official doctrine*. It really is so clear that societies that insisted on a state religion were imposing beliefs that social order should be static. And modern societies that make utility the test of ethics, whether things are useful as each separate individual judges them to be useful, are committing or dooming themselves to a perpetual competitiveness for a perpetually receding horizon of expectations about the possession of material goods. Good for industry and technology but bad for a humanity that does *know* better. The pre-capitalist world did have conventional limitations on acquisitiveness, imposed by ruling classes; but could not an educated society impose

such beliefs on themselves? Some of us do, either from principle or from indifference to what is commonly thought to be 'the good life' (however good our schools, the media and the advertisers prove far more effective as shapers of values—not just the popular press; consider the *Observer* as the priest of conspicuous consumption, the preacher of trendiness and the keeper of a residual, centre-page Sunday conscience).

Socialism begins with scepticism about all official doctrines, but it should not descend into a belief that therefore all ideas are ideological, instrumental. If there were less class interest and competitive individualism, autonomous moral principles would be more important as guides for social policy, not less: the dialogue of liberty, equality and fraternity. Political and moral speculation is likely to flower, not to wither away, in a classless society.

3 *Many believe that the rise and fall or stability of societies is best understood in terms of their social structure.* The theory of class determination (surely 'condition-ing', not determination) is a truth, but a limited and an ambiguous one: status, wealth or office can all compound class, it can be each or blendings of all three in different times and places. Perceptions of race or of nationality complicate matters and severely limit the practical application of classical Marxism. A classless society would still have subgroups, a plural society rather than a mass society; but simply that the conceit, constraint and discrimination of class would vanish. I find this the least ambiguous piece of socialist ideology and am puzzled why even cynical leaders of the Labour Party do not see its persuasive value.

What would a classless society be like? I suspect that culturally it would be more bourgeois than either proponents or opponents believe. 'Proletarian culture' is a debasement of human potential, and indeed of actual achieve-ment, a product of oppression, not the pointer to the future. Avoid inculcating standard accents and competitive commercial values, oh ye radical teachers (do *not* 'educate for industry'), but think that most of the things that you and they want in a better society are those skills and tastes that the bourgeois have already achieved in their leisure. Perhaps the young in their leisure, but only in their leisure, and only while they are young, are experiencing a classless culture through Pop, Rock, Punk and New Wave. But a classless society need not have a common culture, only non-economically determined cultures. And 'youth culture'[a] is largely an exploitative fraud, though a dangerous one to the system, for the possibilities of social mixing it has revealed may not be lost or limited purely to the time of youth. Regional cultures should flourish.

4 *Many believe that the rise and fall or stability of a society is best understood in terms of the nature of the elite groups.* Should socialists talk about no elite groups or only about no permanent and self-perpetuating elite groups? To deny the existence of elites within the movement can be as silly as the Tory who says 'I

---

[a] The original had 'youth cult' here, which seems much less likely, but choose it if you prefer.

don't believe in social classes'. Only by believing in the existence of elites can we control them. Those who talk a lot about democratic election of leaders also need to talk about their control. I grow more interested in the Jacksonian or populist paradigm: obviously not all necessary functions can be made so simple (Illich does go too far) that anyone can do them; but many can. Many more than we suppose. Elites tend to claim both general competence and to exaggerate difficulties. Socialists should not get trapped into attacking all authority, or 'moderate socialists' into defending all authority. The eighteenth-century *philosophes* knew what they were about in attacking the abuse of authority, or its extension into areas where its skills were irrelevant. We must think, interrogate and polemicise to keep each authority within the narrowest limits . . . Yet socialists should not fool themselves that they can govern or that the people can all govern without some experts and some people of exceptional ability. I distrust talented political leaders who affect not humility but ordinariness, who claim they are exactly as others. 'Penetrable elites', 'mobile elites', 'circulating elites', these are serious moral terms, not merely bits of descriptive sociological jargon.

Why concentrate so much on fears of my own side rather than attack the contemptuous elitism of the English ruling classes? Because we have more persuasion ahead of us. Because our left-wing leaders don't understand that when they/we say 'socialism', most people think of Russia and Eastern Europe and do not produce sophisticated, relativist excuses for 'the betrayal of socialism', but condemn them for what they have done as socialists. And are the present Labour Party crazy to clamour for more nationalisation until there is a generation of socialist engineers and middle management? Of course people trained in nothing but politics get taken over by their civil servants, even if they are firm and principled. Thus the country is governed. The bureaucracy is the continuing state.

5 *Many believe that the rise and fall or stability of societies is best understood in terms of the institutions of government.* We worry too much about institutional forms and reforms. This kind of theory is almost always put forward in defence of a market economy to imply that the visible evils or drawbacks could be repaired or limited by better institutions. Consider the great fit of institutional tinkering that ran through this country in the 1960s and early 1970s, until the economic crisis worsened and people rediscovered the primacy of political economy. Unexpectedly Conservatives found their version first. How much time utterly wasted on parliamentary reform! *Mea culpa*. I wonder what Dick Crossman really thought about it—just another move in the power game? What does it matter?

Socialism scarcely has a distinctive theory of institutions. Perhaps it is enough for socialists to be knowledgeable about institutions and law. Almost any set of institutions can be turned to unexpected uses; but none can furnish an alibi for failure (*vide* the Civil Service in his and her memoirs), nor, however rational, shades of the Webbs, nor, however *democratic* (the reborn

Benn) can institutions guarantee success. That is if we are talking about the way of the state. James Cornford's alternative-lifers may be right and perhaps we should observe more closely the anarchist tradition (back to Proudhon! both too much Marx and anti-Marx?) Laski once made a specifically socialist critique of sovereignty and advanced a theory of political power as inherently federal. The Scotland debate showed what narrow lip-service to devolution even the Labour leaders gave. Even in relation to Northern Ireland we English cannot face thinking federally. How strange Americans, Germans and Australians find this. Consider the Common Market debate. I once heard Mr Peter Shore telling a puzzled German audience, though they are supposed to be the greater metaphysicians, that the British people were determined not to lose their sovereignty. I wanted to go looking for it. Buried as *Rheingold*?

Perhaps democratic Socialists, if that is the name, should consider the only authentic institutional innovations of the Socialist movement, short-lived though they were: the Commune and the Soviet. This takes us back to industrial democracy, even in the teeth of the trade unions; or to housing cooperatives, even in the teeth of local Labour oligarchies ('our tenants', as I heard in Sheffield, or 'our housing stock', as I heard in Camden). Even at a considerable price in efficiency? I think so, or else all-out, capital intensive efficiency, set middle management free from the bureaucrats *and* the gentleman in the Boardroom, but tax the product to the hilt for public expenditure. Progressive income tax is fundamental to any socialist strategy: when Callaghan or Healey could find no words to explain this, I saw the emptiness.

6 *Many believe that the rise and fall or stability of societies is best understood in terms of the economy.* To many this is a banality, both to classical Marxist and Hayekian. Engels said: 'We make our own history, but in the first place under very definite presuppositions and conditions. Among these the economic are finally decisive.' Surely, if we must be Talmudic or hermeneutic, the first clause and the last are of equal importance. 'Finally decisive', certainly. Marx said: 'The mode of production in material life conditions the general character of the social, political and spiritual processes of life.' If he did say, as he did, 'general character' and 'conditions' rather than 'specific features' and 'causes', who can disagree? The folly that Marxists are prone to is to think the theory self-sufficient. Economic factors do not determine everything nor anything specifically; and nor does the market necessarily provide the optimum distribution of resources nor fair wages. To believe the contrary though is not to give licence to any kind of fancy. The theory of Marx and Engels is surely correct for industrial society, but less easily applicable to pre- and post-capitalist formations. Alone it is so abstract; other theories are needed before entailments can be drawn for policy and practice. Popper on Marx was an odd mixture of the silly and the profound; but this should not discredit his and Mannheim's general notion of hypothetico-deductive method as the logic of planning. To influence economies one has to think systematically, but work indirectly and tentatively. Keep a line of retreat open when you plan

'irreversible changes', otherwise if you fail to influence men, you fall into massive violence to force them into the preconceived mould.

Consider especially the preconception that in a socialist state there would be no private property. We are not talking about toothbrushes, of course, but we may be talking about heart-pacers and even about clothes, if they are used as indicators of class or of dissent. Private schools, but what about houses and cars? Some things that I mix with my labour, I should surely be allowed to keep. The stunting of other lives and freedoms only arises when I can use my property to deprive others, directly or indirectly, of the substantial minimum of a new conventional, but less acquisitive and competitive, good life. Odd that there has been so little socialist thinking about minimal justifications of property. And it does affect our views about the organisation of an economy. All kinds of small things may be done better if people have a strong sense of possession. (Am I really against the sale of council houses?) But we need to understand better when it is that possession does not imply exploitation or unfair hereditary advantages. The beginning of socialist humanism should be to know why Plato thought that the family must be abolished, but to understand also why it cannot.

If we live with property at all and even say 'large-scale public', 'small-scale private', we live in a mixed economy. But that is simply a description, neither a slogan nor an understanding, neither doctrine nor theory. Probably better not to ask earnestly or tauntingly 'what should the mixture be?', as if general economic criteria could ever be produced. The political dimensions are dominant, but need they hinder efficiency? Ownership as distinct from control is a dogma. Often 'why not public ownership?' (in some form), but often 'why kill the goose that lays the golden egg?' In a world economy with multinational companies, a socialist economic strategy for a country has to be opportunistic. It must either generate or tolerate increased productivity. Socialist values must be imposed on the working of a mixed economy, but state ownership and state control by themselves are either not necessarily socialist, or not the socialism I thought that the English Left wanted to see. The critique of the injustice of the capitalist system used to contain a critique of its inefficiency, precisely for not involving the working class itself in decision-making and the technicians in management. It also questioned whether incentives are in fact primarily economic, certainly at the higher margins. Even the empirical basis of the Conservative case about taxation and incentives has gone unchallenged by Labour leaders. Have *they* not heard of job satisfaction?

7 *Many believe that the rise and fall of societies is best understood in terms of attitudes to law*. Not many socialists go far with this view, but many overdo attempts to expose all law as simply the instrumentality of class exploitation and oppression. And similarly police power. Socialist societies will need law and police, too, but seen as social services, not as 'awful majesty' or as 'the power of the state': they will be demythologised and disarmed, respectively.

Isn't the necessary arming, in the present context, of the police an interesting index not simply of the inadequacy, but of the rottenness of some central feature of our present society? Socialist societies will need public law if we are to avoid what Jack Common and George Orwell once called 'negative socialism': the integration of the one Party with the one State. Diffusion, decentralisation and possibly federalisation of both political and economic power will need new networks of tribunals and arbitration, more 'administrative law'.

Conservatives have seen law as embodying tradition; Liberals have seen law as statutes passed by representative assemblies but enforceable independently of either Parliament or state; and socialists have tended to see law simply as policy, as the necessary relations of the interests of the state—hence tests of 'party spirit' or 'will it help the state?' are applied to particular judgements. But the baby of justice must not be thrown out with the bathwater of liberal capitalism. If 'independent judiciary' as we know them is a myth, judges none the less cannot be servants of the state, even of a socialist state, nor appointed like British magistrates for party services: they must be free citizens in an egalitarian republic. 'Citizen judge' is the only proper way for a judge to be addressed: 'Comrade' is as conniving as 'Your Lordship' is servile.

8 *Many believe that the rise and fall and stability of societies is best understood in terms of attitudes to knowledge.* 'History' is the key to Conservatism, 'the diffusion of useful knowledge' to Liberalism, and Science was to Socialism, not simply the social sciences. Socialism seemed committed to social research. Recently there has been a negativistic outbreak; the word 'epistemology' is scattered through student essays to imply that all forms of knowledge are part of a social system of class control. The answer is obvious, both in polemic and logic, *tu quoque* brothers; but the rubbish goes on as a closed world of its own—a flight from empiricism. Not Science but the sciences should be asserted, or simply that socialism and the sociology have, indeed, a common ancestry and a parallel path. Socialists are committed to prediction, which Conservatives hold to be impossible in principle, dangerous in practice. Liberal theories of justice start from positing (as in Locke, Mill and Rawls) a hypothetical equality of starting-point, contractarian myths, or the social democrats' 'equality of opportunity ': the grounds of just actions are found in, as it were, a reformed past, what it would have been if . . . But socialists do believe in progress, not simply in fairness, therefore good actions must be the outcome of understanding the future consequences of policy. The 'ought' cannot be derived from the 'is', even a future 'will be'; but a socialist ethic is a speculation on what men would be like in better and more equitable conditions. So socialists must have a special interest in those forms of knowledge that seek to predict social change. A socialist argument cannot proceed simply by analogies drawn from the past: future possibilities and the deliberate creation of them are canvassed. But to be sceptical about the degree

195

of probability of predictions is necessary, aware of the multiplicity of conditioning factors, and shrewd enough not to confuse predictions of what is likely to happen with arguments about what ought to happen. The ethically desirable must be the sociologically possible, but not necessarily the immediately probable.

9 *Many believe that the rise and fall of societies is best understood in terms of attitudes to information.* Autocratic societies believe in official information only and in strict censorship; Liberal societies believe in a competitive flow of information, from a privately owned Press; and actual so-called socialist societies believe that all the media should be party propaganda. Socialists are right to consider alternative forms of ownership, but the plural is essential. Socialist politicians are wrong, out of wounded *amour propre*, however great the provocation, to give currency to one arbitrary application of radical escapist epistemology: that all the press simply serve the interests of the capitalist system: (a) it isn't that systematic, (b) some of them don't know what they are doing, and (c) some journalists don't and survive. I am worried that left-wing politicians get obsessive about criticism, rationalising it as a concern for a flow of objective information. Theory and knowledge are far more important. If by clear argument we can change the terms in which people consider problems, reportage will follow. Harold Wilson was plainly a victim of 'the age of information flow' and confused information with knowledge: public relations took over from reality. A socialist public relations won't change reality either . . . Example may, a revival of socialist ethics, but the legislative programme of a new government that would move towards a less unequal, a more free and fraternal society is likely to need much more thinking than can come in three or four years from subcommittees of the NEC or anyone else. The first sign of seriousness will come with a sense of time. Government has to be carried on. Nothing to be done next time that makes future socialist programmes less likely, but to remember that 50 years of English Fabianism exhausted its content in the legislative programme of 1945–50—a real advance along a dead end. As important as expenditure on the Welfare State is, we should devolve administration into the hands of ordinary people, even if it means challenging NUPE as well as Whitehall. 'Self-help' needs socialising. 'Self-government is better than good government', as Balfour once said of the lesser breeds within the law. We still play at governing ourselves in the imperial manner, and a few tribunes won't make much difference; a few thinkers might.

So to learn to think in terms of different time-scales (not wings or factions) simultaneously. They do not contradict, they complement each other and politicians are useless who live in one dimension alone. We have to react to day-to-day events realistically and pragmatically, respecting people's opinions as they are—but not mere pragmatism. We also have to pursue middle-term policy for the eradication of poverty and other injustices—consistently, which means winning elections and changing opinion slowly, as well as determining long-term priorities. And socialists have all the time to practise a code of morality based on fraternity which we can believe will be natural to all in the long-term future condition of an egalitarian society in which all men are free—in the present world, so few are genuinely free. Socialists must not treat other people as if they are already living in the future; to do so is fantasy or oppression. But socialists themselves must carry a testimony that some better, more fraternal and cooperative type of human relations is possible. Otherwise what does it matter who can manage the declining economy best?

14 The Future of the Labour Party

Vol. 54, no. 4, October–December 1983

ONLY time will tell. Has Labour's recent defeat and the collapse of her traditional vote been a sobering bucket of cold water? Or will it reveal that many local Labour constituencies have now become sects, not parties—that is, people more concerned with doctrinal purity and the details of the party programme than with winning the country and one day forming the government?

Those who want to bring 'the purists' (as Roy Hattersley calls them) down to earth will find the going rough; for many of them prefer 'to plant both feet firmly in mid-air'—to steal an old phrase of Laski's.[a] The battle between utopians and pragmatists who tend to aid and abet each other in squeezing out the middle ground is perennial in *any* socialist movement. But this problem is now worse because, paradoxically, the Labour Party has rarely been in better shape from the point of view of young and new members: the decline in membership of the 1960s made it easy and exciting in the 1970s to join and 'win over for socialism' moribund local parties. And this became an enjoyable and satisfactory end in itself, a passionate leisure time activity in which the worst to be feared was a seat on the local council. Benn spoke to these new folk, not to get them to grapple through socialist theory with the hard problems of egalitarian aspirations amid a capitalist world and a hostile or sceptical public, but to flatter them in a Chartist or populist manner that every hard issue and dilemma of policy could be turned into a question of democratic control by the people. And they were 'the people'—not the actual British public nor even individual members of the party. For the 'activists' were the 'real people' because they freely gave their leisure time and energy to politics. And often it wasn't even politics. Many new members saw any kind of compromise about 'our programme' as 'playing politics' or, even worse to the new generation, 'hypocrisy'. In the tradition of Rousseau not Marx, the new Bennites confused innocence with virtue and experience with corruption.

Many party members will actually say that they would rather lose than compromise. And *Tribune* immediately after the election told them what they wanted to hear in two main articles—'Don't Mourn, Organise' and 'Guilty Men' (10 June 1983): the election was lost because the leaders did not believe in the programme. The psychological analogy is irresistible: internalisation can go no further. But Labour's leadership must develop at least a normal degree of the reality principle: to recognise the existence of the outside world. Realists will have to argue within the party, of course, in terms of 'winning over the voters back to socialism'. In truth they were never there. And almost

---

[a] And one of Bernard's favourites, to be found several times throughout this volume.

worse than that: many members of the party seem incapable of talking to any but themselves. The defeat was so great—and more great for being the culmination of a long *process*, not an irrational event—that it is almost as if the Labour Party has to begin all over again. If it holds to its pre-election course it is doomed.

The nature of the defeat

Labour activists who do wish to resuscitate their reality principle could well begin by re-reading Peter Kellner's 'Anatomy of the Landslide' in the *New Statesman* for 17 June; or Ivor Crewe's preliminary analysis of the results in the *Guardian* of 13 and 14 June. If the Labour Party is serious about 'political education' within the party, it should begin by distributing these widely—good shock therapy. Traditionally the Labour Party has stood mainly for and been led by the skilled working class who this time gave Labour only 32 per cent of their vote. Eight per cent more actually voted Conservative and only 6 per cent less Alliance. And it has been a process, not an event. The figures in 1974 were 49 per cent to Labour and in 1979 41 per cent. Only among the unskilled working class did Labour get 41 as against a Conservative 33 and an Alliance 24 per cent, and even then with a similar fall over the last three elections. Kellner picked out one figure particularly: Labour's greatest support occurs among that 24 per cent of the electorate who are council tenants, who give them 49 per cent support; but among home-owning working class voters (28 per cent of the electorate and rising) Labour and Alliance each took 26 per cent and the Conservatives 47 per cent. And geographically we all know what has happened: at the moment in electoral terms Labour is scarcely a national party.

Looked at overall, of course, the Conservatives won their huge majority of seats on a minority and slightly diminished vote, of 44 per cent as against Labour's 28 and Alliance's 26 per cent: a substantial anti-Conservative majority. But it would take at least another defeat of this proportion before any Labour leader would dare to try to persuade the party that some policies (helpful to people) could be gained by a coalition based on electoral reform or electoral alliances, always assuming that Alliance and Liberal voters would stay put if allied with Labour. The message of the figures should be obvious, but the Party has yet to face the fact of its profound unpopularity.

The basic reasons for its unpopularity are clear, but to assess their relative importance is difficult. No one explanation alone will serve.

1. Labour has not adjusted its policies or its image to changes both in social structure and perceptions of class and group loyalty and interest. Root and branch opposition to sale of council houses is a case in point. And its natural concern with poverty and unemployment has plainly scared most skilled working people in jobs and who pay income tax. Many of them can be persuaded that the unemployed are either scroungers or too lazy to

199

borrow Mr Tebbit's magic bicycle. Perhaps only when unemployment was marginal could people be rational about it: mythologies are now invoked to obscure the terror of becoming unemployed and to make those still in jobs believe that they are so because of their own individual virtue. The *Sun*, the *Mail* and the *Express* can be held responsible for part of Labour's decline, not by their direct attacks (which are easily discounted) but by their constant stirring up of tales of scroungers, dodgers, layabouts and moon-lighters: 'what your taxes are spent on'.

2. Labour's post-1979 civil war was conducted openly and without inhibition. Those who blame the press for stirring it up were usually the first to use the press as a way of communicating to fellow party members. And certainly the hard Left and the Bennite Chartists were more to blame than centre Left and Right for talking as if nobody outside the party was listening: all that obsessive preoccupation with the programme, thus tying the hands of a future Labour government rather than winning the public's trust back again. 'First catch your rabbit', said wise Mrs Beaton. Between 1979 and 1983 the Labour Party ceased to look as if it could govern anything. 'Holding the party together' became an end in itself. And it didn't hold together. It was the Social Democratic secession that proved electorally lethal. And yet I met ever so many party workers who said 'We're better off without them'. Well, I felt the same about several power-hungry princes spoiled by high office; but their supporters and voters?

   If pure socialism is not going to win the next election, it was indeed no socialism at all under Wilson that broke the heart of the party. I once pursued his awful books so obsessively in these pages and in the *Guardian* reviews because they revealed a purely pragmatic mind without even a gesture of socialist rhetoric. The party has spent its energy in the past four years as the British army is wont to do: preparing to fight the last war; only in this case to make sure that we would never have a Wilson government again. Small wonder the party now welcomes a man (the very least of his virtues) untainted by office in that era.

3. The Conservatives campaigned on Labour's programme. So often said, but so true, so many hostages to fortune. So much energy was expended, both from within the party and from pressure groups, whose *primary* loyalties are *not* to the party, but to get their plank in the programme—be it CND or Animal Rights. Many pressure groups are now happy with the Labour Party. The Labour Party has far less reason to be happy with all of them: all these minorities do not add up to a majority. In fact programmes or manifestos do not win elections, but they can lose them; and even then not with their detail, but with the general impression they can create if they are overcrowded, uncosted, incoherent or vastly expensive to the wage-earner, whether in terms of taxation or inflation. This may not be entirely fair, but it seemed so.

4. The Tories fought a good campaign (beginning in 1978 and not stopping) and beat Labour at its own, old game, played to Labour's strength and

won. The Labour Party used to be the party of ideas and ideals, of national conscience and public persuasion, of policies and social change, and the Conservatives were the party of responsible and experienced government—the old gang: 'vote for us 'cos we know how'. Wilson changed images in mid-stream and Margaret Thatcher took up the challenge: she developed a *popular ideology*, going back to where Edward Heath began, but with much greater vulgarity, tenacity and empathy—a suburban version of Hayek's political economy as mediated by Sir Keith Joseph. She had no doubt that most people are more worried about inflation than about unemployment. It is no use arguing that this new ideology is as full of holes as a sieve. Austerity, frugality, hard work, self-interest, value for money, getting government out, freeing capital, grandmother's virtues and licensed xenophobia[1] make a psychologically compatible popular ideology for those in jobs.

A public philosophy

The Labour Party, on the other hand, is still tarred with the 'winter of discontent' brush of being a party of government and high taxation, of state and local council interference, preservationists of run-down industries, defenders of obsolescent working practices, a self-preservation society of professional dispensers of welfare. And its leaders seemed to have lost any public rhetoric, only internal codes and celebrations for the party.

Labour needs to recover its grasp on simple persuasive ideas and principles that can imply policies without always needing to spell them out in advance of events and opportunities. This is now becoming recognised by the middle generation of Labour MPs. Robin Cook (who has managed Neil Kinnock's leadership campaign) wrote in the *Guardian*: 'Too many on the Left have suffered from the naive delusion that it is more important to obtain a commitment to policy from the Labour Party than to build support for that policy in the electorate'. And looking at the crowded and often quite unrelated components of the manifesto, he remarked that Marx would have seen it as 'a parody of all the faults to be expected in a reformist party'.[2] Labour must rid itself of manifestoitis and must be able to state clear principles which speak to people outside the party. This possession of a popular ideology used to be Labour's envied strength, what Walter Lippman once called a 'public philosophy'; but now it is its weakness. Several rival modes of discourse exist within the party, mostly not even designed to persuade rivals within the party but simply to mark off tight territories already occupied; and none of them is comprehensible to the public at large, or if so they are irritating or alarming. It has for long been a sick joke that those who talk most about '*the* working class' and 'the *people*' do so in

[1] 'Argie-bashing' to be historically specific.
[2] *Guardian*, 15 July 1983.

incomprehensible special vocabularies; but now the farce could lead to tragedy for the Labour Party and, if there is no effective opposition to this cruel and crazy government and no alternative to its economic policies, for the country as well. Wilson and Callaghan and the leaders of the old-style Labour city machines (those of the era of Dan Smith), abandoned any public rhetoric except vague, empty words like 'care', 'concern', 'equitable' and 'fairness'. When they debated with opponents, a kind of statistical rhetoric emerged, much favoured in BBC political debates: 'we built in our last year more than you in the whole period of . . .' or 'the increase in inflation in October 1978 was the lowest of any month except . . .' All this does is convert anyone who happens to be listening to Churchill's view of statistics.

Labour politicians at every level need to and can make a great conceptual shift: to move from thinking and talking about *what we would do when in office to what people might want to put us in office to do*. I am not advocating opportunism nor abandonment of theory or principle. On the contrary, if the Labour Party is serious in its democratic socialism, it has got to engage in a dialogue with all of the electorate who are not totally committed, through thick or thin, wet or dry, Conservatives. It will do this from its own socialist perspective, seeking to persuade; but then persuasion in a democracy, and in a democratic manner, must be a two-way process. The leadership must create a far greater sense of short-term realism; but the party will only accept that under leaders whom it is convinced have middle-period plans and long-term ideals. Small steps can have high risers. A serious socialist will not merely have a sense of time, but also work out a theory of stages in terms of a specific and actual society. The man who compromises some things in the short term for higher, larger future purposes is not a hypocrite; he is a statesman.

Labour's principles

Labour's principles are not arcane or technical: they simply need rescuing from bad Marxist verbiage, on the one hand, and from neglect and cynicism on the other. People are self-interested, but in any society and culture they construe their interest in the context of general moral beliefs. Beliefs about work are among the most important, particularly in what is still basically a Protestant and a capitalist society. The Labour Party began to lose its way when it became seen simply as a redistributionist party of welfare and lost its early rhetoric and image as a party of production. Perhaps it was never very precise, but the belief was deep that capitalism wasted human and natural resources and that socialist modes of production could be more efficient in producing wealth. In the simplest terms, perhaps socialism said no more, or no less, than that great enterprises go best when people want to work together cooperatively. The value asserted was fraternity, but the belief was that cooperation was economically superior to competition. This was believed with a now astonishing specificity: both Shaw and Wells, for instance thought that the new polytechnic institutions would create a generation of socialist engineers. But now all this has become bureaucratised: socialist economies appears to mean state control and nationalisation, not a genuine mixed economy of cooperative production and more food for any goose that lays a golden egg. The polytechnics have sent into the Labour movement not socialist engineers, but social workers.

Socialism must claw back this lost ground. Socialism began, after all, as a theory that the rise and fall of societies is to be understood in terms of their productive base: the creators of the new wealth, skilled industrial workers. I believe it was called the labour theory of value (which may not work as theory of value in the sense of explaining prices, but does point to the fundamental location of social stability or progress in industrial societies—just as the Conservative used to believe that it was an experienced elite who determined the rise or fall of societies, and it was a Liberal belief that it was invention and initiative by individuals).

Egalitarianism can then be presented not as an argument about redistribution, but as the condition for the creation of new wealth: people working side by side with equal responsibility and in roughly equal conditions. The popular way of putting it is that most people in factories and offices think that if they put their heads together they could do it better than the boss, and that they are usually right. Literal equality has, in any case, never been a socialist belief (give or take a few anarchists): rather, to paraphrase John Rawls, that all inequalities should be challenged and need justifying in terms of the common good is a socialist idea. And democratic socialists would never sacrifice liberty for equality; indeed, like Tawney, they see the one as a condition for the maximisation of the other. And socialists think in a more republican tradition of liberty than do liberals or the new social democrats: they believe that liberty is not just being left alone, but something to be used actively and aggressively. However difficult it makes government, we want active *citizens* making their own decisions cooperatively; not simply well-treated *inhabitants* or *subjects* voting for welfare, still less a nation divided between depoliticised unemployed and workers in employment fearful of political activity in case it destroys their jobs or attacks their earnings.

As I have argued elsewhere,[3] liberty, equality and fraternity are the obvious and primary socialist values, when taken together, not separately, and when applied realistically to actual circumstances and policies. These should form the heart of a socialist rhetoric. But always, of course, actions—or rather practical example—speak louder than words. Rhetoric, said great Aristotle, must enunciate simple principles, be based on empathy with the actual audience addressed, and must find the forms appropriate to persuading that audience. If the Labour Party is to save itself, it must practise rhetoric in that sense, not premeditated propaganda: it must come out of its internal

[3] A Footnote to Rally Fellow Socialists', a long addendum to the third edition of my *In Defence of Politics*, Penguin, 1982.

debates and talk to ordinary people everywhere—at every level, on every occasion and through every medium.

Stages

Idealism and realism can be combined if a new leader can persuade the Labour Party to think in terms of stages, not to repudiate its present programme—though events and second thoughts will make some changes—but to see that the programme is an agenda for a generation, not for 'the first hundred days' or even for the life of a single government. Everything we know about social change and changes of values argues that the task set is far more formidable and needs far more time than the new activists have allowed. But being long term, it must be begun without delay. The long-term objectives are not too difficult to define, just more difficult to reach. In the short term, leaders must have their hands free to respond tactically to opinion as it is, to the economy and to the outside world: above all to what will defeat the Conservatives and restore trust in Labour as a party of government. The next election will be make or break for both Labour and the Social Democrats: disliking the Tories more and more (their troubles are about to begin), a majority of the electorate will not go on splitting their votes.

Middle-term politics is the time for planning, for institutional changes and for getting new ideas established; but it can only be done by a government in power. I suspect that the character of a future Labour government's planning will be far less centralised and *étatist* than in the past, far more concerned with stimulating local and regional initiatives, less concerned with a uniform national equity. The Labour Party should rival Mrs Thatcher's clamour against bureaucracy, not appear to oppose it. Only in the long term can institutional and attitudinal change coincide: a generational perspective which really could lead to a transformation of values towards a fraternal, egalitarian society with both a highly developed work ethic and sense of welfare rights.

If the Labour Party does not move in this direction, its members will pull down its parliamentary leaders or vanish back into sectarian groupuscules, and Alliance will replace Labour. But if it moves too fast, the electorate and many of the trade unions will reject it with the same result. There is a vacuum to be filled. The Tories have polarised the nation, have forced extreme measures on any future government that wishes to restore industry against the city; and they are themselves heading for civil war. The Social Democratic leaders may be motivated by nostalgia for the busted consensus of the 1960s, but their voters are mainly protesting at Labour's follies. To gain them back calls for empathy, patience and time. Neil Kinnock is a socialist with a broad perspective. If anyone can talk to both party and country, restore argument from principles rather than programme and stimulate serious debate about the time-scales and stages appropriate for different goals, and convey both purpose and realism, it is he. In his recent John Mackintosh Memorial Lecture on 'Democratic Socialism' he quoted R. H. Tawney's advice in 1931 that the Labour Party's rethinking in defeat must be:

related to the practical needs and moral traditions of plain men and women, as history has fixed them. It must emphasise primarily what is common with their outlook, not the points at which it differs with them. It must not dogmatise and browbeat, but argue and persuade. Its spokesmen must produce the impression of responsibility and consistency which working class organisations expect in the conduct of their own affairs, and which the public demands from a prospective government. It is too late for the Labour Party, at this time of day, to conceal its socialism, even if that were its wish. What it requires is to create the conviction that it can make a good job of it.[4]

The old historian, of course, like the new political leader, would have been fully aware that the working class of 1983 is not that of 1931. But are the party activists and the trade union leaders so aware? That is the question.

15 The *Observer*

Vol. 56, no. 2, April–June 1985

I have spent a most dismal day, first in going to church, then in reading the *Sunday Times* which grows duller and duller . . . then in reading through the rough draft of my novel which depresses me horribly. I really don't know which is the more stinking, the *Sunday Times* or the *Observer*. I go from one to the other like an invalid turning from side to side in bed and getting no comfort whichever way he turns.

> (From a letter of Eric Blair written on a Sunday in 1932)

IN THE October 1984 issue of this journal,[a] Hugo Young began this occasional series on newspapers with a most interesting inside account of the internal politics of the *Sunday Times*, the struggle for control between owner and editor and its changing policies. All this could be done for the *Observer*, indeed. But I want to essay something simple but rare and difficult, to read the newspaper as a product, to read it closely and externally as an entire and self-contained text. The proof of the pudding is in the eating—as our mothers taught us before the colour supplements' cookery inserts; just for once to look at the thing in itself and not how it came to be, or what it *should* be doing. And to look at it in its entirety. Hugo Young created the impression that the *Sunday Times* is mainly composed of political matter! Did he ever read the whole astonishing artefact?

My quotation from Orwell is a little self-indulgent and external to the text, but it does serve to bring out two basic structural factors. The first is that for most educated, thoughtful, lively and well-informed people, there is only the choice of the one Sunday or the other—or both.[1] No wonder that, hunting for the same market, the two rivals look so like each other, embodying the same kind of 'improving consensus' as the two main political parties used to do in pre-Thatcher days—and for much the same reason. 'Like Tweedledum and Tweedledee', it was often said, which still looks largely true, by content, make-up and values, apart from the *Sunday Times*'s lurch to the Thatcher camp in its few political pages. The second structural factor shown by Orwell's sardonic agony is that Sunday newspapers are designed to be read on *Sundays*, originally to fill the yawning gaps of the Protestant sabbath and now, more and more, to assist people in planning a day of leisure—either in fantasy or reality: what to do, what's on, DIY, vicarious pleasures, fashionable loves and hates, or a score or more of varieties of medical scares and hopes, and a certain amount of catching up with the week, including but by no

---

[1] Certainly just as some people vote Conservative in order to appear to be middle class, so some may read the *Sunday Times* / *Observer* in order to appear educated, thoughtful, lively, well informed and attractive.

[a] Vol. 55, no. 4, 1984.

means predominantly politics. Both papers contain a few controversies of a kind suitable for discussion at a family dinner table, or for couples who have breakfast in bed, often swapping from one 'stinking' paper to the other. For solitaries and lonelies, the Sunday papers are, of course, like Radio 4: a whole culture and surrogate society.

My procedure was this. I took the first issue of each month in 1984, if that was not available substituted by another. Then I read them closely and in their entirety, except for the small ads, but including the larger advertisements which form part of a newspaper's meaning, inescapably. Now, in fact I read the *Observer* every week except when I am abroad, but I 'read' it in a very different way: selecting things that interest me, very much guided by headlines and subheads. I often ignore some sections entirely: skip and dip.[2] Perhaps I have done something now that nobody does, not even the editor, in reading the whole thing.

The issue of 1 July 1984 had about 99,600 words in it. That excludes advertisements, headlines, captions and the colour supplement. To talk only about what I normally read, or what I speculate about other people's choice from the 'magazine', would beg the question. All newspapers nowadays are, in fact, magazines containing varying proportions of news or reports of recent events. It could well emerge from this series that the very term 'newspaper' needs redefining, both as to the main content of the dailies and the probable motives of their readers. On those rare occasions when news is both important and pressing, urgent and changing rapidly, most of us turn to radio or television, don't we?

Overall structure and up-front

The make-up of a paper is revealing. With occasional variations as for a Travel section in February, the paper has settled down into the front section, Review, Business and Weekend sections and the colour supplement. The proportions are interesting. In my sample, the front section varied between 14 and 20 pages—four issues were 14 and three 16 pages. Review is always 8 pages, Weekend always four pages, and Business varied between 14 and 20 in almost exactly the same way as the front section (Business includes the four Sports pages). The colour supplement varied between 40 and 128 pages, according to the seasonal supply of advertising.

The front section could be loosely called the political section. Most people who write regularly for it talk about this section as the policy end. They play an old-fashioned role which stoically ignores what is happening in the rest of

---

[2] In fact I read the headlines on p. 1 quickly, then more slowly the Football League Division One results to see how badly Arsenal and QPR are doing, and then the evening television recommendations in order if necessary to make a pre-emptory joint policy statement over breakfast. Then I start skimming any section anyone else hasn't grabbed. Does anyone read a newspaper sequentially like most books?

the paper: whether the overall content could also, in any possible sense, be a political factor, contradicting or affirming their own proffered values. The front section carries domestic news, foreign news (relatively well covered), editorials, usually two feature articles on the leader page, and a single, long article on the right-hand inside page; also a 'personality column' immediately before the leader page (during the year it was Conor Cruise O'Brien, replaced by Katharine Whitehorn, who joined the paper in 1963 as Fashion Editor); a 'Political Diary' by Alan Watkins (more and more a personality column), and a more traditional column headed 'Politics' by the political correspondent, Adam Raphael, commenting on the most important events of the week. What I mean by 'personality column', by the way—and all papers have carried them since the 1930s—is writing that the editors believe the readers like for characterfulness, forcefulness, quirkiness, unpredictability, rather than for regular and responsible coverage of a subject: the campaigning essayist as it were. The Levins, the Watkinses and the O'Briens are usually better writers than their American counterparts, but they do not appear to have research assistants: they write from the top of their heads, a quirky or forceful view on the same stock of news. The *Observer* has never been much taken with 'the investigative columnist' or 'the Whitehall correspondent', let alone an 'Insight team' given time to dig, as the *Sunday Times* attempted before the money ran out and the iron heel came down.

The leader pages are obviously written with seriousness, perhaps a mite too solemn, for unlike the political columns there is every sign that too many cooks dilute the broth. They obviously favour Alliance,[b] not so much as a policy decision but as temperamental believers in what Arthur Schlesinger once called (without intending the least self-parody) 'the vital centre'. But they are careful not to break with Labour entirely. It probably doesn't matter very much. I suspect that the underlying belief of their leader writers, now that Alliance-boosting has abated, is that the real differences in British politics lie within the two main parties rather than between them. The editorials are all very sensible and decent, but somehow 'wet', in the sense of dealing in generalities never thought through into consistent and practical policies. This middle of the road, considered, overcompromised framework somehow infects as well as selects the signed feature articles on the leader page: not having a decisive set of policies, just decent and predictable values. The *Observer* could open up its leader page to the full range and strength of political and social viewpoints argued outside in our society—as the *Times* imagines it is doing. But, with a few exceptions, the diminishing number of outside contributors all sound as if they have been exposed to the remorseless drip, drip of friendly *Observer* consensual pressure, so that the forceful ideas of a Tuesday become presentable to the majority of readers by the Sunday (who, to judge by the rest of the paper, are little interested in politics anyway).

A fifteen-hundred word 'Profile' each week maintains a very high standard

---

[b] This the SDP–Liberal Alliance, the electoral pact of the 1980s.

of, so to speak, living obituaries of the famous. It is a speciality of the house, as is the Pendennis column which forms the back page of the front section, less room for advertisements which take up half. It deals largely in the personalities of public life. What becomes clear on reading closely the whole front section is that there is a house style, and its basic philosophy is still profoundly liberal in the way they look at the world and the presuppositions they accept—and never bother, of course, to argue. And liberalism in its broadest sense: that events (both historical and contemporary) are to be explained basically by the initiative, enterprise, talent and originality of individuals. The front section is linked to the other sections by the belief that events, whether in politics, art or sport, are to be explained primarily in terms of individual performance and motivation. All issues have to be personalised, which does not mean the writers are writing down to the readers; it is obvious that they themselves believe this. Not for them 'long-term factors', social and economic trends, 'impersonal forces', 'the structuration of society', etc. (Or perhaps for no one on a Sunday.) But this obsession with personal achievement does make their perennial concern for the decline of the British economy and the breakdown of consensus politics (which I have read every Sunday of my adult life) perpetually impotent, trivial and short-sighted. But they are liberal, indeed, so they do not adopt a conservative epistemology either, as the *Times* does so naturally, and as the proprietors are trying to impose on a naturally *Observer*-like *Sunday Times* staff: by conservative I mean experience, tradition, hierarchy, the skill of a traditional elite (plus socialising the best of the creeps, climbers, thrusters and gallopers). The *Observer* is cheerfully radical about mocking 'the Establishment' despite the pleasant voyeurism of the colour supplements glimpses of showbiz people and other personalities. But, of course, it is also a very conscious provider of the information that people think they need to rise in the world; for the upwardly mobile (just as the *Sun* is certainly the paper for those who think they have got stuck down unjustly or unluckily).

If the back page of the front section has to be half advertisement, editorial belief in the primacy of the political (even though their practice denies it) comes across strongly on the front page: only 16 inches of advertising matter is allowed out of 118 column inches. The front page has a good, clean, fresh design, and tries hard to find and feature some exclusive and important-sounding political story not already run in the weekly press. Dubious spy stories may now replace the old 'Impending Cabinet Reshuffle?' as the perennial first reserve for this eye-catching position. 'MI5 Double Agent Defects to the *Observer*' was a good one. Medical scares are another standby; 'Secret Deal over Britain's First Test-Tube Quads.'

The front page carries a selective index to the four mainly political / serious special features, yet much more prominence is given to a two-inch strip right across the top of the front page under the title. This picks out with illustrations special features obviously highlighted to reassure the reader at once, despite the traditional political front page, that the *Observer* caters brightly for 'the whole of life', as it sees life. I pick out three issues at random just to remind you of what kind of things are thus featured. On 11 March 1984: a major new magazine partwork, British cookery; Katharine Whitehorn on alternative living; Germaine Greer, Eunuch into Mother; the Other War, Gulf (on the oil industry) and Little White Hope (on Zola Budd). On 5 August: Yoko Ono, life without Lennon; Clive James and the Big Guns (reporting the *Observer*'s own celebrity shooting contest); Seaside Britain, the Kent Coast; Chariots of Gold, Hugh McIlvanney at the Olympics; and Living the Life (on conspicuous consumption). On 4 November: Paul McCartney talks about his new film; America's Other Election (beauty queens); Castle Battlements, Roy Jenkins on Barbara Castle's diaries; and Heroine of the Wightman Flop (tennis).

The Review section

'The Review' used to be thought of as 'the literary pages', but that was never really true. Reviews of books take up two pages out of eight. The issue of 2 September, for instance, had about 165 column inches of book reviews, 16 inches of book advertisements and 108 inches of Holiday and Travel ads on these two pages. Not much is published in July and August. But on 4 November there were 176 inches of book reviews and 154 inches of book ads. 15 April saw 44 inches of book ads, but then 'What's On' ads moved to take up two-fifths of the left-hand book page. Long gone are the days when Gollancz used to advertise his books on the editorial page of the front section. Publishers' ads are highly seasonal anyway and these figures suggest some doubt in their minds about whether readers of the newspaper buy books for themselves and not just for Christmas presents. And the books advertised show little congruence with the books reviewed. The selection of books for review seems a curious running compromise between a good old-fashioned view of Literature with a capital 'L', a frame of reference that only intellectuals will share, and a belief that readers of this part of the section are interested in almost any biography, whether of a literary figure, a general or a royal princess. It is good on modern English and French novels, poor on literary criticism and academic Eng. Lit. and surprisingly good (if, of course, terribly selective) in doing one general or academic history book a week. It tries hard to keep its literary readers abreast of modern poetry. But either because the literary editor, Terence Kilmartin, who has done the job for 32 years, has no personal interest in pure philosophy, moral or political philosophy, even the best of books in what is after all quite a strong national hand rarely get reviewed.

And again, with rare exceptions, it is as though the social sciences did not exist. But for some book ads, readers would not know that important works get published that need popularising. And the feature writers or serious columnists up-front don't seem to have time to read even the best of social science, though *New Society* does all the gutting for them. Space, of course, as every literary editor knows, is terribly tight; but some are less defensively purely literary than others. The *Guardian*, with less space, throws its net wider.

A few people do nearly all the reviewing. Any editor must rely on trusties. But the number in the *Observer* is so few that the close reader suspects that the ideology of personality is at work again. A commissioning editor believes that readers read for the personality rather than the subject matter. 'What's old AJP on about this week?' Or what mixture of great sense and perverse provocation will flow from Anthony Burgess's pen'? 'What a pity they never really found a substitute for Philip Toynbee (or was it Cyril Connolly?) whom I used to enjoy every Sunday.' Specialists are a nuisance and cannot write English. Also one suspects that once in the family, the reviewers to a large extent pick their own books—which makes for lively writing, but also eccentric coverage and occasional blatant nepotism.[3]

A few political books get reviewed by staff writers from the front section—either a sign of economy or an editorial concern with trying to make precise the necessarily nebulous or consensual '*Observer* editorial line'. Statesmen's memoirs tend to get reviewed by other statesmen, so are rarely given a serious critical appraisal.

The tension between politics and literature (and a very narrow view of each emerges) is made plain on the front page of the Review section. This page carries a single article which normally carries over. It is the big read of the week. My sample was divided between broadly political topics and broadly literary, even if 'literary' usually means the 'private life' of some leading personality. Typical was the headline 'Get on that stage you little bitch', and the box 'Garry O'Connor ends his study of the tragic, doomed marriage of Laurence Olivier and Vivien Leigh'; or 'Blind Boy on a Bicycle. Ved Mehta . . . tells how he struggled for the right to a normal childhood.' And I now know a lot more than I want to about the sex life of H. G. Wells, Rebecca West and the psychology of Anthony West by-lined as 'their illegitimate son'; but it won't stop me reading them. And Eliot's private life ran a strong second to Lawrence's this section. The 'political' features tend to be dominated by excruciatingly intricate and boring spy stories, wives of great men, and Second World War battles (the last of which I oddly enjoy. *De gustibus*. They do have to spread it wide).

Film, theatre and music reviews strike me, overall, as extremely good: they contain some of the best writing in the paper, giving a mixture of reportage and critique—but usually fairly clear which is which. Many of us rely on their excellent 'Briefings' as well as the advertisements for news of cultural events.

---

[3] Just by reading the whole text it is clear how much they puff each other, not out of vanity, I'm sure, but from a professional belief that readers are more interested in personalities than in ideas. I will stray outside the text to recall the colour supplement of 8 May 1983, which celebrated their 10,000th issue. The main feature was 'The Paper's People'—a definitive list of the personable among the inner family.

For dance and art reviews I cannot judge: blind spots. But it is obvious that in all these performing arts the reviewers or columnists are allowed to assume a degree of prior knowledge and cultural reference in the readership which would neither be assumed nor tolerated in the political pages.

And that is unfortunately another way of saying that the level of political writing in the front section is lower than that in the Review section. One can see how this occurs. The good liberal conscience says that the paper's political writings must be accessible to everyone, but that the rest of the pages cater to special interests, often demanding a degree of specialised knowledge in the reader. That political knowledge can be made public and that the public should be involved in politics is a great liberal cultural ideal. But to reflect thoughtfully on that process is not the same thing as involvement in that process: political discussion on a level which matches the best on art and sport need not be exclusive. Shakespeare, after all, solved the problem of talking to different levels at once, often with less space. Good teachers do it. Good doctors move easily from one patient's level of understanding to another's.

Business and Weekend sections

The length of the Business section tells a tale. The amount of reportage of company news, developments and new issues is about equal to political news reportage. There is a similar love of personalising issues and also some really dramatic writing about boardroom purges and take-over bids (it was a treat to see how well they described the bitter struggle for the control of Harrods between their proprietor and that professor),[4] yet the issues never vanish into middle-of-the-road generalities. Their readers, like punters, want precise suggestions and good judgement. If their front section columnists are sometimes diffuse, the named writers in the Business section are admirably urgent and concise, and so write good English into the bargain, nearly as good as in the *Economist* or the *Financial Times*. They run a lot on computer developments: section editors talk to each other apparently, for the colour supplement also ran a good series during the year on the uses of computers.

Most of the Business section is taken up with advertising, but its quality (or to be less sweeping, its cost) shows that insurance companies, investment trusts, mortgage companies and airlines have a greater faith that they influence people with money to spend than publishers show in the book section. Travel and holiday advertising appear in the back of this section, for obvious reasons, even if that may be the only thing that brings some people into it at all. People like myself who previously never read the main Business section are missing, I have discovered, a good deal of much more specialised material on the state of the economy, economic policy and industrial relations

---

[4] Though the stories never reminded readers of who he was. But I know a lot of ordinary readers who don't know a Rowlands from a Murdoch—that is specialised knowledge.

than one can find among the more generalised, general-reader politics of the front.[5]

Rather incongruously, perhaps because they both have to be printed late, the Sports section is tacked on to Business. Here, too, is some of the best writing and photography in the paper. The level of knowledge assumed is higher than in the more popular Sundays which give proportionally more space to sport. A technical phrase like 'primary election' or 'single transfer-able vote' up-front has to be explained (or fudged in a general haze about 'PR'); but 'off-side trap' or 'double fault' get by every time. An historical allusion in a political column to, say, 'Mrs Thatcher playing the Opposition so differently to Baldwin' would need explaining and therefore (counting words) be dropped; but 'like Arsenal played the wings in the 1930s' is rightly assumed to be part of the knowledge of anyone who cares for the sport at all. An interesting sign of social change is that football reportage clearly exceeds rugby reportage, both in column inches and in quality.

As the *Observer* is so reader-conscious, it is surprising that 'the whole of human life' as sport gets such relatively short shrift in pages. Not merely sport in general, but so many sports. Yet 'market-conscious' may be the more fruitful concept. There is little big advertising directly related to sport, so often the sporting section has three clear pages.

'Weekend' evolved out of the Women's pages. And though Katharine Whitehorn moved up front during the year to take O'Brien's column, 'Week-end' is still very much her kind of thing: 'intelligent woman' giving personal opinions on everything from fashion to tokenism to PTAs and what to do about dog droppings. Indeed, like the colour supplement, this section tries to be ahead of fashion whether in cars, clothes or cookery: to play the game of 'spot or start the trend'—literally trendy, but slightly ironically, as if one knows all along that it is a joke and that one day one will be serious again, and not wish for electric can-openers or 1930s French knickers until every child is fed in a world beyond the notional 'NW1' in which the section is set.

'Weekend' always begins with a feature of some seriousness, but again heavily personalised: 'Family Writer: Ann Chisholm talks to Hilary Spurling about her biography of Ivy Compton-Burnett and how she combines having children with her career.' (This may also be a case of building up a relative newcomer to the *Observer* family in order to offer another 'personality' to its readers.) Or 'To Prove a Villain' . . . Antony Sher, who plays Richard in the current RSC production, puts Shakespeare's character into historical per-spective.' He is a fine actor, but one might just as well have Olivier on the history of Cyprus, or the decline of the music hall. This section ends with a half-page 'Notebook' essay by Michael Davie—thoughtful, varied and socio-logical and not needing the hype of personality to keep my interest.

---

[5] Perhaps there could be a box on the leader page signalling advanced political readers to items in 'Business'. Some good may come of this article.

The colour supplement ends it

What really struck me about the *Observer Magazine* is the photography. No wonder so much of it ends up as collage on bathroom or bedroom wall, let alone on Anthony Powell's famous ceiling—itself once featured. The contents are remarkably like an illustrated 'Weekend'. There doesn't seem to be much more to say, only that the cookery is now in colour. And a famous politician, artist, performer or writer shows 'A Room of My Own', something for us to criticise, emulate or envy. There is the odd serious piece embedded in all the good living and how the other half copulate or contracept sort of stuff. One of the best tabular presentations of regional unemployment statistics appeared between lingerie and car ads on 7 October. I hope schoolteachers found it. Roy Hattersley's '100 Years of the Fabians' did get a caption on the cover alongside 'Putting the Skates under Starlight Express', 'Heyday of the Horror Comix' and 'British Cookery—East Anglia'. If one is very clever or pedantic one can find on pages 5 or 7 a table of contents to the magazine. But from the catchpenny cover right through to 'Peanuts', the design of it is as a lucky dip, difficult to extract what one wants and get out quick: one has to turn all those pages of colour ads wondering if there might be something interesting; there sometimes is. It has to be done; one might be at a loss for the subtext on a Sunday night in some unexpectedly specific conversation. Talking points. Here one sees the graphic breakdown of any attempt, which both the political and the literary pages still try to make, at rational discrimination: a kaleidoscope of consumer delights and instant issues are put before us. Or is that what we demand? 'Who the rider, who the horse?', as Yeats remarked.

What emerges is a clear picture of what is best and what is worst in the culture of modernity. 'Have we come all this way for this?' What is best is the sheer lively range of choice, open to those in employment. What is worst is the cynicism or self-deception needed to put all this together week by week to please everybody and offend no one; and for the reader to take it seriously. There is a kind of modem eunuch who is brilliantly expert in mentioning issues as if by so doing they are resolved. Just as most of us now are political voyeurs more than actors, and are grateful for the weekly magic theatre.

The *Observer*'s writers have a clear, common epistemology: that there is true knowledge, but that it is always and only about people's motives. Psychology is king. In the world of competing individualism even 'character' is now replaced by 'personality'. The paper also has an ontology: that the world consists of nothing but momentary pleasures and stimuli—technically Hobbesian sensationalism. Said the master, 'Felicity is a continual progress of desire, from one object to another . . . I put for a general inclination of all mankind, a perpetual and restless desire of Power after Power, that ceaseth only in Death.'

So at the end of the day, reading the whole of the actual text, the difference between the *Observer* and its rival and other downmarket Sunday papers becomes one of degree, not kind. John Stuart Mill attempted to escape from Hobbes, Bentham and his father by distinguishing (or asserting that there was a distinction) between higher and lower felicities: yet even his argument suffers the fatal flaw and anti-humanistic horror of any utilitarian culture, that 'the greatest happiness of the greatest number' whether high or low can indeed be achieved, economically, culturally and politically, while leaving the lesser number outside—even if they number millions— if they are an electoral minority or cannot influence the market. And these millions have no other values than these put before them, useless though they are. The highest aspiration becomes individual escape if you are worthy enough, or in truth lucky enough, to rise into the wonderful narcissistic solipsist, hedonistic world of the Weekend section and the colour supplement (not to mention its own new monthly pull-out section called 'Living Extra'). If one could not laugh, as if in a theatre, one would howl as if with Lear on the heath.

16 The Fundamental Condition of Labour

Vol. 58, no. 4, October–December 1987

THE LABOUR PARTY is back in the ring and on its feet, bloodied but unbowed; yet to look like a party of government again it will need brain as well as blood, sweat and tears. The king of the pollsters, Robert M. Worcester, put the difficulty ever so clearly in the June newsletter of MORI, *British Public Opinion*: 'The 1987 general election saw the most professional and well presented Labour campaign in the party's history. Despite that, it also saw, for the first time in this century, the third successive election of a British Prime Minister.'

All Labour's best efforts have still left the Conservatives with a formidable lead. Although the Alliance's challenge of 1983 to be main opposition party has been fought off, yet anti-Conservative votes are hopelessly split. Yes, 53 per cent (ignoring Plaid and the SNP) did not want a Conservative government; but 65 per cent did not want Labour! And it would be the craziest assumption to think that, even if Labour negotiated an electoral pact with 'Alliance' (or whatever emerges as the third party), Alliance voters could simply be delivered by their leaders to the Labour Party as is. And if Alliance were to collapse tomorrow, survey evidence suggests that twice as many of their voters would go Tory than Labour.

Labour was simply not trusted, or not yet trusted enough. The wounds of the past are too deep to mend quickly. And this despite winning the arguments. Mrs Thatcher won; and with her party as it is, with she as she is and with our country having no entrenched constitution, she can do pretty much as she likes, She won, not because a majority endorse her distinctive policies, but because Labour is still distrusted; and because double-headed Alliance was not taken seriously as a party of government.

The alternatives before Labour if it wishes to be a governing party ever again are not between *either* modernisation *or* electoral alliances. The only realistic inference from the figures, the results, the record, the public mind and the sociology of contemporary Britain is that *both* would be needed, or at least that while Labour pursues the former it must not affront the common sense of the electorate by saying 'Never, no never' to any talk whatever of realignment, alliances or constitutional reform. Peter Kellner in the *New Statesman* has pointed to the fact that Labour's undoubted revival under Kinnock's leadership (and the sobering effect of two defeats) has now restored its votes to precisely the same proportionate share of each of the five main social class categories as it held in 1964. Once again a majority of skilled workers voted Labour, removing the disgrace of 1983. But the absolute numbers of both the skilled and unskilled working class have declined; not the consciousness and life-style of being working class, but the sheer damned numbers. And a grim bonus has come to the Tories: the unemployed and the very poor are significantly less prone to vote.

To win next time Labour will need to claw back a hundred seats, nearly all of which must be in the South since in the North Labour's cup is already full to overflowing. This would need a change of historical dimensions. Now there are, of course, two ways of looking at fundamental electoral change: historically and rationalistically. Rationalistically we can only think of what we can rationally try to do to influence events. But historically, looking back, we know that governments, indeed regimes, more often change because of internal conflict or ineptitude, not because of what their opponents do. Some stronger term than 'accident prone' is needed to characterise the riskiness of Thatcher's autocratic style of government. It is so strong in its sense of main purpose, but so brittle when it encounters unexpected small obstacles—like Mr Michael Heseltine or Mr Peter Wright. It is worth taking a bet that the Tories will tear each other to pieces. But such hopes give no rational ground for sitting and waiting like old Marxists for the inevitable breakdown—'The Coming Crisis of Thatcherism', etc. It could take an awful long time.

The Fabian post-mortem

In the meantime, what is to be done? Even before the party conference, there were two interesting post-mortems. One was a special conference of the London Labour Party. The debate was more open, at times sounding even puzzled, marginally more tolerant than in the past. Events had made some people's responses less predictable and less tied to stereotypes of comprehensive and consistent ideological positions. But in the main it was an old-time punch-up between the 'more socialism' and the 'more realism' brigades. 'Rather than that we desert our socialist principles to win elections . . .' against 'If we can't win elections, what price principles?'

The other post-mortem was summoned by the Fabian Society and was more genuinely reflective. Some voices other than full-time politicians were occasionally heard. The hard Right shares at least one characteristic with the hard Left, a habit of using 'academic' pejoratively. But occasionally thought is needed as well as instant policies or blind loyalty in defence of prepared positions. If an attack is to be mounted (against the enemy for once), the enemy's lines have to be closely studied, tactical opportunities seized which may not be part of a preconceived grand strategy (so long as they do not actually negate or hinder it), and above all one has to be sure that one will be followed if one goes over the top. 'What the people really want' has to begin, alas, with some rough understanding of what they actually want. So the more 'academic' occasion was more fruitful. Much of what follows comes straight from that discussion; but as it was held under 'Chatham House rules' there can be no attributions.

The Fabian post-mortem was a surprisingly cheerful affair. When a death is long expected, funerals can become family reunions. One met people one hadn't seen for quite a time and there was an air of faith vindicated as well as hope frustrated. At a similar meeting in 1983 things were really quite tense: one waited to see who did or did not come into the room, who was alive and who dead. 'Thank heavens Peter is still with us.' 'Sarah must have passed over' (or 'gone to David' was the euphemism for apostasy). But now the Great Secession or the Limehouse Fault seems far away and downstream. Our faith was vindicated to have fought out the Last Fight where it had to be fought, and absent friends who couldn't stand the heat could be viewed now with pity rather than contempt. There was almost a Christian air of 'Come home Shirley, all is forgiven'. Hers had been a bad error of judgement about the nature of the Labour Party rather than malign ideological schism or the power-hunger of a de Gaulle without a France.

Discordant voices, certainly; strange old right-wingers defending public corporations out of the Webb–Robson books of long ago, and one big bouncy Bennite, presumably there for fair play, admitting that the old 'alternative economic policy' was not viable, but then demanding another. The word 'alternative' can be put in front of almost anything. Mainly, however, there was astonishing and sensible agreement on image and policy.

Yes, the Labour Party must modernise its image, and changing the image does mean changing the policies. The burden of proof now has to be made for public ownership, not against it. There was no enthusiasm for nationalised industries, either as a slogan to warm the blood or as a rational administrative response. A speech about the efficiency of British Rail as a model for the future was heard in stunned if nostalgic silence. 'Control' and 'regulation' were the watchwords. No one pleaded passionately for the renationalisation of Telecom, but several urged more control and criticism to ensure its quality, performance and accountability. If the early polytechnics had fulfilled the excited hopes of Shaw and Wells, and had produced socialist engineers and managers, it would have been different. But as they didn't, Gaitskell and Crosland had to be right: don't kill the goose that lays the golden egg; tax it— discover empirically and cautiously the highest marginal rate of taxation compatible with investment without causing a flight of capital.

That one of the greatest freedoms for any of us is owning our own house seemed now taken for granted, even if a council tenant—so great is the speed of social change, and political adjustment. There was a lot of talk about helping poorer owner-occupiers. Actually, wasn't that being done at the end of the Wilson–Callaghan era, the relative shift in funding from new build to doing-up and rehab, all those small and useful improvement grants? But where to draw a radically new line: still large numbers, not merely the homeless, whose main need is subsidised public housing. Both never so much as before and never again, however much we defend local government, so immobilising a system. Some young people cannot find homes where they've always lived; some would like to get away: a good idea to ask them. Ideas about popular consultation are not new. All that was supposed to happen after the Town and Country Planning Act 1967 and the Skeffington Report on participation. But it didn't, at least not on any scale that caught the public imagination; and some Labour councils were among the worst foot-draggers and offenders in knowing 'what our people really want'.

As Neil Kinnock often says, we don't at all like Thatcher's version of individualism, but we do want individualism. We actually like people doing their own thing, and we actually laugh rather than rage when the architect's aesthetic for the building is ruined by a riot of unmatching curtains and china dogs. But we used to put the bye-laws on them: any colour paint so long as it's green, and no dogs or pigeons. An egalitarian individualism needs personal example, and it needs a clearer theoretical basis from which homely examples can be deduced. (Whatever his own life-style, Crosland in print was wise on these things.) Individualism and sociability, not crass competitiveness, is the idea. Example and examples are needed, not the abolition of sports or interschool competitions, or the purging of the language of anything sexist or racist, or thought to be so.

More stress on democracy, genuine popular participation and consulta-tion—even when results are not always immediately pleasing to advanced socialist susceptibilities. Some of these policies could be quite cheap and (let us avoid rhetoric) at least not obviously harmful to production and efficiency. Yes, for instance, to parents and teachers together having far more say in the running of schools (and giving kids a visible lesson in democracy); but a voice elected and democratic, not the Thatcher facade democracy of a few appointed 'good' parents with the head as general manager and DES policing a uniform system. (Perhaps they will send delegations to France, Japan or East Germany.) There was too much acceptance, for my taste, of the idea of a national curriculum. Baker means 'curriculum' not just syllabus, not just what is to be taught but how it is to be taught too. I see opposition to this as a test case of whether the new thinking in the Labour Party about a pluralist rather than a 'statist' model of society is to be taken seriously.

Pluralism

The conceptual shift to pluralism was otherwise dominant at the Fabian post-mortem. Most speakers were very clear that to defend local government against the centralising tendencies of Thatcher's State means democratising both local government and the local parties. The Press is disgracefully biased; but by God we've given some hostages to fortune. Someone testified that he had been on the Greenwich party's General Committee but had now seen the light. And there was no longer shyness in saying what we mean by 'we', that some forms of comradely behaviour are simply not acceptable to democratic socialists, No, we don't abandon. Why should we? We stand in a very old tradition of democratic socialism, less theoretically structured than Marxism but with far more explicit and clear moral doctrines. Marxists have mis-represented the very history of socialist thought. Our socialist theory does point to the primacy (but not the omnipotence) of work and to the problem of the paradox of poverty amid plenty; and our doctrine leads to egalitarianism

219

(not literal equality), sociability and community, liberty and democracy. There's a great deal of overlap with radical liberalism, but in the long run it is a different picture of an ideal society.

'Democracy' and 'liberty' must fly at Labour's masthead and be principles applied to public policy; but for all of us, which means gradually raising the millions in poverty, who are thus virtually outside the polity, to a level at which they can exercise citizenship. The old 'universal' versus 'selective' benefits argument hardly arose, but a massive realisation kept surfacing that for all the 'need for new policies' the mere defence of the NHS and the common schools was popular with nearly all the electorate, and may be the Achilles' heel of Thatcherism.

Empirical policy needs some theoretical framework so that entailments for policy can be made by different people yielding more or less the same, or at least not incompatible, results. Such a framework has given Thatcherism its coherence and *élan* both as an intellectual and a popular doctrine. Wilsonian make-it-up-as-you-go-along or reactive pragmatism just leads to incoherence, and nothing to say to the public except 'trust me' or 'judge by results'. But what if the results are bloody, perhaps because of factors beyond control? Thatcher has survived unparalleled failures of policy, if one judges by unemployment and deindustrialisation, because she has convinced people that she is following courageously 'laws of economics'.

I didn't need to say again at this Fabian post-mortem—others said it forcefully—that the Labour Party needs both a fundamental statement of Values and Principles (which is not as difficult to produce as people believe— it is all in Cole and Tawney, and parts of Morris, Laski and Crosland) and a topical statement of general policies. It is getting more and more clear what should be in it, and most people in the party would accept that it is what they always stood for. The intrusion of Trotskyism on the one hand and of New Left highbrow Marxism on the other will prove to have been temporary, if at the time damaging, episodes in the history of the party. A contingent policy statement, a deduction from a statement of lasting principles, written as an outline programme to guide us for a decade or at least a Parliament, is already needed urgently because, as we all know, the election campaign, for all its effort and drama, cuts little ice, changes few votes. The campaign is continuous. It has to be based on ideas, not just on attack. Until the Labour Party has clear aims and clear policies and habituates the public to their existence in steady state, not recurrent annual clamour, a majority will not trust us, however much misgovernment there is, even callous and cruel misgovernment.

There was a great deal of talk about reforming the party. One person one vote. That was common ground, despite the London Labour Party. The reasons are well known and obvious. Distinctions were implied between the democrat and the activist; activists can be so active that they get almost totally out of touch with ordinary people. But there was less willingness to look at the block vote. Some warning shots that the country doesn't see it as 'democratic', but it could hardly see the Conservative annual conference in that light either. The issue is one of both image and fundamental policy. Unhappily the unions as such are unpopular among the very voters who would need to be won, let alone won back (for times are changing), to gain those 100 seats in the south. Scargill and the Miners' Strike have a lot to answer for. But it goes far deeper. Such is the loss of membership in trade unions and the decline of traditional industries that now almost 50 per cent of union members are in the public service unions. To less affluent, non-union white-collar workers that is what makes the whole Labour Party, especially some city majority Labour parties, look like a kind of public employment society at their expense.

The political folly of NUPE heading the fight against Health Service cuts with slogans of 'save jobs' was almost unimaginable—unless you are such a good public sector socialist that you cannot imagine how the suburban lower middle classes think. Should the link with the unions actually be broken? It is almost inconceivable; a few years ago it would have been inconceivable—but they need reform.

Not one word was said at the Fabian think-in about devolution. There were some Scots present. Why were they silent, or were they just aghast at all this talk of pluralism and decentralisation that did not raise the most pressing priority for Labour? Speaker after speaker said how constitutionally conservative the Labour Party had been. After the destruction of the GLC by simple majority, we must think again about a Bill of Rights and a written constitution. Yes, judges are conservative; but haven't we learned the lesson yet, on our own doorstep as well as from an occasional embarrassed glance at the whole of Eastern Europe: that there are some advantages to 'checks and balances', however imperfect the judges, however perfect the socialist majority in a unicameral popular assembly? Here the rethinking is only beginning. Scotland must force the pace. The United Kingdom is administratively already a quasi-federal state. Might Labour not lead it towards being a formal federal state?

Tactical conclusion

It should not be too difficult for the Labour Party to produce fairly soon, officially or unofficially, a fundamental statement of 'Aims and Values', to be followed shortly afterwards by a statement of 'Policies for the Next Parliament'. Time-scales need sorting out. Bennites were foolish to suggest that 'irreversible social changes' could be legislated for in 'the first hundred days', let alone that they should be in a democracy with the rule of law. We can only proceed towards an egalitarian or classless society through the people and the society already here, with patience and time. From everything we know, mass attitudinal change takes decades and is generational, not triggered by the short term of parliamentary timetables.

This takes me back to the beginning. However much Labour modernises, can we really hope for an outright victory next time? On the record and starting from 32 per cent of the vote and needing three million votes more, the cool, honest and unwanted answer must be sadly clear.[a] Can the party and the country survive one more failure before the leadership and the rank and file are ready to grasp that the choice is between a majority constitutional conservatism which will keep us from office and an electoral agreement with the Liberal Party or a new Alliance? Of course their terms would be electoral reform. But if Labour aspires to be a national, not just a regional, party again, PR has positive attractions. We might never form a majority government, but the people are not likely to vote for one anyway. Yet we could be the dominant partner in a Lab–Lib coalition for a very long time. And would the electorate ever forgive us if the Conservatives got in again with a minority vote because we refused an electoral arrangement? Yet such an arrangement would only work if Labour's policies are much closer to what the country wants.

If one begins to look for common or mutually agreeable policies, there is the whole range of restoring and reforming of the Welfare State, local government and schools, the democratisation of institutions, training and continuing education, reform of the tax structure, and potentially constitutional reform. What is most repellent to Labour Party members about the present Alliance may well be solving itself. And one of the two things most repellent to Liberal activists about the Labour Party is beginning to be tackled by the Labour Party forthrightly: the unrepresentative eccentricity of a few city Labour parties. But the other is the difficult problem of the power of the unions, not just the use they make of it. But we owe it to the country, which would otherwise suffer even longer under Thatcher or her chosen successor, not to shut our ears to negotiations with the Liberals or a new Alliance. But in order to bargain sensibly both parties need to be more clear about their own strength and identity.

---

[a] This paragraph makes interesting reading now. The next general election was Major's victory of 1992, and it would be a full ten years before Blair's first landslide and Labour's eventual return to power, albeit in the guise of New Labour.

17 The State of Our Civil Liberties

Vol. 60, no. 3, July–September 1989

BY CIVIL liberties I mean those things that we need to be able to do without interference by the state in order to maintain what we ordinarily call a free society or, following J. S. Mill's usage, representative government. This kind of system and society is not easy to define precisely; indeed all precise definitions are over-precise, are morally or politically contentious. But we know the cluster of meanings associated with the usage of the concept, and we have a fair idea of its tradition and history; indeed, we are the fortunate products of that history. We need civil liberties to live well and properly in the kind of society we want to live in, so paradoxically we often take civil liberties for granted: we usually assume that fellow citizens have much the same feelings and beliefs, that there is a kind of procedural though not a substantive consensus. It is a sign that something is rotten in the State of Denmark if we feel a need to define civil liberties precisely.

By civil rights I mean something rather different and more formal. 'Civil rights' implies either the need to encode civil liberties in law, or else invokes existing entitlements, guarantees or restraints in law (restraints on actions of government, groups or individuals that incapacitate the equal opportunity of all citizens to exercise civil liberties).

Civil rights can sometimes be confused with human rights. Perhaps freedom is a human right, but it is somehow odd, if human rights are thought to be universal and somehow inherent, to think of all that we expect under civil liberties, the complex institutions of representative government, a free press, freedom of information, toleration of minorities etc., to be inherent rights rather than cultural achievements. All kinds of things may be desirable, but it is a misleading rhetoric to call them all 'human rights'; it is bad enough to blunder into thinking that all remedying of injustice or assertions of majority political will should be legislated as rights. There are, after all, many other mechanisms of social control as well as law. And if we truly believe that some rights are inherent in the very condition of being human, we had better not overload this argument (as Amnesty International well knows) if we are appealing to a dictatorship not to violate basic human rights. Overloading concepts can make messages become mere noise, as in any communications system.

So I wish to discuss the state of civil liberties as the republican tradition of citizenship—I mean not 'no Queen!' or 'Tom Nairn as Philosopher King', but the tradition of active citizenship associated in the history of the West with the Greek and Roman republican tradition. This has let the conceptual cat out of the analytical bag, for it is plain that while all Western governments (and now some East bloc governments too) pay lip service to this tradition, they also take more than occasional nostalgic backward glances to the good old days of an at least equally entrenched concept of civilisation, that of 'the good subject' and 'your station and your duties', or the artful catch-all phrase 'the law-abiding citizen'. 'Good citizen' is usually an exact if unfortunate synonym for 'good subject'. 'Active citizens' can threaten 'law and order' it (or her) self, and at best they are difficult to control.

Of course, morally, 'rights are correlative to duties'. But that does not take one very far. Thatcherites say that, but so did Tawney, three times a day. The content of each term in the equation needs careful examination in any particular context, and my ear tells me that people who use it often without further explanation seem, in practice, to want to imply that it takes an awful lot of duties to earn rights. Good behaviour can earn special privileges. That is one reason why I find the concept of civil rights difficult to apply without begging the question one is trying to answer: with the exception of rights in the narrow but precise sense of legal positivism, what are rights at law? But the laws may be bad laws. One should be law-abiding and perhaps one should teach 'the rule of law' (as I was once told by a government minister should be the case if there was to be political education in schools at all). That assumes, of course, that values can be taught; and the evidence is very contradictory. But citizens, or inhabitants of a citizen culture, seek to change laws, and it should not be made too difficult, or too fortuitous or irrational a process, however indirect, for them to be able to do so.

I don't want to digress into discussing whether our political tradition has room in it for justifications of law-breaking, civil disobedience or in extreme cases rebellion, or is actually based on mythologies of a Socrates and Cranmer defying the law and the sons of Brutus or the Whig Lords chasing out tyrant kings. But I will be watching eagerly to see how the new national history curriculum (since it is abolishing the common people) deals with Magna Carta (signing under the sword), the Long Parliament and the Great Rebellion, and 1688. That is, I suppose, part of 'Our Glorious Heritage'; but Mr Baker will have to rule, like any continental ontologist, that history has stopped—no more rebellions or fundamental changes in the constitution. It stopped in 1688 to be precise, the Act of Settlement, the Protestant succession, the Act of Union and the Sovereignty of Parliament. The arguments for this, by the way, may be found in Edmund Burke's *Reflections on the Revolution in France* and in his *Appeal from the Old to the New Whigs*. The matter worried him.

Against promiscuity

So we should consider civil liberties as a culture and a tradition, not as inferences from abstract ideas of human or natural rights, still less as creatures purely of positive law. Civil liberties are freedoms to criticise (even governments), to publish and publicise, to assemble and to organise corporate action, to worship as one chooses or not to worship, to come and go as one chooses (even from one's country), and to elect representatives to local and national government. They exist far less as the creation of law than through a lack of legal prohibition, or through laws removing obstacles, such as the gradual enfranchisement of adult males and then of women. But, of course, there are restrictions on such legally undefined liberties, largely of a kind justified on grounds of public interest to 'keep the peace' (somehow I prefer that old phrase to 'law and order', now so often invoked, like 'national security', widely and needlessly against actions one simply disapproves of); or a mutual interest in preventing our use of our liberties proving mutually damaging. And some now argue that 'freedom of information' or 'open government' is not just prudential good practice but is a civil liberty or right, a logical extension of the publication of parliamentary debates and of ministers being publicly called to account.

There are obvious conditions for the flourishing, or not, of civil liberties—like the law and practice of Parliament and the independence of the judiciary. They affect the exercise of civil liberties, but are not themselves the individual actions of citizens. This distinction is important, for unless civil liberties are firmly attached to the actions of citizens, far more widecast than simply voting in elections, then elected MPs can claim that, by virtue of election, either they embody some kind of corporate national civil liberty or General Will, or that they alone speak for the millions of individual citizens. Another condition for the flourishing of civil liberties has been commonly held to be, in very broad terms, almost as a truism, pluralism—a complex and active set of group structures within any nation state, let alone a multi-nation state. I say only 'almost' a truism, for this picture of society can be challenged. The Prime Minister is not alone. Famous philosophers have attacked loyalties other than to self or to the state—groups were 'worms within the entrails of the body commonwealth' (Hobbes), 'selfish and partial interests dividing the general will' (Rousseau) and 'sinister interests' (Bentham); even before Hayek.

Some see any traditional listing of civil liberties as unrealistically minimal. 'Welfare rights' at least must be added, they say. There is a respectable case that in an industrial society such rights are essential to common citizenship.[1] But I think it both more logical and prudent to believe that the positive achievement of welfare depends on a prior structure or tradition of civil liberties, rather than that welfare 'rights' are of the same kind. 'Welfare' and 'health' are easier to comprehend as human rights than as civil liberties or indeed as 'civil rights'. It is, of course, possible to have welfare rights without civil rights. Communist regimes have claimed this, sometimes quite plausibly. I see no reason to insist that, while desirable and just, welfare rights are a logical extension of civil liberties (in our system) or of civil rights (in systems with written constitutions). There are other justifications of welfare. The danger is that the clarity of civil liberties as procedural rights (as the rules of the game, not as substantive rights or outcomes) can get smothered by a widespread mental bad habit of calling everything that it is reasonable to demand politically a 'right'. Soon we have a right to work, to equal pay for

---

[1] See Bill Jordan, *The Common Good: Citizenship, Morality and Self-Interest*, Oxford, 1989.

equal work, to no discrimination on grounds of gender, ethnicity or religion, to an X-hour day, etc. etc., not forgetting a minimum standard of living, a good state-of-the-art education for all and fresh air. I take all these to be desirable things, worth campaigning for. But to speak of them as rights is largely rhetorical. Their advocacy depends on the prior existence of civil liberties or rights exercised by citizens, unless they were imposed by our old speculative friends the Benevolent Despot or the Legislator. (And there are those who still think that while for an individual, however improbably, to do this would be despotic, for a political party to do it, if elected, would be acceptable—especially if done in the name of 'compassion' or 'caring' rather than as entitlements needed for 'the practice of citizenship'.)[2]

To call everything we want a 'right' diminishes the special function of rights, and creates confusion. It may confuse the substance of what someone is saying with their right to say it. 'People shouldn't have a right to say such things.' Of course people will speak up for themselves, but advocates of highly unpopular causes are seldom the most effective advocates of their right to say the things that annoy or offend the majority. The most effective plea to enter, after all, is not that we must agree, for instance, with what Salman Rushdie has to say (even with such mad provocation from afar), but simply with his right to say it. Indeed a defence is stronger (which some of his friends have been slow to understand) if it registers genuine disapproval of much of what he says, but nonetheless defends his right to say it. (Yes. of course the exercise of such rights should be qualified by prudence and by care and respect for others, but they are not a matter for legal control even if on serious matters like religious belief. It is hard to avoid hurting feelings, though one need not deliberately stir up violence or break heads. Mr Justice Holmes only said that one had no constitutional right of free speech 'to cry "Fire!" in a crowded theatre'; he did not say that one had no right to shout 'what a load of rubbish!') In other words, we must not confuse the case for tolerance with the attempt to reach agreement or to suppress criticism.

It is precisely this confusion that is created when the good promiscuously call everything they want a right. Things may be just, but even that does not make them a right in the sense that there are rights under a Bill of Rights; or in which, in Britain, we can (or could) point to traditional, conventional civil liberties as part of our national culture. An organisation that professes to defend civil liberties, like the National Council for Civil Liberties, should be extremely careful to preserve its image for defending procedural civil liberties (without which free politics declines) and not to advocate all good causes and general social reform by genial votes of democratic annual general meetings. A majority of its membership (or a majority attending and voting) seems at the moment to be demanding that it should attack the fundamental conditions in society that prevent all being able to exercise equally civil liberties, and should

---

[2] To echo and quote Michael Ignatieff's deeply thoughtful 'Citizenship and Moral Narcissism', *The Political Quarterly*, vol. 60, no. 1, 1989, p. 72.

adopt a positive campaigning stance, not a reactive stance, on individual cases. It must make the activists feel good and active, but it does not convince those it needs to convince for the sake of its clients and for the sake of civil liberties (that is the government, the judiciary and the press) that the NCCL is other than simply a socialist pressure group. Of course, it has every right to be such, if that is what the members really want and if they cannot grasp the distinction between procedural rights and substantive justice, and will not settle for some solid victories on the crucial but narrower front. A few years ago Amnesty faced demands from some of its members to campaign for gay rights positively, and from others to attack 'the real causes, not just the symptoms, of autocratic governments'. But it fought them off. Nothing should damage its credibility in seeking to help actual, individual prisoners of conscience.

The NCCL tragically weakened its plausibility as an advocate for civil liberties when three years ago its secretary, Larry Gostin, who was working to build up cross-bench parliamentary support, was forced to resign after there were large votes at the AGM in favour of three motions, all of which he opposed: (1) that no advice, even, should be given to members of the National Front about their civil liberties—no liberty for the enemies of liberty (in contrast to the firm libertarian line taken by the American Civil Liberties Union[3]); (2) that there was no individual right not to strike against an official union decision to strike; and (3) that a report commissioned by the NCCL be rejected because it mentioned that there had been violence by pickets as well as by police during the Miners' Strike.[4] Small wonder that the NCCL has recently attempted a relaunch. It would better have attempted a candid rethink,[5] and have readopted a cross-party stance such as Charter 88 has been careful to do from the start.

The breaking of the old rules

There can be little doubt that respect for the traditional civil liberties and, indeed, the conventions of the old unwritten constitution are in decline. The rate of decline has been dramatic, but it is unfair to lay the blame solely at the door of Mrs Thatcher, Like so many historical accounts, we are beginning to

---

[3] Professor Norman Dorsen's 'Is There a Right to Stop Offensive Speech? The Case of the Nazis at Skokie', in Larry Gostin, ed, *Civil Liberties in Conflict* relates why and how the ACLU defended the rights of American Nazis to free speech under the First Amendment. There were some resignations, he admits; but he claims that the 'Skokie can become a long term asset for the ACLU.'

[4] See Gostin's own account of the incidents and the NCCL's reaction in his *Civil Liberties in Conflict*, ibid., pp. 12–18 and 227–31. See also my 'Politics, Socialism and Civil Liberties' in the same book.

[5] The so-called relaunch as 'Liberty' was marked by the publication of a book by Peter Thornton, *Decade of Decline: Civil Liberties in the Thatcher Years*, London, 1989. It is a capable and concise summary, but simply assumes that the Thatcher years are self-contained and ignores the little local difficulties in the NCCL.

see that a famous date, 1979 in this case, only marks the acceleration (though a rapid, even a reckless one) of tendencies already afoot. It could hardly be said that Wilson and Callaghan were punctilious in playing the game by the old rules; and the Labour Party certainly showed no interest in the rule book. In retrospect it is more than odd that a good many of us had for so long favoured almost any kind of reform except constitutional reform. It was, of course, because 'Labour cared', and thirsted to do good to others by means of the use of centralised sovereign power.

But Thatcherism has certainly proved an education in constitutional thought. As usual, scholars are blown with the winds rather than trying to direct or divert them. The sudden revival of constitutional law, a subject that seemed to be vanishing in the 1960s and 1970s in both Law and Politics departments, has been remarkable. Challenge and response? And neo-Marxists have been rediscovering law; which is nice but not too important. The January 1989 number of *The Political Quarterly* had three remarkable articles whose very titles summed up the problem: Wyn Grant's 'The Erosion of Intermediary Institutions', Mark Stallworthy's 'Central Government and Local Government: the Uses and Abuses of a Constitutional Hegemony', and Dawn Oliver's 'Law, Convention, and the Abuse of Power'. And the general rubric for the issue was—remember?—'Is Britain becoming authoritarian?' I think the conclusion was, Britain as a society, not yet, but the government in its style and mode of operation, yes.

Censorship for peacetime has been dramatically increased, as the Zircon affair and the 'My Country Right or Wrong' broadcasts showed. The government's hostility to the BBC and public service broadcasting is quite open. It is as if 'balance' is not to be tolerated, and, in any case, the ideological mind always perceives balance as tilted against itself. The new controls on broadcasting 'standards' are not directly political, but they are wide open to abuse by the kind of people appointed; and the whole thrust of policy towards greater commercial competition will make good current affairs programmes less and less attractive to the controllers. The government plainly prefers the hearty bias of the popular press to the damaging balance of both BBC and ITV news and current affairs policy. Most modern authoritarian regimes do not, contrary to belief, fill their airwaves with propaganda—it is very expensive and self-evidently unpopular and boring; rather they fill the airwaves with nothing, I mean pure escapist entertainment. Remember that in Oceania propaganda was only aimed at the Outer Party; it was—apart from a little crude 'hate the enemy' stuff—prolefeed for the proles. Trivialisation is the name of the game, with or without satellite TV. The government has less wish to conduct propaganda than to avoid any serious public debate at all.

The so-called reform of the Official Secrets Act has closed up more holes than it has opened. There will be no more Pontings.[a] The restrictions on

---

[a] A reference to Clive Ponting, the civil servant prosecuted under the Official Secrets Act (and acquitted) for leaking details about the sinking of the *Belgrano* during the Falklands war.

interviewing members of Sinn Fein are likely to be as counterproductive as they are an affront to liberty—our liberty. The Home Secretary's thought (he of all people) that 'some people are deeply offended' was a justification for banning even Republican sympathisers from the air. And there has been the GCHQ case; the narrowing of the sphere of jury trials and a radical shifting of rules of evidence to work against those accused; the imposition of a national curriculum on the schools as part of a general centralisation of the educational system; the running down of the ordinary schools; the pushing through of the privatisation of public utilities, even water, with what seemed to be very little preparation or consultation; and the extraordinary dominance of the will and whims of the Prime Minister herself—again, not without precedent, but precedents that were never used so ruthlessly, unless in wartime, and accepted by colleagues so supinely.

But above all else has been the attack on local government. Now there is a capital city without an elected council, and the spectacle of a nation, with only a handful of government seats (not enough even to work the Scottish Select Committee), denied any kind of subsidiary Assembly, and having more and more power removed from its local government and all kinds of public bodies packed with government loyalists. Gone is the old tradition of 'some of each' and a casting vote to the chair (at which Labour long grumbled, even when in office itself).

The attack on local government is not simply fiscal, but in a direct sense ideological: if the government decides that welfare provision must be starkly minimal, back to bare survival for fellow creatures rather than decency for fellow citizens, then no other form of government, that is local government, is allowed to attempt to make even small amends for inhumanity. Red noses will fill the gap. The personal social services are deliberately run down, largely because necessarily they have been under local control. The poll tax was contrived to have that effect, breaking a long established consensus that major taxation would be graduated according to ability to pay.

The GLC and the metropolitan boroughs were abolished without any prior committee of inquiry or any attempt to reach interparty agreement. In the past one would have safely written in a textbook that constitutional conventions were the informal agreements reached by those who wanted to play in order to play the game, that is the senior politicians on both sides. They were the rules of politics if you wanted that kind of politics, a procedural consensus though not necessarily a substantive one. Now the government acts not merely without consulting the opposition on matters commonly thought constitutional, but with an obvious contempt for both the opposition and Parliament. With the slow purge of the old Tories (only Peter Walker somehow holds out beyond Offa's Dyke), the new breed seem to have no sense of or care for the old conventions, which Baldwin so carefully observed and into which, in a very real sense, he socialised Macdonald and the Labour Party. Mrs T. acts as if she and her government expect to last for ever. The normal assumption of our un- or informal constitutional system has been that abuse of the absolute power, so readily available under the sovereignty of Parliament system, is avoided by a rational expectation that the next general election could be lost, and the other side come in.

Three circumstances have conspired against this old, heavy and always none-too-reliable check or balance: Mrs Thatcher does not think like that—she is certain that she will win again, and again; the parliamentary opposition is divided and has proved itself ineffective; and the electorate is divided enough for minority governments, in terms of voting, to be returned quite easily. Indeed she and her cabinet colleagues now seem to think of the state as their property, and of anyone who hinders their use of it as, if not quite a traitor, certainly a trespasser. Her habitual use of the royal plural and speaking of 'my ministers' is no personal vanity: it is a manifestation of a deeper confusion between 'the government' and 'the state'. The 'public interest' and even 'safety of the state' have become confused with the convenience and pride, not even the survival, of the government—as the *Spycatcher* case revealed.

Inevitable conclusion

Whatever happens, I think we are seeing the last decades of the old system. The old system was not, in a broad sense, all that old; it came in after 1688 and 1707 to ensure parliamentary supremacy and then to ensure the unity of the new United Kingdom. Those were the circumstances in which the doctrine of parliamentary sovereignty was forged.[6] The Scots, I think, deceived themselves in the nineteenth century by romantic history that 1707 was a great betrayal; but a revisionist history now suggests that the great majority of lowland Scots thought that a hard bargain had been driven. They gained trade, security, law and order and their national church was established, at a price of the permanent union of the Crowns and the ending of a Parliament seen by most, when compared to the Kirk, as corrupt, unrepresentative and aristocratic.[7] Time plays strange tricks. The decline in the power and authority of the Kirk left Scotland without a representative national institution. And it left England dominating the union from a single and over-powerful centre, a degree of unrestrained central power that lost most of its point after fears of civil war on the mainland had receded, and nearly all after the Ireland Act of 1920 and the quasi-federal structure of Northern Ireland. But the rhetoric and habit of central sovereign power remained, unhappily in the hands of a generation who had lost all memory of, and all the political skills associated with, the major task of British politics for over two centuries: holding the United Kingdom together.

Nearly every new state in the nineteenth or early twentieth century, or reform movements in old ones, linked the demand for self-government to the

[6] See my 'The Sovereignty of Parliament and the Irish Question', in Desmond Rea, ed., *Political Cooperation in Divided Societies*, Dublin, 1982.

[7] See my pamphlet *Labour and Scotland's Rights*, Labour Club, Tranent, East Lothian, 1989.

attainment of a fundamental constitution. All the British white dominions except New Zealand adopted federal structures with constitutional courts. Eire produced a written constitution and a court. Only Britain held to the sovereignty of Parliament and civil liberties. The prestige of the system was enhanced by the accident of victory in two world wars; or in hindsight one might say, as with the economy, that these victories masked the need for reform. The sovereignty of Parliament could coexist with civil liberties so long as the political culture of the government party respected them. Adherence to conventions depends on an odd mixture of self-interest and tradition. To parody, but also to pay a genuine compliment to the old Tories: gentlemen know conventions, conventions need gentlemen. (I use 'gentlemen', of course, in a perfectly non-sexist way; Tory women once knew the political rules too, and respecting them was part of one's status). I could almost call all this 'An Appeal from the Old Tories to the New'.

Has that kind of Conservative gone for ever, or was it all just an accident of Lord Whitelaw's sloth that gave Mrs Thatcher the patronage to run the machine so hard and ruthlessly with the new breed of creeps and careerists, whose minds were set from the start on office not on 'Parliament'? Even if they win again and she goes, and the gentlemen come back to replace the players (they certainly have a more able government in exile, man for man, than in office), I think the old system is discredited. And even the half-hearted adherence to Europe cannot hide that even legal sovereignty has gone for ever. The dismal record of government defeats under the European Convention on Human Rights tells a new story, but the reluctance of Parliament to take the bit by the teeth and incorporate it into United Kingdom law tells another.

The Labour Party, whether in office or defeated again, will find that the country has had enough of unlimited sovereign power, however used, and however benign, concerned or compassionate are the hands that grasp it. The debate on proportional representation and on a Bill of Rights is already opened up within the Labour Party. Old taboos are being broken. Some kind of holding operation is being cobbled up on high. The Prince of Weathercocks swings round a bit, just a bit, and Mr Hattersley thinks out loud all over the place, an awesome portent. The Leader leaves the door to PR not open, exactly, but not fully closed. The Home Affairs Committee studies options secretly. Be prepared.

The Labour Party could, of course, transform the political scene overnight if it came out for electoral reform and a Bill of Rights, and a temporary coalition to bring in these two measures, together with Scottish devolution as common ground, and a Royal Commission on the Constitution. But it is unlikely that it will. The leadership wants one more crack at the winner-takes-all stakes. Sad for the country, but at least if there was a hung result it stands ready to move quickly. The old ideas have dwindled into vested interests.

The real significance of the Charter 88 movement is (with respect to former Liberals and Social Democrats who held some such ideas all along) that it

231

represents a flight of Labour's intellectuals (all but two or three) from belief in the sovereignty of Parliament and the magnetism of the central state. All sorts are there. Old Marxists turned straight have not forsaken Lenin's state for Mr Sidney Webb's; they have gone over in one leap (well, at varying speeds and with varying travail, but almost all gone over none the less) to the project of a written constitution and the concept of pluralism. The common ground between socialist and liberal intellectuals is now civil liberties themselves; the contempt for them by the government, the neglect of them, and even attacks on them, show the need for constituting them in law.

May I end on a quotation from one of Britain's most thoughtful professors of public law?

If bad laws are a possibility, and they are, the only remedy is better laws and better legal institutions. That, in a nutshell, is the case for adopting an entrenched and justifiable law guaranteeing fundamental rights and civil liberties. Such laws do not involve giving judges that measure of potentially arbitrary power with which a pure doctrine of natural law necessarily clothes them. For such laws can specify a fairly clear and determinate conception of fundamental rights and civil liberties, and they are not necessarily unamend-able. What is required is only that they be difficult to amend. Then amendment occurs only when there is a strung and well-considered will of parliament and people to change the definition of, or even to forgo, some right.[8]

---

[8] From Neil MacCormick's 'Civil Liberties and the Law', in his *Legal Rights and Social Democracy*, Oxford, 1982, p. 58.

18 The English and the British

Book chapter; vol. 62, no. 5, 1991

As I HAVE said before, I am a citizen of a country with no agreed colloquial name.[1] Its official name is the most rarely used. The Central Office of Information publishes a useful annual with a big overseas circulation amazingly called (if one ever thinks about it) *Britain*—a province of the late Roman Empire.[a] And the Preface admits a difficulty:

Care should be taken when studying British statistics to note whether they refer to England, to England and Wales . . . to Great Britain, which comprises England, Wales and Scotland, or to the United Kingdom (which is the same as Britain, that is Great Britain and Northern Ireland) as a whole.

But is 'Britain' usually used as 'the same as' the United Kingdom as a whole? When I say 'Britain' I mean the mainland and deliberately say 'Great Britain' to include Northern Ireland. In the *OED* early usages of 'Britain' refer to the island. Its summary of early modern usage is unusually confused: 'The proper name of the whole island, containing England, Wales and Scotland, with their dependencies; more fully called Great Britain; now used for the British state or Empire as a whole'—perhaps they simply forgot (as is so helpful to do) about Northern Ireland; or is it one of the 'dependencies'? The COI is surely wrong and the *OED* confused or evasive. And so, most of the time, are most of the English.

The term 'Britain' only became used for the Kingdom of England in Tudor times, partly to cement the Arthurian myth of the new dynasty and partly, as

---

[1] 'An Englishman Considers his Passport', *The Irish Review*, Autumn 1988.

[a] This article is not from the quarterly journal issues but is a book chapter from a 'fifth issue', one of the additional spin-off volumes that became an annual element of *PQ*'s output from around this period—hence the 'vol. 62, no. 5' numbering. Bernard edited the volume, *National Identities: The Constitution of the United Kingdom*, which, like many subsequent volumes in the series, began as a small conference. As volume editor he produced a short Foreword but no standard volume editor's Introduction—this chapter is his only substantial contribution to the book, and incidentally is also the last full-length piece he wrote for *PQ* before stepping down as Chair of the board.

The contributions to the book were written after the conference (at Coleg Harlech in 1990)—they were not conference papers in the conventional sense. This is the normal pattern for *The Political Quarterly*: special issues of the journal and fifth issues normally grow out of seminars or conferences and in such cases are written after the event; the journal doesn't recycle already-delivered conference papers.

There are one or two references to the other conference contributions in this piece, but they are minor and it is perfectly readable as a free-standing chapter. I have not included the Foreword in the current volume because it mostly covers the provenance and terms of reference of the collection.

the great Queen grew old, to build a bridge to her heir. He was proclaimed as James VI of Scotland and 'James I, King of Great Britain', king of two realms, not one, although one had changed its name.[2] The same formula was used in the text of the Act of Union of 1707; and throughout the eighteenth century ministerial writers made unsuccessful attempts to establish as colloquial usage 'North British' and 'South British', as if the English and Scottish nations had gone out of business. There was a brief attempt, amid facetious derision, to call all kinds of Irish 'West Britons'.

English statesmen finally hit on a better tactic to close the old back door, not political and cultural integration but a state-fostered cult of a depoliticised Scottish identity: the 1822 state visit of George IV to Edinburgh, commissioned by the cabinet, orchestrated by Sir Walter Scott himself (the clans were reborn—or invented—as Unionists).[3] And Melbourne encouraged the young Queen to visit Scotland, not at all for her health. Luckily she liked it. Her children wore plaid just as children of Viceroys of Ireland were to wear the green. Many of the old English Tories had a clear and politic sense of the diversity of the United Kingdom. In India too they came to practise a politics of cultural tolerance, not assimilation; indirect rule, not administrative centralism as in the Spanish and French empires. Unlike the new breed of self-made men and women, they had some sense of history; and, unlike most socialists, a sense that discontinuities between sociology and government were possible, given political will and skill. They took for granted that the main business of domestic politics was the conciliation of Scotland and Ireland (the idea that Wales was any threat to the unity of the United Kingdom came much later), was holding the United Kingdom or 'Britain' together. They were ruthless in maintaining English political dominance; but, on the whole, let numbers, wealth and territorial advantage take care of that. They had little desire for cultural hegemony, and they viewed Scottish and Irish culture either with a cynical tolerance or with a romantic attraction. It was Tory administrators on the ground who defended native customs against the rationalising, liberal zeal of the Benthamites in the East India Company's offices.[4] Also the English aristocracy were accepting of Scots and Irish with talent and manners getting a share of the patronage. The empire was useful in that respect, and the reformed Civil Service.

[2] Brian P. Levack. *The Formation of the British State: England, Scotland and the Union 1603–1707*, Oxford, Clarendon, 1987, pp. 1–8.

[3] Hugh Trevor-Roper, 'The Highland Tradition of Scotland', in Eric Hobsbawm and Terence Ranger, eds, *The Invention of Tradition*, Cambridge University Press, 1983; and John Prebble, *The King's Jaunt*, London, Collins, 1988.

[4] E. T. Stokes, *The English Utilitarians and India*, Oxford University Press, 1959.

Englishness

The sense of identity of the English is almost as difficult to specify as the name of the state. Perhaps the minimum definition of a nation is a group who think they have the same general characteristics. The difficulties begin when one looks for actual characteristics. It is actually easier for the other nations in the British Isles. There are objective differentiators: in Ireland and Wales religion and language; in Scotland a national history. But there is also, to varying degrees, a helpfully integrative anti-Englishness; or at least a pleasing consciousness of being different from the English.

In all this symposium, the most elusive thing is Englishness itself. Other contributors hint (elsewhere shout) that it is all bad, shouldn't exist or at best that the English are imperceptive of the finest qualities of the others. I think the modern English are often imperceptive. But non-abusive discussions of Englishness are rare. And what is even more odd, they are hard to find among the English. The test is bibliographic. Look at the subject catalogue in any major library under 'nationalism'. One will discover references to shelves of books on nationalism, whether analytical, polemical and celebratory, under American, French, German, Italian, etc., and certainly Irish, Welsh and Scottish, but often none, or astoundingly few, under 'English'. Perhaps a handful of right rubbish written for the Public School prize-giving market of a generation ago.[5] Every year some books of merit appear on what it is to be Scottish and Irish (dozens still on de Crevecoeur's vintage question, 'what then is this American?'), but only a handful of serious reflections on English-ness by Englishmen. Admittedly many novels explore variants of English-ness; but serious studies under 'non-fiction' are few.

Why this dearth? One can pluck from the air conservatively English traits of understatement, taking things for granted, distrust of theory and explicitness, once upon a time a calm contentment that needed no words, and euphemism and suppression; and all those characters in V. S. Pritchett's short stories who never finish sentences, the cult of the social hanging participle. But such explanations are circular. A better one may be political, as I have already hinted: that the old governing class knew that the main business of politics was holding the United Kingdom together. And once, for whatever reasons, the tactic was adopted of tolerating, even stimulating, national cultural identities (so long as state power was not challenged), then it would follow that any deliberate cultivation by the English (as happened everywhere else in nine-teenth century Europe) of a cult of nationalism would be disruptive.

As Burke had argued over the American question, the preservation of power most often involves restraint of power: sovereignty must be tempered by prudence and magnanimity. What even a Boston Anglophile (A. L. Lowell) was to call 'a certain condescension in the English' often caused offence, but historians, statesmen and publicists by and large tried not to make matters

---

[5] Please enter your own references to taste.

worse. Of course, there were notorious exceptions—the Victorian cartoon character Ally Sloper loathed, like Alf Garnett, all foreigners including Scots and Irish; but the evidence of bibliography is clear. And there is another and a related explanation: imperialism became the substitute English nationalism, and the cult of service (and spoils) in Empire was something that could be shared and was shared among the other nations; not merely shared but celebrated in song and story. The Empire was not simply Cobbett's 'system of outdoor-relief for the indigent sons of English aristocracy'. Think how so many of Kipling's imperial tales include figures from each of the four nations (however hierarchically at times). It was the *British* Empire.

This political explanation fits a common stereotype of Englishness: *tolerance*. It is not an attribution at all common before the eighteenth century, but then seemed part and parcel of a consciously sought new era of political stability. 'Fundamentals are dangerous: there are some issues in life which are better left sleeping', said George Savile in *The Character of a Trimmer*, 'we will raise only the issues on which we may disagree without imperilling our country; and even on them we will disagree with buttons on the foils'. Toleration is to be taken seriously, warts and all. After all, it was pursued as policy of state after 1688 and as an Anglican theology of latitudinarianism, trimming between Romanism and Calvinism (the Aristotelian *via media*, I mean, as advocated long before by the judicious Hooker). Protestant toleration still involved discrimination against Roman Catholics, but the motives were mainly political; all things in history are relative and all toleration has limits. Voltaire's image of the tolerant English had another side to the coin, *Albion perfide*. That could almost be a summary of the mental attributes needed to hold the new United Kingdom together: on the one hand toleration; but on the other Machiavellian guile or force against any threat to the unity of the kingdom, perceived as order itself. Hence there was not merely the defeat of a bold, lucky but hopeless foray in 1745, but the savage destruction of the clan system that had made it possible.

Certainly Englishness is to be found more in the specific circumstances of her history, like the reaction to the fear of renewed civil war in both England and Scotland in the 1688 to 1707 generation, than in the 'this sceptred isle' school of thought. Lord Blake's *English World* is a coffee-table book, but a superior one with real matter in it. Yet he says in his Introduction:

England's coastline has helped to shape both the history of the English nation and psychology of the English character . . . The long centuries during which the land was free from invaders meant that there could be a continuity of tradition impossible on the war-torn continent. . . . Some characteristics on which both natives and visitors have tended to agree have to do with national psychology; egoism, self-confidence, intolerance of outsiders, ostentatious wealth, social mobility, love of comfort and a strong belief in private property. . . . We come back to the cliché that Britain is an island, a fact that has been subtly decisive in so many aspects of her history.[6]

---

[6] Robert Blake, ed., *The English World: History, Character and People*, London, Thames and Hudson, 1982, p. 25. Sir Ernest Barker's symposium, *The Character of England*, Oxford,

Notice that he suddenly becomes aware that 'England's coastline' has the slight hiatus of Wales and Scotland, so while the sense of his argument cries out for John of Gaunt's 'England, bound in with the triumphant sea', yet even though he is an English historian and not a geographer he has to say, on sad point of fact, *'Britain* is an island'. Having gone so far he might have noted that before 1688, and spasmodically afterwards, the Celtic periphery was often as 'war-torn' as the continent (some connection with English history?). And more 'subtly' (if he were as subtle as Hugh Kearney), he would see that the land was not always free of invaders (don't Scottish, Welsh and royal armies recruited in Ireland count?); and that 'the continuity of tradition' began in times when neither modern borders nor modern configurations of nationality were applicable; and that at all times then and since the inter-mingling of the people of these islands, their interaction with each other, culturally, socially, economically and militarily, is far, far greater than his (I dare to say) somewhat Little Englander account allows.

Any deep exploration of Englishness must begin by seeing it as a relationship.[7] There is the familiar protest literature of English intrusion, oppression or 'the Englishing of Scotland'. But there is very little that acknowledges frankly the benign effect of the common English language; just as from English thinkers and writers there is little reflection on how much that we call English is a product of dealings with the other peoples. Nonetheless, and here I agree with Lord Blake, a 'strong sense of individual-ism' is remarkable. Alan Macfarlane in his important *The Origins of English Individualism* (1978) sees its roots far earlier than the capitalist market, as Weber, Tawney or C. P. Macpherson had all argued. He sees it in the absence, compared to continental Europe, of a peasant class in the early middle ages, so that even rural society from at least the thirteenth century was remarkably more of a money than a service economy, more mobile and more individualistic, less tied to family and clan. His account of the relative mobility of social class ties in with Namier's famous perception that England at the accession of George III was a highly class conscious country, indeed, but one with a quite unusual and almost infinite gradation of social classes, through which people could rise or fall almost imperceptibly. And Tocque-ville saw in the English concept of 'the gentleman' a bridge between bourgeois and aristocrat lacking in France.

The cult of 'the gentleman' would repay serious study. It was an English product and much emulated. It encapsulated many clichés about the English character: love of property but respect for persons; a certain *savoir faire* going with no great intellectuality; wanting to know what's going on but distrust

Clarendon, 1947 is interesting, but no contributor discusses the 'British' dimension or sees any interaction with 'the others', also the flaw of Gerald Newman's otherwise excellent *The Rise of English Nationalism: A Cultural History, 1740–1830*, London, Weidenfeld, 1987.

[7] As Philip Dodd put it: 'the definition of the English is inseparable from that of the non-English; Englishness is not so much a category as a relationship', in Robert Colls and Philip Dodd, eds, *Englishness: Politics and Culture 1880–1920*, Beckenham, Croom Helm, 1986, p. 12.

of ideas and of aesthetic (as much as of religious) enthusiasm; a love of style but a dislike of ostentation; a refusal to let experts decide but willingness to take advice; a certain respect for amateurishness; a love of leisure and sport and thus a limited capacity for sustained work; a cult of good manners— which, after all, has implications for the parliament house not simply the private house; a social tolerance of the upwardly mobile from trade or industry, but aversion to any obsessive commitment to making money; not to forget, something genuinely and oddly English, a belief that a good life moves back and forth from town to country, country to town; and from all this a conscious cultivation of a somewhat conformist code of behaviour, but resulting in a self-satisfied inner security that allows for a great deal of cynical toleration of eccentricity or even of verbally threatening behaviour. However odd this seems to nationalists today, the cult of the English gentleman had a great integrative or restraining effect (depending on one's viewpoint) on the actual and potential leadership elites of the other three nations. But it had a profoundly negative effect on both entrepreneur- ial spirit and on positive citizenship—it marginalised any putative repub- lican tradition of citizenship in England in marked contrast to Scotland and Ireland.

Orwell's bold attempt to characterise Englishness in *The Lion and the Unicorn* and in *The English People* deserves attention. He sees not the gentry but the lower-middle class as the backbone of an England which, if he sentimentalises it at times, he asserts that he has every right to care for and love as much as Welsh, Scottish and Irish celebrate their countries. And he has no easy answers for what he dislikes in it. He blames these on the English themselves: their snobbishness, the conceit and constraint of class, the greed of the rich—the famous image, 'a family with the wrong members in control'. He cannot take the easy path out of the other nations' intellectuals; to amend Yeats, 'whatever wrongs this country's got the English brought to pass'.

Some of Orwell's insights are eroded by time: 'the gentleness of English civilisation is perhaps its most marked characteristic. You notice it the instant you set foot on English soil. It is a land where the bus-conductors are good-tempered and the policemen carry no revolvers.' And some were truer of the masses than of the classes: 'the English hatred of war and militarism . . . the songs the soldiers made up and sang of their own accord were not vengeful but humorous and mock-defeatist. The only enemy they ever named was the sergeant major.' Orwell assumed a communal fellow- feeling or an habitual fraternal morality, 'common decency', in the lower- middle class and the working class (his 'common man' was close to Kant's and Jefferson's); whereas he thought that the morality of the upper classes had become degraded by a purely competitive individualism. But his common man's morality may well have been attrited by ten years of Thatcherite bombardment in the popular press. Yet his picture of the '*privateness* of English life' still rings true: 'all the culture that is more truly native centres around things which even when they are communal are not official—the pub, the football match, the back garden, the fireside and the "nice cup of tea".' Orwell's celebration of ordinary, commonplace objects, much like H. G. Wells in his early novels (the observations on the proles in *Nineteen Eighty-Four* echo the great description of the bar and of 'the plump woman' in Wells's *Mr Polly*), these show in secular form a kind of Puritan pietism. The ordinary is sacred, whether it is a well-laid brick or a blade of grass: a certain attitude of reverence to nature.

Orwell failed to see that the English character might be affected by, or even itself affect, the other national identities. But in 'Notes on Nationalism' (1944) he made an important distinction between patriotism and national- ism. Patriotism is simply a love of familiar institutions and one's own native land, so that anyone who grows up with these values or beliefs, or adopts them as an immigrant, can be a patriot. Nationalism, however, is the belief that one's country or culture is superior to others. The distinction is useful, even if we use different words to make it or want to use 'nationalism' with qualifying adjectives to cover both cases. At least it could lead one to say that patriotism is natural and as such harmless (unlike too many English left-wing intellectuals who are suckers for everyone else's nationalism while either denying their own obvious Englishness or enjoying rich guilt about it); and also to say that while nations, like persons, are plainly not equal by objective criteria, yet they are, like persons, worthy of equal respect.

It by no means follows, however, that for every nation there must be a state. Such a view is (strong) nationalism as distinct from national sentiment. Or if one must be a nationalist (and certainly in Scotland the word and the feelings associated with it are too important to be surrendered to the separatist SNP), then there is both a strong separatist nationalism and a gentler, open and non- exclusive nationalism. There are multinational states whose unity does not depend on manufacturing a single national consciousness.[8]

Britishness

The English are now very prone to mistake patriotism for a strong nationalism and to forget that the United Kingdom is a multinational state. To try to revive the early Hanoverian 'British nationalism' is futile and is to abandon history for mythology. No assertion of such superiority, whether strident, covert or accidental, is acceptable. And we are, indeed, dealing with overlapping, cross-cutting, interactive but none the less signific- antly different cultural identities. If English nationalism is at least a cultural

[8] A good overview is Walker Connor, 'Ethno-nationalism and Political Instability', in Hermann Giliomee and Jannie Gagiano, eds, *The Elusive Search for Peace: South Africa, Israel, Northern Ireland*, Cape Town, Oxford University Press, 1990. Johannes Degenaar, a political philosopher at Stellenbosch, has written a profound series of reflections on artificial one-nation nationalism as integrative forces, as against a pluralist perspective—for example his *The Roots of Nationalism*, Pretoria, Academica, 1982.

identity, it cannot be shouting in the wind to reprove the Scots for being Scottish (as Thatcher seemed to do, as if it were just a strong provincial modulation of Englishness and need have nothing to do with high politics). Such behaviour is politically provocative and likely to prove self-defeating. Alternatives are not exhausted by the conceptualisation that the present government and the SNP have in common: either the United Kingdom as it is or separation.

It is this confusion of a legitimate if paradoxically under-expressed English-ness with *Britishness* (as Englishness for all) that Tom Nairn and Neal Ascherson acidly call 'Ukanian'.[9] I only differ from them in believing that it is not an inherent aspect of the British state. To prevent this folly cementing itself will need agitation and institutional reform, but the folly was far less in the past than they suggest; and the Conservatives even, as well as the Liberals, once understood this better, through much of the first half of this century, in fact, than the centralising Labour Party. 'British' is a political and legal concept best applied to the institutions of the United Kingdom state, to common citizenship and common political arrangements. It is not a cultural term, nor does it correspond to any real sense of a nation. And nor should it. If in that foreign hotel register I am asked my nationality, I do say 'English'; but if my citizenship, obviously 'British'. To be British demands a kind of loyalty, but a pragmatic loyalty limited to those civic institutions we have in common. (It is rather as Roman citizenship was for peoples outside Latinium). I am a British citizen but I am also English. It happens that I live in Scotland by choice and many of my political and social sympathies are Scottish. If my children had grown up here they could have been Scottish, feeling such and accepted as such. But that cannot be for me at my age; the need for a long period of acculturation is one sure sign of a nation. All this gives me an intellectual and moral conviction that Scottishness is to be taken quite as seriously as Englishness (and both kinds of Irishness too, not to mention that my actual children have a Welsh mother), but taken no more seriously (unless some historical recompense is thought due).

Most Scots I know think of themselves as Scottish and British, perhaps a dual sense of identity, perhaps a more functional differentiation. Some make a great bother of this duality and its due proportions, others wear both coats easily. Most wish to see the terms of the Union revised, but are British in the sense that they still want a union. Most modern English, however, have no sense of this duality at all; to be British is simply to be English. The ignorant and irresponsible under-reporting of Scotland in the London media both illustrates vividly and reinforces constantly this self-deception. And the few English who do see this duality in others find it hard not to sound patronising themselves.

[9] Neal Ascherson, 'Ancient Britons and the Republican Dream', *The Political Quarterly*, vol. 57, no. 3, 1986, reprinted in his *Games with Shadows*, London, Radius, 1988; and Tom Nairn, *The Enchanted Glass*, London, Radius, 1988.

John Mackintosh[b] saw both points when he once spoke of 'two ways in which one can feel Scottish':

One . . . is to feel a resentment against the assumptions of superiority, of absolute standards, so evident in the older British universities, in London media circles, among Whitehall civil servants and so on. The other, when one has been through all these groups and their activities, is to be reasonably confident that the best of what is done in Scotland and by Scots is as good as anything these guardians of proper standards can produce.[10]

And so should the sober Englishman look at the thistle (the leek and the shamrock too). But when he argued the case for devolution, Mackintosh pointed out that it would be all 'self-awareness' but exclude 'nationalist extremism': 'it keeps Scotland in the United Kingdom on the explicit grounds that Scots have a dual nationality; they are English [sic] as well as Scottish'.[11] Surely for once he nods in this minefield of nomenclature. He could have meant what he said: a dual Scottishness and Englishness, but it is a highly questionable claim—even if he were only speaking of himself. He was liked in London and felt thoroughly at ease with the English, but that is not the point. He was so much more Scottish than English, unlike some Scots who spend their working life in the South but visit relatives back North frequently, and become not assimilated but genuinely bicultural. Most Scots are not like that. He surely meant 'British'.

Part of John's true Scottishness was his ease in mixing when a constituency MP with all kinds of classes, whereas his London circle were nearly all from the London professional social classes, those involved in maintaining (well or badly) Britishness, indeed, but notoriously uncertain of the many other class and regional modulations of Englishness. And suppose that he meant what he said (the old way to read a text), his claim to be both Scottish and English; this would have implied deafness to clearly Irish minor themes in Scotland, discordant to his Glasgow ears.

More often the English make this confusion. Some years ago a New Zealand historian of political ideas, J. G. A. Pocock, wrote a remarkable article, 'British History: a Plea for a New Subject', an attack on Anglocentric history as a misreading even of English history and a plea for 'a plural history of a group of cultures'.[12] The new and official National [English] History Curriculum notes the twin difficulty, that English is not British and

---

[10] Henry Drucker, ed., *John P. Mackintosh on Scotland*, London, Longman, 1982, p. 149.

[11] John P. Mackintosh in a pamphlet, *The Case for a Scottish Parliament*, East Lothian Labour Party, Tranent, 1977.

[12] J. G. A. Pocock, 'British History: a Plea for a New Subject', *Journal of Modern History*, no. 4, 1975, p. 603.

[b] John Mackintosh, academic and MP, was for three years Bernard's coeditor on *PQ* but died in office in 1978. For more detail see my note a to Article 25 below, and for an introduction to his life see Tam Dalyell's *ODNB* entry.

yet is much affected by the whole context of these islands, but then passes on doing nothing to remedy it.[13] And Keith Robbins, President of the Historical Association, no less, gave the Ford Lectures at Oxford for 1986–87 on a specifically British approach to nineteenth century history. His published chapter on 'The Identity of Britain' is excellent, except that he talked of a 'Britain' of three nations, not Great Britain, thus excluding Ireland, which sitting as he does in Glasgow made it doubly odd that, in the face of the facts of economic history, he failed to go the whole way. (I completely fail to understand what concept he has of 'integrative' that can exclude Northern Ireland.) Hugh Kearney has given us the only fully integrative account.[14]

After 1920 when the Irish question dropped out of English politics for almost fifty years, both public and official opinion began to lose the old familiarity with 'the United Kingdom question'. After 1950 the end of Empire obviously caused greater psychological problems for the English than for the others. An exaggerated sense of power continued amid visible symptoms of decline. This transformed what had previously been a political virtue into an open wound: the English reluctance to consider a clearly English sense of national identity rather than continue to confound it with a British and, once, an imperial persona. There is now a tendency to put upon the British dimension alone a burden that should have been shared between 'English' and 'British'; but this sharing would have involved for the first time not merely a truly critical self-examination but a far greater empathy for Wales, Scotland and Northern Ireland.

If the distinction can be drawn more clearly, the new immigrants may come to feel more secure—securely British rather than English. (Interestingly people speak of 'Black Britons' not Black English, Welsh or Scottish.) It was the English who seemed (a) to demand of the newcomers that they should become English, and (b) to tell them that it was too difficult. But there is no particular reason why they should become English, unless from individual choice. Like Scots, Welsh and (after all) a majority in Northern Ireland, they could relatively easily and quickly gain a clear British identity—indeed were under some quite proper legal obligation to do so. Enough is enough.

The English ideology

An oddly specific aspect of the English national tradition is usually and unequivocally put forward as British. In times gone by it was needed to

[13] See my review of the National History Curriculum and other books on the United Kingdom question, *The Political Quarterly*, vol. 61, no. 4, 1990, pp. 86–94. [Reprinted in this volume. *Ed.*]

[14] Keith Robbins, *Nineteenth-Century Britain: Integration and Diversity*, Oxford, Clarendon, 1988; and Hugh Kearney, *The British Isles: A History of Four Nations*, Cambridge University Press, 1989.

ensure the unity of the United Kingdom, but today it begins to threaten that unity: the theory of parliamentary sovereignty.

It is uniquely English. That we are the only country in the European Community without either a written constitution or a Bill of Rights demonstrates this. This does not by itself invalidate it. We English may be right that it is uniquely fitting to British conditions. Once it was. It was born in men's minds out of the philosophy of Thomas Hobbes and the experiences of the civil wars throughout the three kingdoms. But its unequivocal assertion in public law was part of the post-1688 settlement, no earlier. Until then everyone had known that power was divided in England between King, Lords and Commons (like 'the trie Estates' in Scotland; and some authorities treated the Church and the Law as quasi-autonomous estates. 'If there had not been an opinion received of the greater part of England that these powers were divided', railed Hobbes, 'the people had never been divided and fallen into this civil war.' But that was the opinion, and the fatal arguments were not about who should wield an unlimited sovereignty but about the relative balance of powers. And, in any case, there were under the same crown, with their own parliaments, Scotland and Ireland. When James I and VI had argued for 'an incorporating union', it was the English Parliament that refused. The Revolution Settlement and the Act or Treaty of Union were crisis measures intended to prevent for ever civil war.

Some Scottish writers need to remind themselves that there are stronger grounds for Scotland's 'Claim of Right' than the belief that Scotland lost its sovereignty through treachery and bribery. (There are democratic arguments, for instance.) In 1707 a majority in the Scottish Parliament, the Scottish Commissioners and almost certainly a majority in the Lowlands (though opinion was divided) saw the urgency for a single overriding authority: to keep the succession in the same hands, to preserve the Protestant religion, to get into the English imperial market, and—very evident as one looks north through Edinburgh streets and sees the Highlands—to preserve peace and order, to end endemic civil war. Federal solutions were discussed but rejected as too speculative, and unlikely in the conditions of the time to provide the security and integration wanted. But most Scots thought that a hard bargain had been struck. All the other important Scottish institutions had been left intact, indeed protected, in the Treaty. There was almost as much difficulty getting the Act through the English Parliament as through the Scottish because the bishops bitterly opposed the intended establishment of the Church of Scotland. The Kirk with its selected ministers and its annual assembly was seen by most as a more representative and national institution than the landowner-dominated and unreformed Parliament of Scotland. The law and the local government (which was nearly all the government there was until the nineteenth century) remained in local hands, with the Kirk vastly influential. It seems to me that the irrefutable historical case for a Scottish Parliament today is less that Scotland was robbed of one in 1707 but that the authority of the Church of Scotland has withered away, leaving

Scotland without any expressive, integrative and policy-making national institution.[15] I am too sceptical of the use of 'sovereignty' as a universal concept to have much sympathy for either the 'give it back' or the 'there was a uniquely Scottish tradition of popular sovereignty' school of thought. To be a good nationalist and a democrat one does not have to be a bad historian.

There was, of course, always a paradox about the new theory of parliamentary sovereignty. Like its intellectual progenitor, Hobbes's *Leviathan*, it was a gigantic bluff. The potential powers were not intended to be used, except to prevent civil war and to preserve law and order. The eighteenth century state was not strong; it was extremely weak and limited in its functions. Indeed the personification of Hobbes's sovereign-Leviathan had not been some English Tamburlaine but one of his own patrons, Charles II, the author of the Act of Oblivion whose main object of policy was 'not to go on my travels again'. The actions of his brother and successor upset such humane or cynical minimalism, and revived fears of religious persecution and civil war.

Even deep into the eighteenth century the new doctrine was not universally accepted. Blackstone intoned that Parliament 'was the place where the absolute despotic power, which must in all governments reside somewhere, is entrusted by the constitution of these kingdoms'. But the rhetorical exaggeration was deliberate, and everyone must have known it. Even so, the young Bentham seized on that passage ten years later in his *Fragment on Government* of 1776 and rudely asked whether Blackstone thought that 'the Switzers and the Germans lack government?', and the great director of the Seven Years War, Chatham, had famously dragged himself to the House of Lords for what proved his dying speech to declare that the Stamp Act was unconstitutional: 'that this kingdom has no right to lay a tax upon the colonies, to be sovereign and supreme in every circumstance'. Chatham's view, of course, did not prevail. Burke, while in equal fury against renewal of American taxation, did not deny the rights of sovereign power; he argued the gross imprudence of exercising them:

I am not going into the distinction of rights. . . . I do not enter into these metaphysical distinctions; I hate the very sound of them. . . . Leave [such arguments] to schools; for there they may be discussed with safety. But if intemperately, unwisely, fatally, you sophisticate and poison the very source of government, by urging subtle deductions and consequences odious to those you govern, from the unlimited and illimitable nature of the supreme sovereignty, you will teach them by these means to call that sovereignty into question.

Like many a practical man, or woman, however, Lord North's mind was programmed with unappraised metaphysical distinctions: he said that 'sovereignty cannot be divided', and thus went away the last chance of conciliating the Americans. Our leaders today should consider Burke's

[15] See my 'The Sovereignty of Parliament and the Scottish Question', in Norman Lewis, ed., *Happy and Glorious: The Constitution in Transition*, Milton Keynes, Open University Press, 1990.

argument deeply. Ministers moved with great speed and some overkill to conciliate Welsh nationalism after 1970 (revealing that Plaid Cymru's priorities lay with the preservation of language and culture by external guarantees more than for Home Rule which—considering that the non-Welsh speaking Welsh are a majority—could actually threaten the language). But Conservative inflexibility over Scotland now leads more and more Scots 'to call that sovereignty into question'.

Pluralism

Blackstone was plainly wrong, and all the English positivist lawyers too. This is important to grasp. It is simply not the case that there 'must in all governments reside somewhere' an 'absolute despotic power'. This view confuses sovereignty with power. Sovereign bodies often lack power, and there can be much power, sometimes more, elsewhere. The theory of sovereignty may have two residual if far from comprehensive applications: (1) to explain and settle jurisdictions: a law is not a law unless it has been passed by a 'sovereign', in our case Parliament (though the sovereign body may, of course, choose to give some other body a superior jurisdiction for defined purposes—as in the Treaty of Rome and the Single European Act); and (2) to remind that in times of emergency concentration of power is essential and ordinary laws may have to be swept aside if a state is to survive. 'When the very safety of the state is in danger, no consideration of good or evil . . .' said Machiavelli; but the republican took that 'when' very seriously as 'only when'. Otherwise, as John Adams said in 1775, 'sovereignty is very tyranny'.

The confusion of sovereignty with power is common, but mainly rhetorical. Further, there is no necessity behind the belief that the more that power is concentrated the more powerful a state can be. Sometimes so, sometimes not. The United States government has great power, internally and externally, without a doctrine or reality of sovereignty (except in time of war and the specific enjoinment on the President to enforce the laws). Many now argue that in the United Kingdom power is so concentrated in Westminster and Whitehall that policies are not merely unresponsive to regional and local needs, but are difficult to implement. The devolution of decision-making is practised by big companies and armies as a way of applying power; but modern British administration is stuck in a time-warp of Blackstonian concepts.

It is not just the case empirically that the United Kingdom is both a multinational state and a highly pluralistic society (regions, religions and different ethnic groups cutting across national boundaries even), but that theoretically we all need to see that political power is always pluralistic; Harold Laski went so far to say in his *Grammar of Politics* that 'all power is federal'. To formulate policy there are always different groups to be con-

245

sidered and conciliated, and to carry out different policies different kinds of agencies are needed, and affect the outcomes.

My theory is that the idea of parliamentary sovereignty had an historical origin (it is not a necessary truth about the nature of politics). That origin was at the time of the union of the three kingdoms. It had some function so long as the main business of British (English?) politics was holding the United Kingdom together, and it worked so long as the governing class understood and tolerated the high degree of actual administrative autonomy in the other nations.[16] But it is now actually a threat to the Union. Ireland might have remained within the Union if Gladstone's Home Rule Bill of 1886, essentially federal, had been passed. And the laws and institutions of the EC now make the theory of parliamentary sovereignty not merely an intellectual nonsense, creating misleading perceptions of reality, but an obstacle (as Charter 88 and many others now argue) to any real constitutional reform. We now need institutions that recognise the diversity. We need, in some sense, federal institutions—though in the facts of the case, the very different circumstances of Scotland, Wales and Northern Ireland, it would neither be a uniform federalism nor merely a dressed-up version of English regionalism as the Labour Party now seems to promise, or threaten.[17]

Under political pressure fixed minds can prove flexible. Both the Northern Ireland Constitution Act of 1973 and the intergovernmental *Agreement* of 1985 pledge the British government to legislate for a united Ireland if a majority clearly wish for and formally consent. Sovereignty is at least not inalienable! The *Agreement* also made the exercise of British sovereignty over Northern Ireland subject to consultation with the Irish government! And it is worth remembering that the old Colonial Office negotiated and freely dispersed federal constitutions to all the old components of the Empire (except to New Zealand, and then only after strong local protests). They understood their business, but federalism was for the lesser breeds within the law, not for the homeland. In the homeland the English ideology thoroughly muddled the concepts of parliamentary government and of the sovereignty of Parliament (Mr Hattersley and Mr Major should visit Canada and Australia urgently for a conceptual jolt).

Federal ideas were common in the old Liberal Party and they now enter the discourse of the Labour Party, even if the leaders are still under the fatal spell of 'winner takes all' power (which is also, as Robin Cook points out, 'loser takes nothing'). Roy Hattersley is by no means the most conservative in his John Bullish defence of parliamentary sovereignty and opposition to electoral reform or a Bill of Rights; he simply talks about it openly. But I can think of no prominent Labour intellectual outside Parliament who does not now argue for some kind of constitutional reform (except John Griffith). And their

[16] See my 'The Sovereignty of Parliament and the Irish Question', in my *Political Thoughts and Polemics*, Edinburgh University Press, 1990, pp. 57–76.

[17] My 'Northern Ireland and the Theory of Consent', in *Political Thoughts and Polemics*, ibid., pp. 77–93.

theoretical framework is now generally pluralist; both the Leninist and the Webbian or old Fabian sovereign, central state are discarded.[18]

The old informal, conventional constitution has outlived its usefulness. Our lack of constitutional law embroils us more and more with the European court and allows a concentration of power that actually restrains the energy of the country. I return to questions of cultural identity. I believe deeply (here I would differ from Christopher Harvie) that the best energy and inventiveness, entrepreneurial spirit as well as the civic spirit, lie in (a great theme of the English novel) 'roots', the provinces and regions, even in England.

We English must come to terms with ourselves. There is so much that is positively good or enjoyably peculiar in our tradition. But we prejudice it by trying nostalgically or sourly to hang on to everything 'that made us great', once upon a time. There is need to shed much dead wood and, above all, not to try to infuse everything that is English into the common property of British. To continue with that bad habit is to make some want to leave home and others, though legally citizens, not feel at home.[19]

[18] For example Mike Rustin, *For Pluralist Socialism*, London, Verso, 1985.

[19] Bhikhu Parekh argues well for taking 'a plural view of British identity' and that 'being British is not a matter of sharing a body of values, for no values are common to all Britons' in 'Britain and the Social Logic of Pluralism', *Britain: A Plural Society*, London, Commission for Racial Equality, Discussion Paper 3, 1989, pp. 58–76.

19 Ambushes and Advances: the Scottish Act 1998

Vol. 66, no. 4, October–December 1995

WELL, 'For a' that, and a' that, it's coming yet for a' that.' 'The Parliament you mean?' 'Aye, I hope so. But there's to be a Bill first. Maybe someone's working on it who means it well; maybe not. We'll have to see what comes out of the mincing machine.'

Labour was pledged by John Smith and has now been pledged also by Tony Blair to legislate for a Scottish Parliament in the first session of a new Parliament, and on the broad lines of the Scottish Constitutional Convention of 1990. The unregenerate might think that report stronger on symbols than on details; but the importance of symbols is not to be denied—for the right audience. 'Aye, there's the rub.' Pledges have a way of coming out in the wash or at least fading badly; but however large or small the majority, Labour will depend on its Scottish MPs and they, even the few private sceptics, feel the breath of the SNP down their necks; after all, the second party in Scotland. 'Remember Govan!' Scottish public opinion is highly volatile. Many Scots vote Nationalist to keep Labour up to scratch on the national question. About a third of Labour voters say they favour independence, and about the same number of SNP voters say they favour devolution.

A new Scotland Bill will have a rough passage through Parliament whatever size majority Labour enjoys, even with Liberal Democrat support. It may be a boon to Britain in the long run, but its importance and complexity will be the bane of Labour's Chief Whip in the run-in of a new government's programme. If the majority is large, the unregenerate and unrewarded will feel free to amend the Bill—not to defeat it, mind, and endanger the government, but to water it down to a degree below proof tolerable in Scotland, perhaps to something as weak and uninspiring as the present proposals for Wales. And if the majority is small, a few English Labour MPs aided and abetted by the Laird o' the Binns[a] may try, just like the Conservative Euro-rebels, to hold the government to ransom. In either case the Tories, in whatever shape, or shapes, will embrace such a potentially destructive issue with hooligan relish; one thing they can all agree on. The Bill will stand and fall on its own. It will have knock-on consequences for constitutional reform, but it will not be presented as the beginning of such a programme. The party is not yet as one on that. How far in these respects the modernising zeal of the leader stretches is by no means clear. While the Scottish project is an example, indeed, of what is meant by devolution in general (and of the alleged swing in Labour thinking from statism to

[a] Tam Dalyell.

pluralism), it is an example, however, very particular and peculiar. Labour has a lot of thinking still to do about general principles for devolution, let alone for a legislative programme. Regionalism could fade away and the city region thinking of the 1960s may yet be Labour's consensus, and the country's. If regionalism comes at all, then it will be as in Spain, with different powers and different speeds for different regions—and with more real content for some than for others. So, because the Scotland Bill will have to be pushed through on its own merits and for Labour's political necessity, it is worth trying to rehearse what is the minimal case from the point of view of the good government of the United Kingdom as a whole.

The minimal case is democratic: a large majority of people want it in a part of the territory of the British state that sees itself, and is seen by the other parts, as a nation. True, to be a nation does not always constitute an especially rational case to be a state. The dangers of such nationalism in the modern world are flagrant, and the possibilities of meeting national aspirations short of separation are many; and that is what the majority of Scots want. The latest ICM polls in the *Scotsman* show only 15 per cent in favour of the status quo, 44 per cent favouring a devolved parliament with some taxing powers, and 35 per cent wanting independence. The case is democratic both in the sense that citizens want it and in the sense that there is need to impose direct public accountability on an already devolved system of government, itself the historical legacy of special treatment that has been needed ever since 1707 to secure Scotland to the Union. The old Tories knew that one of the main businesses of Westminster politics was holding the United Kingdom together.[b] They had some real sense of history; but most of the Thatcher breed live in a myopic blue haze of, as Neil Ascherson acutely observed, 'heritage', an unhistorical construction of English patriotic myths. Not least of these is that parliament has always been and must always be sovereign. If in some narrow legal sense Parliament is sovereign (no laws can be made except by or by consent of Parliament), yet this is, of course, no guide to what can be done or should be done; and the rhetorical use of sovereignty becomes confused with power, tends to assert that we are a socially homogeneous unitary state, and blinds the English political elite who use it to the fact that we are[c] a quasi-federal, multinational state, not at all a simple unitary one, and have been so since 1707.

The argument of *A Claim of Right for Scotland* was basically democratic, namely, what citizens want is to hold government to account.[1] This forceful

---

[1] *A Claim of Right for Scotland*, Campaign for a Scottish Assembly, Edinburgh, 1988, was a document that, despite some unrevised history, stands comparison as a civic utterance in everything but fame with some of the best writings of the American Revolution; there has been little like it since in British politics.

[b] Bernard makes this claim a few times through the articles and reviews in this volume—sometimes even more forcefully than this by saying that it was the principal concern of British politics, at least until the early twentieth century.

and moving document did not depend on what it was at times guilty of: the recycling of bad history. 'Give us back our Parliament!'—and what a feudal relic that parliament was, far less expressive of the commonality than the Church of Scotland; or an imagined medieval Scottish doctrine of sovereignty of the people; or a belief that no good at all came from the Treaty of Union, which 'has always been, and remains, a threat to the survival of distinctive culture in Scotland'. That culture has, in fact, proved admirably hardy, as the authors of those words themselves splendidly epitomised.[2] And as for 'the independence lost in 1707', the union of the crowns in 1603 had at least severely tempered it. But, of course, there is the force of national feeling behind the modern democratic claim. That is where the 'general devolution' argument comes unstuck. No English region even comes close to anything that could reasonably be called in any tortured sense a 'nation' or to having a 'national identity'.

What the Scots don't want

Separation or independence is not the real issue. Even the SNP's recent policy of 'independence in Europe' disguises from most of its followers a more realistic recognition by the more thoughtful among its leadership of a confederal speculation. Just as there is no full independence in Europe, if by independence one means a fully sovereign national state, what is really at issue is the kind of relationship, not the ending of it, between Scotland and the rest of the United Kingdom, a matter for adjustment or even formal renegotiation. If there were some kind of formal independence, some formal legal sovereignty, then economic and social ties alone would make the actual power that the sovereign could hope to exercise far less than what nationalist purists imagine. Ultra-nationalists make the same mistake as the English Eurosceptic Tories: they confuse sovereignty with power, and think by maintaining formal sovereignty they have an unchallengeable ability to carry out premeditated intentions. For once, let the loose cannon term 'power' be defined. Governments can be 'in power' and yet be singularly powerless.[3]

The majority of Scots want devolution or home rule. 'Home rule' implies a *parliament* with more power than a devolved *assembly* and powers somehow, it is at least hoped, entrenched. John Major's claim that devolution or home

---

[2] See Lindsay Patterson, *The Autonomy of Modern Scotland*, Edinburgh University Press, Edinburgh, 1994, for a most thoughtful study of the degree of independence or autonomy that Scotland has long enjoyed. Patterson removes the practical case for a Scottish Parliament from the mists of historical melodrama.

[3] Professor Neil MacCormick, a long-time member of the SNP, has recently written a shrewd demolition of the concept of sovereignty: see 'Sovereignty: Myth and Reality', *Scottish Affairs*, Spring 1995, and 'Beyond the Modern State', *Modern Law Review*, vol. 1, 1993. See also Bernard Crick, 'The Sovereignty of Parliament and the Irish Question', in *Political Thoughts and Polemics*, Edinburgh University Press, Edinburgh, 1990, and 'The Sovereignty of Parliament and the Scottish Question', in Norman Lewis, ed., *Happy and Glorious: The Constitution in Transition*, Open University Press, Milton Keynes, 1990.

rule will lead inevitably to 'the break-up of the United Kingdom' and is 'one of the greatest threats in our history' is a rhetorical invention, not a serious piece of political thinking or social analysis. Teachers will value it as a fine example of that 'fallacy of the excluded middle'. As many have said, the real threat to the United Kingdom lies in not meeting Scottish demands at least half-way, somewhere in the middle, by political compromise. The Prime Minister's folly or opportunism could even be a self-fulfilling prophecy, though it is more likely to be simply water off a duck's back. For the joke is that the English public, at whom this battle cry of 'Save the Union' is aimed, tell the pollsters that they mildly favour Scottish devolution. In so far as the English voters think about it, they appear tolerant and affable; showing no signs of Mr Major's imperial panic. Perhaps they are confused by the government's contrary and more politically astute policies in Northern Ireland. Over there a devolved, indeed a power-sharing, parliament is policy, with even a right to opt out, set down in statutes and joint government declarations, if the people so vote in a referendum.

Some difficulties for the Conservatives are conceptual rather than political. They confuse being English with being British and think that all true Brits should act like the English—their version of English, anyway—whereas most people in Scotland have a sense of double national identity; with constant adjustments and some real tensions, but nonetheless they live with it, are often pleased with it. The identity is, of course, not Scottish or English, but Scottish and British. 'Scottish' connotes a culture, whereas 'British' has a more limited if important legal and political connotation—to be a British citizen. Immigrants sum this up sensibly, and we them, in saying that they are British Hindus, Moslems, Asians, Black, whatever, not Black English, etc. I do not argue against a developed sense of Englishness, quite the contrary—its suppression may have led to an almost paranoid chauvinism; but that sense means accepting Britishness too as a set of historically derived particular relationships with the three other nations, though relationships lacking any democratic institutional clarity.[4]

The other great conceptual confusions that befog this whole question, not only for Tories, attach to 'nationalism' and 'unionism'. Both terms have been hijacked by extremists: on the one hand, the SNP saying that Scottish national identity will wither away without a state (which it has not done for three centuries); and on the other hand, the Prime Minister saying that the devolution project threatens the Union—despite the fact that its supporters wish to stay in the Union. Mr George Robertson MP is as much a unionist as the Prime Minister and as much a nationalist as anyone in Scotland. 'The Union' never implied a centralised, unitary state (quite the reverse), and strong national sentiment does not necessarily imply a separate state. To hold

---

[4] See Bernard Crick, 'The English and the British', in Bernard Crick, ed., *National Identities: The Constitution of the United Kingdom*, Political Quarterly / Blackwell, Oxford, 1991, and 'The Sense of Identity of the Indigenous British', *New Community*, April 1995.

the contrary is either genuine muddle or irresponsible rhetoric. The old Tories had some knowledge of and took some pleasure in the diversity of the United Kingdom; the new Tories, none.

What is being asked

What is being asked is less drastic than most imagine, even if enough, as we will see, to involve real problems—albeit resolvable problems, if faced in time. To summarise the Convention's report:

1 The parliament should be directly elected by an electoral system other than 'first past the post'.
2 Its structures and procedures should enable equal representation of women and men and fair representation of ethnic and other groups, and ensure the transparency of its work.
3 The parliament's powers are to cover all functions of government except defence, foreign affairs, central economic and fiscal responsibilities, and social security policy.
4 A parliament office should be opened in Brussels.
5 A single-tier system of local government was foreseen.
6 The Islands areas require separate constitutional consideration.
7 A charter of rights should guarantee fundamental rights within Scottish law.
8 Revenues should be assigned to the parliament, which could vary the rate of income tax (to plus or minus 3p in the pound).

And from a supplementary report by the Scottish Constitutional Commission, chaired by Joyce McMillan:

9 The parliament to be 112 members, 72 elected first past the post in the ordinary constituencies and 40 taken from party lists according to the proportion of the vote in the eight Euro-constituencies, with each voter voting both for an individual and for a party list drawn up in each Euro-constituency.
10 Failure to agree on how to achieve in law the Convention's objective of 'equal representation for women', so only voluntary measures suggested to the parties, but a series of useful proposals to make parliament user-friendly to women.
11 That the Enabling Bill should commit the Scottish parliament to observe the principle of subsidiarity in relation to Scottish local government.[5]

The powers demanded are those exercised at present by the Secretary of State for Scotland. What will happen to that office when there is a Scottish executive responsible to Parliament and with a Prime Minister elected from it was left unclear. Some link with the United Kingdom Cabinet is needed, even if different parties or coalitions might control Edinburgh and Westminster. Perhaps when different forms of devolution are in place in Wales and

[5] Since few people south of the border have a clue what the actual commitment is, see *Towards Scotland's Parliament: A Report to the Scottish People by the Scottish Constitutional Convention*, 1990, and *Further Steps Towards a Scheme for Scotland's Parliament: A Report to the Scottish Constitutional Convention by the Scottish Constitutional Commission*, 1994, both published by Scottish Constitutional Convention, £2.50 each at Rosebery House, Edinburgh EH12 5XZ.

Northern Ireland, a single Secretary of State for the United Kingdom or for constitutional affairs might in time replace the present three.

Notice that the Scottish Labour Party was won round to a compromise form of PR, but PR nonetheless. The example may prove important and make it more and more difficult for Labour as a whole to continue to hedge and dodge the issue. The Scottish Labour Party was wise to recognise that the prospect of one-party government would deter some popular support for a Scottish Parliament, and canny enough to see advantages in being majority partner in what could be long-lasting coalitions rather than to run the risk of the customary all or nothing, in or out lottery. This penny has not yet dropped into a good many Labour skulls at Westminster, but will as the popularity of a new government almost inevitably begins to decline.

The Convention produced only a few thoughts on how the parliament might operate, beyond a strong hint that it should not be a mini-Westminster—as was plainly envisaged in 1978—and should be more democratic and consensual. There are opportunities for innovation in many respects. Parliament could have a fixed term and could only exceptionally meet outside normal working hours or in school holidays. The timetable could be set by a cross-bench business committee. In a smaller parliament the chairs or conveners of committees could work more closely with ministers, and the number of ministers be kept small—hence no payroll vote. Questions could be answered and debates initiated in response to public petitions. A state-of-the-art computerised parliamentary *and* public information service could be set up from the very beginning. All that Nolan wants and more could be built into Standing Orders so that substantial outside involvement and interests would be a bar to membership. Best foreign practice could be adapted. In scores of ways, great and small, the new parliament could not merely break from the Westminster mould but be a proving ground and example both for future reforms at Westminster and for any future English and Welsh regional assemblies. At last there is a chance to break out of the straitjacket of traditional British institutions and parliamentary practices, so ill-defined in public law and so stultifying not just to particular innovations but to any general spirit of innovation.[6]

Problems: the Tamnable question

Yet the Bill will have a rough passage. Over-representation of Scotland in Westminster will be raised (and is a real problem), and so will the West Lothian question. The Tamnable question is by itself meaningless if it takes the form of asserting that something is unconstitutional; but it does raise some

[6] See *Making Scotland's Parliament Work*, John Wheatley Centre, Edinburgh, 1991, and a revised version to appear later this year [1995] as *To Make the Parliament of Scotland a Model for Democracy*, compiled by David Millar and Bernard Crick and trailed as 'A Democratic Model' in *Fabian Review*, June 1995.

constitutional dilemmas. To say that it is anomalous for Scottish MPs to be able to vote on English matters whereas English MPs cannot vote on Scottish matters is to beg the question, anomalous to what? Presumably to some purported rule of the constitution ('natural justice' might be safer but vaguer): that it is wrong for some MPs to be able to vote on some matters and others not; or for some to have a general competence and others not. There is force in that if some component of justice is the generality of a rule's application. Even Mr Robin Cook was reported as saying, with rash spontaneous sincerity, that it would be wrong for him to hold responsibility for or vote on English health matters when health boards in Scotland became responsible to a Scottish Parliament.

But this is to forget two things. First, it is to forget the fifty-odd years of the Stormont Parliament when the question was never raised against the twelve Ulster MPs (nor will it be if power-sharing comes in a new Northern Ireland parliament; just a huge sigh of relief in the Commons), not to mention the hundred-and-one other anomalous particularities that have been thought necessary to hold the United Kingdom together without provoking nationalist troubles. Consider the anomalous status of the Welsh language in public law, and how unjust, some say, to English immigrants to North Wales. If there were a written British constitution, the West Lothian question either would have to be resolved or would never arise. But just these anomalous concessions needed to hold the Union together were crucial elements in the old, unreformed, informal constitution. Consider that the old 'dependency culture' welfare state, attacked by Thatcher, despised by Portillo, still chugs along grinding out goodness in Northern Ireland for rather obvious political reasons—or, if 'politics' should not sully the constitution, then say for clear reasons of good government.

Secondly, it is to forget that even Scotland's over-representation, while it did not arise as a deliberate guarantee that its national institutions would be respected, yet can be justified as helping to serve that constitutive purpose in the absence of entrenchment in a written constitution. While there is not such a constitution, one's choice of offensive constitutional anomalies is likely to be a wee bit partial. Constitutional purism is found only in school textbooks where an exact answer is needed to every question. Tam Dalyell was against the Scotland and Wales Act anyway, remember? So was Enoch Powell, who coined the phrase in tribute to Tam's forensic skills. But constitutionally one thing is reasonably clear: that Westminster is the *United Kingdom* Parliament, so that elected Scottish MPs can debate and vote on any United Kingdom matter. If English MPs don't like that, the rational answer is a federal constitution with an English parliament as well as a United Kingdom one. James Cornford recently said that 'the problem here is that none of the answers which are constitutionally coherent are politically acceptable'. But this is really an argument for a coherent constitution, such as he (and I, and many others) advocate in principle (though in practice it is going to be one thing at a time and sort out the consequences later). Meanwhile Professor

James Kellas's words are wise: 'It is a mistake to look for a one-dimensional answer to the territorial politics of the United Kingdom. What matters is a correct perception of what the constituent nations want at this time. Once that is known, then the system should adapt to accommodate their wishes.'[7] Why should it adapt? The answer is the same as that Dicey and Ivor Jennings gave to the question why governments should not break *conventions* of the constitution when by law they may, namely the political consequences of so doing; or, to paraphrase Geoffrey Marshall, conventions are what those who want to play a game agree as the rules needed to play that game.

Westminster would still be able to debate anything it likes about Scotland (there was the occasional adjournment debate on Stormont matters), just as the Scottish Parliament should be free to debate and pass resolutions on reserved matters; all that the two Speakers would rule out of order is asking Questions and moving Bills on devolved or reserved matters. But what can never be ruled out in the absence of a constitutional court is Westminster passing a Bill amending the Scotland Act 1998, even abolishing it—as Stormont was first prorogued and then abolished. The Scottish Constitutional Convention demanded that powers be entrenched and subject to change only with the consent of the Scottish Parliament. But under our good old constitution the best brains can suggest no sure way how this can be done; only delays through parliamentary procedure. Here, indeed, is the residual meaning of 'sovereignty of parliament'. But equally, if the sovereignty of parliament doctrine is invoked against the anomaly, the logical reply is that with this very sovereignty parliament can devolve or renounce its authority, and even legislate to surrender it entirely, for instance, to the result of a referendum. And the response to that reply is that 'any future parliament' (why not the same parliament?) could then legislate to repeal the Act and annul the unfortunate result of the referendum. And so on, in circles. 'Logic', says Kellas, 'has never been a feature of the British Constitution.' Conservative objectors 'on constitutional principle' should realise that such is the constitution we have got, rather than inventing new conventions as election cries, especially when they have felt somewhat free of late to break old ones. Such uses and abuses discredit what they wish to honour and preserve. But the Labour Party, especially its Scottish MPs, while knowing that a Scottish Parliament will have to live without entrenchment, should consider what might happen if a Conservative government comes back in 2002. These night thoughts could lead to considering either comprehensive constitutional reform or simply electoral reform to achieve the same safeguard politically. But once in power and elated by power Labour will probably gamble once again on winner-take-all next time round in the tradition of sporting gentlemen. Constitutional reform can only take place by consensus or from commanding power, not as a belated reaction to fear of its loss.

[7] James Kellas, 'A Decision Best Made by Trusting the People', *Parliamentary Brief*, February 1995.

The West Lothian question is usually raised simply to discredit the whole devolution project; but the alleged abuse will continue so long as entrenchment of devolved powers is impossible. In any case it is unimportant by comparison with more positive reasons for or even against the project. The anomaly will be lived with until such time as our anomalous constitution becomes numinous.

Other problems

The over-representation of Scotland is not something that the Conservative Party will let go away long after they have forgotten what the West Lothian question was, let alone that it had no answer. Nor has Labour always been entirely happy. When the party first converted to devolution, more or less, in August 1974 at the special conference in Glasgow, John Smith said that it would be 'dishonest' for Scotland to expect an assembly and yet retain the same number of seats at Westminster.[8] The present number of seventy-two Scottish MPs would be reduced to fifty-seven if the two boundary commissions worked to the same criteria. This imbalance could be said to be Scotland's 'guarantee', in the terms James Callaghan used to try to justify his notorious increase in the Ulster seats (the surrender of a valuable political bargaining counter for what proved to be nothing). But it is unlikely that any future Conservative government would accept both over-representation and the continuance of Scottish devolution. They could use either as a weapon against the other. They are unlikely to let sleeping dogs lie as in the old days. We are in a time of heightened political passions and the breakdown of old conventions. Hard bargains will have to be struck at some stage, even if the Scotland Bill 1998 is silent on the matter. What bargains will be struck will depend at least as much on political circumstances as on constitutional imagination and inventiveness. The bargaining counters may reach into other matters: electoral reform, House of Lords reform, powers and composition of regional assemblies, even radical parliamentary reform,[9] some kind of constitutional court, perhaps.

There will inevitably be grey areas between powers devolved and powers retained. Formal structures will be created to try to resolve disputes between either the two executives or the two parliaments. Such uncertainties and disputes are familiar to many workable systems of government elsewhere and are not entirely different from how town hall and Whitehall used to negotiate before ministers turned Draconian rather than Socratic. Objections on grounds of uncertainty cannot in logic be objections in principle, though they may be symptoms of objections in principle. To say that many

[8] Quoted by James Mitchell in his astringent 'Pitfalls for Labour', *Parliamentary Brief*, February 1995.
[9] I have in mind proposals like Graham Allen MP's *Reinventing Democracy: Labour's Mission for the New Century*, Features Unlimited, London, 1995, that go beyond an internal tidying-up as in Derek Fatchett MP's *Reforming the Commons*, Fabian Discussion Paper no. 19, 1995.

boundaries are uncertain by the criteria is not to say that the principle of having boundaries is self-contradictory. Where to draw the line (or, if the line is clear, whether to respect it or not) is always a pragmatic and negotiable problem; but having lines is a matter of principle. Even the most extreme sovereignty-of-parliament Europhobes, for instance, must believe that there are some things both that Parliament cannot do and should not do.

What is more interesting is what will happen if many disputes over powers raised by affected individuals or organisations come to the courts, perhaps even disputes that are really between the parliaments. The 1978 Act envisaged the judicial committee of the Privy Council as a final Court of Appeal. Depending on the volume and complexity of litigation, this could lead to a constitutional jurisdiction, at long last. The extent and nature of possible appeals to the European Court against UK legislation and decisions of ministers on Scotland is another enigma, even if no longer a novelty in other fields.

The demand of the Convention for a charter of rights 'for special protection . . . over and above the protection afforded by ordinary legislation' was admirably brief but ingenuously evasive as to whether the parliament itself could be held in breach of the Charter by the courts, and if so what remedy there would be to a plaintiff. Proposals for a UK bill of rights or incorporation of the European Convention on Human Rights face a similar difficulty or point of no return. If either parliament legislates to allow its legislation to be overruled, then we are half-way to a written constitution. They could, of course, legislate to overthrow a court's decision, and far more easily than when in the USA a constitutional amendment is needed. But at that point the European Court could also become involved. Enoch Powell is right. We gave away our sovereignty on that fatal day so long ago (not all of it, exactly). But it is quite right that we did.

The greatest parliamentary struggle is likely to be over financial provisions. The Convention said that it sought 'an arrangement for financing Scottish expenditure which will give Scotland's Parliament the kind of independence and flexibility it would require, while retaining an element of equalisation based on Scotland's needs and disadvantages'. This, they said, would be based on a system of 'assigned revenues', that is revenues 'assigned . . . as of right on the following basis':

(a) There should be assignation of all Scottish income tax to Scotland's parliament and if possible the assignation of all Scottish VAT (or a reasonable estimation thereof).
(b) There should also be a power for Scotland's parliament to vary the income tax rate, but there should be some range defined so that the variation in income tax up or down cannot be misunderstood as being by a wide margin (3p up or down now seems agreed between Labour and the Liberal Democrats in Scotland).
(c) Equalisation should continue to be based on assessment of needs starting from the present formula basis (the Barnett formula that succeeded the Treasury's Goschen formula).

And this, they added, should be reviewed on a regular basis (a hostage to fortune they could live to regret).

Alarming funny figures have been launched by government ministers about either the taxes that would be needed or the huge shortfall there would be once the cable were cut. They would make the flesh of many Scottish voters creep if believed. But the intention is not to cut the cable. Scotland will remain a real and active part of the Union. The funny figures are all based on the premise that the equalisation grant would cease. That is a very odd assumption or threat, especially coming from unionists. The public finances of nearly all civilised states have provision for transfer payments or equalisation grants to help poor or special regions.

In fact Scotland pays about 5 per cent less in taxation to central government than the UK average, but that is because of lower per capita income. Scotland receives a noticeable 20 per cent in public expenditure above the UK average; but this is due not to public subventions to keep the Scots happy and the Union, nor, as is widely believed, to the size and dispersal of the population, but mainly to social security entitlements. Perhaps, short of stimulating employment, the government has some more Swiftian solution to the problem of the Scottish poor? But, of course, these aggregates conceal, as they do for England and Wales, some dramatic regional variations. Under devolution both these variations and the whole Scottish budget would be more visible, and more contestable. An economist warns that 'there can be little doubt that the democratic gain achieved from devolved power for Scotland would entail some economic cost which might exacerbate sectional conflicts within Scotland'. But he then points out that there would be economic gains in the great scope for a partly independent economic policy adjusted more closely to local needs.[10]

With genial cynicism the Chancellor has said that £600 a year per Scot would be needed to keep present standards; leave alone playing with 3p up or down, Jonathan Aitken presents that as a 16 per cent rise in income tax. But both these projections apply only, in Aitken's own words, if 'a devolved or independent Scotland were no longer underpinned by the present UK public expenditure formula'. This may be a good case against independence but not against devolution. Again they play the fallacy of the excluded middle. Is this just electoral rubbish or do they believe that if Labour brought these things to pass and they then returned to power, they would abolish the formula? Why? To punish the Scottish electorate or to drive Scotland out of the Union? Quoting these figures in an acute analysis of the politics of Scottish public expenditure, Professor David Heald pointedly digressed into Northern Ireland to cite the 1982 White Paper *A Framework for Devolution*: 'under full devolution the level of public expenditure in Northern Ireland would be determined, through existing PES arrangements, in the light of Northern

---

[10] Clive H. Lee, 'If Edinburgh Found Itself Paying the Bills', *Parliamentary Brief* , February 1995.

Ireland's particular needs and the public expenditure policies of the United Kingdom as a whole, taking account also of the views of the Assembly'.[11] No government, he commented, will ever succeed in convincing the Scottish electorate that obvious differences between Northern Ireland and Scotland are relevant to the principles of equalisation in public finances. Tory back-benchers will, of course, succeed in convincing themselves; and perhaps a few northern Labour MPs will be tempted to cause trouble to extract concessions, American-style.

The Tories should stick to the 3p. That will be worrying enough to some and Scottish Labour is brave to face it, to say to their voters that if you want real differences, if you want better public services, you will have to pay for them. They are saying this, indeed, more clearly than the party south of the border. Undoubtedly, as in the past, when the anti-devolution argument gets put in a general election (or perhaps in a referendum; for if the parliamentary going really gets tough, that escape hatch could be uncovered again), especially when it gets put in such terms, the present size of the pro-devolution vote will undoubtedly diminish. But it is inconceivable from the present size of it and the national sentiment behind it that it can collapse.

The Tories seem on a hiding to nothing, or very little, in Scotland itself, and there is no sign that opposition to devolution stirs middle England; but nonetheless they will seek to raise the greatest possible clamour and do any damage possible to the Bill in Parliament. Even if their capacity to do such damage is severely limited by the election results, they will try hard on the one negative cause that can help them to reunify. A more imaginative leader would have long ago embraced devolution, but on unfavourable tax terms and with a radical diminishment of parliamentary representation. That was Mrs Thatcher's initial plan when first in opposition, a line of thought going back to Edward Heath in 1968 and Sir Alec Douglas-Home in 1970.

Two things could aid the passage of the Bill greatly: a procedural technicality and a style of public discourse. The technicality is to have a short Bill transferring the powers of the Secretary of State for Scotland to a parliament in Edinburgh and setting out financial provisions, but then stating that all previous statutes and orders stand amended in light of that transfer of powers. The Scotland Bill of 1977 was ill-prepared and badly drafted, but the main problem was that it was drafted as the parliamentary counsel will, in terms of black-letter common law: every clause of every Act that ever there was that would be affected was set down in endless schedules to stand amended one by one; an unprecedentedly lavish and generous dog's dinner, as it proved, for endless debates and amendments, gruelling procedural obstruction and delay. An enabling clause could, of course, lead to many challenges in the courts about conflicts of law, just what the extensive drafting

[11] David Heald and Neal Geaughan, 'Financing a Scottish Parliament', paper presented at the conference 'Beyond Westminster—the Practical Issues', organised by the John Wheatley Centre and the Institute for Public Policy Research, April 1995.

of statutes seeks to avoid. But these would come from real litigants with real interests, not from parties or factions of MPs using antique procedures to frustrate clear mandates and popular will. (All this must be drafted or be indicated before office; the Civil Service does not work that way.)

Scottish spokesmen must beware that the advocacy used for the project in Scotland does not always go down a treat in Westminster. The style of popular discourse that would aid the Bill's passage will be for the party leader and other English frontbenchers to seize every opportunity to assert our own patriotism, British and English: to stress that the Bill invites us English to think again about the real nature of the United Kingdom as, at its best, a proud partnership of nations (not an extended English state) who deal with each other robustly but respectfully, enjoying and celebrating national differences. This is true unionism; true nationalism, even.

20 Hannah Arendt and the Burden of Our Times

Vol. 68, no. 1, January–March 1997

MANY have written more clearly about the dynamics of modern despotisms, about the causes and nature of the concentration camps in both Germany and the Soviet Union, and about the fundamental conditions of European civic republicanism and its seeming decay into individualistic consumerism.[a] But no one other than Arendt has tried so hard to see the links between these different phenomena and to set up a mirror by which European civilisation can recognise its faults and perhaps seize a last chance to renovate its house before some other great disaster, or at best a gradual decay of civic spirit and public values, a privatisation of all concerns, comes about. (That is, if that disaster has not already occurred: what does it bode for the future that the Bosnian 'cleansings' and the massacres in 'far away' East Africa were allowed to continue so long, and that the former Soviet Union has been left to rot rather than helped to the hilt to establish and stabilise free institutions?)

However, until at least a decade after her death in 1975 Hannah Arendt's reputation stood far higher in the United States than in Great Britain. Perhaps this is due to the greater openness of American higher education to thinkers who do not fit easily in the procrustean beds of academic disciplines, and the consequently greater interchange there between academia and quality or intellectual journalism; and also to the greater openness of New York than the Oxbridge–London triangle to the ideas of the refugee generation from Germany. In the USA there have for a long time been more people willing and able to cross what here in the UK is still that great editorial divide (despite Orwell, or why he is still held in despite by some) between politics and literature, not to mention a certain lingering intellectual parochialism. Consider that in New York Arendt's closest and most understanding friend, literary executor indeed, was the late Mary McCarthy, novelist and critic; and W. H. Auden knew and admired her too (bizarrely he wanted to marry her, presumably wanting a nanny with intellectual and cosmopolitan class).[1] Only recently have Arendt conferences broken out here—in the States they have

---

[1] Elizabeth Young-Bruel's biography, *Hannah Arendt: For Love of the World*, London, Yale University Press, 1982, is excellent on both thought and life. Arendt would, of course, have denied the disjunction, up to a point.

[a] The article was written as part of the occasional 'Reputations' series current in the journal at the time. Bernard was effectively *PQ*'s Arendt specialist: see his reviews of *The Human Condition*, *Eichmann in Jerusalem* and *On Violence* in this volume.

been legion[2]—and probably the best of many books and symposia about her, certainly the best for clear exposition and good judgement, has come from an English author.[3]

The first British edition of Arendt's famous *The Origins of Totalitarianism* (New York, 1951) was titled *The Burden of Our Time*. That title could hardly have seized the attention of historians and political scientists, nor was Fred Warburg known or knowing among scholars. Secker & Warburg had sprung to prominence and prosperity as Orwell's last publisher, and as having the English rights of Thomas Mann and Kafka. But Warburg was not entirely wrong to see her as keeping the company of such writers and thinkers (who are probably more influential in directly shaping the concepts by which we perceive the world than are social scientists and historians). So the book, as well as being long and difficult and by an unknown author, appeared in Britain with a title of ambiguous connotation that in some way made better sense than the American title—but only when one had got into the book. Only a literary reviewer, Al Alvarez, was fully perceptive as well as unreservedly enthusiastic about what she was trying to say. She was writing, indeed, about the dreadful burden of guilt and horrified astonishment of our times. *How* could such things be done at all that were done so deliberately and in such cold blood in the camps? After all, most people in the wartime USA and UK, hearing rumours or reading unconfirmed underground reports, simply did not believe what was happening; and it is facile to attribute this simply to anti-semitism or scepticism about Zionist propaganda. We did not believe that human beings could do such things to other human beings, deliberately, cold-bloodedly and *en masse*.

Arendt was not writing primarily as historians and some sociologists thought (and then faulted her because of this thought), about *why* this happened—an historical, empirical account of the causes of totalitarian-

[2] The commentator of an Arendt symposium at the American Political Science Association's 1996 annual conference, George Kateb, who himself has written well and not uncritically about her (*Hannah Arendt: Politics, Conscience and Evil*, Oxford, Martin Robertson, 1984) demanded a five-year moratorium and complained that all kinds of people and causes, for which she had little sympathy or to which she gave little attention, such as environmentalists and feminists, anarchists and New Right conservatives, were now trying to claim her by arcane deconstruction of obscure or peripheral texts. May and Kohn (see note 3) in their bibliography cite 324 articles and 21 books about her in English alone.

[3] Margaret Canovan, *Hannah Arendt: A Reinterpretation of her Political Thought*, Cambridge, Cambridge University Press, 1992. Differing viewpoints can be found in M. A. Hill, ed., *Hannah Arendt: The Recovery of the Public World*, New York, St Martin's Press, 1979; Bhikhu Parekh, *Hannah Arendt and the Search for a New Political Philosophy*, London, Macmillan, 1991; Gisela T. Kaplan and Clive E. Kessler, eds, *Hannah Arendt: Thinking, Judging, Freedom*, London, Allen & Unwin, 1989; Philip Hansen, *Hannah Arendt: Politics, History and Citizenship*, Cambridge, Polity, 1993; Lewis P. Hinchman and Sandra K. Hinchman, *Hannah Arendt: Critical Essays*, Albany State University of New York Press, 1994; Lisa Disch, *Hannah Arendt and the Limits of Philosophy*, Ithaca, Cornell University Press, 1994; Larry May and Jerome Kohn, *Hannah Arendt: Twenty Years After*, London, MIT Press, 1996; and, to mention only one article, Judith Sklar, 'Hannah Arendt as Pariah', *Partisan Review*, 83, pp. 64–7.

ism—but about how it *could* happen at all. Many were, indeed (and still are), sceptical about the very concept of totalitarianism that then appeared to be, following the American title, the subject matter in all subsequent editions and revisions.[4] I know of no political theorist in Britain who reviewed the original *Burden of Our Time*. When political theorists did come to look at it, the then prevailing tone of logical positivism or linguistic analysis would have inclined many to share Isaiah Berlin's *ex cathedra* judgement. He once said to me, apropos of kind words about my *In Defence of Politics* (the second edition of which, he noticed, carried an explicit acknowledgement, or dawning recognition, of Arendt's influence): 'We seem to agree on most things except your admiration for de Jouvenel and Miss Arendt. Could you summarise either of their arguments for me in brief propositions?'

'That's a tall order.'

'Indeed, can't be done. Sheer metaphysical free-association. Fairy gold, Bernard, fairy gold, I beg you to notice.'

But I still beg to differ.

Arendt certainly irritated Berlin mightily, for when the *Observer* sometime back in the early 1960s ran a mischievous one-off feature, 'Most Over-rated Authors of the Year', Berlin contributed not with a paragraph of more or less reasoned denunciation, but with two words: 'Hannah Arendt'. And there are things to irritate. She could be verbose, repetitive and eager to say everything at once, and every time; as if, when she started writing and the writing appeared in different journals, she was unsure, understandably whether she had a continuing readership. I think she was primarily an essayist and a speculative, contemplative thinker. *Between Past and Future* (1968), *Men in Dark Times* (1970) and *Crises of the Republic* (1972) were, indeed, all collections of essays. I think her least successful books were those in which she tried to be a fully systematic thinker, as in her final and unfinished purely philosophical volume *The Life of the Mind* (1978). Even her most ambitious book, *The Human Condition* (1958), is less systematic than it appears, more like a set of variations on two great and profound themes, some harmonising well, others discordant and thus 'unsuccessful', but all provoking what she valued and gave us above all: active thought. Even her two most contentious books, *Eichmann in Jerusalem: A Report on the Banality of Evil* (1961) and *On Revolution* (1963) are long essays, far from even attempting to be fully systematic or comprehensive treatments. Only her short book, *On Violence* (1969) achieves the symmetry of form and content of great political writing. Berlin, who writes as well as Conrad, might make some allowance for the more usual difficulties of writing English as a second language in maturity. So, in the image that he popularised, she is a supreme example of fox appearing to be hedgehog. With

---

[4] Elsewhere I have argued that while the concept does not work descriptively—no 'totalitarian' system has ever exercised total control over society—yet the ideological attempt to do so was real and accounts for most of the ruthlessness and lack of normal political and human restraints of Nazism and Bolshevism, not to mention Maoism and Pol Pot's Khmer Rouge. See my 'On Rereading *The Origins of Totalitarianism*', in Hill, ed., *Hannah Arendt*, pp. 27–47.

Berlin, I think that the story of human freedom is one of many foxes, the plurality of thoughts and thinking in a civilised, civic context, rather than the invocation of one or other of those hedgehogging, all-consuming big thoughts; but I would like to persuade him that she was a great fox for freedom, if her more than occasional vices of exposition can be forgiven and the reasons for her inconsistencies understood. Her pretensions can at times irritate: for example, a bad old Germanic habit of appearing to think that the original meanings of concepts should be returned to through philology—in fact she knew better, but liked to parade her erudition (pretending to be a hedgehog). And it took a long time before those in the British empiricist tradition could see that her existentialism, taken pure from Jaspers and tainted for a while by Heidegger, was more than the card-castle of neologisms that passed for philosophy in Sartre and was closer to the humanism of Kant (ever moving between Newton and Rousseau: 'the wonder at the starry heavens above and the moral law within').

Return to the *Origins*

One step forward, two steps back. *The Origins of Totalitarianism*, Arendt's first published book, looks the most systematic, but it is not. Part One on 'Anti-Semitism' and Part Two on 'Imperialism' are somewhat loosely connected to Part Three on 'Totalitarianism' which contained her basic concern, our common burden of failure and guilt: how the Holocaust could ever have happened. She saw this as not necessarily a unique event, if measured by numbers and suffering over the whole sweep of human history (she was irritated at arguments that treated it 'as a Jewish possession'), but as a unique horror and shame for our times in that it negated, came near to destroying, the liberal hopes of progress ascendant in Europe and America before the First World War. Not that, as we will soon see, she thought these liberal ideas unflawed, even if they could not be held responsible for what happened in the camps simply because of their alleged 'emptiness', or by their deification of the self-contained individual (in some strained sense 'lonely' or 'anomic'), as some conservative and even a few social theorists maintained.

Her explanation begins with the breakdown of liberal expectations of a rational and peaceful international order. The First World War, she argued—whatever its causes, profound or contingent—smashed the old system. The idea of total war could come to be applied to social change; and the Great War released two irrational demonic-like forces destroying civic structures and rational expectations, especially in Germany: mass unemployment and hyperinflation. The peace settlement was based on nationalism rather than constitutionalism and, in turbulent conditions, nationalism could easily turn to racialism as scapegoats were sought for economic and political failure. Racialism and anti-semitism explained much of what then happened, providing the impetus to scapegoat and exterminate hated minorities, and one particularly large minority, not just in Germany.

Part of Arendt's bold explanation has led to misunderstanding. She was not saying that English, French, Belgian or even German imperialism was a direct cause of Nazism, but that, first, the dream of an imposed universality created a new type and scale of thinking (she quoted Cecil Rhodes saying he 'dreamed in centuries and thought in continents'); and, second, such incidents as the Congo massacres and exploitation-to-death showed that a contempt for human life could coexist with modernity, or, more subtly and terribly, that such lives were thought not to be human. It then became 'proved' to the Nazi racialists in the extermination camps (no longer mere concentration camps) that Jews were not human: for they did not revolt, some dug their own graves, and individuals when degraded and rendered utterly desperate lost all mutual care and sociability which, to her, is the very mark of humanity.

Part of the 'totalitarian thesis' was, of course, the perception that there was something held grimly in common by Hitlerism and Stalinism. Arendt was not the first to have had this idea, and was a little cavalier not to have noted (or even noticed, perhaps) that certain intellectuals and political writers, all outside the academy, had had this dark thought even in the 1930s: notably Borkenau, Gide, Koestler, Malraux, Orwell and Silone. Certainly the book is gravely unbalanced between a detailed treatment of Germany and a general-ised and sketchy treatment of Russia. But the thesis was sound in one vital respect. She could deal with the seeming irrationality of the irrational by invoking, in a special sense, the concept of ideology: how crazy ideas of the gutter or the library desk could become state policy in both regimes. Never before had two sets of ideas claimed to be comprehensive and predictive explanations of human conduct and become state policy And there were only the two such ideologies, both modern: that of racial determinism and that of economic determinism. All other purported ideologies—better to use another word, say 'doctrines'—were in fact (thank God, or common sense), however good or bad, partial. Some reject this 'partiality'; others accept it as part of the good plurality of existence. As Arendt wrote in the first edition:

While the totalitarian regimes are thus resolutely and cynically emptying the world of the only thing that makes sense to the utilitarian expectations of common sense, they impose upon it at the same time a kind of supersense which the ideologies always meant when they claimed to have found the key to history or the answer to the riddles of the universe. Over and above the senselessness of totalitarian society is enthroned the ridiculous supersense of its ideological superstition. Ideologies are harmless, uncritical and arbitrary opinions only as long as they are not believed in seriously Once their claim to total validity is taken literally they become the nuclei of logical systems in which, as in the systems of paranoiacs, everything follows comprehensibly and even compulsorily once the first premise is accepted. The insanity of such systems lies not only in their first premise but in the very logicality with which they are constructed. The curious logicality of all isms, their simple-minded trust in the survival value of stubborn devotion without regard to specific, varying factors, already harbours the first germs of the totalitarian contempt for reality and factuality.[5]

Both Margaret Canovan and I have argued that *The Origins of Totalitarianism*, for all its faults, its bold but discomforting and alarming—not only to the empiricist—leaps from history to sociology to philosophy, and its mixture of factuality and speculation, is still Arendt's key work, possibly her masterwork. It is a magisterial if untidy mixture of deep passion and cool analysis; many or most of her other works are like huge footnotes constructed to resolve difficulties left behind in the postwar urgency and immediacy of its exposition.[6]

Political man

The Human Condition is the clearest account of Arendt's political philosophy of how political action is the absolute antithesis of totalitarian systems. But it is also an account of the decay of that tradition. Once there was the Greco-Roman idea of citizenship as the highest attribute of human excellence, free men acting together in concerted action reached by public debate. (And in our times women too, of course; but she did not labour the point, nor see the source as tainted by the age-old gender ostracism.) To her the essence of the human condition is the *vita activa*, where citizens interact, not the *vita contemplativa* of the philosophers or the religious, still less the view of man as *animal laborans*, the *mere* creature of necessity We must *labour* to stay alive; but there is *work*, too, which she defined—leaning too much on a special definition which, if it works at all, only appears to work in English and German—as things that we make with our hands to last as if for their own sake, not simply to consume out of biological necessity. She noticed that John Locke had spoken of 'the labour of my hands and the work of my body' and typically appropriated his lesser meaning to her great distinction. But the distinction is not always clear. Works of art can obviously both be made and certainly traded as consumer goods, and can go out of fashion very quickly. Think of what Thorstein Veblen once had to say about 'conspicuous consumption' and class differentiation. But the important thing is that she saw political action as part of the *vita activa*, not of the necessity of labour. Political acts are free acts, they are spontaneous interactions; their value lies in themselves. To act freely is good in itself, keeping in mind that political action is always in concert with others. And her special distinction between labour and work, even if it can jar with ordinary usage, enabled her to see (whatever words are used) that both Marxism and *laissez-faire* economics are variant restless and illimitable forms of worship or sanctification of labour for its own sake, rather than limiting its space to what is necessary for a fully

---

[5] *Origins*, 1st edn, New York, Harcourt Brace, 1951, pp. 431–2.
[6] Canovan, *Hannah Arendt*, pp. 6–7 and 17–23.

human life of action in the public realm: creative work, friendships and contemplation—all higher values than mere labour. (In terms of her definitions, the present British Conservative Party could well be called the Labour Party, except that New Labour might see no need to change its name either.)

She attacks modern liberalism for overvaluing the realm of privacy as against the public realm, just as she spoke carefully of civil rights rather than individual rights or even natural rights. Protection by law from state intervention never lasts unless individuals are willing and able to busy themselves in the making of those laws. The 'price of liberty' is not simply 'eternal vigilance' but perpetual civic activity. Her *Eichmann in Jerusalem: A Report on the Banality of Evil* angered many of her fellow Jews greatly. For, quite apart from the misunderstanding that she meant that evil was banal, rather than that evil men acted as if it were, organising mass killing bureaucratically not flamboyantly, she angered them by her sad historical point that there was virtually no tradition of political action in the stateless people that might have led to resistance; and also by her seemingly heartless view that while resistance was highly unlikely to succeed, it should have been attempted—attempted precisely to demonstrate human freedom and dignity in defiance even of necessity, somewhat as the Stoic faces death. She recounted that Cicero held that a free man, if captured and enslaved with no possibility of escape, then *should* commit suicide—the last free action possible, when possible—rather than see his humanity inevitably debased. The religious may hold suicide to be a sin, though a rationally calculated sacrifice likely to save another's life is always permissible. But Arendt's free-thinking or even pagan existentialism saw our very sense of unique and individual human existence as being in social relationships, how we interact with others, others with each of us. If these conditions of sociability are removed, we cease to be human. So we should assert at least our basic freedom while we can, even if hopelessly perhaps to set an example; but in a totalitarian state we have little hope that the brave example will be remembered, therefore honoured or possibly even effective in the future. Arendt was not a utilitarian. It is a hard doctrine to swallow, or for many to understand. But to try to make an ethic out of the contrary is even harder. Any duty of action or resistance that depends on guarantees of or belief in calculable success is a poor defence in desperate times. It is all too like the crass view that morality must depend on hope of salvation and divine reward.

Thus, though she is often thought of as a modern Aristotelian, she rejects his teleology—even a polis with well-ordered institutions will not necessarily increase in betterment; so much depends on free human action (and sometimes accident, Machiavelli would add—say, Cesare Borgia's sudden death or, for example, John Smith's)—and she rejects what is perhaps his instrumentalism: that free political action in the long run ordinarily succeeds (he might have noticed, under the pikes of Macedonia, that it didn't). She astonishingly sees political action as valuable in itself, each individual volunteering but then enriched by fellowship in common action. Quite

267

simply, she thinks we should live with that astonishment of delight, as when faced with works of art. We do not always say 'What's the use of this?' or 'How much is it?'[7]

So she stands in a tradition of classical republicanism and has profound worries that this citizen spirit is being eaten away by consumerism, and that even representative government and the rule of law can be an invitation to leave politics to others (smiling leaders speaking for us), or to see politics as simply a matter of voting in elections. Like Jefferson she worried that the formal constitution, even of the United States, left too little space for political participation. She viewed referendums, for instance, as inherently manipulative, not especially democratic, as ways of containing, managing and narrowing, not encouraging and broadening, debate. Ernest Gellner once expressed this more simply and scathingly as 'the binary view of politics'. He proclaimed himself 'at least a trinitarian, or else there is always some excluded middle'; well, say 'other', not necessarily 'middle'. Therefore a rash appendix was added to an edition of *The Origins* just after the Hungarian Revolution which saw hope in the what was the old utopia of Proudhon socialism, the spontaneous creations of workers' councils rather than parliamentary or representative democracy. So some topical essays showed interest and a degree of sympathy with the student radicalism of the 1960s, but only because they were challenging 'thoughtless' institutions; that is, institutions simply carrying on without thought as to what was their real purpose, or what they could do better. She quickly saw that most of the students knew no better, and came and went like Edmund Burke's 'flies of a summer'.

So the Left could not claim her; but nor could the Right—though both still try. If she showed a deep understanding of the strength of tradition, it was often in a pessimistic mode—how difficult it is to invent and implement new institutions. And to her the American Revolution was a revolution, not just a rhetorical term for a war of colonial independence: it had been the 'world's best hope', indeed, for civic republicanism, perhaps the 'last hope'. If she could sound like Oakeshott for a moment when arguing that the idea of starting with a blueprint and putting it into practice was preposterous, it was not because tradition determines or is always the major conditioning factor, and therefore political invention, let alone revolution, is impossible, but precisely because the invention of new political institutions is needed. If they are to last, however, they must arise from a plurality of political actors debating among themselves publicly until they can reach a consensus to act together, and to continue acting together.

Hannah Arendt can give some comfort to contemporary communitarians or radical pluralists, so long as the community works politically and within a political tradition, and so long as individuals have the conscious courage to

---

[7] As notably Ronald Beiner has pointed out, she sees political judgement, even action, as much closer to Kant's aesthetics than to his concept of practical reason; see his *Political Judgement*, London, Methuen, 1983.

act alone should the community seek, except in terms of direst and immediate emergency, to stifle public debate—as actual parties so often do. In *The Human Condition* she remarks that nothing in nature is more unique and unlike every other than one man from another, but also that nothing is more like each other. What most generally can resolve this metaphysical paradox is not, say, a belief that we are all children of one father, but that we can all act like, indeed be, citizens.

The life of the citizen and the life of the mind are pre-eminent, and the greatest fault is quite simply not to think what we are doing and to think that we cannot think otherwise and thus act otherwise. Her own position is never quite clear. Certainly it is anti-Platonist; there are no final solutions or simple rational imperatives of any kind. But there are some moral limits and imperatives on *how* we should act in politics as well as acting politically, and these she seems to draw from Kant and Jaspers, a refined modern humanism. Canovan well says that 'it is not so much a position as an internal dialogue, continually going back and forth between alternative standpoints'. In a literal sense this is free-thinking. Perhaps this makes her rather careless of her philosophic presuppositions in essays on current problems, although in other essays she can parade them somewhat pretentiously. In more than one place, however, she expresses her preference for the 'political writer' who has had some experience of the political world, rather than 'the political philosopher'. She herself took on the role of a 'public' intellectual, and that got her into many scrapes when activists, unfamiliar with her writings, could not understand her special use of terms (she was not careful to start each time again as if from the beginning). But what was always important to her was the thinking mind offering reasoned justifications for actions based on reflection. And 'justifications' could never be (to get close to the present) mere sound-bites or appeals to self-interest or a politics dominated by unwillingness to pay for any public improvements.

Thinking to her is, quite simply, the antithesis of thoughtlessness, of accepting things as they are; of speaking, acting or voting as we are expected to, by order, by custom or by appeals to personal loyalty. Yet freedom is not breaking from tradition, whether in a society or a party, but understanding the tradition one is in as a preliminary to action. If radical breaks are needed, they are then more likely to be successful. We do not reach final conclusions, but by debate and activity and the dispersal of power (she sees the very concept of 'sovereignty' as inimical to freedom) a plurality of voices can achieve not The Good, but always some betterment. Not necessarily continual betterment, mind. Our own 'dark times' have seen quite as many downs as ups. Colonial liberation, indeed, but then new tyrannies. Mass enfranchisement and much economic progress, but still dehumanising poverty and dehumanising indifference to it, growing consumerism and neglect of the opportunities of citizenship. Is it her possibly too idealistic and demanding concept of citizenship and human nature that makes me stress her pessimism? I think not. There are many reasons for pessimism if we think of all that is happening to trivialise and bypass the political tradition and to corrupt the institutions of free politics. It is clear how worried she would be when, as I write, the leaders of both main parties in two great countries have been bending much of their energies in election campaigns into persuading their colleagues *not* to debate matters of public interest except by rote. Arendt would see great dangers in this deliberate debasement of political culture by those who should be able and strong-minded enough to thrive on open debate, and have a civic duty to encourage, not suppress debate (perhaps to say from on high, for instance, that 'you gets what you pays for'). But she certainly can help us to put such contingent events (not to use words like 'trivial' or 'thoughtless' again) in a broader context of the nature of our civilisation—to see, in William Morris's homely words, 'what it is around us and what could be'. At least she helps us to struggle when we sometimes wonder what good it does to look the facts squarely in the face. We should read or reread her, both for memory of what is lost and some hope for what still could be so, as we suffer the grotesque, distractive and trivialising plans to celebrate the millennium.

21 Still Missing: A Public Philosophy?

Vol. 68, no. 4, October–December 1997

IT WAS a famous victory. Let me be quite clear, lest my very title suggests squeezing, however gently, sour grapes: I stayed drunk with celebration, without needing to drink very much (unlike on some previous occasions), for several days afterwards. Everyone I spoke to was full of joy at having 'got rid of that lot at last'. Normally civilised and somewhat noncommittal neighbours showed savage exaltation watching the box as familiar face after face at the declaration of poll tried to put a brave face on it, sometimes failing spectacularly, sometimes achieving more dignity in defeat than they appeared capable of in office.

No need, surely, to remind us what everyone knew, from psephologists in demand to my homely neighbours, that the Conservatives had imploded, had earned themselves an almost unprecedented unpopularity (perhaps paralleled only by the popular hatred of Neville Chamberlain after the fall of France, from which not even Churchill could save them five years later), and had signally failed in what they had always given themselves and been given credit for: 'strong government'. They had, like their former colleague, Jonathan of Arabia,[a] fallen on their own sword—and how.

With hindsight we now realise that the election was over long before the official campaign began; there was little change of opinion from within two months of the 1992 result, as if Conservative voters had suddenly realised what they had done, as if they had each trusted to others to mitigate the unwanted consequences of their habitual, but now somewhat excessive, loyalty. Edmund Burke's dictum had again proved sound: general elections are 'decided on the conduct of the late ministry'. (And, as their leadership election has shown, they have not learnt any lessons from the reasons for their defeat; but that is another story, and Labour cannot count on that for ever.)

Labour, New Labour I mean, fought a brilliant tactical campaign. Even if there was (thinking of the future, as we occasionally must) an ominously low turnout for such a great event, it did show that many Conservatives who could not bring themselves to vote against their party could not this time bring themselves to vote for it either. Broadly speaking the Great Tactic consisted in giving as little target as possible to the enemy, making manifesto promises small but perfectly formed and realisable, persuading the public that there had been a clear, if not always clean, 'break from the past', a break almost as spectacular as that one encountered in the 1950s among young Germans—in whose country the phrase originated. That break, of course, was really a continuous process of modernisation begun by Neil Kinnock (whose defeat showed how great was the burden of the past to be overcome in the

[a] Jonathan Aitken.

public mind) and continued by John Smith so positively that Tony Blair could be elected to the leadership among few illusions that he meant to accelerate the process, albeit amid some uncertainty about quite where he was going. (Cromwell remarked that 'an army never goeth so far as when it knows not where it is going'.)

Ideas in politics

Animating ideas are important in politics. The Old Left believed that passionately, but many of their ideas were the wrong ideas. They confused means with values and ends. If equality was both a value (better say 'egalitarianism in conduct') and an end (always better to have said 'an egalitarian society'), then nationalisation was plainly a means and not an end, and the wrong means at that; yet it became treated not merely as a value, but as a shibboleth. Even Marxists seemed to have missed Marx's assertion that socialism could only follow the economic expansiveness of capitalism.

The Old Left were right to realise that the capitalist market, when applied to wages, without considerable public control or mitigation of the consequences by a state dedicated to welfare, does not yield a just and socially tolerable result, as is now seen all over the former Soviet bloc; but they were wrong to see the answer in terms of ownership more than control. They paid little attention to other theories or realities of public finance and, above all, taxation. Well, they were, of course, in favour of taxing the rich to help the poor, but they were so vague that perhaps they actually helped discredit, rather than fortify, graduated income tax as a fundamental principle of social justice. The assumed link between politics and economics was never adequately theorised. In the 1960s very few of the Old Left were bold enough to advocate and attempt to theorise incomes policy in face of political opposition by otherwise—and what an 'otherwise'!— left-wing trade union leaders.

Thatcher, however, taught us all that pragmatism is not enough. She may not have actually read Hayek, but friends, creeps and courtiers, had. Keith Joseph habitually referred to 'the noble philosophy of Professor Hayek'. She peddled an effective populist version of market liberalism, which also served to discredit the vague economic paternalism of the old grandees, the old Tories. Unhappily for the party, it knew no bounds and so served as a rationalisation for an unmoralised, unrestrained, man-on-the-make individualism (not what that former Professor of Moral Philosophy at the University of Glasgow, Adam Smith, was talking about at all); and this even penetrated more than the back benches of the parliamentary party.

Tony Blair clearly saw, as Carlyle famously told Margaret Fuller, that the universe had better be accepted, indeed not ungraciously. Capitalism has brought unique prosperity to much of the world. Perhaps, like Kinnock, he had read (or read about) Hobsbawm Mark II; or more likely it was clear-minded common sense. But how was the growing gap between rich and poor to be bridged, especially without frightening the electorate by any criticism that the Conservatives had lowered income tax far too much, hence in large part bringing about growth in the Public Sector Borrowing Requirement? Better focus instead on the excellent PR polemic that the Conservatives had actually raised taxes—many taxes, if one looked at indirect taxation. And indirect taxation, thundered the opposition front bench, is regressive. But what is progressive? The answer to that simple riddle is widely known, but is taboo in the Inner Party—as shown in the July 1997 Budget, whatever its other considerable virtues. In the Outer Party (and among the proles) there is still a suspicion that the Labour Party, old or new, cannot in public plausibility long compete with the Conservatives as being the party of purported lower taxation and static income tax.

Tony Blair made speeches in opposition that seemed to be working towards a reasonably coherent public philosophy,[1] difficult to name emotively on the hustings, but something modern historians might well call radical liberalism—a liberalism attempting to theorise the somewhat contingent provincial roots of British liberalism by taking on board, or sharing, the pluralist, decentralist tradition in British socialism. There was always a tension in the thinking of the British labour movement between the centralists, whether Fabian or quasi-Leninist advocates of a party-led state, or the decentralists, the pluralists, the municipal and local government tradition—or, more idealistically speaking, the small group, cooperative, community tradition. When Blair talked of 'social-ism' he seemed to be not rejecting the democratic socialist tradition but coming down in favour of that latter side of it. Man is, indeed, a social animal, and to stress this is not entirely banal politically when we have been told, *ipsa dixit*, that there is no such thing as 'society'. Blair had a brief encounter with *Spirit of Community*'s Amitai Etzioni, whose publishers claim on the dust-jacket of the sequel (*The New Golden Rule: Community and Morality in a Democratic Society*) that the author has been 'very influential on New Labour'; indeed, they generously reprint in their press release the new Clause Four. There were even references to Tawney in Blair's speeches, but more for his Christian socialism in general terms than for the fiercely egalitarian inferences for policy that Tawney drew from it in *Equality* and *The Acquisitive Society* (which are not now books to be seen on your shelf when the Leader's men come to tea, unless like me you are known to be interested in the history of ideas). But too often, when Blair spoke about restoring a spirit

---

[1] 'The basis of such socialism lies in its view that individuals are socially interdependent human beings—that individuals cannot be divorced from the society to which they belong. It is, if you will, social-ism. It contains an ethical and a subjective judgement that individuals owe a duty to one another and to a broader society—the Left view of citizenship.' Tony Blair in *Socialism* (Fabian Pamphlet 565, July 1994). There is no real need to mock, as some have done, that hyphen: it is a worthy explication. But what worries me a little is that 'citizenship', to be meaningful, not just rhetorical, must imply devolution and strong local government, philosophically even pluralism—in practical terms, there must be something for citizens to do; but there was no specific commitment to that elsewhere in the speech: it has to be optimistically inferred from the logic of what he said.

of 'community', he linked community to 'society' and to 'nation', as in Clause Four as amended. They are rather big as communities go; in fact they are not communities at all in the pluralist, decentralist and, indeed, sociological senses of that key concept. Etzioni himself is extraordinarily muddled on this point. The sense of solidarity that a whole nation or society can feel is a different thing from the 'community feeling' of a group small enough to maintain an informal, traditional or voluntary moral order, as distinguished from 'society', which may or may not have a moral consensus, but needs central and general legal restraints and procedural consensus to maintain order.

Slogans and themes

It is too early to judge whether the actions, even if not the words, of the new government are based on presuppositions that may come to constitute a new and coherent public philosophy recognisable in the public mind. 'Modernisation' was an effective slogan, but was never defined as a theory, except negatively as 'not Old Labour'. Its most concrete manifestation was not in ideas but in campaign tactics and organisation. Blair had, of course, to be circumspect in the long election campaign and in the still longer run-up. He had to embody concern for obvious social problems, but also reassurance to Middle England that he wouldn't go dipping into their pockets for the sake of other people's consciences. Since he has been in office we have not heard much of 'community' so far, and 'stakeholding', which had a little run, is now, handicapped by the many different weights and meanings, strong and weak, which were heaped on its back, quite out of sight down the field.[2]

Far from 'community', it is 'individual enterprise' and the creation of the conditions for 'equality of opportunity' that are now stressed. But individualism and individual enterprise may destroy real communities; and 'equality of opportunity' can actually work against both egalitarianism and any actual lessening of the gap between rich and poor; that is, unless there are strong anti-poverty policies to sustain, even to create, communities *as a prior condition for* the results of equality of opportunity to prove reasonably just.

The public sector

To attack poverty in the way that not merely Old Labour but all Labour dreamt of, is now either off the agenda or postponed far into the future, thanks to pledges given during the election not to raise the PSBR, not to step

[2] Nonetheless, one can tear the 'stakeholding' prescription right out of Will Hutton's books *The State We're In* and *The State to Come* and still leave the most brilliant and comprehensive diagnosis of our social and economic problems, even if they are out of favour, one gathers, with the Inner Party. Not that they look for second opinions. They have little use for intellectuals and do their own thinking entirely (the Count Frankenstein's children of postwar university expansion).

outside the old government's expenditure targets (both overall and in each department) for two years, and not to raise income tax.[3] The campaign tactic on taxation has made the budgetary limits for manoeuvre extremely tight, and therefore exaggerated importance is given to one-off and relatively small matters that cost little or nothing, and even to some prime red herrings. Harold Wilson made the mistake, let it never be forgotten, of abandoning any clear public philosophy or general policies in favour of simply ticking off triumphantly a list of manifesto pledges fulfilled, many or most of which rapidly proved irrelevant or unadaptable to changing circumstances—if not simply a product of electoral rhetoric more than the needs of government in the first place.

Take the case of the two sectors that are not merely part of Old Labour's dream but of current public, middle-class concern; two factors that helped in the Conservative debacle. Who seriously doubts (except, apparently, the two front benches) that our common schools and the health service are grievously run down, not primarily by maladministration or by their organisation (though faults there are in both), but by being under-resourced (the polite word for under-funded). Since the expenditure required in both cases— beyond the immediate palliatives in the Budget—would involve tax rises including increased income tax, whether they meant to or not ministers have, by concentrating on cheaper or no-cost problems, perpetuated the impression that the methods and ability of teachers, and the greed of hospital adminis- trators and high-tech doctors, are to blame. There are problems, especially with the costs of the internal market in the NHS. Teacher training has been neglected by both the universities and successive governments, then run down deliberately by the last government in favour of learning on the job—as if teachers were garage apprentices. A book by Philip Turner, reviewed in this issue (*Second Class Ticket: The Neglect of State Education*)[b] persuasively argues that a succession of Conservative ministers, ignorant of conditions in our common schools, determined to make a name for themselves by doing— doing *something*, or *anything*. The somethings have been products not of consultation and research, but of prejudice fortified by will power and a craving for publicity in the manner of the Lady of so many of our sorrows. Then the next minister has done something else, something big—and equally disruptive to the good business, on the whole in such safe hands, of teaching our children and grandchildren. Labour will not make that mistake, but it will have to concentrate on matters that need relatively little money; and likewise in the health service.

---

[3] Things get very confusing. I for one am not Old Labour—I polemicised against the Bennites and the Footites hard, and had no tolerance for either the infiltrating wreckers or the Social Democrat deserters—but I am not sure that I am New Labour either. I rather think not. I rather think that the Inner Party have not heard of 'the fallacy of the excluded middle'. Much of the party, I suspect, is excluded middle.

[b] Actually reviewed by Bernard, so reprinted in this volume.

The poverty question touches both these great services. Intellectually Labour sees this. A new committee is being set up to go back over the ground of the suppressed Black Report on Inequality and Health (1980) that demonstrated correlations between high levels of ill health and poverty. But with the taxation pledges tying our hands, and the political fears behind them, there will be depressingly little the government can do, except say 'told you so' with solemn gravity to the Tories. The Budget was, indeed, politically very astute: because they were led to expect no funding increases at all, the media missed the inadequacy of the actual increases. If schools were to be properly resourced and teachers properly paid and thus respected, it is likely that crime could be reduced and economic potential enhanced.

Politically both these services serve most of the middle class as well as the poor, and survey evidence has been impressive that the Liberal Democrats were right in that people could and should have been asked to pay more through income tax for those two great good common causes, and would have done so willingly enough. It is a long argument and a matter of political judgement, but I find the belief of Labour's inner circle that the 1992 election was lost on the taxation issue at least unproven. It was at least as likely that, in a broad historical view, if any one factor can stand alone, Kinnock needed a year or two longer, after having brought the party back to a sense of reality, to convince the public, or rather to let it see for itself, that the Labour Party had put behind it the left/right years of disruption. It is too late now; but with the lead the party had in the polls for almost the whole period of John Major's feeble second innings, surely the tax question could have been taken head-on rather than evaded?

Political popularity is not just basking in sudden sunlight but an opportunity to persuade and change opinion. A popular leader can and should use his position, however gradually and carefully, to bring the public as well as his party to a sense of reality. Lincoln, Lloyd George, Churchill and—sorry to mention it—Thatcher were bold enough to bring public opinion round, as were many lesser people on lesser occasions. Does the modern technology of opinion research somehow inhibit rather than arm the capacity for political change? Certainly we don't like paying more income tax, but we may like the decay of our schools and our health service still less. Leadership is striking some balance or creative compromise, not dropping one of the terms of the paradox. To have accepted Ken Clarke's allegedly tight and realistic, but in fact crudely optimistic, figures may now be cause for regret even in the Inner Party—even now that responsibility for higher interest rates has been shuffled off. Suppose the bull had been taken by the horns, and that the margin of victory had been less. With a smaller majority and its hands not tied, the government would have been stronger and more likely to retain its popularity.

Even given the tied hands, one might hope to hear more of a rhetoric, not, indeed, of socialism (what's in a word?) but of *public service* and of restoring, even enhancing, *public services*. 'Public interest' and 'public spirit' are concepts worth restoring to old prominence in new contexts. This leads straight into another problem, of both a theoretical and a practical nature.

Pluralism and devolution

When the leader was new to his leadership he talked much and well about Britain and British government being overcentralised, about the need for devolution and subsidiarity as paths to better government and more public involvement. This was one key link between old and new in the Labour Party, and also a bridge to Liberal Democratic opinion. I do not hear this now as one of the major themes of office. Yes, elected government will be restored to London, and the capital will have an elected mayor; but there has been no major speech or statement so far on restoring or, as many had hoped, enhancing the powers of local government. Talk of English regions seems to have been quietly dropped. And yet the very roots of the Labour Party's ethos were in civic and municipal government. The new English MPs seem to be for the most part professionals who see London as the sole centre of real power.

When in the 1970s and 1980s so many *marxisant* intellectuals of the New Left began to adopt a more realistic attitude to politics (I would even say, to think politically for the first time), they drifted into the Labour Party, reinventing the wheel as they went along. They wrote about democratic theory and the need for constitutional law and often, quite literally, joined Charter 88. (I remember Neil Kinnock in animated conversation naming several of their leading spirits as 'Trotskyites', and my attempting to persuade him that they were now rabid ex-Trotskyites and born-again democrats.) They were also, almost without exception, pluralists. They had not given up the Leninist theory of the state to embrace easily either Mr Sidney Webb's Fabian centralisation or the English obsession with the sovereignty of parliament. Many of these 'last of the Labour intellectuals' are now in what would once have seemed unlikely alliance with right-wing activists in the constituency parties to resist the implied centralism of the NEC's proposals, published in *Party into Power*, for allegedly 'reforming' intra-party democracy.[4]

Even five years ago I felt confident that this decentralist theory of administration and pluralist theory of power had penetrated to anyone at all thoughtful in the Labour Party leadership. It seems I was wrong. Even the whiff of victory, let alone the reality of office, threatens to bring back the old instinctive, unthinking centralist beliefs. They mean to do good for us all in the localities, so long as we do not want to do different kinds of good for ourselves. Scotland and Wales are now, of course, exceptions to the general rule of central sovereignty. They are not seen as the extreme cases of a general desire to devolve as much government as possible from Whitehall and

---

[4] As seen in the rapidly growing Labour Reform Movement and its series of consultation papers, notably Rebuilding the National Policy Forum (PO Box 5219, Birmingham B13 8DY, or on http://www.zynet.co.uk/ecotrend/LabRef).

Westminster but, as far as most English Labour MPs are concerned, simply as exceptions born of political necessity. That many people in Scotland argue for devolution on democratic grounds—meaning 'republican' ideas of citizenship and participation—not primarily on nationalist grounds at all, is almost always missed in England, largely due to the London-based media. Easier to treat the Scottish demand as purely nationalistic, for then it does not challenge what seems to be the easy acceptance in England of the continued derogation of local government.

Take one key example. Even in opposition, Labour accepted the principle of a national curriculum for schools. Little thought was given to why there should be one at all, or to the dangers of opening the door to political intervention in the curriculum (as has happened). Sensing that the Conservatives were trying to make it a popular political issue, bizarrely arguing and assuming that centralisation would raise standards, Labour said, in effect, 'me too'; and now shows little sign of wishing to return education to local control. Local control should be reformed, made more democratic indeed; but the matter is not even raised. And if we are content or condemned to have a national curriculum, because presumably pluralism has lost out to centralism as the implied public philosophy, consider what a curriculum it is, with no place in it, once again uniquely in Europe, for civic education, education for citizenship itself. That should be a priority for a Labour government, unless the modernisation of New Labour is simply concerned with education for industry, neither for citizenship nor for leisure as part of the quality of life itself. Are these old values lost? Consider also the direct, highly prejudiced and fatuous interventions of Conservative ministers into the detail of the History and English curricula. Again, better not to have a national curriculum at all, especially in education, especially if the public philosophy of New Labour has concern for subsidiarity, devolution, pluralism: better that as much as possible should be done by citizens in localities, not by ministers and civil servants in Whitehall—even if that leads or reverts to different standards and practices and (not unheard of in central government) to some gross mistakes. The price of liberty is astounding variety, even in an egalitarian society. If a nationally controlled curriculum is maintained, then it should be reformed into a flexible set of guidelines only (somewhat on the German model for *Politischesbildung*), in terms of which local authority advisers would have to publish curricula within which teachers would create syllabuses (or syllabi if they care).

In conclusion

Many of us had hoped for three broad elements in a public philosophy of New Labour. First, indeed, a full-hearted acceptance that the production, physical distribution and pricing of goods are best handled by free enterprise and the market, and that the immediate institutional form that the market takes (all markets need a framework of law) is the EU. So far, so good. *But also* that it would use the powers of the state and enable powers in local government to mitigate, if not remove, through the taxation system, unjustifiable inequalities and poverty, whether arising from low wages or unemployment. Yes, that will take time: 'patience and time' as Tolstoy's General Kutuzov said to his young officers, too eager for immediate battle; but the process has to be seen to be beginning,[5] and the agreeable and ingenious device or expedient (I will not say gimmick) of the one-off windfall tax is, indeed, one-off: a fitting punishment to the privatised utilities, but more likely to be a gift soon spent than a lasting pump-primer for the young unemployed. We hoped that New Labour would have had some formulated intention (I will not use the discredited word 'plan') to avoid the permanence of the underclass already with us, and would have begun to argue the ill consequences for society, as well as the moral shame, of such a permanence, which could come about unless public revenues are increased in a fair (see Rawls and Runciman on justice and fairness) manner.

Here even a symbolic increase in the top rate of taxation would have sent a message of more than symbolic importance, intention and hope. The public rage in the pre-election period, even in the Conservative tabloids, at the salaries and bonuses of the 'fat cats' could still be worked upon. The readers of those papers know sardonically and bitterly that their bosses are overpaid and that there are many in the firm quite able to step into their shoes if they do emigrate to purer points of capitalism like Hong Kong or Moscow. The argument that a few pennies in the pound on top incomes would discourage leading entrepreneurs is fatuous, the kind of thing that is said in letters to *The Times* and the *Daily Telegraph* but which no sensible person believes. They are just being greedy—I mean individualistically acquisitive within the law. New Labour has surely well earned the trust of business without such unnecessary and potentially self-defeating concessions. The unconcern of the Stock Exchange at Labour's advance, victory and first Budget was proof and tribute to that.

The second element in the hoped-for public philosophy of New Labour was the democratic impulse: to open up and devolve the processes of government, and to try to create a positive culture of active citizenship. There are some signs of this both in the promises of constitutional reform and in the greater informality and openness of Labour ministers; but so far these seem to be piecemeal responses to outmoded habits of office and particularly gross anomalies (like the peerage in the upper chamber), not guided by any as yet discernible and announced general principles. Scottish and Welsh devolution are, indeed, big steps forward but are not, as yet, being presented as part of a general policy of devolution (underpinned by a philosophy of pluralism, not merely the growing irrelevance of sovereignty theory). The key to the link between comprehensive constitutional reform and a positive citizen culture is, of course, electoral reform—some form of genuine proportional representation (as *is* part of the Scottish proposals). There is the political paradox that

---

[5] See my *Socialist Values and Time* (Fabian Tract 465, March 1984).

while most of the new Labour MPs say they favour PR, older MPs point out that they are the winners in the great and disproportionate swings of the first-past-the-post racetrack gamblers' excitement system. But it is swings and roundabouts. On the Glorious First of May the electorate took the electoral law into its own hands by tactical voting: better for Labour to institutionalise and stabilise this by PR, rather than trust the Conservatives to carry on rendering themselves so spectacularly unpopular.

The third element should be a clear annunciation of aims and values. We are already a highly libertarian society. We need to be, should aim to be, a more egalitarian society and a more democratic society, in both manners and procedures, at every level; and one in which the values that shape our behaviour should include not only respect for individual talent but also encouragement, through education and example, for sociability (we can no longer say 'fraternity'), a concern for the well-being not merely of friends and neighbours but of strangers. The palpable decency, honesty, good intentions and competence of the new government compared to the last has already created something of this atmosphere, but comparisons will fade in memory; and it must not appear to depend *too much* on the personality of one man but rather on the example from above of observable collective will and behaviour and from below of a revitalised civic democracy in the constituencies—local government indeed—energised by a clear public philosophy.

22 Introduction to *Citizens: Towards a Citizenship Culture*

Book chapter; vol. 72, no. 5, 2001

The aim of the ancients was the sharing of social power among the citizens of the same fatherland: this is what they called liberty. The aim of the moderns is the enjoyment of liberty in private pleasures; and they call liberty the guarantees accorded by institutions to these pleasures. (From Benjamin Constant, *The Liberty of the Ancients Compared with That of the Moderns*)

How CAN we become a citizen culture, a country whose inhabitants think it normal, right and even pleasurable to be concerned with and actively involved in public affairs?[a] If ever sections of society were once going that way, we are now—for a multiplicity of reasons—drifting away fast. And by public affairs is not just meant the relationships of inhabitants to the state and government, but also to all those institutions intermediate and mediating between the individual and the state which we call civil society—on which in a free society the power and authority of government ultimately depends.

Each of the contributors to this book was asked to attempt an answer to this question in relation to an important sphere in which they were expert or greatly experienced. They were asked not to be concerned with the short-term issues of what is politically feasible in this next term of a new government's term of office, but to help lift all our eyes by offering middle and long-term proposals for how to realise a vision of such a culture looking towards the middle years of this new century. So to try to define some practical vision or realisable ideal of a more democratic and genuinely inclusive society.

The editor shared a thought with all the contributors without wishing to commit them to a reply: if the old 'forward march' of Labour as a democratic socialist project now seems either halted, indeed, or even abandoned, or at least no longer realisable in its former terms, that then in Britain we can at least, some say at best, aim to achieve a radically more democratic, inclusive and outward-looking society; and that this should reach all the way down from top to bottom, from the practices of central government and the parties to devolved national, regional and local institutions and practices. I suspect that the strange search for a 'Third Way' (either by people too busy to think or too prudent to commit themselves to anything specific)[1] was itself a title

---

[1] See for example Anthony Giddens, *The Third Way: The Renewal of Social Democracy*, Polity Press, 1998, a book of well-meaning abstract generalities curiously or cautiously avoiding any inferences to policy.

[a] Like Article 18 above, this article is from the by now annual fifth (book) issue of the journal, hence its numbering in the normal *Political Quarterly* volume sequence.

decided for a play before a script had been written, that this will settle down into what was perhaps implicit from the beginning: New Labour taking on the old mantle of radical democracy, stealing the Liberals' clothes (and they are good clothes—up to a point, that point being the pinch of poverty), even if not wishing openly to share a common cloak or mantle (which, of course, would imply electoral reform—which is why we lead with that).

Not to beg the question

However, do we beg the question? Is the case really so overwhelming that this is a worthy cause, a social transformation—for such it would be—devoutly to be wished? Others would say that the greatest happiness of the greatest number is to be gained simply through the uninhibited working of the market, now indeed the global market, and that active citizenship or radical democracy would be too interventionist towards the economy, both on the state and the local level. Also one contributor to this book has serious doubts that the public accountability of government would be helped by a citizen culture, indeed I think he thinks it would be hindered; that a clear line of legal accountability and ministerial responsibility could get blurred by populist pressure. These are powerful arguments. And, of course, no sensible person should press the contrary arguments to extremes. Purely market values, total privatisation, would indeed destroy much of what is most valuable in the sociability of human life: that ultimately individual human identity is a relationship with others, mutual recognition and respect. But unqualified democracy can go too far. Beatrice Webb once remarked that 'democracy is not the multiplication of ignorant opinions'. Nor is the person who with passionate intensity gives their whole life to public affairs necessarily to be admired or trusted more than any other in the exercise of office.

So do we beg the question? Yes, we do; or at least we do not here aim to repeat yet again the arguments that there is a democratic deficit in British society and that market pricing need not involve market values. Three books in this same series have argued all this already.[2] We want to build on that and all the large bodies of writing, part the academic on 'civic republicanism' or on 'social capital' and part that of the finest columnists of the broadsheets, which have both been concerned with the broad and basic arguments of principle, but now to try to show in specific instances the case for a citizenship culture and then, perhaps less successfully, how it might operate. The latter is difficult to envisage for the clear reason that the free actions of free men and women are difficult to predict. Elsewhere I have mused[3] that it is curious, if

[2] Colin Crouch and David Marquand, eds, *Reinventing Collective Action: From the Global to the Local*, 1995; Paul Hirst and Sunil Khilnani, *Reinventing Democracy*, 1996; and Andrew Gamble and Tony Wright, *The New Social Democracy*, 1999, all published by Blackwell for *The Political Quarterly*.

[3] Bernard Crick, *In Defence of Politics*, 5th edn, Continuum, 2000; and *Essays on Citizenship*, Continuum, 2000.

commendable and perhaps hopeful, that governments of any hue, obsessed as they are with control and occupationally concerned with citizenship mainly as voting in public elections (and even that is qualified by private musings as to whether high turnout is helpful or not to the party), nonetheless support citizenship being taught in schools ('active' as well as 'good'); and they promote in many a speech 'volunteering' (perhaps secure in the knowledge that most volunteers will be told what to do, that most of our great national voluntary bodies are somewhat negative models of democratic participation). And different ministries sponsor different episodes of local community development, usually as 'pilot projects' (few of which ever fly) rather than as consistent national policy. Nonetheless, all of this may be, I hope, stimulating trouble for the future.

There is another sense in which the question can be begged, as already hinted. Many of us point to the dangers of a society more and more dominated by consumerism linked to an aggressive revival of the Victorian work ethic. You work harder but you spend harder—thrift and savings have got lost somewhere along the road of unpremeditated social change. Family life as well as concern for public affairs suffer when, as survey results confirm observation, hours of work have increased and shopping and sport are people's main preferred activities in reduced leisure time. However, to affirm the primacy in the good life of concern for others and for public values is not to say, as some of us thinking in the Aristotelian and civic-republican tradition of European political thought have come near to saying, that the good man and woman *must* be an active citizen. A moral philosopher, Mark Philp, has written in a recent essay, 'Citizenship and Integrity', that it is not difficult to see the appeal of citizenship in the civic republican or classical mode, and why people should (like ourselves) seek to restore it: 'The vision of a virtuous, active citizenry, engaged in deliberation on the proper ends of their association and taking turns at ruling and being ruled—especially when coupled with the assumption that civic virtue provides the natural comple-tion of the broader moral virtues.' But he points out that this positive view of *citizen* has little moral significance for most people, almost wholly immersed in private concerns, however selfish or predatory. 'It is entirely possible to believe that [some of] those who live private lives may live more virtuously.' His first point is what we now seek to change, but to do so must involve accepting his second point. Perhaps the civic ideal had best be stated as the will to lead both a rich public and a rich private life, and the opportunities and skills to move easily from the one to the other. Indeed having made his humanistic or 'sceptical caveats', he does assert that 'modern democratic states will be politically stable only if most of their citizens see compliance with their civic responsibilities as a requirement of personal integrity'.[4]

[4] Mark Philp in Alan Montefiore and David Vines, eds, *Integrity in the Public and Private Domains*, London, Routledge, 1998, pp. 20–1.

What is to be done?

Do or you are done by. The obstacles to effective doing are, however, great. Much of the nearly free daily entertainment of the popular media seems a form of bread and circuses, either consciously or unconsciously designed to divert people from real issues. There is something in the theories of the old Marxists of the Frankfurt School that capitalism controls not by force but by cultural degradation. Orwell somehow picked this up in his grim satire *Nineteen Eighty-Four*: the Ministry of Truth itself produced prolefeed for the masses including 'rubbishy newspapers containing almost nothing except sport, crime and astrology, sensational five cent novelettes, films oozing with sex, and sentimental songs which were composed entirely by mechanical means on a special kind of kaleidoscope known as a versificator.' But our present press is not uniquely to blame. The tactic of *panem et circenses*, bread and circuses, is as old as fears of the potential power of the people:

From sunrise until evening, in sunshine and in rain, they stand open-mouthed examining minutely the good points and the bad points of the charioteers and their horses. And it is most remarkable to see an innumerable crowd of plebeians, their minds filled with a kind of eagerness, hanging on the outcomes of the chariot race. These and similar things prevent anything memorable or serious being done in Rome. (A fourth century AD writer in *Res Gestae*, XIV, 7, 25f)

Today it is tax cuts, Domes and spinning wheels. But perhaps the noble Roman missed the point. To prevent anything serious may have been the point.

What is to be done? The contributors will speak for themselves. But before I underline or gloss a few points: let me name and briefly explain some key dimensions that we have ignored, mainly because we all take them for granted or because they are part of the problem that we believe a citizen culture could, if not wholly cure, at least abate. Even the Countess of Wessex is aware that prime ministers are increasingly adopting a presidential style; and were she even brighter she might have pointed to a growing American-isation of campaigning techniques and media manipulation among the inner circle of the younger political advisers. Quite specifically many of them had a common experience in following, even participating in, Clinton's first presidential campaign. They then longed to do that here. The machinery of government is now used more for central control or for popular show than for functional efficiency, certainly not to ensure responsiveness to informed opinion. The Treasury and the Home Office are in the first category and the weird range of functions under the magic word 'Environment' is meant to impress, just as Department for Education and Employment was meant to imply that there will be jobs for all if everyone has the right training, and so the emphasis shifts to training rather than (so they say) outmoded ideas of education.[5] Perhaps the two biggest problems are the appallingly low

---

[5] Apart from IT, medicine, engineering and law etc., how do we know in such a 'rapidly changing economic environment' etc. what we are training for? That's a difficult one, so the idea

standard of political debate set by the leaders of the main parties—sound-bite recrimination rather than reasoned exposition of principles and policy;[6] and, not unconnected, the growing alienation of young people from public and political commitments. The first could begin to change if a prime minister or a leader of the opposition by personal example willed it to change, despite the popular press; even by challenging the popular press. Many of us had a hope of this that has been dashed. The second will only change if public expectations rise to demand a lasting uplift of debate and far greater provision for and trust in participation. That is our concern in this book.

The questions of electoral and parliamentary reform are plainly linked. John Maxton's Parthian shot as an MP sets out strongly what MPs could do for themselves to make Parliament a more effective check on the executive and to restore its credibility as the voice of the nation, now so much by-passed both by No. 10 and the media. What price 'modernisation' when it comes to Parliament? But is the power of the whips ever likely to be broken unless electoral reform, meaning proportional representation, not just the window-dressing of the Alternative Vote, gives individual MPs greater security in selection in their own constituencies and makes the business of carrying votes in the Commons as uncertain as it is and will be in any acceptable reformed second chamber? Nonetheless, Martin Linton's acceptance of the 'Jenkins system' as a realistic *first step* has much to commend it, especially if coupled, as he proposes, with a two-question referendum, as was done in the Scottish referendum. Once 'first past the post' is modified, however inadequately, the greater matter will never rest. That is precisely why many of 'the turkeys who fear Christmas' are against any move whatever (except where political necessity forces, as in Northern Ireland, Wales and Scotland already). The political difficulties are great, as if 'the body politic performing open heart surgery on itself. It is awkward. It is painful. But I think it will be done.' If it is not done, it will be next to impossible for New Labour to move (as I suspect its leaders wish) from an ideology or public philosophy of muted social democracy to a strident radical democracy; or move they may try, but they will not be taken seriously.

Several pressure groups within the Labour Party itself see reforms to party democracy as the key to democratic reform in general. They are by no means all 'Old Labour': some have the Charter 88 new liberal faith that constitutional reform by itself can set all to rights—economic questions are either secondary or will inevitably follow. Matthew Taylor challenges such thinking. He sees the problem of 'civic disengagement' as arising from the very control that

---

of 'key skills' has been invented that all in pre-18 education must follow (except that the academic streams pay little attention to these well-meant abstractions—they are for the others). If you don't know what key skills are, the three 'hard' and the three 'soft', it would take too long to explain. I just mention it.

[6] See my meditative polemic, 'The Decline of Political Thinking in British Public Life', in *Critical Review of International Social and Political Philosophy*, no. 1, Spring 1998; reprinted in *Essays on Citizenship*, ibid.

parties themselves exercise over the democratic process. While party leaders may go on about parties getting closer to communities, this 'belies their desire to maximise discipline'. For 'the voice of local communities will tend to be loudest when opposing public authorities'. He points out that community activists 'are increasingly unlikely to see political parties as the most fruitful channel for the pursuit of their interests'.[7] The better role of local parties is 'not to act as a closed shop' (as if they know what people want simply by virtue of being elected—because they wanted to be elected, gave endless evenings to it and were elected, moreover by very small numbers), but 'to offer support to those in the community who share its broad values'. I think local parties have to face these truths unpleasant to them, just as MPs must come to see that the despite into which they have fallen has much to do with their grim addiction to party loyalty on all major issues.

Scottish devolution admittedly arose—and in the strong form that it did—because otherwise, as the late Donald Dewar pummelled into the heads of his Cabinet colleagues, ignoring all fancy arguments, the SNP might have come to dominate Scotland. But being there, for whatever reason, the United Kingdom constitution and its politics can never be the same again, as Joyce McMillan argues. In fact it works pretty well, despite many believing the contrary thanks to the London media (either from ignorance, laziness or economy) taking most of their views on Scotland from the strongly anti-devolution *Scotsman*, doing everything it can to discredit the parliament, rather than from more balanced and open pages of the *Herald*. But here is the spectacle of PR and a coalition government working in a parliament whose procedures have been, like those of the Welsh Assembly, a radical break from Westminster—more democratic, more open and more efficient in its use of time. If regional government comes at least to parts of England, it is likely that rules of procedure will draw a great deal on the Scottish and Welsh experience—unless they are centrally imposed from the start as last-ditch attempts to appear devolutionist and democratic while seeking to retain a centralist uniformity.

If one accepts that now the United Kingdom has to be conceived and managed as a multinational state, the problems raised by how best to deal with racism and to what degree the idea of multiculturalism should be mirrored in legislation and education become manageable. Yasmin Alibhai-Brown sees 'the vocabulary of citizenship' as a linking factor. She is plainly aware of the dangers of the language of 'group rights' as if groups can have the same rights as individuals, which would, for one thing, imply that groups should have rights against their own members who may wish to leave, perhaps to marry out or to prevent others marrying in. Some of the advocacy

---

[7] The concept of 'community activist' still worries some. A recent government advisory committee wishing to advise that FE colleges should be specially funded to run training courses in citizenship for community activists was officially advised to call them 'community leaders'. What's in a name? Quite a lot apparently.

of 'multiculturalism' as a new overriding reconstruction of Britishness has been more demanding than thoughtful. We can, indeed, and should celebrate diversity but within the context of a citizen culture. She quotes admirable words of Gordon Brown: 'As the Tebbit "cricket test" and the Stephen Lawrence case illustrate, there are those who would retreat from an expansive idea of Britishness into a constricted shell of right wing nationalism. My vision of Britain comes not from uniformity but from celebrating diversity, in other words a multi-ethnic and a multinational Britain—outward looking, open, internationalist with a commitment to democracy and tolerance.' May one respectfully ask a Chancellor of the Exchequer to be sure to put some money where his mouth is? Celebrations and democratic institutions (if that means devolution) do not always come cheap. Neal Ascherson similarly links a recognition of diversity in our own midst to a citizen culture that can rise above a narrow nationalism to see that what we share with Europe is a respect for free institutions. And one must not rub salt into Europhobic wounds by noting that the idea of a positive, political citizenship is stronger in most of the EC states than in a Britain still bound by traditions of the law-abiding subject of the Crown. I begin to see why nearly all of those who opposed citizenship education in schools were against the Economic Community in principle. Traditionally we have not needed these kind of things and therefore we do not need them now.

Education, media and community

Anthony Everitt writing on the liveliness of the multiplicity of local Arts groups as themselves examples of people acting together as citizens, says that the problem is 'how to support without smothering'—a problem of which both Isobel Lindsay, writing on the voluntary sector, and Henry Tam, extolling community action as the very root of citizenship, are both fully aware.

There is a real danger that voluntary bodies and charities, sometimes even more informal community groups, can end up tied by grants as virtual agents of the state. And not all the democratic credentials of these bodies are impeccable. However, they are main vehicles for any realistic hopes to create a citizen culture. Funding my membership subscription is inadequate in deprived areas, where need is greatest, and even in mixed areas usually reduces organisers to fundraisers. Appeals are at the mercy of fashion, and giving, while good in itself, seldom responds to rational criteria of need. Ways of central funding must be found that are under local control other than, *vide* Matthew Taylor's argument, by party caucus in town hall. Core funding for Civic Forums on the Scottish model could be the answer who might then break down the pounds into useful pennyweights precisely targeted to local needs. Lots of little sums are needed for which central control is always too cumbersome. As with some Foundations, central government too often finds it cost-inefficient to dispense small grants.

Accountability need not, like school inspection, be annual unless there are real problems; and accountability certainly should not demand uniformity of practice. The press attack central bureaucracy in one breath and then raise alarms in relation to medical procedures about 'the lottery of where you live'. But the answer to that is to lead a more intense civic life where you live. (As again both Henry Tam and Isobel Lindsay argue so cogently.) Politicians should defend diversity of practice. Devolution cannot mean uniformity. Local democracy does not mean that all public services should be the same everywhere. A few hard cases will inevitably occur. The press can have it both ways, all too easily: 'government interference!' and 'scandalous anomaly!' Michael Brunson sees the faults of the media but also the dangers of thinking that there are radical solutions. There may not be solutions by routes of public controls, but that is no reason for governments not to answer back. He does not share my view of the popular press as the great dis-educator of our times. He sees signs of improvement, although he deplores 'life-style' rather than policy reporting and sees the need to give high quality explanations of the facts as well as the facts. But improvement is not a chicken and egg problem. He argues that if people want better newspapers, they will eventually get them. That leads us to education.

The 1998 report *Education for Citizenship and the Teaching of Democracy in Schools* ambitiously stated:

We aim at no less than a change in the political culture of this country both nationally and locally: for people to think of themselves as active citizens, willing, able and equipped to have an influence on public life and with the critical capacities to weigh evidence before speaking and acting; to build on and to extend radically to young people the best in existing traditions of community involvement and public service, and to make them individually confident in finding new forms of involvement and action among themselves.

Richard Pring endorses the subsequent decision for Citizenship to be added to the national curriculum, but rightly sees that on its own it is bound to fail in its full aspirations unless there are changes, over which admittedly it could itself have some influence, in the character of the whole curriculum—still too rigid and still either too vocational or too academically orientated at too early an age. A genuine citizen culture will be based, as the whole western tradition of civic republicanism has been, on humanistic as well as technical values. The idea of a liberal education has taken a hard knock in the maintained sector but is essential for a free society not entirely either work or entertainment dominated. Tom Schuller and Karen Evans both argue the need for opportunities for education in general, for citizenship in particular, to continue lifelong and to influence the world of work, not to be its instrument. Business itself is not entirely unaware that claims to be left alone and a lack of a dialogue about the other claims on the lives of employees and managers could soon prove counterproductive. If things were once over-regulated, now cultural images of work-to-consume coupled with devil-take-the-hindmost may have gone too far, and harsher political reactions can set in if ordinary people are not brought more into thought and participation.

We have been fortunate that the first results of the huge ESRC financed 'Citizen Audit' conducted by Patrick Seyd, Paul Whiteley and Charles Pattie could be reported in this volume. Overall the audit reveals relatively strong social capital: one in three of their respondents devote more than an hour a week in *some form* of voluntary activity. There is thus a base to build upon. But also one in three are dissatisfied with democracy.[8] They conclude that we are, indeed, 'right to be concerned about the levels of public disillusionment in the formal body politic'.

The answer must be found in stimulating democracy in the grass roots and local communities. The state would then have to adjust itself to these new and less manipulable pressures.

[8] See also Alison Park, 'Young People and Political Apathy', in Roger Jowell et al., *British Social Attitudes*, vol. 16, Ashgate, 1999. And Colin Crouch, *Coping with Post-Democracy*, London, Fabian Society, 2001, offers a cogent and comprehensive analysis, much in tune with the themes of this book.

23 Justifications of Violence

Vol. 77, no. 4, October–December 2006

OUR PRESENT government seems commendably obsessed with denouncing domestic violence, but less fastidious about international violence.[1] But let me begin by disposing of the most obvious justification of violence via a personal incident, and then as a political philosopher with a taste for history—before reaching terrorism—the intermediate case of tyrannicide.

In the proud moral arrogance of youth when a student, I spoke for the Peace Pledge Union from a soapbox in Lincoln's Inn Fields. A gentleman in a black jacket, pinstripe trousers and bowler hat—so obviously a solicitor—waved his rolled umbrella at me and shouted, 'Call yourself a pacifist! What will you do if I hit you with my umbrella for spouting such treasonable nonsense?' I replied that I would take his umbrella from him and hit him back with proportionate force: 'I'm not that sort of a pacifist.' That is all that needs saying about violence in self-defence, which is well established in common law even if 'proportionality' is often arguable in court.

But as John Wilkes Booth leapt from the box on to the stage, having shot Abraham Lincoln, he shouted what he thought to be an appropriate Latin tag: 'Sic semper tyrannis'—'That's the way with tyrants' or, more literally, 'Ever thus to tyrants'. The phrase would have been associated by the well-educated in the audience with Marcus Brutus, the most famous of tyrannicides (who had been carrying on a bit of a family tradition), yet the phrase was familiar to most of the Washington audience as the state motto of Virginia, framed in the days of rebellion against King George and the British. But now it was invoked simply for vengeance at the end of the Civil War—all hope of Confederate victory long gone—not to make a violent but perhaps merciful end to the fratricidal carnage of civil war. He was reviled as a mad villain by Unionists, but glorified as a hero by many Confederates.

Glorification and tyrannicide

Now, in our green and pleasant land it has just become a criminal offence to glorify terrorism. But how far will the new offence stretch? I hope not retrospectively, or I would be a very worried old thinker. For on the night of Bobby Kennedy's assassination in 1968 a good friend phoned me up, her voice quivering with emotion: 'Bernard, the killing of the two brothers is so terrible, so wrong; but we must not let go of the doctrine of tyrannicide. We must draw distinctions.' The late Irene Coltman spoke as if we were members

[1] This is the edited text of a public lecture given at Birkbeck College, London University, on 14 June 2006.

of a small sacred (if secular) order, preserving ancient truths about the origins and condition of political freedom: 'When you write your intro to Machiavelli's *Discourses* you must remember that he praised the sons of Brutus.' 'Ah, yes. OK Irene, I will.'[a] The world of classical republicanism was very close to her. She and her husband Roland Brown, then Attorney General of Tanzania, had been close to President Julius Nyere when he had instigated a translation of Shakespeare's *Julius Caesar* into Swahili, so that if he ever acted like Julius Caesar . . . the message was clear.

Actually, I did better than recall the sons of Brutus in the Pelican edition of the *Discourses*. On Monday, 7 April 1969 (this will save Special Branch searching), I broadcast on the BBC Third Programme a talk with the title 'Should Tyrants Be Killed?', subsequently printed in the good old *Listener*; but I've lost my copy. If charged, I will only have the script to produce in court.

Now, my title was rhetorical. The plain answer in the tradition of Western political thought was 'Yes', tyrants should be killed. I said so clearly. I did not have to rely only on the thinkers of Greece and Rome, who honoured tyrannicides but denounced assassins. Many of them took for granted that their fellow citizens would understand that distinction without need for formal definition—just as Tony Blair scorned quibblers in Parliament and said that 'ordinary people understand what is meant by the glorification of terrorism'. But to do better than that I turned to St Thomas Aquinas, who, in the *Summa*, echoed Cicero's praise of tyrannicide, albeit on four strict conditions: (i) that the man to be killed had usurped power violently; (ii) that he had broken the divine and the natural law, and was a threat to the lives and morality of his subjects; (iii) that there was no other remedy; and (iv) that his killing would lead to some better state of affairs—it must not be done for vengeance or for punishment, because those matters were in God's hands.

Of course, in the modern world so much power is now in the hands of party, military or state bureaucracy that the killing of one tyrant usually clears the way only for another. Clause (iv) above is difficult to apply. I would be hard put to name contemporary examples, even from Africa; and silence is more prudent (as George Galloway might learn), even if after all, the criminal charge would be one of glorifying tyrannicide rather than actually causing it. If, that is, the courts reject, to the rage of Blair, Clarke, Reade and my old friend Blunkett, synonyms. A. P. Herbert's good old Mr Justice Cocklecarrot may well say that 'tyrannicide' is 'not terrorism' within the wording of the Act, and so I, if charged, would have to agree with such a shabby line of defence, perforce. For, of course, the Act will be interpreted by the courts and not by Mr Blair's 'ordinary people'—thank god. Populism can go too far.

Now, classical learning would have seen Lincoln, indeed, as a 'dictator'—a consul holding absolute powers constitutionally for the time of the emergency—but not as a tyrant. Yet he might have been. Sometimes it is hard to

---

[a] Here we see Bernard's talent for dramatic reconstruction in full flow, outdoing the milder instance of the conversation with the violent solicitor in the previous section.

judge which is the marvellously poised dramatic and moral problematic in a good production of Shakespeare's *Julius Caesar*. Much of our thinking about the relationship of ethics to politics was shaped by long- or half-forgotten theological dispute and debate about the justification of killing tyrants. There was and is this ultimate justification of personal political violence. Not so long ago in historical time, a Pope opined that it was a moral duty to assassinate a Queen of England, salvation guaranteed. Does that sound familiar? And there was also a Protestant theory of tyrannicide. A great man who invoked it in England—Oliver Cromwell—has his statue right outside the public entrance to the House of Commons. Reformers modified Thomas Aquinas's first qualification for they were all too aware that even a legitimate ruler could turn tyrant, threaten the lives and even wage war against his own people. So off with King Charles's head.

Thomas Hobbes, of course, would have none of this. The master of baroque prose burst out against young men 'reading the books of policy':

From the reading, I say, of such books men have undertaken to kill their Kings, because the Greek and Latin writers, in their books and discourses of policy, make it lawful and laudable to do so; provided before he do it, he called him a Tyrant. For they say not Regicide, that is killing of a King, but Tyrannicide, that is, killing of a Tyrant is lawful.

But if Hobbes disliked the individual intentionality of the word, he sweepingly argued that 'Leviathan' (whether a man or a corporate body) simply loses his authority if he threatens the individual lives of his subjects; and loyalty dissolves in battle when it is plain that the cause is lost. Like Falstaff, he sees that honour is a great killer of men (which is the difficulty that the born-again realist Gerry Adams has with the old guard in the IRA).

So it is important to try to be precise about the quality of our horror at the death of, for instance, a Kennedy. Why should we all appear to have been more shocked by the death of two rich young men lusty in and for power (or by the latest murder emblazoned across the tabloid headlines) than by the premature death of millions by malnutrition and poverty or the failure to stamp out by force, when necessary, endemic local wars and even geno-cides—Rwanda, Bosnia and so on. Surely our horror at 'mere' assassination or murder is because of the meaninglessness of the acts or their irrelevance—like the recent bombings—to the aims and effects intended, rather than because of the killings or bombings by themselves. In his 1980 book, *Violence for Equality*, Professor Ted Honderich went beyond Hobbes to claim that violent revolt was justifiable not just if the state killed its inhabitants arbitrarily and abruptly, but when it was killing them slowly by deprivation, malnutrition and gross economic differentiation, as measured by huge differences in life expectancy between ruling elites and subject populations. Perhaps the 'for equality' of Honderich's title was a rhetorical error. What he really meant was degrees of inequality that lead to gross inequalities in life-span and perinatal mortality—good measures of social justice indeed. For if any individual premature death can be accepted as a natural fatality, yet large numbers comparative to other societies are attributable to and can be remedied by state action, or else the state will face justifiable rebellion. Honderich speaks of 'a want of seriousness in a refusal to distinguish, say, between violence with the aim of achieving a fair distribution of food, and violence with the aim of defending the special privilege of an elite, class, people or race'.[2]

Political violence and terrorism

Some good souls think that they object to any kind of murder or killing. Absolute pacifists reject both capital punishment and war of any kind; and they presumably forsake even killing in self-defence, such as our common law allows; or rebellion against oppression. But political violence differs from individual self-defence or heroic self-mortification; for it involves widespread human relationships and has widespread causes and consequences; and causes can be many and complicated, and consequences often unexpected. In fact, there will always be some unexpected consequences with so many people directly indirectly *affected and involved*.

Honderich has recently argued, in his *After the Terror*, that although it is obvious to us all how we, in the United States and the United Kingdom, were affected by September 11 and the London bombings, we fail to recognise that we are all complicit in injustices of foreign and social policy that must, in common sense, have had something to do with the motivation of the killers.[3] Our leaders, defending their failed policies in Israel/Palestine, Afghanistan and Iraq are fools, knaves or hypocrites by denying any connection and traducing those who do. *Tout comprendre n'est pas tout pardonner.* Bush, Blair and their spokesmen accuse those who dare to try to understand why some Palestinians resort to terrorism as themselves justifying and tolerating terrorism. The tabloid press howled at Cherie Blair for showing understanding and at the brave Jenny Tonge (Baroness Tonge) who, when an MP, lost her position as a party spokesman. But toleration of anything does not mean either agreement or permissiveness: it means disapproval, but a disapproval limited either for moral reasons, if a clash of values is involved, or for political or prudential reasons, to try to leave lines of possible compromise open—and, of course, toleration is needed for understanding. Understanding is needed, indeed, to combat terrorism effectively. I was once told that Arthur Koestler said to George Orwell—or was it Orwell to Koestler?—'Know thy enemy as thyself.'

Terrorists, however, commonly choose methods unlikely to advance or justify their cause except among themselves and their sympathisers. Often the struggle becomes an end in itself. There can even be a cult of honour and reckless heroism—Shakespeare's 'Yours in the ranks of death'—or a touch of

---

[2] Ted Honderich, *Equality for Violence*, Penguin, 1980, p. 198.
[3] Ted Honderich, *After the Terror*, Edinburgh University Press, 2002.

full-blown nihilism, as if deadly violence is a form of knowledge, as in William Butler Yeats's so-called last poem 'Under Ben Bulben'. (Students of Yeats are divided on whether those famous lines show a distanced empathy or a spasm of crazed possession with Patrick Pearse's myth of 'the blood sacrifice'.)

Justifications of terrorism

There are more rational justifications of terrorism. When armed resistance in the field or even in the mountains is impossible, neither civil war nor guerrilla warfare, then true terror is resorted to—the random, the unexpected but recurrent acts of lethal violence intended to create, yes, terror among a population. This terror then can make ordinary people feel that their government is impotent, or it can tempt a government—and some don't need much tempting—into repressive acts and curtailments of customary liberties. Terrorists can set out to undermine confidence in and practices of constitutional virtues. Anti-terrorist repression can make people wonder which is worse, supporting their government or surrendering to demands of the terrorists—assuming that their demands are precise enough and feasible.

But can such terrorism ever be justified ethically? Three years ago, Michael Ignatieff gave the Gifford Lectures at the University of Edinburgh on 'The Lesser Evil: Political Ethics in an Age of Terror'. The doctrine of 'the lesser evil' must, indeed, be reckoned with in the real world and can take us so far: terrorism can be justified as the last resort of the weak against strong, implacable and hostile government. But Ignatieff added another condition that is more contentious: that for terrorists to have any possible justification, they must only target institutions of the state and never civilians. I recall that the IRA began to lose the support of their community, especially women, when bombs killed civilians indiscriminately; they soon learnt to target only the police and the army. So Ignatieff's two *possible* justifications for terrorist violence are 'last resort' and 'civilian immunity'. Now 'civilian immunity' is a good, nice liberal prescription. But the trouble is not just that terrorists are not liberal-minded, but that any clear distinction between civilians and the state is rarely possible. For, as Honderich would argue, we are all complicit to some degree in being so law-abiding that we give tacit support, at least, to the very acts of the state that excite and anger the terrorists, in supporting governments that oppress their people towards violent or early death. Take the invasion of Iraq, for example, or failure to try to check the Palestinian policies of the Israeli government—I just mention these in passing. The terrorist, however, strives to put pressure on the state not just by killing one or two of its officials, like the Mafia in Sicily, but by creating enough widespread fear in the civilian population so that they put pressure on the state or withdraw everyday cooperation—anything for a quiet life.

My objection is not always to terrorism as such as a tactic of the oppressed in terrible circumstances but, rather, to the common failure of terrorists to define their aims clearly enough for political solutions (although by us rejecting all their aims out of hand, rather than analysing their writings and utterances carefully—yes, even those of Bin Laden—we often close the door against any negotiation or conciliation). In her book *On Violence*, Hannah Arendt argued that violence *can* be justified to remedy precise grievances, but not world-changing abstractions such as 'revolution', 'historical inevitability', 'the classless society' or 'equality'—here I part company with Honderich and would rather say, with John Rawls, 'no unjustifiable inequalities' than full-blooded equality. Were she alive today, Arendt would surely add both Bin Laden's 'holy war' and George Bush's 'war against terrorism' to her examples of compelling grandiose nebulosities. She sees violence as the breakdown of political power, not as an extreme form of political power. Violence arises from a failure to pursue political or diplomatic solutions.[4]

Violence (she says) is rational to the extent that it is effective in reaching the end that must justify it. And since when we act we never know with any certainty the eventual consequences of what we are doing, violence can remain rational only if it pursues short-term goals. Violence does not promote causes, neither history nor revolution, neither progress nor reaction; but it can serve to dramatise grievances and bring them to public attention.

Well, of course, it all depends on what one means by 'short-term'. The short term can be a lot more than dramatising grievances. It can be the defence of the state in times of emergency or it can be the overthrow of an unjust and oppressive state, and while all rebellions against oppressive regimes, tyrannies and dictatorships hope to be short term, even in South America, they can often become somewhat protracted. Her 'short-term' criterion for any justification of violence is better applied to clarity of precise and limited objectives than to actual time.

To return to my armed solicitor in Lincoln's Inn Fields, my response was a parable of proportionate threatened violence, well within our common law. But scale that up to the defence of the realm in times of war, and then dilemmas begin. Lincoln asked at the beginning of the American Civil War 'how a government can ever be strong enough to defend the liberties of its people but not so strong as to threaten them'. There is no universal or formulaic answer, except to be aware of the perennial dilemma. We had Emergency Powers legislation in both world wars. Machiavelli, the republican, had said that 'when the very safety of the state is threatened, no consideration of good or evil should stand in the way of its defence'. But by 'safety of the state' he meant the complete collapse of order due to rebellion or rapacious invasion by another state. The safety of the state and the realist doctrine of 'reason of state' are not to be confused with the convenience of governments or over-reaction to spasmodic terrorism, even such as the twin towers on September 11 or the London bombings. Such acts can in no way

[4] Hannah Arendt, *On Violence*, Allen Lane (The Penguin Press), 1970.

destroy either the state or, indeed, the normal life of society, unless a government over-reacts or uses threats of violence as an excuse to justify unusual and repressive measures to its own political advantage. Some suggest that this is happening. Certainly, the temptation grows greater by the day, but there is always a price to be paid for liberty.

I have chosen this theme of justifications of violence because in times of relative peace and prosperity we liberals often cannot face up to the reality of violence, both the legitimate use of force in our own society and the complexity of motivations of those who feel themselves driven to use it against us. We need more of the spirit and insight of what historians of political thought have called civic republicanism and less of the complacency of liberalism. Let me explain—or, rather, since this is no new argument, let me allow Benjamin Constant to explain in his once famous essay of 1820, 'The Liberty of the Ancients Compared to that of the Moderns':

The aim of the ancients was the sharing of social power among citizens of the same fatherland: this is what they called liberty. The aim of the moderns is the enjoyment of liberty in private pleasures; and they call liberty the guarantees accorded by institutions to these pleasures.

If that sounds like a prophecy of the consumer culture rather than a citizen culture, it is. A citizen culture is one in which a people are both active in defence of the state against public enemies, but also active to restrain the state if it threatens their liberties or those of others; and in extreme cases, active even to overthrow it—as in the English Civil War, 1688, the Dutch Republic and the American and French revolutions. In losing the sense of how to glorify active citizenship, we risk losing the sense both of how to understand the motivations for violence and how to discriminate between justifiable and unjustifiable violence.

24 Do We Really Need Britannia?

Book chapter; vol. 78, no. 5, 2007 (published 2009)

... this sudden sense of knowing her all at once much better was not simultaneously accompanied by any clear portrayal in my mind of the kind of person she might really be. Perhaps intimacy of any sort, love or friendship, impedes all exactness of definition.

(Anthony Powell, *Dance to the Music of Time*)

So say I about intimacy with Britannia. To try to define Britishness can be both philosophical and political folly. The philosophical folly arises from the fact, as Arthur Aughey has argued in his profound and searching book *The Politics of Englishness*, that 'a straightforward definition of Englishness' was not required for his study, 'nor is it the precondition for saying something intelligible about contemporary England'.[1] And so, say I, about Britishness, although to seek to explain why Britishness has suddenly sprung into political and academic prominence is, indeed, worthy of explanation—and I suspect that many contributors to this book[a] will see this as the main object of the enterprise. But I will argue that it is political folly for politicians, or anyone else, to attempt to *define* or redefine such a protean concept which most of us take for granted rather than want to see explicated, particularly as a party matter—on which the parties can never and should never agree.

Britishness does not explain why the United Kingdom has held together, nor does it validate the recent and topical belief that by lack of clarity and intensity about Britishness the UK may fall apart. Aughey invokes Michael Oakeshott to suggest that Englishness (and the same goes for Britishness) is not so much a preface as a postscript: it is the exploration of the 'intimations' of a tradition that has many different intimations. He quotes Oakeshott that 'a tradition of behaviour is a tricky thing to get to know' because while everyone agrees it is there, it has diverse modulations and interpretations and each changes through time. Does it need saying that Britishness today is, for instance, very different from the stiff collar-and-tie kind of my youth in the late forties and early fifties? And I am grateful that Aughey quotes me as saying in 1991, before the present fervour and fashion for Britishness, Englishness and identity studies got under way, 'that the identity of the English is almost as difficult to specify as the name of the state'.[2] I am no late

[1] Arthur Aughey, *The Politics of Englishness*, Manchester, Manchester University Press, p. 6.
[2] Aughey, ibid., p. 6, quoting Bernard Crick, 'The English and the British' in Crick, ed., *National Identities: The Constitution of the United Kingdom*, Oxford, Blackwell and *The Political Quarterly*, 1991 [and reproduced in this book as article 18 above, *Ed.*].

[a] This was a chapter in the *Britishness* collection edited by Andrew Gamble and Tony Wright, a journal fifth issue that came out in 2009 (though for technical reasons it has a 2007 volume number). Hence it is the only one of Bernard's *PQ* pieces to be published posthumously.

Published by Blackwell Publishing Ltd, 9600 Garsington Road, Oxford OX4 2DQ, UK and 350 Main Street, Malden, MA 02148, USA

convert to some aspects of Oakeshott's thinking: long ago I described myself as a 'left-wing Oakeshottian', perhaps echoing Edward Thompson's *The Making of the English Working Class* or Raymond Williams's *The Long Revolution*.[3] Aughey also quotes Garton Ash reflecting that 'the very nature of Identity Studies' means that rarely is a definite, clear finding ever arrived at'.[4] However, Bhikhu Parekh has wisely said: 'While the concept of national character is problematic in a culturally diverse society, that of national identity is not. Immigrants can be expected to share national identity but not national character. Ethnic nationalism equates the two: civic nationalism keeps them apart.'[5]

Much ado about nothing?

So attempts to give definitions of Britishness, Englishness or indeed almost any other national identity are what Oakeshott meant by rationalism, or arbitrary 'arrests of experience'. Both concepts are sentiments, feelings drawn from an ever changing historical tradition. So it is surprising that these concepts, being sentiments, are taken so seriously politically in what has been basically (some say notoriously) a British (English and Scottish) empirical tradition of thought. Is not what holds us together mainly interest, practical judgement, utilitarian concerns on continuing advantages and the sheer convenience of a political or civic culture based on compromise and the avoidance of civil war? Of course, this only may explain why we hold together as one state; such a utilitarian view says nothing of the morality of political policies and individual behaviour within the state. But it is odd how much the sentiments of nineteenth century romanticism have recently infected pragmatic political thinking: the belief that systematised shared sentiments or definable common feelings are necessary. They are not. Have we forgotten in England Thomas Hobbes, Jeremy Bentham and John Stuart Mill; or in Scotland David Hume and Adam Smith? There is nothing ignoble or strange in between fifteen and twenty per cent of Catholics in Northern Ireland who vote for Sinn Fein but none the less say that they wish to retain the union. They probably prefer unity in their hearts, but in their heads as sensible family men and women they may first want to know what is in the unity package, how it might change their quality of life, life-chances or whatever. Some may simply favour *good government* and power-sharing where they are. They are not for 'unity above all else'. The same could be said of Scotland and Scottishness.

In the outburst of serious scholarly writing in Scotland on the three-hundredth anniversary of the Act or Treaty of Union, opinion has swung

[3] Bernard Crick, 'The World of Michael Oakeshott', in his essays *Political Theory and Practice*, London, Allen Lane / The Penguin Press, 1972, pp. 120–34.

[4] Timothy Garton Ash, 'Is Britain European?', *International Affairs*, vol. 77, no. 1, pp. 1–13.

[5] Bhikhu Parekh, *A New Politics of Identity*, Basingstoke, Palgrave Macmillan, 2008, p. 284.

away far away from Robert Burns's eloquent, much quoted but silly 'bought and sold by English gold', to seeing that the votes in the last Scottish Parliament were predominantly swayed by calculation as to what was in Scotland's best interest: the opportunities of a relatively poor country getting inside the English imperial trade barriers; the seeming guarantee against a Stuart Catholic restoration and civil war; and all this in a hard-bargained agreement that left Scotland with its own ecclesiastical, legal, local government laws and establishment, the seeds of a famous educational system, and entry into the English now British imperial trade system.[6]

Much has been made of Linda Colley's *Britons: Forging the Nation 1707–1807*. She set out vividly and conclusively the evidence for the deliberate and well orchestrated Hanoverian campaign to merge Englishness and Scottishness into Britishness: henceforth neither Scotland nor England but Great Britain and later the United Kingdom. However, while it succeeded at the level of political institutions (more or less, for Scotland was largely left to govern itself, and the Argylls and the Dundas who managed government business would have been no use to Whitehall and Westminster had they lost their standing in Scotland by becoming Anglicised or only British), at a popular level Britishness does not seem to have caught on. I can find no folk songs in the last great age of folk songs that hail Britain or Britannia (*Rule Britannia* and *Hearts of Oak* were government sponsored theatre songs): it is ever 'old England' or 'auld Scotland'. Scottishness was the popular culture just as Englishness, albeit until recently in a lower register of explicitness, predominated over Britishness. Britishness was a common, primary identity in the white settler colonies of the nineteenth century. Today it is strong as a dual self-description of most immigrants: British Muslim, say, or 'British Asian'. 'English British' is not used in common parlance but could characterise those English who feel a wider attachment to 'Great Britain' or to the 'United Kingdom'. However, many English still confuse Britishness with Englishness. While very few Scots express their primary identity as British, a majority are 'Scottish British', with the emotional weight on the former but legal allegiance still on the latter. Consider that from the beginning of the British military need to recruit Scots in the American War of Independence and the Napoleonic Wars, the prohibitions following the 1745 rebellion, and right through the two world wars to today, no one in Whitehall was foolish enough to try to integrate Scottish soldiers into British or English line regiments rather than specifically Scottish regiments. Even FIFA still recognises, perhaps surprisingly, four national football teams from the one United Kingdom rather than one British team. Finally, who ever talks about 'British novels' or poetry, rather than four distinctive national modes? Britishness

---

[6] See T. M. Devine, 'Three Hundred Years of the Anglo-Scottish Union', in Devine, ed., *Scotland and the Union: 1707–2007*, Edinburgh, Edinburgh University Press, 2008, pp. 1–19; also Christopher A. Whatley, 'The Making of the Union of 1707: History with a History', in Devine, *Scotland and the Union*, ibid., pp. 23–38.

political and legal institutions are real, but there are four recognisable cultures. Yes, each influenced by and interacting with the others, but in distinctive national ways.

Concluding a summary of their series of opinion surveys on perceptions of national identity in England and Scotland, Frank Bechhofer and David McCrone say: 'Englishness, Scottishness and Britishness may be more cultural than political'. Their figures show a relatively weak association between identity and party political support, suggesting that 'it is difficult to mobilise national identity in a straightforwardly political way', even for independence. 'The material we have presented thus suggests strongly that these matters are by no means as clear cut as the political rhetoric would have people believe, and that any or all of these arguments could backfire.'[7]

Mr Brown of London town

Britishness has figured greatly in recent speeches by Gordon Brown. Simon Lee, with deadly scholarly precision, found that in these speeches the only examples he gives of our glorious liberties etc. were *all* from English history![8] There was nary a mention of the Declaration of Arbroath or the signing of the Covenant, nor of course of Bannockburn, these as firm in Scots mythology as Magna Carta in English. Plainly Brown has either become Anglicised through long weeks in London reacting each morning to placate the Scotophobic London press; or his target was the almost equally mythical 'Middle England'; so an almost fatuous attempt to impress that he wore his obvious Scottishness very lightly: 'British Scottish' not 'Scottish British'.

Brown's banging on about Britishness is both mistaken and irrelevant.[9] In his 2007 speech to the TUC annual conference, according to the *Guardian*, he used the term 34 times and in his speech to the Labour Party conference the BBC counted about 80 strikes—not all to define it, of course, but 'our British' attached to this and that almost promiscuously (including the unfortunate and notorious populist 'British jobs for British workers').

This is a profoundly mistaken rhetorical tactic if it is aimed at the SNP, for while nearly all Scots are strongly nationalistic a majority are not separatist (even a quarter of SNP voters favour the Union). There is nationalism and Nationalism. But the trouble is that Gordon Brown really does seem to believe that unity of the United Kingdom is in danger if there is not a strong and common sense of Britishness. Consider the mission statement or

[7] Frank Bechhofer and David McCrone, 'Being British: A Crisis of Identity?', *The Political Quarterly*, vol. 78, no. 2, pp. 251–60.

[8] Simon Lee, 'Gordon Brown and the "British Way"', *The Political Quarterly*, vol. 77, no. 3, pp. 369–78.

[9] The paragraphs to the end of this section are taken from my Mackintosh Memorial lecture, 'The Four Nations: Interrelations', as printed in *The Political Quarterly*, vol. 79, no. 1, 2008, pp. 71–9 [and reproduced in this book as article 25 below, *Ed.*].

sloaghan[b] he had drafted for a conference hosted by HM Treasury back in November 2005:

How 'British' do we feel? What do we mean by 'Britishness'? These questions are increasingly important in defining a shared purpose across all of our society. The strength of our communities, the way we understand diversity, the vigour of our public services and our commercial competitiveness all rest on a sense of what 'Britishness' is and how it sets shared goals.

Not only the global economy makes these assertions in the last sentence, in Bentham's phrase, nonsense on stilts. And must Britishness express a 'shared purpose' and shared 'goals'? Do states really have 'purposes' and 'goals'? Such teleological language is a pale rhetorical echo of the old destructive nationalism of central Europe and the Balkans. Is this really how states hold together, especially in the modern world, whether we like it or not, of a global economy and of all notions of national sovereignty needing to be so qualified as to be almost useless in understanding actual politics whether national and international? This idea of national purpose is what Goethe called 'a blue rose'. And the search for it has proved damaging already as well as frustrating. Both Thatcher and Blair openly spoke of restoring our sense of national importance, to put the 'Great' back into Great Britain. This was a hangover from the old days of Empire and the Second World War—which, of course, we won, albeit with a little help from the USA and the USSR. And this search has meant the American alliance, with—considering the Iraq war—too few questions asked or reservations made.

We do not need a heightened sense of Britishness and clear national purpose to hold us together. Perhaps we just need good government and social justice. National leaders should be careful when they invoke 'our common values'. Perhaps our main common value has been to respect, on the whole, the values of others. In July 2004 Brown gave the British Council Annual Lecture on Britishness and invoked *values*, our British values:

The values and qualities I describe are of course to be found in many other cultures and countries. But when taken together, and as they shape the institutions of our country these values and qualities—being creative, adaptable and outward looking, our belief in liberty, duty and fair play—add up to a distinctive Britishness that has been manifest throughout our history, and shaped it.

'Liberty, duty and fair play'—well, some Scots are beginning to play cricket, of a kind, even if 'fair play' is still a wee bit marginal in the Old Firm encounters. I think Mr Brown plants both feet firmly in mid-air.

[b] Bernard uses this rather affected spelling in his last few articles. It is impossible to say whether he'd always done it but was previously edited back into conventionality or instead this was a new trait. See my note d to Article 25 below.

For citizenship education

Brown told readers of the *Daily Telegraph* that 'I am certain that the teaching of British history should be at the heart of the modern school curriculum, and the current review of the curriculum should root the teaching of citizenship more closely in British history.'[10] His first point is a good one. History was in both Key Stages 3 and 4 in the first national Baker curriculum for England, but Baker's successor Kenneth Clarke took it out of KS 4 *ipse dixit*; so there is no compulsory history after the age of 14. But Brown's second point was either a misunderstanding or a repudiation of the thrust of the citizenship curriculum. For that was based on the knowledge and skills needed to be active citizens, not just good citizens; what was enjoined was *learning* by discussion of real issues and by participation in school and community affairs, not just *teaching* from the front about institutions. David Blunkett backed that from the beginning, even under the eyes of a nervous and traditionalist Blair. We said (I was chair of the advisory group): 'We aim at no less than a change in the political culture of this country both nationally and locally: for people to think of themselves, willing, able and equipped to have influence in public and with critical capacity to weigh evidence before speaking and acting.'[11] (I did not feel the need to tell the group that this was civic republican theory, but they liked the language and the aspirations.)

We wanted to leave teachers as much flexibility as possible to adjust to local conditions, so the prescriptions are both short and general. On Britishness and diversity the national curriculum simply said: 'Pupils should be taught about ... the origins and implications of the diverse national, regional, religious and ethnic identities in the United Kingdom and the need for mutual respect and understanding.' But that was written before the London bombings, and some ministers began to think that a revised citizenship curriculum could help greatly against recruitment to terrorist organisations. I thought that most unlikely. But Brown's *obiter dictum* on citizenship did lead to a review[12]— fortunately in the sensible hands of a retired head teacher of a successful multi-ethnic school, Sir Keith Ajegbo, assisted by Dr Dina Kiwan.[13] In 1998 there had seemed less need to elaborate on diversity than in 2007. But now they proposed adding a fourth leg to the citizenship stool, previously: *social and moral responsibility*, *community involvement* and *political literacy* (what you need to know to get something done usually working with others). This

[10] Gordon Brown 'We Need a United Kingdom', *Daily Telegraph*, 13 January 2007, p. 23.

[11] *Education for Citizenship and the Teaching of Democracy in Schools*, London, QCA, 1998, para. 1.5, p. 7.

[12] *Curriculum Review: Diversity and Citizenship*, DES, 2007.

[13] Sir Keith Ajegbo was head teacher of Deptford Green School, a multi-ethnic school with an outstanding reputation for citizenship education. Dina Kiwan is lecturer in citizenship education at Birkbeck College. Previously she was seconded to the Home Office as the Head of Secretariat to the Advisory Board for Naturalisation and Integration (ABNI), on the implementation of the recommendations of the 'Life in the UK' advisory group.

fourth leg was called *Identity and Diversity: Living Together in the UK*: that all pupils in England, would be taught about 'shared values and life in the UK. This will be informed by an understanding of contemporary issues and relevant historical context which gave rise to them.' But the emphasis in guidance papers is on *discussion* of what are or may be shared values and also *discussion* of what is Britishness. Few teachers would have any confidence about teaching *the* values of Britishness, whether from their common sense or from a book; so in practice discussion is in the spirit of the rest of the citizenship order. Early in the report they noted from their wide consultations: 'The term "British" means different things to different people. In addition, identities are typically constructed as multiple and plural. Throughout our consultations, concerns were expressed, however, about defining "Britishness", about the term's divisiveness and how it can be used to exclude others.' So one does not have to be Aughey, Crick, Oakeshott or Popper to believe that definitions do not settle arguments.

For new citizens

The 'Living in the United Kingdom' advisory group set up by David Blunkett in 2002 (which I chaired—fifty–fifty old Brits and new Brits) reported the following year as *The New and the Old*.[14] Its remit was to propose what 'sufficient' should mean following the Naturalisation, Immigration and Asylum Act 2002 that required United Kingdom residents seeking citizenship to show 'a sufficient knowledge of English, Welsh or Scottish-Gaelic' and 'a sufficient knowledge about life in the United Kingdom'. For once, officials were wise enough not to try themselves to tease out in statutory terms what was 'sufficient'. The Home Secretary accepted most of our recommendations, even if sufficient funding for fully effective implementation was not forthcoming from the Treasury.

Those who thought they had sufficient English[15] could take a machine readable test based on a handbook *Life in the United Kingdom: A Journey to Citizenship*,[16] and the others had to attend classes given by professional ESOL (English as a second language)[c] teachers and make progress by one standard level. However, the media, led by the BBC, insisted in calling these two tests—as if they were one—'the Britishness test'. They were no such thing. *The Journey to Citizenship* (now in a second edition), written mainly for ESOL

[14] Home Office, 2003.
[15] Technically, ESOL Entry level 3, which is the ability to talk comprehensibly on an unexpected subject (that is, not just one's trade or job) and to read instructions. Writing is not tested.
[16] Produced by ABNI in cooperation with the Citizenship Foundation, published by the Stationery Office.

[c] Normally 'English for speakers of other languages'.

teachers and those preparing for the machine readable test,[17] contains useful information about settling in and integration. There was and still is no element of testing for Britishness. Certainly there was a short history, 'The Making of the United Kingdom', at the beginning as background for teachers and others, but specifically not to be part either of the test or the ESOL programme of studies.

The BBC instantly called it 'the Britishness report', possibly in haste and error (trying as so often to anticipate a report, rather than waiting to read it or even the official press release); but the popular press followed suit either by false expectation or malign design. Many newspapers had asked their readers what they wanted in a test, with responses—the date of Magna Carta and Nelson's last words etc.—that would have failed nearly all applicants and most of the native population. I put the matter more cautiously in a Foreword to ABNI's 2005–6 annual report:

There were some [sic] press comments that the programme of studies was not historical and too little concerned with Britishness, but we were unanimous that people become British by learning about the laws, institutions and customs of our country, essential for settling in with mutual understanding.

For the report had taken the view that a sense of Britishness, however perceived, felt or defined, would grow on immigrants through time by their becoming citizens and living in a civic culture and being decently treated. On platforms I would say that we assumed the oldest and most basic contract: that immigrants give their loyalty to a country in return for the protection of its laws.

Well, we did feel the need—and pressure—to say something about Britishness in the report, even if it did not (and has not) carried forward into either the ESOL certification for naturalisation or the machine test. Here is exactly what we said, carefully (in both senses of that word):

Para. 2.6 Who are we British? For a long time the United Kingdom has been a multinational state composed of England, Northern Ireland, Scotland and Wales, and also a multicultural society. What do we mean by a multicultural society? We see a multicultural society as one made up of a diverse range of cultures and identities, and one that emphasises the need for a continuous process of mutual engagement and learning about each other with respect, understanding and tolerance . . . Such societies, under a framework of common civic values and common legal and political institutions, not only understand and tolerate diversities of identity but should also respect and take pride in them—Australia, Canada, India, South Africa and the United States of America are examples of multicultural societies.

And we pointed out that identities are never fixed in every respect, they are always changing, and that many people in the UK have a sense of dual

---

[17] Journey to Citizenship is now, after I left ABNI, somewhat watered down from the more realistic tone of 'how it is' rather than 'how we'd like you to think it is'. See Patricia White, 'Immigrants into Citizens', *The Political Quarterly*, vol. 79, no. 2, 2008, pp. 221–31.

identities. Then in para. 2.7 we took John Bull by the horns as we finessed the problem gently:

To be British seems to us to mean that we respect the laws, the elected parliamentary and legal structures, traditional values of mutual tolerance, and that we give our allegiance to the state (as commonly symbolised by the Crown) in return for its protection. To be British is to respect those over-arching specific institutions, values, beliefs and traditions that bind us all, the different nations and cultures, together in peace and in a legal order. For we are all subject to the laws of the land including Human Rights and Equal Rights legislation, and so our diversities of practice must adhere to these legal frameworks.

Even the even more cautious revised version of the *Journey to Citizenship: Life in the United Kingdom* said: 'The UK has been a multinational and multicultural society for a long time, without it being a threat to its British identity, or its English, Scottish, Welsh or Irish cultural and national identities.' Interestingly, in the traditional oath still to be sworn at the new citizenship ceremonies ('I swear by Almighty God / do solemnly and sincerely affirm that, on becoming a British citizen, I will be faithful and bear true allegiance to Her Majesty Queen Elizabeth the Second, her heirs and successors according to law') and immediately afterwards a new Pledge ('I will give my loyalty to the United Kingdom and respect its rights and freedoms. I will uphold its democratic values. I will observe its laws faithfully and fulfil my duties and obligations as a British citizen'),[18] the only mention of 'British' is in that purely legal context—in which even Mr Alex Salmond is undoubtedly a British citizen, at least for a guid while yet. Any mention of 'Britishness' as a traditional bundle of values, beliefs and traditions was realised as provocative to much Scottish and Welsh sentiment, and very difficult to define; it could run the risk (I naughtily suggested) of being overwhelmed by undiluted enthusiasm in Unionist Northern Ireland. All this was, I think, a wiser approach to 'Britishness' than some ministerial speeches and many editorials.

A note on Scottishness

Paradoxically, to consider 'Scottishness' might set to rest some fears that without an explicit strong Britishness the United Kingdom implodes. As many surveys show, the awareness and sense of being Scottish has been stronger than that of being British or English, though now the salience of Englishness in England is growing, as Aughey has charted and flags of St George testify. Scottish nationalism is strong and almost universal. But we

[18] Brought in, I was told, when the Queen and Tony Blair refused to alter the Oath to mention such things. Some existing citizens object to others taking the Oath at all, by no means all writers in the *Guardian*; but surveys have shown that immigrants like the feeling of being associated with the Queen as head of state.

need to distinguish carefully nationalism and Nationalism. The one is a strong national consciousness, just as Englishmen may have it without wishing to break up the United Kingdom; but Nationalism implies separatism, even though now Alex Salmond's New SNP speaks of 'independence in Europe'; and he reassuringly says that 'independence is a political not a social matter'.[19] And certainly the SNP has been remarkably successful in attracting immigrant votes and even members. The old ethnic party of twenty-five years ago now sees itself as a multicultural national party professing a common civic culture. 'Muslim Pakistanis identify strongly with Scotland rather than Britain—and do regardless of whether they were born in Scotland or not.'[20] But surveys suggest that only three out of ten Scots support independence (a figure that has altered very little since before devolution) and that in the 2007 elections to the Parliament of Scotland only 63 per cent of those who intended to vote SNP supported its core policy of independence.[21] There were other reasons to vote SNP. And Bechhofer and McCrone's surveys[22] also show conclusively that intensity of national feeling and even dislike of 'Britishness' does not, for a majority, lead to a desire for independence. Britishness hardly enters into it.

Presumably, to end where I began, a tacit but strong pragmatic loyalty to the United Kingdom based on habit, tradition and interest underlies strong feelings of national identity and even immigrant identities. We don't need a Britishness campaign to ensure holding the United Kingdom together, just good government. If there are changes they will come through political events, misgovernment and economic mistakes, not through heightened Scottishness or Englishness.

---

[19] Quoted in Crick, 'The Four Nations', ibid.

[20] W. L. Miller, 'The Death of Unionism', in Devine, ed., *Scotland and the Union*, pp. 186–9. But his title implies the death of an ideology not of the Union.

[21] Devine, ibid., p. 18.

[22] Ibid., pp. 258–60.

25 The Four Nations: Interrelations

Vol. 79, no. 1, January–March 2008

So MUCH has been said about the different cultures of the four nations, and always more to be said about how these cultures change, but also something to be said about their interrelations which are so obvious both socially and economically once we cut through the heavy rhetoric of 'independence' or 'the Union'. Any approach to interrelations must begin with history before turning to politics, for so much politics is an evoked memory of past history, true and false, researched or imagined.[a]

Once upon a time, indeed almost yesterday, histories of each of the four historic nations of the British Isles could be written with only glancing reference to the others; some of those glancings are piercingly hostile, others are loftily disdainful. Fair enough that the great *Oxford History of England* was a history of England from earliest times, but it now seems more than little bit off for A. J. P. Taylor to have said in the Preface to his *English History: 1914–1945* volume: '[The] use of "England" except for a geographic area brings protests from the Scotch [as he provocatively called the Scots].' 'They seek to impose "Britain",' he said, 'the name of a Roman province that perished in the Fifth century.' He proposed to stick to English history as his assignment. That Scotland had a different established church and so on, was 'none of my concern'. So it was apparently of no concern to him that the Scottish Church question was the trigger to the English Civil War, or as modern historians now say 'the civil wars in three kingdoms'.

But at least A. J. P. Taylor was teasing, being deliberately provocative or malicious, not ignorant. The case of another Oxford professor is somewhat different, someone who specialised in sounding authoritative in an irritatingly Oxford way. In 1982 Lord Blake, no less, edited an upmarket coffee-table book, full of lovely pictures and distilled prose, called *The English World: History, Character and People*. In his Introduction he pontificated:

England's coastline has helped to shape both the history of the English nation and the psychology of the English character. . . .The long centuries during which the land was free from invaders meant that there could be a continuity of tradition impossible on

---

[a] The original article carried the following 'provenance' footnote: 'This is a lightly revised text of the twenty-fifth John Mackintosh Memorial Lecture given at the University of Edinburgh on 2 October 2007. Many Scottish journalists believe that the 1978 devolution referendum, amid a then bitterly divided Scottish Labour party, would have been carried had he lived another year.'

The reference is to John P. Mackintosh, who died at the age of 48 on 30 July 1978 while a serving MP and coeditor (with Bernard) of *The Political Quarterly*. Willie Robson's immediate successor at *PQ*, he is the only editor of the journal to have died in office. In Mackintosh's *ODNB* entry Tam Dalyell portrays this powerful advocate of Scottish devolution as a man of 'demonic energy' and 'arguably the most compellingly persuasive parliamentary orator of his generation'. His paths linked with Bernard's in a number of ways.

the war-torn continent. . . . Some characteristics on which both natives and visitors have tended to agree have to do with national psychology: egoism, self-confidence, intolerance of outsiders, ostentatious wealth, social mobility, love of comfort, and a strong belief in private property. . . . We come to the cliché that Britain is an island, a fact that has been subtly decisive in so many aspects of her history.

Notice that as Lord Blake rolled on he suddenly became aware that 'England's' coastline has this slight hiatus of the Welsh and Scottish borders. So while his rhetoric cries out to quote Shakespeare's John of Gaunt's 'England, bound in with the triumphal sea', yet even though he was an English historian and not a geographer, yet on this sad point of fact he has to concede, as a scholar, in the last line I quoted, that '*Britain* is an island'. And having gone so far he might have noted that Scottish historians would not so easily accept or recognise the contrast between 'a continuity of tradition' of a mythically peaceful isle of Albion and the 'war-torn continent'. The Scottish seventeenth and early eighteenth centuries were either war-torn or ever fearful of a return of war. And as for England not suffering invasion for long centuries, somehow the victorious Scottish army of the Covenant occupying Newcastle in 1640 did not count, nor the Dutch fleet and army of 1688. Oh, and of course this common English confusion of 'English' with 'British' in this myth of the peaceable kingdom must be forgotten—repressed not even oppressed for its own good.

Revisionist history

Now there is a belief, no older than the mid-eighteenth century, that every nation must constitute a state, or that multinational states are inherently unstable. Nationalist histories supported this view. In the nineteenth century this was thought to be the main purpose of professional history, but there has been a remarkable recent change in the way most historians have come to look at the relations between the four nations, looking at interrelations as well as conceptual or political separations. This actually began in the late 1950s in the very hotbed of nationalist history, the Republic of Ireland, where history had previously been held to have no other serious subject matter than to illustrate and celebrate, in Parnell's famous teleological phrase, 'the march of a nation'. But that march didn't always go straight. Eamon de Valera famously believed in the days of struggle that the future Irish republic would be an Irish-speaking, devoutly Catholic, peasant, agrarian culture remote from the industrial and capitalist world. So the uproar was considerable when historians, first at Trinity College, not surprisingly, but then at UCD, the national university, began to assert that the Easter rising, the civil war and independence could only be properly understood in the context of British imperial history, and that the great events were contingent, could have been otherwise, not a necessary unfolding of destiny. This revisionism was reviled by nationalist intellectuals, but it gradually won the argument not just in academic history, but in the writing, authorisation and teaching of history textbooks in schools.

A similar change took place, to generalise widely but not too wildly, in the academic writing of Scottish, Welsh and lastly even in English history. But it was the Irish historians who showed that you could be a good nationalist without being a bad historian. There are still some popular historians in Scotland who seem to believe that the case for independence rests on proving that the Act or Treaty of Union was nothing but bribery and threat. And it was a New Zealander who first attacked the Anglocentric dominance of English historians. In 1975 John Pocock wrote a truly seminal article entitled 'British History: A Plea for a New Subject'.[1] And the first fulfilment of that plea (and in many ways still the best) was to come in 1989 with Hugh Kearney's *The British Isles: A History of Four Nations*.[2] Both stressed interconnections. If there was a fault in Pocock it was that his thesis fitted high politics best, the two and a half centuries in which the dominant concern of English high politics was that of holding the United Kingdom together. It does not fit social history so well, what used to be called the 'history of the common people'. Under different systems of land tenure, the Irish peasant was not the English agricultural labourer, and different parts of Scotland were different again. British history, like Britishness as a concept or belief, is an overall, umbrella category, mainly political and legal, within which national cultures not merely coexist, but influence each other.

To see Britishness thus is to take issue with the main thesis of Linda Colley's otherwise vastly suggestive book, *Britons: The Forging of the Nation, 1707–1837*.[3] She brilliantly uncovered and portrayed the Hanoverian state cult and, as it were, hearts and minds campaign to persuade that 'We are all Britons, no longer Scots and English'. But I don't believe that it diminished Scottish national consciousness; rather it created a sense of dual identity. And Colley had to exclude Ireland from her narrative to make her claim, although it was a crucial part of the British political agenda for three centuries. Many Scottish aristocrats and placemen did indeed see themselves as British and some even happily or lazily called the United Kingdom 'England', but the common people in both countries were largely untouched, remaining stubbornly and noticeably Scots and English. No folk songs invoke 'Britons' and 'Britannia'; they are all 'old England' or 'auld Scotland'. *Rule Britannia* was a government-sponsored, authored theatre song, not a folk song. And those London journalists today who think Britishness completely overrides and subsumes national identities should complain to

---

[1] J. G. A. Pocock, 'British history: a plea for a new subject', *Journal of Modern History*, vol. 47, no. 4, 1975, pp. 601–21.

[2] Hugh Kearney, *The British Isles: A History of Four Nations*, Cambridge, Cambridge University Press, 1989.

[3] Linda Colley, *Britons: The Forging of the Nation, 1707–1837*, London, Yale University Press, 1992.

FIFA that the United Kingdom alone among all other states is allowed to field four different football teams.

Nationalism not necessarily separatist

Colley[b] was courted by Blair in Downing Street seminars. Her Britishness thesis was used as an argument against nationalism. But there is 'National- ism' and 'nationalism'. Over many years I have fought a losing battle to impress on subeditors the use of an upper case for separatist 'Nationalism' and lower case for cultural 'nationalism', for strong national consciousness that is not necessarily separatist. Gordon Brown in the 2001 general election attacked fiercely, as he said, 'nationalists' in the name of the advantages of the Union. I was pompously moved to write to him to suggest that he either gave the SNP its real name or firmly polemicised against '*separatist* nationalists'. For I humbly pointed out that, to my old English and new Scottish immigrant eyes, nearly all Scots were nationalists, in the sense of having a strong feeling of national identity: the majority were not separatists. I suggested that attacking nationalism as such, lumping separatism and patriotism together, could cause offence as well as confusion and drive some cultural nationalists into separatist politics.

From intellectual history comes a broad point that affects all our percep- tions but often gets forgotten by politicians, indeed by most of us. National- ism and romanticism arose hand in glove. But once we can escape from the conceptual blinkers of romanticism, that local sentiments of the heart must always override the general reasoning of humanity (as exemplified in both the French and Scottish enlightenments), we can see that most peoples' calcula- tion of their interests and of common interests are as important as their perceptions of national differences and divergences. For example, surveys tell us that about a quarter of those who vote nationalist in Northern Ireland say they favour the preservation of the Union! They may favour, in principle, the unity of Ireland, if that is the only question asked; but they sensibly want to know what is in the package for themselves and their families: how will it affect their day to day interests—welfare, unemployment, schools, health benefits, employment rights and so on. This is not contemptible, except to an ultra-nationalist or passionate romantic. Interest, or the theory of utilitarian- ism, is not to be scorned or ignored. The word 'interest' figured largely in the debates of 1706 and 1707. Robert Burns's famous 'bought and sold by English gold' was a later populist rant, foolishly used by nationalist historians as evidence; most of the commissioners on both sides were bargaining from interest expressed in alternative political compromises, above all how to ensure peace and, through commerce, prosperity. The Lowland Scots struck a not-at-all contemptible economic and political bargain, especially as Scots law

---

[b] The original journal version had 'Coltman' here (cf. the mention of Irene Coltman in the early part of article 23), but it is clear that the reference should be to Linda Colley.

remained and there followed the establishment and entrenchment of the real national and popular institution of the day: the Kirk, the Church of Scotland itself and the disestablishment of the Anglican bishops. Again, one does not have to be a bad historian to be a good nationalist.

Brown should know better

So the widely read Gordon Brown should have known better than the London media in attacking nationalism undefined and unqualified. London journalists, with an ignorance that is often wilful, interpret the strong national feeling of Scots as necessarily on a primrose path to separatism (although a few of the journalists favour that path themselves, for somewhat different reasons, as if the revival of a more overt English nationalism is also a case for separatism). Puzzlingly they don't see Welsh nationalism in this light, perhaps not taking the Welsh as seriously.[4] Publicists should at least know, as Alex Salmond well knows, that today there is nowhere near a majority for independence, and that even a substantial number of SNP voters favour retaining the union. There are, after all, several other reasons why people might vote SNP. Many old Labour[c] voters find in him a version of social democracy that seemed lost in Blair's New Labour and is so far unclear in Brown. And back in the 1970s there were other powerful reasons, besides nationalism, for supporting devolution. John Mackintosh's powerful polemics in favour of devolution were based on democratic accountability. Scotland to a remarkable extent, he would remind, already had a devolved administration, but undemocratic and unaccountable. It was a strong argument and could sound anti-nationalist, especially in a once well known debate with Stephen Maxwell (then of the SNP) and also firmly against the EU. But it only sounded anti-nationalist if one drew no distinction between nationalist separatism and national consciousness. Mackintosh himself, after all, was so very Scottish. English publicists whom he mauled in debate would stereotypically call him 'the cocky Scot' or 'the stroppy Jock', insults he and his constituents welcomed and treasured.

Joining the devolution or home rule debate in Scotland after the defeat of the first referendum, I was amazed at the common platform rhetoric 'Without

---

[4] London leader writers and columnists may not be sensitive enough to realise that Plaid Cymru are, at heart, more dedicated to cultural nationalism than to political independence. Independence would leave a majority in Wales of non-Welsh speakers who might not respect the language concessions that came from Westminster to buy off separatism. Remember that Neil Kinnock broke ranks to campaign against devolution in 1997 with the terse cry 'You all know what devolution means, don't you? "Jobs for the boyos"!'

[c] This is ambiguous, of course, but seems most likely to refer to people who voted Labour before the coming of Blair, rather than older people who vote Labour or (in spite of party marketing of the day to the contrary) some quaint historical re-enactment group called Old Labour.

our own parliament, we are losing our identity'. I was amazed because those orators had all too obviously not lost their unmistakably strong Scottish identity, even after two and half centuries' wear and tear. Perhaps political institutions were not as important in shaping or maintaining national cultures as most students of politics had believed. Perhaps that democratic deficit was as important as national sentiment.

But I did not need to be embarrassed about deflating this line of argument after reading Lindsay Paterson's *The Autonomy of Modern Scotland*,[5] for there the historical and sociological evidence was plainly stated that the variant cultures of Scottishness had been remarkably resilient and independent of political institutions. He himself favoured home rule both for reasons of democracy and popular national sentiment. The watchword of the Constitutional Convention becomes 'We want democracy in a Scottish way' not 'Give us our own Westminster', like some postwar colony liberated or abandoned. And that is what David Miller (a former high official of the European Parliament) and I tried to do in a dull but influential pamphlet about parliamentary procedure entitled *To Make the Parliament of Scotland a Model for Democracy*. Now one must notice that the SNP itself, since its stormy days in the late 1970s, has, very much, due to Alex Salmond's clarity and tenacity (from the time when he was nearly expelled from the party for being both too left wing and pro-Europe), begun to move from rhetoric of 'separation' to the more relative term of 'independence'. The forceful, wily erratic Jim Sillars was to coin the *sloaghan*[d] 'Independence in Europe'. The SNP old guard under Gordon Wilson had wished to be free of the EU as well as the UK. They were somewhat UKIP in mentality. I remember Jim Sillars arguing fiercely for independence and yet reminding his audience at a fringe meeting at an SNP annual conference in Ayr that there were, however, difficulties to be faced. There were formidable economic and social entanglements with south of the border: pensions, family commitments, investments and employment and multinational companies. All these entanglements must, he roared, be resolutely and realistically faced up to. But he never said how. At the time I did not dare ask two of his then colleagues on the SNP executive, Professor Neal McCormick and Dr Owen Dudley Edwards, if this was not a disguised argument for federalism.

---

[5] Lindsay Paterson, *The Autonomy of Modern Scotland*, Edinburgh, Edinburgh University Press, 1994.

[d] This is another variation of the idiosyncratic spelling of 'slogan' in the later writings of 'new Scottish immigrant' Bernard. *Chambers Dictionary* (which should know, one would think) doesn't include it; but after pointing out during its definition of the conventional spelling 'slogan' that it was originally a clan war cry, it lists *slogorne, sloggorne* and *slogghorne* (and not *sloaghan*) in the etymology.

Entanglements and interrelations

Such entanglements or interrelations can be, on the whole, positive for most people and only negative for separatist nationalists. And although an old Labour man, indeed a wounded and mournful democratic socialist survivor, I usually follow a conservative, Burkean or Oakeshottian reading of history: that our past history shapes both perceptions and behaviour more than we often recognise and more strongly than abstract principles and pure reason. For instance, I have tried to defuse some of the present worries about recent immigration by reminding anyone who will listen that we have been a multinational state for just over three hundred years and a multicultural one quite clearly for about two hundred years as the Industrial Revolution led to large scale internal migration. Henry Coburn in his *Memorials* saw the new railway as cementing the Union but draining high talent from Edinburgh. As late as the 1920 and 1930s internal migration accelerated as workers moved from the shipyards of the Clyde to the new motor factories of Birmingham, Luton and Dagenham.

Certainly there are new problems arising from postwar and more recent immigration, but in historical perspective, no sudden crisis of multiculturalism. For we have been here before. The worries and venomous reactions to Irish and Jewish immigration in the nineteenth century and the 1900s were remarkably similar to those of the last fifty years: racial, religious and class prejudice abounded transcending simple xenophobia. Britain would lose its identity! But Britain did not, nor did those two immigrant communities. Sections of the press today and most politicians want children to learn more about our history, but in these important respects seem to have little real knowledge of it themselves. Too often they favour a mythical history about a socially homogeneous and consensual past, with only occasional references to self-contained, self-service national compartments. That Irish and Jews are now integrated and British enough without losing a strong cultural identity is seldom remarked in debates about Islam in Britain, neither by old Brits nor by the spokesmen of the new Brits.

Even national differences between states in these islands do not always separate the same sort of people. Consider what sociologists call 'measures of social distance'. For instance, it is clear that middle-class Irish in the Republic find far it far easier to get on with the same sort of people in mainland Britain than they do with almost anyone in the north of Ireland, whether Protestant or fellow Catholic. Family visits are from north to south, very rarely the other way round; and visits across the Irish Sea are easy and at ease. To a great extent this lack of social distance is reciprocated, even in high positions. There was that extraordinary few months when Conor Cruise O'Brien, a former Irish minister— and so much else indeed—was made editor of the troubled *Observer*. He was hyperactive, writing signed pieces himself in bold type in almost every section of the paper, but hopeless at team work, thus a very bad editor. 'The Cruiser' was too erratic. He was dismissed. But no one had objected to an

Irishman being appointed to a British newspaper of—back then—some influence. No one cried 'Paddy go home'. It was strictly *ad hominem*.

Identity crisis?

Indeed, I think we wear our national identities more lightly than many editors and publicists suppose. The surveys and analysis of Frank Bechhofer and David McCrone, here at hand, have shown this. If asked to choose one identity, Scots overwhelmingly go for Scottish not British; whereas English respondents are much more divided between English and British. But if survey questions offer dual identities, unsurprisingly most Scots will go for Scottish and British. And the correlation between intensity of Scottishness expressed and political allegiance is relatively weak. Indeed Bechhofer and McCrone at the beginning of a recent excellent summary article in *The Political Quarterly* sound sceptical about the reality of 'the identity crisis'—that 'wealth of books and articles; discussions and programmes on the presumed "death of Britishness"'—'the topical "stuff of British politics and the media"'—is at least partly fuelled, they say, 'by recent government attempts to foreground Britishness'. They conclude:

Paradoxical as it seems, the Conservatives, the traditional party of the Union, may be wise not to appeal to a sense of Britishness in Scotland because, while our data show clearly that people in Scotland are not rejecting Britishness, there is a problem confronting those who wish to mobilise this. . . . [Our] work shows that politicians cannot assume that if they wish to appeal to Britishness, it means the same thing in England as in Scotland, or to different groups in either country. Further Englishness, Scottishness and Britishness nowadays may be more cultural than political.[6]

In England, I believe, Britishness carries much of the baggage of cultural Englishness which only now is becoming sensibly discussed and rescued— together with the cross of St George—from right-wing extremists. But in Scotland Britishness, I suggest, has a far narrower if strong political sense of recent common history, parliamentary government, constitutional law and the crown as an abstract symbol of unity.

Perhaps Alex Salmond is familiar with Bechhofer and McCrone's work; or does it simply reinforce his own good sense of political reality? In the 2007 election campaign for the Scottish Parliament he said something important but so puzzling to the media in its apparent banality that it was largely ignored: 'Independence is a political not a social matter'. Indeed it is a political matter: if the electorate want it, ultimately they should have it and can take it politically. Look back to the Declaration of Right.[7] But 'not a social

[6] Frank Bechhofer and David McCrone, 'Being British: a crisis of identity?', *The Political Quarterly*, vol. 78, no. 2, 2007, pp. 251–60.

[7] Reprinted with commentaries in Owen Dudley Edwards, ed., *A Claim of Right for Scotland*, Edinburgh, Polygon, 1989. John Mackintosh's widow, Dr Una Maclean, was one of the committee and signatories.

matter'? Enigmatic, but I think that was meant to reassure voters that independence would not distance families and friends from each other north or south of the border, nor privilege employment for real or true Scots, still less disenfranchise immigrants (whom Scotland badly needs), even English immigrants like myself. Any idea in SNP thinking of an ethnic test for Scottish citizenship was long ago abandoned—well, long enough ago. 'Independence' is, indeed—compared to 'separation'—a relative term both economically and socially.

Brown's Britishness

This makes, I think Gordon Brown's banging on about Britishness both mistaken and irrelevant. In his 2007 speech to the TUC annual conference he used the term, according to the *Guardian*, 34 times, and in his speech to the Labour party conference the BBC counted about 80 strikes—not always to define it, of course, but 'our British' attached to this and that almost promiscuously (including the now notorious, or unfortunate, populist 'British jobs for British workers').

This is a profoundly mistaken rhetorical tactic if it is aimed at the SNP. But the trouble is that he really does seem to believe that unity of the United Kingdom is in danger if there is not a strong and common sense of Britishness. Consider the mission statement or *sloaghan* he had drafted for a conference hosted by HM Treasury back in November 2005:

How 'British' do we feel? What do we mean by 'Britishness'? These questions are increasingly important in defining a shared purpose across all of our society. The strength of our communities, the way we understand diversity, the vigour of our public services and our commercial competitiveness all rest on a sense of what 'Britishness' is and how it sets shared goals.

So Britishness must express 'a shared purpose' and 'shared goals'? Such language is a pale rhetorical echo of the old destructive nationalism of central Europe and the Balkans. Is this really how states hold together, especially in the modern world of, whether we like it or not, a global economy and of all notions of national sovereignty needing to be so qualified as to be almost useless in understanding actual politics?[8] This idea of national purpose is what Goethe called 'a blue rose'. And the search for it has proved damaging already as well as frustrating. Both Thatcher and Blair openly spoke of restoring our sense of national importance, a hangover from the old days of Empire and the Second World War—which, of course, we won, with a little help from the United States and the Soviet Union. And this search has meant the American alliance with too few questions asked or reservations made.

[8] See 'The sovereignty of parliament and the Irish Question', and 'On devolution, decentralism and the Constitution', in my *Political Thoughts and Polemics*, Edinburgh, Edinburgh University Press, 1990.

Do we need a heightened sense of Britishness and clear national purpose to hold us together? Perhaps we just need good government and social justice. And national leaders should be careful when they invoke 'our common values'. Perhaps our main common value has been to respect, on the whole, the values of others.

In July 2004 Brown gave the British Council annual lecture on Britishness and invoked *values*, our British values:

The values and qualities I describe are of course to be found in many other cultures and countries. But when taken together, and as they shape the institutions of our country these values and qualities—being creative, adaptable and outward looking, our belief in liberty, duty and fair play—add up to a distinctive Britishness that has been manifest throughout our history, and shaped it.[9]

'Liberty, duty and fair play'—well, some Scots are beginning to play cricket, of a kind. I think he plants both feet firmly in mid-air. Worse, when he gives specific historical examples, they are all taken from English history—as Simon Lee showed with cruel dispassion a year ago in *The Political Quarterly*.[10] Brown clearly wants us to believe that a heightened Britishness is necessary to hold the Union together rather than simply a rational calculation of mutual interest and advantage, as Adam Smith would have seen it, or, as David Hume would have it, tradition and habit. So he attacks the SNP in Scotland with the wrong weapon. He plays into their hands by confusing nationalism as tradition and national consciousness with nationalism as separatism. If there is a threat to the Union, I agree with Neal Ascherson, it is less likely to come directly from the Scottish electorate than from English insensitivity or even provocation (if the Conservatives get back in).[11]

Two of Brown's ministers put the matter more clearly than he in a Fabian pamphlet nicely called *A Common Place*: 'Britishness is like an umbrella under which different identities can shelter.'[12] That is a good metaphor. But Brown speaks as if his British brolly can only shelter one identity. He surely doesn't really believe that? He almost denies himself, and what should be a great strength in his public image not a liability—that he is Scottish *and* a resolute British unionist.

---

[9] Speech of 8 July 2004 on 'Britishness', the British Council Annual Lecture. See also his speech of 14 January 2006 to the Fabian Society's Conference on The Future of Britishness.

[10] Simon Lee, 'Gordon Brown and the 'British Way', *The Political Quarterly*, vol. 77, no. 3, 2006, pp. 369–78.

[11] Neal Ascherson, 'Homo Britannicus: Scotophobia', an Orwell Memorial Lecture delivered at Birkbeck College, 13 February 2007; a substantial extract appeared as 'Diary', *London Review of Books*, 5 April 2007, pp. 38–9.

[12] Ruth Kelly and Liam Byrne, *A Common Place*, London, Fabian Society, 2007.

Coda as delivered

Well, I hope that all this has all been very interesting, stimulating and instructive; but you may well ask, where the hell do I stand? I stand in a rather unusual position which will at least make my conclusion a novel bathos. I return to Salmond's remark about independence being a political and not a social matter. Some years ago I was waiting in a corridor of the House of Commons when he happened to come by. He asked me in good humour whether I would return to England when Scotland got its independence. I replied that I would *probably* have voted against independence in the final referendum, but would then want to be near the head of the queue in Glasgow to get a Scottish passport. He expressed pleasure and surprise. 'Well', I said, 'I really don't believe that independence can bring all the good some hope for nor all the troubles others fear.' He laughed. I may be imagining—and I hope I am not misrepresenting him—but it sounded to me more like a laugh of recognition than a mocking laugh, what Brecht once called 'the laughter of free men'.

Interrelations!? They are so many that whatever happens either way nothing is likely change all that much. Let us cool the debate, not stir it.

Part II
Reviews, 1957 to 2008

1950s

Fabian International Essays, edited by T. E. M. McKitterick and Kenneth Younger[a]

Vol. 28, no. 2, April–June 1957

The 129 prefatory words that justify Mr Gaitskell's prominence on the dust-jacket are not as perfunctory as they might appear: for they state candidly and clearly both the weakness and the strength of these essays. 'They are a collection of individual contributions and do not present . . . a consistent theme or policy throughout' and yet 'their approach is objective and realistic', which is 'especially to be desired in a field where . . . illusions . . . are apt to persist and ideas are too swiftly outdated by events.' But there is something in each of us that must feel it hard not to be disappointed that the parts are so much stronger than the whole. Here are seven excellent essays by seven intelligent socialists, but there is not a glimmer of a specifically socialist foreign policy, although 'illusions' are exposed in plenty. And, a fault part of nature and part of editors, the essays are uneasily scattered at different points between the hotly topical and the coldly eternal. Moreover, much that was topical when the book went to press in May 1956 has come to be, indeed, 'swiftly outdated by events'.

Mr Lowenthal's 'Co-existence with the Soviet Union' is a good account of the relation between Soviet totalitarianism and Russian foreign policy, although it could have appeared almost anywhere. He argues that Soviet 'co-existence' is simply their deep belief in inevitable peaceful victory by economic superiority. Therefore, the West is engaged in a 'competitive co-existence' in which it must keep its powder dry, but also fill the granaries and the workshops of the underdeveloped areas. And the true political reason for this often thankless task is for once clearly stated: 'simply to ensure their independent development along non-totalitarian lines'. Mr McKitterick argues the same point in an essay on the Middle East: 'the West should therefore try to ensure that aid from all sources [i.e., even Soviet] is enough, rather than to embark on a process of competitive bidding for exclusive support'. Our true interest should be in Middle Eastern stability, not in unpopular military alliances. The ultimate problem of the Middle East is, indeed, one of using the £360 million oil revenue left in the area to the betterment of all the inhabitants, rather than to provide more king-size Cadillacs for pint-sized rulers.

Mr Balogh's 'Political Economy of the Cold War' puts a convincing case that our startling 'drift downwards' in political influence stems from our

[a] Hogarth, 219 pp, 18 shillings. (Because of its intrinsic interest, I have added the original publisher and price information to each review as a footnote.)

shortage of capital. If we could pursue a 'forward policy of capital accumulation' by at least forgoing increases in our standard of living, we could afford independent policies and arrest the decline that comes from 'doing too much on the basis of too little'. The problem of British foreign policy is thus the problem of capital accumulation. And Mr Balogh is also not embarrassed to dwell upon the overwhelming importance of our relations with the United States. He *talks about* our 'simultaneous feeling of envy and superiority', and shows far more understanding of American diplomacy than is usual on the Left. It is a nice question why there was not a separate essay on the United States as there was on Russia. After all, following the shame, folly and stupidity of Suez, it is a little comic to write essays that speak of our influence here, there and everywhere, unless it is realised at every turn that our greatest influence on world affairs must be made through the still substantial remains of our peculiar relationship with the United States. Britain is still listened to in the United States more than her power alone explains, but she must now learn to listen too. Although the Fabians are now able to exorcise sentimentality towards the USSR, they are not quite ready to swallow a national pharisaism towards the USA.

Mr Strachey's contribution on 'British Defence Policy' is a weighty (but dubious) case that our political influence demands the possession of a successfully tested hydrogen bomb, and therefore drastic reductions in conventional weapons. Mr Younger's essay on the Far East deserves, though may not get, an equally close attention in the State Department and Pentagon. Mr. P. C. Gordon Walker submits a sound and sober brief for the Commonwealth and, as a law-abiding subject of the Queen, is careful to say nothing that could possibly cause disaffection among any of her darker subjects.

Those who had hoped for a socialist policy from these essays will be profoundly (or irritably) disappointed. But such a disappointment should be overcome. Mr Healey's closing essay, 'Beyond Power Politics', pulls the book together; it is full of the ambiguities and ambivalences inherent in the debate about a socialist or a liberal foreign policy, but its self-awareness of these things is its strength. He begins by suggesting that the American writers of the 'rational interest', 'realist' school, Morgenthau, Kennan and Lippman, run the risk of playing 'Nietzsche to some Hoosier Hitler'. But that is a cheap and ignorant smoke-screen. For he does not, in fact, refute the national interest school but rather, like the other disparate essays, shows a broader awareness of what national self-interest is—of how inextricably the ideals and the fears of one nation are bound up with those of another. The stress is all on practical problems. Mr Healey cautions against trying to rationalise drastically the welter of intergovernmental organisations affecting Europe; he deplores a false juridical neatness and points to the surprising success of many of these institutions as being due to 'the patient empiricism of the organic approach'. Of the three ways of looking at international politics, that of the engineer, the lawyer and the gardener, Mr Healey chooses that of the gardener: 'who deals with forms of organic life which are not fully subject to either rational or mechanical control. He must understand and accept in advance the limitations of his materials.' So here is a Burkean methodology of politics with a socialist perspective, a synthesis that could gain great authority. The *Fabian International Essays* are not socialist in the sense that they are applying a theory, but are socialist in the sense that when examining any problem they take into account a far wider range of social interests than any conservative advocate of 'realism' and 'self-interest' seems able to comprehend.

The Crisis of the Old Order, 1919–1933, by Arthur M. Schlesinger, Jr [a]

Vol. 29, no. 1, January–March 1958

This is the first of 'several volumes' that will be called 'The Age of Roosevelt'. The work has been eagerly awaited, for 'What was the New Deal?' has become the harrowing and perplexing 'What am I?' of the American liberal. And the American liberal, whatever his perplexities, at least feels sure that he has rejected the excesses, of course, of American capitalism while remaining true to the essential American tradition of a glad freedom of enterprise, that phrase construed in the widest, most general, and most noble sense. His hero is a man who is held to have saved American business against its own worst enemy, itself, during the fantastic years of the depression. And he sees the Democratic Party as much as possible as the party of the small (business) man against the big (business) guy, even though, while he trust-busts enthusiastically, he sees the advantages of mildly regulating the then inevitable (and efficient) consolidations of business power. In other words, he sees double and—worse—he often sees that he sees double. He positively squints with agony at how hard it is to recognise the all too closely related Philistines, even though he is sure that he is so much David. So it is not surprising that when 1932 has become the 1688 of modern American Whiggery, so many should wait hopefully, the reviewer included, to see whether the first huge history of the New Deal would resolve these agonies, would reveal the clarity of American liberalism to be as great as its psychological conviction. And Professor Schlesinger is admirably equipped for the task: a teacher of the great Harvard history school, a famed publicist, a founder of the ADA (Americans for Democratic Action—the would-be Democratic Fabian Society), and a speech-writer and friend to Adlai Stevenson.

But this volume is a terrible disappointment. It is written in a slick, catch-dollar, aggressively popular style that shows more will to condescend than evidence of the heights vacated. His impressionistic style of social history becomes in fact the 'personalised' morass of irrelevance of the worst political journalism: we are told that John Nance Garner liked lamb chops and fruit for

[a] Heinemann, 569 pp, 42 shillings.

323

breakfast (what character!) and that, when FDR and his economic adviser met Hoover and his man during the interregnum, the one side smoked cigars and the other (democratically) smoked cigarettes. But the two most significant items of social legislation in the 1920s are ignored almost completely: prohibition and the ending of mass immigration. Page 1 gets off to a typical start: '"We are at the end of our rope," the weary President at last said, as the striking clock announced the day of his retirement. "There is nothing more we can do."' And then a footnote, the first of fifty pages of a formidable looking apparatus of notes, which refers to two quite separate sentences on quite separate pages of T. G. Joslin's *Hoover off the Record* (1934)—a work as authoritative as it sounds. Is this point trivial? Unfortunately, no. For his need to ape *Time* style and *Time* technique is a sign of a wilful desertion of scholarly standards for a partisanship at once violent and petty. We reach the Inauguration of 1933 with such a tremendous build-up of promise and emotion that we are left wishing deeply that history had put into the New Deal all the intelligence, the coherence and the preconceived plan that Mr Schlesinger will have to put into his subsequent volumes in order to avoid bathos. The last page should be read by anyone who does not know what is meant by 'teleology':

Roosevelt, armoured in some inner faith, remained calm and inscrutable, confident that American improvisation could meet the future on its own terms. . . . Deep within, he seemed to know that the nation had resources beyond its banks and exchanges; that the collapse of the older order meant catharsis rather than catastrophe. . . . If this were so, then the crisis could change from calamity to challenge. The only thing Americans had to fear was fear itself. And so he serenely awaited the morrow. The event was in the hand of God.

But the book is worth close study. For it is a precise mirror of the worthy sentiments, yet the lack of perspective, of the present-day publicists of American liberalism. Rather than face the fact, obvious from a foreign perspective, that his differences with his opponents are matters of degree and stress *within* a common, indeed almost a claustrophobic, American liberalism, Mr Schlesinger adopts a half-cocked dialectic theory of American history. Amid the overwhelmingly middle-class classlessness of American life and politics, an even diluted Marxism clearly will not do: he quite rightly rejects the view that American politics will never be stable and explicable until an alleged suppressed left expresses itself. But, instead, he sees American politics as a dialectic struggle between the right and, not the left, but, in the title of a book of his—*The Vital Center*—certainly not the dead centre, the vital centre. If you can put all the ills of the body politic completely at arm's length, you have a foe to shy rocks at, not just a contradictory and human self to scratch. Indeed, the American liberal in such a quest for certainty does not even rend a straw man; he barks in a mirror. The truth is, surely, as H. G. Wells once put it, that the ideas of both American political parties could fit comfortably together as different wings of the old British

Liberal Party of Asquith and Lloyd George, the party of industrialism and freedom. But the American liberal for polemical purposes is constantly tempted to sound more radical than he is. The result, as in the speech-writers of the New Deal (if not in the more mundane and empirical course of its legislative history), and as in this book, is to substitute rhetoric for analysis and to make mere activity sound like plan. There is a much-quoted passage from a speech of Roosevelt's in 1932 that Mr Schlesinger does not recall, though it sums up the reasons for the great popular confidence that Roosevelt was able to restore, and yet also demolishes the claim of the New Deal publicists to have really created anything new: 'The country needs and, unless I mistake its temper, the country demands, bold persistent experimentation. It is common sense to take a method and try it. If it fails, admit it frankly and try another. But above all, try something.' After all, a new deal is not a new game.

The House of Lords and Contemporary Politics: 1911–1957, by P. A. Bromhead; *La Chambre des Lords au XXe Siècle: 1911–1949*, by Michel Bouissou[a]

Vol. 29, no. 3, July–September 1958

Here at last is a full-dress study of what is surely the most odd and gently fascinating political rococo in the world: the House of Lords. Mr Bromhead's weighty study will be recognised as authoritative on the composition, powers, and procedures of that House—the 'and contemporary politics' of the title is, however, one supposes, merely a genial deceit by the publishers; for the substantial propriety of Mr Bromhead's purely descriptive approach is itself a testimony to how remarkably little the question of the House of Lords has ruffled contemporary politics. *Mr Balfour's Poodle*[b] does not ride again, but receives a slightly premature post-mortem. It is in fact a very dull and humourless book—which is a pity when considering an institution so inherently peculiar. 'The main theme of our conclusion', Mr Bromhead says, is the 'wonderful capacity of adaptation' by the House of Lords. But this 'wonderful capacity' can also appear a series of ludicrous shuffles—on both sides of the House—to maintain, above all, the connection of the Second Chamber with the Order of Peerage, without making it too unpopular or distrusted to perform the menial tasks left to it by the House of Commons. To demonstrate how necessary are these tasks, to show how usefully the small band of attending Lords spend their time in the revision of the more non-contentious sections of some peculiarly complex legislation, and to show that an occasional general debate is of intellectually respectable standard, all this is

[a] Routledge, 283 pp, 30 shillings (Bromhead); Libraire Armand Colin, 360 pp, 1,300 Francs (Boissou).
[b] BRC's italics, thus presumably intended as a reference to the title of Roy Jenkins's 1954 book rather than to David Lloyd George's original comment.

pertinent, particularly to those of the Old Left who have jacobinical scruples about all second chambers; but the tasks remain strictly menial: the necessary domestic chores for an unreformed Commons.

For the trap into which all studies of the House of Lords and schemes for its reform have, without exception, fallen is to forget that legislation stems from the King-in-Parliament, or what formula one will, not from two separate Houses or Estates. This seems trite, but in fact discussion of the House of Lords has invariably begun by asking how that House can be reformed, not— the question of overriding importance—'how should the Commons be reformed?' or Parliament as a whole. It is glaringly obvious that the Commons are vastly overworked by detail and that in their reluctance to adopt specialised Standing Committees, and in the steady decline of Select Committees, they have abandoned any real hopes of making authoritative criticisms of the complex work of the more technical government departments. If the Commons continues to adhere to its antiquated procedures and is irredeemably complacent about the colossal wastage of its own talents, it could at least get far more work out of an upper chamber; but an upper chamber reconstituted to perform that kind of work.

Both the logic of the actual 'reforms'—or rationalisations—of recent years and the bias of studies about them has been primarily a concern with the preservation of the peculiar connection between the Upper House and the Order of Peerage, only secondarily with the efficiency of Parliament as a whole. Mr Bromhead has no difficulty in demonstrating how the work of the House of Lords is in fact conscientiously and skilfully performed by only the most responsible sort of peers—those of first creation doing, of course, the donkey work that saves the rest. And he shows that a Labour government has little to fear from them in legislative terms. But this is not the point. Even Lord Salisbury in all his post-Suez glory of principle did not wish for more political or legislative power to the Lords; but he is obviously highly aware of the psychological and sociological importance of the constitutional involvement of the Order of Peerage in the House of Lords as part of the wider, more subtle and pervasive, system of social controls that is the real governance of England. It is not a political question in the customary sense; it is a social question in the grand sense; and, as usual, the conservative has proved a better sociologist by intuition than has the socialist by reason. And, furthermore, it is M. Bouissou and not Mr Bromhead who can, in a book otherwise far less original and scarcely authoritative in its research, at least recognise the obvious and expose, with some pleasant irony and suitable style, the pathos of a relic of aristocratic government. If Mr Bromhead was to justify his book's full title he should, then, not merely have looked at the defects of the Commons, but should have described the place of the Lords in the great triad of the Establishment—the other two instrumental limbs of which are, of course, the Public Schools and the Monarchy. In other words, the whole 'question' of the House of Lords is bound up with the conceit and constraint of class inevitable while an hereditary peerage is officially preserved. If the peerage were abolished, the government would be forced to think sensibly about the functions of an upper chamber.

If the carpet were cleared, there would surely be no reason at all for any power of delay or rejection; but the revision and criticism of legislation could vastly more useful, more authoritative, if it came from a kind of *Conseil d'État*—salaried, professional, bureaucratic, and legal (a Chamber of Revision, or House of Correction). An upper chamber (itself in specialised committees) could then perform many of the functions of inquisition and research that were once the task of the great Select Committees of the House of Commons of the nineteenth century; it could create—and why not?—a counter-bureaucracy responsible to the House of Commons and thus an alternative source of specialised knowledge to the bureaucracies in the ministries; and, as well as routine scrutiny of legislation, it could have some special responsibility to scrutinise the conduct of the nationalised industries. And the public interest would be served if, as in the *Conseil d'État*, a legal section acted as a kind of supreme court of appeal to administrative tribunals. Of course, this reviewer will appear to have thrown all shreds of responsibility to the winds in advocating a substitution of a foreign institution for a native palace of prejudice. He owes both authors an apology; why should political scientists be expected to think more imaginatively than politicians? Constitutional reform, in an era when trumpeters of the Household Cavalry in jackboots and cuirasses can assist the TUC to unveil a memorial by Epstein, is the mere nagging of a sacred cow. Mr Gladstone would not get far today.

Oppression and Liberty, by Simone Weil; *The Human Condition*, by Hannah Arendt[a]

Vol. 30, no. 1, January–March 1959

Stocks in the cult of Simone Weil will be little affected by this book. It reminds one more of her friend Gustave Thibon's story about the kindly bishop who wanted to add to the Litany of Saints the invocation, 'From living saints, Good Lord deliver us', than of his wry reminder—after describing, fairly frankly, what an over-intense, neurotic, innocent-ignorant young bohemian she appeared—that the saints are not sent for our comfort. The book is a pedlar's sack of essays, some published before, some found among her papers in London in 1943; they are repetitious, some even self-contradictory and unfinished. The French edition has some critical apparatus which makes clear from her own notes the place in a larger scheme that some of the pieces would have filled, but this has been spared the English reader—as so often, without hint of the favour done him. This might seem a very slender twenty-five shillingsworth, but for the really beautiful dust jacket on which

[a] Routledge, 195 pp, 25 shillings (Weil); Cambridge University Press for the University of Chicago Press, 332 pp, 36 shillings (Arendt).

Sutherland-like thorns suggest that very painfulness of Weil and her writings which makes one skirmish[b] to mock, rather than squarely face her.

For the title essay (written in 1934) is important. The starting point is Marx. Weil was trying to restore to the French Left a sense that the immortal part of Marx's achievement lies in his sociological concept of 'alienation': the 'subordination of the worker to the material conditions of work', the famous 'reversal of the relationship between subject and object'. 'Work is no longer done', she herself laments, 'with the proud consciousness of being useful'. The 'no longer' may be a pseudo-historical irrelevance, but the fact of the separation is, after all—whenever we dare remind ourselves of it—obvious and appalling; so obvious and taken for granted, indeed, that it can make her own masochistic plunges into 'being useful'—on the benches of the Renault works and in the grape-picking gangs of the South—appear ridiculous rather than noble. The essay seeks to restore Marx as a superb descriptive sociologist of modern capitalism, though at the same time to show that he was a myth-maker to argue that a mere change in ownership could ever change the oppression of the worker by the machine. Here is a close and delicate sorting of Marx's Marxism into its scientific and its utopian ambivalences; in a smaller space, not Marcuse or Popper in all their glory have written better on Marx. And her own viewpoint must now be sadly recognised to have a truth far broader than any mere polemic against the French Stalinists in 1934: 'The worker's complete subordination to the undertaking and to those who run it is founded on the factory organisation and not on the system of property.' She illuminates brilliantly the greatest problem of industrial-democratic society—far, far more than most of the enjargoned tomes of those 'industrial psychologists' whose study of the problem is an acceptance of its perpetuation. But her remedy is purely formal: she betrays herself by that Hegelian tendency to use the word 'concrete' whenever the argument appears to need—but to defy—securing down to some kind of earth. The 'concrete fact' that distinguishes liberty from oppression is 'thought'. But thought for what? She merely contrasts the 'sorry spectacle' of a production line under the eye of a foreman with a gang of building workers discussing and solving an unexpected snag. But they are more likely to be thinking how to botch the job up quickly and cheaply (*vide* the *Ragged Trousered Philanthropists*) than, as Hannah Arendt would suggest they should, how to build as if for immortality.

For 'immortality', to Miss Arendt, is the curious though obvious object to which toil must be related if there is to be any resolution to the problem of 'alienation' as raised by Marx, a problem and a writer she also puts at the centre of things. Arendt, in a pretentious—though entirely plausible—account of the cultural setting of the Western concept of politics, draws a fundamental distinction between labour and work—*animal laborans* and *homo faber*, or, in

---

[b] This reads oddly; 'skirmish' may well be a mistranscription or misprint for 'squeamish', which would seem to be a better fit though not a perfect one.

Locke's words, 'the labour of our body and the work of our hands'. Arendt would say that Weil's 'proud consciousness of being useful' could only possibly apply to work, never to labour. *Labour* is the mere and degrading business of toil for staying alive which results in the mere immediate consumption of things: to the Greek or Roman, a slave was proved not to be a man precisely because he was willing merely to stay alive. *Work* is toil for some permanent result, man liberated from the necessity of mere transitory consumption of his energies: the public realm, the political, also the artistic. She suggests that the esteem for labour, which Marx shared with the bourgeois economists, has nearly killed the active realm of politics in which men sought to do memorable things. Leisure (the time to do things worth doing for their own sake) is not likely to result from technological progress; on the contrary, the endless multiplication of apparent necessities arises, society is 'caught in the smooth functioning of a never-ending process' and is 'no longer able to recognise its own futility—the futility of a life which "does not fix or realise itself in any permanent subject which endures after [its] labour is past"'. (Her quotation is actually from Adam Smith who, like Marx, was more of a humanist than his followers.) But it is hard to summarise what is in effect a synthesis of Hegelianism with the empirical sociology of Marx and Weber. Her work is a kind of cultural anthropology of modern politics; she takes seriously as causal factors in history types of common mass-desires, such as the mundane hope for a realm in which labour will cease, which are apparently beneath the academic dignity or beyond the imagination of our native blinkered empiricists.

Weil and Arendt thus deserve to be read carefully—and read together— because they are surely correct to see that the increasing alienation of man from the possibility of real work and of real leisure is the great problem of modern civilisation. Weil's straining[c] to analyse the problem finally became overwhelmed by her pain at its touch and she fled from the Greek view that politics is all to the Christian view that politics alone is nothing. Arendt, however, appears as the analyst of such views, someone aware of their actual importance—as she showed in her great *Origins of Totalitarianism* (weirdly disguised in its English edition as *The Burden of Our Times*), and someone whose sense of politics is undoubted. If she defends the contemplative life against the cult of utility, she sees it as necessarily related, not antithetical, to the public life. She seeks to show that free politics is based on a dualism of public and private and that this proper dualism is in danger of being subsumed by the modern concept of the social. The state in which everything is social ceases to be political and becomes totalitarian. Thus Weil and Arendt tread common ground, and ground wider and wilder than the gentle pastures of English political thought—at least since Hobbes. But their wilderness is more like the world as most know it.

[c] The original has 'training', but 'straining' seems more appropriate.

1960s

Words and Things: A Critical Account of Linguistic Philosophy and a Study in Ideology, by Ernest Gellner[a]

Vol. 31, no. 1, January–March 1960

For once, with brazen honesty, let the dust-jacket be quoted:

Words and Things deserves the gratitude of all those who cannot accept the linguistic philosophy now in vogue at Oxford. It is difficult to guess how much immediate effect the book is likely to have; the power of fashion is great, and even the most cogent arguments fail to convince if they are not in line with the trend of current opinion. But, whatever may be the first reaction to Mr Gellner's arguments, it seems highly probably—to me, at least—that they will gradually be accorded their due weight.

Thus Bertrand Russell begins his introduction to this very important book; having had some responsibility himself, if parts of the Oxford apocrypha be true, for introducing Wittgenstein into British philosophy, he now endorses an attack, from an apostate—an attack which, if it were nothing else, should be hailed as a sustained feat of literary parody. Let us take Russell's three points in order.

There will be many people whose gratitude might be limited by not being aware of the dragon in the first place. Most readers of this journal, for instance, might appear (certainly to readers of the *Transactions* of the Aristotelean Society) to be 'practical men', at least men concerned with public affairs. But few 'public men' will have forgotten the truth of J. M. Keynes's famous gibe that the ideas of the purely practical man are usually the residue of some 'academic scribbler' of yesterday. As Keynes in his *General Theory* attacked the alliance of academic orthodoxy in economic theory with received, 'practical' opinion, so Gellner attacks linguistic philosophy in relation to social and political opinion: the mood of, not merely, 'there is nothing that can be done about it', but of 'there is nothing worth doing at all'. For the word has got around, at the very least, that the philosophers are saying that they can have nothing whatever to say about social and political problems and that all generalisations, anyway, are suspect. Now this is not surprising to the man who thinks himself the pure politician, the pure administrator, the pure operator, the actor of a given role. But it is surprising to those who think that people do in fact think in general terms, do act, in part at least, according to general theories and moral presuppositions, however much they may try not to. The linguistic philosophers say that there is nothing that can be said outside a particular 'language' (i.e., a set of conventions, however derived), and that the famous 'fundamental' problems

[a] Gollancz, 270 pp, 25 shillings.

of philosophy are only really misuses of the conventions of a particular language. Meaning is only expressible in words and words only mean what people ordinarily use them to mean. Now this would seem very flattering to the 'practical' man. *His* use of words, not that of the 'eagle-eyed metaphysicians', defines and exhausts meaning. But even *l'homme moyen philosophique* has some suspicion that there are choices of which game to play, and that philosophers once had something to do with at least clarifying these choices. Gellner applauds this suspicion. Professional philosophers have not, in fact, destroyed the possibility of moral, social, and political philosophy; they have merely abandoned it—what he calls their 'argument from impotence': the idea 'that philosophy, if it can be concerned with anything, must be concerned with the *how* and not the *what*'. But questions about 'how', the realm of the practical man, are only meaningful on the assumption that there is a realm, a system, which is closed enough for things to work predictably within it. What of the choice and overlap of systems? The 'argument from impotence' says that philosophy is purely analytical, therapeutic at the best: 'philosophy ends in platitude'. But whose platitude?

Yet the more Gellner succeeds in revealing 'the camouflaging of presuppositions and values as procedural rules', the truer the doubt in Bertrand Russell's second sentence. Linguistic philosophy, Gellner shows, is not just a doctrine or technique, it is an ideology—a useful set of ideas for maintaining particular social circumstance. Therefore it is unlikely to be abandoned as a result of rational argument. When he unveils the secret of the universe according to Professor Wisdom and Ludwig Wittgenstein as '*The world is what it is*', he also reveals the social strength of this 'philosophic form eminently suitable for gentlemen'. Its 'neutralism' is in fact conservative (gone are the—largely accidental—left-wing associations of logical positivism); it is esoteric, eclectic, and, as it were, pleasingly *l'art pour l'art*—the 'unpacking' of words, but never the reassembling, is an end in itself; this, in turn, involves 'conspicuous triviality' (as Brillioth wrote of the Anglican Church in the 1840s, 'nothing so suspect as enthusiasm'); it is irrationalist, in that any ideas are acceptable so long as they are made matters of definition and belief, not of rational debate; it is anti-scientific (after a brief bout of panic, engendered by logical positivism, that one would have to learn maths to be a philosopher), and all forms of originality and surprise are ruled out: 'the social idea of imperturbability has been turned into a principle of cosmology: the world must be such as to justify non-perturbation'.

Bertrand Russell chose his words well when he wrote: 'But, whatever may be the first reaction to Mr Gellner's arguments . . .' Not since Keynes's *General Theory* has there been such a frightened flutter of retreat by a man's professional colleagues *away from* reviewing his book—living proofs of Gellner's claim that linguistic philosophy depends on the manners of a closed coterie, not on the contest of open intellectual debate. But even Russell and Gellner could scarcely have hoped for such help as Professor Ryle's returning of the book to the publishers as unfit to be reviewed in the pages of

Mind. Ryle's students will now, presumably, read this book surreptitiously, perhaps wrapped up in the covers of Sir Isaiah Berlin's *Two Concepts of Liberty*.

Polemic is not always the best source of knowledge. But the fashionable philosophers should be aware of a danger in deliberately not replying. The rest of the educated public may grow bored with them and forget about them. If 'metaphysical truths' are no longer fashionable (which has created rather a shortage of straw men for dissection), then there are scientific truths being actively canvassed in the universities and also, growingly, those of social research and speculation. If linguistic philosophy is irrelevant to both these activities, then it is irrelevant indeed. Mr Gellner has not cried '*trahison des clercs*' once again; he has simply shown that linguistic philosophy has nothing to offer him as a sociologist. Its prestige is now shattered. Perhaps political and social philosophy will now pick up the old traces.

Social Principles and the Democratic State, by S. I. Benn and R. S. Peters; *British Conservatism, 1832–1914*, by R. B. McDowell; *The Analysis of Political Systems*, by Douglas V. Verney[a]

Vol. 31, no. 2, April–June 1960

These three books all raise questions of the relations between political principles and social systems. Two of the books announce that 'political philosophy' (one says 'theory') is commonly thought to be dead, but both then humbly offer to raise the buried Leviathan-Lazarus back before our eyes to life, however singed and shrunken. The third book performs a solid descriptive task as if deaf to all the heavenly clamour of philosophers murdering and creating.

The books illustrate that there are perhaps three distinct levels of inquiry which should not be confused. *Political thought* (or opinion) simply treats of the general views about politics that people, whose opinion is of some possible consequence, in fact hold in some particular time or place. *Political theory* attempts to refine the terms of political opinion into theories that explain or comprehend the general character of a particular social system. *Political philosophy* aspires to establish whether any of these political theories are acceptable as general principles transcending, or subsuming, particular circumstances. These are not logical distinctions: they are different degrees of perspective. In our ordinary thoughts about politics they jostle and inter-mingle—'eternity', said Blake, 'is in love with the products of time'. But to separate out these three levels of perception is to state some kind of necessary priority in any serious investigation of the relations of principles to politics. Political theory arises from political thought, and political philosophy arises from political theory (and each must be preceded by knowledge of the other).

[a] Allen and Unwin, 403 pp, 32 shillings (Benn and Peters); Faber, 191 pp, 21 shillings (McDowell); Routledge, 239 pp, 28 shillings (Verney).

Dr McDowell's book is good, plain political thought: the least ambitious of the trio, it is the most successful. He has simply set out to state the political beliefs which an ordinary intelligent Conservative might be expected to hold in the period 1832–1914. Dr McDowell is that rare and valuable bird the historian who is not sceptical about the actual influence of general ideas on political action (he lives in Dublin, not Oxford, which is a help). But he takes his general ideas from politicians and their publicists, not from the few 'set books' of the Pantheon of genteel political philosophy. How often has the brute British empiricist treated of the history of political ideas solely in terms of political philosophy—either out of intellectual muddle, or from sheer laziness in being unwilling to grapple, as Dr McDowell does, with the variety of sources—manuscript, newspaper, magazine and pamphlet, as well as printed book—necessary to comprehend the actual political thought of a period. Dr McDowell's book only errs in being so short that he should have made his principles of selectivity explicit. If the patient scale of a Maccoby or a Cole is ultimately grotesque and finally threatens to obscure as much as it illuminates, yet Dr McDowell's own two superb books on public opinion and Irish politics in the nineteenth century would themselves have been a more ample model for this present book.

Mr Verney quickens hope by claiming that his 'approach is theoretical rather than descriptive or institutional; but it is not primarily philosophical'. There is little discussion, he promises, of great traditional themes—'the method tends to be empirical rather than speculative'. Political theory, then, liveth yet in the form of political analysis. But the analysis, let it be said right out, is bewilderingly diffuse and banal. Who needs to be told that: 'it required considerable finesse' to manage a Tudor Parliament; that Elizabeth I was 'the last of the Tudors'; that 'the following century (1603–1714)' was 'known as the Stuart period'; that Woodrow Wilson was *not* President in 1884; or to be given—accurately, thank heaven—the dates of Queen Victoria and translations of 'primus inter pares' and 'le Roi le veult'? This is, unfortunately, more than a mere uncertainty as to what audience is being addressed; it is a basic failure to distinguish between platitude and theory and between literary example and historical evidence. Englishmen in the eighteenth century, we are suddenly told, 'were members of a free society (as many a . . . ballad such as "Hearts of Oak" and "Rule Britannia" shows)'. And he writes intriguingly, McDowell please note, of 'the time Mr Parnell was sued for divorce on the grounds of adultery'. Clearly many more studies like Dr McDowell's are needed before political scientists like Mr Verney can have enough evidence to generalise on—and a decent chance of getting their facts right when they do. The paucity of secondary works cited in the text (no footnotes—a modern analytical touch) show that there are, however, genuine difficulties facing any work that purports to offer a classification of all known forms of government.

The Benn and Peters is a book in a very different class. Here is a full-scale attempt to deal with genuine problems of political philosophy in empiricist-analytical terms. It contains some brilliant chapters of elucidatory analysis—

notably those on 'Freedom' and on 'Sovereignty'. But there is an ultimate sense of unease left in closing such a book and trying to be clear just how to take it. They steer clear of metaphysics; and they have far more to say about politics than the pure philosophers of the linguistic and analytical school would allow. But still, how is it possible to go so far without evidence? The analysis unpacks and repacks possible meanings of particular and separate terms; but no real attempt is made to see if anyone in politics has ever used them in a systematic manner. Odd realistic cases are brought in as examples to an argument, but no systematic political or sociological knowledge is used. Here is the 'English paradox'; logical empiricists with an apparent distaste for empirical knowledge. Have sociological studies of class nothing to do with an analysis of equality? If political theory arises from the incoherences of ordinary political thought, should not political philosophy arise from the contradictions between various political theories? The analysis of political 'principles' in divorce from political knowledge either leads to a denial that political philosophy has any meaning except the philosophic criticism of political language—as in the late T. D. Weldon's preposterously a priori *Vocabulary of Politics*; or else, as in the Benn and Peters, to insinuating, suggesting, perhaps just taking for granted, a political framework of natural liberalism into which their 'principles' fit.

Thus it is all very earnest, detailed, intelligent, repetitive, brittle, verbal, and slightly—in the approved manner—cranky. In the first page 'woodpeckers in trees' and the 'SPCK' appear as homely examples; but the bizarre homes of the English political philosophers never seem to include many books by people like de Tocqueville, Durkheim, Marx, Sorel, Pareto, the Webers, Mannheim, and—among the moderns—perhaps Arendt, Duverger, Friedrich, Neumann, Parsons, Riesman and Talmon. None of these folk, all concerned with actual knowledge about politics, gets anything beyond a glancing reference, except Marx—and Marx is only used as a stalking horse for the familiar Berlin–Popper attack on historicism: his political sociology is ignored. 'Divorce', strangely, earns three pages—since it is on a London Extra-Mural Social Philosophy syllabus and the book makes the engaging claim to be 'a modern introductory [!] textbook'. And six pages of good liberal zeal are spent in warning students intricately against the doctrines of Michael Oakeshott. This may be a good cause, but it heightens the cranky and parochial character of the book. Empiricist British blinkers presumably also preclude any consideration of works that treat 'totalitarianism' as a new and distinct phenomenon of *anti*-political ideas and organisation. This claim might be thought to raise some questions for political philosophy. But political philosophy in England, it would seem, lives only as a field of examples for philosophical analysis. True political philosophy arises from politics itself, not from philosophy.

The Logic of Social Enquiry, by Quentin Gibson; *Understanding Human Society*, by Walter Goldschmidt[a]

Vol. 31, no. 3, July–September 1960

The story goes that a famous British philosopher once gave a paper at the Institute for Advanced Studies, Princeton, on 'Can the Social Sciences be Scientific?' He delivered the beginning twice, so anxious was he for a late arrival, Albert Einstein, to hear it all. But Einstein's only comment, wrung from him by the speaker's importunity, was: 'What a funny question to write a paper about!' Professor Gibson sets out to convince us of 'the value of scientific procedure in social inquiry'. Alas, as one sets down his book (which bears all the contemporary marks of philosophical brilliance), one is genuinely puzzled as to what possible consequences for social inquiry should follow from either agreeing or disagreeing with him. Whether 'social inquiry' is logically 'scientific' or not surely depends upon the meaning given to the word 'science'; and whatever meaning one gives, social inquiry can hardly be affected[b] (or, indeed, avoided).

Professor Gibson completely begs the question. He adopts a definition of science so broad as to make disagreement almost impossible—except on the score that he actually does less than justice to the distinctiveness of the natural sciences by playing down the importance of 'prediction'. He then plunges straight into a refutation of certain 'anti-scientific' views. These refuted, he shows us in the second half of the book that 'nevertheless . . . there are genuine logical peculiarities in social inquiry, which effect the result to be expected.' This is the Method of the Double Negative: first claim—negatively—then qualify—double-negatively: 'it would seem that we must dismiss as inconclusive all attempts to establish that there is a general failure of objectivity among social inquirers sufficient to render their inquiries futile'. He simply shows that objections to his formulation of science are not tenable; but then with superb scholastic integrity, he resolutely refuses to offer any mundane *examples* whatever of any social inquiry that is scientific. For what really puts one out of patience with this demanding, brilliant, intelligent, intricate, inbred and exhausting genre of writing is its completely a priori character. The only examples of social knowledge advanced are hypothetical ones. The 'logic of social inquiry' somehow exists apart from the problems and fruits of all actual social inquiries. Methodology can only avoid being, in Graham Wallas's words, 'a constant preparation for a journey that never takes place', when it arises from dilemmas about actual theories about society put forward by somebody actually at work on such theories.

Professor Goldschmidt is in such a position. A short test of Professor Gibson's contribution to knowledge is to see whether he discusses *any* of

[a] Routledge, 213 pp, 24 shillings (Gibson); Routledge, 253 pp, 21 shillings (Goldschmidt).

[b] The original has 'effected', which is just possible but on balance seems not to be the intended meaning.

the actual and—to scholars—well-known theories of social change examined by Professor Goldschmidt. Here is a clear, thoughtful and authoritative account of the main schools of thought in anthropological theory, not as a contribution to the *logic* of social inquiry, but towards *understanding* human society. Perhaps as a cultural function of being editor of the *American Anthropologist*, his views are wide, tolerant, and eclectic in the best sense. He dares to believe in evolution (though the logicians will hunt him for this), not in any teleological sense, but in the technological sense of an increasing differentiation of function through time in all observed societies. One suspects that political theory would have much to learn from modern anthropology. Both the 'scientific behavio[u]rists'^c and the 'traditionalists' have yet to digest his simple distinction between custom and actual behaviour. And a lot of the rationalist versus traditionalist debate of contemporary political thought looks rather silly in face of the anthropologist's treatment of 'custom' as something rarely, if ever, static, but rather a creative function towards the sheer survival of any particular society. The student of politics should have far more to learn from a broad cultural and functional approach to the nature of authority than from the subtle analyses of words of the unempirical-empirical philosophers. Professor Goldschmidt's admirable book deserves close attention from all students of society. It maintains, indeed, the old high standards of the International Library of Sociology and Social Reconstruction, in which both these books appear. And it appears in a well-set type, large enough to read without pain, a welcome change from the familiar dense pages of broken type, like crowded tombstones struck by shrapnel, which have so often marked this famous series.

American Foreign Policy, by Louis J. Halle; *A New History of the United States*, by William Miller; *Senator Joe McCarthy*, by Richard Rovere; *The Coming of the New Deal*, by Arthur M. Schlesinger, Jr^a

Vol. 32, no. 1, January–March 1961

American political literature has always been torn between the monumental gesture and the agitated scratch. The Statue of Liberty stands high, but it still gathers flies. There is the never-ending delight in posing and answering the dropsical question, 'What is an American?' and yet there is also the tradition of self-exposure, veritable national muckraking festivals, divine discontent carried on with an almost diabolic frenzy. No country is more nationalistic—even though there is no American 'state', only the Federal Union, yet there is an 'American way' of doing everything, yes everything; but then no nation is more resolutely and honourably self-critical. The answer to this paradox is

---

^c The bracketed [u] is in the original—a deliberate Bernardian touch.

^a Allen and Unwin, 327 pp, 25 shillings (Halle); Faber, 480 pp, 30 shillings (Miller); Methuen, 973 pp, 18 shillings (Rovere); Heinemann, 658 pp, 63 shillings (Schlesinger).

simple: no nation is more exclusively liberal. Affirmation and dissent go hand in hand inextricably. Disraeli once remarked that 'all scoundrels now-a-days profess themselves to be liberals'—which actually proved a false prophecy in Engand. But in America even scoundrels have not had to be insincere in their liberalism. Right from the beginning liberalism was a condition of American-ism, not a doctrine to be taken up or taken down. Imagine compulsory individualism; imagine a middle-class classlessness; imagine a tradition of anti-traditionalism; imagine a nation, as de Tocqueville put it, which did not need to achieve equality, because it was equal already, or was 'conceived in liberty' in Lincoln's precisely measured words; imagine a democratic majority willing to bind themselves against themselves by a rigid constitution; and, finally, imagine an isolationism which could appear as a (white) world-wide ideology by the magic bridge, now broken, of mass immigration—imagine all this and one has the climate of opinion of American liberalism.

Two factors have ensured the unity and self-confidence of Americanism as liberalism: the fact that the experience of free government preceded both independence and industrialisation, and the vanished glory of American isolation from power politics. The first fact will have an enduring influence on American politics—her traditionalism will always be liberalism; but the second fact is contingent and its applicability is dead.

Mr Halle writes profoundly of 'the sense of escape which attended the formation of the American nation'. He is a rare spirit who really does try to face the consequences of the failure of that great experiment of escape. Certainly the world events of the last few years have stirred up a remarkable literature of self-examination. The final eclipse of isolationism as a political force has not, however, so much intensified the debate about new practical policies towards the outside world, as it has re-stimulated the old concern about appearances in the eyes of the outside world. (Mr Halle's book is largely a plea for his fellow-countrymen to worry less what they look like and more about what they do.) Add to this the destruction by Sputnik of, to use Professor Brogan's phrase, 'the illusion of American omnipotence', and the conditions are sadly well made for the emergence of a deeper, more painful and profound, literature of national self-examination. Mr Halle's thoughtful book shows these forces already at work. He is a former member of the State Department's policy planning staff. It is of some comfort that a man with such a shrewd and balanced realism, with such a learned grasp of the 'inarticulate major premises' of American action, could at least have served where he did—and the further example of Mr George Kennan springs to mind. It would be very hard to match such writing in any British diplomatist, ex- or active. In the United States Mr Halle's book, like Kennan's writings and those of Professor Hans Morgenthau, have been bedevilled by the absurd and Procrustean controversy of the campuses about 'realism' versus 'idealism'. But to foreign eyes, at least, Mr Halle seems to gain his point all too obviously that the old idealism of American foreign policy was always too specifically an American idealism to fit the idealism of others. He has also that calmness, which is courage, to remind us, strong and cutting though his attack is on the irrelevance of past American history to present international conditions, that the Russians too have made vast tactical mistakes when blinded by ideology. He does not wallow in that national self-criticism which is sometimes so strong in American liberals as to appear both ludicrous and dishonourable.

If affirmation and reaffirmation will no longer do, neither will the old simple tradition of muckraking. This acts as if there is never need for new thought; there is only the need for the facts to be put before the people. The people's moral calculating machine sometimes gets out of order, but, like Ford's faith in the old Model T, it is supposed never to need replacing. But the mere exposure of 'facts' as an adequate device of political reform depended upon a unity of American values which, in turn, depended upon the plausibility of the vanished isolation. This may seem a ponderous cultural-historical sledgehammer with which to strike books as fascinatingly circumstantial as Mr Rovere's—but nothing less will crack the great, but superficial, attraction of such meaty nuts for any political animal. It is that kind of highly competent and immensely readable, quick and candid, political biography, seemingly really so objective—such as only the top-flight American journalists can do. There is no loaded comment, no too obvious partisan bias, although Mr Rovere does simply take for granted dislike and repudiation of McCarthy. But he loses the wood for the trees. Surely we are only interested in the detail of how the man operated in so far as it suggests how he ever came to have such power? Plenty of men have been clever and dishonest; but McCarthy had an intuition that most ordinary Americans could not but believe, indeed he half-believed it himself, that the vastly threatening outside world must be a product of domestic treason, so used had they been to controlling their own destiny by means of isolation. A conspiracy theory of history is a product of a belief that one can control one's own destinies in a period when the facts have become otherwise, Mr Rovere's book has rightly been highly praised; but it is easier to dissect a dead tiger than it is to explain how ever he came to get there.

Mr Schlesinger's second volume in his huge 'Age of Roosevelt' covers the first two years of the New Deal. This volume is certainly an improvement on the first.[b] The scale of the narrative is better suited to the importance of the events. Some of the material is actually highly original. There is less *Time* style and *Time* technique, less forced personalising of social and economic issues. The sense of period is more sure and is at times superb. Never before has such a clear picture emerged of the enthusiasm and chaos of Roosevelt's first term. But it is still hard to accept the very great praise it has received in most quarters. For it is partisan history at its most flagrant. Undoubtedly FDR was a great man. But Mr Schlesinger attributes to him the kind of greatness which will not wash—a wise all-seeing, affable, democratic Jehovah, a super-statesman, serene and prescient, watching the bitter internal feuds of his lieutenants, but always intervening just in time. But why let them start fighting in

[b] The subject of Bernard Crick's first review for *PQ* three years earlier. See p. 321.

the first place? Why allow them so much political free will (and free expression) if he really had a clear idea of what his slogan, 'the New Deal', was to mean? The most valuable and original part of the book is, indeed, its account of the fantastic conflicts between various departments and agencies. Surely the truth is that Roosevelt, within the system he was operating, could not have stopped them if he had tried. What Mr Schlesinger does not make clear, amid his exaggerated claims for Roosevelt as statesman, thinker and innovator, is his sheer tough achievement as a politician in getting enough order and shape out of an antiquated system to save it from itself amid chaotic conditions. Mr Schlesinger again does not seem happy to praise a man for purely political virtues. He makes heroic claims, suitable as myths of the Northern Democratic Party, but on a level of rhetorical generality hardly acceptable as history. Here is his last paragraph:

The essence of Roosevelt . . . was his intrepid and passionate affirmation. He always cast his vote for life, for action, for forward motion, for the future. His response to the magnificent emptiness of the Grand Canyon was typical: 'It looks dead. I like my green trees at Hyde Park better. They are alive and growing.' He responded to what was vital, not to what was lifeless; to what was coming, not to what was passing away. He lived by his exultation in distant horizons and uncharted seas. It was this which won him confidence and loyalty in a frightened age when the air was full of the sound of certitudes cracking on every side—this and the conviction of the plain people that he had given them head and heart and would not cease fighting in their cause.

If, like the Good Soldier Schweik listening to a sermon at a field mass, one enjoys 'good, thorough flapdoodle', this is all right; otherwise it is sad that a man so full of promise should have devoted himself to pompous reaffirmation rather than to re-thought. He writes more like a speech-writer for President Eisenhower than for President Kennedy.

How good it is to commend a popular history, already highly successful as a paperback in the United States, which does end by arguing that Americans are coming to realise the irrelevance of their past isolation to the present conditions of the outside world. For anyone who wants to re-think about America, or to start from scratch, Mr Miller's book is a thousand times more to be sought after than the thrilling, but soon forgotten, rash of popular sociological muckraking, the books on status, company wives, the 'new suburbia', Madison Avenue, the open and hidden persuaders, which so catch the fancy of our respectable Sunday papers. Mr Miller and Mr Halle join hands, as it were, to reassure anyone—not against the wickedness of Republican warmongers, etc., etc., but against the superficiality of such good intentions as those of Mr Rovere and, above all others, alas, Mr Schlesinger.

The Politics of Upheaval, by Arthur Schlesinger, Jr[a]

Vol. 32, no. 4, October–December 1961

The third volume of Professor Schlesinger's 'The Age of Roosevelt' takes us from the mid-term elections of 1934 to the end of the Presidential campaign of 1936. In four separate sections, each of book length in itself, he treats of the 'Theology of Ferment' (the many popular movements, unconnected with normal politics, which sprang up in the Great Depression); the 'Coming of the Second New Deal' (the collapse of NRA and the growth of huge Federal spending as a compromise between 'reform' and mere 'recovery'); the 'Crisis of the Constitution' (the invalidation by the Supreme Court of the key measures of the administration); and, lastly, the 'Campaign of 1936' (a splendid anecdotal set-piece which makes very clear that FDR's great campaigns were almost as personal as those of General Eisenhower, the candidate not just running ahead of his party, but often running away from it).

There have been until now no two ways about this huge enterprise. The dust jackets now carry almost as many lavish endorsements by famous publicists as the brochure of a new encyclopaedia. But there has been a small band of unreconstructed academic reviewers who have kept their powder dry and have shot away at the targets Mr Schlesinger offers of a partisanship and rhetoric almost unparalleled in a professional historian of a great school of history. However, it must be now clear that, if the lucky author has come to look like an American Macaulay for whom 1688 has become 1932, this at least is precisely the effect he intended. Here is not a historian falling short, but a historian reaching out to beat the publicists at their own game—and the game is, after all, politics. It is fully apt that he should have moved from Adams House, Harvard, to the White House, Washington. For this is history meant to fortify the present—even at the expense of the past.

This is the best volume so far. The confusion of the 'Second New Deal' defies over-simplification. If Mr Schlesinger is an apologist for great principles, he is at least quite openly, and almost unashamedly, more than a little in love with politics. In this volume his zest for actual politics, his delight in telling a complex and—at times—comic political tale, often suppresses his Macaulay complex. The warts are restored to the Great Chieftain's nose—and the picture instantly leaps to life. FDR's confusion and uncertainty early in 1935 are made vivid. His quite Churchillian economic insouciance begins to sink in. The drawbacks of his government by conflict, his positive incitement of disagreement among his lieutenants, have to be admitted. The planners of the early New Deal were, indeed, 'a recklessly articulate lot'. But still nothing can detract from the great political achievement of keeping such a system afloat at all, mainly through the superb confidence which Roosevelt radiated and at most times possessed.

[a] Heinemann, 749 pp, 63 shillings.

The 'Theology of Ferment' is the most original and valuable part of the book. His account of Father Coughlin, the Townsend Plan, the nativism and neo-fascism of Gerald K. Smith, as well as of the tangled fortunes of the much-divided American Left, may well be definitive. Gone is the silly partisanship of his treatment of Hoover. He is for once concerned to understand how these bigoted exotics loomed so important, not—which is easy—to execrate them. The depression had, indeed, thrown many ordinary Americans almost hope-lessly adrift. But if one is impressed by the pluralism of these crazy causes, yet this same pluralism, regionalism and federalism of American life prevented them from ever coming together. They are an impressive index, however, of the devastation wrought by the depression. They deserve some attention from European students of the rise of Nazism and Fascism. The Dictator of Louisiana emerges as one of the most interesting characters in modern politics. Huey Long combined the politics of agrarian protest of an under-developed area with those of the traditional North American machine. He was the only Boss ever to have an ideology as well as an organisation—except perhaps M. Duplessis in Quebec—even if only as vague and compelling as 'Every Man a King' and 'Soak the fat boys and spread it thin'. He had a touch of the Khrushchev, the Lloyd George, the Mussolini, the Bevan and the Nkrumah, all rolled in with the Prendergast and the Tom Watson. He called himself by his nickname, the Kingfish, because, he said, it substituted 'gaiety for some of the tragedy of politics'. He was corrupt, but discontented. He lacked dignity, but the comic buffoon who deflated pomposity appealed to many millions. Roosevelt and his advisers seriously feared that he might prove the catalyst of all the off-beat politics of the hopeful-hopeless. Perhaps it was only a bullet that stopped him.

Schlesinger's account of the Communist Party is, however, a little less well balanced. The mixture of racialism, populism, funny-money policies, pro-phecies, hero-cults and egalitarianism in the off-beat movements evidently puzzled him. But he writes of communism as if he knew the answers before reading the tedious material. There is a little friendly face-saving in his claim that after 1932 'never again would . . . the party as such command much support among serious American intellectuals'. This will leave a little explain-ing to do in the volumes which treat of the mid- and late thirties. A surprising and related omission is that while he notes that John L. Lewis's Mineworkers chipped in half a million dollars to FDR's campaign chest in 1936—the largest contribution by far—yet there is no treatment of organised Labour at all. One sees that the intellectual historian is more alive than the social historian. But the intellectual historian does give an admirably just account of one by no means insignificant source of influence on American progressive thinking at the time—Harold Laski.

Once again, the last chapter is, alas, a collector's piece of over-writing, a logician's choice example of teleology; but generally the style is more chaste than in the previous volumes and all is immensely readable, a great anecdotal splendour of politics.

The Art and Practice of Diplomacy, by Sir Charles Webster [a]

Vol. 33, no. 2, April–June 1962

Sir Charles Webster prepared this book for the press, but he died before it was published. The book consists of some hitherto unpublished general lectures given on special occasions (and Sir Charles was a great lover of such occasions), and of some previously published in historical journals, but likely to be of wider interest. The first group of essays, six in number, covers the 'Art and Practice of Diplomacy', 'The Principles of British Foreign Policy', and some allied topics concerned with international order; the second group, four in number, is an apparent relic from what should have been his great work on Palmerston. There is a pleasant concluding essay on the accession of Queen Victoria.

Let it be said right out that some of the lectures disappoint; Webster's famed and individual mixture of the hortatory and the factual strikes the eye with much less force than it did the ear. There is a touch of banality in his praising of diplomacy for being diplomatic (especially when British—for Palmerston was really a better Metternich than Metternich); and there is even a touch of the politic and evasive in some of his comments on recent diplomatic history (hardly flattering to his own Palmerstonian self-image of a man subtle and painstaking by training, but bold and impulsive by nature). He tells us:

Diplomacy, therefore, is a transaction between individuals and groups and successful diplomacy depends, in my opinion, mainly on three things: first, on producing a climate of opinion in which the desired ends can be most easily obtained; secondly, on devising forms of agreement in which these ends can be translated into practical accomplishments; and thirdly, on creating or perceiving the right moment at which the maximum effort can be applied. For these purposes it is, of course, necessary to possess skill in the representation of argument and a complete knowledge of the facts.

Webster possessed both these last attributes to a high degree, but the oratorical weight of the 'in my opinion' is lacking in print and leaves the definition a little cold and obvious, somewhat bereft of any idea of conscious purpose. The advice he gives is the advice he gave on the technical implementation of policy; there is surprisingly little on the policy itself. Finally, men appear to have been more important than measures, whether in the brilliant account he gives of his dealings with Weizmann in the First World War; of the Council of Ten at Versailles considering his book on the *Congress of Vienna*; or of his midnight skill in tactfully getting Smuts to accept a conflation of his first draft for the Preamble of the Charter of the United Nations with a Foreign Office brief which Webster himself happened to have prepared. 'I am sure you will acquit me of any undue estimate of the importance of the role which I myself played in a subordinate position

---

[a] Chatto and Windus, 245 pp, 30 shillings.

during the two great wars', Webster said in an oration at the LSE, 'if I illustrate my theme occasionally from my own experiences.' Acquittal on this charge is readily given—especially to anyone who tells such good stories so well. But the real charge is the disappointment that his fierce scorn for those 'who have no practical experience of political or military affairs' apparently led him always into the praise and magnification of detail, rarely into consideration of the policies which the procedures should have served. This is the clue to the paradox of Webster. His manner was that of a moralist, so that he often offended those of his colleagues to whom history is a technical discipline as an end in itself and not an attempt to tell truthfully a public story. But since the moral was always personal, specific, and procedural, he disappointed (despite all his superlative gifts) those who think that there were mistakes of policy from which we can learn.

For there is a certain evasiveness in his usual bluff, blunt and 'no nonsense' Palmerstonian judgements when he comes closer to the present. In his lecture on 'The Principles of British Foreign Policy'—which is a masterly summary of the balance-of-power tradition—the thunder suddenly limps when he comes into the twentieth century: 'The Middle East always remained throughout the twentieth century a difficult problem but in spite of all set-backs the route to the Far East was preserved intact and the major British interest thus safeguarded until recent events altered the situation.' Similarly, he is driven to bewailing events rather than explaining them in considering the 'dismal failure' of British foreign policy over the Italian attack on Abyssinia: 'This failure began a period of British policy which I find it impossible to fit into the pattern of her history. It can only be regarded as an aberration, the causes of which are not yet fully explained.' Each reader must judge for himself whether such a statement is the beginning of wisdom or a concession of failure. Webster was sure that 'the basic principles' which we derive from 'our environment and heritage' still apply; the 'balance of power' is 'as important today as it ever was'. And these basic principles have been applied since the war with 'surprising success', except 'for the ineptitude of the Suez incident'—a typically striking and ambiguous remark.

The best—and the very good—parts of the book are the purely historical essays. His account of 'Lord Palmerston at Work' and of Palmerston's dealings with David Urquhart, that greatest of eccentrics ever to plague the Foreign Office from within, reminds us of the very highest standards of historical exposition. His essays on the principles of diplomacy are perhaps not what he should be judged by and are certainly not what he will be remembered for; he will be remembered as a narrative historian who could grip the imagination of any educated reader without vulgarisation and without pedantry.

Wilkes and Liberty: A Social Study of 1763 to 1774, by George Rudé[a]

Vol. 33, no. 3, July–September 1962

The history of popular politics is not to be approached through the 'History of Political Thought', nor through the strange and famous texts of the very few (we are now told) great political philosophers. Few books, indeed, illuminate the meaning of the dominant concepts used by the actors in important historical events. Mr Rudé's book will rank high among these few.

The Wilkite movement marks the beginning of the influence of public opinion on British government on any regular and usable—and hence political—basis. The ideas, the tactics and the milieu of the 'Wilkite patriot gang' contained every element of subsequent liberalism and radicalism. Wilkes 'played the popular engines' successfully against Parliament itself; his political genius lay in being able to appeal at once to the 'middling men', whom he called 'the political nation', and to the 'inferior orders'. Like any leader in a transitional society, he organised the respectable but also made use of a lurking fear of violence by being able, however accidentally and dishonestly, to reach the mob. Had he had a doctrine of any kind, not just personal ambitions, he could have been the English Danton. 'Wilkes,' wrote the *London Chronicle*, 'indigent and profligate, a second Cataline, with quick parts and violent spirits, sounded first the trumpet of opposition and raised combustion over the whole kingdom.' True, once his indigence was satisfied, his radicalism diminished; the mobs who supported Jack Wilkes in the *North Briton* No. 45 controversy and in the Middlesex election riots were much the same people whom Alderman Wilkes fired upon, defending the Bank of England, in the closing nights of the Gordon Riots. Wilkes can only be a hero for the unheroic (Brecht could have made a good *St Joan* out of him). But the movement is the important thing, not the motives of the man: 'I rejoice to see the whole nation taking up my cause as a public, national, and constitutional cause. Have I not dexterously brought this about?' But it is how he brought this about which is important for the history of popular politics. 'The Platform', the pamphlet, the handbill, the demonstration, newspaper propaganda, the reporting of parliamentary debates, the political use of law suits, the cashing in on strikes and industrial unrest, even some mild racialism (anti-Scottish), the open and the covert lobby, the voluntary political society, and the subscribing societies, organised national petitions—all these things came into being or into a new and lasting relationship in the Wilkite movement. And he did show that mass politics—in a developing society— can serve the purposes of individual liberty (*contra* our modern host of learned misanthropists).

Mr Rudé has shown himself as much master of the archives of London as he was of Paris for his *The Crowd in the French Revolution*. At a time when the

[a] Clarendon Press, Oxford, 240 pp, 30 shillings.

archival assiduity of eighteenth-century historians has too often been the Namierite attempt to demote the importance of general issue in politics, by simply ignoring the pamphlet and the printed book, Mr Rudé shows that it is possible to footnote every step, but to write a fascinating and readable text which dares to treat the politics 'without doors' as a necessary part of the politics 'within doors' of Parliament. If only the official history of Parliament for the eighteenth century were in hands just as scholarly but also with Mr Rudé's feeling for politics!

Perhaps some broader conclusions could have been drawn. Had he been able to consult American sources on Wilkes, he would have seen that he was dealing with a common Anglo-American style of politics: it was the middle class, dominant in America, repressed in Britain, which always had more in common (*contra* Marx) than worker or aristocrat. The Boston Sons of Liberty, who can have had few illusions about Wilkes's personal character, wrote to him in 1768: 'Your perseverance in the Good Old Cause may still prevent the great system from dashing to pieces'—indeed, the whole Wilkite movement leads one to suspect that the fundamental reason for American separation was purely political, that Parliament was not reformed. One scholarly quibble: Wilkes did not ascribe the *Essay on Woman* to Bishop Warburton; he only ascribed to him some pedantically obscene footnotes, a parody on his edition of Pope, But, all in all, here is a model of how social history and the study of political ideas as public opinion should be combined. Would that we but had studies of our times like this!

The Appeasers, by Martin Gilbert and Richard Gott[a]

Vol. 34, no. 4, October–December 1963

Here is a brilliantly documented polemic or a passionate piece of research—which it is hard to tell. Two young historians, twenty-seven and twenty-five years old respectively, look back in anger with all the armoured footnotes and acid detail of Namier's essays on Germany. This is a genre rare in English writing, more like the American 'muckraking' at its very good best: the attempt to make out a case by massive documentation—the facts seem to speak (aloud to heaven) for themselves. The case is, I think, made out, certainly against that other—and awesomely unmentioned—deviant-disciple of Namier, Mr A. J. P. Taylor: that appeasement was bound to fail and that it was a deliberate policy—not just muddle and drift, weakness and blunder—pursued with tenacity and conviction. This latter point has never been made more clearly. The ever-astonishing details of Chamberlain and Halifax's by-passing normal FO channels; of their desire not just for peace, but for positive friendship with Germany (against the real enemy); and their refusal even to

[a] Weidenfeld and Nicolson, 380 pp, 42 shillings.

read contrary reports from experienced British diplomats—none of this is new, but the evidence for it is set out together in a clear and telling way. One thing is new, however: the extent of 'Colonial Appeasement'—the attempt to appease Hitler by offering back the former German colonies (not realising then that *Lebensraum* meant colonies, indeed, but in Slavic, not African lands—a point the authors should have made). So this case against the policy centres upon Chamberlain: 'Baldwin favoured appeasement; Chamberlain was determined to put it into practice'.

This, however, is surely to be as narrow-minded as Chamberlain. They have a chapter on 'The Birth of Appeasement', but it is both unoriginal and completely inadequate; by centring on Chamberlain and his friends they begin the long story only as late as 1937. And here the unfairness of this method of factual-polemic becomes flagrant; indeed an alibi is offered to the English public—a public whom they picture as misled by the lies of Chamberlain. So they were, but willingly. It is as wrong in morality and in explanation to lay all the blame on Chamberlain for having misled the people, as it is, in the deeper context, on Hitler for having misled the German people. So they were, but willingly. If the authors had looked at the initial reactions of British opinion to the rise of the Nazis from the September elections of 1930 onwards, they would have seen that every 'unique' feature of Chamberlain's appeasement was present earlier—at a time when something could have been done: the refusal to take Hitler seriously—by both Left and Right; a persistent playing-down of the expansionism and anti-Semitism of the Nazi ideology as rhetoric; a persistent relativising of political crimes; and, in all, an almost complete failure to recognise that Nazism was not just conventional nationalism, nor a normal politics which could be appeased. If there is guilt, it is first a guilt of misunderstanding; and the misunderstanding was general. Here, alas, the authors appear to be not just misleading, but deliberately so. Many a side remark shows that to them the People can do no wrong, though they are strangely gullible—the old Populist myth which has so befogged the understanding of totalitarian aspirations by normal politicians, especially, alas, by socialists. The authors make the case against Chamberlain's policy and, implicitly, against Taylor's history; but like Taylor they revel in anachronism. He argues that Hitler must have been appeasable, *because* the communists today must be appeased; they argue that Chamberlain was guilty because of the fruits of *his* policies. But hardly anyone at the time dared look at the true nature of Nazism, despite abundant evidence, because of the fear of war. If we die, we die; but fear, *contra* Hobbes and Lord Russell, does not always clear the mind.

Futuribles: Studies in Conjecture, edited by Bertrand de Jouvenel; *The Pure Theory of Politics,* by Bertrand de Jouvenel[a]

Vol. 35, no. 1, January–March 1964

Jouvenel is one of those few among the moderns whose very presence contradicts those cynics and pedants who assert that political theory is dead or, in any case, meaningless. Many, of course, write books in a genre indifferently called political thought, theory or philosophy. But most of these writings turn out to be either critical studies of famous texts (which take the genre for granted—I think of Plamenatz, for example), or else attacks on the genre as if it was the only type of political speculation possible, and all based on an accusation that all other political theorists confuse explanation (a proper thing) with evaluation or purpose (whimsical things).

Jouvenel is, however, a true political theorist. While he rejects the idea that politics can be reduced to a science, yet this does not mean that what is left is only the empirical study of unique events. Theories exist as generalisations about matters of importance. Always a theory is put forward for some purpose, implicit or explicit, but always a theory also puts forward some predictions which offer some sort of reasonable guide to future conduct. Jouvenel argues with profound simplicity in the introduction to *Futuribles*.

Any decision we are now taking, any action we are now undertaking, can bear results only in the future, be it immediate or distant: therefore any conscious activity of necessity implies 'looking forward', and it is a telling image, that of Lot's wife, who, as she only looks back, turns to stone.

He and his colleagues offer no synthetic methodology. The beauty of this book is its common sense and, speaking American, *substantiveness*. Each author offers his views about future developments in his field and the grounds on which he reaches them. It is curious that an exercise of mind so common to economists and so talked about by sociologists has been so neglected by students of politics. Of course, the past is prelude. Jouvenel's own contribution is mainly historical, 'On the Evolution of Forms of Government'. But it is brilliantly illuminating. I have never read such a profound and compressed account of the forces at work in modern politics. He deals in theories as the understanding of the situation we are in. In this light theory is a necessary part of action, not an aberration of intellectuals. The most interesting theories are, indeed, those held unconsciously by self-styled practical men. What we seek are explanations of the relationship between aspirations and forms of government, not pedagogic divorce between them. He contrasts the economic optimism with the political pessimism of contemporary thought. He revives the theories of Elie Halévy's masterly but neglected *L'Ère de Tyrannies* of 1938. 'Can we find any phenomena which

---

[a] Droz, Geneva, 321 pp, 40 Swiss francs (*Studies in Conjecture*); Cambridge University Press, 236 pp, 25 shillings (*Pure Theory of Politics*).

seem common to all countries in our day?' he concludes. 'Indeed we can. . . .' And his conclusions are plain to read and should be read.

The most methodologically interesting essay is Edmund Leach's 'The Political Future of Burma'. His four categories of analysis form a framework which does deserve to be applied comparatively and—for once—indiscriminately: factors in a culture with a high degree of stability (such as climate and religion); factors of fairly predictable growth or decline (such as population); cyclic factors (such as the swings of public opinion and the ageing of radical governments); and all those factors 'wholly fortuitous and unpredictable' (those very empirical factors which Machiavelli meant by *Fortuna*). René Servoise's 'Whither Black Africa?' is the most sweeping and provocative— though its strange mixture of St Germain des Prés impressionism and Quai d'Orsay statistics is a bit hard to take. Max Beloff refuses to play the game; his 'British Constitutional Evolution, 1960–1970' rarely gets off the ground from a rather hoary and dated philippic against certain (un)constitutional tendencies in the British Labour Party. We'll see about that one. M. M. Postan also disappoints; his 'The Economic and Social System: the Prospect for 1970–1975' summarises ably, but once again, the incoherence in Marxism between ownership and control. But what of the future? Perhaps the image of a middle-class classless society could be more fruitfully explored than by covering familiar ground to reach a familiar conclusion about the changes in Capitalism and the decline of the Proletariat both as fact and ideology. Perhaps he should have looked to America in economic and social terms as did Tocqueville in political and social terms. (Indeed the omission of the USA and the USSR throughout is odd.) Then Leicester Webb's 'Pakistan's Political Future' is an interesting analysis of the present relationship of dictatorship to political factors in a Muslim culture, but he does not look forward here as brilliantly as he once looked back in his published inaugural lecture, *Politics and Polity* (the same man?). These essays are selections from some fifty-five which have appeared in French in the continuing series called *Futuribles*.

Jouvenel's *The Pure Theory of Politics* is, curiously, the other extreme of the influence of economic theory. If *Futuribles* is Applied Economics, the *Pure Theory* is Analytical Economics, though rather in the Marshallian literary tradition. He attempts to define and to abstract simplified models of typical political situations. I am doubtful if this approach is fruitful—even in economics, *a fortiori* in politics. But this is a long argument. And here, anyway, is Jouvenel not as a theorist but as a philosopher writing in the manner of his *Sovereignty*—of whom someone said 'Fairy Gold'! Indeed, his *Pure Theory* also is beautiful, elegant, stimulating, and written in a wonderfully athletic and precise English; but it leaves me puzzled the morning after as to quite what it was that so delighted me the night before. But 'puzzled' indeed, not feeling tricked. I genuinely want to believe that I have missed something.

Eichmann in Jerusalem: A Report on the Banality of Evil, by Hannah Arendt[a]

Vol. 35, no. 1, January–March 1964

This most controversial book argues three theses. First, that the trial of Eichmann in Jerusalem was inherently unjust: a political trial before the wrong jury since it was a crime against humanity and not just 'the Jewish people'. Secondly, that the role and responsibility of Eichmann himself was vastly exaggerated: he was a mere bureaucrat, not a unique maestro of evil, and the real horror lies in just this, the 'banality of evil' that petty functionaries anywhere can create if they never question the legal orders given to them. Thirdly, that the Jewish communities were mistaken and wrong to cooperate with the Nazis in the organisation of transit to the camps and in the selection of the few promised survivors: wrong in a double sense, that refusal to cooperate would probably have led to fewer deaths, with all the chaos that would have resulted and the sheer administrative difficulty of such a vast round-up in wartime (things were made too easy for Germans to practise 'not noticing'); and also wrong in that cooperation with such evil is itself evil, and even if *some* could be saved by bargains, yet any complicity in arranging the deaths of many or *any* is itself evil.

This is a hard thesis, a bitter one for all the world if they dare think of such things, and for Jews especially who cannot help but be perpetually obsessed by such things. The thesis is made no easier by Arendt's famously complex style, her inability to pursue a firm, clear line of argument without learned digression, and her strange mixture of metaphysical free-association and brilliant sociological insight. She is a great mind of our times, but needlessly and heedlessly obscure in all her works, and here almost irresponsibly obscure. A book for the general reader on such ghastly themes, arousing moral passions in all of us and even some element of pornographic attraction, should have had great pains for clarity bestowed upon it.

But it is an awesomely courageous and honest book, and, to the best of my judgement, essentially true in its three theses. Rarely has a book been so misrepresented, or an author so violently denounced by those willing to cry 'Anti-Semitism', even 'Jewish Anti-Semitism', rather than to face grim facts. For it has been the tragedy of the Jewish people, until the founding of Israel, to be without a tradition of political activity: that persecution and suffering, even the fact of being a nation without a state, had created a psychology of suffering and passivity which precluded active resistance. The Jewish communities of Europe accepted, with few exceptions, the totalitarian premise of inevitability. Suppose resistance was, as it well may have been, utterly futile. But consider what it means if men are then so rational as never to fight against the odds, or never even fight in vain so that there are heroes to be

[a] Faber & Faber, 275 pp, 25 shillings.

remembered in our dark times as well as devils. Dare any man say it who did not go through it? But someone must if even hopelessly oppressed and persecuted men are still to recognise themselves as men, still able to act and make some choices, not just the inert victims of circumstances. Cicero wrote that a free man, if taken as a slave and without hope of escape, should commit suicide. Is this inherently absurd? Yeats wrote of a man on the gallows: 'He kicked before he died, He did it out of pride'.

Paths of American Thought, edited by Arthur M. Schlesinger, Jr, and Morton White; *The First New Nation*, by Seymour Martin Lipset; *American Aspects*, by D. W. Brogan; *Party and Society: Voting Behaviour in Anglo-American Democracies*, by Robert R. Alford; *Interest Groups in American Society*, by Harmon Zeigler [a]

Vol. 35, no. 4, October–December 1964

Dr Johnson's famous remark on patriotism is usually misunderstood. The scoundrels to whom he referred, in his usual precise way, were those who actually called themselves 'Patriots'. They were Wilkes and his allies, the enemies of (Johnson's phrase again, though used approvingly) 'the Establishment', those soon to be called 'radicals', or those who were quite interchangeably called in the politics of the day 'the Friends of Reform' or 'the Friends of America'. Johnson sneered at the 'patriot gang' because they were upstarts who claimed that it was their country just because they lived in it, not necessarily even because they owned it; and because they claimed that citizenship was a matter of virtue, of professing republican principles—that is, acting rationally for the common good, not a matter of that all-important (again Johnson before Bagehot) *deference*. The patriots were the popular party, the enemies of the Tories—and this usage was to continue on both sides of the water until the 1820s at least; and it then expressed something which it is an anachronism to call nationalism. For any man could be a citizen—whatever his antecedents—if his principles and civic virtue were in order. A nation was defined by the possession of a just Constitution, not by history or blood. The whiggish patriot was a man far more civilised in his principles and actions than the patriot of modern nationalism, the man who will stop at nothing for his country. The trouble with Johnson's patriots was, in his eyes, that they stuck at everything: always quibbling whether authority was right or wrong, forever dissenting, so rarely accepting gratefully.

All this first, because one cannot understand how Americans think about politics if one accepts the English identification of patriotism with the political Right. The American liberal is a patriot at least. Schlesinger and White's huge

[a] Chatto and Windus, 614 pp, 50 shillings (Schlesinger and White); Heinemann, 366 pp, 35 shillings (Lipset); Hamish Hamilton, 195 pp, 21 shillings (Brogan); John Murray, 396 pp, 63 shillings (Alford); Prentice-Hall International, 343 pp, 54 shillings (Zeigler).

emporium-symposium is not merely patriotic; much of it, consciously or not, is nearer propaganda than scholarship. American liberals writing about themselves—their favourite subject-matter—have little to learn from Birches and Goldwaters about how to make the eagle scream. There has been some reluctance to say this plainly. Our present-day Friends of America pass this over when reading and reviewing such books in much the same way that the European Left once resolutely ignored the elements of Russian nationalism in Soviet Communism.

This book is meant to be important. Two leading intellectuals—as they say—have gathered together a rare old haul of the fashionable and the solid to produce *the* anthology of American intellectual history to sweep all others from the market. Morton White is an honest analytical philosopher; Arthur Schlesinger has always been the Macaulay of the Democratic Party, the Prince of pop-historians, ever hortatory in tone. Unfortunately his love of 'affirmation' and, if necessary, of 'reaffirmation' has carried his coeditor with him. Let us just 'unpack' one passage from White's introduction: 'While Americans fled from Europe, conquered a wilderness, and freed themselves from foreign domination, they forged a set of beliefs that helped them guide their revolutionary energies and form their new political structure.' 'Fled' indeed!—not many: most left of their own free will to better themselves or to live more congenially; and many migrants, modern economic historians show us, did not view migration even to God's Own Country as permanent, certainly not as a matter of being reborn free or some such pietistic illusion. What 'foreign domination'? It is quite clear that most people on both sides of the water viewed the War of Independence as a Civil War—easy indeed would separation have been if the tendentious word 'foreign' had been accurate. (The worst essay in the book is the first, by a historian, Edmund S. Morgan, fantastic for its anachronistic assumption of an American nationalism in the colonies—the paradox never occurs to him, and for his Wicked Tory Tyranny view of the British, in England he always means. Even fact is wrenched: 'Englishmen, relieved of expenses by American taxation . . .'. The Russians are hardly worse.) And did they 'forge a set of new beliefs'? Were they really 'revolutionary'? And did they form a 'new political structure'? The fantastic effort and pride involved in explaining the newness of American everything might be avoided if a little knowledge were shown of the doctrines of the English Civil War and the structure of English eighteenth-century politics. There is a positively Ghanaian fervour in denying or ignoring the real formative factors of the national experience. The truth may well be that there was nothing new in these United States except the happy circumstances of an English bourgeoisie removed from both aristocratic embrace and proletarian threat. This weird assumption of a spontaneous and blessed national immaculate conception may account for there only being two foreign contributors—Marcus Cunliffe and a tactful Japanese, despite the usual cant of internationalism. The joint editor of *Encounter* (the American one) speaks for Europe on 'Transatlantic Images'—a slick piece.

351

Almost the only person to grapple with the real difficulties is Louis Hartz. He sees clearly that 'the slogans of democratic liberalism . . . were quite as irrational in their appeal as the deferential slogans of European feudalism'. So he can say, with a rare objectivity amid such posturing company, that 'the issue is not one of rationalism in the classical sense, but rather of the behavioral consequences of allegiance to different types of symbols'. And the essential consequence has not been a matter of doctrinal novelty, or philosophy, but simply the style of politics conditioned by the fact that from first foundings in America, not just from the Revolutionary days, politics was a highly public activity. Hartz argued in his *The American Liberal Tradition*, like Gunnar Myrdal in his *The American Dilemma*, that there is an 'American creed', that it is liberalism itself, and that it is so universally held that most take it completely for granted, while those who are self-conscious about it seldom view it objectively, but affirm and reaffirm it. Things that refute its self-sufficiency, like the outside world, must either be ignored or converted; things that contradict its ready application to practical life, which cannot be ignored, like the Negro question, lead to something like schizophrenia rather than reinterpretation or rejection of the American creed. (But surprisingly big things can be ignored as this volume shows—the genocide of the Indians and the ending of any *possibility* of Americanism continuing to appear both national and universal once the doors were closed to mass immigration.) Hartz, who is a suggestive rather than a conclusive writer, has received unexpected support from the most solid, sensible and wideranging of American sociologists, Seymour Martin Lipset.

Lipset—may one murmur quietly?—is not always exciting to read. His method of quoting large passages from perfectly well-known secondary authorities occasionally makes these books seem more immediately desirable than his own great attempt to put them all together. But he does ask important and broad questions and he does succeed in pulling together a host of specialised works. In his *Political Man* he dared to try to assess the scattered evidence on the conditions for 'democratic polity'. The book was marred by being a series of essays thrown together, better in parts than in the whole; and it is a major contribution to modern political sociology—far removed from the rhetoric of Schlesinger et al. (despite the unhappy appearance of the English edition in a patriotic wrapper—when will designers read more than the title of the book they are supposed to characterise?) He does not just assume but he actually tries to demonstrate that values affect social action. And he traces the very great effect in American politics and society of the specifically American combination of 'equality' and 'achievement'. It suddenly dawns on one that, methodologically, he has come near to success in an almost incredible task; he brings the teaching of Talcott Parsons down to comprehensible earth and puts the flesh of history on conceptual dry bones. By doing this he refutes both the laziness and the methods of contemporary British empiricism—but then the existence of a liberal doctrinaire *tradition* always was a stark factual refutation of both—may one say?—Oakeshott and Popper.

His conclusions do not suffer from being familiar. After all, something that should not exist, so plainly does exist that it needs scholarly explanation. Where Lipset is particularly rewarding, however, is in his balanced appreciation of the universality of the symbols of Americanism, and yet in the peculiarity of its incidence. Because there are all sorts of moral wrongs in America, he does not see the system as unstable; but it is not universal either. Britain leans towards elitism, the United States towards equalitarianism, but both are stable democracies. What he has done has been to take the whole sweep of the American social sciences and, with splendid eclecticism, pillage them for anything of relevance to the great and unavoidable questions—what is an American and how peculiar is the American experience?

Far too many books have either affirmed without explaining, all comprehensiveness and generality (both in a scientific and a moral sense) or have followed that great escape mechanism of American social thought, 'pure social science', attempts to take the politics out of politics which, at the best, even when not just conceptual vapours, have been unrelated studies in skilful but unrelated depth. Perhaps the time has come when some of these can be put together, made use of to ask more concrete general questions. Both Professors Alford's and Zeigler's books have this nature. They are not, emphatically not, college texts—we all know what that means. They are genuine works of synthesis, far more alive to criteria of political importance than most previous offerings in American social sciences, but still more scientific in their use of evidence—and more perceptive that much evidence does now exist—than almost anything in English social science.

Political rhetoric, scholarly comparison of monographs and established authorities, these are two types of study; but there is a third which, while it will offend the adepts of[b] both, yet will, one hopes, never perish: the kind of impressionism of which Professor Sir Denis Brogan is master. His latest collection of essays would not get him into the next Schlesinger anthology: too carping and close to the bone—as in his somewhat great essay 'The Illusion of American Omnipotence' (in which it was first clearly stated that 'only American boys have Mothers'). Messrs Lipset, Alford and Zeigler might be a[c] little worried at the lack of clear evidence served up in suitably sterile conditions in his 'A Fresh Appraisal of the American Civil War'. But Brogan catches the mood, the feeling, the character, the significance of American politics like none other. To be an inferior impressionist is to be worse than the dullest methodologist. But to be a master is to have all forgiven. In Brogan nothing is ever really explained, everything is anecdote; but sheer fantastic width of comparison, the depth, range and peculiarity of instances either illuminate a hundred familiar things in a new way, or, as the case may be,

[b] This 'of' is missing in the journal version.
[c] The journal version lacks this 'a' and simply reads 'might be little worried'. The 'a' seems called for by the context, but I am flagging the change here because its addition does completely change the previous sense.

make the bizarre appear quite ordinary. He, too, takes seriously the fact that America is the country of an idea. But he simply warns against the dangers of disillusionment: love's young dream is to be enjoyed, but the avoidance of anger and folly in middle life calls for a scepticism and a realism which Americans have not always shown. Brogan is himself a living refutation of the absolute uniqueness of Americanism. His sense of the inwardness of the American experience is, of course, part of[d] his creative genius, a true exemplification of Coleridge's 'critical sympathy', that momentary 'suspension of disbelief' which enables unlike minds to comprehend each other. But his artistic awareness is helped by a simple social fact: he is a Scot from Glasgow—they are much *more like* the Americans than the English are. Americanism is the ideology of the North British middle class without either the vices or virtues of being squeezed by aristocracy or proletariat.

Men and Work: The Autobiography of Lord Citrine[a]

Vol. 36, no. 2, April–June 1965

It even takes pride of place on the dust-jacket. Self-help and evening education for this young union official in 1914 included learning short-hand—and not Pitman's, but the Gregg system 'with its shapely curves and absence of shading and positioning. . . . My proficiency increased to the point where I was made a member of the Order of Gregg Artists, which was limited to those capable of writing artistic shorthand'. This is far from irrelevant to the character of both the man and the book. Lord Citrine himself explains: 'Why did I take this trouble? It was patent to me that when my colleagues saw that I was writing everything down verbatim, they were almost certain to make me a member of various delegations to meet employers and others.'

So, long verbatim extracts of important interviews or—though carefully distinguished—detailed accounts written up immediately afterwards, these are a distinguishing mark of the book. But Citrine never seems to realise that extracts are but extracts, whether verbatim or not: sometimes a short précis gives a fairer picture of the divisions of opinion in a meeting than a long series of authentic snippets. The impression created is of some kind of 'don't you believe me?' claim to authenticity since 'I did it all myself'. The author by this device turns many an issue of opinion into one of fact. This is not irrelevant to the manner in which he built up the scope and power of the office of Secretary of the TUC. This proud and honest autobiography is almost an instructional manual in how secretaries of large institutions can take over policy formulation from nominal directors while hiding behind the files.

---

[d] This 'of' is missing in the journal version. Another possibility is that the 'part' should be 'partly', but that is far less likely an error than an 'of' omitted from the transcription of what was probably a handwritten original.

[a] Hutchinson, 384 pp, 40 shillings.

Citrine pursued a twofold policy at the TUC: to increase the power of the General Council within the trades union movement, and to expand the activity of the TUC outside its obvious spheres so that it would have to be consulted by every government in nearly all aspects of economic and industrial policy. No one except Bevin did more to shape the policy and character of trade unionism between the wars. His account of the deliberations of the TUC during the General Strike are fascinating but add little to that in Bullock's masterly *Life and Times of Ernest Bevin*, though useful details are added. The government was, indeed, deceitful, provocative, and determined to force a general show-down with organised labour; the TUC was, indeed, fighting by accident and without any clear aims; but the solidarity of the strike was a remarkable feat of spontaneous social organisation. Of more questionable value are the long accounts Citrine gives of 'highly confidential' talks with Neville Chamberlain. Chamberlain appears to have strung him along with all kinds of platitudes and political gossip, all current in the newspapers, nothing really confidential at all, but helping to silence—by then—Sir Walter, the Prince of Discretion, happy for the prestige of the TUC that its officials should be treated with such honour and such empty confidences. Trade union officials are now more leery of this kind of thing. But we now have academics so proud to be 'in the know' or 'close to the government' that their lips are always sealed even from saying the most obvious things.

No, what really emerges is something of prime interest not to political history, but to social history. Citrine's autobiography is perhaps the last monument to the old tradition of self-help, to much that was good in it, to some things that were bad. He plainly owes more to Dean Farrer and Samuel Smiles than to either Methodism or Marx (before the days when three A Levels meant a public pension). There is scarcely a word about poverty, only of personal success in avoiding it. We see the Edwardian 'working man' not 'the worker' of the 1920s. Herbert Wilson's voluble outpourings about the young Harold have somewhat of the same mixture as Citrine's of splendid pride and damnable priggishness. Citrine comes out best from an interview with the great Leverhulme: 'As things turned out, I never again lost my self-confidence'. 'I had never shown any desire to become a Labour Party candidate . . . , but I allowed myself to be persuaded'—which was, of course, a mistake. 'I started work at the Trades Union Congress on Monday, 20th January, 1924. When I reached Euston, contrary to my usual practice, I took a taxi to the TUC headquarters.' The world of brass bands—'his favourite encore was 'Drinking', in which Paley obtained phenomenally low notes almost unknown on the cornet'—and of 'Eugene Sandow's system of dressing myself immediately after a cold bath without drying myself with a towel'. A world of temperance and character, of personalities rather than of social forces: Snowden disliked him, we are told, for having accidentally expropriated his own special jug of orangeade at a Parliamentary Labour Party dinner. Citrine's brilliant future was foretold precisely in 1920 by 'Mrs. Procter, the widow of the well-known phrenologist. Her son was a member of the Electrical Trades Union . . .'

I do not wish to imply that the book is unduly discursive, only that it is not quite as precise as it seems. But this is its virtue. The organisation of the TUC appears so much in terms of the man that we are reminded that great disputes about policy are the almost lewd obsession of intellectuals writing history. The true character of British trade unionism, for good or ill, is better revealed in the honest egotism of Citrine's autobiography, showing who worked the system and for what purposes, than in a dozen of those zealous Socialist accounts of—not what happened, but of what policies there might have been.

English History: 1914–1945, by A. J. P. Taylor[a]

Vol. 37, no. 2, April–June 1966

Would a modern Isaac Disraeli include an account of Mr A. J. P. Taylor, one wonders, in his *Curiosities of Literature* or in his once equally celebrated *The Calamities and Quarrels of Authors with Some Inquiries respecting their Moral and Literary Characters*? The sad thing is that any really great quarreller is likely to transcend the limitations of the latter volume and find a rightful place in the former as well.

Mr Taylor, having been attacked by nearly everyone for his view on the ordinariness of Hitler, now intrudes it everywhere. To picture Hitler as 'a skilful, though unscrupulous, tactician', and not as 'either a madman or as set on a world war all along' may originally have restored a balance against those who saw it as 'all Hitler', a foolish Great Man theory of history in this country; and often, in Germany, a damnable excuse (and Mr Taylor will accept no excuses from Germans, not even Hitler). But now even a political devil can be given no due. Take the question of British propaganda in the First World War. We are told confidently that it 'probably did not do much to shake enemy morale—certainly less than enemy writers later alleged'. No footnote or reference is given. The reader may need reminding that the most famous tribute to the effectiveness of British propaganda was paid by one Adolf Hitler in his *Mein Kampf*—a book whose utility in understanding Nazism Taylor regards as negative. Hitler's judgement and importance have to be demolished even in this—even when he is not to be named.

And Mr Taylor's well-known desire to rescue the word 'appeasement' from ignorant scurrility and special pleading also intrudes everywhere. History is all circumstance and human action; no iron laws, inflexible trends or parallels and repetitions for him—quite rightly. But then why be so patently worried that abuse of Baldwin and Chamberlain will strengthen the hand of all those in the Pentagon and NATO who threaten CND's manner of defending Great Britain? Time and time again Taylor recurs to the theme of our exaggeration of German war-potential in the 1930s and of the probable effects of bombing.

[a] Oxford: Clarendon, 709 pp, 45 shillings.

He points to the clear superiority of the RAF Fighter Command over the ill-directed forces the Luftwaffe could deploy in 1940. Soon, as in Mattingly's *The Defeat of the Spanish Armada*, we will wonder why the foreign squadrons ever took off at all. We were over-prepared, it is implied, and the Germans—which is quite true—never mobilised their economy in the totalitarian way that we were able to in wartime. But never does he hint that it was a jolly good job we were less badly off than we thought in 1939 and 1940. There is an implicit nostalgia for a balance of power.

And at most times Taylor's affable pose of 'gruff Cobbett' or radical John Bull does, for such a great historian of the late Hapsburg Empire, create a surprising insularity. More space is given to the abdication crisis than to the Spanish Civil War. The retrospective evidence on the reality of Nazi ideology of the opening up of the concentration camps is ignored—the Nazis must have blundered into that too, just as they blundered into war. The Jewish question only really arises in some sarcastic sentences which explain how a 'moral feeling' against Germany grew up which made 'English people less reluctant to go to war'—for 'even city bankers became champions of freedom when a Rothschild was imprisoned in Vienna'. Again, he rides his corrective thesis of the essential isolationism of all sections of British public opinion between the wars to absurd extremes. For public opinion was simply wrong: Britain was in fact involved in a system of power relationships. So he ignores all those authors in the 1930s who said so. They were unrepresentative—even if correct. Particularly he ignores any evidence that some people were aware that Nazism represented from its first electoral successes a new type of ideological politics threatening all European order, both in its anarchic irrationality and in its purported rationality. The bibliography deals with a serious book which argues just these things about British opinion and the rise of Nazism, Dr Brigitte Granzow's *Mirror of Nazism*, by ignoring it (which D. C. Watt has called 'the most important study of this subject'). Taylor had, indeed, reviewed her book, which contained a temperate criticism of his underestimation of Nazi ideology—an adjective which could not be applied to the review. These curiosities and suppressions made one distrust Taylor's writing profoundly. 'The Whig dogs' are not even named.

But the book is a masterpiece. It is not quite fully baked, hasty in parts, ill-balanced and hardly to be accepted on authority—as the Oxford histories have sometimes pretended. Mr Taylor does not confuse neutrality with objectivity. Contemporary history and contemporary politics are too close to be separated without emasculating one or the other. His prejudices are like hypotheses which, whether true or false in the final testing, do succeed in creating coherence and order. If he does not warn us enough, well—he is writing for an adult audience who are presumably old enough to look after themselves. Perhaps it should be kept from the hands of children, but it makes it all the more enjoyable for adults. If schoolmasters use it for sixth forms then, at last, they will have to begin where they should: that history is not facts piled upon facts, but the ordering of evidence by critical concepts.

Not just manner, though that is superb: the set-piece of the first two pages which begins: 'Until August 1914 a sensible, law-abiding Englishman could pass through life and hardly notice the existence of the state, beyond the post office and the policeman' and which ends 'the history of the English state and of the English people merged for the first time'. And the character sketch of Asquith on page 34, behaving at Cabinet more 'like a referee in a boxing ring' than a 'national leader'; or that of Lloyd George who 'aroused every feeling except trust'. But the matter in fact contains a precise, and in its extent at least partly novel, thesis which should revolutionise our understanding of the period between the wars.

Here one relishes the paradoxical nature of Mr Taylor. If he is a pacifist, he is also able and willing firmly to say that the Welfare State owes its implementation to the mobilisation of British society by the state in the two world wars. War has been the great accelerator of social change. There is a schoolbook and textbook theory that Asquith's and Attlee's first ministries mark the points of departure from the negative to the positive state. Even a glance at Civil Service statistics, solemnly printed in books which maintain this, show its falsity. The big increases in numbers take place in 1914 and 1939—and then post-war things never get back to 'normal'. Modern war creates the need and the demand to nurture the whole of a population; and it creates the statistical basis of inquiry on which this can be done. War stimulates practical, administrative knowledge of how a society actually works and of the sub-groups who compose it. Our success in two wars of total mobilisation went far to create those habits of secrecy, confidence, dispatch and conceit which mark sections of the Administrative class.

Political consequences follow from this. Taylor, adding to rather than refuting both Pelling and Poirier on the rise of the Labour Party, shows how Labour gained by its role in the war effort both the prestige which brought it into office under MacDonald, but also its somewhat excessive sense of responsibility. Lloyd George was thus a natural wartime leader: his ability both to reach back down and high up the social scale gave him an intuitive knowledge of how hard various sections of society could be pressed. Taylor's account of politics in wartime is original and brilliant. His mixture of irony and involvement is like that of his 'beloved friend' to whom the book is dedicated: Max Aitken. Perhaps a better mixture—but engaging and full of home truths just because it is a very personal mixture.

'The Luftwaffe was a powerful missionary for the welfare state', he writes. Only when the evacuation of London was planned, in fear of total destruction by bombing, did British civil servants begin to realise who and how many they were dealing with; and only then did the state take up again those responsibilities of employment and health which had been taken up so successfully in 1915 and 1916, to be run down, more than relinquished, between the wars. For all the time there was both the realisation that it was possible, which came from the experience of war, not from socialist agitation; and that there was the administrative machine to do it.

This is (since reviewers are supposed to pass one judgement on a book, not two—that it is wildly biased *and* a masterpiece of historical writing) a very English book; the kind of thing that fascinated the elder Disraeli in English authors—a truculent honesty in some things going together with an almost wilful blindness in others. It reads like an account of one side of a family quarrel, but given with such passion and realism that one can surmise the other, and one's sympathies are torn almost in proportion to the sharpening of one's understanding.

The Politics of Financial Control, by Gordon Reid [a]

Vol. 38, no. 2, April–June 1967

This excellent little book on the meaning of the kind of financial control exercised by the House of Commons was the product of a year in England in 1963 (a good year for such matters) spent by the Professor of Politics in the University of Western Australia, but obviously also of a long and deep reading of the basic printed sources. He acknowledges the help of the late Professor Bassett. As in his writings there is, at the end, a curious mixture of complacency and despair about the nature of our institutions and the trends of our times, but at the beginning and all the way through there is a similar biting intelligence and rare devotion to plain facts.

His thesis is that financial control cannot be looked at apart from the whole process of political leadership and control which centres on Parliament, whether radiating from the Cabinet office or from the parties. Looked at objectively, in this plain and untinted light, the British House of Commons does not do so badly as many of its critics suggest—not so badly, at least, in all that it can do, while not, for the sake of rationalising or reforming a part, changing the whole system.

He stresses the primacy of political considerations at every stage, and can quote pleasantly diverse authorities. Bagehot, he reminds us, did not accept that the House of Commons had any special function with regard to finance 'different from its function with respect to other legislation'. Laski had contended that 'the examination and control of finance is not a separate and special function of the House of Commons. . . . By deciding what to do in other spheres, the House largely decides by inference what it is to do in the financial sphere'. And he cites Sir Ralph Hawtrey, formerly economic adviser to the Treasury, as placing 'a high price on words' in saying: 'financial policy is a function (in a mathematical sense) of all other policies'. In other words, there is no point in trying to get Estimates procedure back to estimates, and Supply Days back to the details of supply (as Sir Edward Fellowes and others appear to hanker after). 'If the House looked after policy the fiscal millions

[a] Hutchinson University Library, 176 pp, 27s. 6d; paperback 11s. 6d.

would look after themselves.' Well, not quite, Reid implies; but the controls over details are simply the established controls against exceptional abuses.

Certainly Professor Reid is not entirely happy with existing procedure. It is hideously complex and needlessly arcane in both the deed and the word. He quotes the Plowden Committee's realism: 'what is important to Parliament is to have the opportunity to express a view on the scale and direction of big blocks of expenditure which are not suitable for detailed and individual parliamentary control'. But, he correctly stresses, critics of gibberish, jargon and the archaic are 'noticeably reticent when it comes to advancing alternative methods or substitute "rules"'. Do they object simply to the obscurantism, or do they think that they can get 'genuine control'? In which case they are, indeed, wanting a radical change in legislative–executive relationships all the way down the line. He quotes the frustrated utterance of a former chairman of the Public Accounts Committee, Mr Harold Wilson: 'These committees cannot do much, indeed the House cannot do much, to control the general volume of public expenditure'. But he contrasts this with Prime Minister Wilson's window-dressing, evasive or backpedalling remarks on parliamentary reform.

He concludes that if parliamentary control of finance is characterised by mythical qualities, it is not itself a myth. The myth enables the Executive to cloak the degree of control it exercises over the financial-legislative process; but the going is often rough and should be so. And if it is a complicated course to get to know and to comment upon, this is largely because back-benchers will cry out in one breath 'legislative freedom' while they breathe in party discipline with the next. 'Possibly it is trite', he ends, 'but there is enormous truth in the aphorism that Members of Parliament get the financial procedures, and the financial committees, they deserve.'

Trite, alas, indeed. For it is not a tautology which binds one to the internal coherence of the present system taken as a whole, but a truism that can cut both ways. Two obvious criticisms arise of this astringent and beautifully argued exercise. First, does anyone deserve such a lack of rational connection between—even taking them as they are—the two established means of financial control: the legislative processes which stem from the Bill of Rights concept of a 'grant in Parliament', and the more modern use of Select Committees? He himself admits that the 'actual interdependence' between these two means is 'tenuous'. But if these two processes could be geared into each other, much worry would be abated. Is this base rationalism? And, secondly, to grant his major thesis—that it is all political anyway—may be the greatest possible encouragement to genuine reform, not its chastening. Once the myth of the constitutional sanctity of financial procedure is eroded (a task which this book helps greatly), the minds of MPs and of civil servants may become much more open to bringing into the House of Commons modern techniques of financial investigation which are even now beginning to be used in Whitehall. Here it is simply depressingly conservative to ignore even semi-technical discussions of 'cost-effectiveness' analysis—although granted that Normanton's fundamental work on *The Audit and Accountability of Governments* must have been in the press when Reid was correcting his proofs. But was it so unexpected that a Labour government, albeit torn internally on the issue, yet would nonetheless bring in a few new Select Committees—and appear to commit itself to more—on basically political grounds? The electorate does trust the parties with the control of legislation; but the public is beginning to get worried, in times of economic stringency, about getting value for money. And the point is beginning to get across that an improved parliamentary control of the administration is a more possible and needful task than the pretence to control legislation.

Four Essays on Liberty, by Isaiah Berlin[a]

Vol. 40, no. 4, October–December 1969

This book reprints with some slight revisions Sir Isaiah Berlin's *Political Ideas in the Twentieth Century* (1949), his *Historical Inevitability* (1953), his *Two Concepts of Liberty* (1958) and his less well known Robert Waley Cohen Memorial Lecture to the Council of Christians and Jews, *John Stuart Mill and the Ends of Life* (1959). His prose marches briskly forward, heavy matter carried on short quick legs, but with sudden digressions and deft and amazing changes of tone and pace. The matter is heavy, solemn and leisurely, but the manner is brisk, witty and urgent.

Down the historical High he struts or trots, a quick and friendly word on the run with Tocqueville and Constant—a good beginning to the day; he stops for a moment to talk to Spencer with deliberate tolerance but some boredom and pity too; raises his hat to Comte, not quite cutting him dead; contrives at the next corner to talk to Hegel and Freud at once, suddenly leaving them, angry in each other's company, aware that he has gone but puzzled how; with a sideways lurch and roll down he goes into some dark cul-de-sac where poor Dostoevsky holds down a job as a college porter, then back to the main street— 'Good morning, De Maistre, no no, too kind; but have you managed to reach agreement with Acton yet about not attending the same Church?' 'Hello Schiller, my dear fellow, indeed, indeed, so beautiful and so true, but can't stop now, a thousand apologies, promised to meet Count Tolstoy for no coffee at Oxfam'—until he nearly collides with Marx, perhaps sharp and testy in what he says, 'Yes, yes, I'm afraid I haven't read the last volume of *Das Kapital* yet, but tell me briefly, if you could, what is it precisely that you are trying to say?', but perfectly polite in manner, indeed inquiring softly after his boils and family, warns him solicitously against the traffic and new friends in sports cars, but then is visibly relieved, for once, by the distractive importunities of a small cosmopolitan crowd of disputants and petitioners, *Raisonneurs*, *Idéologues*,

[a] Oxford Paperbacks, 213 pp, 15 shillings.

Intelligenz and *Intelligensia*, to whom he throws a jolly, a cutting or a temporising word to each in his own language, before he hails Condorcet and Spinoza across the street, holding them for a second together in profound conversation, until wheeling from them too and pausing only slightly longer outside Christ Church to prove to a suspicious Coleridge and Carlyle that he has read their latest—but he has his reservations, as he remarked only that morning over breakfast at All Souls to Burke; he triumphantly completes his purposeful walk, ignoring the taunts of a rather ill-mannered mob in the Broad outside Balliol led by Jean-Jacques Rousseau, Gracchus Babeuf and Tom Paine (though pausing to throw from his pockets a few life-belts and sweets in their direction), and now finally in the company of Immanuel Kant and John Stuart Mill sweeps past the Bodleian—urging them both not to take umbrage at Popper, 'He means well by you both'—and surprisingly reaches, although he appeared all the time to be going forward in a straight line and with great definiteness, the admirable enough place from which—just like Mr Auden around one of his English lakes—he first set out. Have our eyes deceived us, is it a miracle or a natural event, or is the impression he creates of moving forward in circles really some sort of parabolic parable aimed in reproof at both Conservatives and Socialists, for he is, after all, a liberal?

But what does it matter if he doesn't appear to get anywhere? The world, after all, is round and so many who believe otherwise have, in fact, succeeded all too well in falling off it. His literary walks bestow recognition or reproof, but never punitive judgement, on a host of intelligent people, both the well-meaning and the malign, who appear either in too much of a hurry or too conceited to walk with anyone, to be going in the wrong direction, or to be—when looked at closely—standing on one leg in a thunderstorm or waiting for the last bus with their eyes shut.

Berlin's genius is for the long critical essay, and one really asks for no more—except that in this book one does get one more than the advertised four, for his remarkable Introduction is as long as any, in which, with incredible patience, tolerance and courtesy, he answers his many critics, but always with a proper and swift self-defence of left–right to the heart when once he thinks the exhibition has gone on long enough, that he has given both the apes, jackals and parasites and the lions, foxes and hedgehogs of learning sufficient dignity and display at his own generous expense. It is hardly odd that some of us enjoy being knocked down by Berlin more than being hoisted on the shoulders of the rest of the philosophical Fancy. And no one can ever accuse him of not boxing to the rules, even though even he cannot dispel some lingering uncertainty as to quite what they are.

1970s

On Violence, by Hannah Arendt; *Violence*, by Jacques Ellul; *Why Men Rebel*, by Ted Robert Gurr[a]

Vol. 42, no. 2, April–June 1971

An incredible amount of pretentious rubbish is being written about violence. The Princeton strategic social scientist grinds away at what he oddly regards as new subject-matter, full of models, data and speculation, all mixed up together like the worst of economics: a new field for value-free research, equally acceptable to rebel and establishment, but long-winded and over-priced! The French theologian finds it necessary to write a terse and agonised attack on a specific and ingenious cult of violence among, not infidels or sceptics, but fellow Christians—doctors so tolerant of the sick that they have embraced the disease gladly, rather than simply suffering it when necessary.

The pampered, spoilt-child student revolutionary cries that violence is liberating (which is what happens to the belief that personality is God when so many come to hate their own home-made images) and is unmasking ('Look, that broken pane of glass was only made of glass, and that broken skull was only made of flesh and bone'). And the socially conservative come to deplore violence in general, exposing themselves as either idiotic or hypocritical, feeding the worst fantasies of their enemies, so that both—oddly refuting their own arguments—then demand more violence against their opponents: that is good violence or legitimate violence, not just any old violence. For you can get hit by that. Only a very few really say that all is violence and that only through greater violence can the good future come (why should the future ever come?—here they forget about the BOMB which is going to destroy the world), and then set fire to themselves. Most enthusiasts for more violence (as such), or more counter-violence, only wish to set fire to other people, or to urge others to start fires. In the 1930s there was the International Brigade; today we have street theatre or occasional punch-ups with the police.

Particularly mad are those on the right who link the growing rate of crimes of violence (although it rather depends from when you start counting) with a propensity to civil disorder. And these good folk are equally matched on the left by the literary cult of the criminal, the theatre of cruelty and all that strange and (fortunately) highly elitist tosh.

So perhaps one should be a little nervous at a new book by Hannah Arendt. But no need. Here is perhaps the clearest, shortest, most straightforward and profound thing she has written. Some moral passion to be understood, or

[a] Allen Lane, Penguin Press, 106 pp, £1.25 (Arendt); SCM Press, 179 pp, £1.50 (Ellul); Oxford University Press for Princeton University Press, 421 pp, £6 (Gurr).

some firm editor or friend, has at last made her come to the point, stick to the point and avoid those famous and vast philological digressions which, in the past, have overawed the layman and angered the scholar.

Her passion is simply for clarity in our use of concepts, above all to distinguish between power and violence. Power is the ability to act in concert, which to her is the essence of all government. Violence 'is by nature instrumental; like all means it always stands in need of guidance and justification through the end it pursues'. Power is to be seen as an end in itself, not something that needs justification. Governments, of course, commonly pursue policies, in the modern world almost invariably, and these need justification; but 'the power structure itself precedes and outlasts all aims, so that power, far from being a means to an end, is actually the very condition enabling a group of people to think and act in terms of the means–end category'. Such power plainly depends upon opinion. Some old ground is covered again, and richly. The strongest is never strong enough unless he has followers. Violence cannot explain any exercise of power (only some changes in its exercise). Dr Arendt could also point out that there are physical as well as political limitations on all 'pure coercion'. Even in cultures whose literature nominally ascribed all power to the physical prowess of heroes, these men were commonly overthrown by women and sleep. Since power rests upon numbers and opinion (far from necessarily democratic, but simply numbers larger than can be frightened by one man twenty-four hours a day), therefore tyranny, she quotes Montesquieu, is the most violent and the least powerful form of government.

It is both very abstract and very immediate to attack the view that violence can be justified as a necessity of power, or that all power should be attacked as necessarily involving violence. And how naive, too, to see oppression as depending always on violence. Instant and perfect obedience, she says, can grow out of the barrel of a gun, but never power. The two terms, power and violence, are in fact opposites: where one rules absolutely, the other is absent.

Violence is simply an instrument. No one denies we have grimmer instruments of violence than ever before. But men use or abuse them. These instruments cannot themselves generate power. They are not all to be despised, but none of them are to be glorified. She deals with the well-known and lurid views of Sartre and Fanon on violence with a slow and careful seriousness; but reveals them as either rhetoric or sheer melodrama. It would be so easy if injustice and exploitation simply depended upon violence. Such short-cut ideologies utterly miss the plausibility and the appeal to opinion of their opponents' doctrines; and hence are impotent to deal with their opponents by any means except violence, or more often by fantasies of violence, since both boots are on the other's foot. People feel driven to violence, she suggests, because power seems to have become so impotent in the modern world. Far from there being too much power, there is too little. The classical capacity for political action seems frustrated. 'Every decrease in power', she concludes, 'is an open invitation to violence—if only because those who hold power and feel it slipping from their hands, be they the government or be they the governed, have always found it difficult to resist the temptation to substitute violence for it.'

Her many reflections on all these problems deserve the most serious reading. Here is a very rare book indeed. It is not, in fact, difficult. If anything, it is too simple, but only simple in the proper sense of basic, abstract and unspecific, yet more relevant to understanding the dilemmas of our times than a wilderness of books on specific protests and discontents.

Only one major worry. Her conclusion that violence most often springs from lack of power is not helped by her definition of power as an end in itself. She needs to distinguish between power as the precondition of any concerted action, with government as that which is challengeable in anything which can be conceived as a society, and power as the ability to achieve an intended and premeditated effect (to paraphrase Bertrand Russell). Power in the modern world necessarily takes the second form, and in the highly systematic and specific form of policy. Power as an end in itself is a sufficient but not a necessary condition for maintaining power. Odd then to object to thinking in terms of 'ends of government', such as 'to realise a classless society or some other nonpolitical idea, which if tried out in earnest cannot but end in some kind of tyranny' (pp. 51–2). Cannot but end in tyranny, that is, if people have not first accepted that government must rest on opinion not mere coercion, or if people think that a classless society would see the end of all disputes and conflict. Perhaps some do. I still believe that a classless society is the most generalised and the truest political aim, but it can only be achieved in political terms (which may not exclude the deliberate use of violence, only not its deliberate maximising); and yet while the constraints, conceits, oppressions and hypocrisies of class are great human evils, they are not the only ones. She should object to the belief in any one single solution as being itself the whole of government, not to single-minded policies towards unimaginably greater human equality as being part of government. Otherwise it is quite clear that the world, with its new smallness and its new instruments of violence and its new mutual knowledge, hence far greater sense of injustice and of jealousy, will destroy itself or reduce itself to barbarism as the technology of the hydrogen bomb spreads into more and more unstable small sovereign states. We are living at the moment in a lull or respite arising from the accident of a very few Powers possessing such weapons. But they show no signs of being willing or able, in terms of conventional power, to enforce their monopoly. One can share Arendt's faith in political action of the classical kind, agree that such politics is the precondition of any solution, but suggest that without the canvassing of solutions (or even belief in solutions? I'm not sure) she will not be read by those she now desperately wants to reach. Power must produce policy if more and more people are not to lose all care and concern for politics, the very loss that weakens power and provides the conditions for violence.

Kingsley: The Life, Letters and Diaries of Kingsley Martin, by C. H. Rolph [a]

Vol. 44, no. 3, July–September 1973

No excuse is needed for reviewing here at some length this already much noticed and much praised book. For Kingsley Martin was joint editor with William Robson of *The Political Quarterly* from the first number in January 1930 until the summer of the following year by which time he had become, after being sacked as a leader writer on the *Manchester Guardian*, editor of the *New Statesman*. He was succeeded by Leonard Woolf but remained an active member of the Board until his death in 1969. And in the 1940s and 1950s Woolf would often act as editor of the *Statesman* when Kingsley was away. Rolph tells how Martin walked across in 1954 to Woolf's neighbouring cottage to tick him off (Woolf was then 74) about some articles which had been published when he was away; Woolf listened in silence, then icily told him that he had assumed his visit was to thank him, but since this was not so, he would tell him what else he had to do besides look after Kingsley's shop; and Kingsley (for he was among the first to use first names publicly) burst into tears, and apologised. He was like that, hasty, full of rages, but generous, sentimental and always racked with remorse. The other excuse for writing at length is that a long and unhurried reading and review can reveal things hidden by the speed and space of the dailies and weeklies.

Some fine reviews appeared in the week of publication. And the reviewers were unanimous in praising Rolph's book as a very fine character study indeed, and in noting how astonishingly objective it was coming from someone who had been a close friend and had worked on the *New Statesman* for twenty-five years. Rolph, indeed, has not just painted a living portrait of Kingsley Martin, but has shown how his guilt-complexes, his remorseless self-inquisitions, his constant revisions and indecisions, and his remorseless energy, all helped to make him a great editor. The *Statesman* nagged the British Left, old 'naggers and staggers', but it did not, at least with any consistency, pontificate; if it was self-righteous, one *saw* it wrestling with the truth—and letting it slip away; if it sounded pontifical in any one week, one could bet one's boots that the next piece by the pontiff would be agonising about the fallibility of the last week's encyclical. But like the Pope, he was married to the Church—only his great affair with the *Statesman* was properly consummated among his many, sad and extraordinary loves. Martin's personality was the journal: he was always Pilgrim, but never escaped from the dialectic agonies of being at the same time also both Mr Valiant-for-the-Truth and Mr Worldly-Wiseman. I mix my metaphors deliberately, for he was the Puritan Pope of the 1930s and 1940s. He practised both a highly intellectual journalism (unlike the front half of the journal since his time) and virtually invented the personal thinking-out-loud column (which now so

---

[a] Gollancz, 431 pp, £4.00.

over-dominates journalism, particularly when the content is not policy and ideas, but the who-did-what-to-whom political or publishing gossip). 'Kingsley seems to have known nearly everyone, while the small remainder felt as if they knew him.' The ordinary *New Statesman* reader enjoyed the prejudices of the editor on gardening, all night public lavatories, this and that, as much as he enjoyed or reacted fiercely to his opinions on world politics. And Rolph discloses the passionate desire of his later years, sad but not surprising, to be a 'television personality' like so many of his friends, and his bitter humiliation that he never quite made it. If he had, then *everyone* could have known him.

As in Boswell's so-called *Life of Johnson*, a remarkable and a remarkably clear and just sense of character emerges. But a serious review should ask, is this really a biography? Richard Crossman remarked, in a perceptive and generous review (considering how shabbily and mistakenly Martin ignored his claim to the succession), that in some respects it was a hasty biography. I suspect that it was rushed to be available for the recent 60th birthday party of the journal. But I could also question the sense in which it is a biography at all. Certainly a biography must get the character of a man right, and must not assume that great men—any more than great books—are ever wholly consistent. This Rolph has done well. But a biography must also be a 'life', that is it must explain how the subject's character is related to the main events of his or her life and to his or her principal achievements. And on this score, there is much room for criticism.

The difficulties facing Rolph were great. I admire the book so much as a 'character of Kingsley Martin' that in criticising it as a proper biography, I must be willing to stick my own neck out and, as they say in Parliament, declare my interest. For like Mr Rolph, I am faced with the problem for the first time of not merely the writing of an authorised biography (that of Orwell), but of deciding what sort of biography is best and how to go about it. Rolph's first difficulty is that Kingsley published two volumes of autobiography and left a third unfinished. My problem is in some ways less, for Orwell only wrote a few biographical passages in essays, although in other ways it is more difficult, for he wrote them in the middle of his writings, not consciously towards the end of his life: hence they are inherently suspect as dispassionate autobiography (if such a model could exist even in heaven); they must also be read as setting the tone for or partly explaining major writings of the same period. Rolph does not accept his subject's autobiographies as unquestionable primary sources, far from it. He draws attention specifically to the large element of self-justification in them and to their partly touching, partly exasperating, mixture of vanity and self-torment. How different, for instance, from Leonard Woolf's great volumes—except perhaps Woolf's famous dispassion was part of his self-imposed image, and did not exclude a great deal of utter silence on sexual things, whereas Martin hid nothing, or very little, but coloured and distorted most of it. But faced with autobiographical writing, the biographer must surely identify clearly what are, in his view and on what evidence, the important distortions, and try to

367

explain them. The main themes of the autobiographical writings have to be clearly, even pedantically, identified, listed even, then measured up by the skills of the contemporary historian. Rolph has simply not attempted to do this.

Rolph's task here was, admittedly, doubly difficult, for Kingsley Martin also left behind him a mass and mess of diaries and letters. Orwell left very little and most of it, if not all, has been published already. Now faced with a mass of unpublished material, the biographer must surely, even if he is primarily concerned with a character portrait, attempt to read right through, sort, order and even number material. Only then can he and we be sure that nothing essential has been missed, so that the job does not have to be done again, and so that he can refer to key passages in such a way that another writer can find them—wherever they are and wherever they will become publicly available (in the University of Sussex library, I gather; but Rolph says nothing about this). Admittedly I am fortunate—Orwell's papers have already been put in order and listed at University College, London; but Rolph gives the clear impression that he only wandered through this mass of letters and diaries at random, and has taken out occasional odd and revealing nuggets, hence the subtitle of the book. There is no consistency and no dull archival references. This is more than academic carping. Sometimes it is hard to determine what he is quoting from. And he admits himself that the handwriting is often very hard indeed to read and that dating some of them 'involves much chronological coin-spinning'. Why? Perhaps some very trivial short notes are hard to date, but for any diary entry or letter with a clear subject matter there should be no difficulty, if one goes to enough trouble, in dating anything by a famous contemporary figure (we are not dealing with Shakespeare's landlady). I've found some very suspect dates of small things, which makes me wonder about larger things. It is just possible, for instance, that 'by 1929' his editorial work on *The Political Quarterly* was 'giving him a further interest' and that Olga, 'a proof reader in a thousand', would 'read and correct the proofs of it as they came from the printer'. But since the first issue only appeared in January 1930 this is much more likely a year later. And in February 1922 he has Martin at a Socialist weekend conference at Dunsford where the company included Bertrand Russell, the Webbs, W. H. Rivers, George Orwell, Hugh Dalton and Barbara Wootton. 'Beatrice lost her temper', he quotes from a diary, 'bullied Blair, and wouldn't let Russell get a word in edgeways. . . .' It is physically possible that nineteen-year-old Orwell, swotting in Suffolk for his Imperial Police exams, could have gone, but most unlikely, indeed sensational if true, for he showed no interest in socialism as such until very much later—much later than many supposed, and he was, to put it mildly, not precocious enough to be noticed and bullied by Beatrice even if there. Indeed, can we take even Kingsley's diary as immune from fantasy? I would want some external evidence that there was such a meeting (otherwise where were Laski, Catlin, Tawney and the Coles that weekend?). I will gladly eat my hat if Mr Rolph can show me this. But the only other reasonable assumption, without seeing the diary, is that either Rolph has got his dating wrong by ten years at least, or that this Blair is some other Blair (perhaps like Mistress Lanier's second-best lover).

Unhappily I am left with the sad feeling that a definitive biography of Kingsley Martin, such as Noel Annan's life of Leslie Stephen or Quentin Bell's life of Virginia Woolf, has yet to be written. And such a book will have to grapple not merely with many inaccuracies in Martin's autobiography, but also with many suspect attributions in Rolph's half-biography, and with the additional problem that accounts of the man and his life's work have been treated separately—in this book and in Edward Hyam's *The New Statesman, 1913–1963*. Hyam wrote a remarkably readable and honest book, but also, in a basic sense an unscholarly one and anyway, however great the honesty, an inside job, a sponsored work, 'company history'. Rolph could at least have maintained a critical running commentary on Hyam's book, rather than virtually ignoring it, at least to give himself a clear structure.

For the structure is very loose. As biography in the full sense, the first 150 pages work best, his youth, wartime service, career at Cambridge, Princeton and LSE. But as soon as he leaves the *Manchester Guardian* and enters onto Rolph's familiar territory, the narrative becomes confusingly discursive. Even the previous chapter, 'Teacher Turned Writer', begins with a one-and-a-half-page potted history of the Fabian Society, and then plunges into Kingsley's appointment at LSE. Does Rolph imply that the reader will best understand the spirit of the LSE as it then was by being reminded of the early Fabians? If so, he is wrong. Beveridge was Director even then, and quickly set himself to remove the Fabian image. And oddly, although we get ten or twelve pages on Kingsley at the LSE, there is no clear account at all of what he taught. A university teacher today may feel that his lecturing is likely to have little to do with the significant things in his life, but was it so even then, to such a young political tiger as Martin, colleague of Laski? What we get instead is an account of the fall of Ramsay Mac's first government. The corrupting 'Life and Times' formula creeps in too often, alas, either as padding or as chatty discursiveness. Chapter 13, 'War and Truth', gives a very good picture of what life was like at Great Turnstile in wartime, but no coherent account emerges of the paper's policies and Martin's influence. 'Of Kingsley's editorial campaigns over the next four years, once he had decided against a stop-the-war movement, there is no space here to write . . .'; why not, when there is a lot of background padding in the 400 pages? Nor lack of space, I suspect, but lack of time: that damned 60th birthday deadline. Indeed the chapter on the war steps, almost at once, smartly backwards into a long account of 1938, in which Kingsley's attitude to Czechoslovakia is candidly shown as hardly different from Neville Chamberlain's. But the war, after all, was the forcing ground of the welfare state and the condition for Labour's first majority government. What socialist journals were saying at the time is important to know.

The lack of clear structure, the discursiveness and the failure either to integrate or to redo in brief Hyam's book, all these make it hard for him to focus on some key issues. Only in the Introduction on p. 18 do we get a brief chronology, for Ralph obviously recognises the difficulty, even though he does not solve it. A much larger chronology would have left him more free to concentrate on themes through time. Especially difficult to follow are the fluctuations of Kingsley's 'fellow-travelling'. He deals with the Orwell incident well and does not attempt to defend Martin's moral stance, although I might mitigate a little the importance of the rejection of the article on Catalonia by wondering whether Orwell ever seriously thought that the *New Statesman* would accept it, or by hinting that he cannot (quite obviously) have been reading it very much while in the trenches of Catalonia. More serious than the isolated Orwell incident is surely his backing of the 'Second Front Now' campaign which the British Communists began as early as 1942. It speaks a lot for either the tolerance or the cynicism of the British establishment that this dangerous rubbish was allowed free expression at such a time. David Caute's recent book *The Fellow Travellers* would have helped him, but the difficulty goes deeper: a certain deliberate superficiality in using his sources. 'All of them are on record in the files of the New Statesman; and it has to be admitted that without a prolonged course of reading in them no one could truly assess their editor's position in the war, or his likely influence on the public and private attitudes of others. I must however return to the private man.' Mr Rolph must pardon me, but I doubt if there was a private man in that sense, and I believe that the least one can expect of a standard biography is that the author has done the essential reading and employed a competent researcher to get all the paper into order, if he cannot do it himself.

Yes, a *serious* (i.e. long) review must conclude, so good on the character, but not good enough on the life and achievements. And rarely have being a 'private man' and being an editor been so closely integrated. Only a great character could have kept alive the excitement of reading the *Statesman*, week after week; its weird mixture of boldness and folly, of ideas and gossip; and when Martin was at his best, which was not during his last few years of editorship, its refreshing avoidance of any replay of the political events of the week, for it was a 'viewspaper' and not a weekly commentary on the events with a week's nominative and a-socialist TLS stuck on the back. So a biography that separates the private and public man is not likely to work in such a case. Again, to risk one last comparison. Quentin Bell could write his life of Virginia purely, he said, about her life, not about her writings—not quite, but nearly, and with a highly self-conscious, stylised, definitely literary writer as subject, it can work, or if still a second best, be a very, very good second best. And with Orwell I suspect that my major task is to explain how he could come to hold the highly original ideas of *Homage to Catalonia, Animal Farm* and *Nineteen Eighty-Four*. His private life is less relevant to an understanding of his stature as a great writer than was Martin's to an understanding of his stature as a great editor. But there is also, however, with Orwell the problem of assessing his influence as a socialist polemicist and moralist, the author of the second half of *The Road to Wigan Pier, The Lion and the Unicorn* and all those weekly columns in *Tribune*. And here these two antagonists had something in common. They were both exemplars as well as shapers of the consciousness of what is to continental eyes such a strange English phenomenon, a strong left-wing non-Marxist tradition. Orwell's socialism, if neglected or misunderstood by his literary friends of the last, brief years of fame, is fairly easy to describe, whereas Martin's is far more difficult, simply because he wrote so much, changed his mind so much, and left books which are only tangential to the main question.

One point of Rolph's admirable character sketch does arouse scepticism. 'Kingsley as a reporter could be careless about facts which got in the way of what he saw as a colourful picture' (p. 203). 'When he was not surrounded by arguing friends he was talking to one of them on the telephone: he spent more time on the telephone than any man (or even woman) I have ever known. Some of his friends thought that he wasted too much time talking and listening to those he judged to be well-informed, and that he should have spent more time reading *Hansard*, blue-books, current literature and the foreign press' (p. 163). And his '. . . rather endearing aptitude for getting a funny story all wrong' (p. 146). But, says Rolph directly, '*I never heard him make the smallest pretence to knowledge for which he had no backing*' (my italics). Well, yes and no. But 'the backing' was all too often the last person's opinion he talked to. And he could abuse confidences. When Martin began on the *New Statesman* he continued to use regularly the LSE senior common room, then smaller, more informal and friendly, and not very worried about rules of membership; but that Martin provoked a tightening up of those rules, simply because he picked everybody's wits over Tuesday or Wednesday lunch, and there on Saturday it would appear in the *New Statesman* personalised, distorted, recognisable but ruined—so the picked-wit thought anyway. His idea of 'expert opinion' was often odd and his use of evidence was often not very proper.

I had met Kingsley only a couple of times before, when as a young lecturer at LSE I was immensely flattered by his phoning me up one day. 'Come and have dinner with me at the Savile, I want to pick your wits. You know my old *Magic of Monarchy* book? I'm so glad. Yes, I think it stands up well, too. But I'm going to revise it and update it. I want to pick your wits on the changing role of the Crown in the Commonwealth.' I told him I didn't know *anything* about that at all and that he should talk to either so-and-so or so-and-so. 'Oh not them, lawyers! Thoroughly dull people. No, it's *you* I want to talk to—I'm sure you'll be bubbling with ideas.' Quite honestly I didn't get a word in edgeways. But I had a wonderful evening. He talked about what *might* have happened to the Crown in the Commonwealth, a speculation in which a few members of the Savile cheerfully joined, and then took me back to his flat for coffee and brandy and talked with wonderful animation about interesting and famous people he had known. I just uttered single prompts like 'Webb' or 'Shaw' or 'Wells' or 'Keynes' and off he would go. Then, the first point, he suddenly felt tired and so thanked me warmly and genuinely for the 'many valuable facts and ideas you've given me'. And I literally had not said a

371

coherent sentence on the Crown and the Commonwealth; but I'm sure he believed that I had—I externalised half of his internal discussion. But there was a sequel, which is the second and more worrying point. Months after-wards his publishers rang me up; he was away in America, they were almost in despair, very grateful that I had 'agreed to read the proofs' and they had a cable from him confirming that I could make any corrections I thought fit. I genuinely believe that he must have imagined that he had asked me. I said I would look at them. Part of me said, 'go to hell', but I was also amused and flattered to be put upon by the great editor, so I said I would look at them quickly, but that I hadn't time to read them line by line. I read one chapter and then, fascinated, I read the whole thing overnight. Then there were cables and letters to and from Martin, and a good fat fee was arranged for a competent young woman I knew to check every quotation in the book. Three-quarters were inaccurate by any possible standard, in at least a quarter of them the words had been distorted so as to strengthen the case he was making, and in six cases the meaning of the original was flatly contradictory to the passage used by Kingsley. For a long time I thought this mess was a product of his relying on his memory (*almost* photographic), but on reading Rolph's book I now see that the more likely source of error was his, let alone Rolph's, inability to read his own handwriting, coupled to his reckless refusal to check things. He did not ask me to the launching party, but he did write a very nice acknowledgement in the book.

Surely—I ask Rolph—was this sort of thing happening all the time on the *Statesman*—or didn't anyone notice or care? In this respect alone, I think Rolph has evaded a great flaw in Martin's character that perhaps, like his admirable characteristics, had *something* to do with his being a great weekly editor. He really didn't mind if something wasn't true or precise so long as it wasn't reactionary and was lively and controversial. In an odd sort of way he was, indeed, a television personality before television. How sadly dull are the antics of the little devils trying to copy him. He was of a kind we will never see again: the puritanical, secular, preacher-mountebank. Lapsed Quakers are the very devil in politics and journalism.

Contemporary Thought and Politics, by Ernest Gellner[a]

Vol. 45, no. 4, October–December 1974

Here is the second of three volumes of Ernest Gellner's major essays which are being edited by I. C. Jarvie and Joseph Agassis. The first was called *Cause and Meaning in the Social Sciences* (1973), mainly on key conceptual issues in the social sciences, and the third will be called *The Devil in Modern Philosophy*, advertised as being Gellner's thinking on philosophy and life. Any volume

[a] Routledge & Kegan Paul, 207 pp, £3.95.

such as this contains better and worse pieces and, what is at times slightly bewildering, pieces written at different levels and for different occasions—which the editors have not always clearly identified. The attributions are tucked away at the back of the book in a highly abbreviated form. For instance, an interesting essay on 'The Dangers of Tolerance' is only attributed to *Government and Opposition*, vol. 6, 1971, pp. 211–18. No one would realise that it formed part of a symposium, indeed perhaps is fully intelligible only in that context. And a piece written for this journal's special number on 'Protest and Discontent' is not identified as such, nor is it mentioned that it was reprinted in a corrected version with the rest of the symposium as a Pelican book. This is sloppy editing. It is puzzling why Gellner has left it to others.

But this is cavilling. For the two volumes reveal him as among the most profound and stimulating of contemporary social theorists, a rare and almost great mixture of the original theorist and the critic. He is an unrepentant rationalist, a believer, if not in 'Reason', certainly in reasoning. Whatever he is writing about, one feels sure that he knows the empirical material, is concerned not just with the nominal meaning of concepts (like the linguistic school whom he so famously attacked in *Words and Things*), but with the meaning derived from the *working* of concepts in practice. He is, not to be too paradoxical, a highly independent intellectual disciple of Popper, and he brings out the social democratic implications of Popper's methodology which is so often, hastily and vaguely, regarded as conservative or 'simply liberal'.

None of the essays are technical. Some, however, like 'Democracy and Industrialisation', deal with highly technical issues, and Gellner's witty and polemical style must conceal to the ordinary reader a great deal of gnomic, at times esoteric, reference. Perhaps his social philosophy is clearest in an essay about the Czech Spring, 'The Pluralist Anti-Levellers of Prague':

In stressing the need for a stratificational base for political plurality and hence freedom, the authors may be more realistic than the starry-eyed Western progressive, who thinks he can without strain love both liberty and equality. They can certainly cite Tocqueville as well as Marx in support of their fears.

He himself, of course, sternly and subtly loves both liberty and equality (or, at least, dislikes all non-justifiable inequalities). But he is determined that no one will mistake the strain. Perhaps it is mostly a matter of defending and amending, of attacking folly and showing that we already have good goals and good means if only we had the will to pursue them consistently. New social philosophies are not needed or would not be noticed if they were new. But, nonetheless, I have a hope that now having published his diverse essays, brilliant and compelling but almost each written for some particular occasion and to some particular audience, he will perhaps sit back and reflect on all he has written so far, and produce (even if he has to repeat himself a bit) a comprehensive and coherent political and social theory such as an old rationalist social democrat would recognise. This would be a truly great and lasting book rather than a continuing series of immediately important and brilliant essays. The wood could get lost for the trees. Probably this is pot calling kettle black. The pot blushes at such a routine reviewers' reaction. Perhaps I have missed the whole point. Perhaps even Gellner, who insists so strongly on the relevance of theory to practice, without adopting any of the easy opiates of one of the 57 varieties of fashionable Marxism, yet must eschew synthesis and systematic prescription, must remain critical-empirical, even if not linguistical. Can one really ask for anything more than a sceptical humanism?

Gollancz: The Story of a Publishing House, 1928–1978, by Sheila Hodges [a]

Vol. 49, no. 4, October–December 1978

Everyone had their favourite stories about meeting Victor Gollancz. I was just in time. H. L. Beales first introduced me to the presence about 1957, I think, at a big party in the US Embassy. 'You know that man holding court there surely?' 'No, who is he?' 'Ah, Victor! I want you to meet a very interesting and promising young man who doesn't appear to have heard of you' (which was not what I said). Then, as V.G. scowled, 'No, on second thoughts you wouldn't be interested in him. He's neither very good, nor very bad, really quite an ordinary, sensible person.' Later he must have forgiven or forgotten me, for he received me warmly as the editor of a German friend's book that had been sent to him. 'I know what you are thinking. No carpets and all this cheap, cheap furniture. First things first, I say. No frills! Every penny into the pockets of the authors!'[b] That was a very old routine by then. Three years later I debated against him at the Oxford Union, and he was simply too old[c] to take banter and irony. When he told the House that the last time he had debated there, hundreds of people had crossed the Floor as soon as he sat down, I rudely heckled, 'Which way?' Though he gave me a lift back, having given me a lift up, not a single word was spoken between Oxford and London, except from Lady Gollancz, 'Cold weather for this time of year, Crick'; and from me, like a character in C. P. Snow, 'Yes, cold weather indeed, Lady G.' Conversations with great men. Did Goethe really go on so much to Eckermann? Perhaps Dr Johnson had his silences too.

Sheila Hodges joined the firm in 1936 and was Assistant Managing Director from 1943 to 1954, so this is, as it were, a company history of a company town. However, it is surprisingly good. The 'inside story' is usually either disgruntled polemic or loyalist apologia. The keynote here is 'surprising

---

[a] Gollancz, 256 pp, £7.50.

[b] This first and last paragraphs of this review contain some fine examples of Bernard's 'reconstructed dialogue' narrative device, right down to the exclamation marks awarded to Victor Gollancz hereabouts.

[c] He would have been about 67; perhaps irony/banter capabilities deserted one earlier in those days. Bernard Crick would not have considered himself past it at that age.

frankness', in the circumstances. Sheila Hodges does admit that 'V.G.' could be a difficult person. Some of the leading figures in contemporary British publishing were for short periods his unequal partners or possible successors. She admits that he could be both mean and demanding. His achievement was, however, so great that there is no need for piety. I would not say that she paints a picture of Gollancz himself 'warts and all', but neither are the few warts she does paint pure tokenism.

He was often autocratic in his relationships with authors, and towards the end of his life was inclined to be too paternalistic towards some of the talented young writers who came to the firm, tending to behave as if he had himself written their books (to their fury). But he was a sensitive and perceptive critic, took endless trouble over points that needed alteration, and above all had respect for what each book was trying to say.

Which is fully just, as is—though less explored—'Victor saw others in stark and uncompromising terms, white woolly lambs who could do no wrong or horrid black sheep who could do no right.' Her account of his relations with Colin Wilson (was there ever a more difficult 'white woolly lamb' and a more difficult publisher thrown together?) is richly comic. (Indeed, who was Colin Wilson?) But she is more balanced and judicious on V.G. himself than on some other of his and the firm's black sheep.

V.G.'s *obiter dictum* that Orwell was '*enormously* overrated' is quoted, but the smell of sour grapes is heavy upon it. True, he did not make a publishing mistake about turning down *Animal Farm*; he decided on principle that he did not want it for what it so inopportunely said about our Russian ally of the time. He would take risks with books he believed in politically or morally, but equally he turned down some potentially high selling books of which he disapproved. T. S. Eliot had, indeed, expressed the same *politique* view about *Animal Farm* on behalf of Faber's, as did Cape. (Gollancz's by 1944 had caught up with the publishing Establishment.) Gollancz's real failing was to turn down *Homage to Catalonia* sight unseen because he knew that anything likely to be so critical of the Communist Party would damage the Left Book Club. Sheila Hodges' account of the working of the Left Book Club is interesting in respect to its size and mechanics, but very guarded about its selection processes. In fact, Laski was a mere figurehead, V.G. worked hard at reading manuscripts, and so did the third selector, John Strachey, who cleared everything with Harry Pollitt and King Street. It is wholly fair to point out that the second half of *The Road to Wigan Pier* is not as good as the first, but odd to repress the tale of how Gollancz tried to publish the descriptive first half without the politically 'difficult' second. He trimmed to his selectors' objections by writing an introduction to it himself, to the surprise of the author, saying that the first half was the work of a genius and the second of a class-conscious eccentric ignorant of the labour movement; and he allowed Laski, in his most Marxist phase too, to savage it in *Left News*, the Club's journal. On the other hand, though Gollancz refused after that to publish

375

Orwell's main political writings, he had great, perhaps even exaggerated, faith in him as a novelist. He backed Orwell heavily in his early days, with little return, and always hoped that the next novel would really sell. None did until *Animal Farm* and *Nineteen Eighty-Four*. Orwell is a sore point. The firm never found a political best-seller to rival the solid mother-lode of Dorothy Sayers' detective novels.

The book is excellent on Gollancz's genuine originality in the design and advertising of books. The illustrations of early advertisements and jackets would make a good pamphlet on their own. Both his energy and his eye for detail were extraordinary. Other publishers hated him for the way he pushed his books, but booksellers loved him for the way he made many publications newsworthy. While advertising skills, commercial acumen and a sense of values were together in one man, things went well. Gollancz was a valuable goad to the publishing establishment of his day. He can hardly be blamed if some of the bigger firms now appear to have separate departments for publicising, accounting and thinking—not always in balance with each other.

Histories of any big publishers are themselves full of the most fascinating internal politics, so many liberal-minded, clever, ambitious and conceited men contending for power. C. P. Snow could have written *The Publishers* as (yet another) companion piece to *The Masters*. And a history of a political publisher (in the sense that for a long time, before he turned holy, politics were V.G.'s main interest—even if detective novels kept it all afloat) has the added interest of showing what political themes counted as important for a general readership in a given era. For political publishing, indeed political writing, in both Gollancz's and Orwell's sense, is now in sad decline. The safe pickings of the university and polytechnic social science market, producing so much needlessly technical, internalised, neologistic, a-political bad writing, have led most publishers to abandon the kind of general reader who was the target on whom Gollancz's eyes were set. Even Penguin, which in a sense replaced the Left Book Club, now seem to assume that the readers of their Specials are social science graduates. This has been a great loss to the permanent or continuing politics education of the nation. The range of Gollancz's politics list in the 1930s might have been a little narrow, but its level was admirable.

Sheila Hodges has, all in all, written a very interesting and a reasonably candid book. It is as good as an inside job can be, written by an honest person who yet knows that compromises have to be made. But our leading publishers should treat themselves more seriously. Their histories should be part of twentieth-century history, so they should open their archives (at least as fully as their authors demand of the government) and commission independent and experienced scholars to write their histories. When cupboard doors are open, no skeletons appear as bad as when the doors are known to be locked. We need more good histories of publishers as we do of newspapers. For the firms, it is a minor form of risk taking and one that professionally they should be committed to. The result might be more interesting than all these political biographies.

To end, however, on a biographical note. 'Your German friend's book', he said to me, 'is really very academic. If you took it to a university publisher you would get respectful reviews that would sell but few copies. If I bring it out, people will think that it is a sensational exposure of how the British Press reported the rise of Nazism, important but unsound. Then when they read it, finding it a little dull, unexpectedly coming from me, they will be all the more impressed that it is "important and sound", even "reliable" they will say. How right you are to bring it to me.' As good books should find a readership, I admired—what should one call it?—V.G.'s 'moral cunning'. But, alas, poor Brigitte's thesis didn't do very well. Sheila Hodges' book deserves to do better than it probably will.

1980s

Rose of England[a]

Understanding the United Kingdom: The Territorial Dimension in Government, by Richard Rose; *The Territorial Dimension in United Kingdom Politics*, edited by Peter Madgwick and Richard Rose; *The English World: History, Character and People*, edited by Robert Blake[b]

Vol. 54, no. 3, July–September 1983

Walter Bagehot's polemic on the reform question of 1867 was called, as every schoolboy knows, *The English Constitution*. And when the President of Harvard, A. L. Lowell, wrote in 1908 the first big, comprehensive, modern textbook, he titled it *The Government of England*. In the Preface he said:

The British Constitution is full of exceptions, of local customs and special acts with which town clerks must be familiar. They fill the path of these men with pitfalls, but they do not affect seriously the general principles of government, and no attempt is made to describe them here. Even the institutions of Scotland and Ireland, interesting as they are in themselves, have been referred to only so far as they relate to the national government or throw light upon its working.

And not much light did they throw apparently. One can hardly blame Lowell for not foreseeing that the return of the Liberals would lead to the break-up of the political unity of the British Isles, but he was obtuse not to understand why as recently as 1884 a Secretary for Scotland had been appointed to buy off Home Rule sentiment; and still more in not giving any account of how the four nations came to be under one crown and how holding them together was a major preoccupation of politicians throughout the eighteenth and deep into the nineteenth century. But almost every textbook since Lowell's has followed suit in ignoring the formula 'the United Kingdom', treating it as synonymous with the English constitution, government or politics, and moreover describing this system as centralised and unitary under a sovereign Parliament.

Even Richard Rose called his first book *Politics in England*. There was perhaps a technical reason for this (the less generous might say an ideological reason). Perhaps he could only make British politics as simplified as his structural functionalist methodology demanded by limiting them to English politics—even then he tended to make the Labour Party sound alien in their own land, rather as Bob McKenzie portrayed them, rather than a traditional body of men and women with the smell of Cromwellian and Covenanting powder always in their nostrils. Now Rose, of course, in the 30 books that he

---

[a] Some reviews had titles by this time.
[b] Longman, 228 pp, £4.50 (Rose); Macmillan, 256 pp, £25 (Madgwick and Rose); Thames and Hudson, 268 pp with 306 illustrations and 221 photographs, £14.95 (Blake).

has written or edited since then (a record which breaks Harold Laski's but not Douglas Cole's) has made great and famous amends, as in the work of his Centre for the Study of Public Policy at Strathclyde and in the United Kingdom Politics Work Group which he founded and still manages. From himself, his disciples, research officers and assistants a stream of books, articles and useful bibliographies on the local institutions and politics of Scotland, Wales and Northern Ireland have appeared, culminating in this joint volume and in his own volume which he clearly regards as, if not a final statement, at least a comprehensive statement of his views on the nature of the United Kingdom. And successive editions of his *Politics in England* have taken in more and more material from the 'Celtic periphery', and in each he has progressively modified the rigidity of his old 'political culture' approach.

His finest achievement, where his energy and organising ability showed off at its best (organising both empirical surveys and the mental concepts on which to thread a vast amount of disparate material), was his book on *Northern Ireland, Government without Consensus: An Irish Perspective*. But some might say, however, that it was a theoretical problem that he had invented to solve, that he was still in the grip of the old Easton and Almond, neo-Parsonian concepts: for some people never dreamt that human government necessarily rests on consensus. 'Consensus' itself was never properly defined. Did it mean values or simply a pragmatic acceptance of procedures and institutions? And did even the narrower sense of 'consensus' imply any positive acceptance of rules, or simply a passive, habitual, prudent, perhaps even a fearful, acquiescence? No one disputes that Northern Ireland is exceptional, but is it exceptional because it lacks consensus or because it does not share it with the rest of the United Kingdom? And the subtitle was odd, for it was not an Irish perspective but a Northern Irish one. Indeed little work on Ireland has come out of the Rose school. They take very seriously the formal, constitutional separation. They seem to ignore their own rules in neither trying to grasp the political relations of the British Isles as a whole, nor in examining the degree to which formal separation has and has not changed common elements in the style and behaviour of politics in both parts of the island of Ireland. Say, to put it very briefly, the common populism. Nor do they examine or see significance in the continuation of so many British administrative practices and assumptions in the Republic.

These two new books begin to show why Rose is unhappy about stressing the economic and political interdependence of the two parts of Ireland; or in going much beyond a very thorough and scholarly set of descriptions of the peculiarities of Scotland and Wales into seeing, what surely follows from his own evidence, that we have for long enjoyed a kind of quasi-federalism. Historically there has been an astonishing restraint in the exercise of parliamentary sovereignty towards Ireland, Scotland and Wales, a kind of informal compact of the nations: consider Irish voting rights in the UK, the Northern Ireland, Scottish and Welsh educational systems, for instance. Or if interdependence is too much to swallow, the old behaviourist should at least see how some of the most characteristically English political institutions and habits have been shaped by the compromises needed to keep the four nations together. Now with the great interest of this Strathclyde school in the Scottishness of Scottish government and politics, I have always been surprised at Rose's lack of interest in the devolution movement. I had put it down seriously to his desire to keep political science and politics apart, and more trivially to his odd attitude to his predecessor in the then new Strathclyde chair, the academic most associated with the devolution movement, the late John Mackintosh (whose important writings on just these themes are not referred to once by Rose in either book).

But what now comes out, quite unexpectedly, is a passionate opposition to devolution which he calls unionism. Indeed he seems to take the Northern Ireland usage of the term and apply it to the Scottish scene where it is far from appropriate. Most, in a strict sense all, Scottish devolutionists are unionists, that is wishing the Union to be preserved; and some indeed were devolutionists mainly for this reason, fearing otherwise a growth in the vote for the genuinely separatist Scottish National Party (well, most of the Nats are genuine, though some strongly if privately believe that by going for separatism they will get federalism). Rose concludes:

The principle of concurring consent rests upon a pair of political conditions. The first is that Unionists [his capital] will continue to be the dominant political force in Scotland, Wales and Northern Ireland. *Unionists are politicians for whom protecting the Union is a first claim upon loyalty.* . . .

The devolution debate at Westminster, like the challenge of Republican violence in Northern Ireland, has shown that Westminster does not put commitment to the Union first . . . The policy of the 1974–79 Labour Government . . . showed this by the way in which it adopted devolution as an electoral policy without regard to its constitutional consequences. . . .

Political authority is not to be won once and for all . . . it must be reaffirmed every day. In the largest part of the United Kingdom, this reaffirmation occurs *faute de mieux* in the absence of any real challenge. In Scotland, Wales and Northern Ireland, consent is active but not inevitable. It requires renewal by the conscious commitment of Unionist politicians and by actions at Westminster that do not undermine the commitment of Unionists to maintaining the United Kingdom.

I thought regular readers would like a taste of the new *engagé*, polemical and rhetorical Rose. But I was never one for replacing the head by the heart; both are so necessary. Converts to the old tradition of political theory and practice must be viewed cautiously. For whatever one wants, it is not likely that 'As goes Ulster, so goes Scotland'. And if he has become, as he is entitled to, a stern Unionist in the context of Ulster politics, he should not use this as a stick to beat Scottish devolutionists. The English need re-educating just on the point at which Rose at last joins in our politics in order to deny. It is very unlikely that Ulster will long continue as a normal part of the United Kingdom, but that does not mean that it could be governed as a normal part of Ireland either. Since it faces both ways, as Rose's earlier evidence suggested, it will have to develop institutions that face both ways, stimulated by a joint desire of both the British and Irish governments to compromise the nationalistic issues.

The normal theory of the sovereign state will not help much here, any more than it is helping to understand what is happening in the EEC. But Rose in the book of essays questions even whether the United Kingdom can be a 'state' at all if it cannot impose its will and territorial integrity on Northern Ireland when the majority wish it. He produces old-fashioned definitions of 'state', as once he had new-fangled definitions of 'process', to strengthen this argument. I would stay with empiricism, personally, and change the definition to fit the reality.

None of the other essays in the Madgwick volume raise such mock-profound issues and all are interesting and able as contributions to a genuine study of United Kingdom, not just English, government and politics. Alan Alexander, incidentally, recently wrote a book on *The Politics of Local Government* which is the first book I know that successfully looks at local government throughout the system as, without labouring the point, an interactive *whole*. In some ways the centre–periphery image can be misleading, for much that we regard as 'typically English' is itself conditioned by interrelations with the other three nations in these islands. I include Lord Blake's posh coffee-table book in this review because there is a great and serious need to characterise Englishness, whether in politics, religion, literature or art. There have been few serious attempts since Orwell's eccentric *Lion and the Unicorn*. But Lord Blake's contributors, who range politically from Edward Norman to Max Beloff (with Hugh Trevor-Roper in the middle) either completely confuse the English and the British, or else ignore the effect of the Celtic on the English. He must be held editorially responsible for the kind of not always unconscious chauvinism that is both offensive to the Scottish and Welsh and a useless way to study United Kingdom history. I venture to commend J. G. A. Pocock's '*British* History: a Plea for a New Subject' [my italics] in *Journal of Modern History*, no. 4, 1975 to Lord Blake for study.

Lastly it should be said that the price of the Madgwick volume is a tragedy, for it would be a good book from which to teach United Kingdom politics, even though a symposium. Rose's essay in it repeats the main theme of his own book, but the rest of his book, despite the price and appearance, is not an authoritative, new textbook but a hasty rehash of his old material to which has been added, like chalk to cheese, an eccentric and polemical reading of a few standard textbooks on constitutional law.

The Diary of Beatrice Webb, edited by Norman and Jeanne MacKenzie. Volume One: 1873–1892, *Glitter Around and Darkness Within*. Volume Two: 1892–1905, *All the Good Things of Life*.Volume Three: 1905–1924, *The Power to Alter Things*. Volume Four: *The Wheel of Life*[a]

Vol. 57, no. 2, April–June 1986

Now that all four volumes are out and can be read through at leisure and continually dipped into for pleasure, there can be no doubt that they are not merely a major source for modern British social and intellectual history but also show that Beatrice Webb must be numbered, however unexpectedly to some, among the great English diarists.

Sidney Webb, the socialist, dined here to meet the Booths. A remarkable little man with a huge head on a very tiny body, a breadth of forehead quite sufficient to account for the encyclopaedic character of his knowledge, a Jewish nose, prominent eyes and mouth, black hair, somewhat unkempt, spectacles and a most bourgeois black coat shiny with wear; regarded as a whole, somewhat between a London card and a German professor. To keep to essentials: his pronunciation is cockney, his H's are shaky, his attitudes by no means eloquent, with his thumbs fixed pugnaciously in a far from immaculate waistcoast, with his bulky head thrown back and his little body forward he struts even when he stands, delivering himself with extraordinary rapidity of thought and utterance and with an expression of inexhaustible self-complacency. But I like the man. There is a directness of speech, an open-mindedness, an imaginative warm-heartedness which should carry him far . . . [14 Feb. 1890]

They cover an amazing time-scale of seventy years and she herself constantly reflects on time: her hopes for the future, memories of the past, wry and candid admissions that not all social change pleases her, and her fears that increasing bodily debility could spread to the mind; but the very last entry is a rational account of the ending of personal time. There are a few mundane passages, certainly, and the MacKenzies have sensibly printed little from their foreign travel and world tours—out of her British environment she could be banal—but generally her profundity of observation, both of events and of people, and the mixture of light malice towards others and honest, even torturing self-criticism, make this both an authentic and a great diary.

It is an authentic diary. Beatrice supervised the typing of most of her diaries late in her life, but the editors have checked them against the originals, and there is no rewriting for the sake of hindsight. Only some spellings and punctuation are altered. The editing is truly exemplary. Some diaries are almost certainly touched up in an author's lifetime, with perfect hindsight, to reflect the interests and tastes of present readers and thus make them more publishable. The diaries of her nephew, Malcolm Muggeridge, for instance, have not been reviewed critically and authenticated, to my knowledge, by historians or biographers professionally suspicious of the 'provenance' and

[a] Virago: 386 pp, £20 (vol. 1); 376 pp, £20 (vol. 2); 460 pp, £20 (vol. 3); 519 pp, £22 (vol. 4).

dating of records. Literary reviewers generally take diaries at their face value. But some, even if not revamped, are begun with future profit and publication in mind: the suspicion that attaches to so many of even the youthful intimate diaries as well as private letters of the Bloomsbury group. Beatrice's diaries genuinely seem to have been written from the first not for publication and posterity but to help her memory in later years, and to offer a running account, like many a Puritan, with a dead or dying censorious God. Certainly in middle life she was aware that she might write autobiography, first *My Apprenticeship* (that made people realise, with surprise, that she was a considerable writer) and then the unfinished *Our Partnership*; but this did not change the essential private informality of the diaries: they were to be a source for published autobiography, not a substitute.

It is a great diary because of its mixture of objectivity and subjectivity, the public world and the worried heart, the mixture of record and reflection, and the tension between writing to keep herself up to scratch, to craft an ideal self-image, and the self-doubting, at times almost destructive, reproofs at her own pride, even arrogance, sometimes snobbery and always an exaggerated public certainty. Nothing that could be said against the Webbs as people cannot be found as harshly in Beatrice against herself. Looking back, she wrote of 'disabling gaps' in their knowledge of Victorian England:

. . . of sport, games and racing . . . foreign affairs, generally speaking were a closed book to us . . . owing to our concentration in research, municipal administration and Fabian propaganda, we had neither the time nor the energy, nor yet the means, to listen to music and the drama, to brood over classical literature, ancient and modern, to visit picture galleries, or to view with an informed intelligence the wonders of architecture. Such dim inklings as we had of these . . . reached us second-hand through our friendship with Bernard Shaw.

In fact, she did herself, even Sidney, less than justice—as the editors properly comment. The diaries themselves show this: they were not even averagely philistine, they were only averagely cultured. She judged themselves by Shaw's extraordinary standards and versatility or by analogy with her own work. Some reviewers have taken her at her face value and have been unable, or politically unwilling (like Shirley Letwin in the *Listener*), to break from the caricature stereotype of unfeeling Webbs, and have used her own accusations against herself literally, rather missing the significance of the fact that they use her own words which are often contradicted by her own behaviour. Perhaps some reviewers simply struck back at her repeated explicit scorn for those who are so cultivated and sensitive but have no effective human sympathies for poverty or deprivation. And Enoch Powell in the *Spectator* found 'an obsession' in the first volume with 'unrealised womanhood' and 'fear of spinsterhood' which 'sometimes verged on nymphomania', a view that tells one more of his lack of experience than of hers.

A celebrated cartoon of Max Beerbohm's once showed 'Mr Sidney Webb on his birthday', playing toy soldiers with real people. Such stereotypes of the

Webbs are, indeed, hard to avoid, indeed a wider stereotype: that all political activists (and some would generously add all social scientists) are philistines. The culture of so many English literary intellectuals, who make such assumptions, is itself notoriously narrow. To them all politics is activism, occasionally to be condoned for its sincerity ('dear Stephen in the Thirties'), but part of a world of indiscriminate telegrams and anger. Freedom is choosing and defending friends not working the Republic. Politics is a world that one may visit for a moment of crisis (or for a lark, or for experiences from which to write a book), but not one of permanence, hence not of 'culture' in either sense of the term, certainly not a world (as in the Aristotelean tradition of politics) of speculation and reflection. In other words, most English, unlike most American, French, German, Italian, Czech, and even Irish, Scottish and Welsh literary intellectuals are politically ignorant and insensitive, say 'philistine'.

Beatrice Webb certainly believed that an intellectual elite must lead social change. 'Democracy', she once remarked, 'is not the multiplication of ignorant opinions.' And they both took a long time to be convinced that socialism was best promoted by commitment to a single mass party. As late as 1925 she thought that Sidney 'in his heart of hearts . . . still believes in Fabian permeation of other parties as a more rapid way than the advent of a distinctly socialist government'. But that permeating elite were to be people of, as it were, 'two cultures' not one. 'One wonders when a generation of leaders of the people will arise who will have learnt that love and pity for the downtrodden cannot achieve its end', she wrote in 1920, 'unless the emotion is accompanied with honesty of reasoning, careful and accurate statement of facts. Religious ends and scientific methods are indivisible if mankind is to rise above the brute's battle for life.'

Her observations can be acid but culturally acute. '[John Morley] and Sidney anxious to be pleasant to each other. A charming person for a talk on literature but a most depressing spectacle as a Liberal leader . . . a pitiable person as a politician—all the more so because he is conscientious and upright. It makes one groan to think of that moral force absolutely useless.' And in July that same 1897 she heard H. W. Massingham call Chamberlain 'no more than a great political artist'.

'Surely', I rejoined, 'we shall look back on the last fifty years . . . as the peculiar period of political artists: we have no statesmen—all our successful politicians, the men who lead the parties are artists and nothing else: Gladstone, Disraeli, Randolph Churchill, Chamberlain, and the unsuccessful Rosebery, all these men have the characteristics of actors—personal charm, extraordinary pliability and quick-wittedness.'

Her view of the world was far from mechanistic. She did not argue against 'artists' in politics, only against 'mere artists'. Her exasperation with Shaw's recurrent frivolity and his 'outrageous behaviour' towards women (outrageous not because he was a seducer, like Wells, but because he was merely a pretend passionate flirt) arose because, when at his best (or her idea of his best), she saw in him a unique combination of the artist and the social engineer. The friendship of Shaw for the Webbs was also no accident.

Beatrice ceased to be a Christian when a young woman but a sense of religious awe and duty never left her. She could work with religious organisations, appreciating their dedication and usefulness, if they were equally tolerant. She resigned in 1897 from the National Union of Women Workers because 'the bishops wives' defeated her resolution that meetings should not begin with prayers. But she noted:

Louise Creighton has distinctly a statesmanlike mind, and the group of women who now control the policy are a good sort—large minded and pleasant-mannered. The 'screeching sisterhood' are trying to invade them but Louise's battalions of hard-working, religious and somewhat stupid women will, I think, resist the attack.

She described the Derbyshire miners as 'A stupid, stolid lot of men characterised by their fair mindedness and kindliness.' Some things never change and are never to be said, except in diaries. That is why authentic diaries can be so entertaining.

Heroes of the early Labour movement get short shrift. 'Keir Hardie, who impressed me very unfavourably, chooses this policy as the only one he can boss. His only chance of leadership lies in the creation of an organization "agin the government"; he knows little and cares less for any constructive thought and action.' But with Tom Mann, she noted, it was different: 'He is possessed with the idea of a "church"—of a body of men all professing exactly the same creed and working in exact uniformity to exactly the same end. No idea which is not "absolute", which admits of any compromise or qualification, no adhesion which is tempered with doubt, has the slightest attraction to him.' And for fair measure she adds Shaw's opinion that 'stumping the country, talking abstractions and raving emotions, is not good for a man's judgement, and the perpetual excitement leads, among other things, to too much whisky' [23 Jan. 1895]. 'What [Josiah] Wedgwood demands is fervent partisanship. Unless you are a partisan you must be a scoundrel' [28 Nov. 1929]. Against such views she put forward not just Sidney's 'the inevitability of gradualism' (if coaxed, poked and pushed continually) but her own 'policy of inoculation, of giving to each class, to each person, that came under our infiuence the exact dose of collectivism that they were prepared to assimilate'. 'There is some truth', she admitted, 'in Keir Hardie's remark that we are the worst enemies of the social revolution. No great transformation is possible in a free democratic state like England unless you alter the opinions of all classes of the community' [23 Jan. 1895].[b]

Some of her portraits are, indeed, etched in acid but remarkably timeless. She describes Susan Lawrence, MP for East Ham North, in the General Strike:

---

[b] The original journal article has an incorrect '1985' here followed by a '?'—presumably a proofreader's query that was not picked up.

... the amazing change in [her] mentality—from a hard-sensed lawyer-like mind and the conventional manner of the moderate member of the London School Board, whose acquaintance I had made five-and-twenty years ago, to the somewhat wild woman of demagogic speech addressing her constituents as 'comrades' and abasing herself and her class before the real wealth producers. Today Susan is a victim to spasms of emotional excitement which drive her from one weird suggestion to another. She lives in an unreal world. In order to keep in touch with what she imagines to be the proletarian mind she has lost touch with facts as they are. And yet she is a real good soul, devoted and public-spirited. It is a bad case of the occupational disease so common among high-strung men and women who come out of a conservative environment into proletarian politics. [14 May 1926]

Ten years later, with the publication of *Soviet Communism: A New Civilisation?* (from which the question mark vanished in the Left Book Club edition of the following year), this might seem a case of pot calling kettle black, apart from the calmer tone of the 'work of supererogation' by the 'two aged mortals, both nearing their ninth decade', as they said in the Preface. A more flagrant case was her comment on Beveridge and his report: 'He agrees that there must be a revolution in the economic structure of society; but it must be guided by persons with training and knowledge—i.e. by himself and those he chooses as his colleagues.' By then they obviously did not think that Beveridge was the right person, even morally, to have been at the helm of 'their' good ship LSE. (Yes, it all comes out, in Beatrice's entries and the MacKenzies' ever accurate but unobtrusive commentary, what Sir Sidney Caine so carefully avoided discussing in his history of the LSE.)

I remember Beveridge delivering the Webb Memorial lecture at LSE in 1959 and, being senile, unhappily devoting nearly all of it to praise of 'my Jane' without whose good management of the house and the servants, he told us, he would have never had the time to write the great works that had so changed the course of our national history. Of course, as I remember telling puzzled students afterwards, both he and the Webbs were 'Whigs' and not self-made radicals: their incredible industry depended, albeit fairly modestly by the standards of their friends, on having domestic servants. Foundations can give one a research assistant, whom one spends half one's time training, but never a housekeeper.

Beatrice's handling of the great and the not so great are equally entertaining—the mark of a true diarist. She comments that 'Malcolm is rabidly abusive of the USSR . . . he has discarded the *Manchester Guardian* and taken on the *Daily Telegraph*. Apparently his revulsion against Communism began on the boat out, as he "watched the expression on the faces of the crew".' She suggests that 'if you see so much of the devil and the idiot in human society, you had better believe in a god to set it right. And confession and absolution would suit poor Malcolm's complexes; he needs spiritual discipline, and would find peace in religious rites. "Malcolm would do well to join the Roman Catholic Church", I suggested' [21 Oct. 1933]. Forty years later he took the advice. He caricatured the Webbs, incidentally, as Mr and

Mrs Daniel Bret in a novel, *In the Valley of the Restless Mind*. Beatrice commented that 'these pages are one amusing and quite harmless episode', although 'What distresses me about this strange autobiographical work is the horrid mixture of religious strivings and continuous amatory adventure'— but then, she is said to be no judge of literature.

Larger prophecies did not come to pass. They both died in the belief that 'collectivism' had become the common property of all the main British political parties. 'Collectivism' to them certainly meant centralism. Despite their forays into the field, theirs was always a London-centred view of England; and it was always 'England' never the United Kingdom. It meant bureaucracy, but a civilised as well as a trained bureaucracy. It first meant municipal and then came more and more to mean state ownership, where rationally applicable; but until their Soviet delusion, influence and control over industry would ordinarily be enough. But it was, for England if not for Russia, always a democratic and parliamentary collectivism. Fortunately the Webbs brilliantly exemplified the accuracy of David Caute's definition of 'fellow travellers'—those who believed in socialism in somebody else's country. And mostly 'collectivism' meant to them no more nor less than common responsibility for common interests, less clearly attached to any single method than defined by its contradicting the vision of a wholly individualistic society leaving all major decisions of policy and welfare to natural selection and market mechanisms. This theory and sentiment they believed had lost its plausibility for ever, perhaps with the death of that tetchy old family friend Herbert Spencer. There are no references to Hayek in the book and only glancing references to Lionel Robbins: but the enemy was already in the gate at their beloved LSE.

Englishness: Politics and Culture, 1880–1920, edited by Robert Colls and Philip Dodd [a]

Vol. 57, no. 4, October–December 1986

I am a citizen of a state with no agreed colloquial name. What do you put in the 'Nationality' box in a hotel register? Of course, the question is badly put— or at least particularly difficult for us to answer. It plainly means to establish our legal citizenship, in which case 'British' is correct: yet that is the least used name colloquially, except in the expletive form of 'Brits' as Australians and, now, both Prods and Provos refer to us. There is no adjective corresponding to what is in our passports, 'United Kingdom of Great Britain and Northern Ireland'. But some of us write, I've noticed, 'Welsh' and 'Scottish' rather than 'British', since the question does ask 'Nationality?'. And when those with addresses in Northern Ireland write 'British', one immediately knows their

---

[a] Croom Helm, 378 pp, £25.

religion and their politics. And a few with similar addresses and identical passports boldly write 'Irish'. The majority write 'English'. The majority of UK passport holders are, of course, English, but I have a prickly feeling that many of them write 'English' not as an assertion of nationality, as do those who write 'Welsh' or 'Scottish', but out of a belief that 'English' is the adjective corresponding to 'citizen of the United Kingdom of Great Britain and Northern Ireland'.

Left-wing authors used to regard any discussion of national identity as subversive of the purity of the Word and a digression from spreading the Good News of class struggle, and I believe that right-wing historians who celebrated 'England' had a just reward in their large sales of unread books produced for Public and above all Grammar School prize-givings. Yet even today, as we begin to explore what went wrong with various triumphalist myths, whether conservative, liberal or socialist, of Great Britain's unique way and purpose, there is a paucity of serious studies of English identity. Look at any subject index of books: shelves on Irish, Scottish and Welsh identity, very few, mostly rubbishy, on this England and Englishness.

So this thoughtful and serious, scholarly yet speculative book of essays is to be warmly welcomed. None of the authors are as openly patriotic as, say, Edward Thompson or myself, but they are not disinclined to admit that there are alternative traditions of Englishness to that of the establishment. Their book is of political as well as intellectual importance. If the English cannot sort themselves out, learn to live with themselves with tolerable myths of fraternity and without myths of imperial mission, there is little hope of Scottish devolution, nor of North and South Wales agreeing on a common policy, nor of Northern Ireland finding, first, an agreed form of devolution, second a form of dual citizenship, an institutionalised 'facing two-ways'—of which the present Inter-Government Agreement is only a hint, not even a real threat.

Philip Dodd reminds us that Matthew Arnold's *Culture and Anarchy* and his lectures *On the Study of Celtic Literature* were composed at much the same time (1866–69). The first had argued that high culture had to be carried to the masses to enlighten and stabilise a new philistine, industrial England: and that the Church and the ancient universities should, as national institutions, take up this mission. The latter had argued that there were other cultural traditions in the British Isles, to be studied, tolerated and even encouraged; but it happened that the Celtic peoples had had literary genius, but not political. His essays were a form of what in the 1930s in Russia came to be called 'cultural politics'. Dodd comments that Arnold's two sets of lectures 'are a reminder that the definition of English is inseparable from that of the non-English: Englishness is not so much a category as a relationship'.

That remark is brilliant and should be set as a compulsory examination question. But in what subject? I'm going to be lavish in my praise for this book for I suspect that, falling between English, Social History and Politics, it will get struck by all in the wretchedly narrow professional journals. And Dodd applies the same thought to the Gaelic movement of the 1890s in Ireland: 'The search for a "pure" or essential Ireland—which legitimised and was in turn legitimised by an essential England—often led the nationalists away from weighing the complex relationship (subordination) of Ireland to England and towards a Gaelic Ireland.' Again, there is a literature (much of it muddled and dishonest) about the destruction of an authentic once-upon-a-time Gaelic culture by Shakespeare and Cromwell, but little on the effect on the English of their relationship with Celts and Scots. I have two criticisms only of this admirable book, and one of them is that the authors see this interrelationship, but they do not explore it in any depth. D. G. Boyce writes extremely well in a chapter called 'The Marginal Britons: the Irish'. But there is no corresponding Scottish or Welsh essay and while he says that 'the Irish challenge to an English dominated British State had profound effects on the political char- acter of the British Isles', he only spells out the more familiar Anglo-Irish dimension, not the Irish-Anglo. I sometimes wonder if the paradoxical stereotype of the English held by the French, that we are both fair and tolerant and perfidious and hypocritical, is not a product of what was once the major business of English politics: holding the United Kingdom together. In this the ideas of the romantic movement were useful: a genuine as well as a political interest in cultural diversity and peasant roots—if they did not rock the boat of state power. Like Arnold, most of the English governing class saw no reason why politics and culture could not be separated. He thought they neglected culture, that the two must be in balance: equal but separate.

My second criticism is that they claim too much for the period they study. Their 'transformation of English national identity' was already under way before 1880. George IV's (one) visit to Scotland was the great nineteenth century episode of a managed cultural politics, a cultural revival commis- sioned by the cabinet and stage-managed by Sir Walter Scott himself. The English encouragement of Irishry in the 1890s followed much the same pattern, even if with less political success. The authors rightly attach great weight to the English Public Schools as a conscious embodiment of national identity (though they show less knowledge of or care for the Church of England); but that process too is old news by the 1880s. And coming in so late to the story, they miss part of the wood for the trees: the creation, or rather the final shaping and sanctifying, of the image of 'the gentleman' as the national stereotype. 'Gentlemanly behaviour' was recognised, all over Europe and South America, to be a uniquely English product, but it could be copied and learned, particularly by Scottish and Irish middle classes. 'Imperialism' was English nationalism for the socially mobile 'other (white) breeds'.

It was the culture of the English gent that was taken to the masses. Brian Doyle writes of 'The Invention of English'. A new academic discipline arose to embody the national consciousness in examples of high literature and correct speech. Consider the Oxford-founded Federation of Working Men's Clubs. The young Oxford missionary, Doyle quotes, must develop 'the knack to be on terms of personal equality with men, while by some *je ne sais quoi* in

389

himself' preserving 'their freely accorded social homage'. 'Colonisation by the well-to-do', said the First Annual report of the Oxford House Mission of 1884, 'seems indeed the true solution to the East End question'; and it went on to claim that working men could only be taught 'thrift and prudence' by men actually associating with them, 'the imperishable youth of Oxford' who could induce them to face 'the elementary laws of economics'.

Some resisted the assumption that there were clear standards to be imposed on the working classes and, with some mutual flattery, on the Celts. When James Murray, the editor of the *NED* (to become the great *OED*), negotiated with the syndics[b] of the Oxford University Press, he found himself under great pressure, notably from Benjamin Jowett, to make the dictionary a source of cultural authority. Murray said that the syndics could not grasp that it was not the function of an historical dictionary of language to establish correct usage and proper standards. As a Scot he was all too used to having been scolded at school for 'bad grammar' for using constructions that were 'guid Scots' but 'bad English'.

The question of whether or not there was a single correct and authoritative English was much the same as whether or not the United Kingdom was an English state (albeit such a tolerant, prosperous and peace-keeping one). Was it an 'Act of the Union' or a 'Treaty of Union'? In law it is almost certainly an 'Act', but in reality it has many elements of a treaty. Now, of course, the language battle by the English state, as the embodiment of class culture, has been well and truly lost for ever. It was lost in the BBC in the 1960s though some complaining listeners from Tunbridge Wells still cannot accept defeat gracefully and hate but everything from the drama department. Alun Howkins's chapter on 'The Discovery of Rural England' makes clear that the rural England was the South-East and not the North—and until Housman there were no fields and dales, lads, in the Midlands. But if English culture has now been revitalised by rediscovering and exalting provincial and regional roots, and if several English vice-chancellors now openly use provincial accents,[c] English politics is still, despite that other, older tradition of socialism, grimly centralist and statist.

Stephen Yeo, in his thoughtful 'Socialism and the State', ranges through all time and space to end: 'Everything which is "voluntary" has been abandoned to the Right rather than being nurtured by the Left. And even the fractions of the Party itself, its constituency parties and constituents, are still seen as a more pressing problem for labour than capitalism, let alone the embarrassment of the unions. Why?' Why indeed, but perhaps as we have, to some notable extent, despite Sir Peter Hall, decentralised and de-Anglicised our culture, there is some hope yet for a popular and participative citizen culture.

[b] The term is incorrect, of course. Oxford University Press has Delegates as the link between university and publisher, whereas Syndics belong to the press of another place. It seems unlikely that Bernard was deliberately using 'syndics' as a generic term for both.

[c] In some readers this may induce nostalgia for a time when the worst you could say about vice-chancellors as a species was that they openly used provincial accents.

But, as Robert Colls points out in his 'Englishness and the Political Culture', after 1688 'the English State took the same view of revolution as the Catholic Church took of miracles'—it believed in them, so long as they were in the past. Over the long haul, he opines, the modern British state has escaped the despotism of monarchs for that of Parliament. Socialism might yet rediscover constitutional law if people go on thinking and writing like this.

Making Trouble: Autobiographical Explorations and Socialism, by James D. Young[a]

Vol. 59, no. 4, October–December 1988

Good for the Clydeside Press! But with all respect to the author, it is quite obvious (and I happen to know) that he had some difficulty finding a publisher; and with all respect to the publisher, this should have been taken by a leading general or literary publisher. Not even the literary editors of the *Guardian* or the new *New Statesman* comb through the large output of 'alternative publishing' worried that they may unjustly miss a buried jewel. Yet this is a small jewel of a book, from a literary as well as a moral point of view.

I should have said 'moral' when writing to at least one famous publisher about it, for 'political' now is not in fashion, unless something very provocative from the Radical Right or very strident from a really famous left-winger (which gives, in terms of such publicity values, a choice of no more than half-a-dozen, already largely written-out or clapped-out, intellectuals). The English literati have no sense of or feeling for politics as a speculative discourse, as concerned (like drama) with conflicts of values and interests. They think of it only as argued solutions, strident annunciations and denunciations—the extreme case of Morgan Forster's unwanted 'world of telegrams and anger'. The only other kind of 'politics' regularly sent out for review by literary editors are auto-biographies by Big Fellows (reviewed uncritically by others of the ilk).

I must declare an interest. I had met the author on several occasions, both academic and political. I was not exactly overjoyed when he asked me if I would read an autobiographical manuscript to advise on its chances of publication. I had read his *The Rousing of the Scottish Working Class* (1979), which I found, for my taste, somewhat pietistic in content and laboured in style. When joint editor of this journal in years gone by I had printed one of his articles,[b] after some rewriting, but not others. As a young man I had been awed at the trouble that Leonard Woolf would take with rewriting an article

---

[a] Clydeside Press, 129 pp, £4.20.

[b] I have been unable to find any article by James D. Young in *PQ* during the years of Bernard's coeditorship, or immediately before and after it. Perhaps Bernard reviewed and edited a paper that was eventually rejected; or, more probably, he has misremembered refereeing a paper by Young for another journal, such as the latter's 1983 piece in the *Journal of Contemporary History*, vol. 18, p. 141.

when someone, he said, 'had something to say but can't write'. His standards were so high, he could forgive. William Robson, on the other hand, who wrote well enough for his didactic purposes, no better, no worse, had no patience with anyone who 'couldn't write'. 'If you *really* want to take the trouble with this, my boy . . .' Only rarely one could, or did.

Yet in writing an intense autobiographical reflection on the troubles of our times, James Young has discarded all Marxiological and sociological neologism and encrustation and found a plain, direct style and a quirky insight that make this unlikely book a little classic. The word is merited in two precise senses: first, that if the book becomes better known, people will turn back to it in future years with the pleasure that comes from the apt description of a mythologically important but now vanished era through the eyes of an adult who can recreate childhood; and second, as an explanation (or do I just mean a graphic example?) of the move from minority proletarian socialism into a reflective, tolerant but still morally committed libertarian-egalitarianism. One could almost say that this is a perceptive account of a personal odyssey from revolutionary socialism to socialist realism.

Nowadays when I meet rich, naive and intolerant men and women in the universities who insist that the coming of socialism will solve everything, I inform them that I am not so sure. To drive the lesson home I attempt to explain that, though socialism would abolish economic exploitation, it will not necessarily end human beings' emotional exploitation of each other. But whether emotional exploitation in a socialist society will be qualitatively different or not must remain an open question.

And I *think* he means that last sentence seriously not as conscious irony.

He grew up in a railwayman's tied cottage in Grangemouth. His mother had begin to get 'a real education' at Linlithgow Academy, but poverty forced her to leave: 'With an extensive vocabulary, a good command of the English language and a fine line of invective, my mother hated injustice, hierarchy and unfairness more than economic inequality.' Some of the views James Young learned at Ruskin and were typical of his articles contained a view of class that he now sees was not the reality of his parents' world.

Although both my mother and father saw themselves as being very working class, there was nothing inherently political about their sense of class identity. Human beings' basic attitudes and world-outlook are cultural, not political. As a matter of fact, in the Depression years working people's sense of being working class was at least partly imposed on them by those in authority. Moreover, some working people in Grangemouth accepted the fact that they were working class in a fatalistic, almost apologetic way, a sort of original sin; and others, a minority like my parents, did so with pride because they saw themselves as decent, hard-working producers of wealth.

He relates how when his grandfather was crippled in a mining accident in 1911, reducing his family to dire poverty, a gathering of his uncles, 'God-fearing, honest Presbyterians to a man', decided heavily to forge his father's birth certificate to send him out to work. Behind both the determination and the determinism of the old Scottish left wing there was Calvin as well as

Marx. Yet at Newbattle Abbey College, where he studied before going to Ruskin, he was taught English by Edwin Muir. Some seeds can find fruition decades later.

About most political and sexual matters the working class of Grangemouth had 'a culture of silence'. He interestingly relates this to language: 'We were taught a stiff, very formal, stultifying, standard English. The Scottish words, phrases and idioms we used naturally and creatively at home and in the streets were not permitted in the classrooms . . . the colourful, rich and informal language of the community—a language full of metaphors, euphemisms and allegories—had no place in the school curriculum.' Small wonder he says that so many Scots find national identity a problem in face of 'the local bourgeoisie's schizophrenia towards the use of Scots': banned at school but spoken richly in public and private by ministers, doctors and policemen.

Only the first chapter is pure autobiography. Each other chapter is about the intellectually important problems of his life, each taking, symbolically as well as actually, a geographical form: Scotland, of course, Poland, Israel and Palestine and the USA. Perhaps Katowice in 1982 marked the turning point in his journey. 'I was informed that military rule had eliminated queues for food and other necessities of life. Yet enormous queues such as I had never seen before in my life were standing before my eyes.' On asking how 'intellectuals could reconcile the irreconcilable' he was told that Polish intellectuals 'existed "on different levels of consciousness without being intellectually dishonest"'. Nevertheless, one could almost smell the fear in the streets.' This is a book of unusual intellectual honesty. Only the title could mislead. What made some academics so angry with him, and act so unfairly, only emerges by implication in this reflective and perceptive book.

1990s

National Curriculum History Working Group: Final Report; The British Isles: A History of Four Nations, by Hugh Kearney; *Britain: A Plural Society. Report of a Seminar; Patriotism: The Making and Unmaking of British National Identity,* edited by Raphael Samuel, 3 vols; *Games with Shadows,* by Neal Ascherson; *The Enchanted Glass: Britain and its Monarchy,* by Tom Nairn; *The Divided Kingdom,* by John Osmond[a]

Vol. 61, no. 4, October–December 1990

The matter of Britain has suddenly taken the concrete form of a national curriculum. Too late for reservations about the idea of a national curriculum at all. The pass has been sold. The Labour Shadow for Education endorsed the general idea while reserving the party's position on details etc. Personally I wish that such a response had not been made on the hoof or the wing and that the party had had the chance to consider the dangers of a national curriculum, especially in History, and at the very least the further whittling away of local powers and of pluralistic institutions that it represents. Comparability of standards between examining boards was the main problem, and actually a relatively minor and a technical problem. But too late for that. The political will was there and the Opposition cried 'Me too!' fearing to be marked as soft on standards. So our complex history is now set down in black and white as official History, although not a detailed syllabus, in fact, as most of the leader writers wrong-ended it as usual, not strictly speaking a curriculum even, but a 'framework' for teaching History in schools from 7 to 17. The remaining examination boards will produce curricula under the guidance of the Secondary Education Council and the DES for schools to make syllabuses and choose books, but the framework when finally approved will have statutory force for the first time in this country's history. The event deserves to be studied as part of the History it has created.

Let me say straight away that it is not as bad as many suppose; indeed it is quite good. Far from lacking in facts and being riddled with concepts and irrelevant 'skills', as Robert Skidelsky has led the cry with his ad hoc and ad lib History Curriculum Association (some of who backed out when they actually read the proposals), it seems a reasonable balance. Best brute British blinkered empiricism is avoided without going potty for either 'concepts are knowledge' or 'all education is socialisation'. History is a recognisable chronological narrative and it will be taught for the first time in a systematic

[a] HMSO, 205 pp, £7.95 (NCHWG report); Cambridge University Press, 236 pp, £17.00 (Kearney); Commission for Racial Equality, 78 pp, £1.50 (CRE report); Routledge, vol. 1 330 pp, vol. 2 300 pp, vol. 3 298 pp, £11.95 each (Samuel); Radius, 354 pp, £7.95 (Ascherson); Radius, 402 pp, £8.95 (Nairn); Constable, 278 pp, £6.95 (Osmond).

framework to all our nation's children. Keith Thomas wrote a wise rebuttal of Skidelsky's panic, 'The Future of the Past' (*TLS*, 8 June 1990), in which he remarked that some of his senior colleagues were evidently unfamiliar with conditions in schools and curricula in general. Even (why 'say' even?) Ralph Samuel, in seeking to allay contrary fears of left-wing teachers, has paid ironic tribute to a Conservative government for stopping the rot. Not a rot of rotten methods or new bias, but in too many schools the sheer squeezing out of compulsory History from what should be, indeed, a prime position in the crowded timetable.

Perhaps what has panicked some historians and politicians is sheer unfamiliarity: being faced for the first time with *any* detailed curricula scheme, let alone one that has to state Attainment Targets for four levels from five to fifteen. Not even the Open University faced such an elaborate task; in distance learning so much has to be spelled out in detail to students, and to tutors and examiners as well, which can be taken for granted, is so often taken too much for granted, in face-to-face university teaching where the syllabus is, at the end of the day, simply what an individual teaches and then examines. Many university History syllabuses have been composed god knows how—well, out of Tradition sired by Good Judgement (which we all have) rather than from Reason out of Reappraisal. OU course books are often mocked by Skidelsky's new friends for pedantic and spoon-feeding over-specification, etc. In fact, they have created new standards for curriculum development ('what's that?') only rivalled by Polytechnic degree structures which, in order to get approved by external monitors, had to explain how and why they reached their conclusions about course content, teaching methods and assignments. In other contexts this would be called accountability.

As I have said, the report looks formidable, bureaucratic and rigid only if one is not used to such animals, or cannot appreciate that the knowing informality that may be appropriate for a university department with a hundred students cannot work as guidelines for ten different age levels of hundreds of thousands. Each subject, say 'Life in Tudor and Stuart Times', has in tabular form a 'Purpose' stated, its 'Focus' and the 'Concepts' whose use must be understood. 'Essential Information' is stated under four heads, 'Political', 'Economic, Technological and Scientific', 'Social and Religious' and 'Cultural and Aesthetic'. The concepts are specified as 'parliament, monarch, aristocrat, gentry, yeoman, merchant, labourer and civil war', and the essential information required in the 'Economic . . .' column is: 1 Agriculture. 2 Towns, trade and transport. 3 Exploration, Drake, Raleigh. 4 Scientific discovery: Isaac Newton.' And this is for the second level (aged 7–11). God save the mark, it is not soft! Many teachers have been complaining that it is overloaded with facts. The Prime Minister herself said: 'When we first started on this, I do not think I ever thought they would do the syllabus [sic] in such detail as they are doing now' (*Sunday Telegraph*, 15 April[b]). And add to this the

[b] 1990.

concepts and skills differentiated in the Report's Statement of Attainment by levels. These are not, of course, to be learned by the pupils but are only guides to teachers and examiners as to what abilities are to be developed and assessed. They do not replace facts. They suggest how 'facts' are to be used and interpreted. And actual assessment procedures and examinations will always involve choice. The dangers in over-prescription in national, mass guidelines (once the decision was taken to centralise) are less than in uncertainty and vagueness.

The choice of core papers and the many options offered (there are many options, and much more freedom of choice than appears at first glance at an unfamiliar and worrying kind of document) are infinitely debatable. An 'India and Pakistan: 1930 to 1964' option will please some and panic others, and ditto for what rattles Ruskin, 'The British Empire at its Zenith: 1877 to 1905' (but 'march to the sound of the guns', say I: attack the question to wake up the examiners. It worked for me). Arbitrary decisions must be made for the sake of clarity. Para 4.3 states the problem: '*It is impossible to teach or learn everything about the past*: it is therefore necessary to select from the vast stock of what might be studied about the past. Making such a selection tends to affirm the importance of what is included, even though what is excluded is not necessarily of lesser importance.' So I don't want to enter into all that. And if there was panic in our ranks at news that a retired naval Commander was to be the man-in-the-street or ordinary parent to chair the History Working Group, yet any 'Gad sir' or 'Yes madame' proclivities he may have had were plainly and properly subordinated to the prejudices of a modern service officer for rational order and explicit system. I've followed the *TES* and the educational Press closely over this, for the matter is nationally so important. Overall the teachers' reactions are like those of the Prime Minister, a fear of overload and too much detail. But as for the content, the consensus seems to be that it could be far worse and is *not* a vehicle for patriotic indoctrination, and is to be defended against last ditch attempts to get ministers to turn it that way. They have struck out the main references to multicultural education, or use of English in other cultures, from the English Report (see *TES*, 8 June 1990). They have such power and have used it, over the protests of the working group's chairman Professor Brian Cox (of Black Book fame, no radical he). A literate and proud man, not a bigot or a creep, he is aware that just as English English has been enriched by Irish, Welsh, Scottish and (come to mention it) American, so it may be by recent immigrant dialects.

My worry *is* about the Report's content as reflected in uncertainty about its basic subject matter. Scotland, for the moment, goes its own way and Northern Ireland likewise. A Welsh group was set up in parallel which will produce, in effect, Welsh variants to the same basic structure and content. So the Report has the usual problem about identity, and yet it says that History is essential for any clear sense of identity. 'To help give pupils a sense of identity' is the third stated purpose of having compulsory History at all. 'Through history pupils can learn about the origins and story of other groups to which they belong, of their community and country, and of institutions, beliefs, values, customs and underlying shared values.' But what if not all values are shared? What if some are in conflict or if some of us live in two cultures, perhaps even have a double sense of national identity?[c] For the first sixteen pages on the principles behind the Report it goes on about 'Britain' and British, never once using the correct constitutional name 'United Kingdom'. 'Britain', A. J. P. Taylor once mocked, was only ever unambiguously the name of a Roman province. It has no clear legal or cultural significance. Sometimes the Report uses 'Britain' as if it is a nation or a common culture, but often as a geographical expression—and then evades whether this includes Northern Ireland. Is only 'Great Britain' comprehensive'? (In 'An Englishman Considers His Passport' in a recent volume of essays[d] I've shown that even the full *OED* is confused on this; or that usage simply is confused.) And their 'British' could often be more honestly rendered as 'English', though History must deal with both clearly.

They are right, in my opinion, to insist that understanding must begin by explaining the origins of the familiar. An imposed internationalism would be skin deep for the uncomprehendingly rootless. (The Secretary of State's intervention to change the overall proportion of British History from 40 to 50 per cent is not crucial, and was probably a placatory bone thrown to his own worried ranks.) But who are we? What is the subject matter of British History? They try to face the difficulty:

4.23 In placing Britain's history at the centre . . . we have recognised that England's role in the history of Britain, though often dominant, has by no means been exclusive. While it would be optimistic to expect that a basically *English*-orientated approach to British history (in further and higher education as well as in schools) should be replaced at a stroke by a truly *British* history syllabus, the National Curriculum will provide a clear opportunity to take the first steps in that direction. Essential elements of Welsh, Scottish and Irish history have therefore been included . . .

4.25 The bed-rock British component of the National Curriculum history course is therefore to be guaranteed as follows:
(i) by including adequate and clear reference to some of the major episodes, figures and trends in English, Welsh, Scottish and Irish history;
(ii) by illustrating major episodes of British history, where appropriate, by example drawn from English, Welsh, Scottish and Irish history; and
(iii) by doing justice to the rich diversity of the political, economic, social and cultural history of the British Isles where these serve to enhance historical understanding . . . .

Unhappily 'Britain's role' of 4.23, if it does mean 'the British Isles' of 4.25 (iii) is not 'at the centre' when one comes to look at the units in detail. The

[c] By this time Bernard Crick was living in Edinburgh.

[d] 'An Englishman Considers his Passport', published in the *The Irish Review*, 5, 1988, pp. 1–10, and later as pp. 23–34 of the volume mentioned here: N. Evans, ed., *National Identity in the British Isles*, Harlech, Coleg Harlech, 1989. See also note a on p. 233 above for another Harlech-based venture from the following year.

'Irish question' is not in fourth level (14–16 year old) core beyond 1914 when there is a jump to 1929 ('Crash!'), so the founding of the Free State and the Stormont regime are out; and if one turns with hope to the Great War option for the same age group, neither the Easter Rebellion nor the Irish conscription crisis are billed. There is a *third* level *option* (11–14 year old) 'Culture and Society in Ireland up to early C20th', which gives 'Easter 1916', 'Partition 1922' and 'Eamon de Valera' under 'Exemplary Information', but at the end of a long journey over thin ice from 'Celtic Christianity' and 'Viking towns' to 'Yeats', 'Joyce' and 'Synge'! Scotland and Wales do better in a third level core 'The Making of the United Kingdom c1500 to c1750'. But the confusion between Britain and England against which the Report warns is still endemic in the study units.

Why should a National History syllabus only take 'first steps' towards teaching the real history of the United Kingdom as a whole, the unit of legal citizenship of us all? Is this English complacency or mental muddle? What is offered is, overall, better than many of the old GCE board syllabuses, but it is still basically an English History with a few respectful asides to famous episodes of Scottish and Irish History thought of in isolation.

Suppose we boldly ask the missing question, the great inarticulate pre-supposition, 'What is Englishness?', the basic question of national identity. Welsh, Scottish and Irish so frankly and persistently raise the question, should we not? And then begin to discover that part of 'Englishness' itself is formed by the relationships with the other culture and nations? The others have no hesitation in studying their own distinctiveness, and how much earlier cultures in their areas have been affected (for good or ill, for good and ill) by the growth of English power. There are few such studies of the English. I believe the explanation is reasonably clear. The invention of 'Britishness' and the revival of the concept of 'Britain' in the early eighteenth century was a political device to create common loyalties to political institutions and a common citizenship— everything that Tom Nairn, with zestful exaggeration, attributes to the cult of the Crown. But before 1707 there was already a common Crown. The whole point of Union was that that was not enough. The cult grew up of parliamen-tary government, whose positive virtues Nairn ignores, if its vices of uncon-trolled sovereignty are now obvious; even though he gives no credence to romantic Scottish nationalism which sees the Scottish Parliament of 1706 as the voice of the people, a view certainly not held at the time.

For the sake of clarity I would rather develop a sense of Englishness as a culture every bit as distinct and definite as Tom Nairn's and Neal Ascherson's sense of Scottishness (neither of who are, incidentally, separatists; both are bitter critics of the SNP). Englishness we'll have with as many or more subcultures as in Scotland, and a similar tendency to polarise into a radical account of history (as in the left-wing patriotism of some of Ralph Samuel's authors and in the spirit of 'Scottish Democracy', shown as still alive in the Campaign for a Scottish Assembly and in the journal *Radical Scotland*) and in an English Tory or a Scottish Whig right-wing version. If Englishness is then a cultural nationalism, among others in 'these islands', 'Britishness' best refers to the common elements of a specifically political culture. The concept of 'Roman' had a similar function amid the cultural and ethnic diversity of the Roman Empire, and the great movement 'to Americanise the immigrants' from the 1870s to 1920 was *not* somehow to transform Irish, Polish, Jews and Italians into White Anglo-Saxon Protestants, but to teach them the practices of the specifically civic elements of the host culture—'Americanism'. It happened that the general culture gave an unusual prominence to the values of a civic culture (as in Rome and as in England and also Scotland, not to mention the Dutch Republic), so broadly speaking the education succeeded. Its class-bound limitations are obvious from the point of view of an ideal of universal republican citizenship, but it was civic enough, as in the United Kingdom after the Reform Acts, for a civic based unity to hold—except for Ireland.

My prescription for the rectification of terms has a grave complication. 'Britishness' is also used and useful to point to undoubted common elements of Scottish, Welsh, Irish and English culture, only in part explained by political hegemony, as shown by the dominance of the English language in the Republic of Ireland despite Eamon de Valera's best efforts. But the History Curriculum overdoes the search for elements in common. I see no need to look for the guiding hand of Thatcher behind this; rather the committee shows a spontaneous good liberal, almost social democratic, zeal to find consensus: a political quest. But an historical quest must also show conflict and real differences as well.

Why cannot the illuminatingly obvious be recognised? Hugh Kearney put it in a recent paper to a History Workshop conference: 'the United Kingdom is not a nation-state like say France, but a multi-national state like Belgium, Switzerland, Yugo-Slavia, the Soviet Union.' Like myself, he is a tremendous pedant. He wants us to say 'United Kingdom' instead of 'the British State'. The state is the United Kingdom (or 'Great Britain' if you must) and it is a multi-national state. English dominance has tended to obscure this simple fact, and now a residual English fear grows that it really is true that every nation should naturally have its own state, so that if it doesn't, it isn't a real nation. (This must be the logic behind the Thatcherite abuse of Scottish aspirations to devolution or Home Rule. Either one thing or the other, no half-way houses.) Since the United Kingdom is a multi-national state, it is bad history, indeed a politicised history, to teach British History as a kind of extension of English History. For the Working Party to have faced the question, but temporised and passed on, is to perpetuate historical error and self-misunderstanding by the English.

A lot of the polemic in Nairn, Ascherson and John Osmond's book of a TV series against English arrogance and imperception is just and funny; the Druids and the Ukanians wallowing in heritage, more often Surrey gnomes than Shakespeare. But both Nairn and Osmond allow polemical rage at the harm the English have done their cultures to blind them to any understanding of the complexity of English culture, the tolerance as well as the calm conceit.

By their principles they preach that nations should respect other nations. Not all are equal in power and resources, but like human individuals, all are to be equally respected. Not for them, alas, the hard task of sorting out the good from the bad of Englishness; and in Osmond radicalism and nationalism seem completely confused and if one didn't know Wales one would think that Welshness was simply a response to abuses by the English Establishment. Too much anti-English rant (though some is sado-masochistic fun) argues some basic insecurity or lack of clarity in his own position.

Nairn seems to deny that there is an English nation, 'only a Southern-lowland hegemonic bloc uniting an hereditary elite to the central processing unit of commercial and financial capital'. (Some of it is very well-written, however; but his writing is quite remarkably uneven, perhaps unrevised.) In many ways he seems typical of the Sixties *English* socialists who gave automatic credence (I mean credulousness) to the virtues in every nationalism but their own. On the contrary, what is needed is for the English to come to terms with themselves as English, not (and here Nairn and Ascherson are right) as an imperial heartland. Only then can there be mutual respect between the four nations, indeed a positive enjoyment of the interrelations involved. Perhaps I enjoy the diversity of the cultures of Wales, Scotland and Ireland so much because I do not feel threatened in my very English identity. I am constantly surprised and saddened that friends in the three other nations can still feel threatened, or say they feel threatened, in their identity by Englishness. To be secure in one's own identity is to be able to treat others as moral equals. William Bloom has recently argued from psychological theory in his *Personal Identity, National Identity and International Relations* that this is as true for nations as it is for individuals; and yet he is aware that individual identity can be soured by exclusive nationalisms.

My theory is that the lack of an intelligent literature on English national character (Orwell was an exception of the Left) was an almost conscious suppression in the nineteenth century. A strident English nationalism would have made the business of holding together the United Kingdom more difficult; and that was, after all, the main business of British politics from 1688 to 1920 (though is not mentioned in the National Curriculum). Imperialism was a kind of substitute English nationalism which allowed for the other nations of these islands to play their part in the Great Game. Patriotism is surely less exclusive than nationalism. Must we not all give some love to familiar and local things, not always weighing them up to the abstract standards of a rational or a perfected humanity? An immigrant can be a patriot. Only his or her children can be nationalists. Raphael Samuel's contributors argue among themselves as to whether the whole concept of patriotism is to be accepted, in a radical, populist version, or rejected as inherently hierarchical and corruptive of enlightenment values. But the argument is more open than it was, largely thanks to Samuel's own huge and creative ambivalences, having put both sides of the argument both fiercely and well on different occasions. The Society for Labour History, the

History Workshop, many of Edward Thompson's writings proclaim the authenticity of a radical English patriotism against the school of Paris Marxists. For this Englishness Ascherson seems to have more respect than Nairn (though one loves him for the enemies he has made). But Samuel and his contributors are mainly tone deaf to the 'English/British' confusion, just as is the otherwise serious and sensible discussion of pluralism as an ethic as well as a theory in *Britain: A Plural Society* (Britain is wholly England, pluralism entirely a matter of the new immigrants, and the other nations vanish!).

The respectable excuse for the National Curriculum Working Group's belief that 'the English orientated approach to British history' can only be phased out gradually ('Lord make me chaste but not yet') is that there are no comprehensively British Isles books to orientate teachers. Professor Kearney has removed that excuse dramatically. His *The British Isles: A History of Four Nations* is a brilliant demonstration that in this strange and shifting configuration of cultures national histories hardly exist except as ideology: all is interrelationships, and in the light of the whole history of these islands nationalisms (and the historical myths they created) have come very late. And who says that history has ended—a crazy fellow in the State Department? Hugh Kearney (a Liverpudlian who has divided his teaching life almost equally between Ireland, Scotland, England and the United States) has done exactly what the New Zealand intellectual historian and political philosopher J. G. A. Pocock said was needed in his seminal article, 'The Limits and Divisions of British History: In Search of an Unknown Subject' (*American Historical Review*, 1982). Because Kearney was a leading historian of the sixteenth and seventeenth centuries, when he offered a short account of the whole of the history of the British Isles in 216 pages, Cambridge University Press concluded that it was a kind of coffee table book, such as Jack Plumb and John Roberts sometimes effortlessly produce, rather than a challenging masterpiece of narrative synthesis. So they padded it out with nice photographs and priced it up accordingly. If they had thought of the National Curriculum for one minute they should have paperbacked it and priced it low to reach every serious history teacher at any level in the two states and the four nations. It should be the book of the new curriculum in a schools edition. It undermines conventional English historiography. It provides an historical framework to examine the question of *identities* at any level. The National Curriculum raised the problem, started to face it, but then walked away. Needless to add, 'British Politics' textbooks in schools are just as Anglocentric, often even worse, and therefore demonstrably false or partial accounts.

The Future of Northern Ireland, edited by John McGarry and Brendan O'Leary; *Interpreting Northern Ireland*, by John Whyte; *Inequality in Northern Ireland*, by David Smith and Gerald Chambers; *Northern Ireland since 1945*, by Sabine Wichert; *Northern Ireland: Politics and the Constitution*, edited by Brigid Hadfield; *The Northern Ireland Question: Myth and Reality*, edited by Patrick J. Roche and Brian Barton[a]

Vol. 63, no. 3, July–September 1992

Some of us recently met to discuss whether (I think *why*) there has been a gradual decline in political publishing in Britain aimed at the general intelligent reader as distinct from academics. That is, of course, just what *The Political Quarterly* aspires to do in a small but real way (in fact most of our readers are academics[b]). That there is a highly intelligent reading public is shown by the sale of difficult and demanding modern novels, the kind in which one can lose the thread easily or never quite twig what's up. But novels, of course, are more entertaining. And newspapers and broadcasting can keep one abreast all too easily of current events, even if more rarely with why things are happening and how one should judge alternatives.

Of course our discussion wandered. Opinions varied sharply as to whether the problem lay on the supply side or the demand side. We might have got somewhere had we concentrated on Northern Ireland as an example. Two of the books listed above are obviously intended to be available for student purchase and use. Therefore they are priced at what now passes for 'reasonably cheap' in paperback, but not printed, of course, in runs long enough to match Penguin's, Fontana's or Picador's prices. The other books have given up hope long before publication of more than a handful of individual purchases, so small runs have to cane libraries hard. However, one thing is striking about each of the books under review. For books by social scientists they are on the whole well written and have all taken pains to avoid disciplinary jargon and circumlocutory neologisms.[c] This is so unusual as to demand explanation. Perhaps the late and greatly lamented John Whyte is a special case. He seemed incapable of writing an unclear sentence. If he ever had any sins, God should pardon all of them just for that.

---

[a] Clarendon Press, 376 pp, £40.00 (McGarry and O'Leary); Clarendon Press, 308 pp, £35.00 (Whyte); Clarendon Press, 401 pp, £45 (Smith and Chambers); Longman, 229 pp, £21 hb, £8.99 pb (Wichert); Open University Press, 208 pp, £35 hb, £12.99 pb (Hadfield); Avebury, 207 pp, £32.50 (Roche and Barton).

[b] A difficult claim to substantiate. Although publishers can conduct surveys to find out who reads their products, and nowadays have download or 'hits' data for any electronic access that goes through their own portal, when these are taken together a journal has, even now, only such partial information to add to subscriptions (which is who *buys*, rather than who reads). Back in the distant past of 1992 there were only subscriptions and anecdote. 'Most' may yet be true but 'many' would be safer.

[c] The journal article had the (probably unintended) neologism 'neulogism' here.

Even Brigid Hadfield's somewhat routine-looking balanced anthology, with its Londonderry Air of publishing opportunities for local lads and lasses, mainly Queen's Belfast in fact, comes across with rare clarity. And the gathering of Unionist academics in the Avebury Press book (again defeated by price before ever it looks for readers) all write with the urgency of a neglected minority (among writers on Northern Ireland, of course, not among its inhabitants) wanting to reach the educated mainland public. And presumably publishers, to give them unexpected credit, keep on taking losses in publishing books on Northern Ireland, because the matter is important and still neglected in the British public mind. The Oxford University Press can, of course, offload some of the risk on libraries; but nonetheless they stubbornly and properly think that the matter is important and the thought and scholarship on offer proportionate. In other words, even academics write clearly and not just for themselves when they have something to say and want to be heard. Even so, alas, they seldom are. These books rarely if ever get reviewed even in the quality Press.

McGarry and O'Leary include one non-academic contributor, Charles Graham of the New Ulster Political Research Group (the spiritual arm of the UDA). He fills in ably for John McMichael who was murdered before finishing his contribution. At least I got a Christmas card from McMichael, arriving three days after his death. His murder was probably not directly connected with his new conciliatory views, but because to be received at the table he knew that his organisation would have to clean up its share of the protection rackets. However his death is emblematic of the practical difficulties faced by any leader worthy of becoming a textbook example of consociationalism.

For McGarry and O'Leary are happy to have a Preface by the self-confessed inventor of consociationalism, Professor Arend Lijphart, which they wisely follow by a 'List of Abbreviations and a Glossary of Key Concepts'. 'Consociation', however, is the only one on which the intelligent non-academic might stumble: the others are 'co-determination', 'confederal', 'devolution', 'equal citizenship', 'federal', 'independent state', 'integration', 'joint authority', 'majority rule', 'partition', 'power-sharing' and 'unitary state'. 'Co-determination' and 'power-sharing' are admitted to be virtual synonyms of 'consociation', which simplifies the matter admirably (the minister can understand that); but the full gloss on the solvent word is:

A political system used in divided societies to share and divide governmental power and authority. Political power is shared by rival subcultures on a proportional basis—in the executive, the legislature and public employment. Each sub-culture or segment enjoys rights of veto and autonomy in the organisation of its culture. Public expenditure can also be allocated on a proportional basis. Consociation is the antonym of majority rule and unlike integration does not endeavour (immediately) to assimilate sub-cultures.

Lijphart notes that the book contains forceful and persuasive statements of diverse political views, indeed; but he claims that consociation must be a first

403

step in any progress, even 'the best hope for assimilation is to start with power-sharing as the first step' (which is precisely why all of Roche and Barton's and some of Hadfield's crew won't put their feet on that ladder). Brendan O'Leary and Paul Arthur, indeed, in a joint chapter, note approvingly that the Irish government has moved from a purely rhetorical nationalism into committing itself in the Anglo-Irish Agreement 'to achieving a united Irish nation by consent'. And they end by stating that the arguments all matter 'because as long as they remain unsolved Northern Ireland has no worthwhile future'.

'No worthwhile future' should be added to their glossary as a synonym to Charlie Haughey's 'failed entity'. But if our two political scientists were strict in their definitions they would note that 'not worthwhile' and 'failed' are prescriptive statements not descriptive, and only arguably predictive. Let me suggest something far more alarming and likely about the future: that the future will resemble the past. Even outside Northern Ireland the streets are full of tragically failed entities who will live quite a bit longer whatever the doctors say.

What seems to me badly lacking in the prescriptive element in all these books is any real sense of time-scale and functions. What kind of things can and should be changed in what time-scale? Most attitudinal changes touching deeply held values or prejudices presumably take at least a generation to work. Does not social science have anything to say about that? Both Lijphart and the editors seem to assume that we are dealing with two coherent systems that should be integrated; the fallacies of scientism and of nationalism happily combine—that everything is necessarily related to everything else (rather than conditionally and contingently); and that for every nation there must be one state (and in this case the myth that there was once a politically united Irish divided only by British conquest). There may not be 'a way forward' but many dimensions of integration and diversity, some of which are more open to control than others by public policy. I am not even arguing for a functionalist approach to integration (why should everything be integrated?). A functionalist approach can be read or misread as a series of small steps, just as the Anglo-Irish Agreement *can* be presented as big step, necessarily pointing in a fixed (the grim pun is deliberate) direction.

Rather than that, one could swap hypotheses and surmise that if the majority in Northern Ireland were given a greater sense of security in what they want to continue to enjoy (that anyway counts for less, thanks to the EC), citizenship of the United Kingdom, then their leaders would be more free to cooperate with the Republic. They could then add to an already interesting list of common institutions, some state, some private, that already link North and South and the Republic and the mainland more than is usual in relationships between legally sovereign states, and far more than foreign observers of 'the troubles' usually notice. One does not change buses and trains at the border. Power-sharing in a parliament in Northern Ireland will inevitably be seen as an irrevocable step to 'unity by consent', rather than as a sensible device for gaining peace and justice in the North.

The theoretical bias which is a political bias comes out strongly when Lijphart quotes Richard Rose's aphorism 'the problem is that there is no solution' and calls it 'as provocative as it is wrong'. And McGarry and O'Leary declare that it is one of the three main objects of the book 'to counter [this] facile, thought-stopping and pessimistic article of faith which has come to dominate academic, administrative and intelligent journalistic commentary on Northern Ireland'. But Rose is right; one must gently insist that only puzzles have 'solutions'. In my opinion any one with 'a solution' to the Northern Irish question should be locked up (with a prison library of history books only, nothing on consociationalism, Belgium or Switzerland). To be humane, one must be a little pessimistic, not reckless with time or too mandatory with models. 'Patience and time' as Tolstoy has Kutuzov say to his impatient young officers. If one must talk the language of solutions, then at least try to sketch out, since state coercion cannot be the answer, how long a path integration would be, even granted the will, and identify clearly the social institutions that can best be supported in the hope that indirectly they will create the conditions for the minimal political trust in which real bargaining can work.

The criticism is familiar that the theory of consociationalism implies that elite groups must bargain on behalf of their communities. The consociationalists answer this as if it were a moral objection to ever acting undemocratically at all, and they point out correctly that all democracies have political elites. But the objection is practical. In precisely the kind of situations of inflamed communal distrust for which the theory seeks to find a formal solution, or a framework in which to seek solutions, leaders all too often cease to be leaders once they start to bargain, to make normal political compromises with the other side. The recent history of Northern Ireland is full of reformers cut down by their party followers, and of moderates forced out of politics. It is not especially objective to think that this difficulty is only found on the Protestant or Unionist side. John Hume once clearly favoured a power-sharing parliament with, for this generation, only a token Irish dimension. Ten years ago it could be calmly discussed in the SDLP leadership whether, in retrospect, it had not been a mistake to insist at Sunningdale on an Irish dimension. Would it not have been better to get a power-sharing parliament working, and at a later date, when trust could have been built up cautiously and slowly, either to revive the idea or point to its practical existence in a network of intergovernmental cooperation? But if these ideas were to be revived now, he would risk splitting his party; just as much as if a Unionist leader (naming names does not help) was to say 'what's the harm?' in a symbolic Council of Ireland.

Smith and Chambers remind us of the depth of the problem, and how strong the case is to remedy the continuing gross discrimination against Catholics in Northern Ireland. Only then will the counter-economic arguments of Arthur Aughey and his Unionist friends (in the Roche and Barton book) gain the hearing over here their merits deserve. Who is pretending that the Republic could take on the North economically, any more than impose or magic law and order? A good account of how a pluralistic Northern Ireland could emerge is found in Rick Wilford's thoughtful essay, 'Inverting Consociationalism? Policy, Pluralism and the Post-modern' in Brigid Hadfield's book. He means let everyone deconstruct the old bloody texts as they choose, is sceptical about *any* overarching solutions and *the* cause and *the* rights and wrongs. Inter-church groups begin to work on the right level; they at least try to alleviate the hatreds that they did so much to cause or exacerbate. Sabine Wichert, a German historian resident in Northern Ireland for twenty years, has written an elegant short history very much aware of the positive values in both traditions, not laying blame or pointing to easy answers.

Britons: Forging the Nation 1701–1837, by Linda Colley; *Myths of the English*, edited by Roy Porter[a]

Vol. 64, no. 2, April–June 1993

There is little doubt that there is a British State, but is there a British nation? Yet one must footnote 'little doubt' with passing references to, say, Tom Nairn, Dafydd Ellis Thomas and John Hume who each plausibly claim that it is in reality an English State posing as a British State. Part of the conceptual confusion is that we English take ourselves so much for granted. There is little serious scholarly writing on the nature of Englishness. English character, behaviour and standards are so implicitly assumed, are such fixed and inarticulated prejudices that it has long been recognised as quite un-English to talk about them, except in the distancing guise of novels. Social scientists are embarrassed by such questions. There are now some very good books by English scholars on the origins, conditions and nature of nationalism as a general ideology, but few serious attempts to characterise Englishness. And the English Left have, broadly speaking, been intellectual apologists or suckers for any nationalism but their own. But it should at least be recognised that there are nationalisms and nationalisms. If all nationalisms have functional, even structural, similarities, the contents do rather vary. A good examination question would be 'Compare and contrast the content of American and of Serbian nationalism', but few of the examiners could answer it. Hannah Arendt once sensibly remarked that while the Communist and the Nazi parties both had totalitarian ideologies, their content, and hence their policies, were somewhat different.

Many of us now believe that English standards are declining. I don't mean among overburdened teachers or that the young no longer quote a witty tag

[a] Yale University Press, 429 pp, £19.95 (Colley); Polity Press, 276 pp, £39.50 (Porter).

from the Bard when ordering their takeaways, but more obviously standards of probity and competence among government ministers and civil servants (firmly not to mention the Royals). They now act in ways that would not so long ago have been clearly seen as un-English. The great English eighteenth century cultural invention and export, the concept and cult of the gentleman, is now in terminal decline.

As Hegel said, the owl of Minerva flies at dusk. Now when 'the great game' of Empire is up, now when nationalism in the other nations of the United Kingdom grows more and more restive, now that the economic and military power of the British State can effect nothing by itself, and now that the crisis of our relationship with the rest of Europe is upon us, a few books of thoughtfulness and merit begin to emerge (perhaps among them two years ago *Political Quarterly's* own *National Identities: The Constitution of the United Kingdom*).[b]

Linda Colley, an already distinguished Anglo-Welsh historian at Yale, now offers a clever answer to the English/British puzzle. After the Act or Treaty of Union of 1707 a sense of British nationalism was invented precisely to bind England and Scotland together. In the eyes of ministerial writers and Scottish Unionists the Scots became 'North Britons'. Further, she argues that this new British nationalism became genuinely popular—that is, shared by the populace not merely the political class. She convincingly argues, albeit mainly by implication (she gets on with her narrative rather than taking issue with all other accounts), that left-wing historians, piously searching for ancestors and early martyrs, got the balance badly wrong. Patriotism was overwhelmingly popular. Why? Not because government propaganda changed opinion, but because it worked on two great fears, already widespread between all classes in England and Scotland: fear of a French invasion and fear of a reimposition of Catholicism. Anti-Popery and Francophobia arose from the long wars between 1688 and 1815. War has never been a popular motive among left-wing historians.

The thesis is clever and plausible and the book is well-written, beautifully and copiously illustrated, based on much original research in popular and local as well as state sources, and yet is wholly accessible to non-specialists. But I am not convinced. The sense in which people felt themselves to be British or Britons was surely different to that in which they still felt themselves to be 'English' or 'Scottish'? Indeed, as she demonstrates, a British *patriotism* emerged and Scottish younger sons of the aristocracy and adventurers from below (the socially mobile) gave to and took from the growing Empire disproportionately. Even on her own examples, the manner and content of British patriotism in Scotland was very different from that in England. In both countries popular prejudice against job- and place-hunters

---

[b] This was a 'fifth issue' of the journal—a set of specially commissioned articles published as a book, annually from the late 1980s onwards. The *National Identities* collection was edited by Bernard Crick and published in 1991.

from the other grew throughout the century. The situation is surely better conceived not as the victory or forging of a new nation of Britons, but as the growth of a sense of *dual nationality*. (Acton was to maintain in his once celebrated debate with J. S. Mill that multi-national states were a 'higher form' of civilisation than nation states—well, usually more tolerant.) But it is also important to notice two things: firstly, that this sense of dual nationality is, indeed, far more Scottish and British, rather than Scottish and English; and is Welsh and British rather than Welsh and English; and, secondly, that 'British', if a cultural term at all, defines a specifically political culture, whereas Scottish, Welsh, Irish and under-studied English refer to general cultures. It would be more clear to speak of British *patriotism* but of English and Scottish etc. *nationalism*.

'British', it seems to me, implies the Union itself, the laws, the crown and parliament, so much and yet no more; not a whole way of life. Tom Nairn was ungenerous and, for once, imperceptive when he argued (in his *The Enchanted Glass*) that without the crown there is no English identity; but he was wholly right to see its vital role as symbol of the unity of the United Kingdom (the Americans, of course, can somehow get by with a Constitution). Neal Ascherson, in some of the essays in his *Games with Shadows*, more generously suggested that the English problem is not an excess of explicit self-consciousness but a lack of it. I suspect that there was a deliberate suppression of English nationalism in the nineteenth century when all other states were either developing it as a state cult or trying to reconcile rival national aspirations. This suppression was in the interests of the major business of English politics since 1688, that of holding the United Kingdom together; so instead of nationalism 'imperialism' was cultivated as a cult and a practical opportunity open to all the four nations.

Colley takes the fact that 'Britons never will be slaves' was sung in taverns not just on theatre stages as evidence that the singers thought of themselves as Britons. It is far more likely that they still thought of themselves as English, Scottish or Welsh except in such contexts of singing patriotic songs, united against the enemy. And even then the covering tarpaulin could slip in the heat of action. Nelson's signal was 'England expects . . .' And by leaving Ireland out of her account completely and underplaying how long the fear of the 'Forty-five' lingered among both English and Unionist Lowlanders, she can underplay domestic political and utilitarian pressures for dual identities within a common political and legal framework; and she has, in restoring a balance, put too much weight on foreign wars. The fear of civil war recurring was always greater. The Whigs had read their Hobbes before their Locke.

Colley, in other words, is right to see the urgent reasons behind the State cult of Britishness after 1707, but she exaggerates its success and misunderstands its nature. Her book raises big theoretical issues without facing them. The political impetus to create an overriding sense of Britishness was so strong. And yet a sense of Scottish identity, with a reasonably sensible body of books characterising it, has survived—even without a parliament, indeed evolved, changed, much more clearly than for the English, despite their political dominance. Cultures can be very resistant to political management. To be fair, her conclusions recognise the consequences of some of this. 'We can understand the nature of the present crisis only if we recognise that the factors that provided for the forging of a British nation in the past have largely ceased to operate.' She says that the British are more inclined than the Germans or the French to view Europe 'as a threat. This partly because they have so often fought against Continental European states in the past; but their apparent insularity is to be explained also by their growing doubts about who they are in the present.'

So one turns to Roy Porter's book with hope, but recoils like a moth drawn to a candle. For his Introduction to a group of essays on English myths uses English and British as if synonyms, has no suspicion even of how much 'Englishness' may have been affected by interrelations with the other nations. Neither he nor Colley seem aware of Hugh Kearney's *The British Isles: A History of Four Nations* (1989),[c] with its systematic demonstration of how strong are interrelations, how historically anachronistic modern nationalism made us. Porter makes no attempt whatever to define what is meant by 'English'; nor do any of his scholarly contributors, even though they are all good writers and aim (despite the hideously misjudged price of the book) to reach the general educated reader. Each of the essays is interesting—among them David Cannadine on Gilbert and Sullivan, Marina Warner on Mother Goose and 'the Old Wife's Tale', David Cressey on 'The Fifth' and Bob Bushaway on the cult of the dead of the First World War. The trees are fine but offer no clue as to what is the nature of an English wood compared to any other, beyond pointing to it. Only Ian Pears comes at all close to the expectation raised by the title and the reputation of the publisher with 'The Gentleman and the Hero', a study of contrasting images of Wellington and Napoleon. But even then Arthur Wellesley was Anglo-Irish. Porter like Colley ignores the Irish question. One of the major problems of British (English?) politics for over two hundred years just doesn't fit their conceptual frameworks.

[c] This title, and those by Nairn and Ascherson mentioned earlier in the review, feature in Bernard Crick's review in vol. 61, no. 4 of 1990, reprinted above.

Two Laskis

Harold Laski: A Life on the Left, by Isaac Kramnick and Barry Sheerman MP; *Harold Laski: A Political Biography*, by Michael Newman[a]

Vol. 64, no. 4, October–December 1993

None of us who heard him lecture will ever forget the experience nor have thought to hear the like again. But did the printed page or his political influence ever live up to his power at the podium? Not only those who did not hear him have doubted that. Now at last we are able to see in perspective and context the true stature of Laski, and with, like the portrait Cromwell wanted from Lely, 'roughnesses, pimples, warts, and everything'. Both books quote Max Beloff, no friend of Laski at all, calling the period 1920 to 1950 'The Age of Laski'. Both books are well written, a pleasure to read as biographies, scholarly and judicious—if in somewhat different ways. And amazingly, considering the contentiousness of the man and the period, there is no substantial disagreement between them either in their assessment or, as far as I can see, in their accounts of particular events. I hope they can respect each other's work; that is not always the case with biographers.

That two real biographies should appear at once is neither tragedy nor farce: Harold Laski was born 1893. These books are the centennial celebration, forcing on LSE, where Laski taught from 1920 when he left Harvard until his death in 1950, a reluctant and minimal notice of its most famous or notorious teacher—an evening organised by the Government students' society with a platform of three voluble old Laski students, and one public lecture by Isaac Kramnick with Professor Kenneth Minogue in the chair, not the Director. The memory of Laski must seem the same kind of incubus to Dr Ashworth as the living Laski had seemed to William Beveridge (and also to President Lowell of Harvard) in the main academic business of raising money from business. ('Seems, madam! nay, it is.') The wheel has gone full circle. Who talks of progress now? In some ways we are back in the 1930s. So it was modestly brave or shrewdly politic for John Smith MP to give a reception for his fellow MP's book, and the Indian High Commissioner fielded on another night his Vice-President, a most thoughtful old Laski disciple. Bad luck for Professor Newman that Macmillan's publicity machine was, for a rare once, outplayed. And their price suggests a bad underestimating both of the book's merits and potential readership.

Professor Kramnick of Cornell (who has written on Burke and on Paine) did the research in America where Laski was almost as famous as in Britain. Barry Sheerman (whose idea it was) did the British digging, although he seems to have used a narrower range of sources than Kramnick. Kramnick did the writing, and he contextualises sadly but firmly like the good historian of ideas

[a] Hamish Hamilton, 669 pp, £25.00 (Kramnick and Sheerman); Macmillan, 438 pp, £45 (Newman).

he is: 'Laski's life speaks to a lost world. If we are now living through what some see as the twilight of socialism, then Laski's life speaks to its morning.' But at times I think I hear the rumble of muffled drums, perhaps from Barry Sheerman (who just missed Laski at LSE), playing a cautious recall for intellectuals to come back to the Labour Party (if any are left), but only after reading his book with its salutary secondary themes of the dangers of rocking the boat and the disappointment of hoping for direct, personal influence. Sometimes they beat the drum too hard. To get a small niggle off my chest, they exaggerate the role of Laski in the founding of this journal (true, he had a *finger* in every pie) and they have the first two editors as Leonard Woolf and Kingsley Martin rather than William Robson and Martin. But the bigger niggle is that in their division of labour Laski's French connection, his intellectual affinity, visits, friends and fame are almost forgotten. Newman is far more aware of how deeply Laski was influenced by French rationalism, enlightenment and *les philosophes*—even if he does not explore it biographically.

The one book is a full biography, and Laski's life is fascinating. The other is slightly mistitled: 'intellectual biography' might have better conveyed its strength and deliberate limit. Kramnick deals with Laski's ideas equally sensibly, but the very scale and chronology of full biography and political events makes it hard to grasp Laski's ideas as a whole, scatters shrewd analysis throughout a wide wood. (And it is no help to have a nominalist indexer who names names but not concepts.) In Newman the ideas, both academic and popular, come together in a thematic treatment that correlates well enough with understanding of the main events of Laski's life; so he never loses the wood for the trees and can make a clearer assessment of Laski as thinker. Those more interested in the history of ideas will turn to Newman and those more interested in the history of the Labour Party and the international socialist movement to Kramnick. But, of course, it was always Laski's claim that his politics derived from his ideas: that theory must relate to practice. This was always one respect in which his Marxism of the 1930s was only skin-deep, even if a thick and glowing skin. Ideas were not a product of material conditions: they are the principles that drive us on to try to reform those conditions. Oh, of course, as he was fond of saying, 'Men who live differently, think differently'; but his whole life testifies to his belief that some intellectuals can cut through the oppressive natural habitat of social conditioning, at least enough to see ahead or to create new paths and relationships.

He was born, we all knew, into a well-off and orthodox Manchester Jewish household. But few of us realised, until Kramnick and Sheerman's researches, just how wealthy and how orthodox. Nathan was a cotton king alright and a leader of the Manchester Jewish community with political influence. He found the dispossessed young Liberal Winston Churchill a Manchester seat to nurse in 1904 which he won in 1906. Churchill stayed at the house quite often, had met the precocious Harold who then *did* have access to Churchill in later times. Both biographers agree that in letters, conversation and lectures Laski often stretched the yarn wide, but never spun cloth from an empty spool. Lord Haldane, Mr Justice Holmes, Felix Frankfurter, Louis Brandeis, FDR himself, all enjoyed and sought Laski's company—even Baldwin and Attlee, for a time, found something in it. Canards at 'that liar Laski' (such as the late George Catlin launched) won't fly any more. (Alas that neither Roy Jenkins nor Roy Hattersley, reviewing Kramnick and Sheerman in the *Sunday Times* and the *Observer*, appeared to have reached or gone back to that part of the exposition.) The problem now appears more that of a storyteller's exuberance, or the highly embellished anecdote-from-life so typical of the pulpit or 'Thought for the Day'. Both biographers are understanding of Laski's half boastful, half didactic but always entertaining foibles, if, quite rightly, not wholly forgiving.

He broke from home spectacularly by eloping in 1911 at the age of eighteen with a gentile PT teacher called Frida, eight years his senior. His parents saw him through Oxford on condition that they did not live together, something that they pragmatically accepted, mostly. From then on she was his constant support, a lifelong love affair. Newman quotes him writing to Frida when she was over sixty (they wrote constantly whenever apart): 'I can't bear to think of what I might have been if I had not found you. As it is, after all these years, I feel with all more heart that I begin to love you afresh every day. And to have you believe in me is the rock on which I build my truth.' His dependence was deep, but also very practical. For in domestic matters, it emerges, he was always hopelessly impractical and unskilled, even by male standards of the day. The 'New Woman' had a lot to put up with when she fell in love, or took on a super-intelligent partner as a good cause.

But at first it was Frida who had an ideology, which he promptly adopted, whereas he had only had a voracious, eclectic intellectuality, based on the dangerous gift of being able to scan, comprehend and retain a page at a glance, as could Sydney Webb, Kingsley Martin and Denis Brogan. Frida's ideology was eugenics. Harold submitted a paper on 'The Scope of Eugenics' to *The Westminster Review* (once J. S. Mill's paper) which they published. Sir Francis Galton wrote to congratulate the unknown author, and was startled to find a seventeen year old Manchester Grammar schoolboy. 'My wonderful boy Jew, Laski by name, came here to tea', he wrote; 'the boy is simply beautiful . . . He is perfectly nice and quiet in his manners. Many prodigies fade, but this one seems to have stamina and purpose, and is not excitable, so he ought to make a mark.' Fortunately Frida began to think that female emancipation could not wait on the long generational breeding processes of the Shavian intelligentsia at summer schools so, instead, following the celebrated breach between Sylvia Pankhurst and her mother Emmeline on direct action and socialism, he planted a bomb for the suffragette cause (if only a small one) in Oxted Station.

At Oxford, proving incapable at laboratory work, he switched from Biology to History, concentrating on the history of political ideas, and became a skilled scourge of the debating chambers in the feminist cause. In 1914 he tried to enlist, despite already having written anti-war editorials for George Lansbury in the *Daily Herald*, but flat feet and a weak heart rejected him, so he took the chance of a job at McGill, and he soon escaped to Harvard for four very fruitful years—fruitful in two important scholarly works, *Studies in the Problems of Sovereignty* and *Authority in the Modern State*. But McGill in 1915 had a reputation far higher than its ability to remunerate its staff (just as I found it forty years later); so with no help from his family and big medical bills to pay when their daughter was born, Laski plunged into serious and continual journalism. He was already gravely workaholic, thinking nothing of sixteen to eighteen hours of 'meaningful activity' a day. There is surely some problem for and with people who preach the cause of humanity but who have no small human pleasures. His only hobby was book collecting and his only idea of a holiday was much like that of Sydney Webb, 'some new and challenging task'. From then on fluent writing became a vice of writing too much, seldom corrected or edited—not even by Frida. Political writing, however, brought him many friends, some already famous, and gained him the fame and notoriety he plainly craved.

His first two books were widely praised both in academic reviews and in, back then, the many serious general periodicals. They criticised the theory of sovereignty and maintained that the strength of society is found not in the state but in semi-autonomous social groups (as was bluntly remarked, the odd spectacle of a rationalist Jewish intellectual applying the social theory of the Anglo-Catholic J. N. Figgis about churches and the medieval historiography of Gierke and Maitland to defend, indeed to make central to the social question, trade unions. The influence of Leon Deguit's pluralism and of French radicalism was less often noted, indeed missed by both biographies.) But the *North American Review* did complain of Laski's tendency to repeat 'essentially the same thought in only a slightly different form'. It became widely remarked that he spoke as he wrote and that this was impressive; but that wrote as he spoke was more the pity. Both authors[b] miss this.

So his essential intellectual habits were set even before he got to LSE in 1920, and his taste for public controversy whetted, sometimes thrust on him, sometimes sought after (his 'intervention' in the Boston Police strike, which soured his relationships with Harvard but not with America, was a bit of both). So too was his love of being in the know and knowing top people. Kramnick produces 'impressive evidence of Laski's skills in who he knew'. Newman quotes from a letter to Holmes about his decision to return to Britain: 'It brings (I dare to hope) some very real political influence within my grasp.' But both authors suggest a vivid mixture of self-importance and a driven conscience to speak out for political reform. Kramnick puts this shrewdly:

[b] Presumably, both Kramnick and Sheerman, and Newman. Bernard increasingly speaks of Kramnick alone as the author of the first book in the remainder of this review.

Respectable Laski was still rebellious Laski . . . His strategic efforts to acquire 'real political influence' in England in the 1920s solidified his ability, forged at Harvard, to deliver sustained and bitter criticism of the ruling class while seeking their embrace. It is, of course, not uncommon for the radical intellectual to take an outside and critical stance, often devastatingly so, like Wells or Shaw, while thriving on the company, support and applause of the very people one has mocked, satirized and sought to topple. Magnify the ambivalence and the marginality in the case of a radical Jewish intellectual in Britain, however, and one can see that while his life strategy was not perhaps unique, its intensity was.

Both books show how Laski's fame grew rapidly as he wrote obsessively at every level from learned journals to the *Daily Herald*. He never lost his pure academic interests, as shown by his lecturing on French political thought from the sixteenth to the eighteenth century and superbly empathetic articles on Rousseau, Machiavelli and Burke. I used to think that his first two books were his best because the most purely scholarly, but Michael Newman is persuasive that the first edition of *The Grammar of Politics* (1925), deliberately written to be accessible to the general, intelligent reader, is his *magnum opus* as well as his most widely read book. 'All power is federal', he declaimed, striking at both Hobbes and Lenin, even if he never fully resolved the difficulties of pluralism in accounting for political order at all. He did not throw the state away entirely, indeed in the Thirties brought it back to create a new social order in the interests of the working class; but nor did he abandon or repudiate this pluralism in the 1930s when Marxism infused his language (Marx's, of course, not Stalin's, nor even Lenin's—'interpretations can differ', he would quip. 'They read Marx in their way and I in his'). Marxism seemed to furnish an explanation of Nazism as late capitalism while liberal thought could only denounce not comprehend such violent and malevolent irrationalism. This was a nearly fatal misreading then shared by nearly all the Left. Indeed some capitalists fell into thinking that Nazism was simply (well, essentially) the only firm defence against Bolshevism. But his liberalism remained. If in any sense he was a fellow-traveller, it was only on his own terms for tightly defined, anti-Fascist international purposes. He wrote several celebrated attacks on the Communist Party for their intolerance, brutality and duplicity. Using our published Index,[c] I find a pungent review in this journal in 1938 of the Webbs' *Soviet Communism: A New Civilisation* in which he chides them for, in that second Left Book Club edition, dropping the famous question-mark of the first edition, and accuses them of a blinkered naivety on questions of civil liberties and human rights.

Laski soon took on board anti-imperialism. The timing of this was spectacularly fortuitous. He wasn't even looking for trouble when summoned for jury service in 1924: the libel action that lasted for five weeks brought by

---

[c] The somewhat idiosyncratic 1979 book-form *PQ* index covering 1930 to 1978, prepared under Bernard's tutelage (see my Introduction to this volume). There are a dozen entries for Laski, starting with 'The Prospects of Constitutional Government' in 1930, the journal's first year (pp. 307–25).

General O'Dyer against an eminent Indian jurist, Sir Sankaram Nair, for accusing him of responsibility for the terrible Amritsar massacre. Jurymen *can* ask questions; it was not in his nature to remain silent and (in trumps) he didn't. He was genuinely, deeply shocked at the blatant racial prejudice revealed, as well as at the verdict. His fame in India lasts to this day. Leonard Woolf moved in on him with his network of Fabian colonial and League of Nations support committees; lasting friendships with Nehru and Krishna Menon resulted, and LSE became the magnet for nationalist intellectuals from the Empire.

Laski's interventions in British politics began in the early 1920s with Lord Haldane as an ally, the Liberal Lord Chancellor in MacDonald's first government, as attempts to forge a Liberal and Labour alliance! But the advent of the National Government and Hitler's rise to power led Laski to think that only a revolutionary transformation of society, albeit by politics, persuasion and parliament, could prevent a new dark age over the whole world. So he became the leading spokesman of the Labour Left and an advocate of the Popular Front, trembling with Cripps and Bevan on the edge of expulsion from the party he favoured; yet soon to be elected to the NEC by the constituency parties. Throughout the war he topped the poll each year. The liberal dictum in the *Grammar of Politics* that 'liberty is the absence of those conditions that prevent me from becoming myself at my best' turned sharp Left, without signalling, into 'liberty is the presence of those conditions that can alone make me myself at my best'. In his lectures he would mock Hobhouse's version of 'the general will' ('I have never seen it walking down Houghton Street'), but an equally metaphysical virus began to infect Laski's writings and lectures, the 'Felt Needs of Our Time'—which happily led to different conclusions at different times. (In my student lecture notes of 1949 I find 'FNOOT etc.' several times in the margin. Psychologically and politically I was under the master's spell—and these good books bring it all back to me, but philosophically I had learnt in Freddie Ayer's seminar at UCL that that sort of argument was meaningless.)

Le Monde said in its obituary for Laski that he had consummated 'a necessary marriage' in the interwar generation of 'Marxism of the mind' and 'liberation of the heart'. It seems rather that this differing couple some-how stayed together in the Laski kitchen, always in tension, sometimes quarrelling, sometimes papering over the cracks for the sake of the neigh-bours, but never seriously intending to separate. Michael Newman is especially interesting on the question of 'Constructive Contradictions' (the title of his last chapter).

The quarrel with Beveridge and the University of London over public confusion between the role of a chair and the power of a socialist publicist, which led him voluntarily to give up his weekly column in the *Daily Herald*, diminished his care to share in the work of the LSE. Once he had made that one compromise, Kramnick and Sheerman show that the balance of left-wing socialism and liberal pluralism in his books and articles swung even more leftwards. But an alienation with LSE never affected his exceptional closeness to his students, his time-consuming helpfulness to almost anyone who came to him for help or just to talk the big questions. I enjoyed both privileges briefly. He made one feel good and big and determined to serve the general will, the public interest or the FNOOT. But sometimes he was generous to a fault; not all his geese were swans: letters recommending 'this most brilliant young man' to his famous friends often needed heavy salting, even binning; and he made too many academic appointments of surprising mediocrity, not even disciples necessarily (as became Oakeshott's habit). No nonsense then about advertising and appointment committees; sometimes it seemed (was old H. L. Beales's view) as if he appointed the first person who came to see him when a job happened to have come up. I think Barry Sheerman must have interviewed too many discreet loyalists among the survivors of the Thirties and Forties to give a wholly accurate picture of the intensity of fratricidal strife. William Robson (this journal's founder) disliked Laski for what he saw as his neglect of the department and incapacity for regular administration. And neither book brings out the full scandal of Beveridge's dictatorial running of the school when the LSE's Secretary became his mistress, a tyranny and duopoly that even brought Lionel Robbins and Laski into temporary alliance to get him out.

Even before the war, Laski tried actively to get Attlee out as Labour leader, albeit relations never broke down completely, even after Attlee's celebrated rebuke in 1945. Attlee thanked Laski warmly for a fierce and brilliant polemic he wrote against the Communist Party when, on the outbreak of war, they defended the Hitler–Stalin pact. And Kramnick shows Laski dutifully writing some briefs for Attlee even when he was trying to get the NEC to assert authority over the Labour members of Churchill's coalition cabinet, especially to come out with a statement of war aims that would involve radical social reconstruction. Laski took the same line as Orwell in his *Lion and the Unicorn* that the war could only be won if there was a social revolution. Rebecca West told him, among others, not to be silly. He caused the Labour leadership endless trouble, but that was what the constituency parties liked, part of why he headed the poll all during the war and so had, in turn and turn about, to be party chairman; most unhappily in 1945. Kramnick is right to air many opinions (though such prejudices feed off each other, of course, not always independent evidence) that there was something 'childish' and attention-seeking in his pulling out the rhetorical stops on everything. His views on politics and policy were serious and profound, but his political judgement often poor.

Yet, having said that, and basically agreeing with Rebecca West, Newman reminds us how prescient were some of his apparent exaggerations. In 1941 in a pamphlet 'Great Britain, Russia and the Labour Party' he wrote that if the three Great Powers failed to agree on a postwar order:

There is the danger, first, that the power of the United States and Britain to provide relief for the peoples of the occupied and defeated countries may be restricted by doctrinal considerations; and . . . the further danger that governments may be imposed on Europe less with a view to the natural evolution of social and political forces in each of the constituent countries than with a view to the receipt of Anglo-American aid . . . conditioned by a desire to make certain that the future of capitalism is not seriously jeopardised . . . Immediately the prospect of Nazi defeat becomes imminent, there will be competitive manoeuvring all over the territory in enemy occupation to secure . . . a group whose purpose may be patronised by London and Washington, on the one hand, or by Moscow on the other. . . . It may mean a return to power politics in a grim form in which the main purpose of Britain and the United States will be to prevent . . . the spread of Bolshevik ideas, while it is the main purpose of the USSR to promote that spread.

During the Cold War he became depressed and dispirited. But even during the Second World War his health began to suffer from overwork. For a few weeks he had a nervous breakdown. But on more-or-less recovering he went back to his old routines in the most difficult and exhausting of conditions, and now separated from Frida most of the week, LSE being at Cambridge and she doing war work in London. (However, not only Laski's tales grew; so do tales about him. Our twin authors were told that Laski was so exhausted in Cambridge, that Lance Beales would wheel him home on his bike. But there are dangers in memory, even Lord MacGregor's; what Beales wrote (*LSE Magazine*, May 1971) was that he would walk with Laski to the lecture rooms putting 'his impedimenta in my cycle basket because I doubted if his strength was equal to carrying them'.)

Frida began to wish that she could restrain him as well as support him: that he did too much in politics, to the cost of the quality of what he could do best—his writing—and that he did not always pick remotely winnable or prudent fights. But she found she could not. He felt passionately that the Labour Party must have democratic control over its leadership; but he also felt passionately that it was his duty to lead that fight. His inflated view of the authority of the party chairman made him an obvious electoral target, despite Churchill's gross exaggeration. But 'the period of silence' that Attlee publicly requested proved impossible, especially when he took up the Zionist cause against Ernest Bevin and the Foreign Office and when his *ex cathedra* views on French and American lecture platforms about anything and everything got reported, not always maliciously, as expressions of Labour Party, indeed government, policy.

There was the libel action following the claim in a local newspaper, but promptly reported by the *Daily Express*, that he advocated violent revolution, rather than that he said there could be violence from the Right if the Labour Party, as he thought it should, tried seriously to dismantle the capitalist system. Some have said that he was foolish to bring the action, arrogantly overconfident. But both authors point out that he had little choice if, with ten days of the election campaign still to go, he had let the libel be repeated. And he plainly thought it dishonourable to let the action drop after the gagging writ had done its work. There was no reproach at the time from the party.

417

Attlee and Morrison instructed Morgan Phillips to organise an appeal to cover the large costs, and an amazing number of prominent Americans contributed. All that was covered. There was no bankruptcy. But he was utterly humiliated. Frida wrote to a friend: 'Harold bore up well till he got home and then wept as I have never seen a man weep, and it just made me feel useless.'

Those who knew him before said that he never fully recovered his zest. But that was a relative judgement. Those of us who heard him lecture in the last two years of his life have to believe that from older witnesses, but it was hard to believe in the high rhetoric and cut and thrust of his lectures, in his enthusiasm for strange scholarly things (that the *Vindiciae Contra Tyrannus* of 1579 should be in the canon of great texts of political philosophy); in his naughtiness ('at least it can be said of Mr Attlee that he is the only Prime Minister of this century who has not committed adultery when in office'); and in his quips and sarcasms, doubtless repeated yearly. 'And finally Rousseau developed persecution mania, for the very good reason that he was persecuted.' 'The Wars of Religion came to an end when Henri of Navarre decided "that Paris is worth a mass", which let me assure you, from my own experience, it is.' Finally he simply brought on a collapse by overexertion in the general election campaign of 1950. Organising the overflow meeting in Red Lion Square, I last saw Laski being supported against falling by Norman Mackenzie and others as they helped him from the car to the platform of the Conway Hall.

Among the tributes when he died Leon Blum, Newman relates, compared him to Montesquieu and Tocqueville, claiming that no one else in Europe or America had ever had such a profound and original knowledge of democratic thought in the period since the seventeenth century. And in Britain Beloff spoke about 'the Age of Laski'. But so quickly after his death his reputation declined dramatically. I think of how Orwell's increased dramatically after his death. Had it all been just the hypnotic magic of his spoken words? Of course it is not the business of biography to discuss what happens after death, or to speculate what might have happened. But the question is interesting and both books touch on it and give much the same answer: the Cold War. His attempt to synthesise Marxism and liberalism, never much more than a rhetorical and emotional synthesis, was pulled apart violently, and not much left useful to either side. And Kramnick shows how in America J. Edgar Hoover's long-kept 'Laski file' (ever since the Boston Police Strike in 1919) began to surface into the hands of predatory senators. Almost any one he had met regularly or had contributed to the libel trial fund, from Eleanor Roosevelt down, became some sort of Communist or un-American Lefty. When James Forrestal, the US Secretary of Defense, went mad, thinking that the Reds were coming through his windows, he mouthed Laski's name repeatedly in paranoid terror. All this is now set down.

But there are other reasons too. The writing that gave him such a public reputation was almost all instant, reactive polemic—even if learned polemic ('theoretical polemic'?)—and the shelf-life of that can be as short as Burke's 'flies of the summer' if its literary merit is not high. His best academic thinking was in the first two books and the associated articles, and his later books were too often repetitive and even tired. *The Grammar of Politics* could have still reached the educated public, but somehow (a large question) after 1950 there was steady decline in political publishing and political writing. The exception to this was the rise of the New Left after 1956 and one might have thought that Laski's attempt to fuse Marxism and liberty would have interested them; but though they talked 'praxis' they had no interest in political practice or in writing that could actually reach working people. The school of Althusser and his Paris rivals saw Marxism as an almost autonomous realm of high theory, so as much as any High Tory they dismissed Laski's writings, if they knew them at all, as mere journalism; and they wrote off the entire history of democratic socialism as bourgeois revisionism.

With university expansion there was a great increase in academic political publishing, but Laski's books were no longer professional enough and the discipline became internalised; almost no one seemed to see the need (except this good old journal) of reaching out to the public (something for extra-mural departments, if at all). And Political Philosophy as a discipline became very much more rigorous under the influence both of logical positivism and then the linguistic school, but just as internalised. Laski was not a real philosopher by those standards, and perhaps only now has enough time gone by to see that he must be an important part of the history of ideas in this vanishing century, if ideas are admitted sometimes to reach, even to reflect, public opinion.

So is there a lasting legacy or was his just a very interesting life at a very interesting time in a bygone past? Both books end by saying something more than a justification for a biography. Both agree that the kind of pluralism that Laski advocated is now becoming dominant in reformist thought, whether some of its advocates recognise the paternity or not. Paul Hirst, an ex-Althusserian turned Fabian, has edited an anthology on pluralism which is half Laski. Newman gives the clearest account of the validity of this, Kramnick and Sheerman incline to think more of the role of the publicist: 'Laski was at bottom a mass preacher and public teacher', a 'public intellectual' they well say. They are kind to quote in their conclusion my opinion on this: 'Laski's greatness was as a teacher and preacher, not as a political philosopher'. But perhaps to split a hair, I think what I meant, or should have said if I had their book then, was that while he is not a political philosopher as academics understand it, yet he was one as the public once understood it and, in principle, could again. So I would have him enduring as not only a 'public intellectual' but as a 'public philosopher'.

Forgive self-quotation but reviewing these two fine biographies has been difficult, a little painful, obviously raising matters close to the bone, revealing my feelings towards Laski as very ambivalent, and revealing almost an anger that he wasted too much of his talents, did not concentrate on what he did best. However, Newman does attach a greater importance to Laski's political thinking than do Kramnick and Sheerman, and he does this by what theatre folk call 'a framing device'. And to my pleasure but slight worry he uses a recollection of mine to furnish that device. He concludes his Introduction:

According to Bernard Crick, Laski's advice to students when studying Rousseau was as follows: 'Do not falter at the formal contradictions of his arguments, which are legion, but endeavour to discover what is the animating inwardness of the man.' As Crick suggested, I have tried to apply the same principles to Laski in an attempt to discover and explain his 'animating inwardness'.

I certainly agree that this 'charitable' interpretative principle should be applied to understanding Rousseau and I was, indeed, implying that it helps with Laski too; but precisely because of his unresolved philosophical contradictions. And Newman does this so well. So it explains Rousseau's and Laski's behaviour biographically and their great appeal historically and psychologically, but it does not warrant a suspension of philosophical standards of judgement, There are some. Logical contradictions are not good for any argument. When he calls his last chapter 'Creative Contradictions' I am worried that some sort of dialectic is implied. That from out of contradictions comes a higher synthesis. No: the dynamic born of contradictions can only construct a life, activities, not a philosophical justification. Biography and the critique of texts are, though they may concern the same person, different activities: 'the life of the mind' is only a metaphor.

These are excellent biographies, of a different kind. But perhaps Michael Newman should now compile, now that interest is aroused again, a big enough anthology of Laski's political thought to show his depth, range and *diversity*. This might meet some of 'the felt needs of our time'—an example for each one of us (and that includes the Labour Party) to start thinking again in terms of principles, never mind that we will never wholly agree.

Political Thought in Ireland since the Seventeenth Century, edited by
D. George Boyce, Robert Eccleshall and Vincent Geoghegan; *Northern Ireland: The Choice*, by Kevin Boyle and Tom Hadden; *De Valera: Long Fellow, Long Shadow*, by Tim Pat Coogan; *Straight Left: An Autobiography*, by Paddy Devlin; *Heresy: The Battle of Ideas in Modern Ireland*, by Desmond Fennell; *Paddy and Mr Punch: Connections in Irish and English History*, by R. F. Foster; *Ireland Today: Anatomy of a Changing State*, by Gemma Hussey; *In Search of a State: Catholics in Northern Ireland*, by Fionnuala O Connor; *Northern Ireland: Sharing Authority*, by Brendan O'Leary, Tom Lyne, Jim Marshall and Bob Rowthorn[a]

Vol. 65, no. 3, July–September 1994

Publishers are not always as venal[b] and calculating as one thinks. When it comes to Ireland, especially Northern Ireland (or the North of Ireland, to please Desmond Fennell, or better a lower-case north) they often seem to lose their wits and act responsibly. There is only one book in the latest offerings whose publishers have clearly decided that no person will buy it, only university libraries—to whom some Houses are more like leeches than chemists. Otherwise this is a bad time for political publishing for the general reader. Well, perhaps some interest in the Balkans, even the Baltic states, and the rain of titles on the break-up of the Soviet Union continues, general and academic. But when did one last see a good book for the general reader on British or American politics? Premature biographies of living statesmen supply most of our political knowledge other than what we do get from the quality media, but they carry the misleading implications that it is all a matter of personalities and connections, not of systems, structures, interests, ideologies.

De Valera is, however, a case where one great man had the kind of influence that Thomas Carlyle preached and L.G. unhappily exemplified. But in some ways Gemma Hussey's urbane book about a modernising Ireland is proof that now twenty years after his physical death, he and his political church-state all but politically dead, whatever the Nationalist writer and resurrection-man Desmond Fennell complexly and confusedly thinks, 'Dev', as John Bowman proved in his study *De Valera and the Ulster Question*, and Tim Pat Coogan confirms in painfully objective biography, beat the drum of anti-partition and Irish unity every year, making it the ethos and shibboleth of Irish politics, but without the least idea of how to achieve it or even any ritual

---

[a] Routledge, 227 pp, £40.00 (Boyce et al.); Penguin, 256 pp, £6.99 (Boyle and Hadden); Hutchinson, 772 pp, £20 (Coogan); Blackstaff, 303 pp, £8.95 pb (Devlin); Blackstaff, 289 pp, £26.00 hb, £9.95 pb (Fennell); Allen Lane, Penguin Press, 382 pp, £22.50 (Foster); Viking, 536 pp, £18.99 (Hussey); Blackstaff, 393 pp, £8.99 pb (O'Connor); IPPR, 155 pp, £9.95 (O'Leary et al.).

[b] The journal article had 'venial' here, which was presumably not intended. Bernard would probably have inclined to the view that publishers' sins were more often mortal than venial.

preparation for its miraculous coming. When Churchill's emissaries dangled baited carrots under his nose in time of war, he picked up his skirts and ran, choosing undiminished independence and neutrality rather than the risk and disruptions of 'unity'.

Bowman and Coogan will think that I have misread them. Diminution of Irish independence was never at issue. Not then, but I suspect that, as the two governments now publicly acknowledge what they have for twenty years agreed in private, that Northern Ireland is a common problem, indeed a common nuisance and tragedy, the reality begins to dawn in Dublin that any form of unity or joint authority would involve crippling costs, both in harmonising welfare payments and in holding down the UDA and their ilk. Only the British government could pay for it; no gain for them, but if they did it would entail them being involved in the finances and administration of the Republic at every level, openly or surreptitiously, perhaps consistently tactful but more likely erratically meddlesome. All thoughtful schemes for sharing authority have implications quite as worrying and muddling for the Irish sense of independence as sovereign power as they do for Unionists. Unionists notoriously only see joint authority as a threat to them, not as a big pill to swallow on both sides of the border. As the British government moves to put some institutional structure—the double referendum of the joint declaration—behind its still somewhat ambiguous tolerance for 'unity by consent', informed opinion in the Republic begins to see that joint authority is not a one-way crossing of the border.

If there comes a time when a unity referendum takes place in Northern Ireland, it would be fatuous (even on the demographic guesstimate that by 2010 there will be an adult Catholic majority) to believe that 'the community' would vote as one irrespective of what is then on offer; what changes had meanwhile been made in the Irish Constitution, what were the provisions for reconciling two very different kinds and levels of social services and welfare? Women have peculiar interests in some of these questions and are a wild card in voting behaviour on both sides of the border. Whether the Republic would really vote for 'taking on' the North is also contingent on events and what would be in the package.

Tim Pat Coogan's magisterial book both helps and reflects the passing of the mythological stage of Irish history. It has long been possible to have a clear sense of Irish identity, albeit a changing identity, as Gemma Hussey and her hero, Mary Robinson, demonstrate without being supercharged with bad history. The Unionist leaders' sense of identity, unhappily, seems bound up with change-resisting myths. No one has yet stood up to the Unionist community and said, as the leaders of the *Broederbond* did in the Afrikaans community six years ago, 'if we try to save everything, we will lose everything'; and they then went on in a widely circulated document to consider thoughtfully 'the minimal conditions for preserving an Afrikaans culture'. No one in the leadership of the UDA has shown that kind of sense, and courage. Glenn Barr might have done, but he pulled out a decade ago. John McMichael wanted some discussion of it, but he was killed by the IRA, probably with the connivance of his own men, possibly for other reasons as well.

Fionnuala O Connor's important and interesting study[c] certainly does not suggest a dramatic sea-change in the dominant consciousness of the Catholic community in the North. She ends by warning against the belief that the armed struggle is a phoney war now rejected utterly by most of the community. The ambivalence towards the IRA is deep, it depends on what is happening, is highly situational; and yet this is true for many within Sinn Fein. Her warning is necessary because the newly differing attitudes she finds to fundamental questions, to unity and what form it might take, to the authority of the church, to the advantages and disadvantages of some British connection, dispel any idea of a monolithic community. But to recognise an increasingly pluralistic community only opens more doors; it does not dictate any clear path towards peace and justice. Northern Catholics still feel threatened, if not as desperately as even twenty years ago; but their sense of identity never depended on threat alone and if its security becomes not inconceivable within a restructured North, this would not ensure the end of Nationalism.

More and more SDLP leaders now think that *they* (John Hume sits on a pedestal beyond all criticism) may have made a mistake in not joining the 'Prior Assembly' and in going all out instead for the 'Irish dimension'. It now looks as if social justice in the North could revive some power-sharing parliamentary scheme. If the IRA will not renounce violence for politics, then the Joint Declaration closes the door on any political (or any other) hopes of even 'some form of unity in an Ireland of the future', as Hume used to say; or rather it closes it for this generation, until a parliament in the North has worked for long enough for the two communities to agree what form of relationship they want with both the British and the Irish states. At that stage the part imaginative and part scholastic 'shared authority' scheme of Brendan O'Leary's colleagues could come on to the political agenda. But it is necessary to be realistic about the time-scales needed for social change to match political invention, and for a new generation of politicians to emerge. Joint authority imposed without the agreement of a common democratic institution could prove as fragile as the present system.

The present generation of political leaders on both sides of the divide manipulate myths of the past against the future. They are as frankly opposed to modernisation as is a basically traditionalist Nationalist intellectual like the tireless Desmond Fennell. He attacks Seamus Heaney for sitting on the fence and for not using (say rather abusing) his poetic powers to illuminate a solution. His popularity he attributes to escapism, not to the accessibility of his language and the wisdom of understanding life as dilemmas and uncertainties. And Fennell's disdain for the great generation of Irish revisionist historians is even greater. He prefers the old mythic stuff. It is almost as if

[c] The book would go on to win the 1995 Orwell Prize—a prize for political writing set up by Bernard Crick with *PQ* sponsorship and first awarded in 1994 (see my Introduction).

he fears for his own identity without the drug of bad history. His type of Irishness, perhaps; but there are others.

Whatever form of new relationship emerges between North and South, whether hard or soft, real or symbolic, the problem will remain of relations between the two communities in the North. Inventive constitutional changes could leave them much unchanged, quite as bad. It is to this question that Kevin Boyle and Tom Hadden address themselves in an updated and concise recycling of their important ideas on communal coexistence. Should the object of public policy in the North be the integration of the two communities based on human rights and common citizenship; or should it be a recognition of the equality of two communities based on the invention of institutions for communal government to enable Catholics and Protestants to govern themselves with minimal need for contact and cooperation? Perhaps the only possible path to the former is through the latter. Toleration does imply recognition and acceptance of differences. Be that as it may, the book summarises all hard evidence on existing degrees of separation, as well as things in common. For a less theoretical feel of 'what it is like on the ground' and a different type of Irishness than Fennell's, Paddy Devlin's autobiography could hardly be bettered: ex-IRA, labourer, trade-unionist, founder member of the SDLP, an effective minister in the ill-fated power-sharing government, and a turbulent jack-of-all-causes once described as 'the coarsest man who ever faced the British government, all in all an unquenchable fighter for peace, respected across the lines not just in ecumenical no-man's land.

The three academic books in this pack stress, doubtless to Fennell's horror, interconnections. There is no true narrative of any national history in these islands that must not deal with mutual influences and with close interactions. How wisely the symposium title their pioneering book *Political Thought in Ireland* rather than *Irish Political Thought*, even if that means austerely sidelining Edmund Burke himself, the greatest Irish, one of the greatest English, the truly British political thinker. Roy Foster's *Modern Ireland* strove manfully, masterly to keep Ireland the absolute centre of the picture, while not ignoring the wider context, culturally or politically. But his splendid new book is unashamedly partisan for moderation: picking cases that show mutual influence, connections and diversities rather than the harsh nationalist tale of oppression and unbridgeable differences. It is not always borders that matter so much as the ease with which people, ideas and loyalties can move across them, back and forth. And it is this that makes good British–Irish relations the real ground for hope, in the long run. 'You've got to understand what it's like on the ground', they used to tell me—which I would repeat in a voice throbbing with realism. It took me over ten years to answer back, 'Yes, but you've got to lift your heads and look at the context which can help you, crush you or abandon you, but cannot solve your problems for you.'

Citizens and Subjects, by Tony Wright; *Politics in an Anti-Political Age*, by Geoff Mulgan[a]

Vol. 65, no. 4, October–December 1994

Tony Wright remarks, in a book that will surely be numbered among the few classic essays on the British constitution, that being redeployed from university to Parliament and seeing it at close quarters 'has done nothing to diminish my belief that here is a system in urgent need of concerted constitutional reform. Quite the reverse'. The diagnosis and prescription are familiar but have never been more clearly put and grounded in a deep understanding of the established theories of the constitution, and their effective hostility to real popular citizenship. They are designed to make us look up and not around. He reminds us that Dicey believed that the absolute legal sovereignty of Parliament was no threat to liberty because of the context of political sovereignty, so that 'speaking generally, a Parliament would not embark on a course of reactionary legislation . . .'

The real restraint was, of course, the political culture, a 'play-the-game political culture' and 'benign because the system was in the hands of gentlemen'. The Old Marxist Left went on about the class system but was seldom precise about beliefs and movements within it. Now the age of the Old Tories, of gentleman, has gone, destroyed or taken over by the new capitalism, the new men and women who have few ethical restraints, other than the criminal law, on what they will do for money or power. The Old Tories valued intermediary institutions and public service and spoke of local government as the school of representative institutions. The new Conservatives scorn all three, and, unrestrained by a constitution, have created a nexus of patronage and corruption which is more like a throwback to the eighteenth century than an advance toward the twenty-first.

Wright sees no perfect answer to the exploitation of the British system, or rather its breakdown as a justifiable and effective system. The complexities of modern society and of the United Kingdom in particular, both territorial and functional, mean that reform will not be 'to embrace a single-channel formula' or a 'uniform method'; he wisely says that 'a certain untidiness is the hallmark of a vigorous pluralistic democracy'. This is a gentle reproof to, on the one hand, a certain ahistorical rationalism in Charter 88 at its worst (oh, at its best . . .), and, on the other hand, to some of his fellow MPs whose minds are still set on a centralised pattern of reform and who might, especially with the precedents set, be as intolerant towards Tory counties as Mrs T. was to metropolitan cities, when in wrong hands. He quotes Dennis Kavanagh: 'The central issue in British politics has not been how to curb the electoral dictatorship but how to capture it.' Yet the answer to this obsession (the religion of the Palace of Westminster) given by Wright is not pious liberalism

---

[a] Routledge, 157 pp, £9.99 pb (Wright); Polity, 215 pp, £11.95 pb (Mulgan).

but a salutary reminder of how ineffective this centralised system has been in the business of good government, the inability to mobilise popular participation for anything other than occasional elections. Instead of citizens we have chartered consumers, and only then at the price of not noticing the unemployed.

Both authors see the need above all else to explore and expand the democratic dimension of politics, and to breathe into it an ethical spirit, both of restraints, of how we behave to others, and of objectives, of how we work with others to define and achieve public goals. Geoff Mulgan begins his analysis with the philosophical worries way back about the compatibility of classical notions of civic virtue, civic republicanism, and the personalities needed to make a success of a civil, trading society. Can there be, as it were, a market economy (for there seems no other method of pricing goods compatible with liberty) without a capitalist personality? Otherwise 'it makes politics little more than a balancing of interests, devoid either of any mission or of any overarching criteria of judgement'. So we need 'a new politics'. But then what he argues for becomes appealing to the ear but extremely slippery to grasp in the hand: this new politics, a postmodern democratic decentralised global order. Too often he stands, as Laski once described the World Government, with both feet firmly planted in mid-air. The difficulty and confusion arises from his definition of politics (or is it only of a corrupted politics?) as 'balancing of interests'. Yes, up to a point; but in politics there are always ethical interests as well as material. The balance may sway, but always both; an absolute contrast is a false disjunction, encouraging melodramatic theoretical polemic in favour of ethics but without definition or diagnosis. And the ethical interests in different cultures need specifying, which is where Wright's generalisations are so much more concrete: the tension between the English gentlemanly ethic and the capitalist ethic, for instance. That is largely why we are in such a mess and do not have a proper constitution.

Now Mulgan's book is a collection of essays rather than a systematic argument. Such speculation is needed. We need to see different paths and some long-term visions beyond the ends of our noses. And now in launching the good ship Think Tank Demos Geoff Mulgan enjoys a kind of holiday creative freedom from the school discipline and short-termism of working for the Party and Gordon Brown, or any other front-bencher for that matter. But I do hope that when his holiday mood is over he will come down to earth for a while and begin to dig, as few others could so well, into the political middle period of policies, quite unrestrained by party prudence and nervousness but voluntarily restrained by realism and the need to convince those who need to be convinced—not just his friends and most of us. Meanwhile if a non-socialist picked up Tony Wright's brisk and cogent book, there is a chance he might be stung to thought; but if Mulgan's abstract discourse—alas, no way could he fathom it.

Townscape with Figures: Farnham—Portrait of an English Town, by Richard Hoggart[a]

Vol. 66, no. 1, January–March 1995

Where are the great Labour intellectual teachers gone? Why are there no heirs in the first division to Laski, Tawney, Cole, and in the second to the Brockways, Brailsfords and Martins? Perhaps odd to call Leonard Woolf 'a Labour intellectual'; *sui generis* sure—I never cared or dared to label him anything in his age to his face, but he edited this journal long enough and sat on or in about every Labour and Fabian committee on the colonies there ever was.

And I ask myself uncertainly if the style of my first paragraph is affectionate irony or loving emulation of Richard Hoggart, his easy mix of the informal and the formal, of cultural references and colloquial tone? Do we fail to recognise great teachers like Hoggart and 'Cherry' Halsey because they merely live and write like exemplary democratic socialists rather than theorise about it all the time? Both Hoggart and Halsey were ignored or scorned by the dandy theorists of the New Left who dominated discussion for so long before harsh events exposed the hollow abstractness and silliness of much of their internalising, self-indulgent, escapist discourse. Common sense, like the novel and parliamentary government, was bourgeois. Indeed it was and is, if one accepts that at the heart of the matter the aspiration of the democratic left and the working classes is towards a middle-class classless society.

It is forty years since *The Uses of Literacy*, which Hoggart had wanted titled *The Abuses of Literacy*. His description of the impact of mass-culture on northern working-class life between the wars carried no grand theoretical framework, was descriptive but none the less invoked moral judgements by the standard of what ordinary people can do in making good things, facing moral dilemmas and reading complex texts. And so the book was, in the language of his critics, 'unresolved'; some good things had gone, some opportunities had been missed but the poor had not been brutalised: amid poverty they still practised neighbourliness and mutual aid and they respected education and wanted good schools. Hoggart's only method, like Orwell's, appeared to be direct observation; but both their observations were tuned to a critical moral sense and wide and deep reading. There was no need to go on and on about presuppositions and theory: they were there well enough in known brands of humanist moralism; or to be posh, varieties of Protestantism without God. (I'm sure Hoggart would agree, out of respect for other people's feelings, to give a capital to a non-existent entity.) And they both saw the lower middle class as the key to the future, either the leaders or the betrayers of 'the common man' (a concept they both preferred to 'the people'). On them depended whether the new literacy of the working class would be a ladder of education or an instrument of trivialised debasement.

[a] Chatto & Windus, 205 pp, £16.99.

Almost by accident Richard Hoggart came to live, stay and retire in Farnham. And now he has written simply from his own perambulating observations an account of the southern middle class under, on the whole, prosperity. He rejects moralising but is proud to be a moralist (a left-wing Leavisite if you want a label). But can he still go back to the supermarket safely? He meditates[b] sadly on the clamorous rudeness of a well-off permed and Burberried woman to an old fellow 'lower in the social scale' who gets his trolley in a twist. Is he being unfair, he worries, to generalise from one horrid woman to a whole class? Allowing for exceptions, he thinks, on the whole, not. Indeed, they ape the gentry but at least the old gentry had some public manners. And can he now stand prudently on the railway platform? He finds the faces of the first-class commuters unattractive, not just because of 'signs of over-eating and drinking'; they are 'watchful, calculating, knowing. They would not use such a vulgar expression as "no flies on Charlie" but they hint at a more sophisticated version of it . . . The range of permitted, accepted, learned expressions is remarkably few.'

Looking at people such as these you may try hard to be as charitable as possible; but it would be a fudging lie not charity to say that the faces and language in themselves suggest comedy lives, the devotion of good school teachers or the disinterested patience of craftsmen, or the selfless absorption of a good scholar or a scientist.

Some reviewers have said that all this impressionistic stuff tells one more about how Hoggart thinks than about—God help—Farnham. True, but they miss the achievement: Hoggart expresses how many of us think, our best prejudices at any rate, far better than most of our theorists, statisticians and— dare one say?—new political leaders, whom we think think like that but are so worried at causing offence that telling examples of foul class behaviour never cross their lips, only of bad policies condemned in bland language.

The book is, of course, a serious impression of the life of a town, and as beautifully and thoughtfully written as his volumes of autobiography, to which it is a worthy pendant. It will get a wider readership than a social survey, and provoke more thought—perhaps thought about how our civilisation could adapt itself to make such places more like communities and less what he calls fractured and porous societies: neighbourliness only practised within class peer-groups and collectively able to absorb most challenges without changing. But could he not have given us, without confusing observation with research, one set of figures that are surely key to his continuous concerns? He is ironical that the Farnham Public Library (which once, together with free schooling, were seen as the key institutions of popular democracy) is now lumped together as 'leisure services' with parks, sports and entertainments. He notes the 'dreadful fear' that like 'earnestness' would be 'divisive and judgemental'. He takes an angry side-swipe at a chief librarian (somewhere else) who told him 'that to insist that some books are better than others is

[b] The journal version has 'mediates' here.

pure cultural elitism' (the ideology that infected his old Birmingham Centre for Cultural Studies); but also hits out at the new managerial ideology of 'getting the maximum reader-value out of available shelf-space'. Yet he doesn't ask the librarian what books people actually read, a question that could be answered thanks to Public Lending Right statistics, whose gathering Hoggart supported in the financial interest of authors.

The literary man and the social observer sometimes pull apart. It is lovely to recall the observations of former Farnham men, William Cobbett and the country novelist George Bourne (George Sturt), in contrast to Farnham today. But that is not direct observation, so why draw the line at using library statistics to ground his hypotheses and fears about reading habits? Otherwise people say, 'Oh that is just old Richard'. No, it is far more than that. Here is a digressive but formidable statement of the cultural values of democratic socialism. I suspect that Halsey might feel the same respect and yet regret—shelter behind his venerability—that his friend has not used shoe leather and notebook a little more. The book has all the virtues of biographies written by novelists, but also a few of the drawbacks.

The *RSA Journal* (July 1994) printed 'The Abuses of Literacy', a lecture in which Hoggart drew the moral of 'Farnham' explicitly and movingly and linked it to a clear restatement of *The Uses of Literacy*. (M. Mowlem should read the book, but must pass the lectures for duty and policy around the front bench.)

Humour and History, edited by Keith Cameron[a]

Vol. 66, no. 1, January–March 1995

Bad government can be controlled by many social mechanisms. Sometimes by law, sometimes by elite or public opinion, sometimes by non-compliance, foot-dragging or strikes by the lower orders, or sometimes by threats or forms of violence—assassination, riot, terrorism, rebellion or revolution. Textbooks classify and reclassify. But I know of no systematic study of what can be and often has been a very obvious and useful element of social control of government: satire.

Any such study would, of course, like others be unsure empirically which is cause and which is effect. Can mockery and ridicule as autonomous forces bring down a government or even a regime, or are they but symptoms of a government or regime already falling into contempt ('delegitimisation', they say)? A few years ago Steven Lukes and Isaac Dhror[b] edited a book *of* (alas,

[a] Intellect, 158 pp, £14.99 pb.
[b] This is an error for Itzhak Galnoor, possibly one of transcription from unclear handwriting as a proofreader would not necessarily recognise the problem. So unless this 'old friend' also went under that other name, it also suggests that Bernard as literary editor didn't check the proof of this final review of that issue—perhaps because it was a last-minute addition and there

not on) political jokes. They were most unfunny on the printed page when removed from any context, and my two old friends were lazy in not trying to establish a provenance of first occurrence and location. The Grandmaster of the Orange Lodge joining the Catholic Church on his deathbed ('If there's any dying to be done, boys, better one of them than one of us') should have been put alongside the version of the Berliner Jew joining the Nazi Party. And 'There'll be dreadful trouble in town tonight, stranger; there's a white girl a-marrying, a-marrying a banker' was heard on the Rand in the 1910s as well as in Tom Watson's ante-bellum Georgia.

So I was seriously hoping that these lectures given at the University of Exeter and now nicely published would be or contain a serious study of power of satire in politics. But 'humour', to be fair, was the theme; and humour, it soon emerges—with 'Humour in the Bible?' (the question-mark is warranted), 'The Devil and Comedy' and 'Psychoanalysis and Humour' etc.—is too broad a concept for any theoretical coherence in Professor Cameron's circus of learned wags, let alone to marshal forces for a methodology of political satire.

However, three contributions might stimulate political scientists and commissioning editors to think how to bring satire into the conceptual frameworks of social control ('Is he serious?' 'Yes, very'). John Wilkins begins his 'Abusive Criticism': 'I begin with a scurrilous [and untrue, *ed.*]^c statement: '"John Major became Prime Minister because he had been buggered by Nicholas Ridley on many occasions." This statement, insulting to both politicians and homosexuals, would be unusual in British culture. In ancient Athens . . . it was a familiar assertion . . .' And what follows is astounding, but different only in degree, I think, not in kind from *Private Eye* habitually and from that one, perhaps yet fatal, misjudgement of the *New Statesman* about the PM and the cook. Susanna Braund's 'Paradigms of Power: Roman Emperors in Roman Satire', however, is an unexpected and uneasy reminder of how satire could be used and controlled by the state. To explain why satire of the state is tolerated today is not, she says, her field; but she provocatively speculates that the satiric impulse today 'is used by those who run the mass media primarily to boost their own popularity ratings'. But that was certainly not the case in the powerful, staggeringly scatological, and apparently effective, satiric attacks by cartoon commissioned by Walpole's enemies—the first chief minister to fall without impeachment or exile—as is shown in Peter Thomson's studious '*Magna Farta*: Walpole and the Golden Rump' (copiously illustrated).

was no time. The book was Steven Lukes and Itzhak Galnoor, *No Laughing Matter: A Collection of Political Jokes*, Routledge and Kegan Paul, 1985.

  ^c The disclaimer is in the original.

The Republic of Letters: The Correspondence between Thomas Jefferson and James Madison 1776–1826, edited by James Morton Smith[a]

Vol. 66, no. 4, October–December 1995

Once upon a time it was possible and actually happened. Affairs of state were, for an all too brief period, in the hands of thoughtful and highly literate men who believed in the power of reason and in reasoned advocacy. Not all were like that, of course, but the intellectual vitality of Jefferson, Madison, Hamilton and Adams was no disadvantage to them when used in public debate. Jefferson and Madison enjoyed among themselves openly an exchange of opinions on everything that seemed important in the world, not just practical politics. Reading this now, and pulling down from the shelf after twenty years the Adams–Jefferson correspondence (printed and edited with an equal high excellence), the impact tears me between exaltation that it was possible at all, and anger that none now can match it. Today only a very few newspaper columnists sustain a reasoned political debate in public.

The letter, the pamphlet and even the book are almost dead as public modes of political thinking. Political thinking of a high quality does exist, but it is almost entirely by and for academics—the appalling cultural paradox of a political thinking divorced and remote from the needs and concerns of public politics. There is now a considerable large and subtle literature about the concept of citizenship and a revival of the eighteenth-century concept of 'civil society'; but none of this reaches citizens. A Harvard historian, Perry Miller, once called the political writings of the late Colonial and early Republican periods 'citizen literature'—a familiar literature aimed at and comprehensible to all literate citizens. Before the Yellow Press, if people read at all they could and did read much more deeply than electors today (to call most people citizens in anything but a legal sense is mainly loaded rhetoric). After all, the book that was read by nearly all the newly literate was the Bible—not (as a casual glance at it will show) an easy read. Good pamphlets had wide circulation and the newspapers carried reasoned speeches and public letters of political leaders in full. The debasement of literacy (what Orwell bitterly satirised as prolefeed) is undeniable. It is hard not to think that trivialisation is a weapon of political control; or it may just be that the market works to give people what they could not possibly want if they could stop to think at all.

Jefferson was the democratic idealist and Madison the republican realist. When Jefferson wrote from Paris, excited by the revolutionary turbulence and innovation, 'no society can make a perpetual constitution', Madison wrote back: 'a government so often revised would become too mutable to retain those prejudices in its favour which antiquity inspires, and which are perhaps a salutary aid to the most rational government in the most enlightened age'. But, on the other hand, the principal draughtsman of the Declaration of

[a] W. W. Norton, 3 vols, 2,073 pp, £100.00.

431

Independence was able to persuade the main draughtsman of the 1787 Constitution that it was, contrary to Madison's first intention, incomplete without a Bill of Rights. We have today no political leaders who can get to the heart of both the theory and practice of constitutional government, and reason with each other (and all of us) over differences. Think of our suited fools in office who confuse legal sovereignty with political power, who rattle the scarecrow bones of 'a federal [sic] super-state', who think the EU principle of 'subsidiarity' stops at Whitehall, and who believe that 'United Kingdom' implies one nation and 'the Union' a uniform and uniformly centralised state. James Wilson of Pennsylvania was reported as saying, when supporting the 'Great Compromise' in the Philadelphia debates, that 'he was for raising the federal pyramid to a considerable altitude, and *for that reason* wished to give it as broad a basis as possible.'

Postmodernism, Reason and Religion, by Ernest Gellner; *Anthropology and Politics: Revolutions in the Sacred Grove*, by Ernest Gellner[a]

Vol. 67, no. 2, April–June 1996

Ernest Gellner will remain one of the greatest voices for truth and reason within the academy of our times. He was little known outside the academy (largely due to the ignorance of most literary editors in the quality press, even though his work is aimed not at subject specialists but at anyone interested in ideas), but within it he ranged—and often raged—free. Original research and thinking in anthropology, original thinking in philosophy and sociology gave him the solid basis for critical assaults and judicial ridings far beyond. Are we not all voices for truth and reason, according to our abilities and opportunities? He thought not, and—if one can face it—he was right: so much in social thought is fashion, professional opportunism and an easy tolerance of other meanings and discourses, a tacit avoidance of questions of truth and moral judgement, or as he tersely puts it: 'Total permissiveness ends in arbitrary dogmatism.'

The permissiveness to which he refers is not, of course, seducing your neighbour's spouse, smoking hash or encouraging single women on welfare to have babies, but rather intellectual permissiveness. In one of his earlier gatherings of essays he propounded a modern categorical imperative: 'social tolerance, always; intellectual, never'. So the main target of both these books, the one his sixth collection of essays, the other a long essay printed as a book, is 'relativism'. Relativism may seem a surprising target for a polymathic, socially tolerant man who found, indeed, nothing human uninteresting.

The argument goes like this. The world dominance of the West in the last century was a product of science, technology and industry, at least partly

[a] Routledge, 108pp, £5.99 pb (Postmodernism); Blackwell, 260pp, £35.00 hb, £19.95 pb (Anthropology and Politics).

caused by a new type of secular reasoning from the previous century usually called 'Enlightenment'. Hardly surprisingly, paternalistic, condescending attitudes were formed towards traditional societies or undeveloped societies. So, properly, if not inevitably, a reaction followed in the thinking of often guilt-ridden Western intellectuals. Anthropologists discover relativism. Irrationalities and superstitions have meanings and work within a social system. Values and beliefs function as self-contained systems. Science becomes a Western set of values (however much everyone wants and uses it, he adds).

Long ago Gellner pointed out that this is all very true, up to a point: the point at which some beliefs—that prayers and sacrifices bring rain to arid land or fertility to women, for instance—hinder the survival or betterment of many communities, let alone shut them off from such ethnocentric, liberal, neo-colonialist namby-pamby stuff as notions of universal individual rights to life, liberty and happiness. (I stumble into Gellner's kind of brutal irony, which is not always noticed by his more wounded readers.) So extreme has this reaction to Victorian ethnocentricism become that it now seems that 'anything goes' so long as it is a coherent system of meaning, or even if incoherent (for coherence entails much sweat), so long as it is an authentic utterance of a liberated individual. That is why postmodernism comes in for lethal side-swipes. In the last essay, 'The Coming *Fin de Millenaire*', he quotes a marvellous passage from Musil's *The Man without Qualities* about the revelling in 'new everythings' in Vienna of the 1890s. That was fun, he sagely comments, but

this time round, however, it is not obvious that there still are any certainties to be undermined. Scepticism or the overturning of truisms by now has an inverse or boomerang effect; by undermining the criteria of all rational criticism, it confers *carte blanche* on any arbitrary intellectual self-indulgence. Total relativism ends by underwriting cheap dogmatism. If anything goes, then you are also allowed to be as utterly dogmatic as you wish: the critical standards which might have inhibited you have themselves been abrogated. What can there be to check you? He who tries to restrain you, in the name of fact or logic, will be castigated as positivist, or imperialist, or both: after all, objectivism was at the service of domination. Total permissiveness ends in arbitrary dogmatism.

The *fin de siècle* was liberating, the *fin de millenaire* may be wilfully destructive.

Relativism is one of three views that Gellner sees as the main contestants for legitimate belief in the modern world. The other two are religious fundamentalism and what he sometimes calls, with a self-deprecatory irony, 'rationalist fundamentalism' or else 'Enlightenment rationalism'. His explanation of why Islam sees a revival of fundamentalism has been hotly debated, but to deny the facts hopefully and accuse him of 'orientalism' does not seem very helpful. His sympathies are with those who suffer because of fundamentalism; but its dominance in modern Islam, compared to the 'facile ecumenical relativism' of most contemporary Christianity, is obvious. It refutes the 'inevitability of secularism' thesis, he says, however much we might wish otherwise. He does not favour living our lives according to

433

'claims for localised cognitive authority, known as Revelation', confessing himself to be 'a full-blooded, committed believer and an intellectual adherent of Enlightenment doubt'. For doubt, discovery and test are the methods of science. The commitment to truth in this perspective is a commitment to unfolding truths, not final truths as in these 'local revelations'. But these local revelations gain in strength amid modernity and relativists must accept them as a package.

Science, however, he reminds us with brusque common sense, is a universal phenomenon, 'doubly transcendent' indeed: first because its laws of nature work throughout the world, secondly because they appear to work in the universe. But it is a commitment to procedures, not to substantive values. Values are relative, up to the point that they do not deny or obscure cognition (or, I think he might have added explicitly, threaten other cognitive beings). Relativism is perfectly appropriate to how we choose the wallpaper and furnishings, but if the house is not built according to scientific principles it will fall down, or at least not last as long as those that are. Life is, of course, a series of compromises between the constraints and opportunities of material nature and the relative choices of society; but viable compromises must recognise this duality, indeed a hierarchy within it with reason on top. Following Gellner, I see it this way. The child challenges an injunction: 'Well, that's what you think.' Rationality begins when the parent demands: 'What if everyone did that?' and didactically points to the likely consequences of pursuing such a course of action as a rule, or even 'just when I feel like it'.

Gellner is at pains to stress, very much as Karl Popper did, the tentative nature of knowledge. No two accounts of scientific method agree, but there is usually a consensus among scientists as to what is knowledge. The only rules are procedural rules, how to proceed. Unlike revelation, they do not beg the question of where we are going, nor, like the relativist, do they say it is all a matter of taste or chance. At this point one might expect him to have related this to the thoughts of his 1994 book *Conditions of Liberty: Civil Society and its Rivals*. Popper had, after all, made a very serious attempt to tie the experimental method of science to a procedural rather than a substantive theory of democracy. But surprisingly he doesn't. It would have taken only a paragraph. Did he take a lofty and impatient 'done that' view—let the reader do some work? Or would it have taken only a paragraph? For there is a big problem that he never faced. It would not affect his moral stance but would modify his sociological account of modernity: that the political, republican tradition preceded modern science, industry, enlightenment—Aristotle, Cicero, Machiavelli, the city-states and all that. Science and republics? As Yeats remarked, 'Which the rider, which the horse?'[b] And is not the idea of constituting a social order to make decisions politically by public debate as much 'Western' as science, and as capable of export?

Of course, unusually among social scientists, Gellner's favourite form was

---

[b] A favourite quote of Bernard's, to be found in several places throughout this volume.

the essay, not the would-be definitive monograph (too often rendered definitive by crushing its borders drastically); so speculative, open-ended, stimulating, critical and shameless in crossing borders; at times a little self-indulgent (but then, that warns the reader that he or she is joining in an argument with a person who thinks ideas are of the utmost importance, not a sermon to others); at times too fond of paradox (as if Bertrand Russell trying to be G. K. Chesterton); but also at times just a little hasty, a little too impatient to get on to the next big theme to bother to consolidate and relate his positions. Others may now try. Two more books, it is said, are in the press. So no final statement—even from those, of course.[c] There are no final statements; there is only the life of reason (or perhaps better, of reasoning). He led that life to the full, to the enlightenment of so many of us.

Hitler's Willing Executioners: Ordinary Germans and the Holocaust, by Erich Goldhagen[a]

Vol. 68, no. 1, January–March 1997

Rarely has a book on any subject so divided expert reviewers from what I will call in a polite way professional reviewers (to say 'journalists' would lump together those whose only knowledge of the subject is that it is important, terrible and always compelling, with those who read serious books on 'the Final Solution'). The difficulty is that here is a book by an assistant professor of Government and Social Studies at Harvard which is based on an extra-ordinarily ambitious PhD thesis that gained the American Political Science Association's Gabriel Almond prize for comparative politics; and a book, moreover, that by size and footnotage (almost 150 pages of apparatus) looks overwhelmingly scholarly but is written with polemical anger and presented by both author and publisher as if intended to be a best-seller (which it has indeed become, on both sides of the Atlantic), showing the public, says the jacket, 'that none of the established answers hold true'.

Let me just say at the beginning that this is, indeed, as many academic and specialist reviewers have already said, an arrogant claim, for the simple reason that if 'none of the established answers hold true' it can only be because *some* of them are also theses of a single cause, a single explanation. Indeed, the claim is false in that most of them do make some useful contribution to understanding and explaining an event that plainly had no single cause and can have no single explanation. The publishers further claim that this is 'a work of the utmost originality and importance—as authoritative as it is explosive—that radically transforms our understanding of the Holocaust and of Germany during the Nazi period'. Most historians review-

[c] Ernest Gellner had died in November of the previous year.

[a] Little, Brown, 619 pp, £20.00; Abacus (pb), £10.00.

ing the book have taken the view, in the words of Wolfgang Mommsen, that it 'sets Holocaust studies back twenty years'. For it revives a view dominant after the war, even among the guilt-ridden and self-flagellating new generation of German historians, that the Holocaust was the product of the long history of German antisemitism, or, crudely, 'the national character'; or, more subtly, of 'the special course of German history', the *Sonderweg*, its exceptionalism in the European tradition.

If the 'overall objective of this book is to explain why the Holocaust occurred', then Goldhagen right from the beginning, and then with endless, angry and passionate repetition, through every source and every atrocity he analyses, argues that it must be found in the nature of German society and beliefs.

The conclusion of this book is that anti-Semitism moved many thousands of 'ordinary' Germans—and would have moved millions more, had they been appropriately positioned—to slaughter Jews. Not economic hardship, not the coercive means of a totalitarian state, not the psychological pressure, not invariable psychological propensities, but ideas about Jews that were pervasive in Germany and had been for decades, induced ordinary Germans to kill unarmed, defenceless Jewish men, women and children by the thousands, systematically and without pity.

The subtitle of the book is portentous, a direct rebuttal of Christopher Browning's *Ordinary Men: Reserve Police Battalion 101*. A strength of both books is that they examine not just the camps but also the far more open and less secretive killings by soldiers behind the lines, probably as great in extent as those in the gas chambers if Russians, Slavs of all kinds, Poles, and Gypsies and other *Untermenschen* are added to the grim account—but this Goldhagen never does: the book is remorselessly, myopically, obsessively about Jews and Germans. Browning's book was a case study based on records and interviews with survivors not of an elite formation but of Police Battalion 101, middle-aged conscripts from Hamburg (notoriously to the Nazis, a Social Democratic town). They obeyed orders to kill thousands of Jews, Poles and captured partisans. Browning finds initial revulsion and reluctance, then a gradual and disgusting brutalisation. But Goldhagen, going through the same material as part of his much wider study, finds a willing acceptance of the task as 'all for Germany' and as the logical culmination of their antisemitism. Browning thinks that 'ordinary men' are capable of being active agents in genocide in such circumstances, namely those of total war. This view of the importance of war as such, brushed aside by Goldhagen, is shared by the Israeli historian Omer Bartov when he speaks of 'the reality of acclimatisation in war' (and I think that is what Pat Barker's recent trilogy of novels about the First World War is about—how decent men can commit inhuman deeds).

Goldhagen, however, thinks that only Germans were capable of the Holocaust, and that the war was only the opportunity; and he assumes, rather than argues, that the Holocaust was a unique event, quite unlike any other genocide (almost as if, as one Israeli historian has said with terrible irony, 'it is a Jewish possession').

Goldhagen sees his 'first task' to be 'restoring the perpetrators' to their proper name 'by eschewing convenient, but often obfuscating labels like "Nazis" and "SS men", and calling them what they were, "Germans"'. He even makes, in a tortured footnote, a 'terminological problem' of how to refer to German Jews, because, he says, 'Germans' when contrasted to 'Jews' seems 'to imply that the Jews of Germany were not also Germans'. Therefore, 'I have, with some misgivings, decided to call Germans simply "Germans" and not to use some cumbersome locution like "non-Jewish Germans". Thus, whenever German Jews are referred to as "Jews", their Germanness is implicit.' It is as if it physically hurts him to write or say 'German Jew'. (His father, to whom the book is dedicated as 'father and teacher', was not German Jewish, it is fair to note—he was in a class I tried to teach long ago at McGill—but a Romanian Jew who somehow survived Treblinka.)

Now, there is no possible doubt about the extent of virulent antisemitism in old Germany, even if a good deal of doubt whether it was inherently, somehow immanently, 'exterminatory' or, as Goldhagen sometimes more cautiously says (without appearing to notice a rather important distinction), a deeply rooted desire to 'get rid of the Jews'. So Goldhagen has some trouble comprehending why so many German Jews who could have left hung on so fatally long, even after the *Kristallnacht* of 9 November 1938; why they thought that violent antisemitism was a Nazi aberration and that enough good Germans remained to protect them with good values, which they, the assimilated Jews, after all fully shared. Several of my best friends are the children of—to Goldhagen—such fools. He is, of course, wiser than they (after the event). But in any case it was a German culture that the exiles, those who did get out, preserved.

The strength and challenge of the book is its range. Goldhagen takes the camps almost for granted. He even admits, assumes or implies that there are plenty of good scholarly accounts of their workings, let alone the literature of the survivors. But he has four chapters on that one Police Battalion, and has no difficulty in showing by many references that these 'ordinary Germans', to him 'willing executioners', were unlikely to have been exceptional. He has three chapters on the relatively neglected 'work camps', arguing plausibly that any idea bureaucrats had that these camps could be efficient and useful for the war effort were hopelessly compromised not just by antisemitism, but by his continual a priori assumption of an 'eliminationist anti-Semitism'. Therefore debilitating and destructive punishment, not production, was the operating ethic.

Two chapters on the final death marches, when camps were abandoned in face of the final Soviet advance, show that the crazy hatred reached new heights of irrationality: the guards marching their charges nowhere until most dropped dead from starvation and exhaustion, instead of, with a rational prudence, abandoning them and losing themselves in the floods of German

437

refugees. He makes a strong case that the skeletal Jews were mocked by many ordinary citizens as they were marched west, and a still stronger one that most bystanders did nothing: they threw no stones but they gave few crusts.

He brings to the attention of the general reader what has long been known to scholars: that knowledge that the concentration camps were in fact extermination camps was far more widespread than early studies had suggested. Granted, he prejudices the reader towards that conclusion by dealing first with the letters to mother, with accompanying photographs of Jews being hung or shot, that ordinary soldiers had sent home from the Eastern Front. It was, indeed, presented as a race war and fought as a race war, against Slavs as well as Jews. But nonetheless he makes a real point about civilian knowledge of the camps too, even if many established scholars of the Holocaust are greatly divided about how widespread was such knowledge. I read the consensus among historians as agreeing that the true purpose *was* known outside the wire, but only locally; and even within the party and the bureaucracy only on a 'need-to-know basis', even if the organisation and resource demands of the 'Final Solution' made that need more widespread than first studies had supposed. But no one doubts the *almost* universal guilt of 'not asking' what had become of neighbours and fellow Germans.

This almost universal guilt as sin of omission is, however, not enough for Goldhagen. Three summary chapters begin the book with a very familiar, if highly contentious and simplified, intellectual history of nineteenth- and twentieth-century Germany. The section heading says it all: 'Understanding German Anti-Semitism: the Eliminationist Mind-Set'. What needs proving he simply assumes from the beginning, so that by the final section, 'Elimina-tionist Anti-Semitism: Ordinary Germans, Willing Executioners', he has accepted his own initial assumption as proof and, therefore, the only explan-ation needed of it all.

An historical debate rages between the 'intentionalists' and the 'function-alists' to explain the Final Solution: was it Hitler's original intent which he could not realise except in time of war? Or was it a ghastly but largely unpremeditated side-effect of ridding Europe of Jews but finding nowhere to put them? The Battle of Britain had made the Madagascar project totally impossible, and the stalemate on the Moscow front removed the Siberian option from the drawing boards, while policy-makers grudged the resources to feed them. Even when social antisemitism had become crazily and wickedly exclusionist, there is still a chasm of explanations to be crossed to reach the final horror of genocide, even within the mentality of some party members and state officials, let alone most ordinary Germans.

Goldhagen, of course, regards functionalist and contextual arguments not just as nonsense but as a modern German evasion, special pleading, distan-cing, obfuscation. And he ignores the reasons why some American, British and Israeli historians, not just Germans, have pushed, in different ways and to different degrees, in that direction. He radiates scorn and contempt over those who would think that any true account must contain elements of both, like

Browning in his *The Path to Genocide: Essays on Launching the Final Solution* (1992) or David Cesarani's painfully judicious introduction to the scholarly anthology he edited on the controversy among historians, *The Final Solution: Origins and Implementation* (1994).

Goldhagen, like all polemicists, seems innocent of any acquaintance with 'the fallacy of the excluded middle', or the more general opinion of historians that great events seldom have a single cause. Not merely is the eliminationist intention of Hitler clear to him right from his first speeches and writings (which is at least highly plausible—how sick at heart one is to recall A. J. P. Taylor and many others dismissing all that as mere rhetoric); it is equally obvious to him that Hitler was preaching to the converted.

This book is a sadly clear case (of a kind discussed in the late Ivan Hannaford's *Race: The History of an Idea in the West*, reviewed below[a]) of falling into the same concepts as one's enemy; a racial account of a particular racism, indeed, what Omer Bartov called in a review 'a bizarre inversion of the Nazi view of the Jews as an insidious, inherently evil nation' (*New Republic*, 29 April 1996).

That is a harsh thing to say, though other reviewers have hinted this more delicately. But to attach eliminationist antisemitism uniquely to Germany is to be anti-German to an unpardonable and irrelevant degree. What of the Lithuanians, the Ukrainians, French and Belgian[b] fascists even, and many others who did their squalid bit? So many of the *kapos* were from the lesser breeds within the law. Certainly 'the Jewish Question' dominated the Nazi theory of race, but it was a comprehensive theory. It graded most of humanity in ranking order; many other groups were classed as degenerative and better off for 'us' to be without. And if the Holocaust was unique, genocide is not. A lot of the author's historical argument depends on an assumption that Germans are specially prone to it and good at it. He might have spared a casual word for the Croats in those happy times, or the Serbs yesterday; or the Congo in good King Leopold's golden days; not to mention Pol Pot. Rousseau once wrote that when he thought of Nero and Caligula he rolled on the floor and howled to think that he was a man.

It is truly astounding that this book in its thesis form could have got the American Political Science Association's prize for 'comparative politics', for there is no sustained comparison in it whatever! Thus its methodological claims are doubly fatuous. They are fatuous in terms of empirical political studies: the book simply ignores evidence contrary to the author's long discredited hypothesis. And they are fatuous in terms of the modern history of political ideas: Goldhagen has no grasp of how complex and subtle the debate has become on distinguishing rhetoric from real intention, or of the many possible relationships there can be between values (good or bad, explicit or implicit) and policy. He is an angry bull in a cluttered china shop.

---

[a] It was the subject of the next review in the same issue, by Andrew Sharp.
[b] The original article has 'Belgium' here.

The questions arise: 'Why the award?' and 'Why the best-seller status?' Well, there are few PhD theses of such a scale, with so many footnotes, so much moral intensity and such sweeping claims to importance. Perhaps there was some nervousness about what would be thought if they did not make the award. But with deliberate bathos may I remark that the Government department at Harvard and the APSA in their turn should have had a subject specialist as one of the examiners, even if it meant crossing disciplinary lines for an established historian of the Holocaust (except that he has attacked nearly all of them).

The best-seller status is due partly to the super-hype of its American launch by Knopf, but this blitz depended on the real need of each new generation for a popular book on the Holocaust. In fact, this is a very demanding book; but it is presented as if it were popular. Actually when the general reader reads it, or more likely dips into it, he or she will find a more balanced account of the whole killing of Jews than in those many books for which the Holocaust means the extermination camps alone, not also the atrocities in the fields, behind the lines, in the work camps and in those final death marches. All that is badly wrong is his simplistic explanation of why it all happened: a unique German eliminatory antisemitism.

Finally two rather different, but equally difficult, issues worry me about the book's publicity and popularity, although I am the last to want to throw stones at any author who tries to reach both a popular and an academic audience. One must doubt if most American readers, including Jewish readers, are as anti-German as Goldhagen appears to be, or take his main thesis as seriously as he would wish. Germany has become, after all, a favoured ally of the United States. Most Jewish readers may have had other thoughts in mind. Some publicists and organisations are, after all, notoriously trigger-happy in asserting that any criticism of the State of Israel is anti-Semitic, or that any criticism of a book by a Jew on the Holocaust is really aimed at the State. By now the old issue of German or Nazi guilt is almost an irrelevance to Jewish opinion; but memory of the Holocaust is, of course, understandably and properly important in maintaining Jewish identity, especially the identity of the non-religious, in a more-or-less secular but nonetheless semi-Christian and still not always fully welcoming society. So passionate remembering achieves a kind of transference into the defence of the State, making criticism of Israel's Palestinian policy untouchable.

My other worry is that the common reader, gentile as well as Jew, will probably skip the intellectual history anyway and go for the vivid accounts of the horrors and atrocities. In the culture of our times the existence cannot be denied, in cinema, television and newspapers as well as books, of voyeuristic attraction to horrific violence. Truths about terror need handling so delicately. Those to whom accounts of the horrors are already familiar must surely yearn for a balanced popular exposition of the many causes and conditions that led to the Holocaust, and the scholarly debate about their overall relative importance. Browning's *The Path to Genocide* has come closest to what is wanted. But, alas, most scholars of the Holocaust are no better than other historians and social scientists in writing mostly for themselves, not thinking of the reading public. So they get the Goldhagens they deserve.

Every decade needs a Holocaust book, and this one may perhaps, in the publisher's 'mind-set' (whatever the author's intention), have ridden on the back of *Schindler's List*, but with the twist (so good for controversy and publicity) not of one good German but of all Germans bad. But this raises quite other large questions about the relationship of learned books to popularisation, and the differences between the culture of university presses and trade presses—issues of moral responsibilities as to method, manner, motives and market.

Second Class Ticket: The Neglect of State Education, by P. W. Turner[a]

Vol. 68, no. 4, October–December 1997

This is an extraordinary book. The author came up through the common schools and started work as a railway clerk at sixteen, but pulled himself up via teacher training and the good old London external degree to become a college lecturer, then an education officer and an inspector of schools in both Devon and London. In 1988 he retired (in near despair, I surmise, at what was being done to the schools even then), but then devoted five winters to teaching in secondary and special schools to prepare for writing this book. From this mixture of knowledge and chalk-face experience has come a grimly well-informed polemic, totally free of jargon, deliberately and well written for the common reader.

I do not wish to disparage the in-house press of Sheffield Hallam University's 'Learning Centre' (except for their pricing policy), nor to exaggerate, but that he could not find a leading publisher for this remarkable and important book, written at times with cool passion and at others with angry common sense, could prove to be almost as great an indictment of the judgement of certain publishers (I burst to name them but won't, not even the one that kept him dangling and then published Melanie Phillips's prejudicial outpourings) as the case of Orwell and *Animal Farm*. But here there is no happy ending; newspapers and periodicals simply will not look at, let alone review, books coming from the in-house presses of the new universities. This may be understandable in most cases, but in this instance it is a major public loss.

The book was written long before Labour came to power. But it is clear that the author would have little confidence that the scale of the problem of run-down and neglect is being faced—or should I more tactfully say can be faced? For he makes clear that there was never a golden age. British society has been

[a] Sheffield Hallam University Press, 156 pp, £9.00 pb.

such that from the beginning of compulsory secondary education in the nineteenth century, it was always going to be a minimal service with low prestige attached to the local authority teacher (it can be different; think of France, Germany, The Netherlands and the Scandinavian democracies). And he may, though I must not put words into his mouth, have little confidence that this government[b] will get off the backs of the teachers and let them teach, concentrating intervention on teacher training rather than on detailed class-room practice. Bad teachers and bad schools are in a minority, but governments find it easier to attack bad teachers (usually following glib press reports) than to give most teachers the support they need.

Phil Turner reminds us that state schools 'started on a shoe-string budget doled out by a grudging government as second class provision for *other people's children*' (my italics). Successive governments cannot, he argues, rise above a determination to ensure that schools are 'good enough rather than good'. But central management has grown because ambitious ministers have to be seen to be doing something. He sees the imposition of a national curriculum as something of a national disaster (and, I add, how quickly we have taken it for granted, as even New Labour appears to do, that the state should control the curriculum—has all that talk and theory of pluralism and of community gone with the wind?); and that this nationalisation arose from the 'need to do something' rather than from any real need in educational terms. Needs were invented to justify policy.

Joseph's successor, Kenneth Baker, seemed equally unacquainted with the facts but determined to do something. What is more, the something in question had to be cheap to implement and had to echo as far as possible the ideological dogma of his party. Not surprisingly, most of the changes that it eventually brought about were at best irrelevant and at worst acutely damaging.

Well, Kenneth Baker did know something. Being chairman of the Hansard Society at the time, he had read and understood the report of a committee I chaired published as *Political Education and Political Literacy* in 1978. Together we argued with Shirley Williams for money for in-service training. But when in office Baker dropped it like a hot brick. Civic education, almost incredibly—and here Britain is proudly alone in Europe again—is not part of the curriculum.

That, however, is a self-indulgent side issue. In a statement that will please no one but is plainly true, Turner says: 'At the centre of the problem lies the fact that our schools have never been given enough money to do the job properly. We have never had an administration with the vision, the under-standing, the moral courage or possibly the desire, to recognise education for what it can be, the primary mechanism of social engineering.' (For the author's sake, I remind that this book was written before New Labour's manifesto.) Social engineering for what? He points out that it would take two

[b] This review would have been written two or three months after Tony Blair's first government came to power.

442

generations in school, but, given enough money (he bluntly avoids the sweeter word 'resources'), crime could be reduced dramatically and economic potential transformed. Yes, it would be expensive; but it is possible. Nibbling at classroom practice and further overloading and confusing the teachers will get nowhere; indeed, intervention without economic investment could, from his experience of teaching in some of the run-down schools, make things far worse. 'Throwing more money at the problem', as Lady Thatcher put it, is not the answer—not the full answer; not a sufficient condition, but a necessary condition.

Turner likes military metaphor. He has written on military history, oddly. 'Defeat at the hands of the Kaiser's Germany', he concludes, 'would have been chastening but would not have destroyed social stability in Britain; the shameful inadequacy of our present education system might do just that.' He could be right. How I wish this book could reach everyone concerned with the education of, in Lady Plowden's once famous phrase, 'all our nation's children'.

The History of Government, by S. E. Finer. Volume 1: *Ancient Monarchies and Empires*. Volume 2: *The Intermediate Ages*. Volume 3: *Empires, Monarchies and the Modern State*[a]

Vol. 69, no. 1, January–March 1998

'The intention of this work is to provide a history of successive forms of government throughout the world from the earliest times to the present day.' This is not a book to be read at one sitting; and this cannot be a real review, only a notice. Your editor[b] resisted the temptation to commandeer all the review space and go to earth for three months to write a proper review: so much to read, so many key references to follow up, so many other views to consider about almost completely unfamiliar territory, so much to argue with; but in the end, whether the review be long or short, whether the work be closely read line by line or (as I had to) skipped and dipped over a four-day 'long weekend', there must be great praise—sadly, of course, posthumous praise—for what may be the masterpiece of postwar British political studies by the liveliest, most wide-ranging and also most methodologically eclectic and personally eccentric of scholars. It is, alas, an unfinished symphony: he died two chapters short of his goal and with some parts unrevised. The main editor, Jack Hayward, and friends who read the full manuscript, notably

[a] Oxford University Press, 1,701 pp, £100.00.
[b] Bernard, in other words—still Literary Editor of the journal, as he was to remain for another two years. Following the policy that had evolved from the days of the first incumbent, Leonard Woolf, the Literary Editor had *de facto* autonomous control over the reviews section of the journal (see my Introduction). Bernard could have given the whole section over to this set of books if he had wished.

Vernon Bogdanor, have been wise to let well alone, only to follow fairly full notes he left and earlier writings to complete the 'Conceptual Prologue'.

So, only a notice: but this is a book to take notice of. Some of us may never finish reading and rereading it. The sweep of it is so vast that many qualifications can and will be made on the parts of which any one historian reviewer has special knowledge; and any political or social theorist worth their salt will feel quibbles or anxieties about its complex classificatory scheme and the general theory of government, not always explicit, that it presupposes. But what must not be done is to doubt the importance of the enterprise, to doubt that it fills a huge gap in political studies. How odd, once one comes to think of it, that there are all those histories of political thought and yet virtually no serious attempts, until Finer, at a history of government. How odd that so many of the writings on the institutions and policies of government are so shallow in historical understanding—say, most of the American school, with Sam Beer as a precious exception—when the most obvious explanation of why and how something occurs (and even a socialist should give a grudging bow to Oakeshott or Burke while saying so) is that something analogous occurred in the past in recognisably similar circumstances. Sir Frederick Pollock's lectures, published as *An Introduction to the History of the Science of Politics in 1890*, long ago pointed to the need for such a history as Finer's, and Carl J. Friedrich of Harvard, in his two uneasy hybrids of textbook and monograph, *Constitutional Government and Democracy* (1950) and *Man and His Government* (1963) showed that he had the capability and the sense of the interdependence of historical and political knowledge to have taken on the task—but didn't. Only Finer saw it through, or nearly through.

Perhaps the missing final two chapters are not total loss. Political science reviewers would have fastened on to them to the exclusion of the unfamiliar histories, which are the point; and Sammy might have been, it is fair to say, grossly tempted to let fly in his polemical mode at his favourite bugbear, 'adversary politics', let alone socialism of any kind (would Blair have puzzled or pleased him?). His polemical side comes out in his completely ignoring Perry Anderson's *Passages from Antiquity to Feudalism* and his *Lineages of the Absolute State*, also an ambitious, if a less comprehensive and more theoretical history of government, but a Marxist (or rather, *marxisant*) history; and even a born-again ex-Communist could come under Sammy's ban, as witness the fate of Karl Wittfogel's masterly if highly contentious *Oriental Despotism: A Study of Total Power*. But I would like to have known his reflections, thinking as he has done on a world scale, on whether the political method and any kind of government we have known can cope with humanity's largely uncontrolled gradual destruction of our habitat. I suspect that he would have been justifiably pessimistic, and certainly not because he knew *he* was dying when he came near to the book's inconclusive end.

The size of this enterprise (Sammy's retirement project and total preoccupation; the word 'obsession' is perfectly fair and non-pejorative to any who knew him) is partly explained by the determined effort that this most cosmopolitan European made not to be Eurocentric. Ancient China looms large. 'We ought, therefore, to bypass European experience and generalise from the entire universe of past politics. We can also forget the preoccupations of the 1960s with development and modernisation. Our interest in state-building goes simply as far as it affects how a polity is governed.' He strenuously seeks to avoid both Eurocentric assumptions and the pretentious teleological nonsense of Fukuyama's 'end of history' or 'contented capitalism'. He does so in the scope of the book but less certainly in his implicit judgements—Enlightenment views of reason, toleration and freedom, albeit in a Tocquevillean mode of conservatism (and 'Why not?', one hears the ghost of Ernest Gellner egging on his friend to ignore both the silly postmodernists and the absolutely value-free positivists).

Now, just a parochial twist of the tail: the editors tell us that Finer was turned down for a grant by the then SSRC, which doubted the project's viability given, for example, its proposed 'combination of historical and analytic typologies'. Happily, the Nuffield Foundation proved more intellectually open-minded than these hidebound idiots of professional social scientists mistaking their demarcations for knowledge. Few of their favourite projects will ever equal this in scholarly importance. Scholarship is sometimes too important to be left to scholars.

Liberty before Liberalism, by Quentin Skinner[a]

Vol. 69, no. 3, July–September 1998

'This essay by one of the world's leading intellectual historians is a major scholarly contribution, with full apparatus, which in its first part seeks to excavate, and to vindicate, the neo-Roman theory of free citizens and free states as it developed in early modern Britain.' For once, zealous and cynical collector though I am of blurb and jacket copy, the above sentence can be wholly endorsed—except that I have tampered with the Cambridge text by adding 'intellectual' in front of 'history'. If I had thought it proper to go further I would both qualify and strengthen by deleting 'one of' and substituting '*the* leading historian of political ideas in the world'. There may be better historians to come, but none in the past has been so well equipped both by his methodology and his analytical subtlety to build on the great progress of historical knowledge and method of recent years. Progress has been especially great in recovering the meaning that past political ideas had to contemporaries. Skinner has been at the heart of this movement and one of its prime movers.

Politicians and even reading journalists don't know it, but we are in a great age of political thinking—of academic political thinking. Elsewhere and often

[a] Cambridge University Press, 142 pp, £19.95 hb, £6.95 pb.

I have railed against the tragic chasm between academic and practical political thinking (if a politics of soundbites and sentimental generalities can be dignified as thinking). This chasm began to open up in the 1920s and 1930s and became deep, on the one hand, with the excessive specialisation and internalisation that went with postwar university expansion, and, on the other hand, with politicians losing belief in rational persuasion in favour of following opinion poll data as if the gospel truth of a *vox populi* who think themselves *vox dei*. But no more of that today.

The blurb stresses 'full apparatus'—a phrase that does not normally warm the blood like wine—and the book is not an easy read for the non-historian. It moves heavily on well-leaded footnotes. Any zest of a true lecture (for this is an expanded version of his inaugural lecture last year as Regius Professor of Modern History) has gone; but the matter is important and Quentin Skinner was obviously determined, once and for all, to show the Cambridge History Faculty that political ideas can be 'true history'. There are two types of inaugural: those that reach out beyond the faculty or department to give others in the university some idea of what another subject is about ('sounds like we've got another journalist') and those determined to show their specialised mastery to their peers ('very impressive indeed, but not quite my field, of course'). Skinner made the usual Cambridge choice. And he uttered reassuring words to those sceptical that any truly scholarly approach to political ideas is possible. He brushed aside any suspicion that 'intellectual historians should turn themselves into moralists' (well, there was another Cambridge tradition): 'My own admiration is emphatically reserved for those historians who consciously hold themselves aloof from enthusiasm and indignation alike when surveying the crimes, follies and misfortunes of mankind.'

But there is a moralist struggling to get out, and the moral has never been more important. Does not the very combed-over blurb say 'vindicate'? Why has he spent, like John Pocock in his great *The Machiavellian Moment: Florentine Political Thought and the Atlantic Republican Tradition*, so much time reviving memory of 'the neo-Roman theory of free citizens and free states in early modern Britain' of his obviously beloved old commonwealth men, Nedham, Harrington, Milton and so many lesser figures, and contrasting their republicanism to modern liberalism? Presumably because he finds something of perennial value, not just a sad memory of good old times gone by in the belief that the state should not simply be the provider and guarantor of each individual's liberties under the law (and then to hell with political activity, or leave it to others), but should be a perpetual public arena of active citizenship. His seventeenth-century republicans believed that political activity by citizens was a school of moral virtue and a guarantee against the abuse of liberty by even the most well-meaning regimes. Liberties granted too easily either create apathy, so that future abuses are harder to resist, or lead to a purely utilitarian frame of mind; if most people are happy, what matter the form of government or whether elections for a new smiling government are all we need care about? Quentin Skinner, indeed, leaps into modern times to attack Isaiah Berlin for believing that liberty can be no more than not being interfered with, rather than also the positive opportunities of citizens to achieve the safety and welfare of the state and a free society.

The nominal presupposition of this historical essay is that the republican tradition is now dead. Certainly it is diminished, but perhaps he is overly pessimistic and categorical on this point only to remove any Cambridge suspicion that he studies the seventeenth-century republicans for any modern motives. His formal methodology must tell us that meaning is contextual to its era, but what he chooses to study is plainly no accident. And when he invokes Henry Sidgwick to show that nineteenth-century utilitarianism had a purely negative view of liberty he breaks his own methodological rules that he has applied so brilliantly to the early modern period. Don't just look for the big texts to understand the political concepts of an era, consider their context, both political and intellectual; who were they writing for and why? If one takes such a wider view of the last two centuries, many, perhaps most, reforming pamphleteers have argued for or assumed the activist, neo-Roman view of citizenship. He allows that the Chartists were a partial exception, as citizen-activists, not seekers for a settled liberal order under which we all can safely limit political activity to an occasional vote. But he ignores both the radical Liberals and the whole of the rank-and-file participative, community-based ideology of the Labour movement until—well, virtually last week; so too early to say with either regret or confidence. Orwell was far from alone in arguing (see especially his *Lion and the Unicorn*) a recognisably republican, not a liberal position. Charter 88 is a fascinating hybrid, some muddle perhaps, but also some sign that the two positions are not entirely incompatible, or can each fit some aspects of government and society better than the other. I came to think (and have said in later editions) that my *In Defence of Politics* was in this tradition; and have recently chaired a most diverse and respectable committee into stating that active citizenship, not just respect for the rule of law and (what tends to be) rote learning about formalised rights, should be encouraged through and even in schools.

It is quite unfair to wish that Quentin Skinner had written another book addressing an intellectual but less scholarly audience; however tightly he claims to have sealed the cork on the old wine of Algernon Sidney's 'the Good Old Cause in which I was for my whole life engaged', there is still a fermenting pressure in the bottle—relevant, important, difficult, not entirely lost; still all to play for, whatever, indeed, the odds. Nothing was or is inevitable. The Whig interpretation of historian was, indeed, as false as the Marxist; but the moral ideal remains, as Quentin's fine obsession with the seventeenth-century neo-Romans paradoxically demonstrates.

2000s

Tailpiece: Clearing Up after Myself

Integrity in the Public and Private Domains, edited by Alan Montefiore and David Vines; *The Sovereignty of Parliament: History and Philosophy,* by Jeffrey Goldsworthy; *The Politics of Nationhood: Sovereignty, Britishness and Conservative Politics,* by Philip Lynch; *Orwell's Politics,* by John Newsinger; *British Social Attitudes, 16th Report: Who Shares New Labour Values?,* edited by Roger Jowell, John Curtice, Alison Park and Katarina Thomson [a]

Vol. 72, no. 1, January–March 2000

What have these books got in common? Very little, except that they are all interesting books that I regret not sending out for review before handing over as Literary Editor to the capable and as yet unwearied hands of Donald Sassoon.[b] A Literary Editor's lot is not a happy one ('Books Editor', really; but the grander title suited *PQ*'s first incumbent,[c] Leonard Woolf). One can dread public occasions like book launches or conferences, when one is haunted by silent reproaches ('You didn't review my book') or the explicit 'I have a book coming out . . .'. Lord Randolph Churchill's aphorism becomes mandatory: 'Never explain, never apologise.' 'Looked a re-run of your last one.' 'So glad you got your thesis published at last.' 'It looked boring.' 'I did send it out but the reviewer defaulted' (a positive critical act? laziness? taking on too much? useless to enquire). 'We can't do everything.' 'A good book indeed but already well covered in the quality press.' 'Too academic for us.' 'Too journalistic for us.' So allow me a sentence or two of appreciative penance on a mixed bunch.

The Montefiore and Vines is tough stuff. Nothing technical at all, but intellectually very demanding, closely reasoned argument about real problems involving a concept or virtue we often refer to but rarely characterise. What does it mean to have integrity? Here is modern moral philosophy at its best. Paul Flather restates the Major Barbara question hypothetically in an essay entitled 'Should Mother Teresa Accept Money from the Mafia? A note on ethical dilemmas raised by fund-raising and giving'. Michael Pinto-Duschinsky provides a detailed case study and commentary on 'Fund-raising

---

[a] Routledge, 342 pp, £60.00 (Montefiore and Vines); Clarendon Press, 319 pp, £50.00 (Goldsworthy); Macmillan, 201 pp, £42.50 (Lynch); Macmillan, 178 pp, £42.50 (Newsinger); Ashgate, 380 pp, £27.50 (Jowell et al.).

[b] This review was set out separately after the main review section at the very end of the journal issue, hence the 'Tailpiece' of the title.

[c] As Literary Editor (from 1958).

and the Holocaust: the Case of Dr Gert-Rudolf Flick's Contribution to Oxford University'. Here, indeed, moral philosophy and philosophers go into action against, on the whole, economists or the excessively market-minded. If there is a moral to this extended Aesopian non-fiction fable it is simply, of course, that *if you sup with industrialist philanthropists, you need a long spoon* (just as they want value for money). In our brave new world of 'partnerships', voluntary sector and business or state and business, the kind of issues raised in this book could concern readers of and contributors to this journal more and more.

Particularly interesting is Mark Philp on 'Citizenship and Integrity'. In a long essay he contrasts the classic Aristotelian, republican view, that acting as a citizen is essential to a good life of personal integrity, with the humanistic view that personal integrity is possible even in an autocracy, and the liberal view that protection for a fulfilled private life is the main object of enlightened legislation. Each viewpoint has its integrity; he sees no moral or philosophical grounds to privilege any one over the other. This is a salutary pin prick, at least, to those of us who push the primacy of the political and the public life too far. 'Yet, not withstanding these sceptical caveats,' he says, 'the arguments advanced here show that modern democratic states will be politically stable only if most of their citizens see compliance with their civic responsibilities as a requirement of personal integrity.' But then he also sees the tension between the idea and practices of a pluralistic culture and the investment of modern states 'in developing a political culture in which citizens see their political standing and its responsibilities as a constitutive component of their individual identities'.This puts me in two minds whether I would have liked him on the advisory group on 'The Teaching of Citizenship and Democracy in Schools'. Alas, one makes progress faster when one does not question every assumption so closely, as from time to time one must.

Goldsworthy's *The Sovereignty of Parliament* is indeed its 'history and philosophy': an immensely learned book, old-fashioned legal scholarship at its best but with obvious contemporary relevance. To whom should I have sent it for review? A political act. Perhaps to Professor John Griffith, who would applaud its defence of the doctrine of parliamentary sovereignty, especially the denial that judges have ever had or should ever have authority to invalidate statutes; or to Professor Neal McCormick,[d] who would say that 'sovereignty' is not a necessary concept either to explain or to ensure social order, and would point out that the claim for 'sovereignty' has no necessary connection with the *effective* exercise of 'power'. Geoffrey Marshall, Warden[e] of Queen's, understands all these issues and might take a balanced view, but then he probably read the book for Clarendon. Difficult to find the right reviewer. Goldsworthy's briefly put view that Parliament could legislate to leave Europe is politically provocative, but then perhaps simply legalistically narrow: if it did so, of course the judges would follow. But at the moment

[d] Presumably Professor Neil MacCormick, then of the University of Edinburgh.
[e] This should be Provost, not Warden, of Queen's.

449

with the Human Rights Act are they not gaining the authority of Parliament to amend Acts of Parliament?

Philip Lynch in *The Politics of Nationhood* has little of the Australian Goldsworthy's depth of constitutional knowledge, but he has a deeper understanding for 'nation' and 'sovereignty' as animating myths of political Conservatism (myths in the sense that they are seen by Conservatives as incontestable and crystal clear, so long as one does not attempt definition). He relates the difficulties that Thatcher got into in trying to find a post-imperial patriotic rhetoric combining 'traditional values' with global market philosophy. Simple as that, really; the difficulties I mean. The more flagrant the contradictions, the more strident the chauvinism. Far easier to assert that we are not European, or 'of Europe', than to say what we are—a difficult business, after all, Englishness and Britishness, as contributors to the last issue of this journal amply witnessed.[f] And what price 'sovereignty' indeed when the Anglo-Irish Agreement of 1985 recognised, on the one hand, that Northern Ireland is an integral part of the United Kingdom until such time (as stated in two previous British Acts) as a majority in Northern Ireland shall vote to the contrary, but that then the government pledges to bring in legislation to effect the unity of Ireland? Lynch's book is short, but sweet and to the point. Old Tories would enjoy it, sadly, pensively. He is too polite to say what seems to me obvious: that the Thatcherite suburbanites have no sense of real history compared to the gentlemen, the old Tories, but only of what Neal Ascherson has called 'the myopic blue haze of "heritage"'. Mark you, the debility goes wider. Two parties were party to building the Dome and neither had thought what to put in it that was distinctively British.

They could have had an Orwell corner or cage; who else so oddly and utterly undeniably—oh, English, of course, not British? (But they could have had one of each: such a rich choice of Scottish and Welsh poets and writers, and for Northern Ireland, by birth, upbringing and education, Seamus Heaney of course, whether real or virtual.) Orwell, so explicit in and reflective about his Englishness (*The Lion and the Unicorn* could be the theme for designers to embellish) and certainly left of centre; indeed, now appearing impossibly left of centre. As *PQ* is partner in the Orwell Prize, I'm really guilty at not sending John Newsinger's book out for review, considering that I read it all through at a sitting (or a bedding to be accurate) and found it the most balanced and sane account of Orwell's politics that I have read. Didn't do better myself. The left has always divided too sharply on Orwell's 'premature correctness' (remember that old fallacy or deviation? He was on to the horror of Stalinism twenty years before the Old New Left broke over Hungary). But the anti-Stalinists have made him too much of an icon at times. He is too protean to be easy to body-snatch. Yet integrity does not always go with sound judgement. Newsinger has sound judgement and a cool head, and is

[f] The January number of 2000 (vol. 79, no. 1) was a special issue on the theme of 'Being British'.

free of those tedious defences of old illusions that to this day, for instance, make a small group of *Guardian* journalists take every chance to snip and snipe at Orwell—as if integrity was not to fight back at Communist infiltration and name names of fellow-travellers. Newsinger has given as good an account of Orwell as a political thinker—never a systematic one, always a stimulating one—as we are likely to find in this generation.

Now, I should have sent out the latest *British Social Attitudes* volume to go together with Eric Shaw's review in this number.[8] For Bob Worcester's obvious message is that the Conservatives lost the last election, rather than that a New Labour image or programme won it. But now we are in New-labourland, do people like it? People are very concerned—morally affronted, indeed—with the gap (the still growing gap) between rich and poor; and yet they share the government's belief that the answer lies in finding work, not increasing benefits (except for the disabled). However, they favour higher public spending (as John Smith rightly sensed) on the obvious targets: health, education and transport; even if it means higher taxation. Ordinary people do seem to see a link between higher taxation and public benefits. Very interesting reading, on a lot of other points too; and with the declining trust in government statistics (a distrust well merited), this annual publication deserves wide support and circulation.

Augmenting Democracy: Political Movements and Constitutional Reform during the Rise of Labour, 1900–1924, by Andrew Chadwick[a]

Vol. 71, no. 4, October–December 2000

As we puzzle at what is happening to the Labour Party right under our noses, sniff for clues in the dailies and digest or throw up big hypotheses from the weeklies, the historical past changes under our eyes in a way that, if it does not solve the puzzle, at least unravels part of today's tangled intensities.

For a long time, unless we were a left-wing student in the 1960s and 1970s and have never thought or read anything since except the *Guardian* (large parts of which seem to be written by sentimental survivors), most of us have realised that the vibrant idea of 'Oh what a falling was there' is historical nonsense: the belief that the early Labour movement was unequivocally Socialist and that parliamentary practices have watered it down, indeed put out the flame. Even if stalwarts realised that it wasn't that way entirely, even if it ought to have been utterly, then old man 'false consciousness' was invoked—a concept that I would explain to unbelievers as like being drunk for a very long time, and not realising it.

---

[8] Eric Shaw reviewed *Explaining Labour's Landslide*, by Robert Worcester and Roger Mortimer (Politico's).

[a] Ashgate, 285 pp, £42.50.

Even in the 1960s I was quoting in lectures, to confuse simple souls, Ramsay MacDonald from his Home University Library *Socialism* of 1911: 'The Labour Party is not socialist. It is a union of socialist and trade-union bodies for immediate political work . . . it is the only political form which evolutionary Socialism can take in a country with the political traditions and methods of Great Britain. Under British conditions, a socialist party is the last, not the first form of the socialist movement in politics.'

MacDonald shrewdly pointed to the future because he knew that false views of the past confused the possibilities of realistic action in the present. Even the author of that *locus classicus* of socialist spin on Labour history, Ralph Miliband in his *Parliamentary Socialism*, began to concede in his last two books that bourgeois liberty was liberty none the less, however inadequate its extent, and that many groups, standing for many different causes, had fed into complex movements loosely allied for reform, or at least for deliberate change from the customary practices of an establishment.

Now historical revisions go much further. The idea of the early Labour movement as a pluralist coalition, even, needs considerable qualification. Many different campaigns tried their influence on the new Labour Party, on the Liberal Party, usually on both, according to opportunity and circumstance: constitutional reformers, electoral reformers, the women's suffrage movement (itself a complex alliance moving at different speeds), educational reformers, disestablishmentarians, the Ireland Home Rule movement, and several majority charities who needed legislation not just money in the tin. The Labour Representation Committee and the radical wing of the Liberal Party commonly worked together after the Gladstone–MacDonald electoral pact of 1903, and some mutual causes survived even after the disruption of the Liberal Party during the First World War.

Andrew Chadwick's opening chapter is a clear and most useful summary of the different assumptions and different preoccupations of recent 'revisionist' writings on the early history of the Labour Party (and is 'revisionism' an 'ism', except in ideologists' eyes, rather than simply sound history as an academic practice? I say to the ghost of Ralph that one does not have to be a bad historian to be a good socialist). Chadwick advances two main theses. First, that the use of 'Socialism' as a yardstick and the notion of an easy transition from simple 'political democracy ("civil" and "political" citizenship)' to 'social democracy ("social" citizenship)', have led to 'an underestimation of the importance of constitutional reform in shaping the left's political identity before 1924'. But 'substituted in their place', he argues, 'should be a number of "yardsticks"—radicalism, labourism, socialism, feminism and, crucially, a discourse whose elements together combined in the form of what I term "radical constitutionalism".' The complexities and contingencies of these relationships need always to be kept in mind, he says (including today, I would add). Secondly, he argues—and sets out the evidence clearly in the rest of the book—that these independent bodies, neglected in the old accounts, were heavily intertwined and had in common a radical discourse and rhetoric of attack on the existing constitutional settlement. He makes his point convincingly that 'radical constitutionalism' brought many disparate causes together.

I think he suspects that this theme has never vanished, even if its continuing existence was obscured by both the weight of socialist writings, stressing and looking for social and economic themes in Labour's programmes, and the kind of centralism associated with the Webbs and the Fabian Society; to put it crudely, how we use the state, not how we change it, is the question.

Perhaps Charter 88 was not as original as its founders believed, but for that reason more likely to be on the right track and to find support despite its perhaps overly ambivalent attitude to the Labour Party, old and new (who else can deliver?) and despite its tendency to use a rationalistic 'all or nothing' rhetoric of either breakdown or a brand-new, systematic constitutional order (some former Marxists cannot live without belief in '*the system*', nor radical liberals neither, growingly unhappy with the workings of the market economy—as it were, 'the System' bad, a new system good).

Perhaps when Pat Seyd and others began in the early 1970s to speculate amid heightened party quarrels and declining membership that a secular displacement from party to pressure group allegiance was taking place, we were looking at too short an historical period—the post-1944 and 1945 expansion of Labour Party membership. Going back a bit, however, the picture is much more as Chadwick's two theses would claim; and coming forward to the present, not so bad a contemporary description either. Most reforming groups, including now the ethnic minorities as well as the female majority, are not fully in either Labour or Liberal ranks, but mostly not fully out either (thanks to the Conservative Party); and they see, however vaguely, hopes for reform as turning not just on party policies but, overall, on constitutional reform.

This badly overpriced book reads well, despite too many noun-clauses and unbalanced sentences that a good copy-editor should have removed (I mean queried). It is a most promising first book; the author seems a person to be reckoned with. We won't have heard the last of him.

In the last special number of *Political Studies* on 'Political Ideas and Political Action' he writes on 'A Public Political Discourse'. Here, once he gets away from methodological matters of puzzling relevance to either action or the public, he asserts that ideas are important in politics but must be found in the ordinary language and presuppositions of political debate and public opinion, not in formal books. This has been said before; but rarely attempted. I suspect that he could do it, and we would then have a very different kind of history of Labour and the groups that have circled around it; a history that would leave all factions chastened and aware that we have to live together, in proportion to need.

Forward to Basics—Back from the Brink: Can Humanity Rescue Itself?, by
J. M. Ross[a]

Vol. 72, no. 1, January–March 2001

Occasionally a serious book of real importance gets shamefully neglected.
Few review editors take time to scan the pages of books coming from small
presses and by unheard-of authors; unheard-of, in this case, outside the
devolution movement in Scotland. As I have remarked before, most book
editors in the broadsheets have little political interest or judgement. It is the
pompous and self-justifying career memoirs of ambassadors and cabinet
ministers that usually get reviewed, and usually favourably—being handed
out with disinterested cynicism to their mates rather than to critical academics
or journalists. The very title of Jim Ross's book might sound glib and crankish,
unless one knew the author. But even to have looked at the customary
biographical note on the back cover might have stirred curiosity, at least: a
career in the Civil Service that ended as Under-Secretary at the Scottish Office
in charge of the legislation and preparation for the might-have-been 1978
Scottish Assembly. Some editors and reviewers might have found it interesting to see what such a senior civil servant thought about the greatest
questions facing us.

Ross is bold and unhappy enough to tackle the big one: 'the risk that . . .
humanity would create a situation demanding changes in behaviour and
organisation which were beyond its collective ability to attain'. His Carlyle-
like anger at the trivialising and short-termism of political discourse does not
spoil a rationality worthy of J. S. Mill. He sets out six problems of which
anyone who thinks at all is aware, but usually suppresses or tries hard not to
face, or at least tries to downgrade.

The first is that humanity has become subject to general stress because the
rate of technological, social and economic change has outstripped the
potential rate of human genetic and cultural adaptation. What ability we
have to shape and control our culture is in fact working against such
adaptation.

The second is that technological change and economic growth have created
expectations of lifestyle which lead 'successful' individuals to demand ever
more space. But these demands, intensifying congestion both of land and
movement, can be fulfilled only by a small minority of the world's population.
Social forces work towards greater inequality, an increasing gap between rich
and poor in all societies, at a time when the rhetoric of nearly all politicians
presumes diminishing inequality, whether by push-up or drip-down.

The third is that the current economic system itself is incapable of
responding to collective wishes in such a way as to limit congestion, over-
population or growing inequalities.

[a] Pentland Press, 101 pp, £8.50.

The fourth is that these problems are compounded by physical and environmental factors: pollution, global warming and the growing danger of the exhaustion of non-renewable resources with so little policy and investment going towards alternatives.

The fifth is that the political systems of advanced societies have created an illusion that electorates can ensure that government deliver the vision they themselves encourage of wealth for all—'room for everyone at the top'. So an obvious side-product is cynicism as ordinary people perceive the difference between reality and rhetoric. (Orwell once remarked that 'the trouble with competitions is that somebody has to win them').

The sixth is that traditional cultures are breaking down under the pressure of global economics and new technologies, and 'no cohesive new cultures are emerging. Hence, in spite of increased administrative resources and improved administrative techniques, societies are becoming less manage-able.' Rather to my own surprise, I find little to disagree with in this brief sketch of six modern horses of an apocalypse—a little dramatic, perhaps, but only for the sake of argument. 'Survival of humanity in the absolute sense is probably not at stake. But a disastrous drop in the standard of life in advanced societies, a severe check and even regression in the less advanced, and a substantial increase in the need for coercion in social management generally, are in prospect, bringing with them a level of conflict that could prove a threat to survival.'

The book is not a series of unsubstantiated assertions by an angry old man, although the author is angry and he is old—old and wise, an earlier age might have said. He has read the stuff on all this, but he has digested it into a tract, not regurgitated it with footnotes as if for research-rating points; and any Greens who read it might note that he has no truck with the anti-science and anti-industrial nostalgia with which they try to make a comprehensive ideology out of a series of good points in what is only a partial analysis.

Ross tries—which is why I liken him to Carlyle—to shake us out of complacent short-termism; but, like the Scottish sage of Chelsea, his pre-scriptions are questionable. His concern to look at humanity as a whole brings him to attacks on religion as escapism and an assertion of Humanism with that capital 'H' as if there is or could be a Humanist movement, rather than a broad, philosophical, secular (hence universal) account of human morality, which indeed needs stirring, and small Humanist Societies that talk seriously but cut no ice and peel no potatoes, As nominally a card-carrying large 'H' humanist I've often tried to get expelled for heresy by noting that religious groups are more likely than Humanist groups to roll up their sleeves for social work. I share Ross's scepticism—and, indeed, there are those who turn to superstition because they cannot face with reason a world acting so irration-ally—but the very divisions of and among religions pose no real threat. If 'traditional cultures are breaking down', the vacuum will not be filled in any single way: that is a minimal hope for freedom, if no cheer to the ravages caused by a politically and morally largely unrestrained global capitalism. But 'breakdown' may be too strong. I have heard Neal Ascherson argue that the culture of global capitalism is, indeed, becoming universal, but it does not destroy strong traditional cultures: it is an often rather thin top dressing, a situational rather than a native culture of nurture; literally a business culture. Two centuries of capitalism have still left the Dutch peculiarly Dutch and the Greeks noticeably Greek. That is not the real threat. Gross economic injustice and environmental despoliation seem the basic threats to civilisation as we have thought to create and enjoy it.

'It is a paradoxical fact that although humanity in the advanced societies . . . has never been in a better position to establish reality, it has probably never been more detached from social, political and economic reality than at present.' As it were, let us enjoy sport, sex and shopping (or, more often, voyeurism on each), but 'let us not face the future'. 'We have created a need for human co-operation and altruism which we seem quite unable to meet.' Everyone should read this tract but, alas, few will; although it is important, short, to the point, well-written, nicely printed and a good price.

The Cunning of Unreason: Making Sense of Politics, by John Dunn [a]

Vol. 72, no. 1, April–June 2001

Who could disagree that 'Politics is the balance of conflict and co-operation between human purposes on any scale on which you care to look at it'? Or that the dominance of 'conflict over co-operation in human interactions . . . will ensure that politics is always a site of danger for human beings, and that the experience of politics, for all but the most egotistical and resilient, will always be somewhat irritating and in the end all but invariably disappointing'? But, of course, the question is often: *How* disappointing?

Thinking of an extreme case, purposive but non-political, indeed anti-political, action (in both Dunn's sense and mine), Orwell once said that 'all revolutions are failures, but they are not all the same kind of failure.' 'Somewhat irritating' is somewhat banal while seeking to be wise. What follows from such remarks, the reader may want to know, and yet not find out after four hundred pages. For this is a Big Book, and presented as such, as if for the general intellectual reader, but lapsing frequently into the internalised world of academic political thought. The cover has a Gillray cartoon of Pitt drawing the cork from bottled heads of Whigs, from which spray out jets of wine labelled as stale jokes, fibs, invectives, abuse, growlings, etc. etc. Presumably this is the author uncorking the cunning of unreason or perhaps exposing folly—which is not very clear; and the inside and rear pages of the book itself are adorned with the Charge of the Light Brigade—which is very puzzling, unless Tennyson's 'dared to do or die' is picked up from the

[a] HarperCollins, 401 pp, £19.99.

encomium that Paul (*The Rise and Fall of the Great Powers*) Kennedy writes for the back cover: 'As usual John Dunn asks questions about politics and the political process that few other scholars have thought of asking (or dared to ask) . . . *The Cunning of Unreason* is a searching intellectual inquiry into the nature of political action; but it is an even more disturbing and acute essay upon the nature of political thought. It is idiosyncratic, brilliant and very original.' The first sentence may be the real enthusiasm of a friend, but it is also the language of a huckster.

The book, if one is not impatient or short of time, has some solid merits. I will come to these. But there is nothing in it that has not been thought of before, indeed thought through, by other scholars, and nothing daring except the over-the-top presentation. Murdoch's men or women may have written on the cover blurb 'very much in the tradition of great political writing', but could anyone other than the author have penned 'clearly and wittily written'? In fact it is turgid and long-winded, and if there is wit it can only be in a Jacobean sense of occasional flashes of sharp insight—nothing funny here, I do warn frivolous readers.

John Dunn earned great respect for his earlier work on Locke. But in the 1990s he became interested in more general themes, writing *Western Political Theory in the Face of the Future* (1992) and editing *Democracy: The Unfinished Journey* (1992) and *Contemporary Crisis of the Nation State* (1995). His reading is wide, but when he comes to write his sense of what is original and what is commonplace, or even banal, is somewhat imperfect. This book is obviously meant to be a *magnum opus*, but in fact it is little more than a learned man telling us what he thinks about the nature of politics. If one thought that this was a last testament, due to ill-health or resolve to leave King's Cambridge for a monastery, one would mute one's criticism. But as the author, as far as I know, is perfectly healthy, one has to say that the book needed reading by friends who would dare to say, 'Why repeat all that again?' or, 'That's good, but wouldn't it come across stronger if much shorter?'

He sees three constitutive components of politics as 'the beliefs and sentiments of a given population, the institutional forms through which that population can (and, for the time, largely must) act . . . and the cumulative consequences of these actions'. That is neat. But he then ponders further, telling us that the 'relation between these components is almost always somewhat opaque', as is the relation between intention and consequence; that 'each component has a conceptually distinctive history of its own, though all also affect one another to varying degree throughout', and that 'each can go well or badly'. He goes on like this for paragraph after paragraph, page after page. It all sounds very wise, but is it in fact saying anything? He seems to plant both feet firmly in mid-air. The only sustained example in the book is a chapter on the coming of Thatcher to illustrate the limits of state power. He is right to stress the limitations arising from the whole situation she inherited, to reprove those who talk of a total break with tradition, who fail to see that she could not move all she wished to move; but

457

that could be said in a paragraph, not in forty quite unoriginal pages which seem new only to the author. Peter Hennessy does that better.

Where he is wise is at the very end, in discussing what space capitalism leaves for political choice. An increasingly 'global' capitalist world sets very different limits to politics from those which were set by its productively more variegated (but also vastly less productive) predecessors. But, like all such predecessors and any possible successors, it itself is, throughout, a world of politics. The limits it sets to politics are limits to the potential efficacy of agency. The institutions of a state have less and less control over their own economy. But in no sense do they limit the content of politics—what we may try to achieve or control. So he ends by asking whether the modern democratic republic, which he sees, indeed, as a great human achievement, can 'replace any or all of [its institutions] in the reasonably near future with other institutions that can serve us better'. Indeed. But he only asks the questions; in a very abstract way he sees the problems, but seems uninterested in even speculative solutions. His early chapters on the origins of political thinking might have reminded him that there is a speculative tradition of political thought, not merely an analytical one.

Such labour and laborious exposition, such a mix of profundity and banality (almost like the writing of a lonely man who gets no criticism before he commits himself to paper), irresistibly reminds me of Oakeshott's review of a forgotten book, the late Sir Walter Moberley's *Crisis of the Universities* (that they were no longer Christian): he read it for its obvious importance and challenging claims eagerly all evening and into the small hours, but then in the morning woke with a headache trying to remember what it was all about.

The Intellectual Life of the British Working Classes, by Jonathan Rose[a]

Vol. 73, no. 1, January–March 2002

Here is an absolute masterpiece of social history that dispels many political myths. The author sets out to discover what working-class readers actually read in the first half of the twentieth century, and how they read it—whether the penny dreadfuls, the classic canon in the Home University Library, public school stories, Shakespeare, imperialist and socialist propaganda alike, and not forgetting the Bible. The author shows that many working-class leaders took all this in their stride, indulging in it as most of us have from time to time or at different stages of life. I twice heard Aneurin Bevan, that proudly self-confessed atheist, speaking at full extempore blast, and his language was saturated with phrases such as 'towards the New Jerusalem' and 'the promised land', and calls to Tories 'to search their hearts and souls and repent'. The Bible to him, as to many others, was literature and language; he

[a] Yale University Press, 534 pp, £29.95.

emerged from early immersion unscathed in conviction but elevated in vocabulary and metaphor.

Jonathan Rose has conducted a mammoth trawl, which he presents brilliantly organised and pointed, through memoirs, letters, library accession lists and registers of borrowing in working men's clubs, institutes and so on. A vivid picture of the eclecticism of 'the common reader' emerges. Socialists were not corrupted by reading Frank Richards's Billy Bunter stories, nor by the fashionable novels of the day; and remarkably few of them, even those who worshipped at the shrine, read Karl Marx. *Das Kapital* might just as well have been in Latin. What is more surprising is that the reading habits of working-class activists were by and large—with some exceptions, of course— much the same as those of the middle class.

There emerges—indeed, the book begins with—a vigorous defence of the idea of literature against that of ideology. Rose could have invoked a comparison, but the book is big enough already. The Soviet system had complete control of all institutions of education, and they had to teach a well-known doctrine. But even Stalin at the height of his power and paranoia did not remove the classics of nineteenth-century Russian literature from library shelves. They were both valued in themselves, presumably, and had the unintended effect of creating alternative worlds for imagination and thought. But Rose has no difficulty in showing that reading and enjoying strictly bourgeois fare did not shake the faith of the faithful in Britain, although perhaps it enabled many to land more softly after 1968.

There is now in postmodernism a nominally non-political ideology that has no time for the autonomy of literature and the ability of the workers to comprehend or, if they do, to avoid being seduced into conformity. He quotes no less a figure than a past president of the Modern Language Association, Barbara Herrnstein Smith, as saying, as if it were so self-evident as not to need argument, that classic literature is always irrelevant to those who have not received an orthodox Western education. It is, she says, an undeniable 'fact that Homer, Dante and Shakespeare do not figure significantly in the personal economies of these people, do not perform individual or social functions that gratify their interests, *do not have value for them*'.[b] Rose sets out to show that this postmodernist theory 'has no visible means of support'. For instance, he cites the memoir of Will Crooks MP, the dockers' leader, who spent 2d[c] on a second-hand *Iliad* and 'was dazzled. What a revelation it was to me! Pictures of romance and beauty I had never dreamt of suddenly opened up before my eyes. I was transported from the East End to an enchanted land. It was a rare luxury for a working lad like me just home from work to find myself among the heroes and nymphs of ancient Greece.'[d] Rose pillories the postmodernists

[b] The italics are as cited by Rose in his book, not Bernard's.

[c] The original journal version has 2p, but it is of course 2d in Rose's book: Crooks died in 1921, half a century before decimalisation in the UK.

[d] I have removed the word 'always', oddly added to the end of this quotation in the journal version.

for asserting, like old Marxists, that reading a text is always conditioned by circumstances (treating a relative banality as an iron law), and yet at the same devaluing the text relative to the autonomy of the reader (well, that is readers like you and me, not the conditioned masses). His first chapter is called 'A Desire for Singularity'—something that reading can give to anyone.

Rose mocks the postmodernists for being so sure that conventional literature conditions its readers that they never undertake the disagreeable hard labour of asking what books people actually read and what they make of them. There are stock theory answers that save all that sweat: 'If we cleave to Marxism, feminism, Christianity, Islam, liberalism, the traditional British class structure to the point where we can no longer step outside it and assume another frame, then we are in the cage of ideology.' He asserts that, 'far from reinscribing traditional ideologies, canonical literature tended to ignite insurrections in the mind of the workers'—much as, he adds, Matthew Arnold predicted in *Culture and Anarchy*.

These last two propositions he demonstrates in twelve fascinatingly detailed chapters on responses to classic literature, informal education and mutual aid, perceptions of fact and of fiction, the conservative canon or 'dead authors', primary education, adult education and the contentions around Ruskin College and the WEA, Marxism and Marxists, the popularity of school stories, cultural literacy in the slums, and Welsh miners' libraries. But then, in chapter 13, 'Down and Out in Bloomsbury', he deals with some working-class figures of the 1930s and 1940s who made contact with Bloomsbury and the kind of sub-Bloomsbury of Fitzrovia that he calls Bohemia. By then the days of the autodidact, those whose university was the free public library, were numbered. I remember around about 1950 someone staggering from a pub on to the top deck of a bus with his arms full of books from the Holborn Public Library. 'It's all here,' he told us all in old Cockney, 'all here. Everything the working man needs to know. All in the books of H. G. Wells'—a figure that Richard Hoggart would treasure as from a bygone age.

Our modern culture, Rose concludes, has 'successfully' reconciled bourgeois and Bohemian values—in the ICA, Channel Four and the Islington Blairites. 'The boutique culture they have constructed involves a process of class formation, where the accoutrements of the avant-garde are used to distinguish cultural workers from the more traditional manual workers. For both these classes the withering away of the autodidact tradition has been a great loss. We forfeited some important knowledge about ourselves when we shut out or forgot the working class observers of Bohemia. Even if they never caught up, they saw, more clearly than any of us, where our culture was moving.'

The Red Flag and the Union Jack: Englishness, Patriotism and the British Left, 1881–1924, by Paul Ward[a]

Vol. 73, no. 3, July–October 2002

In reviewing for this journal in 1959 the three volumes of Arthur Schlesinger Jr's *The Age of Roosevelt*[b] I remarked that one does not have to be a bad historian to be a good Democrat. Never waste a good epigram, said Oliver Wendell Holmes Jr (American politics has often been more dynastic than ours). So in the 1960s and 1970s I re-remarked more than once that one does not have to be unpatriotic to be a good socialist. The old New Left who dominated intellectual discourse way back then seemed to believe in everyone else's nationalism except their own, which I called a very English tradition puzzling to Scots, Welsh and Irish authors. Leave aside that the dandy princes of the New Left were hardly movers and shakers of working-class opinion, still less that of 'Middle England', and that Perry Anderson, Robin Blackburn, Ralph Samuels even and Miliband *père* were only spectral names failing to haunt or affright Surbiton, let alone Europe; but none the less they helped create among historians and political commentators a miasma through which it was difficult to see clearly some aspects of our national past. Their broad view of English nationalism and patriotism was that it was the intellectual property of the Conservatives, a view not unpleasant to Tories if they ever thought in that way. To be fair, Ralph Samuels had begun before his sadly early death to open up an important and wide-ranging debate in the *History Workshop*'s three volumes on *Patriotism* (1989) to a wider and more perceptive reappraisal, albeit one still passionately contested by some.

Now we have a detailed and wholly convincing study of the Labour movement in the key period for the formation of the party that demonstrates it was wrong to view with surprise the overwhelming support of British socialists and the Labour Party for the First World War, including conscription. That was a crucial event; but Paul Ward is able to show that such patriotism was no sudden response to contingent events plus propaganda, atrocity tales and jingoism, but on the contrary had deep roots. Basically, this study turns the accepted view on its head. Patriotism and nationalism were common properties of voters for each of the three parties, even if the Conservatives (through Disraeli's imperialism, Victoria's Diamond Jubilee and the 'victory' of the 'Boer War') made a pretty resolute bid for monopoly. It had its tactical successes but ultimately changed little. What distinguished oppositional Englishness, says Ward, is that 'it attempted to construct a democratic version of national identity'. It is this that got lost in the arbitrary construction of history in the doctrine of the former New Left. Only Tony

[a] Royal Historical Society / Boydell Press, 232 pp, £35.00.
[b] The reviews were actually published in 1958 (vol. 1) and 1961 (vols 2 and 3), not 1959—an informal remembering, no doubt, rather than a check back through the issues or Bernard's files; and the 1979 index does not list them. The reviews are reprinted in this volume—see above.

Benn would shyly confess that at heart 'I am a Chartist'. Ward quotes Anthony Barnett in the 1989 anthology (now perhaps older and somewhat wiser) that the left would be better served 'to insist upon the plurality of national allegiances . . . the diversity of regional differences; the plurality of migrant strain; the importance of gender loyalties; and the conflicting allegiances of class'. Indeed, we are a consciously multicultural state and have been so for a very long time, since at least the Act of Union. But what, pray, holds it all together?

This historical study shows, from the speeches and writing of Labour leaders and thinkers, both national and local, the full complexity of the left's attitudes. Much of that still rested on bad history: the 'myth of the Norman yoke' had a long run for its money. There is a short but admirably concise first chapter on 'Patriotism and Politics before 1881'. Some 'Saxons' even in his later period had teetered on the edge of what we now would see as racism—a curious racism in that the working class, both urban and rural, counted for more by their 'kind hearts' and 'Saxon blood', vouched for by Tennyson, than the wearers of 'coronets', who were cosmopolitan to the marrow, selfish and effete, able to speak *French*. This myth was among the unlamented casualties of the First World War. Attitudes to imperialism could vary. There were 'little Englanders' and 'on to Kabul and the Transvaal!' enthusiasts on left as well as right. Attitudes to France and Germany divided patriotic opinion in the Edwardian era until quite late. (I long to tell Paul Ward about my mother's great-aunt, who must have been at least an emancipated woman because she went on a bicycle tour of Alsace and Lorraine in the 1880s, but then embarrassed her super-patriot daughter in both world wars by being pro-German and anti-French on sanitary grounds.) The *Labour Leader* declared in 1910 that 'no sane politician would dream of opposing expenditure necessary for national defence', which would, of course, ensure that there would be no war.

The heavily documented chapter on the First World War period is a salutary restoration of truth and balance. The heroism of the anti-heroes of the anti-war protests and of the out-and-out pacifists has attracted disproportionate attention. Men of conscience, like Fenner Brockway, defied public opinion, but also in their memoirs had little care to portray it accurately. Most of the anti-war groups on the left couched their arguments in patriotic, not internationalist, terms. Said C. H. Norman: 'I am not pro-German, pro-Russian, pro-French, pro-Belgian; but I am pro-English in the sense that *I know no reason why the British workers should be slaughtered in the interests of Russia and France*.' And the suppression of 'English liberties' in wartime was called 'British Prussianism', just as profiteers were not just profiteers but un-English. 'Most of the left', Ward concludes, 'shared memories of British, mainly English, history with the wider nation, and gave its consent to perpetuate the value of this heritage. The left's concern is only understandable in terms of its development since the 1880s, a development deliberately shaped to make a *British* socialism—a process largely completed by 1924. British socialism must take its place alongside other "invented traditions".'

Just two bones I'd like to pick or share amicably with the author, by no means detractive of this sane and scholarly book. Is 'invented' rather than 'evolved' tradition quite right? And are we really talking about British or not rather a specifically 'English socialism'? He slides over this tricky one. Over the border there are different views. But the usages back then were possibly looser than now. All in all, there is an interesting parallel between this book and Jonathan Rose's *The Intellectual Life of the British Working Classes*, which I reviewed in the January–March 2002 issue of *PQ*.[c] Both, by documentary research, show that, respectively, the patriotism of the left and its reading habits were far more like those of the rest of the country than zealots or enemies liked or were wont to portray. Revisionism in England as well as Ireland is not always a term of abuse.

Cards of Identity

Identity of England, by Robert Colls; *Patriots: National Identity in Britain 1940–2000*, by Richard Weight[a]

Vol. 74, no. 3, July–October 2003

That one famous sentence from a former US Secretary of State, when taken from its context, distorts his meaning utterly: 'Great Britain has lost an Empire and has not yet found a role.' When Dean Acheson spoke those words in the course of an address at West Point on 5 December 1962, he was not counselling Britain to find another such role—on the contrary:

> ... the attempt to play a separate role—that is, a role apart from Europe, a role based on a 'special relationship' with the United States, a role based on being head of a 'Commonwealth' which has no political structure, or unity, or strength and enjoys a fragile precarious economic relationship by means of the sterling area and preferences in the British market—this role is about played out. Great Britain, attempting to work alone and to be a broker between the United States and Russia, has seemed to conduct policy as weak as its military power. HMG is now attempting—wisely, in my opinion, to re-enter Europe, from which it was banished at the time of the Plantagenets, and the battle seems about as hard fought as those of an earlier day.

So, forty years ago, this wise and prescient man, whose liking for English ways did not distort his political judgement, poured cold water on our 'special relationship' and counselled us to throw in our lot with Europe.

The deeper implication is that it is an unnecessary folly to search for any equivalent role to an imperial one. Only imperial powers need trumpet 'a role'. They need a global theme to justify *imperium* over other countries and cultures. For that is what empire is. Can we not be reasonably happy within

---

[c] The previous review in this volume: see above.

[a] Oxford University Press, 409 pp, £25.00 (Colls); Palgrave, 866 pp, £25.00 (Weight).

our own skin without the grandeur of 'a role'? Consider, for example, the Dutch, the Swedes, the Danes, the Norwegians and New Zealanders. If we Brits do have any special role or roles to play, then careful definition is needed, not wild claims—even of the 'best' health service, universities, police, public behaviour, sportsmanship in the world. These claims were current until embarrassingly recently, all too freely and frequently made; at best, careful definition of 'best' was always needed in terms of possible futures relative to achievements of other countries; at worst, we too often reimagined nostalgic pasts amid myths of self-sufficiency (which are never in fact true, whether for nations or for individuals). If the question of 'role' is no longer central, questions of our observed peculiarities or distinctiveness, say 'identity' and 'self-image', are more meaningful, and meaningfully debatable in their variety and modulation.

Here are two remarkable books, complementary not rival, which instantly command respect precisely because neither is obsessed with what should be our role on a world stage (we have had quite enough of that). Richard Weight is concerned to report changing images of Britain and British peculiarities since the beginning of the Second World War (which he rightly sees as undermining the top-down gentlemanly values of two previous centuries); Robert Colls boldly attempts to set down 'how the English have thought about themselves'. Never was the old aphorism more true: 'The owl of Minerva only flies at dusk.' Serious studies of who we are have begun to appear only in the last decade of the twentieth century—I say 'serious' because before then, with very few exceptions, books on Englishness and English character seemed mainly written for Prize Day at first-class second-rate public schools ('public', of course, in that extraordinary English sense, give or take some sad penetration into Scotland too—a sense which is a tale in itself of an Englishness of public service asserted and now decayed into an Englishness of individual and corporate greed). And until recently even thoughtful English historians could confuse 'English' and 'British', as many ordinary people and too many journalists still do. Recently Melanie Phillips accused me of betraying Britishness in the face of immigrants' demands, because I had asserted that we were a multinational state and a multicultural society. I simply wrote on a postcard: 'Dear Melanie, 1707, Bernard.'

In the days of imperial power and during the long postwar delusion that we had won the war (with a little help from the US and the USSR, combined with Hitler's folly and Japan's too), we had little need to be reflective. That suited the English tradition of understatement and dislike of abstract formulations and explicit theories (even if there existed within the once pervasive cult of the gentleman a fairly coherent bundle of implicit presuppositions). But with the loss of power and the sad, obsessive, at times almost crazed delusions that we need to restore it, whether Thatcher's, Blair's or the *Daily Mail*'s, there has gradually grown up an inward-looking curiosity, a kind of ageing adolescent absorption in a 'Who am I?' discourse—a question whose answers do not always have visible effect on actual behaviour.

Concern with identity may be more a product of changing circumstances and changing behaviour than its cause. Concern with identity can be overdone. Perhaps better to look outwards at how others see us, which can have consequences, than to think that there is as much mileage in introspection as too many have recently come to believe.

Robert Colls's book is basically historical. It mixes a history of events with the ideas about those events. The early chapters are a masterly summary of the emergence of the idea of an English nation. He presents it as a history of the emergence of a centralised and bureaucratically competent English state. I find this emphasis on 'the state' questionable. By 'state' he really means no more than central government. Carl J. Friedrich once called the state (following Meineke) 'an abstract corporate halo' around the claim to absolute authority. As Colls himself brilliantly demonstrates, respect for the common law historically had linked the common people to the parliamentary classes and both to the Crown, and limited the powers of the three estates. When a theory of sovereignty was developed, it became one of parliamentary sovereignty; and eventually the powers of the Crown came to be exercised by or in the name of Parliament. Certainly the common law prevented the Crown from becoming the state in the sixteenth-century continental European sense. Henry VIII flirted with the new doctrines of state absolutism, the revival of Roman law, but in the end he found that he could do all he wanted to do through or in Parliament. It was a political order that emerged, as Charles I learnt to his cost when he tried to make the monarch the state. But if talk of an English state without either close definition or comparative analysis leads to ambiguity and conceptual confusion, this does not invalidate the main narrative. His account of the transition from the kingdoms of England and Scotland into a United Kingdom is masterly, using the best of the recent historical writing which has come to stress the interaction of four national histories, not their separate articulation. He sees the Act or Treaty of Union as a blend of Scottish realism and English political skill in balancing contingencies.

Once, however, he has traced the interplay of English and Scottish contingencies and modes of public thinking, interaction somewhat drops out of both narrative and explanation: Englishness seems to stand alone, which plainly it does not. In an earlier book written with Philip Dodd, *Englishness: Politics and Culture 1880–1920* (1986), he shrewdly called Englishness essentially 'a relationship'. I took up this idea avidly, also influenced by then reading John Pocock's seminal essay of 1975, 'British History: A New Subject'. These were the ideas behind the *Political Quarterly* book *National Identities and the Constitution*,[b] which I edited (1991) and to which I contributed an essay, 'Englishness and Britishness' (in a later version, 'The Sense of Identity of the Indigenous British', *New Community*, April 1995)—two refer-

---

[b] Not quite. The book—the journal's 'fifth issue' for 1991—was actually published as *National Identities: The Constitution of the United Kingdom*. Bernard Crick's chapter is reprinted above, p. 233.

ences oddly missing from Colls's otherwise comprehensive bibliography. But after 1707 there is little mention of how the character of the English, or their understanding of their own political nature, was affected by relationships with the others. Surely the dog that did not bark is important; that is, the lack of much writing on English nationalism before the last twenty years, compared to all those catalogue entries under Scottish, Welsh and Irish nationalism (to look no further). This is not just a case of 'for English see British imperialism', but is rather because, if the English ruling class had patronised a state cult of English nationalism, as happened almost everywhere else in Europe, it would have greatly complicated what was their main concern from 1707 to 1914 at least: holding the United Kingdom together.

Colls strangely fails to follow through his own insight of Englishness as a relationship. This weakens his explanations (and would have required a book on the whole British Isles perhaps twice the weight of Weight's 866 pages), but it does not diminish his final understanding. His penultimate section, 'England Now', is a profound and balanced account of how we have come to think of ourselves. His own conclusion is that the deferential nation has gone for ever. Crown-in-Parliament no longer adequately represents the nation. People don't look up, they look sideways, as it were, at each other. 'The idea that the state stands for a homogeneous nation is no longer true . . . The English "gentleman" who tied it all together has changed beyond recognition, as has his constituency, which is far more diverse.' But pluralism works best, he says, only for pluralists. 'It works less well for those who regard English as a uniquely important way of valuing themselves.' But I wonder how many people do uniquely value themselves simply because they are English? Pretty sad to be in that condition, as if national identity were there only to fill a vacuum. No wonder such people so often sound angry and feel threatened. Any such identity is one among others: family, friends, occupation, pastimes, locality, region, religion, ethnicity, European, country of origin—oh, and also this puzzle of 'Britishness'; these all interact, are overlapping and at times highly situational identities. One can overdo this national identity business, unless one does admit a plurality of commitments and allegiances. Colls ends with a flourish that the English people, in Orwell's sense of the people, must learn to trust each other again, and still could do so; but they must also trust, even if to varying degrees, the other peoples of the United Kingdom.

Richard Weight is more inclined to hit the nail on the head hard in his introduction and conclusion. His first sentence startles: 'This is a book about why the people of Britain stopped thinking of themselves as British and began to see themselves instead as Scots, Welsh and English who happened to belong to a state called Britain.' Just a quibble to remind that there is no such state with such a name. The state is the United Kingdom of Great Britain and Northern Ireland. Both authors flinch away (like Linda Colley before them) from the Irish complication, despite the great effect it has had on British politics and political thinking, not to mention literature. But he is right to remind us of a relative shift in identifications in recent times, and he does not confuse national consciousness with nationalism. He has a dour view of the Act of Union—as 'an uneasy relationship' created 'to advance the cause of capitalism, empire and the Protestant faith . . . [and] . . . founded on greed, religious and racial bigotry, fear and contempt'—which is both anachronistic in its value judgements and forgetful that, if one of the main reasons for union was indeed fear, it was fear of recurrent civil war. He wisely gets away from history double-quick, after having the Duke of Marlborough rout the Jacobite army at Culloden.

Back in the home straight of the last sixty years and on his home ground, however, he shows a deep grasp of social history and deploys fascinating examples. He is surely right to identify a growing popular identification with three national cultures rather than with the overarching Britishness. The idea of Britishness has long seemed to me to be only that of a political culture: allegiance to the Crown, Parliament and the laws. If this is of great practical importance—for a desire for order is both rational self-interest and national interest (as Hobbes should always remind one)—yet the connotation of 'British' is nonetheless narrower than that of 'English'. Who talks of a British novel, poem or play? The culture and its artefacts are English, Scottish, Welsh and—yes—Irish. Recent immigrants see this distinction between English and British more clearly than the English. They instinctively call themselves 'British Asians' etc., not English Asians (although some sightings or hearings of Welsh Asian and Scottish Asian identifications seem to be slowly growing).

What Richard Weight has done here is to show, more thoroughly than any other book I know, the changing nature of the national cultures and their components in the last sixty years. Things are now very different and, overall, better. Warriors, Citizens, Viewers, Shoppers, Swingers, Nationalists, Sceptics, Strikers, Hustlers, Tunnellers, Modernisers are the names of well-written and well-evidenced sections. Taking all this on board puts the alleged overriding importance of national identity into perspective, or at least makes it more problematic. Weight is a descriptive sociologist mercifully untainted by the academic wave of fashion for nationalism studies, now moving into identity. He ends by quoting a remarkable plea to Britain by Albert Camus, in a BBC broadcast of 1950, not to stand aside from the European project. 'The facts affirm that, for better or for worse, Britain and Europe are bound up together. It may seem an unfortunate marriage. But as one of our moralists said: marriage may sometimes be good but never delightful. As our marriage is not a delightful one, let us at least make it a good one, since divorce is out of the question.' Weight sagely notes that the marriage of the four countries of the United Kingdom may be an unfortunate one, and separation an attractive and viable solution; but divorce is out of the question. But does he mean political or simply cultural separation? Just thinking of Scotland, if ever there were a divorce, it would be unlikely to lead to a radical separation: both because of economic and social reality and because of EU laws and relations, it would not make as much difference as some would hope and others devoutly fear. The Republic of Ireland and mainland Britain in most respects have closer ties than either does to Northern Ireland, certainly less sense of what sociologists call 'social distance'.

These two books together tell us an extraordinary amount about who we are and what we think about ourselves. But I do begin to think that national identity is not all of life and society. Some thoughts about reason, humanity, the European tradition and international order would not have been irrelevant. Krishan Kumar's *The Making of English National Identity*—which appeared when this review was in proof—has perhaps a greater sense of the wider context.

Multiculturalism and Britishness

Multicultural Politics: Racism, Ethnicity and Muslims in Britain, by Tariq Modood [a]

Vol. 77, no. 2, April–June 2006

Tariq Modood has endured many trials and tribulations, not just to make his career but more so to make his determined point. When he began writing in the late 1980s the human landscape was divided, as both far left and far right saw it, into Blacks and Whites. But the aims of public policy, still less the right policies to achieve even the clearest of aims, are rarely a matter of black and white. He was opposing and exposing racism with the best of them involved in 'race relations', but to his great credit he earned suspicion and unpopularity by also opposing what he well calls 'political blackness'. Anti-racism back in the 60s, 70s and 80s then said that all coloured people should regard themselves as Black because that was how White people (nearly all racist to a degree, of course) regarded them; and that discrimination created an overriding common interest—even, some said, objectively a common culture. Perhaps 'black' was the slogan word, rather than more accurately 'people of (non-white) colour', because it signified both extreme contrast and deep symbolic meanings. Also at that time Afro-Caribbeans were disproportionately active in many protest and community organisations—even if the most famous ideologue of the movement was a Sinhalese Trotskyite.

Modood was one of the first to risk and incur obloquy by pointing out that not all 'blacks' shared the same interests and culture and that Muslims were not a race but shared a religion with a wide range of ethnicities across the Middle East, Africa, the subcontinent and South-East Asia. Also he wrote as a reformer not a pseudo-revolutionary, the fashion of that time before non-Communist Marxists made (to them) the remarkable rediscovery of 'the political'. Thinking politically, Modood could show his co-religionists that they were not threatened by assimilation so long as integration was seen as a

[a] Edinburgh University Press, 240 pp, £16.99 pb and £49 hb.

two-way process of mutual understanding and compromise, not a retreat (either voluntary or involuntary) into segregation. Perhaps underlying all these essays, at last gathered together as a book, is an understanding that the oldest contract concerning immigration known to history is that the immigrant obeys the laws in return for the protection of the laws.

The publication history of this important book tells a tale. An outline was first conceived in 1992 but was rejected by more than fifteen publishers. So the present chapters were all published as essays in different journals (including *The Political Quarterly*). Eventually the University of Minnesota Press took it on, albeit with a thoughtful and enthusiastic Foreword by Craig Calhoun, President of the (American) Social Science Research Council; and this Edinburgh University Press edition soon followed. A conclusion takes in 9/11 but was written before the London bombings. However, he had already seen clearly that the Arab/Israeli troubles were making the British media a little more conscious of British-Islamic attitudes and thought, and that 9/11 suddenly produced Muslim columnists and regular authorities appearing on the *Today* programme etc. (not that all these hastily gathered representatives of 'the community' were particularly representative rather than peculiarly articulate).

Modood uses the discourse of ethnicity. Race, strictly speaking—and what a loosely used concept it is—is only a belief of white (usually but not always) racists. Those who feel discriminated against and raise the cry of 'the equality of races' are really playing into their hands. For strictly speaking there is no such thing as race—if one means that genetic inheritance with visible attributes determines our values and talents. It follows from this belief that races must be kept pure. Intermarriage is a threat, both to 'black' and 'white'. Ethnicity, however, is a belief in loyalty and bonding by extended families; but, subject to all kinds of curious and traditional rules or customs, intermarriage between different ethnicities is thus not an inherent threat. Intermarriage is growing. The customs of ethic communities are constantly evolving, just as those of the majority community change. (Where is the old dominant culture of the English gentleman now—unless that is David Cameron's aim for an English counter-reformation?) Among British born, half of Caribbean men and a third of Caribbean women have a white partner, compared to a fifth of Indian or African-Asian men (among them the author), a tenth of Pakistani and Bangladeshi men, and as yet very few South Asian women. These differences are mainly accounted for by religion and tradition, certainly not by 'race'. The smaller number of Afro-Caribbeans and their less structured community life gives the potential to mix more easily. The salience of black football players helps. There the white working class can make its main vocal protest. Church of England congregations seem to accept male black priests more readily than female white ones—a funny old world. Social class, I suspect, though Modood gives perhaps too little attention to class, makes the big difference between the under-achieving black boys at schools and a small but emerging black middle class in the professions.

469

Perhaps this difference between the social structure of British Afro-Caribbeans and British Asians is what makes Trevor Phillips, of all men, as head of the Commission for Racial Equality, declare against 'the policy of multiculturalism'. It may, perhaps, hold back some blacks, but Modood throughout this thoughtful and well-researched book shows two things clearly: that multiculturalism gives the far larger Muslim and Hindu communities a sense of security; and that it does not involved an ideology of segregation, either voluntary or conditioned by the state. Multiculturalism has not been the result of a policy so much as the recognition of a fact. Many of us live with (at least) two major identities.

Modood is forceful and clear with a wealth of examples as to the kind of petty intolerances by the majority that can offend unnecessarily and even discriminate against minorities (employment practices and even dress codes at work, for instance), but also he points to traditionalist practices that can cut off typically both old and young Muslims from an understanding of the broader culture (those in the world of work are usually more integrated—that is, able to live with two cultures). He would support the government's new restrictions on immigration visas for Imams with neither English language nor knowledge of British ways, and also supports, in principle, the new tests and classes for the granting of citizenship. He values British citizenship, but sees no need—indeed some dangers in—government ministers making a fuss about it, largely to try to placate the popular press. It is the civic culture that holds things together rather than a throbbing patriotism. English understatement has a lot to do with toleration.

But the understandable absorption of most of these essays with contemporary issues and survey evidence does make him, I think, put the cart before the horse and miss the strongest argument against the nativists among the native English. He says, for instance:

The specific shape and texture of British citizenship does not simply vary as an instance of citizenship, but is connected to a sense of nationality (complicated by the fact that 'British' nests Scottish, Welsh and English nationalities, and those various nationalities undergo changes in salience and in their relationship to each other) . . . exactly the same is true of the new migrant group . . . for they too each have a specific character . . .

But I would argue that far from a complication this 'nesting' is itself the United Kingdom and has been since the Act or Treaty of Union in 1707. Scotland was not anglicised. There were Scottish puppets of Whitehall, certainly, but they were left to govern Scotland in a Scottish way under Scotland's (in Burke's sense) peculiar institutions. The main undeclared business of English politics from then until 1922 was holding the United Kingdom together. This is the massive historical precedent long before the *Windrush* and the encouragement of immigration from the subcontinent. Racial and religious prejudice, certainly, as there had been to large scale Irish Catholic and then Jewish immigration; but both within a broad framework of expedient religious and political toleration. Attempts to define a specific content for an overall Britishness and increase the intensity of it for perhaps only short-term political gain, these are likely to unsettle minority ethnic communities. I dare to say that leaders of Islamic and Afro-Caribbean opinion in Britain (and Modood and his Centre for the Study of Ethnicity and Citizenship is now in this category whether he likes it or not) should study and argue from history more to influence traditional modes of thought and prejudices, not just rely on attitude surveys. And British history is not just imperialism and the slave trade.

This takes me to my one worry about this book. He is right to recognise 'the country or polity as a legitimate and irreducible plurality, as a "community of communities" not just a liberal association of autonomous individuals', but I think he is wrong (like his friend and mentor Bhikhu Parekh) to then say that this means 're-imagining or reforming our national identity, our Britishness' now that we are a multicultural society. So we are, but we have been for a long, long time. If Modood and Parekh gave more thought to the history of Irish and Jewish immigration, and Scottish and Welsh internal migration during the Industrial Revolution, they might conclude that not defining Britishness too closely has been most helpful to integration, and that this negative capability was not entirely accidental among the old governing class. Irish Catholics and Jews are good citizens without having lost their identity and by being left to themselves to decide how culturally British (more precisely English or Scottish) they wished to be. To talk of re-imagining Britishness is either as empty or as dangerous as the new ministerial rhetoric of reasserting Britishness. Good laws and good behaviour make Britain a good enough place to live in with always the potential of being a better place; but better through a host of small everyday actions and big public policies.

Perhaps Modood's book is too concerned with stipulative identities and analysing surveys thereon. For identity is often (happily) a poor guide to actual behaviour. People with strongly held different identities may, of course, and do lobby for particular rights and against particular abuses; but it so has happened that in the United Kingdom they generally do so (except a handful of untypical fanatics posturing on a world stage) in a reasonably civic manner. If Britishness is to be reasserted at all it must be seen as something strong but narrow: a political and legal culture, not a general culture as implied by Irish, Scottish, Welsh, English and, indeed, Islamic. How right most immigrants are to call themselves, for instance, British Asians and not English Asians. They do not have to be assimilated to a general culture, only integrated with the economic, legal and political culture. Talk of re-imagining or reconstructing Britishness can be provocative, coming from minorities, or can be dangerous coming from ministers who claim to speak for all of us—but of course they don't.

Eastenders

The New East End: Kinship, Race and Conflict, by Geoff Dench, Kate Gavron and Michael Young[a]

Vol. 77, no. 3, July–September 2006

Last year Tony Blair, in a non-violent glorification speech, said that we were now—thanks to his policies aimed at 'a level playing field' etcetera making it 'possible for all those of talent to rise'—a 'meritocracy' as 'Michael Young had foretold'. This is a fascinating example, to be pedantic and ponderous, of the difference between history and myth, or perhaps more colloquially put, of 'getting it wrong'. Young's book of 1958 *The Rise of the Meritocracy* was, of course, a satirical attack on the growing social ideal that rising up economically was the object of the good life (yes, even then; as so often in social history, Thatcherism only accelerated an existing tendency). But it is nice to think that he has been remembered on high at all, even misremembered.

The positive side of meritocracy goes back to the rejection of social class defined by status; so at least as far back as Napoleon's slogan that both the army and the administration should be a career open to all talents. At first it was in essence an ideal of the professional middle classes, the bourgeoisie. And the route to advancement was through liberal education. Only later did it become, first in the USA after the Civil War (the era of Carnegie's book *Triumphant Democracy*, 1886) and then, indeed, after the Second World War in Thatcher's and Blair's Britain, almost wholly identified with economic success. There was always a problem, of course: that plainly there was not room for everyone at the top. The best answer to this contradiction of capitalism was found in the American genre of 'from rags to riches' popular novels.

In Horatio Alger's *Luke Larkin's Luck*, Luke moves from being a ragged boot black to rescuing and then marrying the millionaire's daughter and getting a seat on the board. 'There has been some luck about it, I admit, but it would not have come to Luke but for his early thrift and virtue.' But the 'lucky break' that sustains both the 'American dream' and the harshness of the new privatisation of public values, the ultra-competitive consumer society, can take the form of a lottery ticket quite as much as sustained hard work and loyalty to disloyal employers.

This new reworking and updating of Michael Young and Peter Willmott's *Family and Kinship in East London* of 1957 reveals a sociological paradox: family and kinship are now stronger among the Bangladeshi immigrants than among the remaining but largely scattered indigenous white families of Tower Hamlets. The moral point that links the fictional satire of *The Rise of*

[a] Profile Books, 274 pp, £15.00.

the Meritocracy to *Family and Kinship*, published within a year of *The Rise*, is that community involves extended family bonds and caring. Left-wing intellectuals have too often been shy of this point, however much they espoused as a cause opposition to the breaking up of communities (of working class others, of course) by well-meant rehousing and slum clearance policies; and right-wing intellectuals saw such ties (among working class others, of course) as holding back the exceptionally talented. This presupposition is beneath the surface of the Dench and Gavron book, writing up what they began with Michael Young before his death, but not so explicit as in his two earlier works.

'Race and Conflict', however, must now mark great changes and a new emphasis for the survey. The residents of the former boroughs of Bethnal Green and Stepney before, during and for a while after the Second World War had lived as extended families. Both private landlords and the council listened when Mum, usually Mum, had 'put in a word' for a daughter about to marry, to be found a place, if not next door, at least in the same street or just round the corner. Long suffering good tenants were thus 'obliged', and the view was that it made for better tenants. The Eastenders had practised self-help and mutual aid in bad times and saw the postwar welfare state as a just reward for their endurance, suffering and patriotism during the war. This comes out most strongly in even the new surveys and interviews. But as rational criteria of allocation by priority of need came in, mainly family size in relation to space as defined by the tape measure of the sociologist Ruth Glass at the LSE, communities were broken up and people began to be rehoused often far away—in those once fabulous New Towns north of London. The new houses were lovely but the Green Line buses to London were crowded at weekends with the lonely family groups trying to keep up connections. After I came back from the USA in 1956, American visitors wanted me to show them, firstly, the East End slums (even then getting harder to find) and then the New Towns as marvels of planning. And as I went drinking with my LSE East End evening students in their haunts on a Friday night, seeing the last of the old tight-knit cockney and Jewish neighbourhoods, I marvelled, living in Hampstead, that at the same time well-off professionals were crowding into converted small artisan cottages or mews flats in Belsize Park and even Camden which were far below Ruth Glass's minimum space per person for public housing, but made desirable and comfortable by well designed and costly integral domestic amenities.

Now, four decades later, Michael Young (before his death two years ago) and colleagues replicated the original study, the same mixture of in-depth characterful interviews, social observation and hard statistics. But the new study is not of the possible fragmentation of a homogeneous community, but of the actual nature of diverse and divided communities. Today the extended family living close together is typical of the Bangladeshi, and all but collapsed among whites. Who now exhibits 'family values' best? Priorities for housing by need worked in favour of the newcomers, so not surprisingly bitterness was stirred

473

among the former white majority. In many parts of Tower Hamlets, the wider area of the new study, they are now the fragmented minority. Family connection now divides the ethnic groups, indeed can fortify racism. The BNP have seized their local opportunities. And this has not been one-sided. The gangs of racist white youths, searching for victims, soon created opponents acting very much in their own image. Mimesis is a strong natural mechanism not confined to the birds and the bees and stick insects.

Geoff Dench and Kate Gavron present their findings clearly and accessibly, with deliberate dispassion and deep empathy for the anxieties of both communities. They do not ignore white racism but they know that simply to rail against it is too easy, too often self-indulgent indeed rather than reflective; they know well, unlike some professional social workers from outside these areas, that to combat white racism effectively social policy and day to day contacts must appear to be even-handed. Yes, it was wrong and mistaken for the older generation of whites to see the former social workers and council officials as 'our people', but the authors are aware that the new generation of social workers can be so anti-racist in principle that they can be imperceptive in practice. Dench and Gavron show the same kind of empathy as Michael Collins in his *The Likes of Us: A Biography of the White Working Class* (which won the Orwell Prize in 2004 but for his Southwark pains got some stick from chat-show trendies). However, the break-up of the white community as extended family is not simply the 'push factor' of incomers (historically no novelty); it is also the 'pull factor' of the changed national culture of consumerism and individualism—as espoused by both Thatcher and Blair. 'It is individuals who are manifestly successful in Britain who are choosing to move on. . . . Hence those who remain . . . are bound to bear some of the marks of failure. They are the ones meritocracy has rejected, so their collective behaviour takes on some aspects of a reaction to rejection.' Conflict is deplorable but its causes are obvious. Some of it may be an inherent racism. One is never sure. But what is clear is that racists' behaviour is spurred on by poverty and a sense of failure.

Surveys and interviews with ordinary Bangladeshis show little sign of the West Indian phenomenon of exaggerated expectations, both economic and social: the idealised version of Britain that several novels have portrayed. They seem more pragmatic and less reactive to hostility if left alone. This poses problems for official policies of integration and the debate about whether multiculturalism is simply descriptive of dual identities or a pejorative description of *de facto* segregation. But their inward-looking pragmatism poses no great problem for law and order, except among the young unemployed when deliberately provoked or exploited by educated outward-looking real or would-be terrorists.

Most immigrants, in fact, obey the laws in return for the protection of the laws. Poverty and unemployment are greater among the Bangladeshi community than among any other immigrant community in geographical contiguity. They certainly suffer from discrimination. But their reference point is not, like the white working classes, others more fortunate or favoured in Britain, but the contrast with back home. The authors quote from Monica Ali's novel *Brick Lane*. The sad heroine Nazneen, with no English but 'hello' and 'thank you', has her new friend Raze explain to her: 'If you don't have a job here, they give you money. Did you know that? You can have somewhere to live, without any rent. Your children can go to school. And on top of that, they give you money. What would happen at home?' But they have no need to quote even a true fiction. One among the many men they recorded says: 'I want to bring my family over but I do not have much money at the moment. The children are growing up and going to school. In our country it costs money to send them to school and to take them to doctors. In Bangladesh you need money the moment you step out of home.' Poor though he is, he sends money home, as most do. But if he could save then he might have the passage money.

However, the authors find evidence of some growing tensions growing within the community. Most Bangladeshis 'are reasonably content to confine their aspirations within their family and community activities'. But they worry that many of the young are beginning to speak English among themselves and are picking up fast the values of the counterculture of modern Britain, inimical to the religious faith and customs of the older generation. The more educationally successful begin to rise on the merito-cratic ladder; so they can and commonly do live in two worlds, in one sense, but no longer actually live in the East End. They are weekend visitors, like the first generation of the Londoners decanted to the new towns. Should we say that they will soon be integrated or that the community is losing its natural leaders?

Both the analysis of this most important study and the dilemmas revealed have implications far beyond Bethnal Green and Brick Lane. Alas, how typical that Tony the Glib, hearing of the title *The Rise of the Meritocracy*, thought that Michael Young of all people favoured a meritocracy. If only he had read Young's once famous short pamphlet of 1948 when head of research at the Labour Party, *Small Man Big World*. Michael gave me one when as a young student I knocked on his door in Gordon Square to collect the monthly party subscription and hadn't a clue, somewhat to his surprise, who he was.

Comrades of the world: you are history!

Comrades: A World History of Communism, by Robert Service[a]

Vol. 79, no. 2, April–June 2008

Here at last is a full account of the rise and fall of Communism, and if tightly packed, yet is readable and overall as objective as seems possible. Robert Service is Professor of Russian History at the University of Oxford, author of

[a] Macmillan, 592 pp, £25.

biographies of Lenin and Stalin, as well as a history of Russia since the collapse of the Soviet Union. It is necessary to state his credentials in this whirlpool of rival perspectives—too many of which still echo controversies of the Cold War.

'Communism, like nuclear fuel, has a long after-life', but now only Cuba, Vietnam and China even pretend to fly the flag (at half-mast); only North Korea claims to be true to the basic tenets of Marxism-Leninism, and even they seem now to be trading off nuclear independence for some fruits of global capitalism. Yet a 'long after-life' indeed—the sentence comes from a *New Statesman* article defending himself from one of the *Guardian*'s subeditors calling him a 'neo-conservative' who underplays 'revisionist history' that some things weren't so bad after all. Well, some things weren't—take full employment—but the price in terms of lives, liberty and despotism was somewhat disproportionate. Robert Service does not give much space to foreign fellow-travellers who often did more than the Communist parties themselves to spread at least the message. Curiously, several old *Guardian* writers still see all anti-communism as tainted with neo-conservatism; even Orwell got the treatment. 'A long after-life' indeed, if perhaps irritating more than crucial in the world scale of things. David Caute defined fellow-travellers in his book of that name as people 'who believed in socialism in somebody else's country'.

Service gets right into the intellectual hard stuff. Right from the beginning, in the times of exile in the 1900s, Lenin was filleting and enhancing the few and somewhat vague passages in Marx on 'the dictatorship of the proletariat' and on revolution as violent (except possibly in Great Britain and the Netherlands). Some of the best criticisms of what became Leninism came from fellow Marxists in this period—Bernstein and Rosa Luxemburg most famously. The theory said that revolution would take place in capitalist Germany rather than in an agrarian and peasant Russia, but the Leninist mentality was able to take advantage of the breakdown of the old regime with a *coup d'état* (the October revolution) while the popular uprisings of the February revolution were censored out of Soviet history. Reading Service makes me recall young Crick's iron law of revolutions: revolutions take place because governments break down not for the reasons that the party that happens to come to power in the chaos hires venal historians to illustrate their foresight.

Nothing in these huge events was necessary. Contingency occurs within social conditions, but can then change them. Stalinism was not a break from Leninism, only a crude form of it. Yet the idea of world revolution was, this book corrects our received views, more often a matter of lip-service than of immediate policy and concentrated effort. Foreign communist parties sprang up fighting poverty and oppression more or less spontaneously, encouraged by the example of the Soviet Union and imitating strong central command and discipline. Rarely were they the creation, as in legend, of heroic Soviet agents loaded with gold and guns; but, once they were in the field, then minimal help had to be given, but more minimal than Western governments supposed. Also we have forgotten that 'the great transformation', the rapid industrialisation of the Soviet Union, creating that image of power that attracted many and alarmed others, depended on Stalin quietly trading oil and grain for technology and capitalist engineers. After the Wall Street crash, 'Stalin's eagerness to trade was a godsend to American industry'. Ford provided equipment and expertise for the huge Novgorod automobile works; the McKee Corporation of Cleveland provided the electric generators and engineers for the new city of Magnitogorsk; and, similarly, the oil wells needed American and Anglo-Dutch involvement.

Pragmatism and paranoia can coexist in one mind. Service confirms the more familiar story of how Stalin's fear of subversion, leading to the purges of the old Bolsheviks and then of the top ranks of the army, desperately weakened military strength, making him desperate for the non-aggression pact with Nazi Germany that was signed on 24 August 1939 to the amazement of the world and discomfort of foreign communist parties. Hitler was free to attack Poland the following month (only postponing his intention to destroy the Soviet Union). That was the first test for blind faith in Moscow that world communism was to endure, long before the suppression of the Hungarian rebels in 1956 and the Czech reformers in 1968. Gradually it became all too much. Khrushchev's speech to the Twentieth Party Congress denouncing Stalinism dismayed hardliners everywhere, but gave those with some socialist idealism remaining a glimmer of hopeless hope; yet it was the slow-burning fuse that was to destroy the brutal authority of communist regimes throughout Eastern Europe. And turning from attempted totalitarianism to a more traditional autocracy could do nothing for the irrationality of the economy.

Yet Moscow had never been as totally in control of foreign communist parties as their enemies believed. Stalin in 1945 urged Mao Zedong to continue the pact with Chiang Kai-shek and the Kuomintang! Moscow had little influence over North Koreans or Vietnamese, and none at all over the genocidal lunatic Pol Pot. The real threat in the Cold War, this history makes clear, was not of communist worldwide victory, but nuclear accident or pre-emptive miscalculation. However, belief in Soviet power and fear could lead to exaggerated reactions. Service recalls Lance Sharkey, the devotedly Stalinist leader of the Communist Party of Australia, and recounts how in 1951 'the Conservatives under Robert Menzies out-McCarthyised Senator McCarthy in the USA by trying to ban the party outright'. The referendum failed, but enough was said about subversion, Stalinist iniquities and close ties with communism in South-East Asia for most Australians to conclude that communism was not for them. Indeed.

Does it now seem 'all so unimaginably different and all so long ago'? Yes and no. Service ends by saying that communism's methods 'will have a long afterlife even when the last communist state has disappeared'.

Scotching the Scots

The Scots and the Union, by Christopher Whatley; *The Union: England, Scotland and the Treaty of 1707,* by Michael Fry; *The Union of 1707: Why and How,* by Paul Henderson Scot[a]

Vol. 79, no. 3, July–September 2008

The London Press is busy Scotching the Scots. Even in the *Observer*: '[I]n 2006 public spending per head in England was £6,762. In Scotland it was £8,265'; then sourly 'every Scot is "worth" 20 per cent more than his English counterpart'. This is true, but no explanation given that the Barnett formula is weighted in such a way that bad health and transport distances in the Highlands and Islands count heavily—even if the variation from the national average is much the same in England's North-East region. Second only to immigrants, Scots are the alien 'other' about whom editors delight, with stirring headlines, to excite their readers into honest, ignorant indignation— much as led the late Sir Denis Brogan to translate the lament of republican politicians in the French Third Republic, 'nous sommes trahis', as 'we wuz robbed'.

Meanwhile, the Scots debate their future seriously but among themselves with deep but fairly calm divisions—a debate at many different levels, one of which involves divergent understandings of their past. So last year, the three hundredth anniversary of the Act or Treaty of Union of 1707, was a bumper year in Scotland for earnest extramural forums and panels, numerous articles high and low, and a few solid big books by historians, both academic and amateur—little of which was noticed south of the border. As far as most English editors and reviewers were concerned, they could have saved their breath to cool their porridge.

Ruaridh Nicoll, however, in the *Observer*, praised Christopher Whatley's careful, detailed scholarly research into the politics and members of the last old Parliament of 1703–1707 for revealing 'the sophisticated politics used by these Scots and reclaims them as patriots', particularly of the commissioners who negotiated with the English. Both Whatley and Michael Fry do, indeed, see the whole process as a negotiation, not as a sell-out, in which the Scots gained greatly as well as losing an independent parliament, or more truly often only a semi-independent after the union of the crowns in 1603. Nationalist popular historians like Paul Scot play down negotiations, bargaining and compromise and quote Robert Burns's ranting rhyme 'bought and sold by English gold' as if evidence. There was bribery and pressure; indeed some heavy metal had to be used on the House of Lords to overcome bishops' resistance to the establishment of the Presbyterian Church, a subsidiary enactment that brought many votes round in the final session of Scotland's

[a] Edinburgh University Press, 424 pp, £25.99 hb and £14.99 pb (Whatley); Berlinn, 422 pp, £8.99 (Fry); Saltire Society, 85 pp, £6.99 (Scot).

parliament, 'the end of an auld sang'. Whatley reminds how 'the political machinery of government—on both sides of the borders—only worked satisfactorily when wheels were oiled by pensions, places and promises of patronage' (no regular inflated salaries and expenses then). Yet overall they were serious men, as concerned for the safety and economic welfare of their country as for 'pelf' and place. They believed that they had made the right decision after long consideration for debatable but sufficient reasons. For if the Scottish Parliament had finally refused the unilateral English legislation for a Protestant succession under one crown, it would have risked, amid Jacobite sentiment, which was then far from negligible, the restoration of the House of Stewart; and there were probably as many or more Episcopalian Jacobites as Catholics. Almost inevitably the largely English war with France would then have led to French intervention in bitter civil war in Scotland and a full-scale English invasion or 'liberation'.

Nationalists like Paul Scot, and even more reflective intellectuals like Tom Nairn and Neal Ascherson, tend to judge the anti-Catholicism of that time by the standards, conditions and politics of today. Then Catholic power, allied to France and Spain, was a military and religious threat to both England and to the Protestant majority in Scotland. The 1688 Revolution Settlement was at stake. Paul Scot, in this short and lively book (summing up much work over many years), has no doubts and revels in rhetorical anachronisms, as when he calls the old parliaments 'spokesmen for the nation'. There was no nonsense about democracy back then and neither parliament was in any ancient or modern sense democratic. His familiar method is to quote impressively from original documents, but mainly passages from anti-unionists, notably his hero, the brilliant but unstable Andrew Fletcher of Saltoun. Like Dr Johnson reporting Parliament he 'does not let the Whig dogs have the best of it'. Whereas Michael Fry, formerly that *rara avis* an intellectual Scottish Tory (now in the SNP like Paul Scot!), and, even rarer, an established scholarly historian outside the university system, in a brilliantly written narrative reaches broadly the same conclusions as Whatley. There is no logical connection between the cause of union in 1707 and where one can stand today. Times change.

Scot has long argued bribery and betrayal as if the case for independence depended on it. I remember saying in my Mackintosh memorial lecture (as in the last issue of this journal)[b] that one does not have to be a bad historian to be a good nationalist. Bad history can indeed, all over the world, put heart into popular movements. Myths and folk traditions have to be considered and placated as well as realities, but it is not only truth that suffers. Dedicated nationalist historians can among fellow intellectuals give the cause an unhelpful air of passionate and uncompromising eccentricity. Truth will come out at some level, just as scholarly history in the last forty years in

[b] Actually in the last but one: vol. 79, no.1, January–March 2008: 'The Four Nations: Interrelations', reprinted above at p. 307.

Ireland has filtered down into the schools, largely replacing nationalist myths. Some recent books on England and Englishness are much like Paul Scot's (as the Ulsterman Arthur Aughey pointed out in his brilliant *The Politics of Englishness*).

Each of the three authors brings out that the final decision for union was without doubt unpopular. Fear of the mob prolonged the debates. Urban riots broke out immediately afterwards, even though they soon subsided into sullen acceptance. However, Whatley argues that the 1715 Jacobite rising was more popular and serious than has been generally supposed; perhaps more threatening to the union, if it had not been so incompetently led, than the more famous and romanticised 1745.

Yes, present politics is mirrored in all history, but it never wholly determines real history. The basic issue in 1703–1707 for Scottish statesmen and church leaders (for the Kirk was the more popular institution in both senses than the Parliament) was could Scotland stand and prosper alone? The answer could be different now. While Whatley says that there never was a time when all Scots were happy with the union, he ends as if from full academic authority and objectivity by invoking 'a framework, that with countless adjustments, has lasted for three centuries', so that '[t]hose Scots who signed the addresses delivered to William of Orange at Whitehall late in 1688 that called for "ane intire and perpetuall union betwixt the two king-doms", would have been amazed and, no doubt, greatly gratified'. Yet Fry, more in the trenches as it were, former journalist as well as scholarly historian, has given serious attention to ultimately impractical compromise proposals in the debates for forms of federalism, and he doubts that the awkward half-way house of devolution can last. He concludes: 'Now we are travelling back from the destination reached at the Union, if along a less bumpy route. But the question poses itself whether we should not make greater haste to the place where we started, as an independent nation.

The question also poses itself, to my mind, of whether independence would bring all the benefits nationalists hope for or all of the troubles that unionists fear. The very slogan of 'independence in Europe' of Alex Salmond's new SNP, as distinct from the out-and-out separatists from everything of the old SNP—from Europe as much as from England—this 'in Europe' tacitly recognises a degree of control that, south of the border, Conservatives resent and kick against. So 'Independence in Europe' is a relative concept. Also social and economic interrelations between Scotland and the rest of the United Kingdom are so close and intertwined that for most ordinary lives independence might make far less difference than is commonly supposed. That, of course, cuts both ways; in the great debate it is not conclusive. Salmond has said that independence is 'a political not a social matter' and that Scotland would still be in the Commonwealth with the Queen still sitting there powerless but pretty. However, the consequences of Scottish independ-ence could be dramatic enough for English politics even without the great temptation for the Conservatives, like the Czechs to the Slovaks, not to make a big fuss about cutting the knot of the union, even to connive in it. Meanwhile the London media and the Labour Party especially should ponder why support grows for the SNP, even when about a quarter of its voters and at least two-thirds of Scots still favour the union. It might just have something to do with the social-democratic, welfare policies of the SNP, which many Scots believe that New Labour have, if not abandoned entirely, fatally diluted— even under Gordon Brown.

Part III
Commentaries, 1974 to 1981

Commentary: Untitled

Vol. 45, no. 2, April–June 1974

Post-mortems are a necessary bore. Think, however, what might happen without them. Anything should be tried to avoid any risks of the mental horrors of the late election campaign repeating themselves. Writing only ten days after the election, one feared that already a deluge of post-mortems would have come from television, radio and press, drowning good and bad points alike, removing any possible need for further comment. And one advantage of a quarterly is that one does not have to editorialise like *The Times* and *Guardian*, even on the morning of the election—which in both cases were collectors' items of punctured platitudes. Just think of the attention any editorial in *The Times* would once again receive if it appeared on a day following no editorial—because there was simply nothing to say, or because the situation was moving too fast.

But the new political situation proved so fascinating, something actually happening day by day of a novel and unpredictable kind, as if to justify the ghastly imperative of news each day having to sound new and of editorial and feature writers having to find some new moral from yesterday, that the post-mortem was short and sketchy. The media dashed on with surprisingly few backward glances. But perhaps not really so surprising, for our whole view of politics has become dominated by day to day news values. This is not to blame the press; perhaps more to blame are the politicians who seem to have nothing better to do than to snatch at ephemeral publicity, few if any of whom appear confident that they can make news, influence events, lead and even change opinion.

There is one man who still has this gift—it does not always come where we would wish it—and who had had this to say:

I consider it an act of gross irresponsibility that this General Election has been called in the face of the current and impending industrial situation. The election will in any case, be essentially fraudulent: for the object of those who have called it is to secure the electorate's approval for a position which the Government itself knows to be untenable, in order to make it easier to abandon that position subsequently.

It is unworthy of British politics, and dangerous to Parliament itself for a Government to try to steal success by telling the public one thing during an election and doing the opposite afterwards. (7 February 1974)

Mr Powell's words deserve getting into the school textbooks. It is a terrible thought that even his bitterest critics, both of his racial views and of his *laissez-faire* economics, let alone of his taste for Nietzsche, cannot deny him an exceptional integrity, indeed use it, just as now, not as an object of admiration in itself, but as a stick to beat the backs of their own purported leaders.

This is the main point lost by the media's lack of post-mortem and by their disease of galloping diurnal myopia. Yes, the polls went up and the polls

Published by Blackwell Publishing Ltd, 9600 Garsington Road, Oxford OX4 2DQ, UK and 350 Main Street, Malden, MA 02148, USA

went down, the polls got closer and at last, thank God, the official polls closed, but few commentators recalled that essentially the polls had presented public opinion as remarkably unchanged since the summer and autumn of the previous year, the beginnings of the 'Liberal revival'—for all the drama of the miners' strike and the almost criminally irresponsible three-day working week. During all that time neither main party was ever more than a point or two above 40 per cent, nowhere near the high forties which has usually passed for 'a mandate for the people', and Liberals were at or just above 20 per cent. Such remained the final result: Labour 37.2, Conservative 38.2 and Liberal 19.3 per cent, with all others gaining 5.4 per cent. All *three* major parties actually lost a little ground in the campaign. The main surprise was the large number of seats that 'the others' picked up, plain evidence that Liberalism is still mainly a protest vote, as seen by the greater attractions in Scotland and Wales of Nationalists as a vehicle of protest. But, the main point to grasp and hold on to tight, the protest must be taken seriously. In the autumn of 1973 it was a commonplace that people were fed up with the leaders of both the main parties. *The Times* even ran its famous funny poll to show that a centre party led by Dick Taverne (or was it Roy Jenkins ?) would sweep the country—if some ahistorical fairy with a wand ever waved it off the ground. The two-party system was plainly getting blamed for many things for which hitherto an esoteric few had been blaming the ill-functioning of Parliament.

The state of public opinion was remarkably little affected by all the sound and fury of the election campaign and the unprecedentedly extensive and boring coverage given to it by radio and television. The broad result had been predictable for some time. May we quote ourselves editorialising in October 1973 about 'The Party System':

The Liberals . . . still only represent a protest vote from people who are plainly angry at the incapacity of either major party to prevent inflation and are disillusioned by the huge and blandly ill-explained changes of basic policies by both parties. Certainly even this protest has now gone beyond a by-election phenomenon. But many people now see the Liberals, rightly or wrongly, as a genuine centre party who for the first time since the 1920s are to be taken seriously in electoral terms.

We could be facing a time of minority or of coalition government. This may not be desirable, but there is no evidence that it need be disastrous. If it did come, it might be what the public wanted. It might even restore confidence in the working of the parliamentary system which could be threatened if the two main parties continue to be so inept and so unsuccessful in dealing with inflation. Certainly it is incredible how out of touch the two main parties seem with public opinion, how grimly internalised their attitudes and disputes have become and how childish and degrading their 'no, you did it first' mutual polemics.

But as one listened to the first post-election utterances of the party leaders, one realised that the point has not yet sunk in. Both Labour and Tory leaders were blaming the electorate for their indecisiveness: they sounded as if they wanted (as Brecht remarked of the East German leaders) to dissolve the

People and elect another one. It will take the failure of another such election campaign to effect any change in public opinion before any reformation of the party system could take place. If it did take place, it would not be *The Times*'s fantasy of a centre party led by civilised good fellows, but more likely a defiance by elected MPs of the internalised world of the two party machines and of the ageing party activists. Nothing in politics is more depressing than the way that the narrow worlds of the party machines, the Palace of Westminster, and the small band of political correspondents all reinforce each other, all regard the other as a source of knowledge or intuition about 'public opinion'. There are, dare one say, the polls. No one wishes to be or need be governed by the polls, but it is common sense to respect their evidence as to how opinion has to be changed if, for instance, a real fair-wages policy is to be undertaken. How crazy that politicians, aided by some men whom they alone regard as 'political scientists', seem to limit their interest in opinion polls to the utterly trivial business of predicting election results. But equally how arrogant it is for the left wing of the Labour Party to believe that 'the people' really want socialism, when the Labour Party is declining in membership, the radical young won't come near it, and so, like a Church that has abandoned proselytising, they turn their enthusiasm inwards on their fellow members. Before there can be a Socialist government, there needs to be a socialist public opinion: the Labour movement needs to go back to the streets and convert people.

Can the leaders of the two parties survive? Probably. Should they? It almost beggars the imagination to think that a man with such littleness of vision that he mistook pig-headedness for firmness, unyielding obstinacy for leadership, could move in one year from a strident belief in a market economy to tying himself to the self-created stake of a rigid incomes policy, provoking a miners' strike, plunging the country into industrial depression, and then snatching at an election to get himself out of the difficulties he had himself created (perhaps more by folly than intent—to be more generous than Enoch Powell), and yet could survive electoral defeat five minutes. And that he could have tried to form a government, nonetheless, without bringing moderate people—indeed!—on to the streets in protest. We are not what we were as a people.

But equally it is no small oddity that an opposition leader who could not win a clear majority in such a circumstance, amid such price rises, such deficits in overseas trade, amid such visible and painful economic misman-agement by the government, was not merely unchallenged to continue, but allowed to continue in precisely the old way of too much personal power used for such narrow political ends, another cabinet riddled with old Bills and Barbaras and self-defeating checks and balances, the very things that led to the economic failures of Wilson's previous administration. The PLP now reaps the fruits of its cowardice in not dropping its shifty pilot four years ago. And Wilson carries on as before. Failure has gone to his head. Power has become an end in itself.

Perhaps there is a faint hope that minority government will restore a habit of collective decision-making among political leaders. When one used to say in the last three years of MPs of *both* parties: 'Why on earth don't you get rid of that man. Can't you see he is such a liability?', the answer always came (well, not always—I was reproved *once* by a Labour MP and *twice* by Tories), 'Who can we replace him by?' No one seemed particularly impressed by the oft-repeated argument of *The Political Quarterly* that that answer embodies the whole problem, the myth of the constitution that we still need a wartime prime ministership, that concentrated power is always more efficient, and the strain it puts on relatively normal men, like Ted Heath and Harold Wilson, to try to act like Lloyd Georges or Winston Churchills. Neither party is short of good No. 2s (which is essentially what Ted Heath was, brilliant as Consul, disastrous as *Princeps*). Many of these No. 2s are even well known in the public eye. To name them is easy but is to do them no service. Perhaps it will not matter quite as much who is Prime Minister. What will matter far more is for there to be a realistic distribution of power where power lies, otherwise for all the seeming powerfulness of the prime ministerial office, little happens if powerful ministers are not given a clear job and left to get on with it.

If we do come to the pass that the country can only be governed by coalitions, then the Cabinet will have to be stronger relative to the Prime Minister than of late. If we do come to the pass that the United Kingdom can only be held together by allowing proportional representation (as proved necessary in Northern Ireland, and would to God we had applied it to parliamentary constituencies there too), then obviously coalitions will be the order of the day.

Coalitions, it is said, would prove weak. 'Strong government' would suffer. One gasps to know what these banalities are thought to mean when, if successful management of the economy were used as a reasonably important test, there has been so little strong government under both Labour and Tory. On economic issues of inflation, industrial relations, prices and incomes, coalitions could prove stronger. They could prove stronger because popular consent, understanding, agreement, compliance, even participation, is needed before any such policies can work, whether 'voluntary' or 'statutory'. Coalition might be able to mobilise public opinion behind a few important measures in a way that the parties have totally failed to do. And a few important measures might outweigh a crowded programme of bits and pieces left over from the great era of party government.

This is not an argument for coalitions. Better that large parties themselves act more like the coalitions they in fact are. But all public confidence in the system could be wrecked if the thoughtful ones in the two main parliamentary parties do not read the election results as a lack of confidence in them both. They are perfectly entitled to say that the results have also disappointed Mr Thorpe, quite apart from the issue of PR; or to say that the Liberals may not really be a party like the others that could be trusted to play follow-my-leader in any kind of government, coalition or otherwise. But that, with respect, is not the main point. In the last election, everyone lost. Prizes for none.

The one place where moderation versus extremism was not a phony issue was indeed a deadly issue: Northern Ireland. And there the calling of a general election, so soon after the elections for the assembly and before the new Executive has had time to establish itself, was more than a mistake; it was a crime. Eleven Ulster Loyalist seats and one SDLP is a nightmarish result, even if five of the Loyalists got in through the divisions of their opponents and even if the turnout was low (66.3 per cent compared to the United Kingdom as a whole, 78.7 per cent). But 59 per cent of those voting supported the Loyalists. Did Ireland not figure at all in discussions of whether and when to hold the election? It was bad enough to have brought William Whitelaw home before his work was done (whatever he thought of the matter) simply to window-dress the hard face of Heath's government—infinitely worse than to have pulled the rug from under Faulkner's and Fitt's feet. The anti-Sunningdale Unionists will now do everything they can to force the British government or the Executive of the Northern Ireland Assembly to hold new elections, to prevent them holding on grimly with three and a half years legally ahead of them. And 'everything' will include physical intimidation and violence. The risk of concerted riots amounting to civil war, no longer mere spasmodic urban terrorism, is now very real, and it would begin from the Protestant side.

One thing, however, should be clear. The power of the Loyalists in Westminster will be a negative one only. Any party that tried to come to terms with them in return for parliamentary support would be damned for ever in the eyes of public opinion. Ordinary people instinctively believe that there are some limits to opportunism. Mr Whitelaw's great public reputation is solely due to Ireland, and people were impressed with how swift and unconventional a British government could be when it had to face a crisis. The late government's Irish policy, both flexible and firm, earned it much respect. One hopes against hope that it will not have been ruined by the premature election. When will we get it into our heads that with so many lives at stake if civil war did break out, no other issue is as important in British politics at the moment—except avoiding economic breakdown which would render all policies impossible.

Will the BBC and ITV think hard about the character of their election coverage? And will scholars begin to study the impact of different types of reporting and current affairs programmes on attitudes and opinions? All that money which is squandered on voting behaviour research and so little to guide the makers of current affairs programmes.

Quite apart from research, however, what should the broadcasting media have been doing? Accurately reporting the campaign? Obviously, and they made a very good job of that. Informing the public on the issues? Here there is great room for doubt. For they mostly concentrated on letting politicians themselves present the issues. And these programmes became, of course, part of the campaign itself; and the press reported them as such. But everywhere one went one found people bored, not just the normally apolitical, but the highly political too; bored stiff at so much repetition and all at the same level of party rhetoric, of childishly shallow charge and counter-charge, petulant and uninformative abuse. Politics is in a debased condition at the moment. Neither main party dares to argue from principle, or seems certain what its principles are. The descent into statistical rhetoric is then inevitable, by people who all too often have little respect for statistical honesty or even statistical competence. Nearly all politicians seem to underestimate both the common sense and the memory of the public. Only a handful of politicians try to explain what the basic problems really are. Most of the leaders think they can change front without having to explain, without then inviting contempt and disgust. They appear to believe that people will accept that only the folly of the other lot has led to the troubles we are in.

Well, perhaps the broadcasting media cannot treat politics in election times more seriously than the politicians do. But they could use elections as orgies of national political education, not just as orgies of political vanity and self-righteousness. Let the politicians establish the issues, but then the BBC should bring in others as well to explore them, and try itself to explain them and to present facts and figures in an impartial way, or to explain why all the figures are slanted. Newspapers in their features sections in election time are better at this than the broadcasting media in the big package programmes. Partly this is for a very mundane reason. Most of the newspapers have reasonably good libraries and research departments. BBC and ITV have 'researchers' attached to programmes, but no continuing group of subject specialists providing a central service—and very few of the researchers know a subject. Their job is to feed interviewers with politically difficult questions, not to brief the public. Most of them care more for making exciting films than for discovering the truth about events or the evidence for policies.

There has been a great decline in the last three years of both quantity and quality in serious current affairs television. Background programmes everywhere are cut in their budgets and instant news is king. Why is this so? Are the media taking their values from the politicians or the politicians from them? One would like to see a serious public inquiry into the nature and objects of current affairs broadcasting. This would not be to smoke out bias or wickedness; most of that is transparent and is much overestimated. What is far more unexplored and worrying is the possibility that serious examination of problems is being swallowed by the daily titillation of instant news—the sort of stuff one watches compulsively and cannot remember a thing about a day later, except that 'Keith was rather good', 'Brian rather bad', or 'Bob was much the same as ever'. All the fears of Austin Mitchell in his important article 'The Decline of Current Affairs Television' (*The Political Quarterly*, vol. 44, no. 2, April–June 1973) seem confirmed by the election coverage.

The worst prophecy about the whole political situation is that things may continue much as they are and that we will all watch the politicians pull the house down, as in Weimar, as in the Third Republic, as in Spain. Well, perhaps never as bad as that—perhaps always only just as bad as at present.

BRC

Commentary: 'Talk of Coalition'

Vol. 45, no. 4, October–December 1974

Most of the talk about coalitions has been fatuous.[a] A 'coalition of national unity'—but for what? Policies must come first. The primary problem is not a constitutional problem. We may just have to get used to living without clear party majorities; minority government is perfectly possible. The primary problem is a political and economic one. Inflation could reduce us to bitter misery, and if there are a very few who would welcome the breakdown of the present system rather than its deliberate change, breakdown indeed it would be, events with totally unpredictable consequences, as likely to lead to the kind of iron regimes that Orwell predicted in 1984 as to anything clearly either revolutionary or Fascist.

There is hardly time to inquire into the fundamental causes of inflation as it approaches a rate of 20 per cent a year and is likely to increase if no firm action is taken. Whether the fundamental causes are of price-pull rather than wage-push, we can but try to control what we can control to the greatest extent: wages. The problem is that this is deemed to be politically impossible after Conservative and Labour have each failed twice, even after swapping clothes. A coalition of national unity could reach restraint to the unions (and the rest of us), but who would take any notice of such ecumenical blather? People in top positions, as Mr Grimond pointed out in a famous letter to *The Times*, have hardly set an inspiring example. They act, as some leading politicians have done in their land deals, as if no one is supposed to be watching. But what has been missed in all this controversy is that there are conditions in which another kind of minority Labour government could be in a stronger position to try again.

Incomes policies have failed because the unions have not been convinced. Now only voluntary wage restraint is thought possible—reaching a parody of nebulousness in the 'Social Contract'. Perhaps it is impossible to persuade

---

[a] This is the central section of a three-part Commentary. The other two parts (on corruption in local government and Labour's nationalisation programme) are by William Robson.

491

some leaders of the largest unions who delude themselves that either there is no crisis or that controls (that is, endless subsidies) of prices can do all that is needed, particularly those few leaders who pretend to be left wing socialists and yet who have in fact given up the original, basic and minimal theoretical perception of socialism: that the market economy does not result in just wages. Never before has this foundation of socialist theory, theory now so often so foolishly and abstractly over-elaborated, been shown to be so relevant and true. But statutory incomes policies have hitherto only appeared to the unions to be hitting at working-class wages, not at all injustices, not at all unjustifiable differences of incomes. A genuinely socialist incomes policy could succeed, one that not merely seemed to hit but did hit high incomes hard, hit them not because redistribution rather than productivity is any great contribution to levelling up, but because in our new conditions high incomes are often not just unfair, but are being rightly seen by ordinary people as intolerably unfair.

A minority Labour government that pursued a new and radical minimum and maximum incomes policy could well count on Liberal support. Only the Liberals are pledged to statutory control of wages and incomes. They have not faced the admittedly terribly complicated implications of how to define and enforce maximums and minimums—particularly maximums. No one has. But as a social ideal it would link the radically minded in both parties. Grimond's note of moral disgust at very high incomes actually hit the nail on the head: the political and moral factors are now much more important than the economic and managerial. We need to recover some of that old puritan militancy that was once a great part of our political tradition. If the business-man cannot work within a ceiling, can anyone offer a convincing theory of why other large groups—public servants and teachers of all kinds, for instance—work within both fixed and known limits? When some leave for higher salaries in America, the replacements are not hard to find. Beyond a certain point, the importance of monetary incentives must decrease rapidly—except for prestige.

The Tribune Group in the Labour Party should be faced squarely with the issue whether it is more socialist to nationalise a few more firms, or to create new institutions to ensure social justice over the whole field of wages and incomes. A Labour government could govern without them if it produced such a radical policy. It would make sense to the rank and file of the unions. Leaders with the courage and clarity to speak to the people over the heads of both the TUC and the CBI would find a great popular response.

How to define maximums and minimums? What kind of institutions to settle relativities within the outer limits? All this would be for debate, bargaining, trial and error. One could even imagine free bargaining much as now, but far less inflationary if the whole society recognised that there was a point beyond which a man must not sink, and beyond which a man need not live, should not live. The Labour Party would want wages councils for every industry, the Liberals would put greater stress on publicity and might begin to believe that if there was complete and compulsory openness about all earnings, many unjustifiable differences would disappear; and many differences people would simply accept. Both as a short-term attack on inflation and as a long-term social ideal, a mini–maxi policy could create, not a new party, but a working alliance between all genuine radicals.

If the radical centre of the Labour Party, so rich in potential leadership, went for such a policy, Liberals would, of course, almost certainly be wise to offer support for a minority government at a price, not hurry to join a coalition of complicity. Their first price is obvious: electoral reform—and it is growing obvious that this may be the only way in which the country can be governed if the two main parties (after the next attempt) still cannot get back to even 40 per cent of the vote apiece. The second price is less obvious in precise form, but to emerge in general intent: agreement not to play politics with the machinery of government and to stop trying to politicise the Civil Service—and this condition almost anyone with the welfare of our poor country at heart should now welcome. Minority governments who keep on changing and re-changing the organisation of government, simply to find or not find jobs for the boys, and who preach—as Wilson and Lady Falkender do—complete distrust of the Civil Service, are very literally betraying their country for a terribly temporary and shallow party advantage. There are different types of socialism than the present leadership recognises, and support for a truly radical policy of social justice on the incomes front could well come from alliance with the Liberals.

BRC

Commentary: 'Opening the Crossman Diaries' and 'The Crisis'

Vol. 46, no. 1, January–March 1975

Opening the Crossman Diaries

In reply to a question in the House of Commons on November 15 about the publication of the Crossman Diaries, the Prime Minister said, 'It would make nonsense of the 30-year rule approved by Parliament for the protection of Cabinet papers if former Ministers were able to evade it by publishing their own accounts of Cabinet Meetings', and to Mr Tam Dalyell, a true friend of the late Richard Crossman, he further said with admirable traditional constitutional rectitude, 'Ministers will not feel free to discuss matters privately in Cabinet or Cabinet committee . . . nor can they be expected to abide by a common decision, if they know that the stand they have taken and the points they have surrendered are to become public knowledge prematurely. . . . In other words, since under the system of Cabinet government the efficacy and the authority of the government depends upon mutual confidence among Ministers and between Ministers and civil servants, the basis of that authority would be eroded by premature disclosure.'

How splendid it is, we must eat some of our previous words, to hear the Prime Minister of our nation speaking with such rectitude—if only someone called Harold Wilson, a former Prime Minister, and someone called Marcia Williams, now ennobled, had not both published memoirs which breach this same rule as clearly as, in the Prime Minister's account, Crossman's Diaries. What has happened to that famous 'British sense of humour' and old-fashioned ridicule that such an utterance as the Prime Minister's could not be howled down in a whoop of derision, laughter and—one can only say—contempt? The sole difference between Crossman's Diaries and the Prime Minister's and his secretary's memoirs is that Richard Crossman was, occasionally, somewhat free in recounting the views of some civil servants about third parties. He recounts that his permanent secretary told him that a certain professor was unsuitable as a specialist adviser for such and such blunt reasons, a record that might reflect on the civil servant's judgement as much as on the professor's competence. Obviously this kind of thing could and should be edited out. But Crossman's own strong judgements on his colleagues? Are they any more undesirable than many of the Prime Minister's and his secretary's remarks in their respective memoirs?

Of course there are genuine worries among some senior civil servants about giving advice if it is to be publicly divulged during their working career. They see this as not so much a matter of the Official Secrets Act (even though its provisions have been used with scandalous opportunism not to ensure the safety of the state, but to avoid political or administrative embarrassment), but of being a basic condition for our system of government. The issue is a difficult one. It may be true what they say; but this could be a weakness of our system. What has happened to the theory of the Fulton Report that more open government would be better government because it would educate people more, enable different experts to speak out earlier and gain a more effective response both from the public and within the whole Civil Service? What is this advice which people would not give if it was to become known in less than fifty, now thirty, years? Assessments of persons? Perhaps, but even then the issue can be the way these judgements are made and presented rather than of them being made at all and even known. Advice on policy, it could be argued, *should* be disclosable. Are we so immature that we do not realise that people differ? And is there not a chance of raising the level of advice if publicity can follow? Why should not civil servants in a democracy have to stand by their professional judgements as to the best means to political ends? The case for discretion is not as obvious as it seems. Our society might be richer, not the poorer, for less of it. 'Mutual confidence' between ministers and civil servants is important, as Mr Wilson said, but more important is mutual confidence between ministers and the public. Secrecy is no way to persuade people in a free and pluralistic society. So while this is in doubt, the case for publishing Crossman's Diaries may be more than a matter of decency and of fairness; the case may be of great public importance. But certainly the Prime Minister himself so breached the rule, if it is a rule we want any longer, that it is wrong and dishonest for him to suppress Crossman's Diaries.

The Prime Minister has said that he does not consider the decision to be his constitutional responsibility, that it is a matter for the secretary of the Cabinet. What humbug for him and his secretary now to place such trust in an official! Why should any civil servant have the responsibility of judging in such matters? Better that the courts should decide the issue rather than an official. And how *can* a Prime Minister surrender power in this way? Where there is power, there is the responsibility. Mr Patrick Gordon Walker recently told his own tale about his own book when, in a dignified and forceful article in the *New Statesman*, he reminded the Prime Minister of something that so rarely needs doing—that he is Prime Minister. For Wilson is not just dodging the issue, he is deciding it.

The situation is fraught with irony. I remember Richard Crossman telling me shortly before his death that one day in the Cabinet both the First Secretary and the Chancellor had to be away at the beginning. 'Harold had put in as a filler a paper proposing to reduce the ban on the publication of state documents from a fifty- to a thirty-year rule.'[a] This was a very modest reform, long overdue. 'Yet only Tony Crosland and I', he said, 'were prepared to support the PM and Gerald Gardiner against civil servants.' He went on to tell me how Michael Stewart and then James Callaghan read aloud to the rest of them the departmental briefs provided for them by their officials. 'Here was a Labour Foreign Secretary objecting that a reduction of the ban on publication to a thirty-year rule might damage the reputations of civil servants active during the Munich crisis while they were still alive. I pointed out that the present ban, quite apart from all its other drawbacks, was rendered intolerable by the permission which a Cabinet minister, particularly a Prime Minister, can obtain to use official documents denied to academic and objective historians for writing his memoirs.' Crossman thought that if they were going to go on exercising the right to turn out memoirs as often as not no better than *plaidoyers*, then there was a powerful case for letting the historians get at the documents as soon as possible. He was hardly surprised to find that not a word of his argument was retained in the Cabinet minutes.[b]

When John Wilkes was arraigned before Parliament for breach of privilege for libelling a fellow Member in his privately printed *Essay on Women*, the single copy stolen by the public hangman from Wilkes's house from among the thirteen printed proved insufficient for circulation to the two Houses to pass judgement upon; so the government printer of the day got to work and

[a] The closing quotation mark here is missing in the original version, but I think this is where it should be—which means that the 'modest reform' claim belongs to Bernard and is not assigned to Crossman. The extensive 'remembered' comments by Richard Crossman in this paragraph provide a spectacular example of Bernard's use of reconstructed dialogue, one of his favourite narrative devices (see my Introduction).

[b] But we do at least have Bernard's retelling—or glossing—of it.

495

produced hundreds. The only surviving copy known is from among those; the government of the day was more effective in publishing it than ever was Wilkes. Something rather similar has now happened. Many copies are now floating around because the Cabinet Office has Xeroxed them to go to civil servants mentioned in the pages to see if they object, presumably to draw up a list of objectors. Human nature being what it is, copies have leaked out with a typically British elitist result. Almost anyone in the know who wants to see it can see it; most television and newspaper offices have copies of it. And yet the public are denied from seeing it. Having leaked so much, even those who may feel hurt by it should see the case for allowing the true and authentic version to be issued by the normal publishers. One can also raise a purely literary and patriotic point: it is one of the greatest and most spontaneous diaries in the vernacular since Pepys, since Evelyn (it really is, the old devil really pulled it off); something that will be thought of almost on the level of Boswell's *Life of Johnson*. I have read no book in recent years more likely to raise the level of understanding of how our system of government works—and does not work. Has not the establishment's tradition of secrecy something to do with the mess we are now in? It worked well enough, perhaps, for keeping the system going when there was no permanent economic crisis, and therefore no need for governments to try to influence the behaviour of ordinary working people, even to understand them, so long as the votes came out right. But now Old Secrecy has made it hard for both ministers and civil servants to persuade the public to turn the rhetoric of 'the social contract' into a condition of everyday life.

The Crisis

The gravity of the crisis is now apparent. Though we go on borrowing abroad, credit is running out. Those who mocked the 'prophets of doom' are now themselves discredited, but they still carry on governing: the Whitehall–Westminster farce. Parliamentary government is not discredited, it has simply been by-passed by the party leaderships and Whitehall, although the ordinary backbench MP should have been the most effective person to bring home to ordinary people—on whose response everything depends—the gravity of the crisis. The October election now seems a light year away when Mr Healey was foolish enough to allow himself to be put up to demonstrate that the underlying rate of inflation was slowing down to a modest 6 per cent, and when it seemed extravagantly brave for Shirley Williams to speak her mind out over Europe and for Reg Prentice not to force himself at all times to radiate cheer and happiness. The government now does everything it can to convince the unions of the dangers of a runaway inflation, and, regarding Europe, Mr Wilson has now climbed back on the fence again, indeed even fallen off on the other side precisely at the point from which he first set out. But all that wasted time. No wonder the new penitence seems implausible to so many!

If only there were better leadership, men who would speak honestly, openly and demandingly directly to the people; for otherwise the conditions for recovery and reform (and the two must go together) are beginning to emerge. For the primary obstacles to more positive political action have been conceptual. First, the belief of the 1950s and 1960s that standards of living would continue to increase (even if not quite so fast as those of some of our neighbours); secondly, the belief that the economy was under control (well, more or less under control, a bumpy journey with odd stops and starts, but basically the direction could be controlled, the economy could be steered); and, thirdly, that low levels of popular participation in government and industry were a positive sign of health and not an actual or potential weakness (voters should vote, investors invest and workers work, but not much more than that).

Each of these abstract, vast but all-pervasive assumptions is now, to borrow a phrase, withering away. As regards the first, we may have to live within our means and the means may not increase—people are beginning to accept this fact and to resent the silliness of suggestions that this 'stop' is just lasting a wee bit longer than the last 'go'. As regards the second, the crisis takes on a national form and there are, heaven knows, local exacerbating factors, but people recognise that there is also a world crisis and one which assumes a particular dimension in Europe: governments will no longer be expected to insure us against all troubles, so will not necessarily be thrown from office if the standard of living falls or if they adopt measures which in the 1960s would have seemed electorally suicidal. People are now prepared to think in realistic terms of relativities and probabilities; politicians should abandon the silly rhetoric of total promises and total blame (those who do so are the most respected). As regards the third, people are beginning to ask what can they do to help, and some politicians are beginning to realise that the price of government-undisturbed-by-the-unpredictabilities-of-participation has been a lack of response from ordinary people when leadership is offered: as was shown in the last war, democracies can achieve at every level far more mobilisation of resources and energy than autocracies when the crisis is evident, the cause is clear and the leadership candid and firm. There is a sense in which the approaching referendum on Europe is the price that the pro-Europeans are having to pay for thinking that it was enough to have carried a majority in Parliament and in Fleet Street and not in the hearts of the people. No wonder that Harold Wilson has been able to empathise so vividly with both sides of this question at different times.

Thus the political situation may be more fluid in this country than is often supposed. Political conditions are beginning to emerge which could prevent collapse. We may even be forced into fundamental reforms and reconstruction, to prevent repetition of this crisis.

We may, in a phrase, be forced into siege socialism, but it can be siege socialism with a human face—which is not exactly a slogan for the billboards, but something to be put in the pipe and smoked of whoever would aspire,

497

through the Labour movement, that is the Party and the Unions, to lead the country out of the mess and into something better. We need more equality (or far less unjustifiable inequalities), more freedom of expression (including particularly leading politicians, even in government), more participation (both for job-satisfaction and efficiency) and more openness and public knowledge about how rewards are arrived at and what they are. The Labour Party could stress six points and find a ready response in the public. They should anticipate the likelihood that the 'social contract' will break down or, even if it can shamble along, will perpetuate, if inflation continues, intolerable inequities.

(i) The need for levelling down and for equality of sacrifice. Both unions and business should accept that it is in the general interest that many differentials should go or grow less. A genuine socialist incomes policy would set a minimum and a maximum income and encourage openness and public debate about jobs and rewards.

(ii) The need to set example and to create a sense of fairness, hence not merely a maximum income but tight control on the perks and privileges of leadership. Political leaders should be puritanical and austere in money matters. They should purge many who are actually corrupt and should discourage careerists. And the same for top business. We should appeal more to job satisfaction and less to ever-continuing personal income incentives.

(iii) The need for workers' participation in all kinds of enterprise as a statutory right, both for the sake of job satisfaction and efficiency. Here Mr Benn is right. But this means the unions surrendering power as national bodies relative to workers organised in syndics. Here Mr Benn is wrong (or can't have it both ways). (I wish the staff would run newspapers, but not the NUJ.)

(iv) The need to encourage the mobility of labour and retraining, which means a dramatic reversal of the postwar shibboleth of both main parties to bring jobs to people rather than people to jobs, and means a national rather than a municipal housing policy.

(v) The need to encourage industry more than the city, hence direct national investment in industry. Again Mr Benn is right. But the question of ownership should never come before the question of efficiency. Here again Mr Benn is wrong.

(vi) The need to cut out all the waste of excessive advertising and packaging. One knows the 'economic argument' against. It might even save little. But the psychological importance of such a campaign would be immense. Appearances do count.

BRC

Commentary: 'Pandora's Box, Sovereignty and the Referendum'

Vol. 46, no. 2, April–June 1975

Once upon a time, it is strange to remember, the British Constitution was regarded as clear, predictable, settled and rather boring to discuss.[a] What opened Pandora's box? It is hard to tell, perhaps long-term historical factors, declining wealth, power and national confidence; or perhaps short-term political blunders, nearly all associated with the pragmatic (that is unprincipled) politics of Mr Harold Wilson, our great national Humpty Dumpty or curate's egg who has done everything but fall off the fence; but that endemic confusion has now been released, there can be no possible doubt whatever.

In wildest fantasy who could have foretold ten years ago that we were about to face a national referendum whether to stay in EEC or not on renegotiated terms which few people can understand any better than the original ones; a Cabinet that has had to agree to divide so that all can hold onto office, but which has already broadened the public disagreements into the whole field of basic economic policy; and, as if this were not enough, to have in preparation a bill for legislative devolution to Scotland and Wales which, if its political effect is misjudged—and it depends largely on the political genius of Mr Edward Short—could lead to the unwanted dismemberment of the United Kingdom? Perhaps simple lack of political courage and integrity has got us into this mess. Wilson's fourth administration is burdened with the mistakes of his second and his own obsession with justifying them. He saw the need back in 1966 for a genuine incomes policy and for trades union reform, prepared the ground but then lost his nerve and took short views; he brought the Labour Party into a pro-European stance, but then in the misjudged hope of overthrowing the Conservative government in 1971, he let loose the devils whom he had tied up, and now they will not grant his request to go back into the sack again; and he talked up devolution of government and Labour's unique sympathy for Scotland and Wales but did nothing, and has now over-reacted and not argued back to the nationalists.

How odd it is that such a consummate politician (so people say, however grisly the results) has apparently lost all belief that opinion can be changed, only that it can be managed.

Since we have the referendum campaign, we have to endure it and fight it with a good heart. Our view is quite simply that whatever economic uncertainties there might have been about the original case for entry, the economic consequences of withdrawal would now be disastrous. 'Britannicus' set this out in *The Political Quarterly*, July–September 1974, with classic clarity. So no more looking backwards, except to note that while sceptical of

[a] This is the second element in a two-part Commentary. The first is by William Robson, on the abandonment of the Channel Tunnel.

the motives and implications of deciding things by referendum, yet perhaps it is the price that the pro-Europeans of all parties have had to pay for pushing entry through Parliament without convincing public opinion. Just as neither the social contract nor statutory incomes policies can work if ordinary people are not convinced, so such an important thing as entry to EEC could not be made to last without great trouble while the public remained unconvinced. The temptation was too great, and if Mr Wilson had not played that card in 1971, who is to say that Mrs Margaret Thatcher or some other would not be playing it now—someone else whose Europeanism is, if radiant, yet possibly skin deep? This is not to argue that entry to Europe should have been made by referendum or a special general election, but simply that nowadays the political elites cannot simply decide among themselves: public support must be gained, not because of the rights of man, but because the economic and industrial behaviour of ordinary people can make or break the best-laid plans of Treasuries and party committees.

How will the issue be decided? Perhaps at the end of the day, it is all a matter of a gut reaction. Amid great worry and uncertainty, not liking either fully, ordinary people will have to decide whether they are more worried psychologically at raving xenophobia or at drivelling cosmopolitanism, or will be more worried economically at going it alone than at being a regulated part of a larger market. Speaking for myself, I am hardly as much pro-European as fiercely anti-nationalist. I love England, I value the political and cultural interdependence of the United Kingdom, but I am depressed at what happens when people believe that the only proper unit of government is one coterminous with a nation. I do not see my Englishery as threatened by Europe so much as by Mr Shore and Mr Powell. 'Self-government is better than good government'—surely not if we have a choice about it, only if the 'good government' is imposed. Difficult though it is, for god's sake let us keep up the old tradition of judging governments by whether they are just or not, make citizens of subjects, do well for them and help them to do well for themselves; not simply whether our rulers share our culture in every respect.

Perhaps because the economic arguments are so speculative, an almost meaningless argument has been substituted. Whether staying in Europe is destroying our *sovereignty* or, equally meaningless, whether it can enhance it.

The concept was just about falling out of the 'Political and Social Thought' third year university papers into 'The History of Political Thought' alone, when some socialist pseudo-intellectuals apparently discovered its existence not merely in the older law books, but also surviving in the correspondence columns of the *Daily Telegraph*; and saw a chance to make dead highbrow theory live vulgar rhetoric. Any who can remember Harold Laski arguing how the doctrine of sovereignty arose to serve the needs of the new centralised capitalist state in the sixteenth century, but how it now contradicts both a pluralistic ethic and the essentially plural distribution of power, both internationally and within society, will be surprised to find that Michael Foot, Peter Shore and Wedgwood Benn have somehow tried to build this most elitist of concepts into the pantheon of socialist ideas. The ideas of democratic Socialism (to capitalise it as Orwell used to do) are now in such a muddle that they can get away with this philosophical perversion. National sovereignty is surely, as Laski argued, the very antithesis of socialism. The context is made too narrow. If economic forms are more important than political, then they transcend particular states; and if there is to be more democracy and equality, independent power must be exercised by primary groups within the state— Citizen Benn rarely needs reminding of that. But he, of course, has gone the whole hog: he has proclaimed that the British Constitution is based on the sovereignty of the People—not even of Parliament—a doctrine which at its best is meaningless, at its worst a rationalisation for the holding of absolute power by 'friends of the people'.

'Sovereignty' is now a poor term with which to understand the realities of political power in a world full of legally sovereign states, of all shapes and sizes, but none so powerful as not to depend on others, none so small as not to have its pride. Parliament is sovereign only in the sense that law can only be made by ministers of the Crown going through certain procedures in Parliament. But this has nothing to do with the realities of power, just as formal claims to monopolise power (as have been made for the office of Prime Minister) often have little or nothing to do with the effective use of power. It depends what one wants to do. If, for instance, one wants to maintain, let alone expand, the prosperity of a modern industrial state or one wishing to industrialise, the most complicated network of dependencies on others and mutual aid to others is inevitable. The EEC may be well or badly organised. It seems rather badly organised at the moment. But it does not exercise the kind of power that could once have been claimed as sovereign—as both its opponents or its more silly advocates assert. And even suppose it did develop by the end of this century into a clearly federal form of government. Even then, I venture the prophecy, the French would remain remarkably French, Germans German, Italians Italian, English English, and the Scottish and the Welsh would be still clearly distinguishable.

The entry under 'Sovereignty' in the *New Encyclopaedia of the Social Sciences* begins:

The concept of 'sovereignty' implies a theory of politics which claims that in every system of government there must be some absolute power of final decision exercised by some body or person recognised both as competent to decide and to enforce the decision. . . .

Ay, there's the rub, the last phrase: which modern state has this? And the entry ends:

Sovereignty is relevant to emergency situations. . . . The practical difficulties of deciding when a state of emergency exists are always great and open to abuse—but they are practical and procedural difficulties; they do not destroy the real difference between the time of sovereignty and the time of politics.

If 'sovereignty' has any relevance to deciding whether we should stay in Europe or get out, it can only be because the referendum itself is an artificially engendered crisis. We could have solved it in more ordinary political ways. But being artificial, it need not prove fatal.

BRC

Commentary: 'Joint Editorship' and 'The Referendum that Was'

Vol. 46, no. 3, July–September 1975

Joint Editorship

The next issue of *The Political Quarterly* will see a change of Joint Editor. Professor John Mackintosh MP will replace Professor William Robson, who becomes chairman of the editorial board. William Robson founded this journal in 1930 and has been joint editor ever since, except for a brief period during the Second World War, when his long-time editorial colleague Leonard Woolf was in sole charge. William Robson told the tale of the founding of the journal in his contribution to the fortieth birthday number of *The Political Quarterly*, and also in his Introduction to *The Political Quarterly in the Thirties* (Allen Lane, 1971),[a] which he edited. He has chosen the time of his eightieth birthday, this 14th of July, to change his role in the direction of the journal. May his continuing editorial colleague thank him deeply for his long editorship and congratulate him warmly on his eightieth birthday, on behalf not merely of the editorial board past and present, but also, doubtless, of all our regular readers. His achievement and influence have been unique.

The Referendum That Was

What a boomerang for those who first picked up the weapon! It could have an important effect on the conduct of British politics in that it shows that a government can appeal to 'the People' above the heads of their self-styled leaders. Those who talked the most about popular rather than parliamentary sovereignty became victims of their own double delusion: the belief of the Tribune Group that they spoke for the 'real people' and that big union leaders could deliver their loyal members' votes. Exceptional use of referendums could be a way of breaking out of deadlocks like the Scottish and Northern Ireland problems and present-day industrial relations, each of which have in common that the elected leaders are commonly more intransigent on key issues than the majorities who elect them. A government should be able to

---

[a] An edited volume collecting *PQ* articles from the 1930s. It was conceived by Bernard as a vehicle for William Robson and Leonard Woolf, but edited by Robson alone following Woolf's death (see my Introduction).

require that leaders of all kinds of representative bodies ascertain whether they are really speaking for their members on matters that gravely affect the public interest.

BRC

Commentary: '"The Good Causes": a New Series' and 'Lament for India'

Vol. 46, no. 4, October–December 1975

'The Good Causes': A New Series

The article in this issue on 'Shelter' by Patrick Seyd[a] begins a new standing feature which has been planned by Mr Seyd in cooperation with the editors.[b] He will contribute two more articles and other commissions have been and are being made.

During the 1960s a variety of new pressure groups were established, primarily in the areas of welfare and environment policy. These groups were new, both in the sense of their concern with issues previously ignored, and in their adoption of different methods in attempting to secure their objectives. During this same period the individual membership of both major political parties has declined greatly and some evidence suggests that these pressure groups have attracted the support which previously would have been channelled into the parties.

A particular group of these could be called, both colloquially and precisely, 'Good Causes', in that they are usually registered as charities, usually enjoy considerable public prestige and while often getting publicity in the press, occasionally having 'house histories' written or friendly accounts by former officers, rarely attract the general suspicion attached to 'pressure groups', both business and union; nor do they attract serious study. And if they are subject to scrutiny by the Charity Commissioners, this is limited to financial audit and to questions of *ultra vires*; they do not ask if they really are doing anything useful, could do it better or give value for money to members, donors or foundations.

So studies in depth of many or any of these bodies, such as, for instance, Shelter, Child Poverty Action Group, the Conservation Society, the Council

[a] That is, 'Shelter: the National Campaign for the Homeless', to give it its full title. This was perhaps an initiative by Bernard, given that he alone introduces it and there's no trace in the editorial board minutes of the day. It's not clear who else was commissioned to write on the theme. An article by Patrick Seyd on the Child Poverty Action Group followed two issues later in 1976 but the initiative seems to have petered out altogether soon afterwards.

[b] These two pieces are the first and third elements of a three-part Commentary. The second element was 'What kind of Labour party?', the first editorial contribution by Bernard's newly appointed coeditor John Mackintosh.

503

for the Protection of Rural England, the National Council for Civil Liberties, the National Trust, Anti-Apartheid, the Festival of Light, National Viewers' and Listeners' Association, Campaign for the Advancement of State Education, Radical Alternatives to Prison, National Association for the Care and Rehabilitation of Offenders and the Disablement Income Group, etc., will be attempted by academics or journalists in a manner comparable to some of the full-scale, that is book-length, studies of major pressure groups. But it is fortuitous which groups get studied in books and the very depth and thoroughness precludes any regular review with priorities of public policy in mind rather than the accidents of access to archival sources.

The aim is not to write complete contemporary histories or political science studies of each or any of these, but to try to establish in a responsible quarterly journal at article length a regular review of the 'Good Causes' one by one. The case is that they should be subject to more public scrutiny and accountability than they are, so that every three or four years there would be a major review of the leading 'Good Causes'.

A common pattern of inquiry will be followed in examining all the groups: to examine the origins of each group, the organisation and structure of each group, the development of each group's policy and their methods in attempting to influence policy in the last five or ten years and, finally, an assessment of each group's effectiveness. The intention is that the examination of a group should proceed along similar lines to the serious article-length book or fair-minded review: i.e. an outline of the subject under study followed by a critical appraisal. The project aspires to combine the best of both the academic study of politics and the investigative manner of responsible journalism, thus appealing to a wide audience when the reports are published. The research will deliberately be more superficial than in an academic study of a single group, but that is the whole point—to cover more ground and to prove that it could be done regularly.

BRC

Lament for India

Those who think that we are still greatly affected by memories and myths of the imperial past had better learn to beat another hollow drum after the lack of interest with which Mrs Gandhi's destruction of democracy in India was received by most of the British press. The night she arrested the leaders of the opposition parties in Parliament, the event got third spot for about half-a-minute on the BBC's main television news. The first test match and a coach crash got more prominence. Now, of course, this is partly a product of the deplorable decline of straight reporting on BBC television (sound is slightly better) in favour of 'we take you to the scene' actuality (which is often quite a long way away, anyway, and the reporter hurried to the scene is often in a worse position to evaluate what has just happened than a central analyst receiving reports both from him and from other centres and sources). The imposing press censorship meant no film, no on-the-spot reports, hence very little news value.

But that is another question—a question we would like to explore in future issues: what constitutes news values and what factors of technique and media-fashion warp rational priorities of political importance? How often does the medium strangle the message?

The question for the moment is why both political leaders and press have been so quiet about India? A feeling of hopelessness? Indifference? Or a silly-cunning-lazy FCO[c] view that open criticism might make matters worse? But matters are very bad. The world will be extremely lucky if it does not have to witness not merely the destruction of democracy in any worthwhile sense in India, but also the beginning of a long period of instability of government bringing with it great risks of international involvement. If there had been a clear emergency, that people in India could recognise as an emergency, then there would be some chance of thinking of the new regime (and of it thinking of itself) as an emergency government which would aim at the restoration of parliamentary opposition and a free press after the emergency had been tackled. But the immediate cause seems less to have been the rather technical electoral offence by Mrs Gandhi which the Supreme Court held would bar her from voting in Parliament, rather than a more general crisis of confidence in her as an honest political leader, the question of hiding from public view her tolerance of corruption by Congress Party leaders. She has now made brutally clear that exposure and criticism earns imprisonment.

After 27 years India has become a dictatorship and it is hard to see how the process can be reversed. The door seems open to that weary and terrible cycle of coup upon coup that has cursed post-liberation Africa and which has nothing whatever to do with efficiency or development, only with personal hunger for power of the oldest and simplest kinds. And to be done by the daughter of the Mahatma Gandhi himself.[d] History has provided few ironies more cruel.

Already one finds in the press that odd unwillingness to call personal dictatorship personal dictatorship which has often marred reporting and understanding of African events. Partly we feel guilty; partly we think it tolerant to accept that things are different over there; but partly it is the old 1930s myth that dictatorship is efficient—what led even such a free-spirit as George Bernard Shaw to praise, in the same breath, Stalin and Mussolini; or which led many to consider solemnly 'the price' in terms of efficiency that was paid for liberty—although wartime experience completely refuted the myth. Considering the problems of governing what is as much a continent as

[c] The original had 'F.O.C.' but it seems almost certain that FCO (the Foreign and Common-wealth Office) is the intended target.

[d] Perhaps the time pressure of producing Commentaries led to errors such as this. There is no room for another interpretation here: Bernard really does say that Indira Gandhi is the Mahatma's daughter. (Her father was Jawaharlal Nehru.)

a country, if by country one means a clear national tradition, it may be that parliamentary government, with all its slowness, changes and indecisions, is the only way to hold it all together, to allow expressions of all regional interests, rather than the very great centralised power that would be needed to do it by force. Mrs Gandhi and the Congress Party do not have that kind of power. The Congress Party cannot furnish enthusiastic cadres, as once in Russia and in China, to take the message to the people with books and bludgeons combined, if the excuse for the takeover were social and economic revolution, a mass-mobilisation towards modernisation and socialism. In fact the Congress Party lacks all such impulse or even ability. Such talk is rhetoric, not an explanation of the rise of dictatorship but routine and shallow excuses for its exercise.

The very size and complexity of India pulls government in one of two ways: either an efficient and thoroughgoing totalitarian autocracy or parliamentary-representative government. Mrs Gandhi will not lead in the first direction but what she has done makes a return to the second solution extremely difficult; so what is sadly most likely is that what will prove her failure to hold the states together will also provide the opportunity for either military or Communist rule. The efficiency of autocracy is a myth—unless it goes the whole way to totalitarianism. None of the old nineteenth-century arguments against the *inefficiency* of autocracy (before ever arguments against its illiberality cut much ice) have lost their relevance. Certainly drastic reforms were needed. But all the reforms she is now instituting could have been done by her parliamentary majority and through Parliament.

The press in India is now silenced. Foreign journalists who will not submit everything to censorship have been expelled. And such men as J. P. Narayan, the land-reformer, the former leader of the Socialist Party, are still in prison without trial—just like the old days. There has been little protest. But we of all people should not be silent. Such a lapse back from even a highly imperfect parliamentary democracy into a highly imperfect autocracy should not go unremarked. It is a tragedy for the whole world that parliamentary institutions have been destroyed by a coup from the top in the third largest country in the world. How fatalistic or purely self-centred we have become when so little is said, even if little can be done. How fragile is democratic citizenship, even in India, when Mrs Gandhi appears to have got away with this coup so easily.

BRC

Commentary: 'Freedom and the Labour Party'

Vol. 47, no. 2, April–June 1976

Mr Roy Jenkins recently told the Oxford Social Democratic students that there might be a case for primary elections to select constituency candidates.[a] And in the same week Lord George-Brown was move to feel that he had had enough of the Labour Party, though whether because of Lord Goodman's fears for the freedom of the Press or Mr Solzhenitsyn's chiliastic fears for the safety of the whole Western world, it was hard to make out.

Tactically, one doubts if George-Brown's new friends will thank him for actually resigning from the Labour Party. His criticisms surely carried weight because he was a Labour elder statesman, proud of his trade union card, not just one of the swan-song chorus like Lord Chalfont, Lord Shawcross and Lord Godot[b] who wait for the coalition that will never come. But, nonetheless, was he right to feel that somehow the Labour Party is now selling liberty short? And is Mr Jenkins right to think that we will need primary elections if the nominating process is not to be taken over by sectarians?

The analysis could be right but the conclusions wrong. Ordinary people have become even more put off from politics—largely, as we have kept on saying, by the failure of party leaders to talk in terms of principles and to exhibit them by conduct and example; by their inconstancy in policy; and by their talking down to the electorate who see through the silly pretence that most of our major problems are 'the fault' of the other side. It is not the Left extremists who have driven moderate Socialists from active membership of *some* constituency parties, it is the feeling of helplessness engendered by the Macmillan–Wilson style of politics, that buying of time, avoidance of hard decisions, weakness in government but jealous strength in preventing genuine collective power. But as membership of the Labour Party has declined, the substantial property gets taken over by squatters or inherited by those sectarians who have always been with us, but up until now have been outnumbered and sat upon. So the Party moves to the left and gets more and more out of touch with ordinary people. The Left should have learned its lesson over the Common Market campaign; but instead it blunders on into the hope of selecting a type of candidate who will infallibly lose every marginal seat and render many safe seats marginal.

Yet there are no safeguards to this happening except people of the broad centre of the Labour movement staying in or joining to prevent it happening. Think of Northern Ireland, where a majority of the people plainly want compromise. But they dislike the extremism of 'their leaders' so much that they will not join the parties, hence the politicians actually frustrate their

[a] This is the second piece in a two-part Commentary. The other is by John Mackintosh on 'Liberty and Equality'.
[b] Probably just a generic reference rather than a swipe at anybody in particular.

wishes with relative ease. We would only get primary elections if the majorities whom Mr Jenkins wishes to see involved were there already to institute these primaries. And if they were, there would be no need.

The Labour Party leadership of the moment does seem insensitive to the freedom of the press and far too sensitive to its criticisms. But if one shares Lord Goodman's diagnosis, one may yet have more faith in Lord Ardwick's prescription (also in this issue).[c] If the NUJ *can* exercise such power, then its sleeping members must/will wake up and speak for themselves. Ditto in the Labour Party branches. Ditto in the trade unions. Ditto in the NUT and in the NUS.

If George was thinking clearly, he should have stayed in the Labour movement and fought it out. We cannot ask for protection from democracy. We can only ask that it is genuine democracy and for more of it. Do leaders represent those they lead? If their claim that they do touches the public interest, is there not always a public interest to verify the claim? It is in this direction that we need to think.

And we cannot hope for our liberties to be protected for us if we don't exercise them positively ourselves. A nuisance to some, but the alternatives are worse; but others will enjoy the fray. If political leaders of the Centre of the Party will stand up and refuse to be muzzled, they have a great potential political following. Liberty is won or lost, contracted or expanded, in particular issues, not by generalised hopes or fears. So this issue examines just some particular issues.

BRC

Commentary: 'House and Nation' and 'Northern Ireland'

Vol. 47, no. 3, July–September 1976

House and Nation

Early June days of 1976. . . . By the time these words appear in print it is possible that our nation will be near ruin as an effective and independent political force; or equally possible that, once again, we will have bought or borrowed some more time—and once again evaded facing long-term problems.

'Resist all cuts in public expenditure', cried some, and even, 'all wage restraint'; and others said 'management is crippled by taxation'—as if it is possible for any government to continue to borrow one-fifth of what it spends,

[c] The Commentary pieces taken together set the scene for a largely freedom-themed issue. Goodman (writing as Lord Goodman, then chairman of the Newspaper Publishers' Association) contributed an opening article 'The Freedom of the Press'. Lord Ardwick (writing as John Beavan), produced his closing 'Westminster Scene', a regular feature at this time, and would join the *PQ* editorial board in the following year.

or for real wages to increase when productivity is stagnant or even declines. Perhaps oil will save us. Perhaps reckless political spending has not overshot a reasonable borrowing on future income. But if we are borrowing a fifth of public expenditure and if the balance of payments is still unhealthy, fantasies of international capitalist conspiracy are not needed to explain why overseas creditors and investors may judge otherwise. The *Tribune* Left seems to suggest that foreign creditors and investors should ignore our present troubles because of the future good prospects of oil. These prospects are great indeed. But so is our myopia if we expect foreigners to take our risks for us. Have not our political leaders the guts to say: 'Massive cuts there must be, we are living greatly beyond our means and even so have fallen behind other Western Europe standards of living; but they will be restored when the oil comes in'? We must tighten *our* belts and live in hope, not on an overdraft.

Is it politically impossible to explain this: that we cannot expect others to take the risk of our anticipating future income? Wilson, and now Callaghan, seem to think so. We think they underestimate the public and that in doing so, and in doing almost anything simply to hold all elements of the Labour Party together, they are actually reducing even further its basis of electoral support. The public are hungry for honesty, and fed up with the internalised discussions of the declining numbers of party members.

Bad luck, indeed, for the Chancellor, after having got, with excellent political management, the 4½ per cent agreement with the TUC, to have had a run on the pound on his hands. Puzzling and undeserved? Yes, if one considers the effective steps taken against inflation. Decidedly not, if one considers the fundamental state of the economy in terms of productivity and investment.

Len Murray has said to the trade union audience: 'Of course we are opposed to waste. But if foreign financiers think we are prepared to slash living standards of worker sections of the community, it's not on. It's the British people who will decide.' They may, indeed, decide not to cut, even to increase wages, but no one can 'decide' to maintain living standards unless foreigners buy our goods and invest in our industries and leave their money in our banks. Mr Benn must believe that foreigners should do just that and as they are told; but they may be forgiven for thinking him, at best, economically stupid and politically demagogic.

If we survive these crisis weeks, we have still to hold inflation down and to begin not just to tackle a technical problem called productivity, but to try to recapture in politics, journalism, education, in our whole culture, something of the spirit of production that was once capitalism, before too many entrepreneurs became gentrified, or was once held to be more effectively as well as more justly done by socialism (though hardly by extending the Morrisonian public corporation).

And we act meanwhile as if no one is watching us. The Shipbuilding Industries (Guarantee of Unproductive Employment) Bill is forced through the House by a minority government, representing a minority (just under 40 per cent) of the voters even (a mere 29 per cent of the electorate), to placate a minority of the PLP. Confidence is an odd thing. Perhaps the famous irrelevance of the Bill to our economic problems escaped the foreign press; but not the trickery and deceit, the misleading of the House, the fight on the Floor of the Commons. I was in Holland when it happened. The amazement, gloom and sympathy made me almost ashamed to be. . . .

And on top of all that, came the Resignation Honours Scandal, the crowning triviality of Wilson's career, than whom few men can have harmed their country more (except all those who supported him, waiting for a chance, not daring to make a chance, and then choosing the same again). Not that the ludicrous elevations matter. We raise no moral issue. But what does matter is the famous letter of Lady Falkender (*The Times*, 31 May) which grimly revealed what one correspondent well called: 'the great satisfaction of a small flattering clique over a catastrophic decline in our national fortunes'. *For she said that he left office 'with concern that it would be inherited smoothly and not in a situation of crisis'.*

That she believes this to have happened is a horrifying revelation of how isolated, both physically and psychologically, high office can be. Wilson's failure ever to tackle fundamental problems, his essential squalid trivialising of politics, has been, alas, not so much a negative personal achievement as an extreme but almost logical product of the internalising of politics at Downing Street.

It must not be too late to remedy this. The Left of the Party with its rhetoric of 'the people' is, in fact, desperately refusing to notice declining membership and increasing unpopularity, just as it hated to have to notice any connection between wages and inflation. The loyalists of the Right are desperately refusing to notice that they kept Wilson in power and, at a time of crisis, have gone for a successor who has yet to prove himself anything beyond a caretaker and, in political style, at least, simply a second Wilson who has yet to learn 'what does it profit a leader to hold the whole Labour Party together if he lose the nation?' They passed over at least four people of national stature—if only they would/could speak out: Healey, Jenkins, Crosland and Shirley Williams. And their votes have sustained absurd Bills—even though no one now believes that a single defeat should bring down a government.

Political as well as economic reconstruction is now needed. It is no use, Wilson having gone, simply to carry on the Wilson style of government: indecisive, short-term politics, cronyism, obsessive concern with party unity and constant reshuffling of not merely ministers but of the very functions of departments. And with both the main parties so much in public disfavour, no use either to follow blindly and to use brutally the conventions of majority, one-party parliamentary government. Primary elections, electoral reform, free votes, 'temporary coalitions for the emergency' (to use an Irish phrase), constitutional divisions of power, all these must be thought of, some almost certainly will have to be used, if public confidence in our system is not to collapse. But above all, more candour and more principle from leaders who will lead, and less pragmatism and time-serving—all these become relevant, as does moral seriousness rather than place-hunting, press baiting and memoir writing. To what depths has our old political genius sunk?

Northern Ireland

Rarely can a book have been more timely than Professor Richard Rose's recently published *Northern Ireland : Time of Choice*.[1] It shows with admirable objectivity, clarity and brevity just what the problem is, giving both religion and nationalism their independent due; characterises the main parties to the conflicts (and their growing complexity); analyses recent elections and sets out, more clearly and frankly than any White Paper has done, the possibilities that there are—some of them very grim. There is no 'solution', he reiterates, if by solution one means a generally agreeable formula. Something will have to give, something will have to be imposed if there is not to be, as well there could be, total breakdown of law and order, not even a clear-cut civil war. As in his previous and more 'scientific' book on Northern Ireland, *Governing without Consensus*, he remains the analyst and not merely stresses that all 'solutions' are dubious, but even refuses, with rare modesty, even after so much labour, to identify his own 'best buy'.

Professor Rose's indecisiveness in policy recommendation actually mirrors with unhappy aptness the present situation. But if 'direct rule' is one of his possible scenarios, much of the evidence seems to point against Mr Enoch Powell's hopes for its continuance and acceptance: provincial nationalism has now gone too far. Some kind of Northern Irish political authority must be created. If an elected Convention could not provide the starting point for it (though I think that Craig's Vanguard Party and the SDLP came closer to a working agreement than Rose acknowledges), then nominated caretaker governments must be formed and tried. The Northern Ireland Office seems to have slumped back into calm unimaginativeness, and its old over-concern with the security problem. No executive will be acceptable to all interests, but one might prove acceptable to most if we just try, try and try again. A local executive must be given time to establish itself *before* elections or be given a fixed term of office. No consensus exists to legitimate a government, but a local government might succeed in legitimating itself—given time and resolute support. And legal safeguards and divisions of power are now (a formal Federalism?) easier in the light of the Scottish devolution proposals which could suit Northern Ireland well.

BRC

---

[1] Published by Macmillan at £6.95 or £2.95 in paperback, 175 pp.

Commentary: 'The Death Wish'

Vol. 48, no. 1, January–March 1977

The government is struggling hard to deal with the mess that it has inherited from Wilson's long neglect of basic economic problems, indeed from the neglect of us all (parties, business, unions, Civil Service and education) to be more productivity-minded. The need for this was seen by cooler heads, but ignored by most politicians ever since it became clear as long ago as in the mid-1950s that our postwar recovery lagged far behind that of our main political partners and our economic competitors.

As if activated by some death wish, the NEC of the Labour Party has chosen this time to launch a campaign of opposition to the government's economic policy, a campaign which is either malign or stupid. Some are malign. They aim to destroy the government not in the name of common humanity but of dogmatic socialist principle (if hardly in the name of realistic socialist policy); and others are malign as a sour emotional reaction to the perennial difficulties of being in power—they aim simply to rid themselves of responsibility and return to the innocent and favoured passions of perpetual opposition. The campaign is stupid for three reasons, the short-, mid- and long-term ones.

The short-term stupidity is that such a degree of irresponsibility will doubly ensure the defeat of the government at the next election. Energy going into internecine strife would better be spent examining why Labour Party membership is declining so drastically—and in seeking a remedy (certainly more inter-party democracy is needed, if it can trust ordinary party members, not just ward activists, with decisions and can reach the ranks of its regular voters). The middle-term stupidity is that the attack on any cuts in public expenditure when we are plainly living so much beyond our means threatens to brand the constituency Labour parties as economic simpletons or primitive distributivists who believe that the more the cow is milked the bigger the udders will grow and the more the milk will flow. In practice this has come to be, of course, simply an advocacy of guaranteed public employment without any sense of or care for productivity. When the NEC organised a lobby of Parliament against the government last November, Mr Alan Fisher, the moderate leader of NUPE, argued at a rally for the nationalisation of all banks and insurance companies—presumably to ensure that all his members remained in jobs until the money ran out. The left wing leads us into the bureaucratic state, following the example of those selfless patriots, the pension-indexers of Whitehall. But it is easy to see why opposition to any cuts can appear plausible when there is so little fairness and equity in relative sacrifices. Does anyone truly believe that high taxation on management is the real reason for the continued postwar inefficiency of most British middle-sized firms?

The long-run stupidity is that *they* are forcing the Labour Party into a choice between social democracy (in the softer sense of a humane management of a mildly mixed economy) and democratic Socialism, aiming indeed at a fraternal, egalitarian and cooperative society, but becoming less and less libertarian and democratic as less and less[a] actual people support it, lapsing into the old and terrible cant of 'forcing people to be free', of serving an abstract People rather than real, awkward, hard-to-move, ordinary people.

If a choice has to be made, it is because the *Tribune* Left want to force it—being at heart always happier in opposition rather than in government. But the choice need not be made. The Labour Party simply needs to sort out its long-term goals and strategies from its short-term necessities and tactics. In any case, socialism is of such a kind—if it is to change society and optimise values of liberty, fraternity and equality—that it can only be achieved through consent. Coercion sours and destroys and breeds coercion. It does not liberate human imagination and energies. The entire history of socialism by coercive central party control in Eastern Europe could, in the long run, prove an irrelevance. Already a reaction has set in and Euro-socialism can now look at Euro-communism, very cautiously but definitely, in ways that might leave the Right of the British Party far behind, but also expose the present Left of the Party as suffering not merely from acute myopic parochiality, but from a self-defeating impatience. If a democratic Socialist society is to be achieved, it can only be on a scale such as that of Europe (indeed Europe provides the most clement and promising conditions), but only on a scale of generations, not of two or three British governments.

BRC

Commentary: 'Jubilee?', 'Penguin', 'Porn' and 'Parliament'

Vol. 48, no. 3, July–September 1977

Jubilee?

One odd thing about the Peter Jay controversy[a] was that he embodies in its most unforgivable form the unwanted virtue of having been right all along about the fundamental state of the economy and not listened to—what the creeps and time-servers of the late Harold Wilson's Cabinet called 'intellectual arrogance' and 'talking the country down'.[b] The press has its knockers,

---

[a] Yes, it should be 'fewer and fewer', but retaining this original form maintains the clearly intended parallel with 'less and less libertarian'—and besides, in this collection I'm allowing Bernard to stay substantially free from the depredations of the anal-triumphalist school of editing.

[a] The reference is to David Owen's appointment of Peter Jay as Britain's Ambassador to the USA. Owen was not only his close friend but Foreign Secretary in the government of Jay's then father-in-law, the new Prime Minister James Callaghan.

[b] This four-part Commentary, which at almost 5,000 words matches the length of an average *PQ* article, is among the longest ever written for the journal—and may indeed be the longest.

513

on grounds sometimes more sensible than the ludicrous evidence that Sir Harold recently presented to the Royal Commission on the Press—revealing a persecution mania without even the excuse (as Laski used to say of Rousseau) that he was persecuted. The press (even without the *Daily Mail*) does silly things. But it was always, as we look back over the 25 glorious years of national history we are celebrating, a handful of professional economic journalists who kept up warnings, from the mid-fifties at least, that our growth rates were falling behind those of our principal competitors, and that both British industry and British finance were picking off the soft home markets in preference to the difficulties of exports. People like Peter Jay, Andrew Shonfield, Alan Day and Michael Stewart, Samuel Brittan and Michael Shanks were saying this in the press long before the TUC, on the one hand, and EEC, on the other hand, became scapegoats sufficient unto all our ills. And political leaders just didn't want to hear, not just Macmillan and his Chancellors, but also Wilson and (until so very late) his too.

Only two years ago the Queen's advisers allowed a passage to be put into her Christmas message deploring those prophets of doom who were talking our country into a depression, etc. I think it was only the BBC who picked this up (who else listens?) to allow one of your editors to make a mildly adverse comment on Boxing Day. I doubt if Wilson had the passage put in. Probably like the 'United Kingdom for ever' passage in her recent effort (which sent a chill of foreboding down the spine), it was a spontaneous offering—or what the Webbs once called, in apology for their *Soviet Communism: A New Civilisation?*, an act of supererogation. It is simply that at that level, people tend to think alike. They take for granted the historical power of the British state (over whose decline she has, in fact, had the ill luck to preside) and they have insulated themselves from unemployment, the effects of inflation and the decline in our public services. Those, indeed, like the Duke of Edinburgh, who can look after themselves, seem perfectly sure that everyone should look after himself.

So a sour note on Jubilee. This journal is supposed to be moderate. But our prejudices are of an old radical, no-nonsense, hard work and the public interest kind (is 'puritanical' the word?) which is, like so many ordinary people one speaks to, disgusted at the cheap vulgarity of royal ostentation at a time of unemployment and hardship. As the football crowds cry, 'What a load of rubbish!' The whole thing, stage-managed to distract people from the crisis, may well—to use a Commonwealth word—boomerang. When will leading politicians realise that calls for wage restraint cannot be expected to work if equality of sacrifice is not seen to be practised by all wealthier classes: drones, businessmen and higher civil servants alike? Their patriotism has severe limits.

Birthday Honours should have gone to a headmistress of a primary school in Sheffield who refused LEA orders to march or bus her flock to join all other Sheffield children in waving flags spontaneously at the Queen in a local park. She says her duty is to educate her children, not to waste their time. The parents support her. Such people are real England.

Penguin

Remember when the *Observer* spread its anti-Suez editorial over the whole of the two inside pages? Not quite as large, but on 11 May 1977, the *Daily Telegraph* allowed Mr Robert Moss to wander over their two inside, feature pages with 'A Story of Editorial Bias', an attack on 'the Left-wing record of Penguin's political book lists'.

He began in cheerfully prejudicial style by telling a tale that after the murder of the Israeli athletes at the 1972 Olympics, an office memorandum in the name of Neil Middleton, their political editor, was circulated about the commissioning of a book justifying the Palestinian action, and throwing them all into a panic until they realised it was a hoax. But, says Mr Moss, inventing a new kind of sub-factual tar-brush, no one seems to have doubted that it could have happened. 'Having recently returned from a visit to my friendly local Marxist bookstore with an armful of the latest Pelican Originals, I can see why', he adds. One has no reason to doubt that this event actually occurred. One might think that this is an odd sampling procedure for someone connected with *The Economist* Intelligence Unit to adopt. Had he gone to a bookstall in a museum, in a stately house, in a tourist centre, in a large church or even in a university, he would find Penguins of very different kinds. And neither Pevsner's guides nor Puffins seem, as yet, to be seriously penetrated; but Mr Moss had better keep vigilant.

However, on a narrow front, he has a narrow point. Penguin's political list is much more heterogeneous and unsystematic than, for instance, their Sociology and Economics sections. A textbook here, a polemic there, books cover all points of the spectrum and at very different standards, including many Marxist books and, of course, the scholarly Pelican Marx Library and the Pelican Classics (which as distinct from Penguin Classics, are their collection of classics of political ideas—of whom only three authors out of 19 published by January of this year appear to be Marxists). Coverage of the Third World does, however, he is quite correct, tend to be heavily Marxist, though none of it orthodox Communist (a distinction that Mr Moss believes unworthy of notice).

I myself complained two years ago, in two batches of mass reviews of political Penguins in the *New Statesman*, about how uneven in quality these books were. Some of the offerings in the South American Library were ridiculous. It often seemed as if facts didn't matter so long as the conceptual framework was correct, and since these frameworks were all very much the same, the books were very boring, predictable and often ludicrously thin in any reliable contemporary history. There tended to be one chapter of Marxist analysis, one of polemic, and then padding from reference books to make weight in what more naturally should have been a long essay in a quarterly or annual. One author, having completed his manuscript on a far-off land, was discovered never to have been there and so had to be hurriedly dispatched for retrospective legitimation (or so his sister told me). But the brute facts are that these are but a small part of Penguin's offerings; that young Marxists tend to be more knowledgeable about the Third World than Mr Moss's friends (except when they set up as counter-insurgency consultants); and that the New Left does conduct its debates mainly in a Marxist framework, although within this, more and more, the style remains more objectionable than the changing content. For every lunatic justifying terrorism in the name of the People ('reified' People, not actual People), there is now a long-winded and anxious libertarian, reinterpreting Marx through Gramsci, believing in Euro-communism, attacking the old Communist practices of intolerance and oppression. *La vérité est dans les nuances.*

Mr Moss's real trouble in openly demanding that the business managers of Penguin, the Pearson group, should purge their beast (which is, indeed, a national institution worth arguing about) is that he accepts no distinctions within Marxist writings and does, indeed, despite the break-up of inter-national Communism after 1956, still believe in a conspiracy theory. He appears to believe that all the dotty and intense students of Marx, who do more harm by withdrawing from real politics into polemic than ever they would do by intruding upon it, are *objectively* agents of the Kremlin. No wonder they regard him as objectively fascist, which he is not, only an authoritarian apologist for dictatorships (as his recent book *The Collapse of Democracy* shows). Mr Moss's oddity is that he seems to think that Penguin should act politically like the BBC and achieve literal balance. Why? Does he exaggerate its importance? They are not the only paperback firm any longer at all at all. He accuses Penguin of not publishing right-wing authors whom they do not print simply because they are authors of firms also publishing paperbacks. He ignores many whom they do print. I must tell him how many reprints there have been on my *In Defence of Politics*, hardly Marxist. And he assumes that Penguin has fallen off of late. The truth is, of course, that Penguin's political publishing was always biased towards the Left; and 'bias' never meant a totalitarian exclusiveness, as he seems to assume and actually wants practised. I take down from my shelf Pelican Books No. 1, author, George Bernard Shaw; title, *The Intelligent Woman's Guide to Socialism, Capitalism, Sovietism and Fascism*; and the first advisory editors, V. K. Krishna Menon, H. L. Beales (may he live for ever!), W. E. Williams (of the WEA) and Professor Lancelot Hogben.

Somewhat inconsequentially, as well as a fall from Neo-Liberal economic grace, Mr Moss also has a 'systematic exclusion of important books from the non-Left' which goes back to their rejection, he says, of Orwell's *Animal Farm* in 1944 as critical of the Soviet Union and exposing 'the defects of the Left'. Why is it that any right-wing polemicist conjures with Orwell's name when he was a left-wing socialist, not a Marxist, true, but an egalitarian as well as a libertarian, friend of Michael Foot and Nye Bevan, literary editor of *Tribune*? This is an invention. Orwell did not offer *Animal Farm* to Penguin in 1944. He offered it to Gollancz, who turned it down, to two conservative publishers, Cape and Faber, who turned it down, before Fred Warburg carried it. Penguin had, in fact, reprinted Orwell's *Road to Wigan Pier* in 1941, which contains his famous polemic against the Marxists!

Penguin's list was always biased in a socialist, progressive and reformist way—and why not? But never, never, then or now, was it exclusively left wing. If Mr Moss appeals to the commercial self-interest of the Pearson group, they should consider the grim and comic history of attempts to form Right Book Clubs or series of a true, impartial, balanced and Robert Moss-like kind.

Bad commercial decisions were made. Their old Education Library wasn't much use to teachers and lacked that judicious mixture of prescription and reliable information that was the hallmark of the old Pelican. But that has been wound up. Reviewers liked to review way-out speculations about education and society, but teachers rarely bought them. There are books like that which review well and sell badly, a sign that their message would be better found in articles and pamphlets. By and very large, however, even in its elephantine growth, the old amphibian is still a national glory. And if there are more Marxists nowadays (I think Mr Moss and I would agree on that), they buy more books than Young Conservatives; and even if Mr Moss could be right that we should stuff our ears to any siren calls that liberty can be debated, defended and extended in Marxist terms, this can hardly be blamed on the management of Penguin. Any yielding to this new brand of right-wing, economic-liberal intolerance could prove intellectually disastrous. Mr Moss does not want speculation, he wants orthodoxy. It is odd that such a tough, sceptical and civilised old Tory as Bill Deedes, the editor of the *Daily Telegraph*, should trim his sails to such a doctrinaire wind. One hopes that this is no sign of the times. Cold winds of intellectual intolerance could begin to blow in unlikely places.

Porn

'Liberal tolerance is always faced with the problem', wrote David Holbrook in his 'The Politics of Pornography' in our January number, 'of tolerating developments which threaten those values in which tolerance is grounded'. He was not attacking liberal tolerance; he was trying to face the problem of by what criteria do we extend or limit tolerance. And in the present number a most tightly reasoned and important article by D. J. Heasman, 'Sexuality and Civil Liberties', ends: 'Some rights, after all, are rather more crucial than others'.[c] Mr Holbrook's article unleashed a small flood of offers to write rebuttals. Shock was expressed that we had printed him. We could have filled the present issue until the bucket slopped over. Some seemed to think that in arguing that the cult of pornographic violence is damaging to values of reason, freedom and liberality (indeed, following Lawrence, of sexuality), that

[c] Full references are: David Holbrook, 'The Politics of Pornography', *The Political Quarterly*, vol. 48, no. 1, pp. 44–53; D. J. Heasman, Sexuality and Civil Liberties', *The Political Quarterly*, vol. 48, no. 3, pp. 313–27.

Mr Holbrook wanted the return of the rack and the gibbet—he never even mentioned censorship, confining himself (somewhat to our disappointment) to moral and psychological aspects, largely ignoring the legal. And some wanted equal space to state the case for the liberating effect of pornography, no holds barred. Several correspondents seemed to confuse him with Lord Longford and Mrs Whitehouse, missing entirely that his argument was put in wholly secular terms and not knowing that he is a card-carrying British Humanist. He does go on a bit, but the counter-attack struck us as far more obsessional; and the fact is undoubted that even a writer of his fame and talent finds it harder and harder to find space to state his case. So many editors of intellectual weeklies and monthlies seem to live in a NW1 world of Radical Chic in which the expression of novelty and the desperate one-up-manship game of being a yet more authentic personality, these are values far more prized than serious discussions of the limits of tolerance and the constituents of human sociability.

So often, indeed, a kind of black propaganda is launched against any who think that pornography is bad or trivial; that they favour general powers of censorship—rather than, perhaps, that they are saying simply that it is bad and trivial; or that a man is accused of hypocrisy if he tolerates something without positively advocating it. Private pleasures or inadequacies seem now, being newsworthy more than furtive, to demand public legitimation. And on both sides, with few exceptions, there is little attempt to try to reason about what kind of things may or may not harm conditions for sociability, thus becoming, on such a line of argument, proper objects for legislation. But even then, legislation is not all of a piece. Arguments for individual rights to be thrust in the face of an indifferent or worried majority (like capital punish-ment reform, etc.) have to be used sparingly, saved for matters of life or death. It is easy to see why local opinion may object to display, for instance, and could have powers, if local democracy means anything, to forbid, limit or licence. But it is easy to see why local opinion should not become involved in censorship of books or journals. The choice is not between repression and free expression, between Mrs Whitehouse and the Institute of Contemporary Arts—the extremes who feed off each other. Some rights are more important than others. Many ordinary people are puzzled when intellectuals say that rubbish is art or therapy, rather than that rubbish is rubbish, need not be touched, should not be touched but need not be legislated against, either, so long as it is not thrust on other people, particularly children. Too many intellectuals are frightened of condemning or mocking pornography for fear of being thought authoritarian. But the struggle for civil liberties was concerned with more important matters than, say, the ICA's obsession with any kind of censorship of sexual artefacts. Socialists should see much of this as a retreat from politics, not 'liberty in danger'. The contrary can sometimes be true.

Parliament

Discussions about parliamentary reform take place in far too narrow a context. Dull stuff about procedure, services and committees has become worse than conventional wisdom; it has become examination fodder. Sixth-formers can reel off five reasons for parliamentary reform and 10 reforms before the examiner has even pulled the trigger. It has now become yet another way of keeping students of politics away from politics. Consider when, however, in the nineteenth century 'parliamentary reform' meant franchise reform in order to change the distribution of political power in the nation. Looking back on the parliamentary reform movement of the 1960s, it now seems to have been (if I may recant) largely a waste of time and effort. The need for it was another of those symptoms that we moderates so easily mistake for the disease. Generally, the 1960s saw an almost obsessional drive to reform institutions: Parliament, the Civil Service, the machinery of central government, local government and education; but far less thought was given to what they should be used for, reformed or unreformed. Rarely was the case made that in order to carry out specified, important policies, institutions had to be changed. The impetus for change came out of a hazy but intense feeling, technocratic but faintly romantic, that given better machinery, better policies would follow and that the distribution of political power would be gently and beneficially changed. It was as if there was a natural political market mechanism which only needed some imperfections removed. No wonder some Tories thought it a waste of time that would change nothing and some Socialists saw it as mere ameliorism.

A second volume of essays from the Study of Parliament Group, *The Commons in the Seventies* (Fontana), edited by S. A. Walkland and Michael Ryle, bring these contradictions of power and procedure to the surface. Many of the essays are the old stuff, how things were done and might be done a little more effectively. Michael Ryle offers an introductory survey which asks people to pull up their socks a bit, transistorise their garters but to remember that the traditions of the good old House really work pretty well, considering, so long as we constantly adjust 'effective and critical procedures to match the power of government'. But 'match' is the rub. Nevil Johnson, however, uses his formidable powers of negation to write a searching essay on how little the new Select Committee system has been able to achieve: 'they have continued to seek quantitative reform without qualitative change'. Faith in select committees, he says, 'seemed to be a way of avoiding the awkward dilemma lying at the heart of the parliamentary reform argument, or at least of softening its impact'. The dilemma is that 'for reform to be effective in the sense of altering relations between Government and Parliament, it seemed to be necessary to challenge accepted views of how the House should operate and of party alignments within it'. No committee system can by itself bridge the gap, he implies, between two different sorts of parliament: that which assumes majority rule (thus 'primarily a place for public debate, for presenting a challenge to a government and for sustaining a government') and a '"bargaining" model, brought into existence by the persistence of several parties, none of which regularly has an absolute majority, or by the presence of parties which are internally divided'. So parliamentary reform by procedures cannot change the political system; but if the political system changes, then radical reform of institutions must follow. Dr Johnson at last convinces me that the cart cannot go before the horse.

Stuart Walkland goes further and, in effect, kicks over the traces of the Study of Parliament Group, which has been officers of both Houses and academics pulling in double harness—so long as they stay in the ruts of the consequences of existing policies and don't challenge the policies. (I could once explain how this wonder worked, indeed had a hand in harnessing these two horses in backwards, but now I've lost the knack or am frightened of the Leader of the House who seems to declare all constitutional speculation disloyal to the Labour Party.) For Mr Walkland repudiates the optimism of the first volume of essays (*The Commons in Transition*) and accuses most of his contributors of still fudging the dilemma:

Less than 10 years has served to demonstrate that neither the Commons nor the country as a whole was, in fact, in any transitional state, except to a worse condition, and the multifarious social, educational, administrative and parliamentary reforms of the 1960s have been ineffectual in securing any regeneration of Parliament, government or the economy, improvements in the functioning of which remain as elusive as ever. . . . What is needed if ground now lost is to be regained is political realignment to the point where no government is in the position to act as the political arm of a powerful minority interest, whether to the Left or to the Right, and where its main allegiance is of political necessity and considerations of survival to a broader based and representative House of Commons. Change of this nature cannot come from Parliament itself—it must reflect the new social and political impulses relayed through the structures of the national party system, although much could be done to facilitate it through electoral reform. Procedural tinkering is in these circumstances irrelevant; the search for it dissipates energies which would be better employed in analysing the political problem. . . .

All except a few Liberals assumed the desirability, even the inevitability, of a largely two-party model of parliamentary politics. . . . Academics and others who shaped reforming opinion had their own political axe to grind. . . . It is not without significance that Professors Hanson, Wiseman, Crick and Mackintosh, with their mentor, Professor Laski, were all Labour supporters who could not be expected to canvass even the possibility of electoral change which might threaten the stability of their own party. . . .

John Mackintosh and the late Harry Hanson would be as surprised as I to find the hand of Laski behind all this. He might well have agreed with Walkland that procedural reform is all 'tinkering': he was stirring a far bigger pot. And there is something comic in the excesses of a Liberal like Mr Walkland suddenly rediscovering the rude facts of political power. For it is at least pot calling kettle black to denounce reforms in procedure as politically unrealistic but then to espouse electoral reform as a super institutional panacea. But half a truth is better than none and Mr Walkland has the rare gift of total relevance.

More and more your editors begin to see the case for electoral reform, or rather the need to be prepared for it if political conditions change in England as they have already changed in Scotland, Northern Ireland and Wales, each of which countries would be more governable, more easy to keep within the Union, if there were PR.

Electoral reform, in my view, can and should only form part of a far broader attempt to reflect in our constitutional arrangements the real dis-tribution of power in our society. One aspect of the real distribution of power, by no means the only one, is shown in a Chancellor publicly bargaining over his budget with the TUC. Surely this is sensible? Some try to make our flesh creep by calling this a 'corporate state', though with the next breath they will probably rabbit on about the virtues of 'pluralism'. Electoral reform by itself would make no difference to the need for any government to negotiate with powerful organised interests of any kind—parliaments cannot do this well; they can only throw more light on the process. Mr Walkland seems to hope that electoral reform would give the popular support for Parliament to reassert its sovereign powers against the interests. Such an individualistic theory of power is, indeed, Liberal. Both Tories and Socialists have more sense of the power and the value of organised groups.

Parliamentary sovereignty and pluralism do, indeed, mix badly. The question is not how to assert Parliament's power both against government and all these groups, but how Parliament can play a leading role (a) in keeping the leaders of these groups accountable to and representative of their own members; and (b) in keeping each group as a whole accountable to the public. (Even in this, Parliament is the focus of several processes, but not the exclusive one: the media and academic research are also important.) In other words, 'extra-parliamentary' is not necessarily 'anti-parliamentary'; and it is extra-parliamentary groups which stand most in need of being made both more democratic and more accountable. The broad and good concept of parliamentary government is one that needs extending far beyond Westmin-ster. If this leads to a relative diminution of central power, does it matter so long as those who have the power to produce or not, or to work hard or not, whether management or men, feel themselves properly represented? In a word, Bullock is as important as Blake.

Parliamentary reform must raise all these questions. Having accepted Johnson and Walkland's critique, the speculation must be pushed further. Certainly, 'parliamentary reform' can no longer be concerned with tinkering with procedure—as is Lisanne Radice's Fabian Tract, *Reforming the House of Commons*, which simply repeats all the proposals of 10 to 15 years ago (with neither theory nor any great sense of purpose), a sad exhibition of the intellectual bankruptcy of the contemporary Fabian Society. She wants a strengthened committee system, pre-legislative committees, more services and facilities to Members and, *sancta simplicitas*, morning sessions. This will make us all better. At least their earlier pamphlet of 1959 with the same title (which I now repudiate) tried to deal with the problem of power and to relate Parliament to the wider political system. But Mrs Radice just pops out stale bright ideas for making life more comfortable and meaningful for backbench MPs. They have, however, the remedies for impotence in their own hands if they wanted to use them: to vote against their own party more regularly and to refuse to become PPSs—useless jobs whose real function is so that a Prime Minister can muzzle his majority with patronage.

The Hansard Society has just produced the report of a working party under Professor David Coombes on the effect on British representative institutions of membership of the EEC (*The British People: Their Voice in Europe*, Saxon House, Teakfield Ltd). Some of it is pretty conventional, intricate and trivial stuff about the failure of Parliament to adjust adequately its procedures to the new challenges of . . . , etc., full of the usual Liberal gimmickry; but some of it is very much better, imaginatively construing 'representative institutions' to include TUC, CBI, other interest groups, the professions and local government. It examines how some of them have organised themselves, not waiting for Parliament, to do or be done down in Bruxelles.[d] What emerges is a mixed tale with the CBI, for instance, acting sensibly but with the TUC sulking about the referendum result and doing little or nothing in Bruxelles, even to the detriment of their own members' interests. But these extra-parliamentary forces are where influence on the Commissions should come from. A companion volume will appear later this year from the Hansard Society called *Parliament and the Public* (the report of a working party headed by John Mackintosh). He will raise the basic question of what should Parliament be doing. The view is taken that neat little schemes to improve public understanding of and access to the House are a bit beside the point until either backbench MPs or the electorate have decided whether majorities in Parliament will move from a supportive role to governments into a bargaining role. There's a lot of procedural reform to be done if they do; but if not, not.

BRC

---

[d] The French spelling is in the original. Given that it's unlikely to be a mistake, readers are free to decide its significance along the spectrum from knowing comment to affectation.

Commentary: 'The Education Service'

Vol. 48, no. 4, October–December 1977

Clearly it is a mouse, even if a very agile and earnest mouse which has had a quick look all over our house, but why, oh why, did the mountain ever need to labour?[a] *The Green Paper, Education in Schools: A Consultative Document* (Cmnd 6869) begins: 'In his speech at Ruskin College, Oxford, on October 18, 1976, the Prime Minister called for a public debate on education. The debate was not to be confined to those professionally concerned with education, but was to give full opportunity for employers and trade unions, and parents, as well as teachers and administrators, to make their views known.' The speech was made against a background of strongly critical comment in the press and elsewhere on education and educational standards. And in by now classic Green Paper style it rabbits on: '1.3 Some of these criticisms are fair . . . ;' and '1.4 Other criticisms are misplaced. . . .' Such an even-handed justice is rendered, 'on the one hand' and 'on the other hand', that it can assuage all anxieties if read aloud in the Secretary of State's best 'I can understand all your problems and up to a point sympathise' voice; or it can confuse utterly if read through journalists' reports who found it, understandably, hard to summarise; or it can irritate if read slowly and in the original on holiday, as many of us have now been reading it. If the conclusions are (as nearly all commentators agree) either platitudes or prevarications, this may be because the problem that led to the enterprise is never defined.

The Prime Minister felt, deeply but vaguely, that there was public worry and that something should be done about it—particularly something that showed that the Labour Party could comprehend the fears of the Silent Majority, not just the threats of shop stewards. And Shirley Williams seemed not unloath to try to educate the press and the public on what secondary education is really about (in fact the descriptive parts of the paper are the best. 'You see, they do know what the real problems are', I can tell my teacher friends, 'even if they think they can't do much about them'). Yet the character of the public worry was never defined. The suspicion remains that DES has been put through a time-wasting operation for image-building purposes rather than to achieve anything lasting. (There are, after all, similarities as well as differences between Mr Callaghan's and Mr Wilson's styles of government.)

Many public worries may be inevitable in times of social change—changes deliberate and unintended, foreseen and unforeseen, welcome and unwelcome. Much of it may be normal parental worry that little Willie or Sandra 'isn't doing as well as she should', perceived in vague but aggressive terms of education as social 'climbing' (i.e. social mobility of a one-way kind). Such

---

[a] This piece is the second element of a two-part Commentary. The first is on the diplomatic service, by Donald Cameron Watt (a *PQ* editorial board member at the time).

worries are now food for *good* (i.e. lively and irresponsible) daily journalism. Amid a decline in family discipline (in some ways so much to be welcomed) and a general fear by the older generation of the younger, many people hope for more out of the schools than they possibly can or should give. Parents who never read a book and rarely turn off the telly expect schools to motivate children even to the extreme and often unnecessary pitch of doing homework willingly. Firms expect schools to produce docile employees with relevant skills and astonishing initiative. Churches who are losing their congregations expect schools to act for them as spiritual truancy officers. And for the popular press, our great de-educator, to make allegations of falling standards and occasional incidents of violence stable themes for feature-page fill-ins, is hypocrisy of a very high order.

If people are worried about methods of education and the organisation of education, rather than about the kind of society into which our children are growing up, there are better ways of pin-pointing these worries than holding public debates (such as one your editor attended) in which representatives of organised groups and interests wearisomely arose, not to debate, but simply to present what their organisations had already put on paper. The government's own Social Survey might furnish more accurate clues both as to what the rank-and-file of these organisations actually think and to what is worrying ordinary people than either such staged debates or Big Jim's antennae. And having discovered them, what then? Should public opinion define the objects of education or even the paths of reform? Or should they not rather point to the problems of implementation if there are new policies to follow any perceptions of new needs?

The curriculum

For instance, one idea constantly recurred in the debate and the Green Paper considers it favourably: that there should be a compulsory core in the curriculum (and a fairly large core) of studies to enhance numeracy and literacy right through the school. 'This seemed common ground among both those who took a liberal view of education and those who took a vocational view. But should this idea be officially encouraged and if so, how? Pay attention!

2.18 Action to improve the planning and development of the curriculum will be successful only if it takes into account fully the division of responsibilities for education in schools. The control of secular education in maintained schools . . . rests with the local education authority. . . .

2.19 It would not be compatible with the duties of the Secretaries of State to 'promote the education of the people of England and Wales', or with their accountability to Parliament, to abdicate from leadership on educational issues which have become a matter of lively public concern. The Secretaries of State will therefore seek to establish a broad agreement with their partners in the education service on a framework for the curriculum, and, particularly, on whether, because there are aims common to all schools and to all pupils at certain stages, there should be a 'core' or 'protected' part.

2.20 In their turn, the local education authorities must co-ordinate the curriculum and its development in their own areas, taking account of local circumstances, consulting local interests. . . .

2.21 As the next step the Secretaries of State propose to invite the local authority and teachers' associations to take part in early *consultations about the conduct* of a review of curricular arrangements in each [sic] local authority area. . . .

2.22 The intention of the Secretaries of State is that, following these consultations, they should issue a circular *asking* all local authorities to carry out the review in their own area in consultation with their teachers and to report the results within about twelve months. The Department would then analyse the replies as a *preliminary to consultations* on the outcome of the review and on the nature of any advice that the Secretaries of State *might* then issue on curricular matters.

The irony-inducing italics in this lovely bit of drafting are all mine. Granted all the sensitivities about state and local control of education, who imagines that any policy—if it were seriously meant—could be so impossibly hedged with the need to get agreement from so many authorities? There is a world of difference in politics between what is agreeable (something almost impossible among so many) and what is acceptable; and the latter calls for national leadership and clear aims. How else—right or wrong—did the comprehensive policy ever come about?

The Green Paper notices in passing that 'the general acceptance of a core curriculum' would contribute to minimising the difficulties of parents whose jobs demand mobility. No one knows how great this problem is. But one suspects that it could be a substantial psychological limitation on the mobility of labour, not as great as that of public housing (the distribution of which is absurdly and rigidly localised), but an important disincentive nonetheless. Difficulties of 'the children settling down in schools in other areas' in part reflect the lack of a national curriculum, or at least national elements in the curriculum. In this respect, particularly when the relationship of the educational system to economic and political leadership comes to be considered, it is absurd to leave out of consideration (as the Green Paper does) the private sector. The 'common core' and 'education for an industrial society' are as much neglected in the private as in the public (or rather local) sector.

Standards and assessment

On standards and assessment the report is sensible and reassuring to those who really worry that standards are falling, rather than that they are becoming interested, for the first time, in how much better things could be. Most standards of literacy and numeracy appear to be gradually increasing, but nonetheless a feeling of relative deprivation is real enough as people's expectations grow—themselves a product of better education. The 'progressive' versus 'traditional' methods of education debate is rightly dismissed as a provocative red herring. There are a few dedicated loonies who pride

525

themselves on 'everything new' or on 'nothing new', but most sensible, even most routine, teachers pick and choose. The Green Paper raises the more relevant issues about how to learn from experience. How is performance to be assessed and the effectiveness of actual methods used in real situations? The idea of leaving certificates for all pupils is rejected (perhaps with too little discussion). Once again the numerous local authorities are exhorted to examine methods of record keeping and assessment other than public examinations, and to report. 'This outline description of the possibilities leaves a number of detailed points for further discussion.' Indeed.

The role of HM Inspectorate is dealt with very briefly, almost dismissively. The whole 'public relations origin of this Green Paper precludes any open thought about the role of the national and the local inspectorates, particularly the growth of local advisory services. Let them be locally based, by all means, but surely subject to clear national standards? In some LEAs advisory services hardly exist and in others are simply a circular, self-justifying mechanism for established local views on what should be taught and how. 'On the whole, inspection tends to be a subjective and qualitative process, though H.M. Inspectorate is increasingly moving towards complementary quantitative analyses . . .' (3.6). Is this really the view of Mrs Williams? Is DES beginning to lose its belief in good judgement and to deflate the qualitative for the quantitative? Certainly the new Assessment of Performance Unit (APU) in DES is much to be welcomed, trying to develop tests suitable for national monitoring in English language, mathematics and science initially. Nonetheless, it is surely a tool to be interpreted and used by a national inspectorate. The national inspectorate should have more powers and greater numbers. Dare it be said this bluntly and simply that we should rather trust the general direction of secondary education to their knowledge and experience than to opinions of local councillors?

Lack of discussion of the role of HMIs may be because of internal differences within DES, where lately the inspectorate have become more influential relative to ordinary civil servants. But the PR nature of this Green Paper precluded, even from appendices, a series of papers on special topics prepared by members of the inspectorate. It has been decided, it seems, not to publish them. So they will not appear—since HMIs are civil servants. Or are they? Should not the inspectorate be in a position to make their own views clear nationally? For them to be silent, amid all this tender excess of pluralism, with the Minister and her advisers acting as if LEAs are the voice of the people or, in any sense, a serious political force, is unfortunate. 'Open government' has its limits, it seems.

Teachers

In terms of Big Jim's[b] trimming politics, there had to be a rap on the knuckles for incompetent teachers. Tough talk flows, hedged with procedural safe-

[b] Prime Minister James Callaghan.

guards, about how they just possibly might ever be dismissed simply for not doing the job they are paid to do (and I would look at some of my dear university colleagues likewise, and wonder how it has come to be under bureaucratic capitalism, to coin a phrase, that the professions have come near to establishing an absolute private property in a job). And there had to be, then, more serious sermonising about the better need for in-service courses, both refresher and retraining. Without the latter, the former would have just added injury to insult in this time of cuts when the crudest and truest measure of conditions for effective teaching is simply a lower pupil–teacher ratio. Only an exceptional teacher can achieve with 30 what the average teacher could with 15.

Excellent proposals are made for a greater integration of teacher training and higher education. Both universities and polytechnics should wince at the unstated implication that they have neglected shamefully their wider responsibilities for teachers' education beyond the mere validation of BEds. And the great importance of continuing in-service education is clearly and strongly stated. But again, 'how shall these wonders come to pass?' By exhortation to local authorities to pull up their socks, report back and then we'll all jolly well have a serious look at it together again! And such vagueness and infirmity of policy as this, despite knowing that: 'provision varies widely from area to area and in some authorities is quite inadequate: moreover there is recent evidence to suggest that existing provision has been reduced' (6.24).

The Paper also notes the problem of induction, that young teachers are commonly plunged in to teach the maximum number of hours with little if any guidance and no time for preparation. It notes that in *two* LEAs, Liverpool and Northumberland, pilot schemes for induction of new teachers have been introduced with government help and that 'several other authorities introduced pilot induction schemes on their own account'. One might suggest both to the NUT and to a Labour Minister that (a) this degree of LEA energy, care and concern makes nonsense of the Green Paper's strategy of reform through agreement among the LEAs (unless this Paper is pure moonshine); and (b) that induction and in-service training should, in minimum amounts and to national standards, be every teacher's right and duty. Teachers need, in all our interests, a national charter to guarantee and enforce their continuing education against local neglect and headteachers' favouritism.

The air of unreality about what actually determines what is taught in schools is briefly dispelled when 6.34 bravely begins: 'The character and quality of the headteacher are by far the main influences in determining what a school sets out to do and the extent to which it achieves its aims'. Or not. So the Paper once again exhorts LEAs to be very careful how they appoint headteachers. The cat jumps out of the bag but is popped back in pretty quickly. In many parts of the country, after all, headships are part of the spoils of local politics. The real issue is ignored. For many reasons of administrative convenience and of politicians' distrust of teachers, local authorities give an absurd amount of power to a headteacher—as they do to heads of FE

527

colleges—in relation to his colleagues. At least universities are better in that respect. No Vice-Chancellor or a head of a department nowadays would dream of making so many decisions on his own, or with only token consultation, as is the common practice of headteachers, progressive and reactionary alike. Experienced teachers are constantly demoralised and publicly shown to have no authority when they are given their timetables, told to try a new syllabus, permitted or not to go on a course—all things that should be a matter of collegiate decision.

Perhaps there are different ideas of what a Green Paper should be. Shirley Williams had the character and originality to have produced a clear analysis of needs and clear proposals for a national policy in England and Wales, even if it meant new powers for the centre or the use of indirect sanctions (as in ramming home Comprehensive policy). And she could have tried to relate secondary to post-experience education, for perhaps we could do with less of the former if the latter were guaranteed as of right. But what in fact we are offered is a very intelligent, Civil Service job of identifying what the main problems of maintained secondary schools are thought to be by the already organised interested parties, and indications of possible broad lines of beginning to come near, sometime (after the next election), to dealing with them, perhaps. It is like a parody of the present state of the Social Contract. Neither a 'common core' nor 'relevance to industry' can be achieved simply by consultation, and even if so the victory would be pyrrhic if the private sector were not also involved. Meanwhile the 'state teachers' do their best, with remarkably little public support or sympathy from either state or the public. Mrs Williams still has it in her hands to raise the morale of teachers, which would do more for standards in education than a hundred such stilted debates and soft Green Papers. Empathy must be a precondition to policy, not a retreat into a bog of excessive consultation.

BRC

Commentary: 'Political Education, Elections and the Media'

Vol. 49, no. 2, April–June 1978

A spectre is haunting the republic of reason. The ghosts of the last few general election campaigns inhabit the unborn spirit of the one to come.[a] The quality of British political debate has never been lower, and it will soon achieve new depths. The image that ordinary people have of political debate is of Tweedledum and Tweedledee screaming abuse at each other. If tomorrow

[a] This is the second element of a two-part Commentary and follows 'The Killing of the Scotland Bill' by John Mackintosh.

the sun were to cease to shine upon the world for 40 days, the Prime Minister and the Leader of the Opposition would both publicly blame each other, if not for the event at least for lack of preparation while in office.

One of the working papers of the Hansard Society's Programme for Political Education (whose final report is to be published by Longman this June) says:

... such political education as there now is usually comes not from schools or media, but from waging of General Election campaigns by leading politicians. A young person could form the opinion that politics is (i) a residual claim to govern on the simple ground that the other side is inherently stupid and tells so many lies; (ii) simply the expression of social interests; and (iii) simply an auction of speculative benefits for probable support. So little reasoning and canvassing of principles enters into current electoral campaigning that politics may seem just a question of 'who gets what, when and how'.

If this is the 'realistic' 'pragmatic' or 'moderate' view of things, can these realists (who say that they know better, but must act worse—like the Healeys and the Whitelaws) explain why both electoral turnout and party membership is declining so drastically (except among the Nats); and why politicians as a class continue to decline in public respect?

Any issue is *raised* that might help to win an election; and issues may be raised without having any policies. Mr Callaghan called for a debate on education, sensing public worry, but offering no policies or guidance, carefully not (himself) implying that teachers are responsible for any alleged growth of indiscipline or decline of standards—only raising the issue. Mrs Thatcher (even more irresponsibly) called for a debate on race relations, sensing public worry, but offering no policies or guidance, carefully not (herself) implying any demagogic prejudice—only raising the issue. And another interesting race is getting under way; who can go furthest on 'law and order' without committing themselves to getting anywhere?

Wilson set the tone in the campaigns of 1970 and 1974, the rejection of rhetoric of principle for a rhetoric of personality—'trust me as a person and look at him/her'. And Callaghan has essentially continued the same tactic, even if far more plausibly, far less ludicrously. Continuities between their styles of politics are as apparent, however different they are as people, as divergencies. Indeed, the leaders of both parties underestimate the public. Both believe that it is skilful rather than self-indulgent to talk down and to personalise every likely issue, rather than to consider basic problems from the perspective of conservative or socialist doctrines. Something more sensible and thoughtful remains in the parties, but the leaderships seem keen to suppress it. To be fair, some Conservative leaders are in a more thoughtful and generalising frame of mind than at least the public face of Mr Callaghan's Cabinet. When that very rare thing happens, a time of doctrinal intensity coming upon English conservatism (perhaps really an internal battle between Burke and Adam Smith, between Disraeli and Hayek), it is sad that Labour

529

reacts officially not by reasserting or defining socialist values and theories, but by playing the pragmatist, the sceptic about ideas, the embodiment of Jim Bull Baldwin's blinkered common sense.

Instead of challenging the whole bluff about economic incentives in relation to performance in top jobs and increasing direct industrial investment, the Labour government looks set to squander all revenues in a political auction of cutting income tax—still the fairest, the most comprehensible and potentially redistributivist of taxes we have (if a wealth tax could be added).

Sometimes one wonders if the parties are that bad or whether a vicious circle in their relationship with the broadcasting media does not accentuate the cataleptic diurnal ding-dong of 'Yes you did!', 'No I didn't!', 'Yah!', 'Boo!' Yahoo politics. An important and interesting study and report by Jay Blumer, Michael Gurevitch and Julian Ives, *The Challenge of Election Broadcasting* (Leeds University Press, £1.50) suggests that it does. Two things seem to happen in general elections. Radio and television give too much time and attention to an essentially repetitive campaign as 'news', thereby provoking the invention of some daily pseudo-event by the parties and inducing the boredom of overkill among innocent viewers. The fear of editorialising reduces the coverage of genuine issues and basic problems to those ludicrous self-conceits, the party broadcasts. How much better, Blumer et al. suggest, if the parties must insist on these broadcasts as well as all that news, that they were immediately followed by discussion or interview. American politicians submit themselves to questioning by three or four journalists of different papers and persuasions. And why should not the real issues of the campaign be treated as informative feature programmes, not dominated by candidates? Doesn't the public have a right to independent information and might not independent features on political issues raise the whole tone somewhat?

The Challenge of Election Broadcasting is moderately worried in tone, unlike our shrill anguish at the debasement of British politics. They suggest practical ways of trying to ensure that the politicians' priority of presenting themselves does not entirely muzzle the media's responsibility to inform the public upon the issues which are the real subject-matter of any politics worth having.

BRC

Commentary: 'Political Reviews'

Vol. 49, no. 3, July–September, 1978

Like the Prime Minister when he launched the 'great debate' on education last year, we too are worried about standards.[a] We have editorialised more than once in the past few years, as it is so easy to do, about the low standards of national political debate set by the party leaders themselves; the tendency of the press to over-personalise events and to under-emphasise theories, principles and issues; the lack of political education in so many schools; and in our last issue we endorsed Dr J. Blumer's mordant study of the mutual feedback of trivialisation between the parties and the television companies in the coverage of general elections. Before that storm breaks, let what Mr C. and Mrs T. doubtless regard as intellectual arrogance turn the knife into its own intellectual ribs to consider an often-neglected dimension of national political education.

Specialised books get written about politics. They are not all good. They are not all equally clear. Often more important are those other books that raise political issues indirectly and need political review, whether about crime, punishment, morality or the environment. But is the general educated public, say those who read the quality press, aware of them? There is reason to think not, partly because of the structure of newspapers in relation to reviewing in general, though partly, let it be granted, because of the books themselves. Quality newspapers and weeklies have what are called Literary or Book pages. 'Literary' usually conveys better what is on most of them than plain 'books'. At least one literary editor sees his main role as defending culture against politics, a battle that he has successfully fought for many years, never losing out on his principles, only on his space. With so little space available, sympathy is called for. One could sympathise more if literary editors of that fine old breed did not, while rarely compromising in favour of political books, compromise weekly in favour of popular biography and shallow memoirs. Political publishing is both under-reviewed and what is reviewed is so often the worst.

Among the literary intelligentsia can be found a philistinism about politics to match anything that politicians can show towards the arts. It usually takes, even in classically minded men, a romantic form: politics is seen as a realm of force and will, mitigated only by personality and sincerity. Most politics in the

---

[a] Alone of all the Commentaries I selected for this collection, this one is unsigned. Against the slight risk that it is not pure Bernard I justify the choice on the grounds of content (many Bernardine themes, including political publishing and reviewing, Orwell, the sterility of much academic writing etc.) and style—not Bernard at his wildest, but sparky enough. Also, Bernard was by now grand enough in his own right, and long past the days of Willie Robson's green ink, so even if he had shown it to his coeditor (John Mackintosh) the latter's influence would be very small.

theatre is of this kind. Therefore they are obsessed with commitment and conviction. Ranting politics or 'authentic statements' by personalities tend to get reviewed, as did all that weary succession of 1950s confessions of poets who were for one week in the Communist Party; but studious works about politics or those that reflect on genuine political dilemmas, rather than urging instant action NOW, get ignored. Editors suffer low standards in the few political books they review, standards they would not tolerate in novels or criticism; or if Wilson or the Crossman Diaries must be reviewed on the literary pages, then they get politicians to review them—almost always hurriedly and incompetently. Faults, indeed, on both sides. If most reflection about politics is written by political philosophers, they tend as writers, with a few exceptions, to be inbred, academic, esoteric and over-technical and as reviewers to be reluctant to write for the general public, seeming rather to worry what colleagues will think. Yet considering that in the last 10 or 15 years there has been a great revival of political theory concerning itself with issues of policy, it is sad how little of this gets picked for review and expounded intelligently and non-technically.

Perhaps literary editors look at books of political theory and say, often correctly, '90 per cent of the paper's readers aren't interested or wouldn't make head or tail of it'. Leave aside that that could be said of most of the books they do review, haven't they a duty to pick out what is important and encourage that growingly rare virtue of old-fashioned reviewing, not the personality essays of the same old lot every Sunday: a patient and clear exposition of what the book is about written by someone who might know about the subject and can write, as is not such an exclusive art, in good clear English prose? A good review always contains three balanced elements: what the book is about, how original it is and who is it aimed at, and is it good as a whole or is its argument made good or the evidence sound? Let the criticism, judgement or even polemic in the third section be as strong as a man cares to make, if—and only if—he has done the proper work of the first two stipulations. But many literary editors seem to find it difficult to know a hawk from a handsaw once they leave literary biography and the novel. This is not to be *ad hominem*, though the actual number of men (no women) involved is worryingly small and the results, whether from the culture or personal affinities, tend to be depressingly similar. Rather we point to a diminished knowledge of and respect for politics in literary culture. Orwell once said that he wanted above all to make political writing into an art.[b] Literary editors will, indeed, look back to anything on politics and literature in the 1930s with pleasure, but anyone trying to be a political writer today finds it hard to get a hearing outside the sectarian little magazines. Perhaps a contemporary Orwell would have gone to a new university and would he

---

[b] Bernard would by now—mid-1978—be in the final stages of writing his Orwell biography. This statement about political writing as an art would become the motto of the Orwell Prize for political writing that he founded.

writing, indeed, in awful social science or Marxist jargon, often in painful combinations of both. Such stuff is sometimes not even meant to be comprehensible outside of the family. Yet not all such are grating handsaws, some are bedraggled hawks: some have something to say that needs, quite simply, translating for the public. Most empirical Sociology and Economics raises the same problem as academic Political Science. There have been polemics enough in *The Political Quarterly* about bad writing and neologistic[c] thinking in the behavioural social sciences and in the Marxist camp (their problems of language are oddly similar) for us not to feel shy of saying that there is more than a little such that needs translating, even a very little that is necessarily highly technical but has important implications both for knowledge and policy. The quality press rails against Marxist writing, for instance, but makes no serious attempt (except perhaps in the *Guardian*) to inform its readers what the theoretical differences within the camps mean in practice. This is especially important since the *TLS* (every book's last hope) seems to exclude even the mildest Marxist reviewers and to perceive political theory largely in traditionalist terms. Book reviews, after all, are about something more than the likelihood that readers will actually buy the book: they are a vital form of publicising knowledge, including knowledge about ideas and ideas about ideas.

Has politics any special claim when space is short? Perhaps 'political science' as a discipline does not unless it has books of literary merit which are being neglected (especially if some books of literary criticism are notoriously badly written). But 'politics' as reflection upon the means and ends of political activity *does* have a special claim. Civilisation and culture, not simply cohesive society and welfare, depend on having the right, at the very least tolerable, political arrangements. We suggest a simple syllogism: the arts depend on human freedom; freedom depends on political activity; and therefore the arts depend on political activity. Of course, it is fallacious to infer that a man or woman cannot be an artist if he or she is not involved in politics. Some can stand outside civic involvements and responsibilities and a few need to do so, as long as a majority do not. If politics is left for a few, the result is autocracy. Autocrats can be great patrons of not *the* arts but only of *some* arts, *the* arts in an official form with censorship and proscription for the rest. Totalitarian regimes actually hold that official art is necessary as propaganda to mobilise the masses. One of the signs that we live in a reasonably free, even if a far from just, society is tolerance of all forms of the arts: so tolerant in fact that some aggressive lads are driven for their provocative pleasures into greater and greater extremes of 'anti-art'. That is another question. Intellectuals, however, do have a special responsibility for treating politics with seriousness, for considering what is profound and thoughtful, not cynically doing a few statesmen's memoirs from time to time, nor a social problem book a month for balance.

[c] The original has the neologistic 'neulogistic' here.

Part of the practical problem is that, while books are so important, space given to them is so derisory. Yet the real trouble is not that literary pages include so little politics, though they should be more serious and discriminatory in much they do review, but that the Political Editors and the Features Editors do not feature enough political books. Many books on practical politics and on social policy should themselves be treated as political events. Political books get lost in the galloping diurnal myopia which is the dominance of news values (the manufactured and the transitory) over features (the structural and the perennial). Political reviewing as an art was once part of our culture. It is in decline. The distinction between feature page and book page in newspapers and weeklies is, in many ways, an obstacle to serious writing about political issues. Symbolically, the front legs and the back legs of the *New Statesman*, each of which still have some kick left in them, could occasionally, with advantage, be introduced to each other. Radio and television, though less inhibited in this way, do badly by books in general and by no means fill the gap left by the decline of weeklies and monthlies. The real problem, however, is that too short term a view of politics is taken. The memoirs of a failed statesman who cannot write good English,[d] even, are treated as an event, but advocacies of policy are buried alive in academic journals.

Commentary: 'Euro-Communism'

Vol. 49, no. 4, October–December 1978

This issue contains two articles on France and Italy and a review of books on Euro-Communism in general.[a] In future issues we hope to study the Communist parties of Spain, Portugal, Great Britain and the far Left in the Federal Republic. Opinions vary. Theory, strategy and tactics intermingle. Ideas and circumstances are all in flux. But can anyone now seriously maintain that the Italian Communist Party is, in the words of an editorial in *The Times* of three years ago, 'a Trojan horse'? Conservatives are, of course, fully entitled to fear and dislike a more libertarian and democratic Communist movement than the old rigid and inept Stalinism. But they are both intellectually foolish and tactically inept to regard it as the same phenomenon. To socialists it is the most significant development of recent years.

---

[d] Unless Bernard is ruling out 'the vernacular' from counting as 'good English'—which seems unlikely—this is puzzling if it is a reference to the Crossman Diaries. Three years earlier he had written 'One can also raise a purely literary and patriotic point: it is one of the greatest and most spontaneous diaries in the vernacular since Pepys, since Evelyn (it really is, the old devil really pulled it off)'. See the Commentary 'Opening the Crossman Diaries' above.

[a] This is the opening component of a two-part Commentary. The other part is on Official Secrets, written by James Cornford.

We make two assumptions: (i) that Russian control over most European Communist parties is now minimal, and unlikely to be restored—unless great mistakes are made by the EEC or NATO or unless great reforms take place in Russia; and (ii) that nonetheless Euro-Communism is a very broad concept; there is no common movement, only common conditions, so that each country reacts very differently. The conditions are broad but tangible. There is the clear fact that few people who call themselves socialists can now regard the USSR as in any sense a model of a socialist regime. In most respects, it is a parody of the idea of a socialist regime: not simply in its intolerance to dissent but also in its class stratification. Milovan Djilas was right. But also there has been the unexpected re-emergence of parliamentary regimes in Spain, Portugal and Greece. If we do not rejoice more, it is only because these re-emergences are less positive than a kind of proof of the difficulty of running modern regimes by centralised autocracy. Some Communist parties have learned this lesson, some not. Some become social democratic, others simply national Stalinists.

Opinions and circumstances, as we have said, vary. M. Leduc[b] argues that the French Communists, while free from Moscow, have not yet settled an internal debate between authoritarians and democrats. Mr Shaw[c] sees the Italian Communist Party as so far broken from the past as now to be backsliding on basic socialism. What will Lord Chalfont think of this? Indeed, recently some members of the Tribune Group have been preening themselves that they are 'far to the Left of the Italian Communist Party'. Perhaps—and far less effective. The European political scene is now far more fluid (confused?) than many suppose.

BRC

Commentary: 'Ten Years in Ulster'

Vol. 50, no. 1, January–March 1979

Few commentators found much new to say last autumn to mark the tenth anniversary of the civil rights marches and subsequent troubles in Northern Ireland. Many newspapers had to make a positive effort not to try to keep on forgetting about it. We take our title, however, from an editorial that Conor Cruise O'Brien wrote in the *Observer* on 1 October 1978, noting that: 'The principal political development in the last 10 years—indeed during the last 58

[b] Author of the first article in the same issue, as mentioned by Bernard: Victor Leduc, 'The French Communist Party: Between Stalinism and Eurocommunism', *The Political Quarterly*, vol. 49, no. 4, pp. 400–10.

[c] Eric Shaw, 'The Italian Historical Compromise: A New Pathway to Power?, *The Political Quarterly*, vol. 49, no. 4, pp. 411–24.

years—has been the substitution of direct rule from Britain for devolved government at Stormont'.

He not merely noted, however: he welcomed. Constitutional issues create strange bedfellows. The Irish eloquence of the O'Brien, as one must say, finds itself on the same side as the anti-devolutionary, parliamentary sovereignty rhetoric of Mr Enoch Powell, who seems to have been so successful in persuading his fellow Unionist MPs to drop or mute the cries they made two years ago for a Parliament in Northern Ireland. O'Brien's argument was, of course, very different from that of Powell's:

... British people today are vaguely unhappy about direct rule. If the British people had been, and now were, better informed about Northern Ireland, that pattern of feeling would have been reversed. The working of devolution would have inspired deep misgiving and foreboding, and the working of direct rule should now inspire sober and cautious satisfaction.

The working of democracy, through devolved institutions in Northern Ireland, meant that the minority community was permanently governed by representatives of the majority—permanent rule of Protestant over Catholic. With Northern Ireland as the unit, and given the tradition of relations between the communities, democratic process cannot give any other result. ...

Fear and resentment are still at work in Northern Ireland but their sway has been notably diminished by experience of direct rule. Neither community now feels itself to be in imminent danger of being at the mercy of the other. The police is no longer seen as an instrument in the hands of one community against the other. In these conditions, support for both the IRA and the Protestant para-militaries has been steadily falling away.

There is no one we like to have lecture us more than Mr O'Brien, and it is no pleasure to note that his cautious optimism about conditions in Northern Ireland in October 1978 have been violently refuted by the bombings in December. The IRA found its own way to welcome Mr Callaghan's granting of extra seats in Westminster to the province—a grant which seems to play no part in any general settlement in Northern Ireland but has simply been squandered away as part of Mr Callaghan's immediate need to keep a parliamentary majority. Proponents of direct rule have nothing to fear from a Labour government. The government never accepted direct rule as policy: it simply stumbled into it through lack of policy. Now it is in danger of rationalising its predicament as a virtue.

O'Brien favours direct rule for quite other reasons. O'Brien can hardly be accused of favouring policies because they are expedient to the British government. Nor does he share the knowing pessimism of his Deputy Editor, John Cole, himself an Ulsterman, whose 'Ulster: the Deadly Fantasies' (in the same issue of the *Observer*) argued so rightly that there are no simple or painless 'solutions', but who then either had nothing positive to say or left the implication that, being stuck with direct rule, we had better reconcile ourselves to it. John Cole's consistent line is one of pessimism—a kind of Hobbesian rational prudence: surrender to Whitehall for the price of peace all provincial liberties and normal practices of citizenship, a relative peace at least. Like Mr Roy Mason, the Secretary of State for Northern Ireland, he is entirely governed by his fears that any new policy initiative would make matters worse. He and his editor are free journalists, so this is their genuine opinion, and it reflects much moderate opinion in the Province, growing sick of all politics. Mr Mason, however, may just be serving out his time and will soon have either no job or a better job.

O'Brien is not a man to be governed by his fears. Courage is a political virtue and he has shown more of it than almost any man in contemporary politics. He reminded his fellow countrymen that in Ireland there were two nationalities (in his book *States of Ireland* (1972)). When in government as Minister of Posts, he let his sceptical views continue to be known (he made 'Posts' cover all communication—refusing to be muzzled) on the language question, the religious question and the 'all Ireland' clause of the Constitution; and he has attacked the IRA more knowingly and bitingly than any. Yet his advocacy of continued direct rule in Northern Ireland is based entirely, it seems, on the need to protect the rights of the minority. He is not insensitive to the rights of the majority: he has reminded the Republic that the Protestant persuasion does constitute a majority and, in some cases, even a national consciousness. He accepts the separation of Ireland. But he can see no way of protecting minority rights except through Westminster and Whitehall. This is not a strange view, in fact, for an Irish citizen to hold: it is precisely the view that Irish citizens would hold, apart from their lapses into the kind of sentimental tolerance for republicanism which he himself has attacked so often and so well.

So long as Northern Ireland does not have its own devolved Parliament, future deals can be made more easily between Dublin and London. These deals are not likely to be as dramatic as some Loyalists fear, neither withdrawal nor sell-out; but rather will give a framework to make marginal adjustments more easy in Northern Ireland by distant managements responding to other problems and opportunities. So many of these now turn on Europe, on energy, agriculture and monetary problems as well as time-honoured migration. Dublin and London wish to manage these problems, including the problem of Northern Ireland, with as little interference as possible from representative institutions in that unhappy province. Easier to deal with them in Westminster. Although no one would admit it in quite these words, a kind of informal theory of quasi-condominium is growing up between the British and the Irish governments. The Unionists have been given their MPs in Westminster to make them feel, like Mr Powell, more important: there will be no Parliament in Northern Ireland forced to set up joint committees on this and that with the Dail, but the ministers and the civil servants will negotiate more freely. And more irresponsibly. If this kind of thing created in Scotland the swell of opinion in favour of devolution, will it not also occur in Northern Ireland again, with its far more recent history of devolved or virtually federal government?

Perhaps it is unfair to impure this as a conscious motive to Conor Cruise O'Brien, but only offer it as a background to show the damage that the *Observer*'s line could do by falling into the same do-nothing categories of thought as official opinion. Only the press seems capable of keeping speculation alive about alternative policies in Northern Ireland. His argument was, after all, based on the discriminatory record towards the minority of the old Stormont; and on the seeming impossibility of the main political parties in Northern Ireland reaching agreement, as the failure of the Convention three years ago is supposed to have shown.

Consider, however, some of the disadvantages of direct rule. Granted that a Parliament in Northern Ireland will not in any way placate the IRA, yet no-Parliament will further alienate the Protestant extremists. No-Parliament will lead to the further decay of the political parties in Northern Ireland, particularly the SDLP which, deprived of an effective political role, loses many of its best members and lapses back into ritual republicanism. If there is an Assembly in Scotland, the anomaly will be gross, not merely in theory but in everyday practice. If there is an Assembly in Wales and not in Northern Ireland, it will be insulting. If there is no Parliament, there will be no hope of joint action between the two communities; action both for welfare and for security against the gunmen.

Few doubt that rule by the Northern Ireland Civil Service is relatively benign, just and efficient. But the Province is reduced to a colonial status (or the informal condominium of two great powers) if the real government cannot be called to account locally. A Northern Ireland Department in London is no substitute for an Assembly in Belfast. Without an Assembly the Province will have many local councillors, more fanatics and no politicians except a handful away at Westminster.

Every general consideration of the theory of free government works against direct rule for Northern Ireland, especially when Scotland and Wales will move differently. Many particular considerations in the Province argue that direct rule is just buying time and accepting that the violence goes on and on but can be contained, possibly by placating the Irish Government more than by police and military means. John Cole is half right: violence is, indeed, unlikely to cease. Before any settlement could be reached it would grow worse, for the simple and obvious reason that the IRA do everything in their power, risk their last man and their last supplies, to wreck any new initiative. If we seek to avoid that, then sporadic violence will drag on for ever. Things will have to grow worse before they can grow better: everyone knows that— surely even Mr Callaghan, Mr Mason and their advisers; but they are all buying time, and the *Observer*'s uncharacteristic and undemocratic advice is welcome to them.

We say 'undemocratic' not in the soft and silly sense that there is some presumed right for every lump of land to have an assembly governed by a possibly intolerant majority, but rather in a fundamental sense, that if people who feel themselves by tradition to be a people are denied an appropriate degree of self-government, things can only get worse: denial of representation creates more extremism than its abuse.

For its abuse can be guarded against. In this issue we carry, for instance, an article on the effect of Scottish devolution on the *English* Constitution.[a] The author argues, rightly or wrongly (we think rightly), that the effect will be federal, despite the intentions. Parliament will want the courts to take up more of the disputes over conflicts of powers and jurisdiction than it originally intended. It will not have laboured for all this only to be stuck with Scottish problems on the floor of the House. During the Northern Ireland Convention the British government demanded, quite rightly, that the main parties including the SDLP should reach 'agreement' as to the form of a new Parliament or Assembly. Mr William Craig's Vanguard Party's negotiations with the SDLP came nearer to success than is often acknowledged. They might have succeeded if more support could have been given to them and if the Convention itself had been treated with the dignity of a future Parliament and less like a gang of political delinquents released on ticket-of-leave for community service. There should have been, and there could be now, a fall-back position if 'agreement' fails. Indeed, the White Paper of 1976, produced almost in desperation before the final sessions of the Convention, which failed to agree to the majority (i.e. Unionist) report, lapsed into talking of the need for more 'widespread acceptance' by the minority. This was a lapse into common sense that should have been pursued.

Many things in politics are not agreeable to minorities but are acceptable, or can be made acceptable. And acceptance can be tacit as well as formal. No one can expect the SDLP to say that they accept the only form of parliament agreeable to the majority, one that could yield a majority government. But it is not inconceivable that they would accept it in the sense of working within it if it were constituted in the framework of a new Northern Ireland Act which created not merely an Assembly but a Bill of Rights, with a constitutional court to rule upon it while the British government still enforced decisions and laws.

The UUUC or Unionist coalition report to the Convention had stuck out for straight majority government, but had talked grandly, patronisingly and vaguely of 'a Bill of Rights and Duties'. Some argued at the time that they should have been hoisted with their own petard: given their 'victory', left to fight elections, but then bound hand and foot by non-discrimination clauses in a written constitution—a 'victory' that the SDLP would not have claimed, implacably wanting power sharing (in many senses quite rightly), but a victory that they might nonetheless have accepted and enjoyed. At the time, those who argued in this way with the Northern Ireland Office were told, with knowing pity, that it was totally unrealistic: 'It would not get past the doormat at No. 10'. The occupant of No. 10 at that time was Sir Harold

---

[a] Vernon Bogdanor, 'The English Constitution and Devolution', *The Political Quarterly*, vol. 50, no. 1, pp. 36–49.

Wilson, buying time as usual, hoping to prevent the coming on of Scottish Devolution. If the Northern Ireland Convention had taken place only a year later, the atmosphere would have been very different—well, somewhat different: Wilson had bowed to Scottish opinion and realised that some form of devolution had to take place. What a botched and unprepared measure that was! Whitehall was unprepared for the business that an earlier generation had understood well: constitutional draughtsmanship, devolution or surrender of power to colonies. In both the imperial and the Irish context, indeed, politicians in the first 25 years of this century had far more imagination and experience in such matters than those in this incompetent and fearful third to final quarter. The mere drafting of such a Northern Ireland Bill of Rights would prove, to the amused eyes of Americans and Germans, unexpectedly difficult for us. Yet surely not impossible. It is time to consider a comprehensive *de facto* even if not *de jure* federal framework for the government of the United Kingdom.

Northern Ireland cannot be denied the rights held by majorities elsewhere to have elections for a provincial assembly which offers federalism or devolution up to the standards of so many other countries in the Commonwealth, Europe and North America. The prejudices of unitary sovereignty have grown dangerous as well as absurd. Political prudence for the long run demands some short-term risks: the risk, for instance, of allowing elections, perhaps even before the *full* details of a new constitutional framework are clarified. The results are no longer predictable. But even with the worst electoral results, we still hold security in our hands and can impose a constitution. *Impose* a constitution? *Impose* direct rule?

Mr O'Brien's arguments for the continuation of direct rule (i.e. no policy) by the British government are well meant for the political situation in the Republic of Ireland. But it is a gift horse that we in England should reject. To be given a present of irresponsible government and to be told how well we do it is only storing trouble for the future. Does *he* really wish *us* to treat Northern Ireland as a colony? Cannot a quarter of the energy that has gone into constitutional innovation to help the problems of the Labour Party be spared for the lives and self-respect of people in poor bloody Ulster?

BRC

Commentary: 'Political Broadcasting'

Vol. 50, no. 3, July–September 1979

We are happy to carry in this issue an interesting and informed account by Mr Mallory Wober of the ITA of the dilemma relating to the direct broadcasting of Parliament.[a] He seems almost to take for granted that the day of the cameras will come. Surveys reveal that an appreciable number of viewers think that the cameras have already occupied Westminster as they hear voices that are not those of Reginald Bosanquet or Angela Rippon rumbling from behind vaguely identifiable stills of politicians. The real dilemma that concerns Mr Wober is whether direct broadcasting of Parliament of either kind, whether sound or vision, should be presented in short measure on the popular programme at peak times, or given much more extended treatment on an alternative channel. The one strategy holds out the hope that something will get across to the inert viewers, while the other not merely offers more and better to those actually interested in politics but also the hope that any act of choice, even by channel twiddlers, becomes fortified by increased attention.

Mr Wober offers us survey evidence that ordinary people say they want direct video broadcasting of Parliament and say that the sound broadcasting of Westminster is a good thing; but he admits to some scepticism about what these replies mean and is cautious not to infer that such attitudes are easily related to behaviour. Certainly more research might show what links there are, if any, between—as it were—thinking religion a good thing and being willing to listen to *Thought for the Day* or *Lift Up Your Hearts*.

However, is he asking the right question? The answer may well be that if you want to get to Biddicombe, you should not start from here. Are we still trying to get to Parliament rather than the broader lands of parliamentary politics?

Is there all that much point in talking simply about Parliament? It is all too easy to confuse, as Mr Robin Day has done, the privilege and prestige of the media with their effectiveness in not simply getting Parliament across but, like Parliament, in the political education of a nation. A free Parliament, debating freely and publicised widely, is a necessary condition of what can be called parliamentary politics, but it is not a sufficient condition. Parliamentary politics is wider than the proceedings of Parliament. Pressure groups, trade unions, professional associations and political parties are all part of parliamentary democracy. Most extra-parliamentary politics is not anti-parliamentary. Even grant that Parliament is the primary or predominant institution in politics, yet it is not the only one. The Press and the broadcasting media contribute to politics in many ways other than reporting Parliament. They also are representative as well as influencing and reporting. Perhaps leaving

[a] Mallory Wober, 'Public Opinion, and Direct Broadcasting as an Aid to the Efficacy of Parliament', *The Political Quarterly*, vol. 50, no. 3, pp. 316–25.

541

all particular faults and failings aside (which are many and gross), the press present parliamentary politics better by being tied to even a reformed parliamentary procedure.

The studio discussion between politicians is, after all, a very economical and concise way of presenting political issues—even if it often degenerates, for lack of an editorial voice or for nervousness about using non-party experts, into presentation of party differences rather than debate about issues and problems. That is easily remedied. Some things are so well suited to one medium rather than to another. It is not at all self-evident that the direct broadcasting of Parliament, however well edited, is the best form of political information and commentary for the public. Do journalists really believe it is? Do politicians?

Consider the BBC's *Yesterday in Parliament*. Audience research figures would be interesting. Why are they so shy? Rumour has it that listening figures are declining and the IBA is happy to escape from such an obligation. If there is research to be done, would someone perhaps examine whether or not there has been a growth in comic items and a decline in political matter in the morning *Today* programme on BBC since the broadcasting of Parliament began? It cannot all be Brian Redhead. One suspects a displacement effect already. One fears a greater displacement effect if Mr Wober gets his way and there is direct television broadcasting of Parliament. Programme planners will not take time from *Coronation Street* for the sake of Westminster. The extra time needed would be at the expense of the existing current affairs programmes and of the political elements in the funny hodge-podge prolecult 'babblebox'[1] magazine programmes.

If the ITA, the IBA and the BBC are in a mood of openness, could their spokesmen discuss publicly the internal threats to current affairs programmes rather than attaching perhaps excessive importance—one suspects mainly a symbolic importance—to the broadcasting of Parliament?

To suggest that some of the lobby for direct television broadcasting are acting purely symbolically (that is, for public relations and prestige) is not to deny that there are others who want it for its 'realism'. Even if it did not gain more air-time for politics, it would be a gain, they argue, for ordinary reports to be *actuelle*. Mr Wober frequently invokes reality. But this, like *cinéma vérité*, is an epistemological delusion. 'A raw slice of life' direct from 'our reporter in the Falls Road' is seldom more meaningful than a report by a central analyst receiving messages from many inputs, including our man on the streets. For all its naturalist dress, it is as prone to bias as anything else. How many of us with a serious interest in politics take our instant news from the BBC Third Programme or the World Service, because they have none of these confusing attempts to grasp 'reality'?

To consider the more general question, the broadcasting of the last general election was as bad as ever. ITA put a huge amount of cash and effort into

---

[1] A prophesy of H. G. Wells in *The Sleeper Awakes* (1899).

having more teams in the town halls on election night. Yet this is all window dressing. Election night coverage is a political irrelevance and more in common with the pre-match build-up for the Cup Final than to political literacy; it simply amuses an already captive audience. The campaign is the thing. And not just reporting of the campaign, but trying to provide a background of information on which the ordinary main channel voter can make up his or her mind; or if made up already, simply inform and educate them better on the issues and the system. It is a great chance wasted. Both BBC and ITA still nervously allowed the politicians a monopoly not merely of establishing the issues—which has some degree of inevitability about it—but also of dominating the discussion of them almost exclusively. Time and time again issues are trivialised and distorted by the 'Yes you did', 'No we didn't' debate, rather than by offering any independent analysis of issues, helpful to the public, to which the politicians could then respond. Politicians could be tempted into having something serious to say rather than 'Trust Harold/Jim' or 'Time for a change'.

This is not a chicken and an egg problem. The broadcasting media have interpreted the impartiality clause of the Television Acts in a lazy and safe way, creating a dialectic ding-dong of immediate confrontation. They could perfectly well sit most spokesmen down in turn, not with each other, with political commentators and experts on the issues under discussion. There is room for experiment here.

Television has responsibilities as well as opportunities. Features must not surrender entirely to News, particularly during elections. It can present political issues, at differing levels, reasonably well—so long as it is not a general election. Will it be any better in 1984?

BRC

Commentary: 'The Two Islands'

Vol. 51, no. 2, April–June 1980

Unless the British and the Irish understand each other's internal politics better they will constantly confuse official utterances with true motives.[a] While any British government must remain firm to its repeated pledge that there will be no basic changes in the position of Northern Ireland without the free consent of a majority of its inhabitants, yet the time has now come when the government must remind all politicians in Northern Ireland that neither 'the Irish dimension' nor 'the American dimension' can simply be cursed and

---

[a] This is the second element of a two-part Commentary. The first is an untitled piece on the Soviet invasion of Afghanistan by the distinguished journalist David Watt, by then Bernard's co-editor following John Mackintosh's death in 1978.

ignored. If the minimal nature of these pressures are understood correctly, they are even grounds for some modest hope.

There is a slight chance, even, that the present Conference could, in a limited sense, succeed. At last we have a government (for better or for worse)[b] with some clear political will. Last autumn's green and white paper, *The Government of Northern Ireland: A Working Paper for a Conference*, systematically dropped the old talk of the need for agreement among the party leaders and substituted 'highest possible level of agreement' and 'reasonable and appropriate arrangements to take account of the interests of the minority'. It spoke about considering 'arrangements for a progressive transfer [of powers] over a period of time' (that is, majority rule subject to tough restraints which would only be lifted if the minority in Northern Ireland was content); and also said that: 'the Government will take whatever decisions are needed to implement any arrangements agreed in the conference provided that these arrangements appear likely to be broadly acceptable to the people of Northern Ireland as a whole' (which means that when agreement is *not* reached on a package, the government will take the HCF or the LCM and put it directly to the people).

That this is no academic exercise in textual exegesis can be seen by Mrs Thatcher herself letting the cat out of the bag when she told the *New York Times* (13 November) 'that she would not permit the squabbling political parties to block her political initiative' and that if they said: ' "you cannot do anything unless we all agree . . .", she would impose a solution'.

She could, not that such a solution would stop the violence. Indeed, any devolution would stir up instant pre-emptive terror from the IRA. But any Provincial government which was acceptable to the rank and file of the minority, even if not agreeable to their leaders, would have some chance of riding the storm and creating, albeit slowly, a climate of opinion in which normal policing could be restored. Any attempt at broadly acceptable devolution is better than the perpetual provocation of continued direct rule (even though it is true, as the *Observer* argues, that this is acceptable already to a large majority in Northern Ireland; but so might better policies be) or Enoch Powell's policy of complete integration. Ian Paisley has long broken with Powell on this issue and while unwilling to concede power-sharing in a cabinet form of government, has grown more realistic about the need for minority involvement and constitutional guarantees in any workable framework of government.

Yet the dilemma about devolution is as great as ever. Paisley now at least does not wish to find 'a solution' that would break up the SDLP and drive their supporters back in the direction of Sinn Fein. In a rather rough and ready way he appreciates that John Hume and others have built up a large overwhelmingly Catholic party which has been willing to work within 'the State' not merely in the brief days of the power-sharing Assembly, but also as a reasonably loyal opposition in the last days of the old Stormont. However,

---

[b] This was Margaret Thatcher's first government of 1979–83.

since 1974, largely from utter frustration during the Wilson and Mason era of no policy, the SDLP has moved noticeably back into the Green. In 1974 they could privately concede that by insisting on 'an Irish dimension' at Sunningdale, they had undermined the acceptability of the new Assembly to Protestant workers. But now John Hume has to insist that Irish unity should be discussed and that the British guarantees to the majority are an obstacle in the way of genuine negotiations. He plainly thinks of a federal Ireland with Ulster enjoying, *somewhat* like Quebec, a special role—perhaps even international guarantees to the Protestants. No one knows better than John Hume, however, the risks of driving the Protestant community back into the militant frame of mind that created partition in the first place. UDA gunmen operating with mass support would be a far grimmer spectacle than the present IRA. The SDLP leaders do not share the chaotic fantasies (or the IRA connections) of the Troops Out Movement. 'We are not asking', said John Hume recently, 'that Great Britain pull out and leave us to it, but that she should join the ranks of those who would persuade the Unionists that their future lies in a stable and firm political association with the rest of Ireland'. Note that he says 'political association' and not 'unity'; but even so the British army can no more 'persuade' Orangemen than it can persuade Nationalists.

Yet some way forward should be found that is broader than or could emerge from mere devolution. There is not merely the blood; there is the money. Consider simply that in 1978–79 public expenditure per head was £919 for England, £1,079 for Wales, £1,138 for Scotland and £1,460 for Northern Ireland. Consider the benefits that the EEC has brought to Southern farmers compared to those in the North. Remember that President Carter promised nearly three years ago that large American 'job-creating investment' would follow 'the establishment of a form of government in Northern Ireland that will command widespread acceptance through both parts of the community'. (Both he and Senator Kennedy are on record in favour of the unity of Ireland, 'with the consent of a majority in the North'—that is, on the Tuesday afternoon before the Second Coming.)

In this context Mr Haughey's speech of 16 February to the Fianna Fail Party is worth reading fully and closely. He, too, is preoccupied with economic problems. Beneath the rhetoric something important is moving. 'Violence can never bring a solution', he might actually have condemned it, but that's not bad. 'For over sixty years now, the situation in Northern Ireland has been a source of instability, real or potential, in these islands', note the last three words. 'The Conference [in Belfast] itself cannot provide a conclusive settlement', indeed. 'Northern Ireland, as a political entity has failed and a new beginning is needed'; certainly the political entity in Northern Ireland has failed. He tries to reassure Protestants that their interests will be protected in 'the Ireland of the future', clearly a different concept from 'the future of Ireland'. 'Northern Ireland distorts official relations between Britain and Ireland', and Whitehall now appreciates this. 'We look forward to some new free and open relationship', he concluded, 'in which Irishmen and women, on their own, without a British presence but with active British goodwill [i.e. cash], will manage the affairs of the whole of Ireland in a constructive partnership within the European Community.'

Of course he overbids. Even so, he implies that a federal Ireland would involve constitutional changes in the Republic. But could one think of a largely self-governing political entity that enjoyed common citizenship and legal as well as economic relationships with two neighbouring states? Federalism is not the concept, neither is condominium; but both countries may simply have, out of common humanity, political need and propinquity, to think of something new. Speculation is needed. The *Guardian* began a remarkable series of articles on Northern Ireland by noting the possibility of dual citizenship, the absence of any preconditions in Mr Haughey's request for a summit and that 'it is more generally acknowledged in Dublin than is often realised that the two islands cannot be thought of as entirely separate units'. The implications need to be drawn: so a long, gradual but necessary process. An 'Ireland of the future' is very long term, but short-term actions must not shut the door on it unopenably, though talk of the British government withdrawing guarantees to the majority in the North will, at the moment, prove totally self-defeating. Specific guarantees of a different kind from a different direction are needed.

BRC

Commentary: 'William Robson (1895–1980)'

Vol. 51, no. 3, July–September 1980

Many tributes have already been made to William Robson as scholar, teacher and reformer. Since he was also this journal's founder, let us limit our tribute to that.[a] Since it was so important to him, let us quote his own words on why he did it and what he thought it was.

I conceived the idea in 1927 of a serious political review in which progressive ideas could be discussed at an adequate length, and shortly afterwards I found that Kingsley Martin had arrived at a similar idea. [We were then junior members of the teaching staff of the LSE][b] We felt the need for a forum where a philosophy and a programme could be hammered out for the socialist movement, which was growing in strength but was lacking a coherent body of ideas. The existing quarterly and monthly reviews were either quite general in their interests, or conservative or right-

[a] Although it is not a Commentary in the normal *PQ* sense, this tribute to its founding editor opened the issue of the journal in the normal Commentary position. William Robson had died on 12 May, only four months after his last article for the journal appeared. His *ODNB* entry, in which he is described as a 'jurist and reformer', was written by Bernard.

[b] This sentence is interpolated in brackets because it comes from a later paragraph of Robson's introduction.

546

wing liberal in outlook, or moribund. . . . *The Political Quarterly* was conceived as a device to provide a bridge between the world of thought and the world of action, between the writer, the thinker and the teacher on the one hand and the statesman, the politician and the official on the other.

'In launching *The Political Quarterly*', Robson continued,[1] 'we were guided by a theory about the structure of public opinion in Britain . . . : that all or nearly all new ideas or progressive policies begin with discussions or writing among a very restricted circle of persons of exceptional ability and concentrated interests. . . . The membership of these elites and the circulation of their publications is very restricted, and perhaps numbers only two or three thousand persons. After intensive discussion in these narrow circles, ideas or proposals which survive and win acceptance are presented to a wider audience through the weekly papers . . . and now through some . . . radio or television broadcasts . . . The number of this wider circle is probably between 250,000 and 350,000 persons. After this second level of discussion, ideas or proposals which survive criticism . . . then break through to the mass audience in the national daily and Sunday newspapers.'

Robson then quoted two appropriate dicta from Leonard Woolf's autobiography (Woolf was joint editor from 1931 to 1958). First, that 'Practically all journalists, from the great Press Lords down to the humblest reporter, suffer from the grossest delusions about the influence of the newspaper which they own, edit or write for.' And, secondly, that: 'I feel some encouragement too when I contemplate the other end of the scale where are journals of small circulation like *The Political Quarterly*. There is no doubt that, if their standards, both journalistic and intellectual, are high, they can have considerable influence. The reason is that they are . . . written by experts for experts.'

Finally, Robson quoted from the original prospectus that: 'It would differ from the existing reviews, partly because the space at its command would enable it to aim at a standard of thoroughness impossible in a short article, and partly because it would be planned by a group of writers holding certain general political ideas in common. . . . [But] it would welcome contributions from persons of different political connections, provided that they were of the necessary quality. It should be realistic and critical in spirit, and should attempt to handle its subject with sufficient authority to attract the attention of all persons seriously interested in political and social questions, whatever their political views. While it would naturally be mainly concerned with questions of topical interest, it should endeavour to treat them in a broad and philosophical manner, and should aim at diffusing thought, rather than at presenting a case.'

For the eight years I was joint editor with William (or William's joint editor) I never found the journal particularly 'broad and philosophical', although

---

[1] W. A. Robson, ed., *Political Quarterly in the Thirties* (Allen Lane, 1971), pp. 9–35.

547

highly relevant to short- and middle-term public policy. Speculative about policy alternatives, yes—Robson was on to that long ago; but first principles were rarely discussed. John Mackintosh, his editorial successor in 1975, argued well in two articles just before his own death that a positive theory of the mixed economy was *needed*, that Crosland's social democracy was, like the Webbs' before it, historically outmoded; the need was perceived but not, alas, the theory developed. To be honest, I did not find originality in Robson so much as uniquely high standards, great learning and an intense sense of relevance and public duty. *PQ*, both in its regular contributors and in articles clearly written specially for us, reflects this. I had some new ideas when Robson retired, but they proved either impossible or ridiculously marginal. The mark of a great journal is the settled weight of tradition in both contributors and readers. Subsequent editors are both ineffective and far less influential than such a founder.[c] Essentially one maintains the standards that were set so well. Bagehot once remarked that in writing for a long-established journal even one's style became affected.

Standards were at the heart of the matter. I admire the professed elitism of Robson and Woolf's theory of public opinion so frankly stated. New ideas do filter down. Mr Benn may deceive himself that he is the *vox populi*; he is simply a tribune among the people—and why not? Robson was well aware that the formation and dissemination of new ideas is only part of politics; they have to prove acceptable to and even workable among ordinary people. His lifelong hope for more participation in local government, his concern for the powers of local government, did not contradict his realistic, elitist theory of opinion formation. It supplemented it, simply the other side of a simultaneous equation.

He had as much scorn for those who pretend that democratic processes can supplant reasoned, rational policy, as for those who say that the experts should rule without interference. In his last years he grew scathing about what he saw to be a decline in the standards of public service of the higher Civil Service: the erosion of the doctrine of conflict of interest when Sir William Armstrong retired to the top of the Midland Bank, above all when the mandarins gave themselves (well, Robson said that) inflation-proof salaries and pensions. Such things saddened him.

The standards related not just to knowledge and expression but also to judgement. 'What is justice?', he would muse. 'Well, considering administrative tribunals, it takes time, "patience and time"', quoting. Every article received, however obviously hopeless, save only the most lunatic or eccentric, would be read by him carefully, analysed into its components and judged on each. At first I resented time wasted, but came to see that he was right. Editors are not 'talent scouts', he once told me, 'We act in a

---

[c] This is an oddly unconvincing claim from Bernard if it is applied to himself, the more so as time goes on and Robson's direct influence (though not his legacy and general ethos for the journal) slips into the past.

judicial capacity'.[d] Standards of knowledge depended on his own wide knowledge. Very, very rarely did he ask for any outside specialist opinion. So I suppose basically the subject-matter of *PQ* became what Robson himself could grasp and criticise. That never seemed much of a restraint.[e]

Standards of expression were formidable. Robson would seek to clarify both the style and the logic of even the most distinguished contributors. He had no fear or favour, although he went far beyond what I thought was right without at least telling the author: 'do it this way or try elsewhere'. Leonard Woolf (quite rightly) thought he was doing a favour to drastically rewrite some contributions when 'they do have something to say but such difficulty in saying it'.

Robson backed me and praised me when a frontbencher complained that I'd changed all his flabby passives into crisp actives; but he was quite distressed to discover that Mackintosh and I had farmed out the proof-reading.[f]

Politically, the Welfare Fabianism that Robson stood for can be seen in two ways: that it was achieved but is not adequate to new conditions, or that it is crumbling away. He left a legacy in the journal that in style, level of knowledge, standard of contribution and readership, is both hard to match and hard to change—even if its influence may be less than he had hoped. Yet one looks back with awe and reverence at his scholarly, public and editorial achievements.

Only this January he made a long, witty and relaxed speech at the 50th birthday party of the journal (indeed, he continued lecturing at LSE until the end of February and attending meetings of the Greater London Group that he founded and which had so much to do with the reform of London government). In the 50th birthday speech he was careful to thank each of the several publishers the journal has enjoyed in its history, first Harold Macmillan himself, and lastly and currently the Thomson Organisation;[g] but stressed

---

[d] This is a decidedly passive view of the editor's function—waiting for submissions to appear and then passing judgement. No present-day academic commissioning editor—and the job title gives the game away—would survive for more than a few weeks if they put this into rigorous practice. Nor would it work as a *modus operandi* even for academics and other non-professional editors acting in editorial capacities on journals. The creation of any lively and coherent publication needs its editors to go out and hunt, not merely sit at home by the fire and wait.

[e] Perhaps not at the time, but in the longer term and if carried on by WAR's successors, this limitation would have helped to drag *PQ* into a small and quiet corner from which it may never have escaped. This is why Robson's journal needed to become Crick's journal to continue to prosper, even to survive (see my Introduction).

[f] Again, see my Introduction. This modest outsourcing was an early stage in the modernisation of the journal and a realisation among the newer editors that the complete 'hands-on' control of its founders was unsustainable.

[g] At that point there had been four publishers; now it is five, counting Blackwell (who replaced Thomson in 1985) and the present Wiley Blackwell as one publisher. Then a junior partner in the publisher Macmillan, the first of those partners, the future Prime Minister Harold Macmillan had advised the founders on its processes, practices and financial terms.

that as regards copyright, title and editorial independence we were still the small, non-profit-making private company of an editorial board that he had founded, with that gift of £2,000 from George Bernard Shaw, in 1930.[h]

To my knowledge, besides himself, only two others then survived[i] of those who had signed the original prospectus from which I have quoted:

P. J. Noel Baker, Ernest Barker, C. Delisle Burns, A. M. Carr-Saunders, Henry Clay, G. D. H. Cole, G. Lowes Dickinson, P. Sargant Florence, Margery Fry, T. E. Gregory, Lynda Grier, Freda Hawtrey, L. T. Hobhouse, J. A. Hobson, Eva Hubback, H. J. Laski, F. Lavington, A. D. Lindsay, C. M. Lloyd, J. J. Mallon, T. H. Marshall, Kingsley Martin, C. S. Myers, Percy Nunn, Olivier, W. A. Robson, C. P. Scott, R. H. Tawney, Beatrice Webb, Leonard Woolf, Barbara Wootton.

It is in such a great company that all of us will finally remember him. As Yeats said in a poem: 'All the Olympians; a thing never known again'.

BRC

Commentary: 'Perspectives on Unemployment'

Vol. 52, no. 1, January–March 1981

We asked most of the contributors to this special number to write on the extent of unemployment in a region of the United Kingdom, on its social effect, and on its probable political consequences.[a] We also asked for certain

[h] An interesting insight into the way this kind of information distorts over time. Shaw's contribution was actually £1,000—generous enough for such a speculative venture—as Robson himself states in various places, including articles on the founding that he wrote for *PQ* in 1951 and 1970, as well as in his Introduction to the 1971 book collection. The sum of £2,000 was what the founders wished to raise in total to get the journal under way, but Shaw only contributed half of this.

And whereas many small journals, especially across the spectrum of the arts and humanities, set out with the honourable intention of making no profit and manage to keep that aim alive, the modern *PQ* of recent decades could not sustain itself and its activities (such as seminars, conferences and event sponsorships) on such a diffident and unworldly basis.

[i] Two who were still living at that point were Barbara Wootton, who served on the *PQ* board into the 1960s, and the sociologist Thomas Marshall, who died the following year. Perhaps these are the survivors that Bernard meant.

[a] This is the last Commentary that Bernard wrote for *PQ* after retiring as coeditor in favour of Rudolf Klein during the previous year. It is more an introduction to the rest of the issue than a normal Commentary, but the acutely current topic of unemployment was a fit subject for a Commentary in its own right.

As I mention in my Preface, the special issue that this Commentary introduced was reproduced as a book, *Unemployment*, published by Methuen in 1981. At the close of the preface to the book he announces: 'I sadly chose this sombre theme to mark my retirement after fifteen years in *The Political Quarterly*'s editorial chair, handing on to David Watt and Rudolf Klein. So I carry responsibility for all omissions, most of all a regret that I did not commission a piece— thinking with hindsight of the Brixton disturbances—specifically on black unemployment. But I special topics to be covered, notably youth unemployment and trade union wage bargaining. Most of the articles are deliberately descriptive and informative. While some in fact contain arguments about what should be done, only two contributors were asked to address themselves principally to what should and could be done, Professor Maurice Peston on the economics and Austin Mitchell MP on the politics of unemployment. Readers will notice one obvious omission from the regions included, the South East. This omission is deliberate.

Consider these figures. In September 1980 there were, according to the Department of Employment, the following percentages of unemployment in the regions—with a national average of 7.4 per cent.

S. East 4.9; E. Anglia 5.8; S. West 6.8; W. Midlands 8.0; E. Midlands 6.6; Yorks & Humber 7.6; N. West 9.2; North 10.2; Wales 10.3; Scotland 9.7; N. Ireland 13.3[b]

What is glaringly obvious is that the further one goes from London the worse the situation becomes. And within some of the worst-hit regions there are area variations, such as Liverpool, Glasgow, Tyneside and Belfast, which reach well over double the national average. This may not surprise people, for such regional variations are part of our economic history. But they are also part of our political and cultural history. The outlying regions are those with the least political effect generally, those most easy to ignore in electoral terms—especially when Conservative governments are in power. And the 'peripheral regions', to give a geographical expression a realistic and terrible moral connotation, are also those which culturally are the least understood and perceived by the administrative, political and opinion-forming elite of the South East, mainly those who work in London.

It has long been thought, not merely morally but also politically and prudentially, that the modern state needs to ensure the welfare of its inhabitants, not merely to provide for their safety and defence and their formal equality before the law. Why is the danger of such vast unemployment not seen, as well as its immorality and social destructiveness? The answer must lie in the fact that in the capital city 4.9 per cent unemployment is hardly perceptible, unless one happens to live in, say, North Kensington or Brixton or Hackney, which most of the opinion-makers and administrators (to put it mildly) do not. When it is so difficult to get a plumber, a charwoman or a window-cleaner in spite of 'so much unemployment', the whole thing, they

am wholly unapologetic at reopening the debate about whether Britain at its best can remain a centralised state based on London and the elite mentality of the London, Oxford, Cambridge triangle.'

[b] For the book version of the special issue Bernard was able to update these figures by six months to April 1981. The substantial increases in revised list are a stark reminder of the employment difficulties of the period. In just over six months the national average had risen from 7.4 to 10.1 per cent, and the regional totals to the following: S. East 7.1; E. Anglia 8.2; S. West 9.1; W. Midlands 12.0; E. Midlands 9.2; Yorks & Humber 10.6; N. West 12.1; North 13.1; Wales 13.0; Scotland 12.0; N. Ireland 16.4.

feel and perceive, must be an illusion. And two decades at least of soft living and easy riding have made those in jobs, especially in the top jobs (like many of our readers), simply not want to know; they wish to disbelieve it, those two million moving towards three million unemployed. The Chairman of the CBI had to make a winter journey (but to his honour he did) before he became convinced that in the experience of the regions there is a depressing danger (quite beyond adjustments of the interest rate and the 'strength' of sterling, etc.) of sheer ungovernability. This may not take the form of demonstrations, riots, civil disobedience (and beyond?). Several of our contributors candidly refuse to scare us in this all-too-human way. It may take the form of these millions of people simply dropping out of the polity, simply ceasing to be citizens: on the one hand, ignored by a tough-minded government, even by self-protective trade unions; on the other, a population removed from the possibility of influence, control, usefulness. Professor Ridley's surmise is all too likely to prove true: that permanently unemployed young people (white and black) will not fall prey to 'political extremists', but rather enter into violent, random, delinquent protest, a *Clockwork Orange* world rather than one of political stirring. Would that they did fall prey to the Revolutionary Socialists or the National Front; that might stir some normal pre-emptive political reactions. What is more likely to happen is that their 'mindless' delinquency (quite rational in their hopeless circumstances) will simply evoke more cries from the employed of the need for 'law and order', for more to be spent on the police force and less on the social services: a vicious circle of irrelevant class aggression. Such will be the social consequence of what the Labour Party and CBI and anti-Thatcher Tories are beginning to call the sacrifice of industry to capital, the all-out attack on inflation, even at the cost of productivity.

Because of the lack of political response to mass unemployment and the flagrant indifference of public opinion, our symposium begins quite simply with an account of what it feels like to be unemployed. Some people are sceptical about Jeremy Seabrook's Orwellesque technique of being the participant observer; they prefer aggregate data instead. But aggregate data do not reveal the qualitative effect, indeed cannot show how people are likely to react. It does not matter precisely how typical some of the people he interviews are: the disturbing point is that they exist at all. And one of his comments on the contrast between the 1930s and today worries like a nightmare and shifts political perspectives:

In the 1930s, those who wanted to work had a sense that they had only to wait before their labour would be required again. . . . Unemployment impaired their sense of worth, assailed their dignity, denied them and those they loved adequate food and comfort. But it didn't rob them of the skills themselves. Now . . . there is a terminal sense of the extinction of work itself. Something elusive and despairing pervades those towns and cities which were built only for the sake of their purpose in the old industrial processes. It is as though working class were being wounded in its very reason for existence, work itself.

Fred Ridley's contribution is of profound importance. It is fair to say that he did not begin his work for unemployed young people on Merseyside with the perspectives he now holds. The best way of avoiding these perspectives, perhaps, is not to look and not to know, deliberate suppression; otherwise one observes, he says: 'passive alienation . . . a generation idle and frustrated because unemployed; rejected by employers, thus alienated; concentrated in certain districts where the environment itself is grim—not revolution, but simply undirected violence and pointless destruction'. 85 per cent of unemployed young people on Merseyside, he reminds us, recently replied to a survey that they had no interest in politics. And Ben Pimlott points out that in the North East there are more than four times as many unemployed for each notified job vacancy as in the South East. It could be that politicians will now arise capable of stirring the unemployed and 'the regions' against the political and cultural dominance of the South East; and they could be, would have to be, as tough towards private property rights as the present government has been towards the (the right?) in their crazy, single-minded, monetarist obsession with inflation—at whatever cost, it seems, to employment or industrial production.

John Osmond, writing on South Wales, where of all places disorder might well be expected, reaches similar conclusions to Fred Ridley. He weighs the present evidence and finds that even as South Wales becomes deindustrialised, rioting and extremist politics are unlikely. He is a responsible political journalist. It says much about the situation in the regions that such matters have to be weighed. And, after all, it is through deliberate government policy (Austin Mitchell scarcely exaggerates) that unemployment has come to that pitch. I find that I myself, supposed by many to be a Paladin of moderates, am beginning to consider the thesis of the philosopher Ted Honderich's recent book *Violence for Equality*. He easily dismisses most arguments for violence, but in so far as most large inequalities are deliberately maintained by government, there remains, he considers, always a residual possibility of violence when such imposed inequalities correlate to different life expectancies among the social classes. The argument is difficult and esoteric, as well as disturbing; but Honderich points out that governments have a greater opportunity (and moral duty) to end misery without violence than most revolutionaries to create justice through violence. Government must come to its senses.

Government policy has brought us to the point where such thoughts cannot be suppressed, unless we never look further afield than the placid and affluent home counties. And when high unemployment and nationalism coincide, it is gross political folly to think that the 'United Kingdom' or devolution question has been settled; contributors from the other nations make that abundantly clear. It is perhaps mildly obsessive of Stephen Maxwell to have treated unemployment in Scotland almost solely in terms of its effect on the fortunes of his own Scottish National Party. Not all Scots will welcome this. (An icily clear statement of Scotland's economic condition

553

is to be found in the October 1980 number of the Fraser of Allander Institute's *Quarterly Economic Commentary*, University of Strathclyde.) But basically Maxwell is right. Scotland is one of the worst hit regions of the British Isles, and special attention is only given to her needs and traditions when she acts, or threatens to act, in—from a United Kingdom point of view—an aberrant political manner.

More gently, Professor Norman Gibson, writing on Northern Ireland, quotes Keynes to show: (a) that state intervention for full employment is possible, and (b) to remind us that this may not be compatible with the highest wage rates possible:

If we decide that the interests of justice and charity require that the income of the working class should be higher than that which they receive from the economic machine, then we must, so to speak, subscribe to that end. Taxation is a measure of compulsory subscription, and the subscription must be spread over the whole community. But if that subscription is to fall solely on a particular body of employers then we must not be surprised if the level of employment and output is below what it should be.

Part of the blame the late Labour government must take is not just for their partial acceptance of monetarism but their political cowardice in not fighting Mrs Thatcher hard enough when she promised tax cuts. If we want full employment and a welfare state, a high, graduated income tax on those in profitable employment is inevitable and justifiable; and if nobody likes paying it even on the margin, that is a different proposition from saying that people will not pay it if they think the cause is just, or even that they would be too frightened of the consequences if they did not. Mr Callaghan failed his party on that—little or nothing to do with the 'Left', 'Right', 'Democratic' or 'Centrist' disputes within the Party. And the Labour Party retreated from an incomes policy rather than try to produce a socialist incomes policy—or quite simply to control the top as well as the bottom (what I long argued for in these columns: a 'mini-max' incomes policy).

Yet things have gone so far that Maurice Peston can argue here that: 'it is a measure of the mess that we are in that with the best will in the world it is hard to believe that unemployment could get down to a million by 1990'. Simply consider, he argues, the number of jobs that would have to be created in each year to get back to old expectations, especially when there is not merely laying off (recession) but now large-scale closing down (depression). (Stan Taylor's article on the deindustrialisation of the West Midlands is grimly impressive on this point.) The political and economic situation is obviously one in which welfare will have to be created from social security for many years rather than from any real hopes of job creation on the scale needed. The Gross National Product will depend more on capital-intensive industry, even if we can get the bankers off our shoulders. And this will mean higher levels of income tax. And the unpopularity of this among new taxpayers—as the last election showed. And the positively weird state of British public opinion about unemployment and poverty.

Four years ago, a comparative study was conducted on *The Perception of Poverty in Europe* (published by the Commission in 1977). Most people in Europe had a fairly dour and common-sense attitude to poverty, that it was caused by involuntary unemployment and by initial poor home conditions. But one category of respondents was labelled 'cynics'. These were people who rarely if ever see poverty: 'If poor people exist, it is because they are lazy or lack will power . . . there is no great need to reduce social inequality and the public authorities are doing enough—if not too much'. Over all the EEC countries, 14 per cent of respondents were 'cynics', but in Britain a massive 27 per cent—10 per cent higher than the next country, Germany. And recent surveys tell us that *most* people in jobs believe that there are jobs to be had if the unemployed bestir themselves! As with their stories of welfare-state scroungers, the popular press have a lot to answer for. Where else could these stupid and distinctively British stereotypes have come from? If there are to be alternative economic policies, political leaders have to establish, boldly and patiently, that unemployment is involuntary, and that we face disaster, either economic or political or both, if people cannot be got back to work. If that is not possible, their life chances must be rendered much the same as for those in work—which means high taxation towards redistribution of incomes.

Keith Middlemas, the Conservative historian, wrote a remarkable article in the last number of *The Political Quarterly*, which was really the prelude to this special number.[c] It concluded:

. . . what will Britain look like after even three years of two million unemployed? Divisions which for half a century governments have tried to abolish will show nakedly, between the two geographical Englands, with Scotland, Wales and Northern Ireland on the periphery, like the Italian Mezzogiorno; between those in work and the unemployed; between the mature and the young, between white and black. They already exist. If they are heightened by the sort of political conflict allied to a capital/labour antithesis which nearly every Conservative leader since Baldwin has tried to prevent, or by an unthinking and indiscriminate assault on trade unionism which confuses structural backwardness with moral turpitude, or by an intolerant repudiation of the post-war consensus rather than a reasoned attempt to find out what went wrong, then it will recall the old tag: *'Ubi solitudinem faciunt, pacem appellant'*—where they make a desert, they call it peace.'

Perhaps it will be more easy to carry out alternative economic policies, if attempted by the reviving Labour Party, than actually to recognise their need.

Bernard Crick

---

[c] It was added to the book collection too.

Part IV
Seventy Serious Years, 1998

Contents

Preface

ALTHOUGH this work is published to celebrate the 70th birthday of *The Political Quarterly*, the reader need not fear a 'company history'. I see it as the biography of a journal and have tried to write with the same critical objectivity and integrity that one should apply to the biography of a person—that is, respect for documentary evidence wherever possible rather than for faded, addled and partial memories (including my own). Like the journal itself under its successive editors, my standards are scholarly but I write for an intelligent general audience beyond the academy, for what we now call 'the policy community'. By this I mean all the thinking and reading members of the public and the media who still read serious books on public issues and problems. The opinions expressed are mine alone. The editorial board have given me a completely free hand.[a]

The contents of such a journal founded in 1930 are surely interesting in themselves, both for what they mirror of the major concerns of the times and for the occasional possibility of pinning down influence, that will-o'-the-wisp: 'Who the rider, who the horse?',[b] as Yeats remarked. But some readers will find two minor themes interesting, since many now study journals and the media closely: how a small journal was founded, funded, survives and runs itself on a shoestring and keeps its independence; and how editors and boards work together or not—although sometimes the evidence is lacking, sometimes flimsy and occasionally embarrassingly full.

I have often scorned the pretensions of biographers of living people (almost always they seek to praise or to defame, to conceal or to expose). So my final judgements about the role of *PQ* in the 2000s compared to the 1930s will necessarily be prudent and inconclusive. There are four living former editors (including myself) as well as the present joint incumbents.[c] And two great figures loom large over the history of the journal. William Robson was joint editor from 1930 to 1975 (except during the Second World War), and then chairman of the board until his death in 1980; and Leonard Woolf was joint

---

[a] Even though its planned publication date was timed to celebrate *PQ*'s 70th anniversary, this was always to be an entirely personal creation by Bernard rather than a jobbing ceremonial work turned out merely at the behest of the board.

The comment about the 'thinking and reading members of the public and the media' betrays Bernard's still strong belief—consonant with the *PQ* founding ethos, of course—in the existence of the educated general reader (or 'the intelligent lay reader' and many other variants). Hard-nosed publishers, and particularly their marketing departments, will have a much more cynical view about the existence of such creatures.

[b] One of Bernard's favourite tags.

[c] The then current editors were Andrew Gamble and Tony Wright, and the other three former editors he mentions are Colin Crouch, Rudolf Klein and David Marquand.

© 2012 The Author. The Political Quarterly © 2012 The Political Quarterly Publishing Co. Ltd
Published by Blackwell Publishing Ltd, 9600 Garsington Road, Oxford OX4 2DQ, UK and 350 Main Street, Malden, MA 02148, USA

editor from 1931 until 1958 (sole editor during the war),[d] literary editor until 1962, and a lively member of the board until his death in 1969. Before there were token women there were token young men: I joined the board in 1966 and was subsequently joint editor, chairman, and lastly literary editor until resigning from the board this year,[e] being of the same age as the journal and aware of how difficult old men can become. Being both author and a small part of the story raises a problem more difficult than what used to be called, in *the* Church and *the* Party, 'self-criticism'; while loyal to and respectful of sources, I decided that while the 'I' must be muted it could not be avoided: it is too strange to write of oneself in the third person.

Following the good custom of the journal not even to look academic, I have kept footnotes to an absolute minimum, while always striving to be true to and respectful of sources. The surviving papers of William Robson are in the British Library of Political and Economic Science, in loose folders with approximate subject headings (in which the *PQ* folders are far from complete). Leonard Woolf's papers, far more numerous, are well catalogued and listed by correspondent in the library of the University of Sussex. I thank both archivists for their help, and above all my old associate and assistant on my Orwell work from Birkbeck days, Audrey Coppard (*PQ*'s company secretary),[f] for finding time to read and help improve these chapters.

Bernard Crick
Edinburgh[g]

---

[d] The precise dates of William Robson's absence on war work vary between different sources, even Robson himself, but in his bibliography they are given as October 1940 to July 1946 (C. E. Hill, compiler, *A Bibliography of the Writings of W. A. Robson*, Greater London Papers no. 17, LSE, 1986).

[e] 2000, when the book was due to be published.

[f] And, more significantly and for longer, she was the journal's Assistant Editor. The formal Company Secretary role was created in the 1980s. Audrey began working for Bernard as a research assistant, originally for him and other senior academics, at Birkbeck in about 1973, but was soon largely appropriated by Bernard alone especially as his Orwell project progressed. He then brought her to *PQ* on both the editorial and later the company sides (see my Introduction).

[g] The proof before first correction had '1 February 2000' here but Bernard struck it out.

Introduction

The function of *The Political Quarterly* is to discuss social and political questions from a progressive point of view; to act as a clearing house of ideas and a medium of constructive thought. It is not tied to any party and contains contributions from persons of various political affiliations.

It is a journal of opinion, not propaganda.

> (From 'The Announcement', a circular drafted by William Robson,
> Kingsley Martin and Leonard Woolf, 1927)

I feel some encouragement too when I contemplate . . . journals of small circulation like *The Political Quarterly*. There is no doubt that if their standards, both journalistic and intellectual, are high, they can have considerable influence. The reason is that they are . . . written for experts by experts, or, from another point of view, they are professional or trade papers. *The Political Quarterly* is partly a technical paper in which the professional politician, the administrator or the civil servant, can find information and ideas of the greatest importance to his work and unobtainable elsewhere.

> (From the fourth volume of Leonard Woolf's autobiography,
> *Downhill All the Way*, 1967)

Most of the articles are written by intelligent experts—not a very common combination.

> (From the fifth volume of Leonard Woolf's autobiography,
> *The Journey Not the Arrival Matters*, 1969)

THE ABOVE extracts[a] make clear that the animating idea of the founders was to create a bridge between experts and generalists. When Leonard Woolf talks of 'written for experts by experts', he assumes not just intelligence but good plain English rather than technical vocabulary; otherwise even experts in different fields misunderstand each other. To pick up quickly his 'unobtainable elsewhere': this had real meaning in the period between the two world wars, but much less by the time he wrote that in 1967, still less today. Many of the think-tanks now do what the *PQ* did almost alone in the 1930s. The reasons for the survival of the journal will have to be found elsewhere, including low costs on the supply side and postwar university expansion on the demand side. Also it was very important, compared to other little magazines, that *PQ* kept going all through the war when Woolf edited it alone, through all the public difficulties of wartime and the private heartbreak and tragedy of his wife's suicide. (I have, by the way, in my possession their

---

[a] In the circulated proof version these extracts were set out ahead of the Preface, effectively as volume epigraphs, and took up most of a page. I reduced them to the present less ponderous length by substantially reducing the material taken from the Leonard Woolf autobiography, and then moved them here to the start of the Introduction where they read nicely into the following text rather than function as epigraphs.

Published by Blackwell Publishing Ltd, 9600 Garsington Road, Oxford OX4 2DQ, UK and 350 Main Street, Malden, MA 02148, USA

own set of the first five volumes, which Virginia Woolf bound and stitched by hand.)[b]

However, before an account of the founding (and Robson's papers reveal a more complex story than he portrayed writing long after the events in the fortieth year special number or in his Introduction to the 1971 anthology, *Political Quarterly in the Thirties*),[c] something needs to be said of the intellectual context of the day. This may help to explain, beyond the accident of personal acquaintance, how two such unlikely men as Robson, the teacher of public administration and administrative law, and Woolf, the joint proprietor with his wife of the Hogarth Press, could come together and work together with mutual respect for almost forty years. And neither, it must be said, was always a particularly easy man to work with.

Around the turn of the twentieth century the discourse of the 'New Liberals' had a real impact on the thinking of leading politicians, some of whom were themselves political thinkers, perhaps not always in terms to satisfy a modern seminar in political philosophy, but certainly thoughtful

---

[b] These still exist. Bernard acquired Leonard Woolf's run of the journal, which he could extend with his own copies after Woolf's death in 1969, and this is now in safekeeping on behalf of the journal. After William Robson died in 1980 his set was acquired by *PQ* and became the 'official' set of record; all of the Robson volumes have been rebound, the first decades retrospectively during the journal's Thomson era, and then later by craft binders on an annual basis.

The five volumes that Bernard mentions—well used and bulky too, with the first year alone running to over 600 pages—have an ochre coloured quarter cloth binding with printed paper covers of a stylised floral design and matching endpapers. (He once asked me, in one of his twinkly moods, 'Do you think they're worth anything?') The title and volume details are hand-blocked in gold on the spine, against a black panel. The outside paper on the covers has faded to a gold and grey, but the endpapers retain much of the original colouring of yellow, orange and violet. There is no outward sign of the binder's signature or other identifying mark, and that she was the binder is the result of Bernard's reporting of Leonard Woolf's testimony (though of course entirely plausible, given the period). After 1934, Woolf's set remains in its original quarterly bindings as delivered.

PQ's entire backstock was digitised in 2005 as a service to researchers and the wider readership, part of a process that is continuing apace across the entire journal publishing spectrum. The creation of a digital version of a journal has many obvious benefits. However, the corollary of this process is that libraries everywhere are destroying or disposing of their printed journal holdings. This may seem to be of little consequence now that the complete run of a journal is a few mouse clicks away, but something is irretrievably lost when this happens. What disappears is much of the publishing context, particularly original covers and flysheets, but possibly endpapers and prelims too, with their advertisements, pricing information, evidence of typographical fashions, and other significant detail—all of it important contextual information, now often studied as 'paratext', of great value to researchers in many fields. This makes the Woolf set, even more than the more functional Robson set, an important subject for long-term preservation.

[c] This is true (the slightly revisionist article in question is Robson's 'The Founding of *The Political Quarterly*', vol. 41, no. 1). In the later versions, and in spite of Robson's immense significance to the journal and its foundation, there is something of the 'I founded the journal' about his later accounts and an ever-present tendency to see *PQ* always through the lens of its 1930s incarnation and influence. I say a little more on this in my Introduction.

about politics, and accustomed to setting out reasoned grounds for their conclusions in the then many heavyweight but non-academic periodicals.[1] These liberals[d] often gave the impression of reasoning themselves into unlikely conclusions. Unlike so many leaders of our times they were not, in Hannah Arendt's simple words, either 'thoughtless' or 'banal'. Modern political rhetoric has not merely become banal, but also routinised and largely thoughtless. The aim nowadays is not to say anything different. But there was then a class of men (it was, of course, in that world, at once so close and so distant, almost all men—Beatrice Webbs were few and far between) some of whom were in the universities, some in Parliament, mostly in the professions, some landowning gentlemen with libraries and intellectual tastes who all read what each other wrote, usually knew each other, or knew of each other, quite well. They were accustomed to a high level of public debate, whether in books, articles or letters to *The Times*, or on the then many alternative platforms, whether in print or at the podium. They gave good reasons for what they said; not just stating opinions with as much appearance of sincerity as nowadays seems natural while spraying soundbites on the box.

These were the 'public moralists' of Stefan Collini's subtle and illuminating study of political thought and intellectual life in the Britain of those days.[2] That was also the time, in the 1900s, when the Webbs (who were to write notable articles for *The Political Quarterly* in the 1930s) were less interested in the founding and fortunes of a Labour Party than in the tactics for permeating an existing establishment, the opportunities of putting their work on social reform directly to political leaders, often over the dinner table.[3] There was, in other words, what Walter Lippmann had called 'a public philosophy'; but already by the 1930s it was in danger of being drowned by a democratic flood, as he saw it, of mere assertive opinion, and opinion deified by being studied scientifically, as he himself in his youth had pioneered.[4] Leonard Woolf grew up in that older world.[e]

---

[1] See M. Freeden, *The New Liberalism*, Oxford, Oxford University Press, 1978.

[2] Stefan Collini, *Public Moralists: Political Thought and Intellectual Life in Britain, 1850–1930*, Oxford, Clarendon Press, 1991.

[3] Royden Harrison, *The Life and Times of Sidney and Beatrice Webb, 1858–1905*, London, Palgrave, 2000.

[4] Contrast Walter Lippmann's *A Preface to Politics* (New York, 1914) with his *The Public Philosophy* (Boston, 1954).

[d] Given Bernard's pernickety and (sometimes) systematic approach to initial capitals I have decided to follow the original copy—safety first, or editorial cowardice if you prefer—unless there's an obvious mistake. Readers should therefore step gingerly over liberal/Liberal, socialist/Socialist etc. An apparent inconsistency may be an actual inconsistency, or it may represent an intended distinction.

[e] In 1930, *PQ*'s first year, Robson was 35 and Woolf was 50.

These men were part of an elite, well-educated and liberal-minded, predominantly but not exclusively a specifically Liberal elite (with some exceptions, of course: there was the Tory Fitzjames Stephen, brother of Virginia's father, Leslie Stephen). If in socialist eyes they were not so much a counter-establishment as part of the establishment; nonetheless, they were a highly literate elite who wrote in an intellectually demanding but, to any who cared to make the effort, accessible manner. Good English was almost the main mark of English culture.

Robson, however, was of the postwar generation of scholars concerned with public affairs, who were much more respectful of the specialist and the expert, and sought to be experts themselves: the beginning of the professionalisation of writing about social policy. Paradoxically, supreme generalists and populists like H. G. Wells and George Bernard Shaw preached the coming of the socially conscious scientific elite and the professional social scientist: the leaders of a New Age were to be the graduates of the Regent Street Polytechnic, Imperial College and Sidney Webb's idea of the LSE. Robson was, in fact, picked up by Shaw—quite literally, for in 1919 the author of *Heartbreak House*, the great rival prophet to Wells of the coming age of air power, realised to his embarrassment that he had never been up in an aeroplane. His critics would mock the mocker. He had read a book published in 1916 on the future of air power by one W. A. Robson (whom he was as astonished as the publishers to discover was only 21). So he asked this young, by then RFC, pilot to 'take him up'. On landing safely, Shaw then, as it were, took Robson up. 'What are you going to do now the war is over?' Robson admitted to be at a loose end. 'Not chicken-farming', said GBS. 'The LSE is the place of the future.' He pulled his big reporter's notebook out of his big tweed pocket and, resting it on the fuselage, wrote 'Here is a note to my friend Sidney Webb'.[5] A long and brilliant academic career followed. Such is chance.

Woolf was always attached to the idea and ideal of the late Victorian and Edwardian generalist, far more than Robson. He saw Robson, sometimes ironically and teasingly, as the 'expert'; but he helped keep Robson's interests wide. Virginia found William boring, but thought it important to meet him from time to time to find out 'what was really going on'. One must not forget how much time and dedication Leonard Woolf put into political matters: he was secretary of both the Fabian Society's and the Labour Party's colonial

---

[5] As related by Robson to the author [Bernard—*ed.*] and others [in fact, this brief biographical information is substantially that in G. W. Jones's Preface to C. E. Hill, compiler, *A Bibliography of the Writings of W. A. Robson*, Greater London Papers no. 17, LSE, 1986—*ed.*]. Robson had to leave school early when his father, a Hatton Garden dealer in pearls, died nearly bankrupt. He worked as a clerk for the Graham-White Aviation Company at Hendon aerodrome. An eye for detail (that only occasionally degenerated into a fearsome pedantry), and great and meticulous organising ability, soon made him assistant manager of the aerodrome at the age of eighteen. While still at Hendon he had written a book, *Aircraft in Peace and War* (1916). He saw active service in World War I as a lieutenant in the Royal Flying Corps—soon the RAF—partly in France and then on night patrol against Zeppelins over London.

committees through most of the 1930s.[6] As early as July 1916 the Fabian Research Department had published *International Government: Two Reports by L. S. Woolf. Together with a Proposal by a Fabian Committee for a Supernational Authority That Will Prevent War*. It contained the kind of ideas behind the founding of the League of Nations and its advocacy became well known. An American edition was published in the same year by Brentano, then a leading house, and not merely had the commendably shorter title of *International Government*, but also an introduction by Shaw!

I can find no evidence concerning when or how Woolf and Robson first met, but Shaw could well have been the marriage-broker as well as providing the dowry for *The Political Quarterly*. Robson, however, was to keep a willing, perhaps slightly masochistic, Leonard to doing at least his fair share of their humdrum work of editing, proofing and managing the journal—no sub-editor slave for them, and a journal full in the main of practical policy articles.[f] The high-minded rationalist, humanist abstractions of Woolf's *Principia Politica* were never trailed or unloaded in *PQ*. His 'De Profundis' article[g] of 1939 is an entirely different matter. One important thing both men had in common—the law reformer and the literary editor—was a devotion to, at times almost a fanaticism for, clear expression. They edited everything themselves, read the proofs themselves and were highly interventionist. One felt it an honour to be rewritten by Leonard, if somewhat tedious to have to argue back against Robson's dislike of colloquialisms (only when he got old did he get more indulgent). 'Good prose need not be unlively', I would often sigh to myself as he toned me down in the 1970s.[h]

Collini ended his story of the 'public moralists' in 1930, as if it were the end of the Golden Age of the gentleman generalist. In the same year this journal began its self-imposed task of bridging the old and the new—in fact, it was three years after the first attempts to define the purpose and raise money in a small elite circle. The old was dying as the new came in: 1929 saw the demise of the once most famous and politically influential of periodicals, the

[6] Hermione Lee's masterly biography (*Virginia Woolf*, London, Chatto, 1996) not merely defended Leonard most sensibly and decisively against some feminist writers who blamed him for neglecting her (in fact, the depth and burden of his devotion was exemplary) but brought out their *mutual* concern with political and public questions, albeit that was his sphere for actual writing and hard labour in committees. The Hogarth Press published many political pamphlets.

[f] This entirely hands-on approach to running the journal survived almost until the end of the Robson era. Bernard was very much instrumental in bringing it to an end, as I describe further in the Introduction.

[g] This article, looking at the deeper causes of the war and the difficulties of winning a subsequent peace, was written during its first week and leads the final issue of 1939: *The Political Quarterly*, vol. 10, no. 4, 1939.

[h] Invisible green ink: the main reason why I was unwilling to include unsigned Commentaries from that period in this collection, even when they deal with roundly Crickian themes in a largely Bernardian way.

Edinburgh Review, and the *Westminster Review* had closed 'for the duration' in 1914 and never reopened. Woolf sought less to perpetuate that world, which he loved and mourned, however modernist he was in literature with the Hogarth Press, than to civilise the new experts.

The first two issues are worth close examination for their odd mixture of the old and the new. Alfred Zimmern led issue 1 with a think-piece on 'Democracy and the Expert', but there was also 'A Political Dialogue' by Goldsworthy Lowes Dickinson, which could have been written as a paper for the Cambridge Apostles at any time in the 1900s. These appeared before Robson on 'The Future of Trade Union Law', Keynes on 'The Question of High Wages' and an anonymous 'The Disappearance of the Governing Class'—in fact by Beatrice Webb,[i] presumably not wishing to embarrass Sidney, who at the time was most uneasily in office under Macdonald. And looking at the first contributors and the first Board, there is a very revealing dog that does not bark. To pick up the phrase in the original 'Announcement'—'from a progressive point of view': just as Collini does not discuss the popular intellectuals of the socialist movement and the Labour movement, so *PQ* from the very beginning takes both an unashamedly elitist and a 'centre Left' or simply 'progressive' stance, broadly sympathetic to but firmly distanced from the internal politics and the leading figures of the Labour movement, however much discussed they were. True, Harold Laski was on the Board, but his deep involvement in the Labour Party came a decade later. J. M. Keynes was also on the Board, had some role in the launch and published some key articles in *PQ*, but still hoped for a revival of Lloyd George's radical faction of the divided Liberal Party, thinking Labour too socialist and, in any case, dead after the fall of the second Labour government. Certainly, Webb published in *PQ* his famous (and misleading) account of that fall but what editor could resist it?[j] (Robson told Peter Self sometime in the 1960s that 'regrettably I must admit that Reg Bassett'—an old Labour teacher at LSE who by then had gone Tory—'has exposed Webb's mendacity').

However, the point is that the word 'progressive' indicated that *PQ* was not launched as a journal of 'the Left', without adding many qualifications to that term or using it very broadly.[k] So perhaps no accident that Robson and Woolf struck a good deal with Harold Macmillan[l] to publish the early numbers: his

---

[i] She wrote under the guise of 'A Political Correspondent'. Bernard leaves out the other two main articles, coming between Zimmern and Lowes Dickinson—'How Far Can a Labour Budget Go?' by J. Wedgwood (a Josiah, from the famous family, whose book *The Economics of Inheritance* is reviewed in the same issue) and 'The Problem of the Mines' by G. D. H. Cole.

[j] This is a reference to Sidney Webb's lead article 'What Happened in 1931: A Record', *The Political Quarterly*, vol. 3, no. 1, 1932.

[k] *PQ* insiders still debate this point today. And even Bernard (as is evident in some of his writings in this collection) takes slightly different positions over time concerning the 'leftness' of the journal.

[l] Actually a deal with Macmillan the publisher, of course, though the journal's contact and professional adviser on its establishment and terms was Harold, then a junior partner in the firm.

progressive Conservatism of the time could find some common links with *PQ*, as with another body founded slightly later for much the same purposes, PEP (Political and Economic Planning). And no accident either that Robson and Woolf chose not to try to realise their aims through the Fabian Society. They were both active in the Fabian Society, but they saw it as too tied to the Labour Party leadership (as ever, some might say) and, at that time, far too far to the Left under the heavy influence of Douglas and Margaret Cole.

I am sure that at the end I will vindicate Woolf and Robson's view that *PQ* was, is and must be, an elite journal.[m] Ideas and policies must be acceptable in a democracy, but they do trickle down, not up. There is much phoney populism in intellectual rhetoric today: too many know-all columnists and presenters who know so little and read so little, but are never at a loss for a striking opinion. But it is now a different kind of elite, more professionalised, more dispersed, and perhaps bewildered by a multiplicity of sources: not clustering to a few, not even to *PQ*.

[m] See my Introduction for more on Bernard and the elite journal.

Chapter 1
The Foundings: Motives and Methods

For the fortieth birthday number of this journal in 1970 William Robson wrote an account of the founding.[1] Why not simply reprint it? If so, it would need heavy footnoting. I have leant on it heavily, but in those footnotes would also have to lean on it a little in a punning sense. Over forty years, perspectives can change and memory, as I warn myself looking back across almost the same length of time, is an active substance, growing as well as decaying, never an inert record. Letters of the period can reveal a story not essentially different but with interesting differences of intention, interpretation and perspective.

Robson wrote 'I conceived the idea in 1927 of a serious political review in which progressive ideas could be discussed at adequate length, and shortly afterwards I found Kingsley Martin had arrived at a similar idea. . . . Kingsley Martin and I took the lead in bringing the idea to fruition. We were then junior members of the teaching staff of the London School of Economics and Political Science.' But in 1951 in an article on 'Bernard Shaw and *The Political Quarterly*'[2] he had written 'Some time in 1927 a few of the younger and more active Fabians began to entertain the idea of starting a serious political review . . . We wanted an organ to serve as a forum for the evolution of a philosophy and a programme for the Socialist movement, which was then stumbling and fumbling along with growing strength but devoid of any coherent body of ideas.' He then repeats that he found that Kingsley Martin, 'then an assistant lecturer. . . had arrived at the same conclusions . . . and was prepared to devote his energies to the task of getting it established. Thereafter we joined forces . . .'

Notice that by 1970 'the younger and more active Fabians' had vanished, and the 'philosophy and programme for the Socialist movement' had been replaced by the more ambiguous but comprehensive 'from a progressive point of view' of the first issue. And the Prospectus circulated to enrol shareholders spoke only, as we will now see, of 'industrial and social reconstruction' and disavowed commitment to any one political party or programme.

One simply does not know. Was the capitalised 'Socialism' of 1951 closer to Robson and Martin's first thoughts in 1927 or a reflection in 1951 that the Labour government, in its fragile second term, needed new ideas—the long legacy of the Webbs expended? Or did second thoughts arise back then, conditioned by the uncertain attachment of programmes to parties in the late 1920s, coupled with practical difficulties of fundraising? In many respects the

[1] 'The Founding of *The Political Quarterly*', *The Political Quarterly*, vol. 41, no. 1, 1970.
[2] *The Political Quarterly*, vol. 22, no. 3, 1951.

economic thinking of both Lloyd George and Simonite Liberals, not to mention their constitutional thinking, was more radical and programmatic than that of the Labour leadership of Ramsey Macdonald and George Thomas. Oswald Mosley's programme for remedying unemployment through public works was a kind of practical anticipation of John Maynard Keynes's general theory, a programme that had already led Mosley from the Conservative to the Labour Party, and soon further into the foul wilderness of fascism. Systematic thinkers, trying to apply the thinking of the social sciences to social policy, could not always expect a welcome in the Labour Party. If they announced their loyalty too strongly, they could soon be accused of disloyalty for speaking out of turn, or whatever was said in the 1920s to mean our 'off message'. When the fundraising began, significantly no approaches were made to unions, but to private individuals who were comfortable enough to each put up a little: in other words, to the old liberal elite, whether they were of Liberal or Labour persuasion or uncommitted in any party sense.

The reference to younger and active Fabians suggests that the idea was in the air; but the initiative was certainly that of the two young men—young men who had already made a mark and whom the older generation were, figuratively speaking at least, willing to put money on, but young men nonetheless. Neither of them sought to be editor. The editor must be a name of fame and probity and not such as to scare non-socialist backers. J. L Hammond was approached, and dithered for almost two years before declining. Hammond (1872–1949) must have seemed the ideal candidate—the famous social historian, joint author with his wife of *The Village Labourer*, *The Town Labourer* and *The Skilled Labourer*; secretary to the Civil Service Commission of 1907–13, a special correspondent of the *Manchester Guardian* since 1919 and a member of the Liberal Party. Surviving correspondence shows Leonard Woolf, not Robson or Martin, seeking to persuade Hammond; indeed Woolf used the argument, knowing Hammond's fear of being overburdened or left to feed the new baby on his own, that 'Robson and Martin have done the donkey-work already', seeming to imply that they might so continue: as assistant editor(s), on the money side, etc.

How did Woolf get involved? Again, we simply do not know what brought him together with Robson. Most probably Shaw, already Robson's patron, at least for that first vital step from a cockpit in the RFC to an eventual chair at the LSE, the two meeting from time to time and in correspondence since at least 1918,[3] but also the author of the Preface to the American edition of Woolf's advocacy *International Government* of 1916. Woolf (1880–1969) was of an older generation than Robson, fifteen years older, and already literary

---

[3] In a surviving letter of 7 January 1918 from Shaw to Robson in Canada (then a flying instructor after completing his quota of active-service flights, partly in France, partly on anti-Zeppelin patrol over London), Shaw responds to a question on what would he have done had he been in his twenties rather than nearly sixty in 1914. The frank and friendly tone suggests earlier correspondence (presumably on the future of air power—see footnote 5 in my Introduction above).

editor of *The Nation*, joint proprietor of the Hogarth Press, and a well known, if not famous, writer on international affairs, secretary of the Labour Party Advisory Committee on Imperial Affairs (from 1924 to 1945), also of the Fabian Society's colonial committee. So it was natural that he should take the lead in the head-hunt. Everyone that Robson and Martin would want to get on board, soon literally on *the* board, would know or know of Woolf.

However, what was the 'donkey-work' the two had done, either themselves or working through whomever? Robson relates in the 1970 account that he and Martin 'enlisted the interest of about 40 or 50 leading intellectuals whom we invited to a private meeting at the London School of Economics to discuss the project. . . . All were persons of intellectual distinction with a keen interest in public affairs.' And after that meeting a prospectus was circulated. So revealing is it that I reproduce it in full for (to anticipate my conclusion) if the circumstances and the relative needs have changed, the reader may consider that the basic aims of the journal have changed little, nor do they need to, so well laid was the foundation stone.

A POLITICAL QUARTERLY

It is proposed to establish a Quarterly Review, which will have as its special object the discussion of social policy, public administration and questions of industrial and political organisation, primarily in Great Britain, but also, from time to time, in other countries. Its aim should be to do for these matters what *The Round Table* has attempted to do for imperial politics. While treating them in a scientific spirit, it would have as its subject current political and social problems, not political science in the abstract. It would differ from the existing reviews, partly because the space at its command would enable it to aim at a standard of thoroughness impossible in a short article, and partly because it would be planned by a group of writers holding certain general political ideas in common.

While its intellectual basis would be an acceptance of the view of the necessity of industrial and social reconstruction it will not be mortgaged to any one political party, nor be committed in advance to any particular programme. To discover truth and promote social well-being will be its only definite loyalties: and as a journal it will know no other allegiance. Thus it would welcome contributions from persons of different political connections, provided that they were of the necessary quality. It should be realistic and critical in spirit, and should attempt to handle its subject with sufficient authority to attract the attention of all persons seriously interested in political and social questions, whatever their political views. While it would naturally be mainly concerned with questions of topical interest, it should endeavour to treat them in a broad and philosophical manner, and should aim at diffusing knowledge and stimulating thought, rather than at presenting a case. It should draw on the experience of the Continent, the USA., and the British Dominions, as freely as on that of this country, and should appeal not only to English readers but to all serious students of political, economic and social questions.

The reasons for thinking that such a journal would meet a demand are as follows:

1. There is no journal in England[a] today which attempts to deal authoritatively with questions of social policy and political organisation. The whole tenor of political

[a] Note the 'England' focus of this paragraph.

discussion in England is at the present time in a profoundly unsatisfactory condition. The national daily newspapers, with scarcely more than one exception, are either controlled by a handful of millionaires who definitely prevent the effective expression of opinions from which they differ, or else are harnessed to the yoke of a particular political party. The weekly sixpenny journals, excellent though they are as commentaries on current events, are unable to devote the necessary space required for the adequate discussion of the larger political and social questions; while the monthly reviews, attempting, as they do, to cover every field of human activity, necessarily do so in a superficial manner. It is a serious matter at the present juncture, obviously a critical period in English history, that there should be no recognised avenue through which new ideas on social and political affairs can emerge for intelligent printed discussion.

2. Political and social questions are occupying an ever-increasing amount of public attention and will continue to do so more and more in the future. Apart from pamphlets and books, the great development of experience and thought in these fields, both in Great Britain and in other countries, has never been made accessible to the man in the street. He will not read a Quarterly Journal, but he will read the daily Press, and the Journal would influence him by supplying the materials upon which the more reputable newspapers could draw.

3. The discussion of all political and economic questions suffers because there is no organ in which they are treated thoroughly, with reasoned arguments and a candid presentation of the available evidence. The result is that the general public is at the mercy of catch-words. There is also a growing number of persons who are not committed to any programme but who are nevertheless interested in a serious discussion of social and economic policy. Consider, in the light of these demands, the almost entire absence of any serious discussion in the Press of the real nature of the coal problem, or of unemployment, or of the problems of combinations and monopolies, or of trade unionism, or of the experience of our own and other countries regarding the possible methods of organising industries under public ownership and of their advantages and defects. There has probably never been a period in which so many political and economic experiments have been made in Europe as in the last ten years. Yet hardly any serious attempt has been made to estimate their significance and value.

Whatever views may be held as to questions of policy, in the sphere of political or economic organisation, it will be agreed that the first condition of a sane treatment of difficult questions is that the relevant facts should be known and should be discussed with candour and impartiality. A Quarterly, such as is suggested, would do valuable work in helping to spread an understanding of the real nature of the problems with which the country is confronted. The probability that within five or ten years a Government will be returned which is pledged to large measures of economic and social reconstruction makes the diffusion of such an understanding all the more important.

The size and format of the proposed Journal would be so arranged as to include, among other regular features, reviews of current English and foreign literature and relevant official publications, and a digest of judicial and administrative decisions of public significance. But the main value of its contents will lie in its special articles. We believe that it will be possible to form a group of contributors sufficient to ensure a continuous supply of matter of adequate quality, and it is believed that the Editor contemplated is one who will command general and cordial approval.

573

The main difficulty to be overcome is the question of finance. It is estimated that an initial guaranteed sum of £2,000 will secure the Journal for a period of at least two years. It is hoped that afterwards it may become self-supporting.

P. J. Noel Baker, Ernest Barker, C. Delise Burns, A. M. Carr-Saunders, Henry Clay, G. D. H. Cole, G. Lowes Dickinson, P. Sargant Florence, Margery Fry, T. E. Gregory, Lynda Grier, Freda Hawtrey, L. T. Hobhouse, J. A. Hobson, Eva Hubback, H. J. Laski, F. Lavington, A. D. Lindsay, C. M. Lloyd, J. J. Mallon, T. H. Marshall, Kingsley Martin, C. S. Myers, Percy Nunn, Olivier, W. A. Robson, C. P. Scott, R. H. Tawney, Beatrice Webb, Sidney Webb, Leonard Woolf, Barbara Wootton.

Here is an almost definitive list of the politically progressive great and good of the time. The two up-and-coming young men, as we would now say, had done their networking. Curiously Keynes did not sign, but almost immediately joined a committee for implementation. It consisted of Woolf, Carr-Saunders, Laski, Keynes, Gregory, Martin and Robson; and Robson was to note that Tawney and Lowes Dickinson 'were also extremely helpful'. The Coles, G. D. H. and Margaret, were noticeably missing—their personal dominance of the Fabian Society at the time would have already set alarm bells ringing with Woolf, Robson and certainly the Webbs.

The next step was, of course, to raise the money. The founding of little magazines with big aspirations is no easy matter. Intellectuals can waste weeks of time in pipe-dreaming, plotting and planning. Nothing had—or has— changed much since Dr Johnson's day. Middle class men of letters reluctantly seek patrons. Foundations understandably fear only to get the blame when projects fail, blame for not letting the projecteers try, try and try again. In fact at that time only the Rowntrees subsidised political journals, and Woolf had had a bad experience in the early 1920s with the Rowntree Trust—for it was then very much a family matter, a little whimsical, somewhat nervous and only liberal to Liberals.[4] So sums were drummed up from friends and acquaintances, varying from £5 to £150; but after about six months only half was pledged of the £2,000 that the inner circle calculated was needed to ensure a three-year run or trial on a shoe-string budget (then and for most of its life). Here Robson's acquaintance with Shaw became the trump card, albeit in a tantalising slow and teasing game over eighteen months. GBS did not just sign cheques; he extracted malicious fun from the process. Robson went to see him in Whitehall Court in early January 1928. A typical Shavian postcard followed:

Whitehall Court,
24 January 1928

Generosity is not a septuagenarian quality; and my recent compulsory munificence in the matter of supertax has left me the meanest of men.

Come! How much have you got; and what is the lowest additional contribution which would enable you to try for a year?

[4] See Duncan Wilson, *Leonard Woolf: A Political Biography*, Hogarth Press, 1978, pp. 120–3, 125–6.

Robson replied that his committee were all agreed that a three-year run was the only fair test: 'if we were to stop after a year such a result would discredit the idea of a serious political paper for years to come'. But he promised to work on real figures.

Whitehall Court
11 March 1928

I think I'll wait and see what happens the first year. Do you realise what a stupendously obsolete thing a quarterly is? It suggests that the Fabian Society, which began fifty years ahead of its time is going to end 50 years behind it. This enthusiasm of young men for old things is ghastly. Are you surprised at my not sharing it? G. B. S.

Robson worked on Shaw's flicker of interest slowly but surely. He knew his habit of playing hard to get, of teasing and badinage. Robson was never a particularly humorous man, but he knew how to humour Shaw. By 5 March 1929 he could write to him:

I really think in the interests of the Review I ought to relieve you of the £1,000 which you have generously agreed to contribute. It is true that we do not actually require the money at this moment because we are still involved in the preparatory stages. But in the first place the money might be on deposit at the bank usefully earning interest for the Review, and in the second place, if you were unfortunately to be run over by one of those super-silent cat motor cars which now steal along the streets, as very nearly occurred when I was walking with you down Kingsway last year, it would be extraordinarily difficult to persuade your executors that I had managed to extract a promise for the sum in question from you.

Then Shaw swung into practical mode. A bank account must be opened in the name of the trustees, 'otherwise there would be nobody to pay the money to but you personally; and though this would not deter me it might deter strangers'. And 'I shall certainly not give you the money as a gift'; whether shares or debentures 'it must be an investment of some sort'. Indeed for years after Shaw's death the public trustee, whom he made the sole executor of his infamously complex will, sent his man along to *PQ*'s annual company meeting to make sure that if we ever made a profit, which then we never did (indeed we have never paid anything on the shares issued), that the state would have its small share. And the sage ended with the sage advice: 'Always keep control in the hands of friends'. Robson took his advice, so by 11 July 'the cheque goes to the bank by this post'. Robson, meanwhile, consulting with legal colleagues at LSE, had created a company structure in which editorial control was vested in non-profit-making shares of a private company issued only to members of the editorial board, and that debenture capital carried no voting rights. This is an admirable device for small journals. It meant that while any management company, constituted by various publishers at various times (five in the history of the journal), could cease publishing us, they could not take over the title nor rights to the

575

backstock.[b] (Years later I urged the wisdom of this model on Ann Smith who founded the *Literary Review*, doing everything herself but neglecting formalities; she took capital for expansion from a wealthy publisher and soon she was out and the title his.[c])

Meanwhile the search for an editor and for other donations or shareholders had continued. Kingsley Martin had left LSE to pursue a career in journalism, becoming a leader writer on the *Manchester Guardian*. He pursues[d] Ernest Simon, later Lord Wythenshawe, Liberal MP, industrialist, philanthropist and former Lord Mayor of Manchester. First of all, Simon says he is supporting too much already, and grumbles why it is that all good things need subsidy; but then he relents and promises £100 if Hammond does, indeed, agree to be editor. But that possibility was slipping; Hammond shrewdly became more aware, the more they pressed him, of the burden and the commitment. Woolf writes to him (19 December 1928) that although a joint editorship is unworkable for a weekly or a monthly, it could work for a quarterly. Keynes and Edgeworth, he reminds him, were joint editors of the *Economic Journal* for years. He put his finger on the perennial problem of a high class quarterly: 'it would considerably lighten the work and responsibility of the editor, which is a material consideration in the case of work done like this necessarily as a by-product of [other] activities, because not a full-time job'. And he might have added—though two gentlemen then would tacitly understand this—paying nothing. (For many years editors were not paid; at the very first board meeting I attended, when the Thomson organisation had just taken over our printing and publishing,[e] Woolf tried to resist—on

[b] This is not quite accurate, in that the publisher partners of the journal—still five, if Blackwell and its successor Wiley Blackwell are considered the same company—are not really part of its management (certainly not as a 'management company') but in the *PQ* form of arrangement are entirely separate, as partners for the duration of a formal and renewable agreement (commonly five years). This is sometimes known as society publishing, not because of any connection with Debrett's but because it is a model adopted by a large number of learned societies. What is true is that if a journal retains ownership of its title, editorial control etc. on this 'society' partnership model, whether constituted as a company or not, then the publisher cannot usurp its editorial policy or close it down (though it could make things very difficult). If things went seriously wrong it would probably either wait for the arrangement to lapse and not renew it, or in more urgent cases just sever relations via a clause in the contract.

In the end, the security and well-being of any journal depends on the integrity and good sense of its board and controlling committees. After all, the board of a hitherto independent journal could decide to sell it outright—which has happened often enough—so that the title passes to a publisher. Once it has complete ownership of journal a publisher can do whatever it likes with it, including replace the editors, radically change the editorial policy or close it down completely.

[c] The publisher in question was Naim Attallah. Bernard added a comment here on one of the few marked proof pages to survive (see my Introduction) that I thought it best not to include.

[d] The present tense is as the original hereabouts, perhaps used to enliven the narrative or just to allow Bernard to use 'Simon says' in the next sentence.

[e] This appears to have been the editorial board meeting held on 4 January 1966 at 42 William IV Street, London, a few months before he was appointed coeditor. Bernard was mistaken about Thomson, however; they had not just taken over the publishing at that point but had performed that role since the first issue of 1963, three years before.

principle—any idea of paying authors, as Thomson assumed must be done even though they would have to subsidise the journal.)

Woolf made a precise suggestion: 'To be quite frank I wondered if you would possibly agree to be a joint editor with Laski'—his own idea, not discussed with the others. 'There is another advantage in it. . . . and that is that the quarterly is to be progressive, i.e. it must include the general outlook of both 'Liberals' and 'Labour'; the combination of the two colourations in a joint editorship would therefore have obvious advantages.' (I read this with an appreciative irony, for so I had rationalised fifty years later in similar terms the defeat by a Social Democrat of a Labour nominee backed by the existing Labour joint editor and myself as chairman.)

This must have been the dawn of the idea of a joint editorship when Hammond finally said 'no', although his immediate response to Woolf was to decline to work with Laski. He had belonged to a little group planning a book together of which Laski acted as secretary and 'it broke down because he always said and thought that he had summoned people when he hadn't. His methods would make the work of his colleague much harder I think than a sole editorship.' He suggested Cole, which went no further and may have worried Woolf that Hammond knew so little about the tensions among the brothers. Laski and Cole were daggers drawn. Woolf now came into play.

Woolf writes to Martin (23 February 1929) to say that Hammond definitely would not take it on 'even in joint editorship with me'. So he had written to Robson and told him '(a) I cannot take it on alone, but (b) will edit it jointly with someone else if a suitable person can be found. I am not very keen on undertaking it as my hands are already pretty full, but if the committee feels it is the best solution under the circumstances, I am prepared to do. I incline to think that of all the suggestions Robson would be best as joint editor with me. I have not suggested it to him as I thought it might come better from you or someone else.' But something changed that spring. A letter from Keynes to Robson of 28 June begins by congratulating him on his forthcoming marriage to Juliette Alvin—the French cellist, later pioneer of music therapy—but adds:

I had a talk with Woolf about the editorship of the new Journal as we walked away the other day. I am sure that on personal grounds he would be perfectly happy if your colleague were to be Martin rather than himself. Indeed his only reason for not withdrawing was the belief that some members of the committee might be a little afraid of Martin's alleged rashness, so that it would help them that there should be at any rate another name in the field. That is to say, his notion was to stand there available in the event of the committee feeling afraid of appointing Martin. But if this was not felt then Woolf does not in the least want the job for himself.

So Woolf can write to Martin without embarrassment in February recommending Robson all as if Martin was not a candidate for joint editorship himself; but by June from Keynes's letter it is reasonably clear that Robson wanted Martin not Woolf, and that Martin was 'not unwilling'. If the young man was as 'rash',

577

indeed, as the old man I knew, then 'not unwilling' is an understatement—this author falling into the conventions of the time he is writing about. None of this figures in Robson's 1970 account. History has been smoothed over a little. Perhaps Robson felt that, despite what would seem obvious temperamental differences between him and Kingsley Martin (the one so rash and dashing, the other so methodical and careful)[f] that it would be easier to work with, or influence, someone of his own age than someone already of Woolf's eminent reputation. He may have feared a bossy nanny for his own baby. On 26 July Woolf writes to Martin: 'There is no need for you to feel bad. I always tell the truth unless there is a very good reason for telling a lie, and in this case there is no need for me to do so. The Quarterly interests me and I like having a finger in interesting pies, but as I said (truthfully) I have not really the time for it and was glad to get out of it.' And he then plunges into professional detail about the publishing contract with Macmillan as if to demonstrate that even if there is a whiff of Martin intriguing against him, yet he is too big for all that and will show that his finger in the pie is helpful to the public good.

The publishing contract was, indeed, with Harold Macmillan, then publisher as well as young politician,[g] who undertook the correspondence personally and gave them what Woolf agreed with Robson, who undertook most of the correspondence, were 'very reasonable terms'. Obviously turning to Macmillan was more than finding a publisher. Robson wrote (in his 1970 article) that he felt it important that a 'periodical of progressive outlook . . . be published by a firm of impeccable respectability and high repute'. Indeed, he may have felt that many a left-wing journal that was self-published or published by a small left-wing firm was doomed to the image of sectarian aggression and introversion before ever it was read. That was not for his journal. But also: 'I recall one incident at the end of my visit to Mr Macmillan. He had not yet published *The Middle Way* but it was already clear that he was at odds with right-wing elements in the Tory Party. I said "I sometimes wonder why you are where you are in political life". He looked at me hard and replied: "I regard the Conservative Party as the only means of achieving reform by general consent in this country".' I think both men were shrewd to see something more than commercial advantage (of which there could have been very little for Macmillan) in their association. The first draft of the contract from Macmillan spoke of 'to be entitled "Social Progress" or some such name'. But the committee, now transmuted into both editorial board and a limited liability private company, preferred the earlier title, *The Political Quarterly*.

---

[f] Perhaps needless to say it is Martin who is rash, Robson methodical, though Bernard has the names and descriptions in opposite order. Through these paragraphs it is sometimes tricky to work out who is writing to whom, but it can be done. The outcome of the story is that the editors of the new journal were Kingsley Martin and William Robson, but Martin stood down the following year and Woolf replaced him.

[g] As I mentioned in an earlier note, the agreement was with Macmillan the publisher not Harold himself, but Harold Macmillan took a personal interest and conducted the negotiations.

Index